INTERNATIONAL CRIMES AND
THE *AD HOC* TRIBUNALS

International Crimes and the *ad hoc* Tribunals

GUÉNAËL METTRAUX

OXFORD
UNIVERSITY PRESS

OXFORD
UNIVERSITY PRESS

Great Clarendon Street, Oxford OX2 6DP

Oxford University Press is a department of the University of Oxford.
It furthers the University's objective of excellence in research, scholarship,
and education by publishing worldwide in

Oxford New York

Auckland Cape Town Dar es Salaam Hong Kong Karachi
Kuala Lumpur Madrid Melbourne Mexico City Nairobi
New Delhi Shanghai Taipei Toronto

With offices in

Argentina Austria Brazil Chile Czech Republic France Greece
Guatemala Hungary Italy Japan Poland Portugal Singapore
South Korea Switzerland Thailand Turkey Ukraine Vietnam

Oxford is a registered trade mark of Oxford University Press
in the UK and in certain other countries

Published in the United States
by Oxford University Press Inc., New York

© G. Mettraux, 2005

The moral rights of the authors have been asserted
Database right Oxford University Press (maker)

Crown copyright material is reproduced under Class Licence
Number C01P0000148 with the permission of OPSI
and the Queen's Printer for Scotland

First published 2005
Published new as paperback 2006

British Library Cataloguing in Publication Data
Data available

Library of Congress Cataloging in Publication Data

Mettraux, Guénaël
International crimes and the ad hoc tribunals / Guénaël Mettraux.
p. cm.
Includes bibliographical references and index.
ISBN 0-19-927155-0 (hard cover : alk. paper) 1. International offenses.
2. International criminal courts. I. Title.
K5301.M48 2005
345'.0235—dc22

2004025881

Typeset by Newgen Imaging Systems (P) Ltd., Chennai, India
Printed in Great Britain
on acid-free paper by
Biddles Ltd., King's Lynn

ISBN 0-19-927155-0 (Hbk.) 978-0-19-927155-9 (Hbk.)
ISBN 0-19-920754-2 (Pbk.) 978-0-19-920754-1 (Pbk.)

1 3 5 7 9 10 8 6 4 2

Contents

Foreword

by

The Hon David Hunt AO QC*

The United Nations International Criminal Tribunals for the Former Yugoslavia and for Rwanda, created by the international community as a challenging new response to intractable conflict and massive violations of human rights, are advancing into their second decade of existence after years of investigations, trials, sentencing, appeals and even acquittals. In doing so, the two tribunals have come into their own as international courts, demonstrating the very real role which international institutions have to play in the administration of criminal justice.

Over this decade, the judges of these two tribunals – with the prosecutors and defence counsel who practise before them – have had to grapple with the interpretation of norms of international humanitarian law in their relatively recent transformation and with their application to international crimes. This process has produced a formidable and growing body of case law concerning the wide range of international crimes within the jurisdiction of the two tribunals and the numerous procedural and jurisdictional questions raised by this new field of law.

The present work, with its comprehensive consideration of the jurisprudence on each of the international crimes within the jurisdiction of the two tribunals, is a timely and invaluable guide to this expanding body of law. The work systematically examines the definitions and elements of each of these crimes as laid down in the trial and appeal judgments of both tribunals. The importance of the tribunals' *case law* in understanding the legal character of these international crimes cannot be underestimated. The drafters of the Tribunals' Statutes drew on a range of prohibitions in the laws of armed conflict and other branches of humanitarian law found in fundamental sources, such as the Geneva Conventions, and in other subject matter-specific treaties, such as the Torture and the Genocide Conventions. The prohibitions and standards in these conventions and in the body of international humanitarian law generally, although plainly established as part of the international legal framework, were directed principally to setting standards and prohibitions which bind States. They include little of the specificity necessary for the application of a prohibition as *criminal* law which binds individuals in their personal capacity, with potentially penal consequences. For example, there could be no serious dispute about the existence and the fundamental nature of the

---

* Judge of the UN International Criminal Tribunal for the former Yugoslavia 1998–2003, presiding judge of Trial Chamber II 2000–2001, judge of the Appeals Chamber 2001–2003; formerly judge of the Supreme Court of New South Wales, Sydney, Australia 1979–1998, Chief Judge at Common Law 1991–1998.

prohibition of rape in wartime. However, the various sources of that prohibition such as common Article 3(e) of the Geneva Conventions have done no more than identify 'rape' as prohibited conduct. These sources do not descend into the detail of the precise conduct which constitutes the crime of rape, and a brief consideration of the extent to which the terms of domestic criminal laws around the world differ in their definitions of the crime of rape demonstrates that the answer to this question is no foregone conclusion. The same difficulties have arisen in relation to a range of other crimes within the jurisdiction of the two tribunals, such as the crimes of enslavement or terror, which were devoid of any clear definition as an international *crime* until they first came to be considered by the Yugoslav Tribunal.

The two tribunals have had to address these questions as they have arisen, sometimes with the assistance of relevant judgments of the Second World War tribunals, sometimes drawing on case law of domestic courts and tribunals and other examples of state practice, and on other occasions by reference to the general principles of law found in the domestic laws of States. In circumstances where there is insufficient state practice or other source from which to identify a precise criminal prohibition, the task of the tribunals has been to affirm that, at the stage of the development of international criminal law relevant to the events before them, certain prohibitions such as the prohibition of 'violence to life and person' were not the subject of any sufficiently specific or accessible definition to be an appropriate source of individual criminal responsibility. The affirmation of the principle of legality or *nullem crimen sine lege/nulla poena sine lege*, stated in fundamental international instruments such as the International Covenant on Civil and Political Rights (Article 15) and now in the Statute of the International Criminal Court (Articles 22 and 23), allows for no other conclusion. This process of moving from the mainly generalized prohibitions imposed upon States by international humanitarian law to the particularity and clarity of legal standards necessitated by the criminal law which binds individuals has been an essential part of the tribunals' development, not simply as international legal institutions but as functioning criminal *courts*.

The body of jurisprudence which has resulted from the progressive consideration and definition of international crimes by the tribunals over the past ten years is now a substantial one, and it has played a considerable part in the identification and development of international criminal law. This jurisprudence has a broader significance than to trials before the tribunals themselves. Many of the crimes over which the tribunals have jurisdiction are now also within the jurisdiction of other *ad hoc* international tribunals such as the Special Court for Sierra Leone. Of potentially broader significance is the fact that the case law of the tribunals as it has developed over the last decade has served as a reference point in the formulation of the Statute of the International Criminal Court and of the Elements of the Crimes within its jurisdiction. The experience of the two tribunals in considering, identifying and applying the definitions of crimes in a range of situations should provide a valuable body of precedent and principles on which the judges and practitioners of the ICC may draw as appropriate. Equally, domestic courts are increasingly involved in the application of international humanitarian law in the criminal law context, and they have drawn on the jurisprudence of the tribunals in doing so.

In this context, a comprehensive work which guides the reader systematically through this extensive volume of jurisprudence crime by crime, and with commentary on other essential aspects of the substantive criminal law, including forms of liability and sentencing, is an invaluable reference point for practitioners and commentators alike.

The author, Guénaël Mettraux, is particularly well qualified to author this book. In addition to his academic qualifications in international law, he has the advantage of having worked within the Chambers of the Yugoslav Tribunal for several of that tribunal's most active years, and he has subsequently been practising as a defence counsel before that tribunal. His background as an international lawyer, combined with his experience as a practitioner, means that he has approached the subject matter from a secure understanding of international law, its sources, and the way in which it develops, and also with a strong recognition of the importance of the need, from a criminal law practitioner's perspective, for clarity in the criminal law.

The careful review and analysis of the jurisprudence of the two tribunals in this work is informed by Mr Mettraux's wide knowledge of international humanitarian law as it has developed over the past decades, extending beyond the jurisprudence of the World War II tribunals to the less accessible case law of a range of other international and domestic courts applying international humanitarian law. He has had almost unique access to the records of those courts and tribunals. This knowledge of international humanitarian law precedent informs this work, so that tribunal judgments are placed in context; appropriate examples are given; and, occasionally, a critical analysis is provided of the extent to which the tribunal jurisprudence is consistent (or inconsistent) with the international humanitarian law precedents and practice which preceded it. The primary purpose of this work is not, however, to be an analytical review of the jurisprudence of the two tribunals; it is first and foremost a practical guide to the law of the tribunals as it has developed over their lifetime and as the law is applied today. It fills the very real need for a text which recognizes the primary function of the tribunals as fundamentally criminal law institutions, albeit operating in an international context and adjudicating the most serious of crimes.

I strongly recommend this book as an essential reference work for practitioners, and as a comprehensive text for students, commentators and anyone else with an interest in understanding the important and rapidly growing body of international criminal law.

Sydney
October 2004

Preface

This book has been a long, in fact, a very long, endeavour. The idea for it was not really mine but that of a dear friend, Professor Salvatore Zappalà. For several years, however, it remained a manuscript well buried from sight, including from mine. It stayed there until another friend and mentor, Professor Antonio Cassese, convinced me to turn the manuscript into a book. Due to professional commitment first as a legal assistant to the Judges of the *ad hoc* Tribunal for the Former Yugoslavia, and then as Defence Counsel, the finalization of this work was long to come. But I hope that the experience acquired over the years in that extraordinary judicial environment will provide the reader with more than the dry recounting of the law as it is being made in The Hague and Arusha.

The *ad hoc* Tribunals are, in many different ways, much more than about the law that they have produced over the years. My ambition when writing this book, however, was limited to providing those interested in the subject of international crimes with an instrument that would allow them to understand the law of the Tribunals a bit better or at least to make it more accessible to them. Others, hopefully, will tell other aspects of the life of the *ad hoc* Tribunals which are missing from this volume.

The principal subject-matter of the book, the law of international crimes as applied by the *ad hoc* Tribunals, was chosen for no other reason that I found it to be a fascinating one and that there appeared to be some interest for the topic. I considered, furthermore, that some of the lessons of the *ad hoc* Tribunals, and its contribution to the law of international crimes in particular, could be lost if not properly recorded.

The law of international crimes as presented in this book is not a fully fledged body of law which has been refined by years of judicial fine-tuning. The Tribunals after all are only ten years or so old and the body of rules and principles that they have built up has come, bit by bit, out of their numerous orders, decisions, judgments, and appeals that make up what is known as the 'jurisprudence' of the *ad hoc* Tribunals. The careful observer will identify many inconsistencies between various decisions and judgments rendered by these Tribunals and may come to realize how much the Tribunals have changed over the years and why.

As a result of its incremental development, the law of the Tribunals looks very much like a large patchwork made up of numerous pieces fitted together over the last decade. The composition of this patchwork has in large part been the result of the random order in which cases came before the Court, but the colour and shape of its pieces were in many instances dictated by those involved in those cases, first among whom were the Judges. Many gaps remain in the body of law of international crimes at the *ad hoc* Tribunals, some of which will be filled by the

Tribunals over the last few years of their existence, whilst others will feed academic discussions for years to come.

Two chapters in this book – the one dealing with forms of criminal liability and the one dealing with sentencing – have been included in order to provide the reader with a comprehensive picture of the subject-matter of international crimes at the *ad hoc* Tribunals and to put this topic into its proper context. These two chapters, however, are merely an introduction to two vast subjects which both deserve books of their own.

As with any such enterprise, writing this book proved a very arduous experience, but thankfully not a solitary one. Many people have contributed to this book, and although I cannot hope to mention them all here, I am sincerely grateful to all of them.

Claire Harris read an earlier manuscript of this book, making innumerable suggestions, correcting many infelicities in my English, and never shying away from telling me I *was* wrong. The book greatly benefited from her remarkable intelligence. This book is also hers.

I am also most indebted to Eve La Haye, Salvatore Zappalà, Norman Farrell, and Amir Čengić who have made many precious comments in relation to various chapters of this book and who have otherwise helped with its finalization. I am particularly grateful to Moya Magilligan who has done an incredible work of editing of the manuscript before submission. Obviously, all remaining mistakes are mine.

My gratitude also goes to John Louth, Louise Kavanagh and Gwen Booth at Oxford University Press who have been the most attentive and patient of editors.

Pauline Thomas, Eva Knutsson-Hall, and Gary Meixner, all superb librarians at the ICTY, have systematically put up with my most thorny requests and provided me with all the material I ever asked them to trace for me.

Mention must also be made of some other colleagues and friends (legal assistants, prosecutors, defence counsel, and others) who have contributed to making the Tribunals what they are, exceptional places: Jim Landale, Nicholas Robson, Brigitte Benoit, Haris Halilović, Daryl Mundis, Vladimir Domazet, Stéphane Bourgon, Michael Bohlander, Ken Roberts, Lola Kavran, Emir Suljagić, Jérome de Hemptinne, Hirad Abtahi, and Thomas Henquet, and the many others to whom the Tribunal is most important and whose commitment I was able to observe from having had the good fortune to work with them.

Institutions are rarely about the individuals who make them work, but they often bear the imprints of the most exceptional among them. Two towering personalities have shaped the *ad hoc* Tribunals more than any others and deserve to be mentioned here. The first one, Judge, and then President, Antonio Cassese breathed life into the Tribunals, working impossible hours, convincing those who did not believe in international justice that an international criminal court had its place and setting out to prove that it could work. Without Judge Cassese, the *ad hoc* Tribunals would simply not have survived.

Another Judge, His Excellency Judge David A. Hunt, took over where Judge Cassese had left the Tribunals. With an incredible enthusiasm and commitment, Judge Hunt has done more than anyone else to transform an adolescent institution into a functioning criminal court, imposing his view that if they were to be respected as courts of law, these Tribunals should operate as normally as any other court and should never compromise upon the fundamental rights of an accused person. On a more personal note, Judge Hunt has been the kindest and most generous mentor, always giving his time to those (big or small alike) who sought his advice or assistance, not least the author. Judge Hunt taught a naïve civil lawyer what the common law was all about, showed him what being fair and just meant in a courtroom, and inspired him to pursue his own thoughts and defend his opinions. For all these, and many other things, I am most grateful and truly indebted.

The Hague, GM
August 2004

Tables of Cases

Any entries without page references are included because of their relevance to the subject.

ICTY

(for full text of judgments/decisions see www.un.org/icty)

Table of Judgments (alphabetical)

Table of Judgments (chronological)

ICTR

(for full text of judgments see www.un.org/ictr)

Table of Judgments (alphabetical)

Table of Judgments (chronological)

ICTY

(Indictments and other Relevant Filings)

World War II Cases and Other Miscellaneous

PART I

SUBJECT-MATTER JURISDICTION OF THE *AD HOC* TRIBUNALS AND APPLICABLE LAW

PART I

SUBJECT-MATTER JURISDICTION OF THE *AD HOC* TRIBUNALS AND APPLICABLE LAW

1

General Remarks – The Creation and Jurisdiction of the *ad hoc* Tribunals

On 22 February 1993, the United Nations Security Council expressed its 'grave alarm at continuing reports of widespread violations of international humanitarian law' in the territory of the former Yugoslavia.[1] Determined to put an end to such crimes, to bring peace and stability back to the region and with a view to punishing those responsible, the Security Council took the unprecedented step of setting up an international criminal tribunal pursuant to Chapter VII of the Charter of the United Nations. The Tribunal thus created was given the authority to prosecute and judge serious violations of international humanitarian law committed on the territory of the former Yugoslavia since 1991. Grave breaches of the Geneva Conventions of 1949, other serious violations of the laws or customs of war, genocide, and crimes against humanity were all crimes which came within its jurisdiction. The Statute of the 'International Criminal Tribunal for the Prosecution of Persons Responsible for Serious Violations of International Humanitarian Law Committed in the Territory of the Former Yugoslavia since 1991', or ICTY, was drafted to provide jurisdiction over any of the above categories of crimes committed anywhere on the territory of the former Socialist Federal Republic of Yugoslavia, including its land surface, airspace, and territorial waters since 1991.[2] And although the jurisdiction of the International Tribunal and that of domestic courts were to be concurrent, the former was given primacy over the latter.[3]

At the time, it was hoped that the establishment of the Tribunal, and the punishment of such crimes, could contribute to the restoration of peace and stability in the region, all other measures having failed. Unfortunately, the establishment of the ICTY did not stem the flow of very serious violations of humanitarian law in the former Yugoslavia. Nor does it seem to have stopped it

---

[1] Security Council Resolution 808 (1993), UN Doc. S/RES/808 (22 February 1993); Security Council Resolution 827 (1993), UN Doc. S/RES/827 (25 May 1993).

[2] See Article 8 and Article 1 of the ICTY Statute. The argument of the Defence in the *Ojdanić* case that the jurisdiction *ratione temporis* of the ICTY did not extend to the events that took place in Kosovo in 1998 was rejected by the Trial Chamber and by the Appeals Chamber (see *Milutinović* Kosovo Jurisdiction Decision). See also *Šešelj* Vojvodina Decision, pars 15 and 17 concerning Šešelj's challenge to the *ex post facto* nature of the Tribunal in relation to the crimes charged against him.

[3] Article 9 of the ICTY Statute.

anywhere else, for that matter, least of all in Rwanda where, in 1994, atrocities on a scale not witnessed for half a century were carried out in the course of a few months.[4] On 8 November 1994, the Security Council once again seized itself of the matter and decided to establish an international tribunal for the purpose of prosecuting persons responsible for genocide and other serious violations of humanitarian law in Rwanda in 1994.[5] The Statute of the International Criminal Tribunal for Rwanda (ICTR) provides for a subject-matter jurisdiction which, apart from slight nuances, is essentially similar to that of the ICTY.[6] Its jurisdiction *ratione temporis* and *ratione loci* is concerned with crimes committed in Rwanda or neighbouring states between 1 January 1994 and 31 December 1994.[7] As had been the case with the ICTY, the Rwanda Tribunal was given primacy over domestic courts in relation to the crimes within its jurisdiction.[8]

Ratione personae, the jurisdiction of both Tribunals is limited to natural persons and excludes any official privileges or state immunities that such persons might otherwise have enjoyed before domestic courts (Articles 7(2) and 6(2) of the ICTY and ICTR Statutes). The individual criminal responsibility of any individual who was sufficiently involved in the commission of a statutory crime might be engaged if he 'directly' took part in the planning, instigating, ordering, committing, or otherwise aiding and abetting of any of those crimes (Articles 7(1) and 6(1) of the Statutes) or if he was the commander of those who committed such crimes (Articles 7(3) and 6(3) of the Statutes).[9]

---

[4] There is a wealth of literature on the events in Rwanda. Only a few books are mentioned here as examples of the many publications on the subject: P. Gourevitch, *We Wish to Inform You that Tomorrow We Will Be Killed with Our Families* (New York: Farrar, Straus & Giroux, 2000); G. Prunier, *The Rwanda Crisis: History of a Genocide* (New York: Columbia University Press, 1995); Y. Mukagasana and A. Kazinierakis, *Les Blessures du silence* (Arles: Actes Sud, 2001).

[5] Security Council Resolution 955 (1994), UN Doc. S/RES/955 (8 November 1994). The resolution expresses the Security Council's 'grave concern at the reports indicating that genocide and other systematic, widespread and flagrant violations of international humanitarian law have been committed in Rwanda'.

[6] The Commission of Experts for Rwanda in its *Final Report* had suggested that the ICTY should simply expand its jurisdiction to include crimes committed in Rwanda (Final Report of the Commission of Experts established pursuant to Security Council Resolution 935 (1994), S/1994/1405 (3 December 1993), (Final Report of the Commission of Experts for Rwanda), par 179; Preliminary Report of the Independent Commission of Experts established in accordance with Security Council Resolution 935 (1994), S/1994/1125 (1 October 1994), ('Preliminary Report of the Commission of Experts for Rwanda'), par 139). Although this solution was eventually rejected, and a distinct *ad hoc* Tribunal for Rwanda was set up, the two Tribunals are closely interconnected in various manners. For instance, the judges that make up the Appeals Chamber are the same in both Tribunals and, until September 2003, the Tribunals had a common Prosecutor.

[7] Article 7 of the ICTR Statute. Concerning the scope of the jurisdiction *ratione temporis* of the ICTR, see, however, *Nahimana* Trial Judgment, par 1044, where the Trial Chamber held that acts of conspiracy (to commit genocide) which had occurred prior to 1994, but which may be shown to have resulted in the commission of genocide in 1994, would come within the Tribunal's jurisdiction.

[8] Article 7 of the ICTR Statute.

[9] See generally Part V below. For the purpose of this book, perpetrators and accused persons will generally be referred to in the masculine form. Traditionally, perpetrators of mass atrocities have been overwhelmingly male; two female accused (Biljana Plavšić at the ICTY and Pauline Nyiramasuhuko at the ICTR) have so far appeared before the *ad hoc* Tribunals.

2

Subject-Matter Jurisdiction and Applicable Law – Customary International Law and Treaty Law?

2.1 ICTY	5
2.2 ICTR	10

The Statutes of the *ad hoc* Tribunals contain not much more than the skeletons of the crimes that are within their jurisdictions. The definitions of those crimes and the application of the law of international crimes in general, therefore, call for further refinements to be made by the Court which has been entrusted by the Security Council with the task of applying the Statute whilst ensuring that it was not thereby legislating new international law.[1] The first problem to confront the Tribunals has related to the body of law which their Chambers must apply to determine the elements of those statutory crimes under international law as well as their very existence as international criminal offences.

2.1 ICTY

The Statute of the Yugoslav Tribunal does not expressly provide for the body of law which the court is to apply to determine the scope of its jurisdiction *ratione materiae* and to define the crimes which come within that jurisdiction. In his Report to the Security Council accompanying the proposed Statute of the Tribunal, the Secretary-General of the United Nations had made it clear, however, that the Tribunal was expected to apply 'rules of international humanitarian law which are beyond any doubt part of customary law' when making that jurisdictional determination.[2] In effect, judges in The Hague were told to satisfy

---

[1] Report of the Secretary-General (ICTY), par 29.
[2] Report of the Secretary-General (ICTY), par 34. See also L. D. Johnson, 'Ten Years Later: Reflections on the Drafting', 2(2) *Journal of International Criminal Justice* 368, 370 (June 2004): 'As

themselves that the crimes with which an accused had been charged were crimes under customary international law at the time when they were committed, that is, that the relevant acts were both recognized as criminal under customary international law and that they were sufficiently defined under that body of law.[3]

Consistent with that general directive, the Appeals Chamber made it clear on several occasions that the subject-matter jurisdiction of the Tribunal needed to be based 'on firm foundations of customary law'[4] and that Chambers of the ICTY were bound to apply,[5] *ratione materiae* and *ratione personae*, customary international law:[6]

[T]he Tribunal only has jurisdiction over a listed crime [in the Statute] if that crime was recognised as such under customary international law at the time it was allegedly committed. The scope of the Tribunal's jurisdiction *ratione materiae* may therefore be said to be determined both by the Statute, insofar as it sets out the jurisdictional framework of the International Tribunal, and by customary international law, insofar as the Tribunal's power to convict an accused of any crime listed in the Statute depends on its existence *qua* custom at the time this crime was allegedly committed.[7]

In other words, the International Tribunal for the former Yugoslavia does not have jurisdiction over violations of treaty law or violations of domestic law unless

the [Security] Council was, for the first (and as far as anyone knew, for the only) time, establishing as a binding enforcement measure a judicial organ, having the power to sentence individuals to imprisonment, it was thought prudent, in spite of temptation, not to use the occasion to advocate "progressive" interpretations, clarifications or additions, but rather to stick as much as possible to what was incontrovertibly customary international law.' At the time of the drafting of the ICTY Statute, Mr Larry Johnson was Principal Legal Officer, Office of the Legal Counsel, United Nations.

[3] See *Vasiljević* Trial Judgment, par 202 ('If customary international law does not provide for a sufficiently precise definition of a crime listed in the Statute, the Trial Chamber would have no choice but to refrain from exercising its jurisdiction over it, regardless of the fact that the crime is listed as a punishable offence in the Statute. This is so because, to borrow the language of a US military tribunal in Nuremberg, anything contained in the statute in excess of existing customary international law would be a utilisation of power and not of law') and *Kordić and Čerkez* Articles 2 and 3 Jurisdiction Decision, par 20 ('The Trial Chamber agrees that the principle of legality is the underlying principle that should be relied on to assess the subject-matter jurisdiction of the International Tribunal, and that the International Tribunal only has jurisdiction over offences that constituted crimes under customary international law at the time the alleged offences were committed.'). See also R. Zacklin, 'Some Major Problems in the Drafting of the ICTY Statute', 2(2) *Journal of International Criminal Justice* 361, 363 (June 2004).

[4] See, in particular, *Hadžihasanović* Command Responsibility Appeal Decision, par 55 (see also ibid., pars 35, 44–46). See also *Ojdanić* Joint Criminal Enterprise Decision, par 9; *Blaškić* Appeal Judgement, pars 110, 139, and 141.

[5] According to the *Aleksovski* jurisprudence, Trial Chambers are bound by the decisions of the Appeals Chamber (*Aleksovski* Appeal Judgment, par 113).

[6] See, generally, *Hadžihasanović* Command Responsibility Appeal Decision, pars 12, 35, 44–46, and 55; *Ojdanić* Joint Criminal Enterprise Decision, pars 9–10; *Blaškić* Appeal Judgment, par 141. See also, concerning the definition of the crime of genocide, *Krstić* Appeal Judgment, par 224.

[7] *Ojdanić* Joint Criminal Enterprise Decision, par 9 (footnotes omitted). See also *Kordić and Čerkez* Articles 2 and 3 Jurisdiction, par 20: 'The Trial Chamber agrees that the principle of legality is the underlying principle that should be relied on to assess the subject-matter jurisdiction of the International Tribunal, and that the International Tribunal only has jurisdiction over offences that constituted crimes under customary international law at the time the alleged offences were committed.'

those conventional or national prohibitions have additionally become part of customary international law.[8] In a number of *obiter dicta*, however, Chambers of the Tribunal had hinted at – but had never actually acted upon – the possibility that it could, under certain circumstances, have recourse to treaty law (in particular, to the Geneva Conventions and their Additional Protocols) and could base a conviction upon such a conventional, rather than on a customary, basis.[9]

Only on one occasion (in the *Galić* Judgment of 5 December 2003) has a Trial Chamber relied upon a treaty to anchor its jurisdiction over a particular type of conduct. In this case, Trial Chamber I convicted Stanislav Galić for, *inter alia*, 'terror' and 'attacks on civilians', based on Additional Protocol I of the Geneva Conventions.[10] In so doing, the Trial Chamber not only set aside the direction of the Secretary-General of the United Nations that the Tribunal should only apply those rules which are beyond any doubt part of customary law, but it also discarded the binding jurisprudence of the Appeals Chamber mentioned above which requires that its jurisdiction be grounded 'on firm foundations of customary law'.[11]

Theoretically, a treaty could very well provide, explicitly or even perhaps implicitly, that a particular conduct should be regarded as criminal. The Statute of the International Criminal Court is a perfect example of the availability of such a mechanism. It is also true that a treaty provision might be self-executing and might apply not only between state parties but also directly to the individuals

---

[8] A good illustration of that point may be found in the *Strugar* Appeals Chamber decision of 22 November 2002 in which the Appeals Chamber made it clear that the basis upon which the accused had been charged with 'attacks on civilians', and could be convicted thereupon, was not the provisions of the Additional Protocols to the Geneva Conventions which provide for the prohibition against attacks on civilians and civilian objects, but consisted of these principles embedded in those provisions as found in customary law (*Strugar* Jurisdiction Decision, pars 10, 13, and 14). See also *Vasiljević* Trial Judgment, par 198, which provides that 'Each Trial Chamber is thus obliged to ensure that the law which it applies to a given criminal offence is indeed customary.' See also *Čelebići* Appeal, par 170, where the Appeals Chamber said that the Tribunal has jurisdiction over crimes which were already subject to individual criminal responsibility prior to its establishment. See, finally, *Blaškić* Appeal Judgment, pars 110, 139, and 141 ('while the Statute of the International Tribunal lists offences over which the International Tribunal has jurisdiction, the Tribunal may enter convictions only where it is satisfied that the offence is proscribed under customary international law at the time of its commission'), where the Appeals Chamber reiterated that its jurisdiction *ratione materiae* depends on the content of customary international law at the time when the acts in question were allegedly committed.

[9] Most famously, in an *obiter dictum*, the Appeals Chamber in *Tadić* held that 'the International Tribunal is authorised to apply, in addition to customary international law, any treaty which: (i) was unquestionably binding on the parties at the time of the alleged offence; and (ii) was not in conflict with or derogating from peremptory norms of international law, as are most customary rules of international humanitarian law' (*Tadić* Jurisdiction Decision, par 143). It added that: 'We conclude that, in general, such agreements fall within our jurisdiction under Article 3 of the Statute' (ibid., par 144). See also, e.g., *Blaškić* Trial Judgment, par 169; see *Semanza* Trial Judgment, par 353 and references quoted therein; *Kayishema and Ruzindana* Trial Judgment, pars 156–157, and *Rutaganda* Trial Judgment, par 89.   [10] *Galić* Trial Judgment, pars 63 et seq.

[11] *Hadžihasanović* Command Responsibility Appeal Decision, par 55.

concerned. Even more explicitly, it may be that the state parties to the treaty have enacted domestic legislation criminalizing the conduct in the relevant treaty, as has been the case in numerous state parties to the International Criminal Court.[12]

The problem as far as the *ad hoc* Tribunals are concerned is that, with the exception perhaps of the Genocide Convention, none of the instruments which they could apply in relation to their subject-matter jurisdiction may be said to provide for international crimes. First, there is no international treaty which could arguably be said to provide for the criminalization of crimes against humanity. Concerning war crimes, it must be noted that neither the Geneva Conventions, nor their Additional Protocols may serve – nor were they ever meant to serve – as a basis for a criminal conviction.[13] As noted by the International Committee of the Red Cross in its *Commentary* to the Geneva Conventions, '[a]ll international Conventions, including this one [i.e. Geneva Convention IV], are primarily the affair of Governments. Governments discuss them and sign them, and it is based upon Governments that the duty of applying them devolves.'[14] The Geneva Conventions and their Additional Protocols are international treaties and as such, in principle, are binding on states only.[15] Even if it were accepted that some of their provisions might be self-executing and would therefore apply to individuals *qua* treaty, none of those provisions, not even their grave breaches sections, were ever meant to be regarded *per se* as an international criminal code the breach of which could entail individual criminal responsibility directly under the treaty regime. When it had been suggested by the Soviet delegate during the negotiation of the Geneva Conventions to replace the expression 'breaches' in the 'grave breaches' phrase with the expression 'crimes', it was pointed out to him that:

an act only becomes a crime when this act is made punishable by a penal law. The Conference is not making international penal law but is undertaking to insert in the national penal laws certain acts enumerated as grave breaches of the Convention, which will become crimes when they have been inserted in the national penal laws.[16]

---

[12] See, for example, the amendments to the Australian Criminal Code Act 1995 (Cth) made by the International Criminal Court (Consequential Amendments) Act 2002 (Cth), which added offences under the categories of genocide, crimes against humanity, and war crimes to the Australian Criminal Code.

[13] At the end of the negotiations, all delegates were reminded that the Diplomatic Conference which led to the adoption of the Conventions 'is not here to work out international penal law. Bodies far more competent than we are have tried to do it for years' (Fourth Report drawn up by the Special Committee of the Joint Committee, 12 July 1949, Final Record of Diplomatic Conference II, Section B, p 115).

[14] See J. Pictet (gen. ed.), *Commentary, Geneva Convention Relative to the Protection of Civilian Persons, Convention IV* (Geneva: ICRC, 1960), p 26 ('ICRC, *Commentary to Geneva Convention IV*').

[15] The Preamble of Additional Protocol I makes it clear, for instance, that this instrument is directed to and binding upon 'the High Contracting Parties, ie, states parties to this treaty'. According to the Commentary of the ICRC, '[t]his unquestionably refers to the States for which these treaties are in force in accordance with their relevant provisions' C. Pilloud *et al.* (eds.), *Commentary on the Additional Protocols of Conventions 8 June 1977 to the Geneva of 12 August 1949* (Geneva: ICRC, 1987), ('ICRC, Commentary to the Additional Protocols').

[16] Fourth Report drawn up by the Special Committee of the Joint Committee, 12 July 1949, Final Record of Diplomatic Conference II, Section B, p 115.

This is not to say that a number of provisions contained in the four Geneva Conventions or their Additional Protocols may not have become criminal offences under customary international law as indeed many have. But that is not the same as suggesting (as the Trial Chamber did in the *Galić* case) that, regardless of its crystallization under customary international law, the treaty *itself* may form the basis of a criminal conviction. Those instruments were never meant to and cannot do so conceptually as they are not binding *qua* treaty upon individuals, but only upon signatory states.

What the *Galić* Trial Chamber appears to have done is to mix up two different issues, as the Nuremberg Tribunal had done in relation to the crime of aggression, and to equate two levels of international prohibitions: illegality and criminality. Because a particular conduct is prohibited under a treaty provision, its breach does not necessarily (and generally does not) entail individual criminal responsibility for the perpetrator for in fact, and as already pointed out, not every illegal act is criminal. Most of them are not. The fact that two or more states have agreed to render a certain act illegal between them, and that a breach by one of them would render that state liable to pay compensation does not mean that those states have decided to render such violation a crime entailing the individual criminal liability of the actual perpetrator of the act.[17] From the point of view of the individual, 'a finding to the effect that a given norm is binding *upon a state – qua* custom or treaty law – does not entail that its breach may also engage the criminal liability of the individual who committed the act, let alone that it may have that effect under customary international law'.[18] Only a limited category of conduct contrary to international law has, thus far, been recognized as international crimes.

In sum, but for this one apparently misguided exception, the ICTY has constantly and consistently relied upon customary international law to determine the scope and the nature of its subject-matter jurisdiction.

It is almost certain that the negotiations of the Statute of the International Criminal Court, and its subsequent adoption by a relatively large number of states, had an important impact on the content of customary international law in this field. Because most of the crimes relevant to the jurisdiction of the ICTY (and all those relevant to the jurisdiction of the ICTR) were committed prior to 1998, the relevancy of the Rome Statute in identifying customary international law at the *ad hoc* Tribunals has been very limited.[19] As a result of these developments,

---

[17] The distinction between the illegality and the criminal nature of an act under international law was raised by defendant Muller in the Belgian case *Prosecutor v. Strauch et consorts* but it was rejected by the Belgian Court de Cassation without motivation (*Strauch and others*, Belgium, Court of Cassation, decision of 22 July 1949, in *Pasicrisie belge*, 1949, I, 561–563. Summary in English in *Annual Digest 1949*, 404).

[18] *Vasiljević* Trial Judgment, f 545, p 77. See also *Kunarac* Trial Judgment, par 489.

[19] See, e.g. ibid., footnote 1210 ('Although the ICC Statute does not necessarily represent the present status of international customary law, it is a useful instrument in confirming the content of customary international law. These provisions obviously do not *necessarily* indicate what the state of the relevant law was at the time relevant to this case. However they do provide some evidence of state *opinio juris* as to the relevant customary international law at the time at which the recommendations were adopted'); *Furundžija* Trial Judgment, par 227; *Tadić* Appeal Judgment, par 223.

however, some of the findings of the *ad hoc* Tribunals as to the state of customary law might already be outdated. Findings of the *ad hoc* Tribunals that a particular principle or a particular crime (or elements of a crime) is or is not part of customary international law must therefore be considered in light of the timeframe in relation to which such findings were made.

2.2   ICTR

On the face of it, the subject-matter jurisdiction of the ICTR appears to have been defined more expansively than that of the ICTY. In his Report, the Secretary-General of the United Nations wrote that the Security Council had drawn the subject-matter jurisdiction of the Rwanda Tribunal more broadly than it had for the ICTY by including not only violations of customary international law but also certain violations of treaties:[20]

[T]he Security Council has elected to take a more expansive approach to the choice of the applicable law than the one underlying the statute of the Yugoslav Tribunal, and included within the subject-matter jurisdiction of the Rwanda Tribunal international instruments regardless of whether they were considered part of customary international law or whether they have customarily entailed individual criminal responsibility of the perpetrator of the crime. Article 4 of the [ICTR] statute, accordingly, includes violations of Additional Protocol II, which, as a whole, has not yet been universally recognized as part of customary international law [. . .].

It is not totally clear whether that position intentionally departed from that adopted by the ICTY or whether it was, as one author has suggested, 'an unintentional distinction'.[21] Based on the Secretary-General's statement, however, a number of Trial Chambers have suggested that the ICTR's jurisdiction *ratione materiae* was defined more broadly than that of the ICTY and that the Rwanda Tribunal was therefore empowered to apply both customary international law and treaty law, insofar as it was binding in Rwanda at the relevant time.[22] Most of those Chambers, however, when defining a particular crime or when determining its content did not limit the scope of their considerations to those treaties on which they claimed they could rely to base their jurisdiction. The Chambers often failed to make it clear what body of law they were *in fact* applying to determine the scope of their jurisdiction.

---

[20] Comprehensive Report of the Secretary-General on Practical Arrangements for the Effective Functioning of the International Tribunal for Rwanda, Recommending Arusha as the Seat of the Tribunal, UN Doc. S/1995/134 (13 February 1995), par 12.

[21] M. C. Bassiouni and P. Manikas, *The Law of the International Criminal Tribunal for the Former Yugoslavia* (Irvington-on-Hudson: Transnational Publishers, 1996), p 458.

[22] See, e.g. *Akayesu* Trial Judgment, pars 604–607; *Kayishema and Ruzindana* Trial Judgment, pars 156–158, 597–598; *Musema* Trial Judgment, par 242; *Semanza* Trial Judgment, par 353.

By contrast, on those few occasions where it discussed that issue, the Appeals Chamber has hinted that the ICTR too should be applying customary law to its jurisdiction *ratione materiae*. In the *Čelebići* case, for instance, the Appeals Chamber pointed out that the Security Council, when establishing the ICTR, 'was not creating new law but was *inter alia* codifying existing customary rules for the purposes of the jurisdiction of the ICTR'.[23] Also, the Appeals Chamber of the ICTR made it clear that it would be both 'unnecessary and unfair' to hold an accused person responsible in relation to a conduct which was not clearly defined under international criminal law.[24] Such definitions might be found in certain treaties, but very few would be of sufficient clarity.

There are, in fact, good reasons why the ICTR should also be applying custom: first, treaties are, in principle, binding upon states, not individuals, and the ICTR must determine what rules are applicable to individuals, not states. As noted above, the fact that a treaty might have been breached is not yet sufficient to conclude that an international crime has been committed. Even if the ICTR were permitted to rely upon treaties to determine the contours of a particular prohibited conduct, it would still have to establish that the violation of that provision entails individual criminal responsibility under international law. And as noted above, at the time relevant to the Tribunal's jurisdiction, and insofar as Rwanda is concerned, there was no treaty applicable that provided for the criminalization of either war crimes or crimes against humanity. Secondly, where treaties regulating certain conduct do exist (as in the case of the Geneva Conventions of 1949), they might be so outdated in some respects that their application in the circumstances of contemporary conflicts would sometimes be all but impossible. In contrast, by relying upon customary international law, judges are able to take into consideration the gradual evolution of contemporary laws of armed conflict without departing from the politically potent legalism necessary to the legitimacy of the Tribunals.[25] Thirdly, treaties might exist in relation to some, but not all of the crimes provided for in the Statute of the ICTR, and where no treaty exists in relation to a particular crime, the Tribunal would generally have no choice but to rely on customary law. Thus, for instance, there is no convention relating to the definition and elements of crimes against humanity and the ICTR may turn nowhere other than custom for its definitions. Finally, applying customary international law at the ICTR would promote a degree of homogeneity in the jurisprudence of both *ad hoc* Tribunals in relation to the definitions of international crimes and would prevent the injustice that might result from two ICTR Trial Chambers which could apply different bodies of law (sometimes treaties, sometimes custom) to different accused who have been charged with the same crimes.

---

[23] *Čelebići* Appeal Judgment, par 170.   [24] *Bagilishema* Appeal Judgment, par 34.
[25] See T. Meron, 'The Continuing Role of Custom in the Formation of International Humanitarian Law', 90 American Journal of International Law (AJIL) 238, 247 (1996).

The fact that the law applied by the *ad hoc* Tribunals is more than mere statutory law gives their pronouncements particular authority and resonance outside of The Hague and Arusha courtrooms. And it may persuade other courts, not least the ICC, to regard their legal findings, if not as precedents, at least as important jurisprudential guideposts.[26]

---

[26] The existence and jurisprudence of the *ad hoc* Tribunals already appears to have had an essential de-inhibiting function with national courts by showing them that crimes such as genocide or crimes against humanity exist in law and that they can be sanctioned in courts. It is significant that a disproportionate number of cases recently taken on by domestic courts relating to international crimes (in countries such as Switzerland, Germany, Belgium, or France) are dealing with violations of humanitarian law which occurred in the very places for which *ad hoc* Tribunals have been set up (namely, the former Yugoslavia and Rwanda), rather than in relation to any of the many other places where such violations are occurring daily. It is also significant that, when doing so, domestic courts have relied so heavily, almost religiously, on the law developed by these two Tribunals. See, *inter alia*, in Switzerland, *Niyonteze*, Tribunal Militaire d'Appel 1A, judgment of 26 May 2000 (www.icrc.org/ ihl-nat.nsf); *Niyonteze*, Tribunal Militaire de Cassation, judgment of 27 April 2001 (www.icrc.org/ ihl-nat.nsf); *In re G.*, Tribunal Militaire de Division I, decision of 18 April 1997 (www. cicr.org/ ihl-nat). In Germany, see *Jorgić, Djajić, Sokolović* and *Kuslić* cases (for references and discussions of these cases, see K. Ambos and S. Wirth, 'Genocide and War Crimes in the Former Yugoslavia Before German Criminal Courts', in H. Fischer, C. Kress, and R. Lüder (eds.), *International and National Prosecution of Crimes under International Law: Current Developments* (Berlin: Berlin Verlag, 2001), pp 769 et seq.). In Belgium, see Cour d'Assise de l'arrondissement administrative de Bruxelles–Capitale (http://www.asf.be/AssisesRwanda2/fr/fr_VERDICT_verdict.htm).

3
Identifying Customary International Law and the Role of Judges in the Customary Process

Penetrating 'les ténèbres du droit coutumier'[1] and identifying customary rules in the field of international criminal law is a truly daunting task, particularly as most instances of state practice will occur 'in juridical outer space'[2] and out of judicial sight:[3]

When attempting to ascertain State practice with a view to establishing the existence of a customary rule or a general principle, it is difficult, if not impossible, to pinpoint the actual behaviour of the troops in the field for the purpose of establishing whether they in fact comply with, or disregard, certain standards of behaviour. This examination is rendered extremely difficult by the fact that not only is access to the theatre of military operations normally refused to independent observers (often even to the ICRC) but information on the actual conduct of hostilities is withheld by the parties to the conflict; what is worse, often recourse is had to misinformation with a view to misleading the enemy as well as public opinion and foreign Governments. In appraising the formation of customary rules or general principles one should therefore be aware that, on account of the inherent nature of this subject-matter, reliance must primarily be placed on such elements as official pronouncements of States, military manuals and judicial decisions.

Locating *opinio juris* will be no easier than identifying state practice. Even where the Tribunal is satisfied that a particular prohibition exists under customary international law, it must still establish that this prohibition applies to individuals (and not only to states), that the standard that it sets out is sufficiently foreseeable and accessible to meet the requirements of the principle of legality, and that the breach of that prohibition entails individual criminal responsibility under customary international law.[4]

---

[1] V. Pella, *La Guerre-Crime et les criminels de guerre: Réflexions sur la justice pénale internationale* (Neuchâtel: Editions de la Baconnière, 1949), p 82.
[2] D. Luban, *Legal Modernism* (Ann Arbor: University of Michigan Press, 1997), p 355.
[3] *Tadić* Jurisdiction Decision, par 99.
[4] In the jurisprudence of the Tribunals, *opinio juris* systematically plays the dominant role (see, e.g. *Kupreškić* Trial Judgment, par 527). State practice often operates more as a way of explaining or justifying the finding of the court that a norm is indeed customary, rather than for that practice to constitute the rule. Customary rules in international criminal law have therefore emerged even where

Because of the difficulties to establish those, and because international criminal law is still a body of law in need of legal precision, international criminal tribunals from Nuremberg to The Hague and Arusha, have had to give it substance and precision and have eased many meta-legal standards into proper legal prohibitions. Without judicial input, such legal standards, in and of themselves, would rarely have attained the degree of precision and certainty required from a legal norm to warrant more than a vain hope of compliance. In the history of international criminal law, international tribunals have done more than merely give jural *imprimatur* to norms in waiting and have been much more than mere 'evidential sources' of customary law. In effect, taking advantage of the plasticity and indeterminacy of customary law, international courts and tribunals, not least the *ad hoc* Tribunals, have often acted as 'customary midwives', 'des accoucheurs de normes coutumières', so that international criminal law may owe more to judges than any other part of international law.

Just as it is for judges of the *ad hoc* Tribunals to weigh the evidence of the facts relating to the alleged crimes when assessing the guilt or innocence of an accused, it is for them to evaluate the extent to which a rule may be said to exist under customary international law in light of existing state practice and *opinio juris*. As with the weighing of evidence, identifying customary international law is no exact science. And the finding that a norm does indeed form part of customary law must merely be the most reasonable conclusion based on the best available evidence of the existence or non-existence of that rule. The problem with custom is that the benchmark used to determine the rule's existence consists of a method, more than – as with evidential matters – a degree of mental certainty such as the 'beyond reasonable doubt' standard. It may therefore depend even more than evidential findings upon the individual judge's assessment of the sufficiency of the material before him or her. Judicial discretion in that regard is not, however, unfettered. First, the court may not ignore state practice (or *opinio juris*) if it exists. It must take those into account and weigh their significance. Secondly, the court must actively look for state practice (and *opinio juris*). And where it decides, for instance, to disregard existing state practice, it must explain why it considers it to be irrelevant. Thirdly, the court must carefully reason and explain its conclusion as to the customary or non-customary status of a norm, in the same way it is obliged to give reasons for all of its material conclusions.

state practice was rare and far from consistent. While the accepted rule is that the existence of a customary norm is established 'by induction based on the analysis of a sufficiently extensive and convincing state practice, and not by deduction based on preconceived ideas' as to what the law should be (Delimitation of the Maritime Boundary in the Gulf of Maine Area, Judgment, *ICJ Reports* 1984, par 111), in international criminal law, Tribunals have frequently turned the customary process on its head, stating the rule first and explaining subsequent state practice in its light. See, for example, *Furundžija* Trial Judgment, pars 162 and 253, in relation to the enlargement of the definition of torture under customary international humanitarian law; *Tadić* Appeal Judgment, pars 163–169, concerning the scope of the 'protected persons' status under the grave breaches regime of the Geneva Conventions.

A statement that a norm is customary is therefore only ever as good as the explanation referred to by the court in support of its finding to that effect. Regrettably, many a Chamber of the *ad hoc* Tribunals has been too ready to brand norms as customary, without giving any reason or citing any authority for that conclusion.[5] A reasoned opinion on this matter is a condition of the precedential value of the court's pronouncements and an element of the fair trial guarantee and the rationale of a judgment must therefore be 'clearly explained'.[6]

'We might wish the law were otherwise but we must administer it as we find it', a military court in Nuremberg since noted.[7] The truth is that the process of uncovering custom is not a purely logical and certainly not a neutral one. What judges find to be customary may be what they are willing or able to find in the practice of states and their *opinio juris* so that customary law has to a large extent been a matter of opinion, rather than one of existing state practice,[8] to a point where it sometimes seems that 'rules laid down by judges have generated custom, rather than custom generated the rules'.[9] Whether custom precedes its judicial acknowledgement or whether its jural quality depends on the court's recognition of it, the identification of a norm as customary has always been accompanied in the field of international criminal law, to some degree, by a judicial *coup de pouce*. Whereas international judges have traditionally shied away from normativism in relation to custom, in war crimes cases, they have tended to see their role within, rather than outside, the process of formation of custom.[10] Often the moral righteousness of

---

[5] So, at times, has the International Court of Justice. See, for instance, Case Concerning the Arrest Warrant of 11 April 2000 (Congo v. Belgium), 14 February 2002, ICJ General List No. 121 ('*Yerodia* case').

[6] *Kunarac* Appeal Judgment, par 42. The right to receive a reasoned opinion is also a recognized element of the fair trial guarantee (see, e.g. *Furundžija* Appeal Judgment, par 69).

[7] *United States v. von Leeb and others*, US Military Tribunal sitting at Nuremberg, Judgment of 28 October 1948, in *Law Reports of Trials of War Criminals*, XI ('*High Command* case'), p 563.

[8] See, for instance, *Prosecutor v. Simić*, IT-95-9-PT, Decision on the Prosecution Motion under Rule 73 for a Ruling concerning the Testimony of a Witness, 27 July 1999, in which one judge disagreed with the majority of the Trial Chamber concerning the customary status of the ICRC's privileges, in particular, in relation to the (non-)disclosure of evidence (Separate Opinion of Judge David Hunt on Prosecutor's Motion for a Ruling concerning the Testimony of a Witness). See also the disagreement between the majority of the Appeals Chamber in the *Erdemović* case and Judge Cassese on the customary status of the defence of 'duress' to murder where both camps reach opposite conclusions about the state of customary law on that point (*Erdemović* Appeal Judgment, pars 46–55 of the majority decision; Separate and Dissenting Opinion of Judge Cassese, pp 13–55). In his opinion, Judge Cassese held that the law on that point was not ambiguous and uncertain, contrary to the majority's view, and he also decried what he saw as the majority's recourse to a 'policy-directed choice tantamount to running foul of the customary principle *nullum crimen sine lege*' (p 52).

[9] J. C. Gray, *The Nature and Sources of the Law* (New York: Macmillan, 1931), p 297: 'It has often been assumed, almost as a matter of course, that legal customs preceded judicial decisions, and that the latter have but served to give expression to the former, but of this there appears to be little proof. It seems at least as probable that customs arose from judicial decisions.'

[10] See *Trials of War Criminals before the Nuremberg Military Tribunals under Control Council Law No. 10, United States v. Ohlendorf and others*, US Military Tribunal sitting at Nuremberg, Judgment of 10 April 1948, in *Law Reports of Trials of War Criminals*, IV ('*Einsatzgruppen* case'), pp 411, 499, concerning the recognition of crimes against humanity as pre-existing crimes under international law. See also *Judgment of the International Military Tribunal for the Trial of German Major War*

a norm has provided a ready justification for its judicial promotion into customary law.[11]

It is true, as one author has remarked, that 'every recognition of custom as evidence of law must have a beginning some time',[12] but the progress of customary international law in this field has at times taken place at the expense of some of the fundamental guarantees due to any accused person and the principle of legality might at times have failed to curb judicial creativity.[13] Arguably, this happened in Nuremberg when the International Military Tribunal concluded that aggression and crimes against humanity were recognized as discrete criminal offences under international law. Likewise, on a number of occasions, the *ad hoc* Tribunals have been willing to do more than merely *state* or identify customary law, by making sense of some of its contradictions and ordaining it in a more coherent and certainly more accessible fashion. Considering the general lack of precision of international criminal law, this may in fact be inevitable to ensure the efficacy of that body of law.

Some degree of law-making on the part of international courts and tribunals may be both necessary to bring precision to international law and, if exercised reasonably and with due regard for the principle of legality, may be acceptable. It could, however, have a number of serious implications if the *ad hoc* Tribunals used their discretion in that regard to do more than to guarantee the law's efficacy. First, the credibility and acceptability of international norms and standards depend to a large extent upon the readiness of states (and individuals) to comply with them and states will not easily do so in relation to norms or standards that ignore their position on a given issue and their practice in that regard. Secondly, international tribunals risk losing the trust that states have placed in them if they are seen to assume too much discretion when determining what the law is, regardless of what states consider it to be.[14] Thirdly, from the point of view of customary

---

Criminals, Nuremberg, 1946, Vol. 1 ('IMT Judgment'), pp 218–222, in relation to the crime of 'aggression'.

[11] See *Furundžija* Trial Judgment, pars 168–169, in relation to the process of criminalization of rape as an international offence. See also *Einsatzgruppen* case, p 497: 'Humanity is the sovereignty which has been offended and a tribunal is invoked to determine why. This [i.e. crimes against humanity] is not a new concept in the realm of morals, but it is an innovation in the empire of the law. Thus a lamp has been lighted in the dark and tenebrous atmosphere of the fields of the innocent dear. Murder, torture, enslavement, and similar crimes which heretofore were enjoined only by the respective nations now fall within the prescription of the family of nations. Thus murder becomes no less murder because directed against a whole race instead of a single person.' See also *Kupreškić* Trial Judgment, pars 515–529.

[12] S. Glueck, 'The Nuremberg Trial and Aggressive War', 59 *Harvard Law Review* 396, (1946) 416–418.

[13] For a discussion of the 'uncovering' crimes against humanity in Nuremberg, see IMT Judgment, pp 253 et seq. and, *inter alia*, J. Graven, 'Les Crimes contre l'humanité', 76 *Recueil des Cours de l'Académie de droit international de La Haye* 427 et seq., (1950), and R. S. Clark, 'Crimes against Humanity at Nuremberg', in G. Ginsburg and V. N. Kudriavtsev (eds.), *The Nuremberg Trial and International Law* (Martinus Nijhoff, Dordrecht 1990), pp 177 et seq.

[14] See B. Cheng, 'Custom: The Future of General State Practice in a Divided World', in R. Macdonald and D. Johnston (eds.), *The Structure and Process of International Law: Essays in Legal Philosophy Doctrine and Theory* (The Hague: M. Nijhoff, 1983), pp 513, 544: 'While those states

international law, judicial intrusion into the process of custom-making is conceptually somewhat awkward. Traditionally, the rule was indeed that only 'state' practice is relevant to the making of custom, and that the practice of legal entities other than states (and other than those whose acts could be attributed to a state) is, as a matter of principle, irrelevant to the making of custom. By expanding the scope of a norm of customary international law under the cover of its interpretation – for instance, when determining that an act is not only illegal but also criminal under customary international law – international courts challenge the exclusive power of states to make custom. Finally, and most importantly in this context, judicial creativity in the field of international criminal law is a direct challenge to the principle of legality. The perpetrator of an international crime need not know when committing a crime that he is breaching international law for him to be convicted for a breach of that body of law,[15] but 'the principle of legality requires that the crime charged be set out in a law that is accessible and that it be foreseeable that the conduct in question may be criminally sanctioned at the time when the crime was allegedly committed'.[16] Considering the difficulties encountered by Trial Chambers in defining some of the offences provided for in the Statutes, one wonders at times how those could be said to have been sufficiently foreseeable and accessible to the accused.

Surely, the principle of legality does not prevent a court from interpreting and clarifying the elements of a particular crime under customary law.[17] Once a criminal prohibition has been said to exist under customary international law, it is therefore not an objection to its application to a specific situation to say that that situation is new if it reasonably falls within the application of the principle.[18]

which accept the jurisdiction of the court are usually willing to recognize a great deal of discretion to the court and to abide by the court's exercise of that discretion, it is also clear that they will not do so for long unless the law as applied by the court corresponds, at least in its main features, with the law as laid down by themselves.'

[15] See *In re Artukovié*, District Court in Zagreb (Croatia), K–91/84–61 (14 May 1986), p 22: 'The perpetrator [of a war crime] does not have to be aware that he was breaking international law. The violation of international law in the description of these acts represents an objective condition of indictability, by which the character and the frame of illegality has been specifically determined in this criminal act in the sense that the act must be unlawful also according to international law' (translation on file with the author).

[16] *Hadžihasanović* Command Responsibility Appeal Decision, par 34 (footnotes omitted). See ibid.: 'As to foreseeability, the conduct in question is the concrete conduct of the accused; he must be able to appreciate that the conduct is criminal in the sense generally understood, without reference to any specific provision. As to accessibility, in the case of an international tribunal such as this, accessibility does not exclude reliance being placed on a law which is based on custom.'

[17] *Aleksovski* Appeal Judgment, pars 126–127; *Čelebići* Appeal Judgment, par 173.

[18] *Hadžihasanović* Command Responsibility Appeal Decision, par 12. See also Judge Shahabuddeen's Partial Dissenting Opinion in *Hadžihasanović* Command Responsibility Appeal Decision, par 9 ('There is no question of the Tribunal having power to change customary international law, which depends on State practice and *opinio juris*. If State practice and *opinio juris* have thrown up a relevant principle of customary international law, the solution turns on the principle. But that does not bar all forward movement: a principle may need to be interpreted before it is applied. This is illustrated by acceptance by the jurisprudence of the Tribunal that the Tribunal may clarify the elements of a crime. In the process of clarification, the Tribunal has the competence, which

The ICTY Appeals Chamber has cited with approval the holding of the European Court of Human Rights in *C.R v United Kingdom*, where it said that 'the progressive development of the criminal law through judicial law-making is a well entrenched and necessary part of legal tradition. Article 7 of the [European Convention of Human Rights] cannot be read as outlawing the gradual clarification of the rules of criminal liability through judicial interpretation from case to case, provided that the resultant development is consistent with the essence of the offence and could reasonably be foreseen.'[19] But too great a shift away from a practice-oriented sort of custom to a more specifically *humanitarian* interpretation of the customary process, as often practised in The Hague and Arusha, carries with it the risk of '[undermining] the certainty and clarity which sources of international law have to provide'.[20] In criminal trials, this risk is compounded by the fact that such a lack of certainty might seriously jeopardize the rights of the accused.

any court of law inevitably has, to interpret an established principle of law and to consider whether, as so interpreted, the principle applies to the particular situation before it. This is so because a court called upon to apply a principle proceeds on the basis of a finding, express or implied, that the principle has a certain meaning, however self-evident that meaning may be. In my view, customary international law in turn proceeds on the basis that, whenever a body is established on the international plane to exercise judicial power, that body corresponds to the central idea of a court as known to States generally; it therefore has competence to interpret a principle of law and to determine whether the particular situation before it falls within the principle as so interpreted. The competence is insep-arable from the judicial function; it does not invite to open horizons, but, within disciplined limits, it has to be exercised') and par 10 ('If [a given factual situation] is capable of being governed by the established principle, that principle must be held to prevail. In acting accordingly, the Appeals Chamber will not be changing customary international law but will be carrying out its true intent by interpreting and applying one of its existing principles', footnotes omitted).

   [19] *Ojdanić* Joint Criminal Enterprise Decision, n 93, p 15 and *C. R. v. United Kingdom*, Judgment, 22 November 1995, Series A 335-C (1995), par 34.

   [20] *S v. Petane*, Cape Provincial Division, 3 November 1987, (1988) 3 South African Law Reports 51, reprinted in M. Sassòli and A. Bouvier, *How Does Law Protect in War? Cases, Documents and Teaching Materials on Contemporary Practice in International Humanitarian Law* (ICRC: Geneva, 1999), pp 959, 963 (a summary in English of this decision may be found at http://www.icrc.org/ihl-nat.nsf/0/50c59239e1b869edc1256b0500490120?OpenDocument).

4

Binding Precedents and Internal Jurisprudential Hierarchy

In ten years, the law of the Tribunals has moved forth with leaps and bounds, pushed forward as it were by enthusiastic judges. To bring some order into a chaotic development which had started to cloud the readability of the Tribunals' jurisprudence and risked descending into complete judicial anarchy, the judges have clarified the jurisprudential hierarchy that prevails within the Tribunals and specified the extent to which decisions of a Chamber may be said to be binding upon another.

Although the Appeals Chamber is not legally bound to follow its own decisions, it has recognized that the need for certainty, stability, and predictability in criminal law required that it should follow them in principle, but that it could depart from them 'for cogent reasons in the interests of justice'.[1] The Appeals Chamber will, therefore, in principle follow the *ratio decidendi* of its own previous decisions and will only exceptionally depart from those 'after the most careful consideration has been given to it, both as to the law, including the authorities cited, and the facts'.[2] By contrast, the *ratio decidendi* of decisions and judgments of the Appeals Chambers is binding on Trial Chambers of their respective Tribunal.[3] Finally, decisions of Trial Chambers have no binding force on each other, although a Trial Chamber may follow the decision of another Trial Chamber if it finds that decision to be persuasive.[4]

[1] *Aleksovski* Appeal Judgment, pars 97, 101, and 107. See also ibid., par 108: 'Instances of situations where cogent reasons in the interests of justice require a departure from a previous decision include cases where the previous decision has been decided on the basis of a wrong legal principle or cases where a previous decision has been given *per incuriam*, that is a judicial decision that has been "wrongly decided, usually because the judge or judges were ill-informed about the applicable law".'

[2] See *Aleksovski* Appeal Judgment, par 109. See also ibid., par 110: 'What is followed in previous decisions is the legal principle (*ratio decidendi*), and the obligation to follow that principle only applies in similar cases, or substantially similar cases. [. . .] There is no obligation to follow previous decisions which may be distinguished for one reason or another from the case before the court.'

[3] See ibid., par 113: 'The need for coherence is particularly acute in the context in which the Tribunal operates, where the norms of international humanitarian law and international criminal law are developing, and where, therefore, the need for those appearing before the Tribunal, the accused and the Prosecution, to be certain of the regime in which cases are tried is even more pronounced.' On the other hand, decisions of the ICTY Appeals Chamber are not legally binding on ICTR Chambers, nor are ICTR appeals decisions binding on ICTY Chambers, although they have had great persuasive force.   [4] Ibid., par 114.

Judgments and decisions of the Tribunals are now in the hundreds and with the crystallization of the law of the Tribunals and with the pressure of time heavy on the Chambers, the almost artisanal and academic approach of some early judgments where the court would go a long way seeking to explain its decisions and to provide external authority for its legal findings and, occasionally, to express views on matters not actually before the Chamber in the relevant case (see, e.g., *Tadić* Trial Judgment, *Čelebići* Trial Judgment, *Furundžija* Trial Judgment, or *Akayesu* Trial Judgment), have been replaced by a more mechanical, almost autarchic, approach to the law of the Tribunal. With some exceptions, the more recent jurisprudence of the Tribunals does not seek to question findings of law made in previous judgments and decisions (even where these earlier judgments and decisions are not binding upon them), preferring instead to adopt them as authority. There is a risk that a Chamber may thereby be adopting and perpetuating a rule that has no or very weak foundations under international law. It remains the case, therefore, that 'it is every Chamber's duty to ascertain that a crime or a form of liability charged in the indictment is both provided for under the Statute and that it existed at the relevant time under customary international law'.[5]

---

[5] *Ojdanić* Joint Criminal Enterprise Decision, par 16.

PART II

SERIOUS VIOLATIONS OF THE LAWS OR CUSTOMS OF WAR: 'WAR CRIMES'

5

War Crimes in the Statutes of the
ad hoc Tribunals

Wars have traditionally been unique opportunities for all sorts of egregious criminal conducts as they foster an environment in which 'the powerful do what they will, and the poor suffer what they must'.[1] Whilst fear and blind hatred for the enemy give some appearance of legitimacy to the use of force as a tool of self-preservation, the relevancy of the law as a traditional inhibitor of criminal conduct appears to diminish with every instance of abuse and atrocities. The laws and customs of war are an attempt to recast the use of indiscriminate violence at war in its true aberrational character, by creating a sufficiently potent disincentive upon that 'perpetual temptation to behave badly' at war.[2] The extent to which the laws of war will be successful in doing so in practice depends not only on the standards set by those rules, but primarily on the consequences that an infringement is likely to trigger for the perpetrator.

The creation of the *ad hoc* Tribunals is an important advance in both respects insofar as their Statutes recognise minimum standards of conduct at war which, if breached, attract penal sanctions and also set up a judicial mechanism whereby those standards may be enforced and the guilty punished. The recognition in the Tribunals' Statutes that certain serious violations of the laws of war entail individual criminal responsibility, and the provision of a clear enforcement mechanism for the trial and punishment of those crimes, gives new potency to the standards. The fact that the United Nations Tribunals were given jurisdiction over various categories of serious violations of the laws or customs of war gives meaning to the idea that such violations as well as their punishment are matters of universal interest and concern.

---

[1] Quote attributed to Mr Arria, Ambassador of Venezuela, during the discussion leading up to the adoption Security Council Resolution 780 (1992), 6 October 1992, S/RES/780 (1992), reprinted in V. Morris and M. Scharf, *An Insider's Guide to the International Criminal Tribunal for the Former Yugoslavia*, vol. 2 (Ardsley: Transnational Publishers, 1995) ('Morris and Scharf, *The Yugoslav Tribunal*') pp 147, 149.
[2] J. Keegan, *War and our World: The Reith Lectures 1998* (London: Pimlico, 1999), p 50.

'War crimes', as serious violations of the laws or customs of war are commonly known, are sometimes understood as involving a different, intrinsically less serious, often unplanned, sort of criminality than either crimes against humanity or genocide. In many ways, war crimes are regarded as the almost inevitable criminal consequence of any armed conflict. A war crime, in its technical, legalistic, sense is, however, both more restricted and more complex than this popular perception would have it. A war crime, for the purpose of the *ad hoc* Tribunals, consists in a serious violation of the laws or customs of war entailing individual criminal responsibility. Within that general framework, the Statutes of the *ad hoc* Tribunals contain a list of war crimes over which the Tribunals may in principle exercise their jurisdictions. Whereas the subject-matter jurisdiction of both *ad hoc* Tribunals is almost identical in relation to crimes against humanity and genocide, their respective jurisdictional framework has been cast quite differently in relation to war crimes.

5.1   War crimes in the Statute of the ICTY

The ICTY Statute contains two articles – Article 2 and Article 3 – which deal specifically with war crimes: Article 2 is concerned solely with a specific category of war crimes, namely, 'grave breaches of the Geneva Conventions of 1949', whilst Article 3 covers other serious violations of the laws or customs of war:

Article 2

Grave breaches of the Geneva Conventions of 1949

The International Tribunal shall have the power to prosecute persons committing or ordering to be committed grave breaches of the Geneva Conventions of 12 August 1949, namely the following acts against persons or property protected under the provisions of the relevant Geneva Convention:

  (a) wilful killing;
  (b) torture or inhuman treatment, including biological experiments;
  (c) wilfully causing great suffering or serious injury to body or health;
  (d) extensive destruction and appropriation of property, not justified by military necessity and carried out unlawfully and wantonly;
  (e) compelling a prisoner of war or a civilian to serve in the forces of a hostile power;
  (f) wilfully depriving a prisoner of war or a civilian of the rights of fair and regular trial;
  (g) unlawful deportation or transfer or unlawful confinement of a civilian;
  (h) taking civilians as hostages.

Article 3

Violations of the laws or customs of war

The International Tribunal shall have the power to prosecute persons violating the laws or customs of war. Such violations shall include, but not be limited to:

  (a) employment of poisonous weapons or other weapons calculated to cause unnecessary suffering;

(b) wanton destruction of cities, towns or villages, or devastation not justified by military necessity;

(c) attack, or bombardment, by whatever means, of undefended towns, villages, dwellings, or buildings;

(d) seizure of, destruction or wilful damage done to institutions dedicated to religion, charity and education, the arts and sciences, historic monuments and works of art and science;

(e) plunder of public or private property.

The jurisprudence of the Tribunal has established a clear 'division of labour'[3] between Articles 2 and 3 of the ICTY Statute: Article 2 is only concerned with those acts and omissions which may be said to constitute 'grave breaches' of the Geneva Conventions. Article 3 of the Statute has been said to constitute a general and residual clause covering all serious violations of international humanitarian law not covered by the other articles of the Statute,[4] in particular those which do not fall within Article 2 of the Statute ('lest [Article 2] should become superfluous').[5] That, in turn, means that whenever an accused person is being charged cumulatively under both articles of the Statute in relation to the same conduct, and if the conditions and requirements of Article 2 are met, he or she may not additionally be found guilty under Article 3 of the Statute.[6] The list of offences enumerated in Article 3 are, as the language makes clear, illustrative and not exhaustive,[7] and it may cover other serious violations of international humanitarian law not explicitly listed in the Statute, provided they are recognized by customary law and do entail individual criminal responsibility in case of breach.[8]

According to the Appeals Chamber, the role and function of Article 3 of the ICTY Statute is to fill those gaps which the legislator, the Security Council, may have left in the text of the Statute, but which were intended to come within its terms:[9] 'Article 3 functions as a residual clause designed to ensure that no serious violation of international humanitarian law is taken away from the jurisdiction of the International Tribunal. Article 3 aims to make such jurisdiction watertight and inescapable.'

When interpreted in such a way, the Appeals Chamber concluded, Article 3 fully realizes the primary purpose of the establishment of the International

---

[3] *Čelebići* Appeal Judgment, par 137, by reference to *Čelebići* Trial Judgment, par 297.

[4] See, *inter alia*, *Tadić* Jurisdiction Decision, par 89–91; and *Kordić and Čerkez* Articles 2 and 3 Jurisdiction Decision, pars 17–23; *Čelebići* Appeal Judgment, para 125; *Kunarac* Appeal Judgment, par 68; *Tadić* Trial Judgment, par 559; *Blaškić* Trial Judgment, par 168; *Jelišić* Trial Judgment, par 33.

[5] *Tadić* Jurisdiction Decision, par 87.

[6] See below, chapter 23. See also 'Article 2 is more specific than common Article 3' (*Čelebići* Appeal Judgment, par 420).   [7] *Tadić* Jursidiction Decision, par 87.

[8] *Prosecutor v. Kvočka et al.*, IT-98–30/1-PT, Decision on Preliminary Motions Filed by Mlado Radić, and Miroslav Kvočka Challenging Jurisdiction, 1 April 1999, par 23.

[9] *Tadić* Jurisdiction Decision, par 91.

Tribunal 'not [to] leave unpunished any person guilty of any such serious violation, whatever the context within which it may have been committed'.[10]

In practice, Article 3 of the ICTY Statute has been interpreted to criminalize several categories of war crimes: (i) serious violations of the Hague law applicable in international conflicts and/or internal conflicts; (ii) serious infringements of provisions of the Geneva Conventions other than those classified as 'grave breaches' by those Conventions; (iii) serious violations of common Article 3 of the Geneva Conventions and other customary rules applicable to internal conflicts; and (iv) serious violations of certain provisions of Additional Protocols I and II to the Geneva Conventions.[11] Also, grave breaches of Additional Protocol I have been held to fall under Article 3 of the ICTY Statute, rather than under Article 2.[12]

Articles 2 and 3 of the ICTY Statute are not, despite their areas of overlap, purely interchangeable provisions, whereby the latter only becomes relevant whenever the former is not. Whereas Article 2 of the Statute may only apply in the context of an *international* armed conflict (or in the case of a state of occupation), Article 3 applies to 'crimes perpetrated in the course of both inter-state wars and internal strife'.[13] Furthermore, Article 2 only applies to 'protected persons' and 'protected properties' (see below) and is limited to grave breaches of 1949 Geneva Conventions. By contrast, Article 3 protects a broader group of individuals and interests. In particular, and as noted above, it encompasses violations of both Hague as well as of Geneva law,[14] including violations of common Article 3, and other serious violations of international humanitarian law.[15]

---

[10] *Tadić* Jurisdiction Decision, par 92.

[11] Ibid., par 89; confirmed in *Čelebići* Appeal Judgment, pars 125 and 136. See also, for instance, *Kunarac* Trial Judgment, par 401; *Kordić and Čerkez* Articles 2 and 3 Jurisdiction Decision, par 22.

[12] See *Martić* Rule 61 Decision, par 8. Proceedings undertaken under Rule 61 of the Rules of Procedure and Evidence serve as a mechanism by which the International Tribunal may react to the failure of the accused to appear voluntarily and to the failure to execute the warrants issued against them. It permits the charges in the indictment and the supporting material to be publicly exposed and allows the victims to use this forum to have their voices heard. Rule 61 proceedings are not a trial *in absentia*, as they involve no finding of guilt and no verdict, and they do not deprive the accused of his right to contest the charges against him. Given the absence of the accused, the 'jurisprudence' which came out of such proceedings is to be taken with caution, and it is exceptional that it is ever cited by any Chamber of either *ad hoc* Tribunal as precedent.

[13] Report of the International Tribunal for the Prosecution of Persons Responsible for Serious Violations of International Humanitarian Law in the Territory of the Former Yugoslavia Since 1991, First Annual Report, UN Doc. A/49/342, S/1994/1007 (29 August 1994), p 19.

[14] *Čelebići* Appeal Judgment, pars 126–127, 132–133. See also *Tadić* Jurisdiction Decision, pars 87–88. Statements by members of the United Nations Security Council certainly support that interpretation (for references see *Tadić* Jurisdiction Decision, par 88). See Report of the Secretary-General pursuant to Para. 2 of Security Council Resolution 808 (1993), UN Doc. S/25704 (3 May 1993) ('UN Doc. S/25704'), pars 43–44.

[15] *Čelebići* Appeal Judgment, par 134; *Kunarac* Appeal Judgment, par 68.

5.2 War crimes in the Statute of the ICTR

The regulation of war crimes as provided in the Statute of the Rwanda Tribunal differs markedly from the regime set out above. Article 4 of the ICTR Statute provides as follows:

Article 4
Violations of Article 3 Common to the Geneva Conventions and of Additional Protocol II

The International Tribunal for Rwanda shall have the power to prosecute persons committing or ordering to be committed serious violations of Article 3 common to the Geneva Conventions of 12 August 1949 for the Protection of War Victims, and of Additional Protocol II thereto of 8 June 1977. These violations shall include, but shall not be limited to:

(a) Violence to life, health and physical or mental well-being of persons, in particular murder as well as cruel treatment such as torture, mutilation or any form of corporal punishment;

(b) Collective punishments;

(c) Taking of hostages;

(d) Acts of terrorism;

(e) Outrages upon personal dignity, in particular humiliating and degrading treatment, rape, enforced prostitution and any form of indecent assault;

(f) Pillage;

(g) The passing of sentences and the carrying out of executions without previous judgment pronounced by a regularly constituted court, affording all the judicial guarantees which are recognized as indispensable by civilized peoples;

(h) Threats to commit any of the foregoing acts.

The scope of the ICTR's subject-matter jurisdiction in relation to war crimes is narrower than that of the ICTY in at least two respects. First, it is limited, from a substantive point of view, to serious violations of common Article 3 of the Geneva Conventions and serious violations of Additional Protocol II. The more limited jurisdictional reach of the ICTR in relation to war crimes reflects the view that, for the purpose of the Rwanda Tribunal, the armed conflict that took place in Rwanda at the time should be regarded as an 'internal' one.[16] The list of war crimes within its jurisdiction *ratione materiae* was tailored accordingly, limiting them to those which constitute serious infringements of rules and provisions applying in the context of internal armed conflicts.

As a result, certain conduct which may be regarded as criminal under the ICTY Statute would fall outside of the jurisdiction of the ICTR, including conduct that

---

[16] See Secretary-General Report (ICTR), par 11.

would constitute a grave breach of the Geneva Conventions (Article 2 of the ICTY Statute), unless they also consitute a serious violation of common Article 3 or Additional Protocol II. Secondly, the Statute of the ICTR does not appear to cover any violations of Hague law, except for those Hague rules which have made their way into Additional Protocol II. As pointed out above, and by contrast, Article 3 of the ICTY Statute extends the jurisdiction of the ICTY to a number of serious violations of both Geneva and Hague law.

On the other hand, the jurisdictional scope of the ICTR in relation to war crimes is broader than that of the ICTY in at least one, though minor, respect: Article 4(h) of the ICTR Statute provides for the criminalization of 'threats' to commit any of the listed offences, whereas the ICTY Statute does not do so (at least not explicitly). Perhaps unsurprisingly, given the volume of crimes *actually* committed during events in Rwanda and the large number of potential accused, the possibility to charge an accused with a mere threat to commit such a crime has not yet been used by the ICTR prosecutor and may in fact never be.

The narrower jurisdictional focus of the Rwanda Tribunal in relation to war crimes appears not only to be the result of the different nature of the armed conflict in Rwanda as opposed to the former Yugoslavia, but also to be a reflection of the fact that the criminal activity in each context revolved around different cores: an attempt to exterminate a whole group in the case of Rwanda and a violent ethnic partition of a country in the Yugoslav context. In turn, the relevancy of war crimes as a criminal idiom capable of labelling the sort of crimes committed in Rwanda appears much less potent than it may be in the Yugoslav context.[17]

As is clear from the text of the Statute of the ICTY, the list of war crimes over which the Tribunal may exercise jurisdiction is not exhaustive and the ICTY has in fact exercised jurisdiction over a number of serious violations of the laws of war which are not expressly mentioned in their Statutes where those violations satisfied a number of substantive and jurisdictional requirements set by the court. The ICTR, by contrast, would appear to have limited the scope of its war crimes jurisdiction to those expressly provided in the statute.

---

[17] It is quite significant in that respect to note that, until the Judgment of the Appeals Chamber in *Rutaganda* (26 May 2003), not a single accused had been found guilty of war crimes at the ICTR. Equally revealing, perhaps, is the fact that this first conviction for war crimes at the ICTR was imposed, not by any Arusha-based Trial Chamber, but by the Hague-based Appeals Chamber.

6

Chapeau Elements of War Crimes

6.1   General remarks

The laws or customs of war may be defined generally as the 'rules of international law with which belligerents have customarily, or by special conventions, agreed to comply in case of war'.[1] The content of that body of rules is not static, 'but by continual adaptation follows the needs of a changing world',[2] so that the determination of what may constitute a war crime (or a serious violation of the laws or customs of war) will depend on the state of the laws of war at the time when that determination is made.[3]

A 'war crime' may in turn be defined as a serious violation of the laws or customs of war which entails individual criminal responsibility under international law.[4]

---

[1] *History of the United Nations War Crimes Commission and the Development of the Laws of War*, compiled by the United Nations War Crimes Commission (London: His Majesty's Stationery Office, 1948) ('*UN War Crimes Commission*'), p 24. In *ex parte Quirin*, the law of war was said to include 'that part of the law of nations which prescribes for the conduct of war the status, rights and duties of enemy nations and of enemy individuals' (*Ex parte Quirin*, US Supreme Court, Judgment of 31 July 1942, 317 U.S.1, 27–28 (also in 17 AILC, 457–485 and 63 S.Ct 87 L.Ed.3 (1942)).

[2] IMT Judgment, p 221.

[3] *Kunarac* Appeal Judgment, par 67. See also Memorandum of the Secretary-General, 'The Charter and Judgment of the Nürnberg Tribunal, History and Analysis', UN Doc. A/CN.4/5 (3 March 1949) ('UN Doc. A/CN.4/5'), p 62.

[4] In 1942, Professor Lauterpacht as representative of the Commission for Penal Reconstruction and Development, defined war crimes as follows: 'War crimes may properly be defined as such offences against the law of war as are criminal in the ordinary and accepted sense of fundamental rules of warfare and of general principles of criminal law by reason of their heinousness, their brutality, their ruthless disregard of the sanctity of human life and personality, or their wanton interference with rights of

From the point of view of the *ad hoc* Tribunals, however, only those war crimes that are stipulated in the Statute (expressly or implicitly) may be prosecuted.

Furthermore, in order to prosecute those crimes successfully under the Statute, the Prosecution must establish in relation to each one of them, that at the time when these acts were committed there existed a state of armed conflict in the relevant area and that the acts of the accused were sufficiently connected to that conflict (sometimes referred to as the 'general' or 'preliminary' conditions) and that the offence allegedly committed constituted a serious infringement of a rule of international humanitarian law that entailed his or her individual criminal responsibility under international law at that time ('Other jurisdictional requirements').

6.2   Existence of an armed conflict and nexus therewith

Whereas crimes against humanity and genocide may in theory be committed in time of war as well as in peacetime, war crimes are intimately attached to a state of armed conflict so that in the absence of an armed conflict and a sufficient nexus between the acts of the accused and that conflict, no war crime is possible.[5] To prove that a war crime, pursuant to the Tribunal's Statute, has been committed in a particular case, whether committed in an internal or an international armed conflict, the Prosecution must first establish that: (i) there must have been an armed conflict at the time when and at the place where the alleged crimes were committed, and (ii) there must be a sufficient nexus between the acts of the accused and the armed conflict.[6]

6.2.1   Existence of an armed conflict

Existence of an armed conflict: micro- and macro-approach

While the first general requirement for prosecution of a war crime that there must be an armed conflict at the relevant time is clear, neither the Geneva Conventions,

property unrelated to reasonably conceived requirements of military necessity.' (See L. Radzinowicz and J. W. Cecil Turner (eds.), *International Commission for Penal Reconstruction and Development*, Proceedings of the Conference held in Cambridge on 14 November 1941 between the representatives of nine allied countries and of the Department of Criminal Science of the University of Cambridge, cited in *UN War Crimes Commission*, p 95. A Trial Chamber of the ICTY defined 'war crimes' in general terms as 'covering violations of customary norms of humanitarian law entailing individual criminal responsibility. It encompasses both grave breaches of the Geneva Conventions and [other] violations of the laws and customs of war' (*Kordić and Čerkez* Articles 2 and 3 Jurisdiction Decision, par 22).

[5] In the *Farben* case, the court acquitted the accused upon count two of the indictment (spoilation as a war crime) insofar as Austria and the Sudetenland were concerned as, the court found, no state of war existed at the relevant time and therefore the laws of war were inapplicable (*United States v. Krauch and others*, US Military Tribunal sitting at Nuremberg, Judgment of 29 July 1948, in *Law Reports of Trials of War Criminals*, VIII ('the *Farben* case'), pp 1096–1102).

[6] *Kunarac* Trial Judgment, par 402; *Naletilić and Martinović* Trial Judgment, par 225 and references cited therein (see in particular *Naletilić and Martinović* Trial Judgment, n 596).

nor the Additional Protocols, provide for a definition of what may be said to constitute an 'armed conflict'. The *Commentary* of the International Committee of the Red Cross rather unhelpfully suggests that 'any difference between two States and leading to the intervention of members of the armed forces is an armed conflict'.[7]

When establishing the Yugoslav Tribunal, the Security Council could have decided, as had been suggested by the United States,[8] to determine that, for the purpose of this Tribunal, an armed conflict existed (in the whole or in part of the territory under consideration) and to establish what the nature of that armed conflict was (an international one or an internal one).[9] Instead, the Security Council left this matter to be determined by the Tribunal itself.[10]

When the issue first arose before the ICTY in the *Tadić* case, the judges were also faced with a choice between two alternatives: should it consider the armed conflict that took place in the former Yugoslavia as a whole (that is, in the whole of the territory of the former Yugoslavia, or possibly, the whole of Bosnia and Herzegovina[11]) and declare it to be either internal or international in character or should it, instead, consider separately the various circumscribed geographical areas to which each and every indictment related? In *Tadić*, the indictment alleged that an armed conflict existed in the territory of Bosnia and Herzegovina between about 23 May 1992 and about 31 December 1992.[12] On that basis, the Trial Chamber (and later the Appeals Chamber) could have opted for a general finding as to the internal or international nature of the armed conflict in Bosnia and Herzegovina as a whole during the relevant period of time, thereby deciding the matter for the

---

[7] ICRC, *Commentary to Geneva Convention IV* (art. 2(1)), p 20.

[8] During the negotiation of the ICTY Statute, the United States had suggested that the matter should be legislated by the Security Council and that it should be concluded that the conflict in the former Yugoslavia was, after 25 June 1991 (proclamation of independence by Croatia and Slovenia), an international armed conflict (UN Doc. S/25575, 6, in Morris and Scharf, *The Yugoslav Tribunal*, vol. 1, p 58).

[9] This was very much the logic followed by the Military Tribunal in Lausanne (Switzerland) in the *G.* case, in which the court held that the armed conflict in the former Yugoslavia had to be assessed as a whole and had to be regarded as international in character (*Grabez Goran*, Switzerland, Tribunal Militaire de Division I, Decision of 18 April 1997, in www.icrc.org/ihl-nat).

[10] *Čelebići* Appeal Judgment, par 135: 'the Security Council in adopting the Statute was of the view that the question of the nature of the conflict should be judicially determined by the Tribunal itself, the issue involving factual and legal questions'. The Appeals Chamber noted the Security Council's 'indifference to the nature of the underlying conflicts' (*Tadić* Jurisdiction Decision, par 78) whilst the Secretary-General said that the Security Council 'clearly intended to convey the notion that no Judgment as to the international or internal character of the conflict [had been] exercised' (UN Doc. S/25704, par 62). See also, *Tadić* Jurisdiction Decision, pars 75–76. The Appeals Chamber said that 'the Security Council purposely refrained from classifying the armed conflicts in the former Yugoslavia as either international or internal and, in particular, did not intend to bind the International Tribunal by a classification of the conflicts as international' (ibid., par 76). The Commission of Experts in its Final Report was also of the view that such a task was better left to the Tribunal (Final Report of the Commission of Experts for the former Yugoslavia, par 43). See also Morris and Scharf, *The Yugoslav Tribunal*, pp 55 et seq.

[11] Insofar as Rwanda is concerned it was established once and for all by the Security Council that the conflict was, for the purpose of the Tribunal, of an internal character.

[12] *Prosecutor v. Tadić*, IT-94-1-I, Second Amended Indictment, 14 December 1995, pars 3.1–3.5.

Tribunal once and for all. Instead, the Appeals Chamber held that the armed conflict in the former Yugoslavia in fact consisted of several geographically more limited 'armed conflicts' which were of a mixed character, internal in some respects, and international in some others (depending on both time and place).[13]

Putting aside the merit of the Appeals Chamber's finding, there are both benefits and disadvantages to its ruling. The prime benefit is that, had it decided that the armed conflict in Bosnia should be considered as a whole, it would probably have concluded that the conflict was international in character due to the involvement of several sovereign states. This, in turn, would have precluded any developments in the law of internal armed conflict, which has turned out to be one of the most fundamental contributions of the *ad hoc* Tribunals to the field of humanitarian law. Furthermore, the narrow focus, or case-by-case approach adopted by the Appeals Chamber, has allowed each Trial Chamber (and the parties in each case before the Tribunal) to limit the scope of relevant evidentiary considerations to the material *directly* pertinent to the case at hand, without having to review evidence not remotely related to the charges.

Such a piecemeal approach to the Yugoslav conflict may, however, blur the reality and historical pertinence of interactions between various events which occurred across the territory of the former Yugoslavia since 1991. Also, had the Appeals Chamber decided once and for all that the armed conflict in the former Yugoslavia (or Bosnia) was an international one, it could have saved the Tribunal many courtroom hours spent on establishing the nature of the armed conflict in relation to each and every case before the Tribunal. It would also have allowed the court to apply a single body of law to all accused appearing before the Tribunal and to assess the criminality of their actions in relation to that one body only, rather than the two regimes now being applied at the Tribunal.[14] The approach of the Appeals Chamber also entails a risk of contradiction between various Chambers as to the nature of a particular conflict occurring in a specific region, depending on the geographical and temporal scope of their considerations, and depending also on

---

[13] *Tadić* Jurisdiction Decision, par 77: 'the conflicts in the former Yugoslavia have both internal and international aspects' (not the use of the plural). The Appeals Chamber is in conformity with the Security Council's intention as the Security Council 'well knew, in 1993, when the Statute was drafted, the conflicts in the former Yugoslavia could have been characterized as both internal and international, or alternatively, as an internal conflict alongside an international one, or as an internal conflict that had become internationalized because of external support, or as an international conflict that had subsequently been replaced by one or more internal conflicts, or some combination thereof' (ibid., par 72). See also ibid., par 74, which lays down a number of statements made by the Security Council supporting the Appeals Chamber's interpretation.

[14] In its Final Report, the Commission of Experts for the former Yugoslavia noted the difficulty of applying different bodies of law to the different armed conflicts in the former Yugoslavia and opted, for its own purpose, to apply one single body of rules to the whole of the conflict: 'the character and complexity of the armed conflicts concerned, combined with the web of agreements on humanitarian law that the parties have concluded among themselves, justifies the Commission's approach in applying the law applicable in international armed conflicts to the entirety of the armed conflicts in the territory of the former Yugoslavia' (Final Report of the Commission of Experts for the former Yugoslavia, par 44).

the evidence presented by the parties in the case in which they make their finding.[15] There is also a risk that, by focusing the court's attention upon too narrow a geographical and temporal framework, the court would be denied a full understanding of the events which form the background to the indictment or even of the acts and conduct of the accused.[16]

The break-up of the former Yugoslavia may therefore be subdivided, for the purpose of establishing the existence of an armed conflict and the character thereof, not only geographically, that is, with distinct armed conflicts taking place in discrete geographical spheres of the territory of the former Yugoslavia, but also temporally, so that the various armed conflicts which might have taken place within that territory may not be regarded as necessarily continuous in nature, but rather as events susceptible of change of nature over time, from internal to international or the other way round.[17] As a result, the extent of the application of international humanitarian law from one place to another on the territory of the former Yugoslavia (and from one time to another) will depend upon the particular character of the conflict with which the relevant indictment is concerned.[18]

A different approach was adopted in relation to the ICTR. 'Given the nature of the conflict [in Rwanda] as non-international in character', the Secreatary-General explained, 'the [Security] Council incorporated within the subject-matter jurisdiction of the Tribunal violations of international humanitarian law which may either be committed in both international and internal armed conflicts, such as the crime of genocide and crimes against humanity, *or may be committed only in internal armed conflict*, such as violations of article 3 common to the four Geneva Conventions, as more fully elaborated in article 4 of Additional Protocol II.'[19] Thus, for the purpose of the ICTR, it was decided from the outset that the armed conflict in Rwanda should be regarded as an internal one and that only certain categories of violations of the laws and customs of war which apply in such context (namely, serious violations of common article 3 and Additional protocol II) shall be within the Court's jurisdiction.

The definition of an 'armed conflict', international and internal

According to the Appeals Chamber, an 'armed conflict' may be said to exist 'when-ever there is a resort to armed force between States or protracted armed violence

---

[15] In order to avoid such risk, Trial Chambers could, for instance, consider the nature of the armed conflict taking place in a given geographical area as an adjudicated fact thereby avoiding contradictory factual findings in relation to the same events.

[16] A Chamber is not, however, bound to limit the scope of its consideration to the immediate area around the place where the crimes are said to have been committed and it may decide, as far as evidence permits, to look beyond those confines where, for instance, events which occurred in a different area are considered to be relevant by the court to the crimes charged against the accused. See, e.g. in *Tadić* Trial Judgment, par 566. In practice, few Chambers appear to have looked beyond the confines of the framework set for them by the prosecution in its indictments.

[17] See, e.g. *Tadić* Jurisdiction Decision, pars 84 and 137; *Aleksovski* Appeal Judgment, pars 122 et seq.; *Čelebići* Appeal Judgment, par 26; *Blaškić* Trial Judgment, par 75.

[18] *Tadić* Trial Judgment, par 571.

[19] Secretary-General Report (ICTR), par 11 (emphasis added).

between governmental authorities and organized armed groups or between such groups within a State'.[20]

The above definition distinguishes between *international* armed conflicts on the one hand (those that occur 'between States') and *internal* armed conflicts on the other ('protracted armed violence between governmental authorities and organized armed groups or between such groups within a State'). Although the laws applying in each context overlap a great deal, it is a fact that certain conducts will be regarded as prohibited in one context but not necessarily in the other.[21]

Such a scenario, however, has become the exception as the jurisprudence of the *ad hoc* Tribunals has witnessed (and has promoted) a systematic rapprochement between the law applying to international armed conflicts and that applying to internal ones, and most of the conducts that are regarded as criminal in one regime are now also generally regarded as criminal in the other context.[22] The Appeals Chamber of the ICTY has explained that the traditional distinction in international law between its response to instances of belligerency on the one hand and insurgency on the other, and a move from a sovereignty-oriented focus to a 'human-being oriented approach' of humanitarian law,[23] had slowly eroded the distinctions which traditionally existed between the two regimes so 'that in the area of armed conflict the distinction between interstate wars and civil wars is losing its value'.[24] Eventually, it is likely (and desirable) that all differences between the rules and regulations applicable to international and internal armed conflicts might disappear altogether, as it seems illogical that an act should be regarded as criminal in one context, but not another, or that a victim should be protected in one type of armed conflict but not in another. For the time being,

[20] *Tadić* Jurisdiction Decision, par 70; *Kunarac* Appeal Judgment, par 56.

[21] It seems quite clear that what is prohibited in internal armed conflicts is necessarily also prohibited in international armed conflicts (see also *Čelebići* Appeal Judgment, par 150: 'Something which is prohibited in internal conflicts is necessarily outlawed in an international conflict where the scope of the rule is broader'). The reverse is not necessarily true, however. For instance, one may raise the question as to whether 'unlawful attacks on civilian objects' as understood under Article 52 of Additional Protocol I (with no equivalent in Additional Protocol II), although probably a crime in the context of an international armed conflict, would also be regarded as criminal if committed in the context of an internal armed conflict.

[22] *Tadić* Jurisdiction Decision, pars 100 et seq. The Appeals Chamber noted a number of mechanisms whereby this process of application took place, notably through common Article 3 of the Geneva Conventions and agreements (or unilateral statements) made pursuant to that provision between (or, by) warring parties whereby they undertook to respect those minimum standards. The Appeals Chamber also noted in that context the action of the ICRC, two United Nations General Assembly resolutions, some declarations made by member states of the European Community as well as Additional Protocol II, and some military manuals (see pars 108 et seq.).

[23] *Tadić* Jurisdiction Decision, par 96: 'The dichotomy [of regulatory regime depending on the nature of the armed conflict] was clearly sovereignty-oriented and reflected the traditional configuration of the international community, based on the coexistence of sovereign States more inclined to look after their own interests than community concerns or humanitarian demands.'

[24] *Tadić* Jurisdiction Decision, par 97. The Appeals Chamber also said that 'if international law, while of course duly safeguarding the legitimate interests of States, must gradually turn to the protection of human beings, it is only natural that the aforementioned dichotomy should gradually lose its weight' (ibid.).

however, differences still exist between the regulations of each category and the characterization of an armed conflict as either international or internal will therefore determine the body of law to be applied in relation to that conflict and, possibly, be determinative of whether particular conduct is prohibited or indeed criminal under international law.[25]

A conflict may be said to be 'international' in character, the Appeals Chamber said, when it is being fought 'between States'. There is no requirement that this armed conflict involves the passage of troops of one country over the borders of another state and a conflict could therefore be international even if the hostilities occur on the territory of a single state.[26] And the hostilities the subject of that conflict apparently need not reach any minimum level of intensity.[27] In other words, whenever the armed forces of two states are involved in combat against one another, even in a minor border clash for instance, an international armed conflict could be said to exist.[28]

An 'internal armed conflict', by contrast, is therefore first and foremost determined by the negative test that it is not an international one. As soon as two or more states are sufficiently involved in the hostilities, the armed conflict becomes an international one and the law regulating such conflicts becomes applicable. An armed conflict which is originally internal in character may therefore develop into an international one if a second or more states become sufficiently involved in the hostilities.[29]

The definition of an internal armed conflict given by the Appeals Chamber ('protracted armed violence between governmental authorities and organized

---

[25] *Tadić* Jurisdiction Decision, par 67.

[26] It would, therefore, include situations of partial or total occupation as provided for in Article 2(1) of the Geneva Conventions. This definition does not refer, however, to 'armed conflicts in which peoples are fighting against colonial domination and alien occupation and against racist régimes in the exercise of their right of self-determination, as enshrined in the Charter of the United Nations and the Declaration on Principles of International Law concerning Friendly Relations and Co-operation among States in accordance with the Charter of the United Nations' (as referred to in Article 1(4) of Additional Protocol I).

[27] It is even possible to imagine situations where no combat would need to occur. See J. Pictet (gen. ed.), *Commentary, Geneva Convention Relative to the Treatment of Prisoners of War, Convention III,* (Geneva: ICRC, 1960), ('ICRC, *Commentary to Geneva Convention III*'), specifically art. 2(1), p 23: 'Any difference arising between two States and leading to the intervention of members of the armed forces (8) is an armed conflict within the meaning of Article 2, even if one of the Parties denies the existence of a state of war. It makes no difference how long the conflict lasts, how much slaughter takes place, or how numerous are the participating forces; it suffices for the armed forces of one Power to have captured adversaries falling within the scope of Article 4. Even if there has been no fighting, the fact that persons covered by the Convention are detained is sufficient for its application. The number of persons captured in such circumstances is, of course, immaterial.'

[28] In coming to this definition, the Tribunal was no doubt strongly influenced by the ICRC, *Commentary to Geneva Convention IV,* p 20, which provides that '[a]ny difference arising between two States and leading to the intervention of members of the armed forces' is an international armed conflict and '[i]t makes no difference how long the conflict lasts, or how much slaughter takes place' (see reference to that Commentary in *Čelebići* Trial Judgment, par 208).

[29] On the process of internationalization of armed conflict, see *Tadić* Jurisdiction Decision, pars 84 and 137; *Aleksovski* Appeal Judgment, pars 122 et seq.; *Čelebići* Appeal Judgment, par 26; *Blaškić* Trial Judgment, par 75.

armed groups or between such groups within a State'[30]) focuses on two aspects of the conflict: the intensity and duration of the hostilities and the degree of organization of the parties.[31] Assessing whether the hostilities are of sufficient intensity does not depend on the subjective judgment and assessment of the parties to the conflict, but on the objective and actual level of violence involved in the confrontation between warring parties.[32] There is no clear line indicating the level at which hostilities may be said to be sufficiently intense to amount to an internal armed conflict. Instead, Chambers of both Tribunals have relied on a number of factors, such as the continued involvement of the United Nations Security Council in events in the former Yugoslavia, the involvement of large amounts of weaponry and troops, evidence of sustained and coordinated military operations, the inability of state authorities to control a portion of its territory, and the scope of the geographical area within which hostilities are taking place.[33] Secondly, the relevant parties must exhibit a minimum degree of organization and cohesiveness which are such as to enable them to plan and carry out concerted military operations and to impose discipline within their ranks.[34] In particular, according to one Trial Chamber, those troops must in all cases be under responsible command and be able to meet the minimum standards of humanitarian law.[35] By reason of those requirements, an internal conflict as defined above will in many respects resemble an international armed conflict.

The Appeals Chamber's definition of what may constitute an 'internal armed conflict' is indifferent to the fact that none of the parties to it might represent or claim to represent the legitimate state authorities. Nor does it require that any of the parties to the conflict must be in control of any sizeable part of a territory (although this fact

---

[30] A very similar definition had been put forward as early as 1989 by Gasser who defined internal armed conflicts as 'armed hostilities which take place within the territory of a State between government forces and armed insurgent groups [. . .] or between] various (private) armed groups fight[ing] each other' (H. P. Gasser, *Im Dienst an der Gemeinschaft* (Basel/Bern/Frankfurt: Helbing & Lichtenhahn, 1989) ('Gasser, *Armed Conflict within the territory of a state*'), 'Armed Conflict within the Territory of a State', in Haller *et al* (eds.), pp 225, 226).

[31] *Tadić* Trial Judgment, par 562. See also *Rutaganda* Trial Judgment, par 93; *Čelebići* Trial Judgment, par 184; *Akayesu* Trial Judgment, par 120; *Milošević* Rule 98bis Decision, par 17.

[32] *Akayesu* Trial Judgment, par 603: 'the ascertainment of the intensity of a non-international conflict does not depend on the subjective judgment of the parties to the conflict. [. . .] If the application of international humanitarian law depended solely on the discretionary judgment of the parties to the conflict, in most cases there would be a tendency for the conflict to be minimized by the parties thereto.'

[33] See, e.g. *Tadić* Trial Judgment, pars 567–570; *Akayesu* Trial Judgment, pars 619–620; *Tadić* Jurisdiction Decision, par 70, and sources quoted therein; *Milošević* Rule 98bis Decision, pars 26–32. For other relevant factors, see also ICRC, *Commentary to Geneva Convention I*, pp 49–50 and ICRC, *Commentary to Geneva Convention IV*, pp 34–36. The non-governmental troops need not be under the command of a civilian authority (*Milošević* Rule 98bis Decision, par 34), nor do these forces need to exercise control over a part of a territory (ibid., par 36).

[34] See, e.g. *Akayesu* Trial Judgment, par 120 mentioning 'hostilities between armed forces organized to a greater or lesser extent'; and par 625; *Tadić* Trial Judgment, par 562 referring to 'the organization of the parties to the conflict'. See also *Milošević* Rule 98bis Decision, pars 23–25, pointing to the extent of organization of the forces involved (KLA), the existence of an official joint command structure and headquarters, the designation of zones of operation, and the ability to procure, transport, and distribute arms.   [35] See, generally, *Akayesu* Trial Judgment, pars 625–626.

might be relevant to the Trial Chamber's determination that the hostilities are indeed more than mere banditry or insurgency).

These closely related criteria of intensity and organization are used mainly, if not solely, 'for the purpose, as a minimum, of distinguishing an armed conflict from banditry, unorganized and short-lived insurrections, or terrorist activities, which are not subject to international humanitarian law'.[36] In the context of internal hostilities which fall short of this threshold, war crimes may in principle not be said to have been committed, leaving such matters to domestic criminal legal systems. As noted by one author, when there are disputes about the existence of an armed conflict and whether humanitarian law may be applicable to that situation, the primary matters to consider should be 'the intensity of the violence and the need for protection of its victims'.[37]

The determination as to whether an armed conflict exists, and its internal or international status, constitutes a mixed question of facts and law to be made by the court. Several defence teams at both Tribunals have, for tactical or practical reasons, challenged the existence of an armed conflict at the time and place relevant to their indictment,[38] or, more often, they have simply refused to agree prior to trial to the fact that such an armed conflict had existed.[39] As a result,

---

[36] J. Pictet (gen. ed.) *Commentary, Geneva Convention for the Amelioration of the Condition of the Wounded, Sick and Shipwrecked Members of Armed Forces at Sea, Convention II* (Geneva: ICRC, 1960) ('ICRC, *Commentary to Geneva Convention II*'), p 33; (ICRC, *Commentary to Geneva Convention III*), p 37; (footnote in the original). *Akayesu* Trial Judgment, par 625: 'an armed conflict is distinguished from internal disturbances by the level of intensity of the conflict and the degree of organization of the parties to the conflict'. The ICRC *Commentary to the Additional Protocols*, Additional Protocol II, par 4341, provides as follows:

> The expression 'armed conflict' gives an important indication in this respect since it introduces a material criterion: the existence of open hostilities between armed forces which are organized to a greater or lesser degree. Internal disturbances and tensions, characterized by isolated or sporadic acts of violence, do not therefore constitute armed conflict in a legal sense, even if the government is forced to resort to police forces or even to armed units for the purpose of restoring law and order. Within these limits, non-international armed conflict seems to be a situation in which hostilities break out between armed forces or organized armed groups within the territory of a single State (footnotes omitted).

See also ibid., art. 1(2) of Additional Protocol II, pars 4471 et seq., in particular pars 4474–4477.

[37] H. P. Gasser, 'International Humanitarian Law: An Introduction', Henry Dunant Institute (Bern: Paul Haupt, 1993) ('Gasser, *International Humanitarian Law*'), p 23.

[38] Duško Tadić, for instance, claimed that there did not exist a cognizable armed conflict at the time and place relevant to the charges laid against him (see *Tadić* Jurisdiction Decision, pars 66 et seq.) Likewise, on appeal, the Defence in the *Kunarac* case tried to argue that an armed conflict did not exist in relation to certain areas relevant to the indictment (*Kunarac* Appeal Judgment, pars 61–65). The Appeals Chamber dismissed that submission, stating that the Prosecutor was not obliged to establish that an armed conflict existed 'in each and every square inch of the general area' (ibid., par 64). The state of armed conflict, the Appeals Chamber said, 'is not limited to the areas of actual military combat but exists across the entire territory under the control of the warring parties' (ibid.).

[39] The Rules of Procedure and Evidence of the Tribunals provide for the possibility for the parties to agree to a number of factual issues, without the need for them to litigate such matters. In some cases, the Defence and the Prosecution have agreed prior to trial that an armed conflict existed at the time and at the place relevant to the indictment. Although not bound by such accord between the parties, the Court has generally given due weight to their concessions on such matters.

in most cases, Trial Chambers of both *ad hoc* Tribunals have had to determine, repeatedly, whether an armed conflict existed at the time and place relevant to each indictment and whether that conflict was internal or international in character.

Proof of the existence of an armed conflict does not mean, however, that the prosecutor must establish that an armed conflict existed 'in each and every square inch of the general area' where military activities are occurring.[40] As far as the application of the laws of war is concerned, the temporal and geographical scope of both internal and international armed conflicts indeed extends beyond the exact time and place of hostilities.[41] Once it is established that there was an armed conflict at the time and place relevant to the indictment, the laws of war will in principle apply to the whole of the territory of the warring states or, in the case of internal armed conflicts, to the whole territory under the control of the parties to the conflict, whether or not actual combat takes place there, and continue to apply until a general conclusion of peace or, in the case of internal armed conflicts, until a peaceful settlement is achieved.[42] A war crime need not therefore have been committed at a time when or in a place where combat was taking place as long as the conduct in question was sufficiently connected with the armed conflict as a whole.[43]

6.2.2   Nexus between the crime and the armed conflict

Role and function of the nexus requirement

A great many crimes are committed in armed conflicts that do not constitute war crimes.[44] To qualify as a war crime, the act or omission in question must have been sufficiently connected to the armed conflict. In the words of the Appeals Chamber, the conduct in question must have been 'closely related to the hostilities'.[45]

The function of the war nexus requirement appears to be essentially twofold. First, it serves to distinguish war crimes from purely domestic crimes over which

---

[40] *Kunarac* Appeal Judgment, par 64. In the *Blaškić* case, the Trial Chamber likewise said that the armed conflict does not have to exist 'within each municipality concerned [by charges]. It suffices to establish the existence of the conflict within the whole region of which the municipalities are part' (*Blaškić* Trial Judgment, par 64.)   [41] *Tadić* Jurisdiction Decision, par 67.

[42] *Tadić* Jurisdiction Decision, pars 69 and 70; *Kunarac* Appeal Judgment, pars 57 and 64. See also *Čelebići* Trial Judgment, pars 209–210; *Tadić* Jurisdiction Decision, par 68; *Blaškić* Trial Judgment, par 64.

[43] *Kunarac* Appeal Judgment, par 57: 'There is no necessary correlation between the area where the actual fighting is taking place and the geographical reach of the laws of war.'

[44] See, e.g. *Kayishema and Ruzindana* Trial Judgment, par 600; *Aleksovski* Trial Judgment, par 45.

[45] See, *inter alia*, *Tadić* Jurisdiction Decision, par 70; *Kunarac* Trial Judgment, par 402; *Krnojelac* Trial Judgment, par 51. In the *Čelebići* case, reference was made to 'an obvious link' (*Čelebići* Appeal Judgment, par 193) and to 'a clear nexus' (*Čelebići* Trial Judgment, par 197) between the armed conflict and the acts of the accused, apparently all referring to the same requirement, but using a different terminology every time. The Trial Chamber in *Blaškić* talks of an 'evident nexus between the alleged crimes and the armed conflict as a whole' (*Blaškić* Trial Judgment, par 69). The *Kayishema and Ruzindana* Trial Chamber boldly talks of a 'direct conjunction' between the acts and the armed conflict which appears to be a very high standard which is not supported by any instance of state practice or war crimes judgment (*Kayishema and Ruzindana* Trial Judgment, par 623).

the *ad hoc* Tribunals have no jurisdiction. Whilst the international laws of war would apply to assessing the criminal character and the gravity of those actions which are sufficiently connected with the armed conflict to be regarded as a war crime, domestic law (whether penal or disciplinary) would normally apply to the latter sort of conduct. Secondly, the nexus requirement serves to exclude from the realm of the laws of war purely random or isolated criminal occurrences which do not constitute war crimes for the purpose of the Tribunals' Statutes. Once again, random or isolated incidents would in principle be sanctioned, not by the international laws of war, but by domestic law.[46]

Meaning of the nexus requirement and indicia thereof

Although the nexus requirement is important for the reasons just mentioned, scant attention has been paid to its substance and exact meaning. What does 'closely related to the hostilities' mean in practice? Must the crime be substantively related to the conflict, or is it sufficient for it to be geographically connected to the armed conflict? Must the acts charged in the indictment have been committed in combat, or can it still amount to a war crime if committed when fighting has receded?

What is clear from the jurisprudence of the *ad hoc* Tribunals is what this nexus does *not* require. First, the armed conflict need not have been causal to the commission of the crime to qualify as a war crime: in general, a similar sort of crime could in theory have been committed in peacetime and the crime in question need not have been the direct consequence of the armed conflict.[47] But the armed conflict must still have played a substantial part in the perpetrator's ability to commit it, his decision to commit it, the manner in which it was committed, or the purpose for which it was committed.[48]

On appeal, the appellants in the *Kunarac* case had submitted that, even if the allegations against them were established (namely, that they were responsible for various forms of sexual mistreatment against non-Serb women), their acts and conduct were not sufficiently connected to the armed conflict to be regarded, for the purpose of Article 3 of the ICTY Statute, as 'closely related to the armed conflict'.[49] According to the appellants, this requirement of nexus implied that the crimes could not have been committed *but for* the existence of an armed conflict, and this must be established in respect of each and every crime with which they

---

[46] Such conduct could also, all other conditions being met, constitute a crime against humanity or genocide.　　　　　[47] See, e.g. *Kamuhanda* Trial Judgment, par 735.

[48] *Vasiljević* Trial Judgment, par 25; *Kunarac* Appeal Judgment, par 58.

[49] *Prosecutor v. Kunarac*, IT-96-23 and IT-96-23/1-A, Appellant's Brief for the Accused Dragoljub Kunarac against Judgment of 22 February 2001, 16 July 2001 ('*Kunarac* Appeal Brief'), pars 8–10 and *Prosecutor v. Kunarac*, IT-96-23 and IT-96-23/1-A, Appellant's Brief for the Accused Zoran Vuković against Judgment 22 February 2001, 12 July 2001 ('*Vuković* Appeal Brief'), pars 50–53. See also IT-96-23 and IT-96-23/1-A Transcript, T 48 and 61–68, and *Prosecutor v. Kunarac*, IT-96-23 and IT-96-23/1-A, Appellant's Brief for the Accused Radomir Kovač against Judgment of 22 February 2001, 26 July 2001 ('*Kovač* Appeal Brief'), pars 35–37.

were charged.[50] The appellants contended, furthermore, that it is not sufficient that there was an armed conflict at the relevant time, that they took part therein as soldiers and that the alleged victims were civilians.[51] The Appeals Chamber made it clear that war crimes need not be so intertwined with the war that whenever identical criminal conduct could have occurred in peacetime they may not be regarded as war crimes when committed at war. The criminality of war indeed overlaps a great deal with peacetime criminality and many of those acts that would qualify as war crimes (such as murder or rape) would often qualify as domestic offences too if committed in peacetime, so that the fact that certain acts or conduct may fall in one category does not exclude that they would also fall in the other:[52]

The Appellants' proposition that the laws of war only prohibit those acts which are specific to an actual wartime situation is not right. The laws of war may frequently encompass acts which, though they are not committed in the theatre of conflict, are substantially related to it. The laws of war can apply to both types of acts. The Appeals Chamber understands the Appellants' argument to be that if an act can be prosecuted in peacetime, it cannot be prosecuted in wartime. This betrays a misconception about the relationship between the laws of war and the laws regulating a peacetime situation. The laws of war do not necessarily displace the laws regulating a peacetime situation; the former may add elements requisite to the protection which needs to be afforded to victims in a wartime situation.

Secondly, the nexus requirement does not imply any strict geographical or temporal coincidence between the acts of the accused and the armed conflict.[53]

---

[50] *Kunarac* Appeal Brief, par 8 and *Vuković* Appeal Brief, par 51. See also IT-96-23 and IT-96-23/1-A Transcript, T 61–63. A somewhat similar argument was put forth by the Defence in the *Belsen* trial which suggested that the only purpose in making a crime a war crime was to secure legitimate warfare and that such acts therefore needed to be directly connected to war or combat operations (*United Kingdom v. Josef Kramer and others*, British Military Court sitting at Luneburg, verdict of 17 November 1945, in R. Phillips (ed.), *Trial of Josef Kramer and Forty-Four Others (the Belsen Trial)* (London: William Hodge and Co., 1949) ('the Belsen trial'), in L. Friedman, *The Law of War: A Documentary History* (New York: Random House, 1972) ('Friedman, *The Law of War*'), p 1501). The mistreatment of prisoners of war, the Defence claimed, did not come within the realm of such actions and could not therefore constitute war crimes. In response, the Prosecution submitted in its closing speech that the mere fact that prisoners came into the hands of the Germans and were interned and imprisoned by them, and that their countries were occupied by the Germans as a result of operations of war, was sufficient to transform crimes committed against them into war crimes (Friedman, *The Law of War*, p 1507).
[51] *Kunarac* Appeal Brief, par 10 and *Vuković* Appeal Brief, par 53.
[52] *Kunarac* Appeal Judgment, par 60.
[53] *Kunarac* Trial and Appeal Judgments and *Rutaganda* Appeal Judgment, par 570; *Tadić* Trial Judgment, par 573. In *Kunarac*, the Trial Chamber held that the acts of the accused (essentially, rapes and other forms of sexual violence) were closely related to the armed conflict despite the fact that they had been committed over a long period of time, including at a time when no military activity was taking place in the region where these crimes were being committed. 'Not only were the many underlying crimes made possible by the armed conflict,' the Chamber said, 'but they were very much a part of it' (*Kunarac* Trial Judgment, par 568). It is irrelevant, the Trial Chamber added, that the actual fighting had shifted away from the town of Foča, where most of the crimes were being committed and that the town was under the control of the perpetrators' group by the time the events charged occurred because, the Chamber said, 'the criterion of a nexus with the armed conflict under Article 3 of the [ICTY] Statute does not require that the offences be directly committed whilst fighting is

And it does not mean that the acts of the accused must be committed whilst fighting is actually taking place, or that it must have been committed at the scene of combat.[54] It is sufficient, for instance, that the acts of the accused be closely related to the hostilities occurring in other parts of the territories controlled by the parties to the conflict.[55] Likewise, the nexus requirement would be met where the crime was committed either during or in the aftermath of the fighting, 'provided that it is committed in furtherance of, or at least under the guise of, the situation created by the fighting'.[56] It would not be sufficient, however, to establish merely

actually taking place, or at the scene of combat. Humanitarian law continues to apply in the whole of the territory under the control of one of the parties, whether or not actual combat continues at the place where the events in question took place' (*Kunarac* Trial Judgment, par 568). It is therefore sufficient that the crimes were closely related, for example, to hostilities occurring in other parts of the territories controlled by the parties to the conflict, or, if they are committed in the aftermath of the fighting, that they are committed 'in furtherance or take advantage of the situation created by the fighting' (*Kunarac* Trial Judgment, par 568; see also *Naletilić and Martinović* Trial Judgment, par 180). And the nexus requirement certainly does not require that the acts of the accused must have been committed in the midst of combat activities or in the general geographical areas where combats are taking place (see, e.g., *Tadić* Trial Judgment, par 573; *Čelebići* Trial Judgment, pars 194–195).

[54] *Vasiljević* Trial Judgment, par 25; *Kunarac* Appeals Judgment, par 57; *Kunarac* Trial Judgment, par 568.

[55] The laws of war indeed 'apply and continue to apply to the whole of the territory under the control of one of the parties to the conflict, whether or not actual combat takes place there, until a general conclusion of peace or a peaceful settlement is achieved' (*Vasiljević* Trial Judgment, par 25; *Tadić* Jurisdiction Decision, par 70; *Kunarac* Appeals Judgment, par 57; *Čelebići* Trial Judgment, pars 194–195). In *Blaškić*, the Trial Chamber applied that very principle to the facts of the case (pars 69–70):

69. [. . .] In addition to the existence of an armed conflict, it is imperative to find an evident nexus between the alleged crimes and the armed conflict as a whole. This does not mean that the crimes must all be committed in the precise geographical region where an armed conflict is taking place at a given moment. To show that a link exists, it is sufficient that:

'the alleged crimes were closely related to the hostilities occurring in other parts of the territories controlled by the parties to the conflict'.

70. The foregoing observations demonstrate that a given municipality need not be prey to armed confrontation for the standards of international humanitarian law to apply there. [. . .]

[56] *Vasiljević* Trial Judgment, par 25; *Kunarac* Appeal Judgment, par 58; *Kunarac* Trial Judgment, par 568; *Stakić* Trial Judgment, par 569. The Appeals Chamber in *Rutaganda* made it clear that the phrase 'under the guise of' the armed conflict 'does not mean simply "at the same time as an armed conflict" and/or "in any circumstances created in part by the armed conflict". For example, if a non-combatant takes advantage of the lessened effectiveness of the police in conditions of disorder created by an armed conflict to murder a neighbour he has hated for years, that would not, without more, constitute a war crime under Article 4 of the Statute' (*Rutaganda* Appeal Judgment, par 570). The Inter-American Juridical Committee said that war crimes needed to have been committed 'as part of military operations or as an incident to the existence of hostilities' (Report of the International Juridical Status of Individuals as 'War Criminals', prepared by the Inter-American Juridical Committee in accordance with Resolution VI of the Inter-American Conference on the Problems of War and Peace held at Mexico City, 21 February–8 March 1945, p 4). The question as to whether war crimes could ever be committed prior to the start of the armed conflict, although they truly should be seen in its perspective, is a difficult one.

that the conduct in question took place whilst an armed conflict was ongoing or that this crime could be committed due (at least in part) to the circumstances created by the armed conflict.[57] If, for instance, a civilian merely takes advantage of the general atmosphere of lawlessness created by the armed conflict to kill a hated neighbour or to steal his property without his acts being otherwise closely connected to the armed conflict, such conduct would not generally constitute a war crime.[58] The line between the two situations is, however, a hard one to draw, but there should be no presumption or fiction that, because a crime is committed in time of war, it therefore automatically constitutes a war crime. No such presumption exists under international law.

Thirdly, war crimes are not limited to crimes of a purely military nature and the category of war crimes has now expanded beyond the limits of the crimes of the soldiery.[59] A war crime may generally be committed by both combatants and non-combatants alike.[60] Hence, for instance, in the case of Mitar Vasiljević, a former waiter who had been loosely associated with a group of Serb paramilitaries, the Trial Chamber made it clear that '[a]lthough he did not take part in any fighting, the Accused was closely associated with Serb paramilitaries, his acts were all committed in furtherance of the armed conflict, and he acted under the guise of the armed conflict to commit the crimes which the Trial Chamber accepted that he committed'.[61]

Fourthly, the required nexus is one between the acts of the accused (as charged in the indictment) and the war itself, that is, the circumstances, events, and consequences which result from the fighting between two or more parties. As already noted, it is not a requirement that the perpetrator should somehow be

---

[57] The ICC Elements of Crimes define the nexus requirement for war crimes as follows (Article 8(2) (a) et seq.): 'The conduct took place in the context of and was associated with an [. . .] armed conflict.'

[58] This illustration was used by the Appeals Chamber in *Rutaganda* (par 570). See, however, *Tadić* Trial Judgment, par 573.

[59] During the Second World War, the sub-committee on war crimes of the Commission for Penal Reconstruction and Development (composed of Monsieur De Baer, Monsieur Burnay, Dr Glaser, and Dr Lauterpacht) distinguished between three categories of war crimes: '(1) Acts connected with warfare and contrary to the laws of war, e.g. use of poisons, attacks on hospital ships, etc. (2) Acts not connected with warfare committed: (a) without authority, e.g. rape, murder, etc. (b) with the approval of or at the order of authority, e.g. mass murder, murder of hostages, deportation, etc. (3) Serious crimes committed against property: (a) without authority, e.g. looting. (b) with the approval of or at the order of authority, e.g. wanton destruction, plundering of art treasures, etc.' (cited in *UN War Crimes Commission*, p 97).

[60] In other words, 'there is no explicit provision in the Statute that individual criminal responsibility is restricted to a particular class of individuals' (*Akayesu* Appeal Judgment, par 436). Anyone can commit a war crime, civilian or military, high level officers or foot-soldiers. See also *Law Reports of Trials of War Criminals*, Vol XV, 58–60. In particular, war crimes may be committed by civilians (see Law Reports and H. H. Jescheck, 'War Crimes', in Bernhardt (ed.) *Encyclopedia of Public International Law* (Amsterdam/New York/Oxford: North Holland Publishing Co., 1982), vol. 3, p 294.   [61] *Vasiljević* Trial Judgment, par 57.

related or linked to one of the parties to the conflict.[62] Nor is it a requirement that his actions be interconnected with other crimes (such as crimes against humanity) committed in the context of that conflict.

Fifthly, the nexus requirement for war crimes is different from the similarly named requirement contained in the ICTY Statute in relation to crimes against humanity. Article 5 of the ICTY Statute provides that, to come within the Tribunal's jurisdiction, a crime against humanity must have been committed 'in armed conflict'.[63] This requirement is satisfied by proof that there *was* an armed conflict – international or internal – at the time and place relevant to the indictment.[64] Contrary to what is the case with war crimes, in the case of crimes against humanity pursuant to Article 5 of the ICTY Statute, there need not be a substantive relationship between the acts of the accused and the armed conflict; the requirement of Article 5 of the ICTY Statute is a purely jurisdictional one and it is satisfied by proof that, at the relevant time and place, there was an armed conflict.[65]

Finally, customary law does not require, despite some initial suggestions of defence counsel, that a war crime must be pursuant to an officially sanctioned practice to commit such crimes:[66]

It is not [. . .] necessary to show that [the crimes were] part of a policy or of a practice officially endorsed or tolerated by one of the parties to the conflict, or that the act be in actual furtherance of a policy associated with the conduct of war or in the actual interest of a party to the conflict; the obligations of individuals under international humanitarian law are independent and apply without prejudice to any questions of the responsibility of States

---

[62] *Akayesu* Appeal Judgment, pars 443–444:

443. [. . .] international humanitarian law would be lessened and called into question if it were to be admitted that certain persons be exonerated from individual criminal responsibility for a violation of common Article 3 under the pretext that they did not belong to a specific category.

444. [. . .] The nexus between violations [of international humanitarian law] and the armed conflict implies that, in most cases, the perpetrator of the crime will probably have a special relationship with one party to the conflict. However, such a special relationship is not a condition precedent to the application of common Article 3. In the opinion of the Appeals Chamber, the Trial Chamber erred in requiring that a special relationship should be a separate condition for triggering criminal responsibility for a violation of Article 4 of the Statute.

The decision of the Appeals Chamber on that point overturned a stream of decisions to the contrary which all found their source in an unsupported suggestion of the *Akayesu* Trial Chamber that, in order to be found liable pursuant to Article 4, the perpetrator had to be sufficiently linked to one of the parties to the conflict (see, e.g. *Akayesu* Trial Judgment, pars 439, 630–634; and *Kayishema and Ruzindana* Trial Judgment, pars 175–176; *Rutaganda* Trial Judgment, pars 96–98; *Musema* Trial Judgment, pars 264–266; see also *Kunarac* Trial Judgment, par 407).

[63] The Statute of the ICTR does not contain such a requirement.

[64] *Tadić* Appeal Judgment, pars 249, 251; *Kupreškić* Trial Judgment, par 545; *Kunarac* Trial Judgment, par 413. See also below, sub-section 10.1.

[65] See, e.g. *Tadić* Appeal Judgment, pars 249, 272, holding that a nexus between the acts of the accused and the armed conflict is actually *not* required. See also *Blaškić* Trial Judgment, par 71.

[66] *Tadić* Trial Judgment, par 573 (footnote omitted).

under international law. The only question, to be determined in the circumstances of each individual case, is whether the offences were closely related to the armed conflict as a whole.

The existence of such a policy or plan to commit war crimes may, however, be evidentially relevant and may help distinguish war crimes from purely domestic crimes.[67]

What the nexus demands, on the other hand, is less clear, and the Statutes of the Tribunals are silent on that point.[68] It is unclear, for instance, whether the perpetrator must know of the existence of the armed conflict and whether he must have been aware that his acts were a part thereof.[69] What is certain, however, is that the nexus should not be understood as 'something vague and indefinite' so that any act committed in the general context of an armed conflict would automatically qualify as a war crime.[70] It is up to the Prosecution to present the relevant facts and to establish, in relation to each and every crime charged in the indictment, that a close connection exists between the acts of the accused and the armed conflict.[71]

There are acts that on their face may appear to be connected with the armed conflict, but which are not substantively related to it and which may not be said to consitute war crimes. Retaliation killings between competing paramilitary groups which fight on behalf of the same party to an armed conflict, for instance, may be facilitated and in a sense 'be closely related' to and occur 'under the guise of' the armed conflict, but such acts may not be said to be such as to qualify as a war crime. Parasitical criminality that opportunistically uses the cover of the armed conflict does not, in principle, satisfy the requirement of nexus.

It has also sometimes been suggested that crimes committed in a purely private capacity or for personal reasons unrelated to the war would not in principle be regarded as war crimes.[72] Rather than excluding altogether crimes committed in a private capacity or for private reasons from the realm of war crimes, such criteria appear to be among the factors that may allow the court to decide whether, in view of all the circumstances, the acts of the accused may indeed be said to have been sufficiently connected to the armed conflict. It has also been suggested that crimes which answer to a criminal ideology or which have their own justification outside of the armed conflict may not amount, *sensu stricto*, to war crimes. Sereny, for

---

[67] See, e.g. *Kunarac* Appeal Judgment, par 58; *Tadić* Trial Judgment, par 573; *Čelebići* Trial Judgment, pars 194–195.

[68] The Statute of the ICC provides that (i) the conduct must have taken place in the context of and be associated with an armed conflict and (ii) the perpetrator must have been aware of factual circumstances that established the existence of an armed conflict (see Articles 8(2)(a) and 8(2)(b) of the Statute).

[69] Although the ICC Statute expressly provides for such a requirement, the existence of that requirement *qua* customary law is less than certain. In any case, from an evidentiary point of view, such knowledge and awareness on the part of the accused will generally be self-evident.

[70] *Kayishema and Ruzindana* Trial Judgment, pars 185–188.   [71] Ibid.

[72] See Inter-American Juridical Committee, *Report on War Criminals*, p 8: 'Such crimes [i.e. those committed in a private capacity] may be designated as "common law crimes", and they should be determined and judged precisely as if the offender were not a member of the armed forces.'

instance, suggested that Nazi crimes against the Jews could not constitute war crimes '[f]or the truth is that Nazi crimes ('NS crimes' in Germany), although their perpetration was facilitated by war, had in their origins nothing whatever to do with the war.'[73] From a legal point of view, such a proposition is difficult to support insofar as the laws of war do not look into the cause or motivations (let alone the political ideology) behind the crimes to decide upon their classification as war crimes, focusing instead on objective indications of their close linkage with the conflict.

Despite the clear position in international law that not all crimes committed during war are war crimes, it appears that, at times, Trial Chambers of the *ad hoc* Tribunals have acted upon a quasi-fiction that, because there was a war raging at the time and because the accused committed his crime during such upheavals, the acts and conduct of the accused were necessarily sufficiently connected to the armed conflict. That, however, is an assumption that no Chamber should make lightly, lest the specificity of the laws of war may be lost. The temptation to systematically depict crimes committed in times of war as war crimes would indeed constitute an undue attraction of international criminality (as well as an undue attraction of international jurisdiction).

What distinguishes a war crime from a purely domestic crime 'is that a war crime is shaped by or dependent upon the environment – the armed conflict – in which it is committed'.[74]

The assessment as to whether the acts of the accused were sufficiently connected to the armed conflict in a particular case will be made *a posteriori* but it must be made objectively (not in relation to the conception of the accused or his awareness of what was happening, although such perception may be evidentially relevant). Acts which, at the time when they were committed, did not demonstrate any apparent relation to an armed conflict may, in retrospect, be found to do so (for instance, preparatory actions and persecution-like war crimes). However, the court must be careful not to frame crimes in a 'war crime light' if, at the time when they were committed, they were not in any way related to past or future events which would come to be relevant to the determination that there was an armed conflict at the time.[75]

There is no hard-and-fast rule that would allow the court readily to distinguish war crimes from 'non-war crimes'. Instead of drawing a strict (and probably unworkable) dividing line between the two, the *ad hoc* Tribunals have therefore

[73] G. Sereny, *Into that Darkness: An Examination of Conscience* (New York: Vintage Books, 1983), p 98.
[74] *Kunarac* Appeal Judgment, par 58; *Rutaganda* Appeal Judgment, pars 569–570.
[75] For *in concreto* illustrations of that requirement, see, *inter alia, Kayishema and Ruzindana* Trial Judgment, pars 188, 604; *Tadić* Trial Judgment, pars 572–573; *Blaškić* Trial Judgment, pars 69 et seq.; see also *Akayesu* Trial Judgment, pars 641–643 as to the Trial Chamber's finding on his relationship to the conflict; in *Krnojelac*, the Trial Chamber found that the acts of the accused (various forms of mistreatment inflicted upon civilians detained at the KP Dom prison in Foča, in Eastern Bosnia) had been committed 'as a direct result, in furtherance of and under the guise of the hostilities' thus satisfying the nexus requirement.

considered a number of factors that they may take into account to determine the nature of the relationship between the acts of the accused and the armed conflict so as to determine the sufficiency of the linkage between the two:[76]

  (i)   the status of the perpetrator (as soldier or combatant);[77]

  (ii) the status of the victim or victims (as non-combatant);[78]

  (iii) the circumstances in which the crime was committed;[79]

  (iv) the fact that the crime was committed in the context of an ongoing campaign to achieve particular military goals;[80]

  (v)   the fact that the crime coincided with the ultimate purpose of the military campaign;[81]

  (vi) the fact that the crime was committed with the assistance or with the connivance of the warring parties;[82]

  (vii) the fact that the crime was committed as part of, or in the context of, the perpetrator's official duties;[83]

  (viii) the fact that the victim was a member of the forces of the opposing party.[84]

A relevant indication that a particular act may constitute a war crime would be found in its being prohibited in existing treaty law, mainly, the Geneva Conventions and their Additional Protocols although, as pointed out above, the fact that certain acts are regarded as illegal under international law does not yet permit the conclusion that their commission would entail individual criminal responsibility in case of breach. None of the above when taken individually may be conclusive, and Trial Chambers must therefore take into account all relevant indications that the acts of the accused are, or are not, sufficiently connected to the conflict before concluding that the conduct in question may be regarded as a war crime.

Because the purpose of the laws of war is 'to protect the human being and to safeguard the dignity of man in the extreme situation of war',[85] the nexus requirement has been interpreted quite broadly by the ICTY, which has resulted

---

[76] The ICTR Appeals Chamber made it clear that, when determining whether a sufficient nexus has been established, the court would generally have to consider a set of factors, rather than a single criterion (see *Rutaganda* Appeal Judgment, par 570; see also ibid., pars 576–579). See, e.g., *Stakić* Trial Judgment, pars 569–570, 575–576.

[77] *Kunarac* Appeal Judgment, par 59 ; *Kunarac* Trial Judgment, par 569; *Furundžija* Trial Judgment, par 65; *Rutaganda* Appeal Judgment, par 570; *Naletilić and Martinović* Trial Judgment, par 180.

[78] *Kunarac* Appeal Judgment, par 59, as civilians captured during or after combat; *Kunarac* Trial Judgment, par 568; *Furundžija* Trial Judgment, par 65; *Tadić* Jurisdiction Decision, par 70.

[79] For instance, in the case of torture inflicted during interrogation, the nature of that interrogation – in *Furundžija*, the victim was asked about the military activities of the enemy (*Furundžija* Trial Judgment, pars 63 and 65).

[80] *Tadić* Jurisdiction Decision, par 70. *Vasiljević* Appeal Judgment, par 27, where the Appeals Chamber noted that the accused had been 'closely associated' with a paramilitary group.

[81] *Kunarac* Appeal Judgment, par 59; *Tadić* Trial Judgment, par 574; *Stakić* Trial Judgment, par 576.

[82] *Tadić* Trial Judgment, par 575.   [83] *Kunarac* Appeal Judgment, par 59.   [84] Ibid.

[85] Gasser, *International Humanitarian Law*, p 16, as quoted by Judge David Hunt in his Separate and Partially Dissenting Opinion, par 22, *Hadžihasanović* Command Responsibility Appeal Decision.

in a rather extensive degree of overlap between those acts which may be said to amount to war crimes under the Tribunals' Statutes and those which are regulated by other bodies of law (in particular, by domestic penal legislation). When interpreting the laws of war, it must be remembered, however, that they are intended to protect certain categories of people against certain consequences of war, not against crimes in general.[86] By contrast, the ICTR has showed great reluctance in making a finding that such nexus had been established.[87]

Breaking the nexus

Once a sufficient nexus has been established between the acts of the accused and the armed conflict, it will last for as long as his actions continue to be sufficiently related to the armed conflict. That nexus might, however, be eroded over time and the court must assess whether the passing of time (or other circumstances) might in fact have resulted in breaking that link altogether. In the *Kunarac* case, for instance, a number of young Muslim women had been captured following the military takeover of the town of Foča by Serb forces and they had been kept in detention, sexually abused, and enslaved during long periods of time, long after combat had receded from the region. Despite the passage of time and the receding of military activity from the area under consideration, the close relationship that existed between the crimes committed by the accused and the armed conflict did not cease to exist.[88] 'The requirement that the act be closely related to the armed conflict is satisfied', the Trial Chamber explained, 'if, as in the present case, the crimes are committed in the aftermath of the fighting, and until the cessation of combat activities in a certain region, and are committed in furtherance or take advantage of the situation created by the fighting.'[89]

There may be a point in time, however, when a close connection between the crime and the armed conflict may dissolve and where applying the laws of war to those acts would not be consistent with the role and function of that body of law, nor with the requirement that the conduct in question must be closely related to the armed conflict to qualify as a war crime.

6.3　Other jurisdictional requirements

In addition to the two preliminary requirements mentioned above (existence of an armed conflict and sufficient nexus of the acts of the accused therewith), there

---

[86] See *Semanza* Trial Judgment, par 368, in relation to common Article 3 and Additional Protocol II.

[87] The *Rutaganda* Appeal judgment of 26 May 2003 is the first judgement of the ICTR in which the Rwanda Tribunal found that the required nexus had been established (see *Rutaganda* Appeal judgment, para. 556 et seq.).

[88] See *Kunarac* Trial Judgment, where the Trial Chamber noted that '[h]umanitarian law continues to apply in the whole of the territory under the control of one of the parties, whether or not actual combat continues at the place where the events in question took place' (*Kunarac* Trial Judgment, par 568).

[89] Ibid.

are four additional – jurisdictional – conditions that must be fulfilled before an alleged violations of the laws or customs of war may be prosecuted under the Tribunals' Statutes:[90]

(i)   the violation must constitute an infringement of a rule of international humanitarian law;

(ii) the rule must be customary in nature or, if it belongs to treaty law, certain conditions must be met;

(iii) the violation must be serious, that is to say, it must constitute a breach of a rule protecting important values, and the breach must involve grave consequences for the victim;

(iv) the violation of the rule must entail the individual criminal responsibility of the person breaching the rule.[91]

6.3.1   Infringement of a rule of international humanitarian law

The expression 'laws or customs of war' has been rarely used in the Tribunal's vocabulary, and the expression 'international humanitarian law' which, some may say, is in fact broader in scope, is generally preferred. International humanitarian law is traditionally understood to consist of '[those] rules applicable in armed conflict set forth in international agreements to which the Parties to the conflict are Parties and the generally recognized principles and rules of international law which are applicable to armed conflict'.[92]

The requirement that a war crime must constitute an infringement of a rule of international humanitarian law is somewhat circular, but it underlines two important factors: first, breaches of other bodies of law, such as human rights law or domestic military legislation, do not constitute war crimes for the purpose of the *ad hoc* Tribunals and do not come within their jurisdiction, unless they also violate international humanitarian law. Secondly, breaches of the *jus ad bellum* do not constitute war crimes, nor do they come within the terms of the Tribunals' jurisdiction. International humanitarian law is indeed not concerned with the (il)legality or (il)legitimacy of recourse to war, nor with its causes. Nor are the

---

[90] See, *inter alia, Tadić* Jurisdiction Decision, par 94; *Aleksovski* Appeal Judgment, par 20; *Kunarac* Appeal Judgment, par 66.

[91] Depending on the basis upon which these acts were charged (treaty law or custom), a number of Chambers have suggested that slightly different requirements could apply. If, for instance, such charges are based on an alleged violation of treaty law, as opposed to custom, different conditions might have to be met, those Chambers said (see *Kunarac* Trial Judgment, par 404; see also *Krnojelac* Trial Judgment, par 52). See also comment above about the possibility to charge an individual for a violation of a treaty (sub-paragraph 2).

[92] Article 2(b) of Additional Protocol I. The Commission of Experts defined 'international humanitarian law' somewhat unhelpfully as the 'rules of international law applicable in armed conflict' (UN Doc. S/25274, pp 13–15).

ad hoc Tribunals concerned in such matters, and their jurisdiction is limited to alleged violations of the *jus in bello*, and does not include, for instance, the crime of aggression.[93]

A priori, there is no limitation (unless otherwise expressly provided) in respect of the manner in which international humanitarian law might have been infringed by the accused, but the conduct in question must be more than simply contrary to the spirit of that body of law to constitute an 'infringement' for the purpose of this definition. But because of the humanitarian character of most of these rules, the court has systematically interpreted quite broadly what could be regarded as an infringement of that regime with a view to furthering its purpose.[94]

6.3.2 Customary or conventional nature of the rule

Before concluding that a certain act or omission constitutes a war crime coming within its jurisdiction, the Tribunal must be satisfied that the conduct in question is contrary to a recognized rule or standard of international humanitarian law. As noted above, as far at least as the ICTY is concerned, that rule or standard, as well as the criminal consequences of its infringement, must be established pursuant to customary international law, for example, because that conventional provision has, through consistent state practice, grown into a customary prohibition.[95] As argued above, the fact that a particular prohibition is provided for in a treaty would not in itself be sufficient for a breach of that prohibition to come within the jurisdiction of the *ad hoc* Tribunals, whether the breach is said to constitute a war crime, a crime against humanity, or genocide.[96]

---

[93] See (First Annual) Report of the President of the ICTY to the United Nations General Assembly and Security Council, 29 August 1994, A/49/342-S/1994/1007, par 19, where the then President of the ICTY (A. Cassese) noted that the reason why crimes against peace were not within the Tribunal's jurisdiction was probably because 'the Security Council preferred to reserve itself competence in the field of aggression and similar crimes against peace'.

[94] See, e.g. a number of occasions when the Appeals Chamber adopted this approach to interpret various aspects of humanitarian law (those cases are cited in n 41, p 13 of Judge Hunt's Dissenting Opinion, *Hadžihasanović* Command Responsibility Appeal Decision); *Tadić* Appeal Judgment in relation to Article 2 of the Tribunal's Statute (par 166), Article 5 (pars 282–285), and Article 7(1) (pars 190–191); *Aleksovski* Appeal Judgment in relation to Article 2 (par 152); *Čelebići* Appeal Judgment, also in relation to Article 2 (pars 67–70, 81). Appeals Chamber decisions adopting this approach in relation to other issues include: *Aleksovski* Appeal Judgment, in relation to the doctrine of judicial precedent (par 98); *Prosecutor v. Milošević*, IT-01-51-AR73, Reasons for Decision on Prosecution Interlocutory Appeal from Refusal to Order Joinder, 18 April 2002, in relation to the resolution of discrepancies between the English and French versions of the Rules of Procedure and Evidence (par 16). See also *Furundžija* Trial Judgment in relation to the forms of liability in Article 7(1) (par 254).

[95] The existence of a conventional prohibition which is said to have crystallized into customary law will be of assistance to the court, however, in order to determine the contours that the rule might have taken under customary law. The difference between conventional and customary humanitarian law should indeed not be exaggerated as their most fundamental rules generally coincide and because they often 'mutually support and supplement each other' (*Tadić* Jurisdiction Decision, par 98).

[96] See above chapter 2.

6.3.3 'Serious' nature of the infringement

Not every violation of the laws or customs of war amounts to a war crime as understood under the Statutes. Some violations that are not sufficiently serious may, for instance, attract a disciplinary response rather than a penal one.[97]

As far as the *ad hoc* Tribunals are concerned, the Statutes expressly provide that only 'serious' violations of the laws or customs of war come within the jurisdiction of the Court,[98] and only those violations may entail the individual criminal responsibility of the accused pursuant to the Statute.[99]

According to the Appeals Chamber, a 'serious' infringement is one that 'constitute[s] a breach of a rule protecting important values, and the breach must involve grave consequences for the victim'.[100] This requirement, one Trial Chamber has noted, constitutes a 'qualitative limitation' upon the Tribunals' competence.[101] An act that may be said to be contrary to humanitarian law, but which does not involve important values, or has only minor consequences upon the victim, would therefore fall outside of the Tribunals' jurisdiction. Most of the prohibitions the breach of which could be considered candidates for war crime status protect the personal, physical, or mental integrity against certain forms of treatment (e.g. torture or cruel treatment) or concern the use of certain methods against them (e.g. poisonous weapons) whilst yet other prohibitions protect the pecuniary, cultural, spiritual, or property interests of individuals or communities. The lesser the protected interest, the more serious the infringement of that interest will have to be for the act to be regarded as a serious infringement of international humanitarian law.[102]

---

[97] The line between those violation that would attract penal consequences and those that would only entail disciplinary measures may be difficult to draw in practice (see *Bagilishema* Appeal Judgment, par 36).

[98] *Tadić* Jurisdiction Decision, pars 90–91. In its proposal regarding the Statute of the ICTY, France had suggested limiting the Tribunals' jurisdiction to 'the most serious war crimes, those committed on a mass and systematic scale, causing particular revulsion and calling for an international response' (UN Doc. S/2566, at 21, 25, in Morris and Scharf, *The Yugoslav Tribunal*, vol. 2, p 59). Likewise, the CSCE report (see Morris and Scharf, *The Yugoslav Tribunal*, vol. 2, p 211, cited in n 201 p 60 of Scharf, vol. 1) suggested that the ICTY's jurisdiction 'should be limited to the most serious crimes, in particular in view of the fact that international proceedings are always more complex, costly and time-consuming than proceedings at the national level. Also the interest of prosecuting serious crimes is greater than in other cases.'

[99] It could be argued that acts that are not sufficiently serious to come within the Tribunal's jurisdiction could still be regarded as 'war crimes', as that qualification does not depend upon such a high threshold; this requirement is jurisdictional only, not substantive.

[100] *Tadić* Jurisdiction Decision, par 94. See also, e.g. *Akayesu* Trial Judgment, par 616; *Prosecutor v. Kvočka et al.*, IT-98-30/1-PT, Decision on Preliminary Motions Filed by Mlado Radić and Miroslav Kvočka Challenging Jurisdiction, 1 April 1999, par 9. The Appeals Chamber said that 'the fact of a combatant simply appropriating a loaf of bread in an occupied village would not amount to a "serious violation of international humanitarian law" although it may be regarded as falling foul of the basic principle laid down in Article 46, paragraph 1, of the Hague Regulations (and the corresponding rule of customary international law) whereby "private property must be respected" by any army occupying an enemy territory' (*Tadić* Jurisdiction Decision, par 94).

[101] *Kayishema and Ruzindana* Trial Judgment, par 184.

[102] See, for instance, concerning infringement of property interests, *Naletilić and Martinović* where the chamber dismissed one count on that basis, and *Kunarac* Rule 98bis Decision, pars 15–16, in relation to plunder.

The gravity of the infringement must be assessed on a case-by-case basis in view of all the circumstances of the case. Factors of relevance to that assessment range from the nature of the infringement, the manner in which it was carried out, the means and methods used, its repeated nature, the interest or value involved (e.g. human life, physical integrity, etc.), the position of the accused at the time of the acts, the nature of the accused's participation, the consequences of the acts upon the victim, the irremovability of these consequences, the motives of the accused, etc.[103] In particular, the context in which the act is committed may render it more serious than it could at first appear: thus, an act of denunciation to authorities may not *per se* appear very serious, unless such denunciation is likely to lead to the criminal execution of the person thereby denounced. Likewise, certain infringements which, individually, would not be sufficiently serious to constitute a war crime may, if repeated, fall within that category.[104]

Some categories of offences appear to be serious enough *per se* to qualify as war crimes within the Tribunals' jurisdiction without further need for the court to consider the circumstances under which these crimes were carried out.[105] These would be likely to include all of those offences expressly listed in the Statute under Articles 2 and 3 of the ICTY Statute and Article 4 of the ICTR Statute.[106]

6.3.4 Individual criminal responsibility

Most humanitarian rules are binding *qua* international law on states only, not on individuals directly. And still fewer entail individual criminal responsibility in case of breach. The Judgment of the International Military Tribunal in Nuremberg remarked, however, that crimes are committed by individuals, not by states, and that no one should be allowed to hide behind this normative illusion. By the time the Nazi leaders were put on trial, only some of its most fundamental provisions had taken penal shape. Since then, however, the number and variety of infringements which are said to entail individual criminal responsibility have multiplied several-fold and the Tribunals have taken stock of this development and have in fact promoted it.

The process by which an international prohibition which might at first have been binding on states only becomes binding on individuals and, furthermore, entails criminal consequences if breached, is one of the murkier aspects of the Tribunals' jurisprudence. It appears that, often, Trial Chambers have been quite prompt in deducing the criminal character of a prohibition from the mere fact

---

103 For an illustration, see *Aleksovski* Appeal Judgment, pars 30 et seq., where the appellant submitted that the acts for which he had been convicted were not sufficiently serious to amount to war crimes pursuant to Article 3.

104 See *Kupreškić* Trial Judgment, par 526 concerning the cumulative effect of attacks on military objectives.

105 Most serious offences addressing the physical integrity of an individual would be of this sort.

106 See, e.g. *Akayesu* Trial Judgment, par 616; *Semanza* Trial Judgment, pars 370–371 and references quoted therein; *Kayishema and Ruzindana* Trial Judgment, par 184.

that the conduct in question was prohibited as between states.[107] An international crime, however, is more than a breach of international law, and not all breaches of international law constitute international crimes. An international crime means a particular conduct which is made criminal directly by international law both as regards the prohibited conduct as well as the criminal responsibility placed upon individuals for such conduct.[108] The criminalization of conducts in breach of the laws of war has traditionally been reserved for the most serious breaches of its fundamental provisions, but with the advent of human rights, international humanitarian law has come to recognize a growing number of such violations as war crimes when commited in the context of an armed conflict. These differ significantly in terms of the values and interests that they seek to protect and in terms of the seriousness of the violations that they sanction. And many obligations that originally were binding upon states only have morphed into criminal prohibitions, modifying at times the very definition or scope of the prohibited conduct.[109]

In practice, what the *ad hoc* Tribunals must establish in relation to every conduct which they say constitutes a war crime is therefore that the conduct in question has become criminal under customary international law by reason that, for instance, most if not all national jurisdictions have criminalized it or by showing that a treaty provision which prohibits certain conduct has come to represent customary international criminal law. It may also be shown that, in the language of the International Covenant on Civil and Political Rights (article 15.2), conduct is 'criminal according to the general principles of law recognized by the community of nations'.[110]

When making such an assessment, the court may take into account some of the following factors: (i) a clear 'intent [on the part of the international community]

[107] In its opening to the discussion of this offence, the *Kordić and Čerkez* Trial Chamber stated that it would 'consider the definition of imprisonment pursuant to which its *legality* will be discussed' (*Kordić and Čerkez* Trial Judgment, par 295 (emphasis added). The Trial Chamber then defined 'imprisonment' as 'arbitrary imprisonment, that is to say, the deprivation of liberty of the individual without due process of law' (ibid., para 302). The Chamber further stated that the *unlawfulness* of the imprisonment would be assessed in light of the following factors: '(i) civilians have been detained in contravention of Article 42 of the Geneva Convention IV, i.e., they are detained without reasonable grounds to believe that the security of the Detaining Power makes it absolutely necessary; (ii) the procedural safeguards required by Article 43 of the Geneva Convention IV are not complied with in respect of detained civilians, even where initial detention may have been justified; (iii) they occur as part of a widespread or systematic attack directed against a civilian population' (ibid., para 303).

[108] See, *Vasiljević* Trial Judgment, par 193 and *Ojdanić* Joint Criminal Enterprise Decision, par 9 (in particular, fn 28), citing the holding of the *Vasiljević* Trial Chamber with approval.

[109] See, e.g. *Kunarac* Trial Judgment, pars 465 et seq., concerning the definition of the crime of 'torture'.

[110] *Čelebići* Appeal Judgment, par 173. See also *Milutinović* Joint Criminal Enterprise Decision, par 42. One author has pertinently insisted on the facts that acts which have been criminalized at the international level are those which cause grave harm to the international community (R. Woetzel, *The Nuremberg Trials in International Law* (New York: Stevens & Praeger, 1960), p 110).

to criminalise' that conduct;[111] (ii) the fact that such conduct may be said to be contrary to 'elementary considerations of humanity'; (iii) the general condemnation of such breaches; (iv) the fact that 'substantive justice and equity' require that such conduct be regarded as criminal; and (v) the fact that there have been a number of undertakings to punish certain actions.[112] Ultimately, it has not always been evident how these factors have been taken into account by international and domestic war crimes courts. It has often been the case that the last step in the process of criminalization of legal prohibitions in international law has been a judicial step, and nowhere more so perhaps than at the *ad hoc* Tribunals.

Once the Tribunal is satisfied that the above requirements have all been met, it must finally determine whether the prohibition under consideration has reached a sufficient degree of precision and accessibility to satisfy the fundamental principle of legality. This principle provides that no person should be convicted for a crime that did not exist at the time of the acts charged against the accused or for which there existed no reasonably foreseeable and accessible definition at the time.[113] It is remarkable, and perhaps somewhat surprising that, with one exception,[114] Trial Chambers of both Tribunals have systematically found that all of the crimes charged by the Prosecution existed under international law at the relevant time and that all of them were sufficiently defined to meet the requirements of foreseeability and accessibility. That, in itself, highlights the important normative role of the judges of those Tribunals in the defining of international offences found in the Tribunals' Statutes.

---

[111] If the intent to criminalize a given course of action is unclear from existing practice, the court should in principle refrain from considering it criminal. 'The fact of the controversial character of some of the rules of war tends [. . .] to impose a limitation upon the scope of offences which may properly be prosecuted as war crimes.' (H. Lauterpacht, 'The Law of Nations and the Punishment of War Crimes', 21 *British Yearbook of International Law (BYIL)* 58, 74 and 75 (1944)).

[112] *Tadić* Jurisdiction Decision, pars 128–137. In their dissenting report, the American members of the Commission on the Responsibility of Authors of War which was set up after the First World War, suggested that in determining the criminality of an act, one should take into account the wantonness or malice of the perpetrator, the needlessness of the act from a military point of view, the perpetration of a justifiable act in a needlessly harsh or cruel manner, and the improper motive which inspired it. Memorandum of Reservations Presented by the Representatives of the United States to the Report of the Commission on Responsibilities, contained in Annex II to the Report of the Majority Commission on the Responsibility of the Authors of the War and on Enforcement of Penalties, 29 March 1919 (also cited in *History of the United Nations War Crimes Commission and the Development of the Laws of War*, compiled by the United Nations War Crimes Commission, 1948, p 36).

[113] See, e.g. *Ojdanić* Joint Criminal Enterprise Decision, par 21.

[114] See *Vasiljević* Trial Judgment, pars 193 et seq. (in relation to 'violence to life and person').

7

Grave Breaches of the 1949
Geneva Conventions

7.1   Grave breaches of the Geneva Conventions as war crimes

Each of the four Geneva Conventions of 12 August 1949 contains a 'grave breaches' section, which specifies particular breaches of the Conventions for which the High Contracting Parties have a duty to prosecute those responsible and in relation to which jurisdiction is recognized as universal.[1]

The 'grave breaches' of the Geneva Conventions constitute a particular sub-category of war crimes. To come within the ICTY's jurisdiction, a grave breach must therefore meet all of the above requirements (armed conflict and nexus therewith and other jurisdictional requirements) in addition to those specific to the grave breaches regime. Although they share the *chapeau* requirements with all other war crimes, grave breaches are characterized from other categories of war crimes, as far as their definition is concerned, in at least two important respects. First, grave breaches only apply to armed conflicts of an international character (or to a state of occupation) and not to internal armed conflicts. A grave breach of the Geneva Conventions may not, therefore, be committed in the context of an internal armed conflict. Because the subject-matter jurisdiction of the ICTR is limited to war crimes committed in an internal armed conflict, grave breaches do not fall within its jurisdiction and the relevancy of the grave breaches regime is therefore limited, as far as the *ad hoc* Tribunals are concerned, to the ICTY.

The second main characteristic of the grave breaches regime concerns the status of those protected by it, in that the protection afforded thereunder is limited to specific categories of individuals ('protected persons') and properties ('protected

---

[1] *Tadić* Jurisdiction Decision, par 79.

properties'). Thus, whereas other categories of war crimes (in particular, those provided for in Article 3 of the ICTY Statute) may apply generally to any civilian or to any category of civilian properties itself, the scope of the grave breaches regime is clearly limited to certain categories of protected individuals and properties. The concepts of 'protected persons' and 'protected properties' are thus technical expressions which strictly limit the categories of people and properties which may enjoy the protection of the grave breaches regime.

There is no distinction between the grave breaches regime and other categories of war crimes, however, insofar as perpetrators are concerned. Any person may, in principle, commit a grave breach of the Geneva Conventions.

Aside from those definitional specificities which will be discussed below, the grave breach regime is characterized by a particular set of procedures and obligations placed upon states that are parties to the Geneva Conventions, which includes, not least a system of universal jurisdiction.[2] The purpose of the Geneva Conventions in providing for universal jurisdiction in relation to its grave breaches only, the Appeals Chamber has explained, was 'to avoid interference by domestic courts of other States in situations which concern only the relationship between a State and its own nationals'.[3] The fact that the Geneva Conventions provide for such an enforcement mechanism over its grave breaches does not, however, have direct relevance to the ICTY, as the scope of its jurisdiction is determined by its Statute (and customary international law) and not, for instance, by any procedural requirements set in the Geneva Conventions or their Additional Protocols.[4] The grave breaches regime, as provided in the Geneva Conventions, also provides for a number of additional obligations binding on state parties to the Geneva Conventions, but those are of limited relevance, if not complete irrelevance, to the *ad hoc* Tribunals.[5]

7.2   General elements of grave breaches

7.2.1   'International' armed conflicts and state of occupation

International armed conflicts

As noted by the Appeals Chamber, although Article 2 of the ICTY Statute does not explicitly refer to the nature of the conflicts to which it may apply, its reference

---

[2] *Tadić* Jurisdiction Decision, par 79: 'for these specific acts, the [Geneva] Conventions create universal mandatory criminal jurisdiction among contracting States'.

[3] *Čelebići* Appeal Judgment, par 79. See also ICRC, *Commentary to Geneva Convention IV*, p 46.

[4] That enforcement mechanism, the Appeals Chamber made clear, had not been imported into the Statute since the International Tribunal itself constitutes a self-sufficient enforcement system for the perpetrators of grave breaches who come within its jurisdiction (*Tadić* Jurisdiction Decision, par 81).

[5] State parties to the Geneva Conventions must, for instance, provide for criminal sanctions for individuals committing or ordering the commission of grave breaches, enact legislation necessary to provide for effective punishment of persons committing or ordering the commission of a grave breach and search for persons alleged to have committed or ordered the commission of grave breaches and bring them (regardless of their nationality) before their courts. See, generally, G. Draper, *The Red Cross Conventions* (New York: Draeper, 1958), pp 20 et seq.

to the grave breaches provisions suggest that the article is limited in its application to international armed conflicts.[6]

The clearest scenario where an international armed conflict may be said to exist is where two states are openly waging war against one another. In addition, an armed conflict on the territory of one state which may at first sight appear to be internal in character may be regarded as international (or, depending upon the circumstances, it may be deemed to be international in character alongside an internal armed conflict[7]) 'where the troops of another State intervene in the conflict or even where some participants in the internal armed conflict act on behalf of this other State'.[8] Thus, an armed conflict may be regarded as international where '(i) another State intervenes in that conflict through its troops, or alternatively if (ii) some of the participants in the internal armed conflict act on behalf of that other State'.[9] The test to be applied in both cases to determine whether the armed conflict is or has been an 'international' one is that of whether the other state has 'overall control' over some of the participants in the conflict:[10]

In order to attribute the acts of a military or paramilitary group to a State, it must be proved that the State wields overall control over the group, not only by equipping and financing the group, but also by coordinating or helping in the general planning of its military activity. Only then can the State be held internationally accountable for any misconduct of the group. However, it is not necessary that, in addition, the State should also issue, either to the head or to members of the group, instructions for the commission of specific acts contrary to international law.

The 'overall control' test therefore 'calls for an assessment of all the elements of control [between a particular state and a party to the armed conflict] taken as a whole and a determination to be made on that basis as to whether there was the required degree of control'.[11] Such a degree of control may manifest itself in many

---

[6] *Tadić* Jurisdiction Decision, par 78 and *Tadić* Appeal Judgment par 80. As noted above, an 'international armed conflict' may be said to exist for the purpose of the Tribunal's jurisdiction whenever there is a resort to armed force between States (*Tadić* Jurisdiction Decision, par 70). The determination that an armed conflict is international in character will not only dictate the body of law which will apply to that armed conflict, but it may also happen that a foreign state which is involved in such a conflict may, under certain circumstances, be held responsible for violations of international humanitarian law committed by individuals acting on its behalf (*Tadić* Appeal Judgment, par 97).

[7] Ibid., par 84.　　　[8] See, e.g. *Blaškić* Trial Judgment, par 76.

[9] *Tadić* Appeal Judgment, par 84. See also *Rajić* Rule 61 Decision, pars 13–32. The ICTY has not specified whether intervention on the side of the state as opposed to a non-state entity involved in the armed conflict could internationalize the armed conflict as when, for instance, a state would call for the assistance of an adjacent state to quash an insurgency within its territory.

[10] *Tadić* Appeal Judgment, par 131. It should be pointed out, however, that the Appeals Chamber appears to have limited the applicability of the 'overall control' test to organized armed groups. As for individuals or groups not organised into military structures, the *Tadić* Appeals Judgment tends to suggest that 'specific instructions concerning the commission of that particular act' need to have been given their actions to be regarded as attributable to the state (ibid, pars 132–137). Alternatively, the Appeals Chamber said, it must be established whether the unlawful act of that individual or un-organised group had been publicly endorsed or approved ex post facto by the State in question (ibid., par 137).

[11] *Aleksovski* Appeal Judgment, para 145 and *Čelebići* Appeal Judgment, par 42 on the determination by the Appeals Chamber that the applicable test was that of 'overall control'. See, generally, *Tadić* Appeal Judgment, pars 88–145 and *Čelebići* Appeal Judgment, pars 10–26, in particular concerning the reasons for the exclusion of the 'effective control' test laid out by the ICJ in the *Nicaragua* case

ways, none of which will necessarily be decisive individually: financial and logistical support; direct or indirect involvement in directing, coordinating, or supervising local troops; planning of operations; transfer, appointment, and replacement of army officers ordered by the controlling state; payment of wages of warring forces; common political or military agenda between the state and the party to the conflict; coordination of operations between the controlling state and the local forces; and other forms of support and assistance are all relevant.[12] The giving by the controlling state of orders or instructions is not a prerequisite of the 'overall control' test, although the existence of any such order or instruction may be relevant to whether or not overall control was indeed exercised at the time.[13] The 'overall control' test could thus be fulfilled even if the armed forces acting on behalf of the controlling state had some discretion in the choice of means and tactics to conduct their operations, although participating in a common strategy along with the controlling state.[14] And the controlling state need not be in overall control of local troops in the whole of the territory in which combat is taking place. Its involvement may be geographically more limited.[15] The Appeals Chamber has found that when the controlling state is an adjacent state, and that the controlling state is attempting to acquire territory in the neighbouring state through the armed forces which it controls, it may be easier to establish that threshold.[16]

(*Nicaragua v. United States of America*, International Court of Justice, judgment of 27 June 1986, in ICJ Reports 1986 ('*Nicaragua case*')). According to the Appeals Chamber, '[t]o the extent that it provides for greater protection of civilian victims of armed conflicts [than the 'effective control' test as applied by the ICJ in the *Nicaragua* case and the 'specific instructions' test], this different and less rigorous standard is wholly consistent with the fundamental purpose of Geneva Convention IV, which is to ensure 'protection of civilians to the maximum extent possible' (*Tadić* Appeal Judgment, par 146; see also *Čelebići* Appeal Judgment, par 42).

[12] See, generally, *Tadić* Appeal Judgment, pars 150–151 and for the factual application of that test, see ibid., pars 152–162. See also *Blaškić* Trial Judgment, pars 95–123; *Rajić* Rule 61 Decision, pars 13–32; and *Naletilić and Martinović* Trial Judgment, pars 189 et seq. and references quoted therein.

[13] See *Aleksovski* Appeal Judgment, pars 141–144. See also *Tadić* Appeal Judgment, pars 137: 'control by a State over subordinate *armed forces or militias or paramilitary units* may be of an overall character (and must comprise more than the mere provision of financial assistance or military equipment or training). This requirement, however, does not go so far as to include the issuing of specific orders by the State, or its direction of each individual operation. Under international law it is by no means necessary that the controlling authorities should plan all the operations of the units dependent on them, choose their targets, or give specific instructions concerning the conduct of military operations and any alleged violations of international humanitarian law. The control required by international law may be deemed to exist when a State (or, in the context of an armed conflict, the Party to the conflict) *has a role in organizing, coordinating or planning the military actions* of the military group, in addition to financing, training and equipping or providing operational support to that group. Acts performed by the group or members thereof may be regarded as acts of *de facto* State organs regardless of any specific instruction by the controlling State concerning the commission of each of those acts.' [14] *Čelebići* Appeal Judgment, par 47.

[15] See, e.g. *Blaškić* Trial Judgment, par 94; *Naletilić and Martinović* Trial Judgment, par 194: 'There is no requirement to prove that HV troops [i.e., Croatian troops] were present in every single area where crimes were allegedly committed. On the contrary, the [armed] conflict between the [Bosnian Muslim Army] and the [Bosnian Croat Army] must be looked upon as a whole and, if it is found to be international in character through the participation of [Croatian] troops, then Article 2 of the Statute will apply to the entire territory of the conflict.'

[16] *Tadić* Appeal Judgment, par 140.

In the *Milošević* case, the question was raised as to the point in time when two states may be said to have become involved in an international armed conflict when one or both of those states were seceding from another state. In its indictment relating to the conflict which took place in Croatia, the Prosecution claimed that the armed conflict in Croatia could be said to have been international in character from 8 October 1991, the date on which Croatia's declaration of independence from the Socialist Federal Republic of Yugoslavia became effective. The *amici curiae* in this case submitted, by contrast, that the conflict only became international at a point in time between 15 January 1992, when Croatia was recognized by the European Community, and 22 May 1992, when it became a member of the United Nations.[17] The Trial Chamber in this case said that the existence of Croatia as a state, as understood in the definition of an international armed conflict, and the moment from which it may be said to have come into existence, could be established based on four elements ('the core principles for the determination of statehood'[18]) drawn from Article 1 of the Montevideo Convention on Rights and Duties of States of 26 December 1933:[19]

  (i)   a permanent population;
 (ii) a defined territory;[20]
(iii) a government;[21]
(iv) the capacity to enter into relations with other states.

In this case, the Trial Chamber said that Croatia met all of those requirements no later than 8 October 1991 and that the armed conflict between Croatia and the Socialist Federal Republic of Yugoslavia could therefore be regarded as international in character since that date.[22]

Just as an armed conflict which is originally internal in character may become an international one, an international armed conflict could develop into an internal one where the overall control of a state external to the territory over local forces ceases to exist. But the mere withdrawal of one state's official forces from the territory of another would not necessarily have that effect where the withdrawing state is otherwise able to exercise overall control over one party to the conflict, or of forces fighting for that party. In the case where a state has apparently withdrawn its forces from another state, the conflict may thus continue to be regarded as international if it can be established that there is 'continuity of control' between that state and the groups or forces that it had been assisting. In such a case, despite the apparent withdrawal of its forces, the state may maintain the 'overall control' of the local armed forces.[23]

---

[17] *Milošević* Rule 98bis Decision, par 83.   [18] Ibid., par 86.   [19] Ibid., pars 85–114.
  [20] The Trial Chamber made it clear that claims to the territory as a whole or to parts thereof would not affect the question, of statehood, nor do the boundaries of that country need to be fully determined (ibid., par 96, and examples cited therein).
  [21] The Trial Chamber noted, *inter alia*, that Croatia had an effectively functioning government, with ministerial and other personnel, which performed all sorts of governmental functions (ibid., par 106).   [22] Ibid., par 115.
  [23] See, e.g. *Čelebići* Appeal Judgment, pars 34–51.

States which are party to an armed conflict may decide that certain treaties or provisions may apply between them, regardless of the actual character of the armed conflict in which they are involved.[24] It would appear however that the Tribunals have excluded the possibility for parties to an armed conflict ever to agree upon the nature of the armed conflict in which they are involved, which might have allowed them in practice to 'contract out' of a particular regime which would otherwise be binding on them 'by reason of the nature of the relevant conflict.[25] The nature of the armed conflict is an issue of facts and law to be determined by the court and the Appeals Chamber has made it clear, in any case, that in determining the issue of the nature of the conflict, 'structures put in place by the parties should not be taken at face value':[26]

Undue emphasis upon the ostensible structures and overt declarations of the belligerents, as opposed to a nuanced analysis of the reality of their relationship, may tacitly suggest to groups who are in *de facto* control of military forces that responsibility for the acts of such forces can be evaded merely by resort to a superficial restructuring of such forces or by a facile declaration that the reconstituted forces are henceforth independent of their erstwhile sponsors.[27]

From an evidentiary point of view, it may be somewhat complicated for the Prosecution to establish the existence of an international armed conflict. This, coupled with the fact that most (if not all) acts, which could otherwise amount to grave breaches of the Geneva Conventions, could also be charged under Article 3 of the ICTY Statute, has led to the slow disappearance of Article 2 charges from most indictments or to their withdrawal where they originally existed.[28]

State of occupation

The grave breaches regime will also apply in those situations where a state of occupation existed at the relevant time. 'Occupation', one Trial Chamber noted, is 'a transitional period following invasion and preceding agreement on the cessation of the hostilities. This distinction imposes more onerous duties on an occupying power than on a party to an international armed conflict.'[29] Pursuant to Article 42 of the Hague Regulations, which is generally regarded as representing customary law on

---

[24] See *Čelebići* Appeal Judgment, par 44 and *Čelebići* Trial Judgment, par 229.
[25] See, e.g. *Blaškić* Trial Judgment, par 82 where the Trial Chamber held that 'the parties to the conflict may not agree between themselves to change the nature of the conflict, which is established by the facts whose interpretation, where applicable, falls to the Judge'. See also *Akayesu* Trial Judgment, par 603; *Čelebići* Appeal Judgment, par 44. The recognition of belligerency by one side would turn the conflict (whatever its nature prior to that recognition) into an international armed conflict. [26] *Čelebići* Appeal Judgment, par 46.
[27] *Tadić* Appeal Judgment, par 154.
[28] The withdrawal of Article 2 charges took place, for instance, in the *Krnojelac* case prior to the commencement of trial (see *Prosecutor v. Krnojelac*, IT-97-25-PT, Motion to Withdraw Article Two Counts, 27 October 2000). Article 2 charges were also withdrawn in *Hadžihasanović* (see *Prosecutor v. Hadžihasanović*, IT-01-47-PT, Amended Indictment, 11 January 2002).
[29] *Naletilić and Martinović* Trial Judgment, par 214.

that point, '[t]erritory is considered occupied when it is actually placed under the authority of the hostile army. The occupation extends only to the territory where such authority has been established and can be exercised.'[30] 'Occupation' is therefore more than mere presence in a given geographical space and more than mere military invasion of a given territory.[31] To determine that a territory is indeed 'occupied', the following elements must in principle be established:[32]

(i) the occupying power must be in a position to substitute its own authority for that of the authorities of the occupied state, which must have been rendered incapable of functioning publicly;[33]

(ii) the enemy's forces have surrendered, been defeated or withdrawn. In this respect, battle areas may not be considered as occupied territory. However, sporadic local resistance, even if successful, does not affect the reality of occupation;[34]

---

[30] See ibid., par 216; and *Kordić and Čerkez* Trial Judgment, par 339, which adopted that definition. It is an interesting question, and apparently an unresolved one, whether a state could ever be said to 'occupy' parts of its own territory. See, e.g. *Tan Tuan v. Lucena Food Control Board* (Philippines Supreme Court, 6 October 1949), which related to a seizure of black market goods on 14 June 1945: 'This phase of the case is controlled by the laws of war [. . .]. The fact that this was not foreign territory did not deprive the US Army of the status of belligerent occupant. Military government may be established not only in foreign territory occupied or invaded in time of war, but also domestic territory in a state of rebellion or civil war.'

[31] See, for an interesting and debatable position upon this matter, W. Hays Parks, Special Assistant to the Army JAG, Briefing on Geneva Convention, EPW's and War Crimes, US Department of Defense, 7 April 2003, www.defenselink.mil/news/Apr2003/t04072003_t407genv.html:

> *Parks*: When you are an infantry company commander, and you're told to take the hill, you physically occupy it. That's military occupation with a smaller – lower case 'm' and lower case 'o'. It certainly does not mean that you have taken over it with the intent to run the government in that area. That's the very clear-cut distinction, that until – usually, until the fighting has concluded and is very conclusive, do you reach the point where technically there might be Military Occupation – capital 'M', capital 'O' – and a declaration of occupation is issued. That's a factual determination; it's a determination by the combatant commander in coordination with others, as well. Obviously, we occupy a great deal of Iraq at this time. But we are not, in the technical sense of the law of war, a military occupier or occupation force.
>
> *Question*: Until hostilities cease?
>
> *Parks*: That's going to be a factual determination by the combatant commander in consultation with others.

[32] *Naletilić and Martinović* Trial Judgment, par 217 (footnotes are in the original).

[33] *Rajić* Review Decision, pars 41–42, quoting A. Roberts, *What Is a Military Occupation?* 53 BYIL, pp 249 and 300 (1984). See also *Manual of Military Law, Part III, The Law of War on Land*, United Kingdom, 1958, par 503; *The Law of Land Warfare*, Field Manual No. 27–10, US Department of the Army, 18 July 1956, chapter 6, par 355; *Interim Law of Armed Conflict Manual*, New Zealand Defence Force, 26 November 1992, par 1302.4.

[34] See *Manual of Military Law, Part III, The Law of War on Land*, United Kingdom, 1958, pars 502, 506, and 509; *The Law of Land Warfare*, Field Manual No. 27–10, US Department of the Army, 18 July 1956, chapter 6, pars 356 and 360; *Interim Law of Armed Conflict Manual*, New Zealand Defence Force, 26 November 1992, at pars 1302.2 and 1302.5. See also *Humanitarian Law in Armed Conflicts, Manual*, edited by the Federal Ministry of Defence of the Federal Republic of Germany, August 1992, par 528.

(iii) the occupying power has a sufficient force present, or the capacity to send troops within a reasonable time to make the authority of the occupying power felt;[35]

(iv) a temporary administration has been established over the territory;[36]

(v) the occupying power has issued and enforced directions to the civilian population.[37]

The law of occupation only applies to those areas actually controlled by the occupying power although it does not require physical presence or control on every square metre of a given territory.[38] In a situation where the Prosecution claims that a state of occupation has been established, the Court will have to determine 'on a case by case basis whether this degree of control was established at the relevant times and in the relevant places'.[39] And just as an armed conflict may be internationalized by the involvement of a foreign power, occupation may apparently take place through proxies, if those who physically occupy a given territory are in fact under the overall control of a foreign power.[40]

Despite the above, one Trial Chamber has suggested that the time at which the law of occupation may become applicable to 'individuals' may be different from the time at which it may apply to 'property and other matters'. According to the

---

[35] See *Manual of Military Law, Part III, The Law of War on Land*, United Kingdom, 1958, pars 502 and 506; *The Law of Land Warfare*, Field Manual No. 27–10, US Department of the Army, 18 July 1956, chapter 6, par 356; *Interim Law of Armed Conflict Manual*, New Zealand Defence Force, 26 November 1992, pars 1302.2, 1302.3, and 1302.5.

[36] See *Manual of Military Law, Part III, The Law of War on Land*, United Kingdom, 1958, par 501. See also, Lauterpacht, in *Oppenheim's International Law*, 7th edn, vol. 2, 1952, par 167.

[37] See Article 43 of The Hague Regulations, according to which '[t]he authority of the legitimate power having in fact passed into the hands of the occupant, the latter shall take all the measures in his power to restore, and ensure, as far as possible, public order and safety, while respecting, unless absolutely prevented, the laws in force in the country'; *Humanitarian Law in Armed Conflicts, Manual*, edited by the Federal Ministry of Defence of the Federal Republic of Germany, August 1992, par 527; D. Fleck, *The Handbook of Humanitarian Law in Armed Conflicts* (Oxford/New York: Oxford University Press, 1999), par 525.2.

[38] See *Tadić* Trial Judgment, par 580, which quotes from the *Manual of Military Law*, which states: 'The fact that there is a defended place or zone still in possession of the national forces within an occupied district does not make the occupation of the remainder invalid, provided that such place or defended zone is surrounded and effectively cut-off from the rest of the occupied district.' *Manual of Military Law*, Part III, *The Law of War on Land*, United Kingdom 1958, par. 501.

[39] See *Naletilić and Martinović* Trial Judgment, par 218: 'There is no requirement that an entire territory be occupied, provided that the isolated areas in which the authority of the occupied power is still functioning "are effectively cut off from the rest of the occupied territory" ' (footnote omitted). The *Naletilić and Martinović* Trial Chamber also correctly pointed out that the Trial Chamber was mistaken in having recourse to the 'overall control' test to determine the existence of a state of occupation (*Naletilić and Martinović* Trial Judgment, par 214; *Blaškić* Trial Judgment, pars 149–150).

[40] See, e.g. *Tadić* Trial Judgment, par 584: 'Such a situation [of occupied territory according to the Geneva Conventions] is not restricted to circumstances in which the foreign Power has occupied a certain territory and then recruits local agents. As will be seen, the relationship of *de facto* organs or agents to the foreign Power includes those circumstances in which the foreign Power "occupies" or operates in certain territory solely through the acts of local de facto organs or agents.' See also *Blaškić* Trial Judgment, par 149.

Naletilić and Martinović Trial Chamber, 'the application of the law of occupation as it affects "individuals" as civilians protected under Geneva Convention IV does not require that the occupying power have actual authority' and ' "[f]or the purposes of those individuals" rights, a state of occupation exists upon their falling into "the hands of the occupying power" '.[41] On the other hand, when the charges relate to 'protected properties', the Prosecution would be expected to establish that a formal 'state of occupation' as described above was in place at the time.[42]

The law of belligerent occupation will generally cease to apply when the occupying power loses effective control of the territory in question: 'Whether, then, this body of law is replaced by the laws of war in the narrower sense or by the law of the former territorial sovereign, depends on the fortunes of war.'[43]

From a prosecutorial point of view, the incentive to establish that a factual situation amounts to an 'occupation' appears to be essentially threefold: (i) a finding to that effect would trigger the applicability of the law of international armed conflicts and, therefore, a better developed, more protective, set of rules than if the conflict in question were to be regarded as an internal one; (ii) it would trigger in particular the applicability of the grave breaches provisions to such a situation which is, in many ways, more precise and detailed than other parts of the laws of war; and (iii) if the Prosecution were to charge an accused as a commander pursuant to Article 7(3) of the ICTY Statute, the existence of a state of occupation would provide for a broader (geographically based) form of command responsibility for the commander who is in charge of the occupied area, whereby he may be held responsible not only for the acts and conduct of those directly subordinated to him down the chain of command but for all those who would commit a crime within the occupied territory, all other conditions of command responsibility being met.[44]

---

[41] *Naletilić and Martinović* Trial Judgment, par 221.

[42] Ibid., par 222. It is unclear whether that interpretation is in contradiction with the findings of the *Rajić* Trial Chamber which seems to suggest that the law of occupation would apply during the invasion phase (and, therefore, prior to the formal establishment of a state of occupation) whether the protected interest is a civilian or properties (*Rajić* Rule 61 Decision, pars 40–42). The finding of the Trial Chamber on that point is, however, unclear and may be open to different interpretations.

[43] *International Law as Applied by International Courts and Tribunals* (Stevens & Sons, London, 1968), vol. 2, pp 174, 176, cited at *Tadić* Trial Judgment, par 581. See also *Naletilić and Martinović* Trial Judgment, par 218: 'The law of occupation [. . .] ceases to apply where the occupying power no longer exercises an actual authority over the occupied area.'

[44] 'The matter of subordination of units as a basis for fixing criminal responsibility becomes important in the case of a military commander having solely a tactical command. But as to the commanding general of occupied territory who is charged with maintaining peace and order, punishing crime and protecting lives and property, subordination are relatively *unimportant*. His responsibility is *general* and not limited to a control of units directly under his command. Subordinate commanders in occupied territory are similarly responsible to the extent that executive authority has been delegated to them.' (See *United States v. List and others*, US Military Tribunal sitting at Nuremberg, Judgment of 19 February 1948, TWC XI (1950) ('*Hostages* case'), p 1260).

May the grave breaches regime apply to internal armed conflicts?

May the grave breaches regime be applied to an internal armed conflict? Duško Tadić, the first indictee ever to appear before the ICTY, had argued that the grave breaches regime could not apply in the context of an internal armed conflict and that the Geneva Conventions had expressly limited its application to 'international' armed conflicts. The Trial Chamber in this case, however, decided otherwise. It pointed out that Article 2 of the ICTY Statute was a 'self-contained' provision and that it did not contain any requirement of an international, as opposed to internal, armed conflict for it to apply. The Trial Chamber held that it was only required to refer back to the Geneva Conventions for one purpose only, namely, the identification of those protected under the grave breaches regime.[45] There is, therefore, no ground for treating Article 2, the Trial Chamber said, as in effect importing into the Statute the whole of the terms of the Geneva Conventions, that is, including the requirement that the grave breaches be committed in the context of an international armed conflict. Tadić appealed the Trial Chamber's finding on that point.

The Appeals Chamber rejected the Trial Chamber's broad interpretation of Article 2. The grave breaches system, the Appeals Chamber held, establishes a twofold system with, on the one hand, an enumeration of those offences which are regarded as serious enough to qualify as grave breaches, and closely bound up with it on the other hand, a mandatory enforcement mechanism 'based on the concept of a duty and right of all Contracting States to search for and try or extradite persons allegedly responsible for "grave breaches"'.[46] Because of the constraining nature of that enforcement mechanism, the requirement that the conflict be 'international' in character, the Appeals Chamber explained, was 'a necessary limitation on the grave breaches system in light of the intrusion on State sovereignty'.[47] 'Grave breaches', the Appeals Chamber continued, may only be committed against those which the Geneva Conventions regards as 'protected persons' (and 'protected properties'), and those persons and properties are only protected by those Conventions if they are caught up in an international armed conflict.[48]

Interestingly, the Appeals Chamber noted that recent trends in the practice of states may be showing a possible change of *opinio juris* indicating that the limitation of the grave breaches regime to international conflicts may be dying out. It noted, in particular, the views of the government of the United States, which had submitted an *amicus curiae* brief on that point in which it suggested that 'the "grave breaches" provisions of Article 2 of the International Tribunal Statute apply

---

[45] Ibid.   [46] *Tadić* Jurisdiction Decision, par 80.   [47] Ibid.

[48] Ibid., par 81. 'By contrast', the Appeals Chamber added, 'those [grave breaches] provisions do not include persons and property coming within the purview of common Article 3 of the four Geneva Conventions' (ibid.).

to armed conflicts of a non-international character as well as those of an international character.'[49]

Were other states and international bodies to come to share this view, the Appeals Chamber said, a change in customary law concerning the scope of this regime might gradually materialize.[50] For the time being, however, and insofar as the ICTY's jurisdiction is concerned, grave breaches provisions only apply in the context of an international armed conflict.[51]

7.2.2 'Protected persons' and 'protected property' – the status of the victim

Only where it is proved that the armed conflict was international in character or that there was a state of occupation at the relevant time will the court turn to the second question of whether the victims are to be regarded as 'protected persons' or as 'protected properties' as understood under the Geneva Conventions.[52] In order to establish whether a person or an object is 'protected', reference will be made to the relevant provisions of the four Geneva Conventions (which each define the persons and property to which their respective provisions apply[53]) with the interpretative assistance of the accompanying ICRC *Commentaries*.[54]

Protected persons

Article 4 of Geneva Convention IV provides that '[p]ersons protected by the Convention are those who, at a given moment and in any manner whatsoever, find themselves, in case of a conflict or occupation, in the hands of a Party to the Conflict or Occupying Power of which they are not nationals'. The limitations placed upon the categories of persons which are entitled to the protection of that regime are essentially twofold: first, the person must find himself or herself 'in the hands of a Party to the Conflict or Occupying Power' and he or she must be of a different nationality from that state.

---

[49] *Prosecutor v. Tadić*, IT-94-1-T, [*Amicus curiae*] Submission of the Government of the United States of America Concerning Certain Arguments Made by Counsel for the Accused in the Case of *The Prosecutor of the Tribunal v. Dusan Tadić*, 17 July 1995, p 35, cited at *Tadić* Jurisdiction Decision, par 83.

[50] *Tadić* Jurisdiction Decision, par 83. See also *Kordić and Čerkez* Articles 2 and 3 Jurisdiction Decision, par 15.

[51] *Tadić* Jurisdiction Decision, par 84. See, generally, S. Boelaert-Suominen, 'Grave Breaches, Universal Jurisdiction and Internal Armed Conflict: Is Customary Law Moving Towards a Uniform Enforcement Mechanism for all Armed Conflicts?', 5 *Journal of Conflict and Security Law* 63 (2000).   [52] *Tadić* Appeal Judgment, par 82.

[53] All four Geneva Conventions and their Commentaries are available on the ICRC's website (www.icrc.org).

[54] Ibid., pars 80 and 81. Concerning the relevancy of the ICRC Commentaries to the Geneva Conventions and their Additional Protocols, see, e.g. *Milošević* Rule 98 bis Decision, par 19.

Subject to Article 4(2) of Geneva Convention IV,[55] civilians as well as prisoners of war (in enemy territory, occupied territory, or the combat zone) who do not have the nationality of the belligerent in whose hands they find themselves, or who are stateless persons, may be regarded as protected persons.[56] Prisoners of war, for this purpose, could be either members of the regular armed forces of one of the parties to the conflict or 'members of militias or volunteer corps belonging to a party which in addition met all of the following requirements: (a) were commanded by a person responsible for his subordinates; (b) had a fixed distinctive sign recognizable at a distance; (c) carried arms openly; and (d) conducted their operations in accordance with the laws and customs of war'.[57]

Civilians do, in principle, enjoy the status of protected persons – all other conditions being met – unless they take a direct part in the hostilities in which case they would, for such time as they take part therein, lose their status as protected persons.[58] The Trial Chamber in the *Čelebići* case pointed out that there should be no gap in protection between Geneva Convention III (relating to prisoners of war) and Geneva Convention IV (relating to civilians) and that if the victim may not be regarded as a prisoner of war pursuant to the Third Convention, 'he or she necessarily falls within the ambit of Convention IV, provided that its article 4 requirements are satisfied'.[59]

As noted by the Appeals Chamber, 'protected persons' pursuant to Article 2 of the Statute must 'perforce' cover the persons mentioned in Articles 13, 24, 25, and 26 of Geneva Convention I, Articles 13, 36, and 37 of Convention II, Article 4 of Convention III on prisoners of war, and Articles 4 and 20 of Convention IV on civilians.[60]

The Appeals Chamber further noted that the Geneva Conventions also intend to protect:[61]

[T]hose civilians in occupied territory who, while having the nationality of the Party to the conflict in whose hands they find themselves, are refugees and thus no longer owe allegiance to this Party and no longer enjoy its diplomatic protection (consider, for instance, a situation similar to that of German Jews who had fled to France before 1940, and thereafter found themselves in the hands of German forces occupying French territory).

---

[55] Article 4(2) of Geneva Convention IV reads as follows: 'Nationals of a State which is not bound by the Convention are not protected by it. Nationals of a neutral State who find themselves in the territory of a belligerent State, and nationals of a co-belligerent State, shall not be regarded as protected persons while the State of which they are nationals has normal diplomatic representation in the State in whose hands they are.'

[56] See, generally, *Naletilić and Martinović* Trial Judgment, pars 203–209; *Tadić* Appeal Judgment, par 164. Those participating in a *levée en masse* would also be protected under that regime (see *Čelebići* Trial Judgment, par 268). The Trial Chamber has defined this category of individuals as 'inhabitants of a non-occupied territory who, on the approach of the enemy, spontaneously took up arms to resist the invading forces, without having had time to form themselves into regular armed units, and at all times they carried arms openly and respected the laws and customs of war' (ibid.; see also ibid., par 270).

[57] See, generally, *Čelebići* Trial Judgment, par 268.

[58] See, generally, Article 51(3) of Additional Protocol I.   [59] *Čelebići* Trial Judgment, par 271.

[60] *Tadić* Jurisdiction Decision, par 81.   [61] *Tadić* Appeal Judgment, par 164.

To be relevant to that issue, the Appeals Chamber stated, diplomatic representation must be 'effective and satisfactory', although it did not lay down the exact significance of this requirement.[62] Thus, the determination of what person may be said to be 'protected' under that regime does not depend solely on his or her nationality, *sensu stricto*, but account must also be taken of the existence or non-existence of actual diplomatic protection in relation to that person:[63]

[. . .] nationals of a neutral State or a co-belligerent State are not treated as 'protected persons' unless they are deprived of or do not enjoy diplomatic protection. In other words, those nationals are not 'protected persons' as long as they benefit from the normal diplomatic protection of their State; when they lose it or in any event do not enjoy it, the Convention automatically grants them the status of 'protected persons'.

The nationals of co-belligerent states cannot, in principle, be regarded as being 'protected'.[64] But before making a finding that two states are indeed co-belligerents for the purpose of applying (or not applying) the grave breaches regime, the court will have to determine, in fact, whether these states are *acting as* co-belligerents. If two states are not in reality acting towards each other as co-belligerents, although they may claim to be, their citizens (and prisoners of war) could in principle enjoy the protection of the regime.[65]

It is unclear from the jurisprudence of the ICTY whether an accused charged with a grave breach must be proved to have been aware of the circumstances that render a particular individual a protected person and, if so, of what exactly he must be shown to have known.[66] What is certain, however, is that the Prosecution must establish in relation to each alleged victim that at the time when the crime

---

[62] *Blaškić* Appeal Judgment, par 186.

[63] *Tadić* Appeal Judgment, par 165; see ibid., par 168: '[Article 4 of Geneva Convention IV's] primary purpose is to ensure the safeguards afforded by the Convention to those civilians who do not enjoy the diplomatic protection, and correlatively are not subject to the allegiance and control, of the State in whose hands they may find themselves. In granting its protection, Article 4 intends to look to the substance of relations, not to their legal characterisation as such.' See also *Blaškić* Trial Judgment, pars 145–146; *Blaškić* Appeal Judgment, pars 172–182.

[64] Article 4(2) of Geneva Convention IV provides that 'nationals of a co-belligerent State shall not be regarded as protected persons while the State of which they are nationals has normal diplomatic representation in the State in whose hands they are'.

[65] See *Blaškić* Appeal Judgment, pars 187–188; *Blaškić* Trial Judgment, pars 134–143. The Trial Chamber noted that, indeed, Bosnia and Croatia had not declared war on each other, that they continued during the conflict to enter into various international agreements and that their diplomatic relations were not terminated by the conflict. The Chamber said, however, that it should not limit its considerations to 'the formal or superficial elements' but instead examine 'the true situation' of their relationship during the conflict (pars 137–139). Although they fought Serb forces together, the Trial Chamber said, Bosnia never saw Croatia as a co-belligerent insofar as their relationship *vis-à-vis* each other was concerned as Croatia was lending assistance to the HVO (Bosnian Croat Forces) in its fight against the ABiH (Bosnian Muslim Forces) over the period at issue (par 139). In coming to that conclusion, the Trial Chamber considered the nature of their relationship in the geographical area (central Bosnia) to which the indictment relates, not the whole of the territory in which they may have interacted (par 143).

[66] In the 'Elements of Crimes' of the ICC, the perpetrator needs only to know that the victim belonged to an adverse party to the conflict (footnote 33 to Article 8(2)(a) of the elements of Crim).

was allegedly committed, he or she was 'in the hands of a party to the conflict or occupying power of which he or she is not a national', as defined below.

'In the hands of'

In order to be 'protected' under the grave breaches regime, the above categories of individuals must find themselves 'in the hands of' a party to the conflict or occupying power. The expression 'in the hands of' must be interpreted broadly as encompassing 'persons finding themselves on the territory controlled by that party or occupying power':[67] 'It is not to be understood merely in the physical sense of being held prisoner, but indicates that the civilian in question is in territory which is under the control of an opposing party to the conflict.'[68] For prisoners of war, in particular, the requirement of being 'in the hands of' means that prisoners of war are protected 'from the time they fall into the power of an enemy and until their final release and repatriation'.[69]

In the case of occupied territories, it has been suggested by one Trial Chamber that the determination as to whether civilians may be said to be 'in the hands of' the occupying party does not depend on the occupying power actually exercising 'effective control' over the area where those civilians are located.[70] According to the *Naletilić and Martinović* Trial Chamber, a civilian could be regarded as having been 'in the hands of' the occupying force already during the invasion phase, regardless of whether the occupier has been able to establish its authority over the territory in question or whether the invasion is still ongoing. The Trial Chamber said that in such a situation, the status of 'protected persons' does not depend, *stricto sensu*, on the actual existence of a state of occupation. It found that civilians could be regarded as being 'in the hands of the occupying power' as soon as they physically fell into its hands or otherwise found themselves in the invaded territory in the intervening phase prior to the establishment of a state of occupation, 'regardless

---

[67] *Naletilić and Martinović* Trial Judgment, par 208; see also *Čelebići* Trial Judgment, par 246.

[68] Ibid., (fn omitted). As noted in the ICRC, *Commentary to Geneva Convention IV*, p 47:

[t]he expression 'in the hands of' is used in an extremely general sense. It is not merely a question of being in enemy hands directly, as a prisoner is. The mere fact of being in the territory of a party to the conflict or an occupied territory implies that one is in the power, or 'hands', of the Occupying Power. It is possible that this power will never actually be exercised over the protected person: very likely an inhabitant of an occupied territory will never have anything to do with the Occupying Power or its organizations. In other words, the expression 'in the hands of' need not necessarily be understood in the physical sense; it simply means that the person is in territory under the control of the Power in question.

See also *Rajić* Rule 61 Decision, pars 13–32.

[69] See *Naletilić and Martinović* Trial Judgment, par 209, citing Article 5 of Geneva Convention III. See also *Tadić* Trial Judgment, par 579: '[The expression "in the hands of"] is not restricted to situations in which the individual civilian is physically in the hands of a Party or Occupying Power.'

[70] *Naletilić and Martinović* Trial Judgment, pars 221–222. By contrast, the *Tadić* Trial Chamber had suggested that '[t]he exact moment when a person or area falls into the hands of a party to a conflict depends on whether that party has effective control over an area' (*Tadić* Trial Judgment, par 580).

of the stage of the hostilities', and regardless of whether the occupying state indeed exercise effective control over the area in question.[71]

'A party to the conflict or occupying power'

In the case of an internationalized conflict, this requirement would be met whether the victims found themselves in the hands of the controlling state or in the hands of the local forces which are under its 'overall control' without any difference in the protection to which they are entitled. The ICTY has not yet had to decide whether peacekeeping forces or NATO forces that were present in the area during the conflict could be regarded, in any particular case, as a 'party to the conflict' for the purpose of the grave breaches regime and whether they could in theory have committed grave breaches of the Geneva Conventions in that context.

'Of which they are not nationals'

Article 4 of Geneva Convention IV was intended to cover anyone who is not a national of a party to the armed conflict or the occupying power in whose hands he or she is.[72] The ICRC *Commentary* to that provision explains that this requirement, and the limitation placed upon citizens of the state of nationality, was 'faithful to a recognized principle of international law: it does not interfere in a State's relations with its own nationals'.[73] But times have changed since the Geneva Conventions were adopted in 1949, the Appeals Chamber has said, and Article 4 of these Conventions 'may [now] be given a wider construction so that a person may be accorded protected status, notwithstanding the fact that he is of the same nationality as his captors'.[74]

According to the consistent jurisprudence of the ICTY that substance should prevail over form, the protected status of an individual should not depend on 'formal bonds and purely legal relations', but on 'the substance of relations' which exists between that individual and a state.[75] Thus, formal national and domestic laws regarding nationality are not necessarily determinative of the question and an international tribunal such as the Yugoslav Tribunal 'may choose to refuse to recognise (or give effect to) a State's grant of its nationality to individuals for the purposes of applying international law'.[76] The Appeals Chamber has made it clear that domestic laws are relevant to determining the nationality of the victims for the purpose of applying the Geneva Conventions only to the extent that they are in conformity with international law and that they are interpreted within its framework.[77] The Appeals Chamber insisted, however, that its finding concerning

---

[71] *Naletilić and Martinović* Trial Judgment, pars 221–222; *Tadić* Trial Judgment, pars 579–580.

[72] See ICRC, *Commentary to Geneva Convention IV*, specifically Article 49, p 46.   [73] Ibid.

[74] *Aleksovski* Appeal Judgment, par 151; *Čelebići* Appeal Judgment, par 57; *Tadić* Appeal Judgment, pars 164 and 169.

[75] *Tadić* Appeal Judgment, par 168; *Čelebići* Appeal Judgment, pars 57, 82–84.

[76] *Čelebići* Trial Judgment, par 258. See also *Čelebići* Appeal Judgment, par 82.

[77] See, in particular, *Čelebići* Appeal Judgment, pars 75 and 76 and references cited therein. See also *Čelebići* Trial Judgment, par 263 (footnotes omitted): 'The provisions of domestic legislation on

the relevance and function of domestic legislation pertaining to nationality was limited to the determination of the status of a particular individual (or group of individuals) as a protected person under the Geneva Conventions and that it did not have the effect of regulating the nationality of these individuals for other purposes, nor did it purport to pronounce on the – domestic – validity of local laws.[78]

The Tribunal has, therefore, consistently promoted what it called a 'broad and purposive, and ultimately realistic approach'[79] to the question of who may be considered a protected person pursuant to that regime, one that would ensure the protection of the civilians (and prisoners of war) 'to the maximum extent possible'.[80] Accordingly, the requirement of distinct 'nationality', as it appears in the Geneva Conventions, must be interpreted as requiring that victims and perpetrators owe allegiance (actual or potential) to different states; this approach was unsurprising in the context of a conflict such as that in the former Yugoslavia where in the minds of the warring parties considerations of nationality were of vastly inferior significance to those of ethnicity. In view of the circumstances that accompanied the break-up of the then Yugoslavia, ethnicity became a factor of great relevance to the determination of protected person status:[81]

This legal approach, hinging on substantial relations more than on formal bonds, becomes all the more important in present-day international armed conflicts. While previously wars were primarily between well-established States, in modern inter-ethnic armed conflicts citizenship in a situation of violent State succession cannot be determinative of the protected status of persons caught up in conflicts which ensue from such events. The Commentary to the Fourth Geneva Convention charges us not to forget that "the Conventions have been drawn up first and foremost to protect individuals, and not to serve State interests" and thus it is the view of this Trial Chamber that their protections should be applied to as broad a category of persons as possible. It would, indeed, be contrary to the intention of the Security Council, which was concerned with effectively addressing a situation that it had determined to be a threat to international peace and security, and with ending the suffering of all those caught up in the conflict, for the International Tribunal to deny the application of the Fourth Geneva Convention to any particular group of persons solely on the basis of their citizenship status under domestic law.'

[78] *Čelebići* Appeal Judgment, pars 99–101.

[79] Ibid., par 95. See also, e.g. ibid., pars 71–73 and 81; *Čelebići* Trial Judgment, par 266; and, generally, *Tadić* Appeal Judgment, pars 164–168.

[80] Ibid., par 168; *Aleksovski* Appeal Judgment, par 152.

[81] *Tadić* Appeal Judgment par 166. See also *Čelebići* Appeal Judgement, par 84: 'The nationality of the victims for the purpose of the application of Geneva Convention IV should not be determined on the basis of formal national characterisations, but rather upon an analysis of the substantial relations, taking into consideration the different ethnicity of the victims and the perpetrators, and their bonds with the foreign intervening State.' See also ibid, par 81: 'depriving victims, who arguably are of the same nationality under domestic law as their captors, of the protection of the Geneva Conventions solely based on that national law would not be consistent with the object and purpose of the Conventions. Their very object could indeed be defeated if undue emphasis were placed on formal legal bonds, which could also be altered by governments to shield their nationals from prosecution based on the grave breaches provisions of the Geneva Conventions. A more purposive and realistic approach is particularly apposite in circumstances of the dissolution of Yugoslavia, and in the emerging State of Bosnia and Herzegovina where various parties were engaged in fighting, and the government was opposed to a partition based on ethnicity, which would have resulted in movements of population, and where, ultimately, the issue at stake was the final shape of the State and of the new emerging entities.' See also *Aleksovski* Appeal Judgment, par 152; *Blaškić* Trial Judgment, pars 125–133.

such as that in the former Yugoslavia, new States are often created during the conflict and ethnicity rather than nationality may become the grounds for allegiance. Or, put another way, ethnicity may become determinative of national allegiance.[82]

Thus, in a situation where victims and perpetrators give ethnic allegiance to different states, Article 4 of Geneva Convention IV would still be applicable in principle and grave breaches could be committed 'even if in the circumstances of the case the perpetrators and the victims were to be regarded as possessing the same nationality'.[83] This was so, for instance, in the *Čelebići* case where the Trial Chamber found (and the Appeals Chamber upheld) that Bosnian Serb detainees could be considered as having a different (albeit unidentified) nationality from their captors, the Bosnian (mostly Muslim) authorities, despite the fact that all of them were Bosnian nationals.[84] They were, therefore, to be regarded for the purpose of Article 2 of the ICTY Statute as 'protected persons'.[85] This was the case too in the *Tadić* and *Aleksovski* cases, where victims and perpetrators were all 'Bosnians' or citizens of Bosnia and, in practice, Herzegovina, but of different ethnicity and different national allegiance.[86]

Protected property

The concept of 'protected property' is not the subject of a specific definition in the Geneva Conventions, nor in the Additional Protocols, but its content is made explicit in various provisions of those instruments. According to the Appeals Chamber, 'protected property' for the purpose of Article 2 ICTY Statute would at least cover the objects mentioned in Articles 19 and 33 to 35 of Geneva Convention I, Articles 22, 24, 25, and 27 of Convention II, and in Articles 18, 19, 21, 22, 33, 53, 57, etc. of Convention IV on civilians.[87]

Although those objects that are recognized as being 'protected' under the Geneva Conventions (and their Protocols) are in principle immune from attacks at all time, the Geneva Conventions 'identify certain highly exceptional circumstances

---

[82] *Tadić* Appeal Judgment, par 166.

[83] Ibid., par 169; *Čelebići* Appeal Judgment, par 83.

[84] *Čelebići* Trial Judgment, par 262; *Čelebići* Appeal Judgment, pars 95–98. The Appeals Chamber said that it 'particularly agrees with the Trial Chamber's finding that the Bosnian Serb victims should be regarded as protected persons for the purposes of Geneva Convention IV because they "were arrested and detained mainly on the basis of their Serb identity" and "they were clearly regarded by the Bosnian authorities as belonging to the opposing party in an armed conflict and as posing a threat to the Bosnian State" ' (ibid., par 98).

[85] Such an interpreation, the *Čelebići* Trial Chamber said, 'is fully in accordance with the development of the human rights doctrine which has been increasing in force since the middle of this century. It would be incongruous with the whole concept of human rights, which protect individuals from the excesses of their own governments, to rigidly apply the nationality requirement of article 4, that was apparently inserted to prevent interference in a State's relations with its own nationals' (*Čelebići* Trial Judgment, par 266). The Trial Chamber rejected the idea, however, that there existed as yet under international law 'a right to nationality of one's own choosing' (see *Čelebići* Trial Judgment, par 256 and *Čelebići* Appeal Judgment, par 93).

[86] See, respectively, *Tadić* Appeal Judgment, pars 167–169 and *Aleksovksi* Appeal Judgment, pars 137–152.   [87] *Tadić* Jurisdiction Decision, par 81.

where the protection afforded to such property will cease'.[88] The real extent of protection afforded to such properties (whether real or personal, moveable or immovable) will therefore depend on the circumstances of each case, and in particular, whether those properties are located in an occupied territory.[89] The jurisprudence of the ICTY has not specified the circumstances under which those objects and properties could lose their protection.

As indicated above, in the case of an occupation, and contrary to what appears to be the case in relation to 'protected persons', one Trial Chamber has stated that objects and properties could only become 'protected' once the occupying forces actually exercise effective control over the territory which they have invaded.[90]

7.2.3 Underlying offences

Article 2 of the ICTY Statute contains a list of particularly serious violations of the laws of war which constitute grave breaches of the Geneva Conventions.[91] The list of underlying offences provided in that provision appears to be an exhaustive one, so that the ICTY has not exercised its jurisdiction in relation to any grave breach not expressly listed therein.

Wilful killing (Article 2(a) ICTY Statute)

'Wilful killing' as a grave breach of the Geneva Conventions has been said to consist of the following elements:[92]

(i) the death of the victim as the result of the action(s) of the accused;
(ii) the accused intended to cause death or serious bodily injury which, as it is reasonable to assume, he had to understand was likely to lead to death;[93]
(iii) the victim was a protected person.

---

[88] See, for instance, in the case of medical units and establishments, Articles 21 and 22 of Geneva Convention I, in relation to the material of mobile medical units, Article 33 of Geneva Convention I, in relation to medical transports, Article 36 of Geneva Convention I, and, in relation to military hospital ships, Articles 34 and 35 of Geneva Convention II (see *Kordić and Čerkez* Trial Judgment, par 336). See also Article 52(1)–(2) Additional Protocol I concerning the general protection due to civilian objects.

[89] See, below, 'Extensive Destruction and Appropriation of Property, Not Justified by Military Necessity and Carried Out Unlawfully and Wantonly'.

[90] See *Naletilić and Martinović* Trial Judgment, pars 221–222. As already noted above, this interpretation might be in contradiction with the finding of another Trial Chamber in the *Rajić* case which seems to suggest that the law of occupation would also apply to properties in the intermediate phase between the invasion and the actual establishment of a state of occupation by the invading force (*Rajić* Rule 61 Decision, pars 39–42).

[91] The list mentioned in Article 2 matches almost exactly the list of grave breaches provided in Article 147 of Geneva Convention IV.

[92] *Čelebići* Appeal Judgment, par 422. See also *Blaškić* Trial Judgment, par 153 ('For the material element of the offence, it must be proved that the death of the victim was the result of the actions of the accused as a commander. The intent, or *mens rea*, needed to establish the offence of wilful killing exists once it has been demonstrated that the accused intended to cause death or serious bodily injury which, as it is reasonable to assume, he had to understand was likely to lead to death.'); *Čelebići* Trial Judgment, pars 420–439; *Kordić and Čerkez* Trial Judgment, par 229.

[93] *Blaškić* Trial Judgment, par 153.

The *actus reus* of this crime is identical to that of 'murder' (as a war crime or as a crime against humanity).[94] The Prosecution must therefore establish that the death of the victim has been caused by an act or omission of the accused.[95]

As for the *mens rea*, all grave breaches must have been committed 'wilfully' which means that the accused must have acted 'consciously and with intent, i.e., with his mind on the act and its consequences, and willing them'.[96] Death which is an accidental consequence of the actions of the accused will therefore not suffice.[97] The required state of mind may be inferred from all the circumstances surrounding the infliction of harm and the resulting death of the victim but it must be the only reasonable inference to be drawn from the evidence.[98] 'The relevant question', the Trial Chamber in the *Čelebići* case said, 'is whether it is apparent from these circumstances that the accused's actions were committed in a manner "manifesting extreme indifference to the value of human life".'[99]

As repeatedly pointed out in the jurisprudence of the ICTY, the definition of 'wilful killing' under Article 2 and 'murder' under Articles 3 and 5 of the ICTY Statute is essentially similar in substance.[100] The only significant distinction between those two offences lies in the fact that their *chapeau* or general elements will be different, depending on the article of the Statute pursuant to which the crimes are charged. This, in turn, could impact upon the ability of the Court to convict a person cumulatively in relation both to murder (pursuant to Article 3 and/or Article 5 of the ICTY Statute) and wilful killing (pursuant to Article 2). Whereas cumulative convictions would always be possible between Article 2 and Article 5 of the ICTY Statute,[101] the same is not true of Articles 2 and 3, when the most specific category of crimes (those provided in Article 2) would exclude cumulative convictions for the same underlying offence pursuant to Article 3 of the ICTY Statute. Thus, as pointed out by the Appeals Chamber, this would mean that, where a person has been charged with both wilful killing under Article 2 and murder under Article 3 in relation to the same conduct, a conviction based on the first charge would exclude a conviction based on the second.[102]

---

[94] See, e.g. *Čelebići* Trial Judgment, par 422; *Čelebići* Appeal Judgment, par 423. See below, subsection 8.13.1.   [95] See below sub-section 8.13.1, and references cited.

[96] ICRC, *Commentary to the Additional Protocols*, Additional Protocol I, par 3474, p 994. The Commentary continues: 'this encompasses the concept of "wrongful intent" or "recklessness", viz., the attitude of an agent who, without being certain of a particular result, accepts the possibility of it happening; on the other hand, ordinary negligence or lack of foresight is not covered, i.e., when a man acts without having his mind on the act or its consequences (although failing to take the necessary precautions, particularly failing to seek precise information, constitutes culpable negligence punishable at least by disciplinary sanctions)' (ibid.).   [97] *Čelebići* Trial Judgment, par 433.

[98] See, generally, on that standard of proof, *Krnojelac* Trial Judgment, par 67.

[99] Ibid., par 436.

[100] See, e.g. *Čelebići* Trial Judgment, par 422: 'The Trial Chamber takes the view that it is the simple essence of these offences, derived from the ordinary meaning of their terms in the context of the Geneva Conventions, which must be outlined in the abstract before they are given concrete form and substance in relation to the facts alleged. With this in mind, there can be no line drawn between "wilful killing" and "murder" which affects their content.'   [101] See below, sub-section 24.

[102] *Čelebići* Appeal Judgment, par 423: '[t]he definition of wilful killing under Article 2 contains a materially distinct element not present in the definition of murder under Article 3: the requirement that the victim be a protected person. This requirement necessitates proof of a fact not required by the

Torture and inhuman treatment, including biological experiments
(Article 2(b) ICTY Statute)

Torture

Concerning the definition of the crime of 'torture' see the definition of torture as a serious violation of the laws or customs of war.[103]

Inhuman treatment (Article 2(b) ICTY Statute)

'Inhuman treatment' has been described, in general terms, as 'acts or omissions that cause serious mental or physical suffering or injury or constitute a serious attack on human dignity',[104] or as 'intentional treatment which does not conform with the fundamental principle of humanity'[105] or, in different terms again, as 'a general, non-exhaustive catalogue of deplorable acts which are inconsistent with it, these constituting inhuman treatment'.[106] More specifically and helpfully, it has been said to consist of the following elements:[107]

(i) an intentional act or omission, that is an act which, judged objectively, is deliberate and not accidental, which causes serious mental harm or physical suffering or injury or constitutes a serious attack on human dignity;

(ii) committed against a protected person.

The act or omission in question must have been:

(i) deliberate and with the intention to inflict serious physical or mental suffering or to commit a serious attack on the human dignity of the victim;

(ii) done by the perpetrator knowing that his act or omission was likely to cause serious physical or mental suffering or a serious attack upon human dignity, but reckless as to whether such suffering or attack would result from his act or omission.[108]

elements of murder, because the definition of a protected person includes, yet goes beyond what is meant by an individual taking no active part in the hostilities. However, the definition of murder under Article 3 does not contain an element requiring proof of a fact not required by the elements of wilful killing under Article 2. Therefore, the first prong of the test is not satisfied, and it is necessary to apply the second prong. Because wilful killing under Article 2 contains an additional element and therefore more specifically applies to the situation at hand, the Article 2 conviction must be upheld, and the Article 3 conviction dismissed.'

103 See below, sub-section 8.13.3.   104 *Čelebići* Trial Judgment, par 442.
105 Ibid., par 543.
106 Ibid., par 532. See also ICRC, *Commentary to Geneva Convention IV*, p 598:

[Inhuman treatment] could not mean, it seems, solely treatment constituting an attack on physical integrity or health; the aim of the Convention is certainly to grant civilians in enemy hands a protection which will preserve their human dignity and prevent them being brought down to the level of animals. That leads to the conclusion that by 'inhuman treatment' the Convention does not mean only physical injury or injury to health. Certain measures, for example, which might cut the civilian internees off completely from the outside world and in particular from their families, or which caused grave injury to their human dignity, could conceivably be considered as inhuman treatment.

107 See, *inter alia*, *Čelebići* Appeal Judgment, par 426; *Naletilić and Martinović* Trial Judgment, par 246; *Kordić and Čerkez* Trial Judgment, par 256; *Blaškić* Trial Judgment, pars 154–155.
108 *Čelebići* Trial Judgment, par 543; *Krnojelac* Trial Judgment, par 132.

This offence encompasses not only acts that would amount to torture and those intentionally causing great suffering or inflicting serious injury to body or health,[109] but also extends to 'other acts contravening the fundamental principle of human treatment, in particular those which constitute an attack on human dignity'.[110]

To qualify as 'inhuman treatment' pursuant to Article 2(b) of the ICTY Statute, the act or omission must have caused serious mental and physical suffering that may, however, fall short of the severe mental and physical suffering required for the offence of torture.[111] But it must reach the same threshold of seriousness as that required for other similar offences, such as cruel treatment and wilfully causing great suffering or serious injury to body or health.[112] 'Ultimately,' the *Čelebići* Trial Chamber noted, 'the question of whether any particular act which does not fall within the categories of the core group is inconsistent with the principle of humane treatment, and thus constitutes inhuman(e) treatment, is a question of fact to be judged in all the circumstances of the particular case.'[113]

In case of doubt as to whether an act or omission is sufficiently serious to qualify as 'inhuman treatment' or in case of doubt as to whether an act that qualifies as 'inhuman treatment' is sufficiently serious to qualify as torture, the doubt should always be interpreted in favour of the accused and he should, in the first case, be acquitted of the charge and, in the second, be convicted for the lesser offence of inhuman treatment.

'Inhuman treatment' has the same function within Article 2 as do, respectively, 'cruel treatment' and 'inhumane acts' in relation to Articles 3 and 5(i) of the ICTY Statute. All three of them are residual or 'umbrella' clauses that capture all violations which are sufficiently serious to come within the purview of those provisions without having been expressly provided for.[114] From a definitional point of view too, all three offences basically require proof of the same elements.[115] 'Inhuman treatment'

---

[109] See, e.g. *Čelebići* Trial Judgment, pars 442 and 544.

[110] *Blaškić* Trial Judgment, par 155. The Trial Chamber in that case was satisfied that the forcible digging of trenches under dangerous conditions and the use of prisoners of war as human shields could amount to 'inhuman treatment' pursuant to Article 2(b) of the Statute (see *Blaškić* Trial Judgment, pars 713–716 and 738).

[111] See, e.g. *Čelebići* Trial Judgment, par 542. 'Inhuman treatment' is also distinguishable from torture by the absence of any requirement that the act or omission causing serious pain must have been committed in order to obtain a certain result (see, e.g. *Čelebići* Trial Judgment, par 542). On the difficulty to distinguish the degree of seriousness sufficient to meet the torture threshold and to distinguish acts of torture from lesser offences, see, e.g. *Krnojelac* Trial Judgment, pars 216 et seq.

[112] *Naletilić and Martinović* Trial Judgment, par 246.   [113] *Čelebići* Trial Judgment, par 544.

[114] Ibid., par 543: 'inhuman treatment is intentional treatment which does not conform with the fundamental principle of humanity, and forms the umbrella under which the remainder of the listed "grave breaches" in the Conventions fall. Hence, acts characterised in the Conventions and Commentaries as inhuman, or which are inconsistent with the principle of humanity, constitute examples of actions that can be characterised as inhuman treatment.'

[115] *Krnojelac* Trial Judgment, par 130 (and n 381 at p 60, and references cited therein). See also: *Čelebići* Appeal Judgment, par 426 ('the sole distinguishing element [between inhuman treatment and cruel treatment] stems from the protected person requirement under Article 2. By contrast, cruel treatment under Article 3 does not require proof of a fact not required by its counterpart. Hence the first prong of the test is not satisfied, and applying the second prong, the Article 3 conviction must be

also largely overlaps with the offence of 'wilfully causing great suffering or serious injury to body or health' as provided in Article 2(f) of the ICTY Statute.[116]

Biological experiments

No charges have been brought before the Tribunal based upon this offence and it is unlikely that any such charges will ever be brought.[117] This underlying offence, in one respect, resembles the crime of torture, insofar as the act which may constitute it must have been committed for a specific purpose, namely, a biological experiment.[118] The elements of its definition have not otherwise been laid down by the Tribunal.

Wilfully causing great suffering or serious injury to body or health (Article 2(c) ICTY Statute)

The offence of 'wilfully causing great suffering or serious injury to body or health' consists of the following elements:[119]

(i) an intentional act or omission consisting of causing great suffering or serious injury to body or health, including mental health;
(ii) committed against a protected person.

The conduct in question must have caused great suffering *or* serious injury to body or health.[120] Contrary to the crime of torture it need not, however, have been committed for any particular purpose.[121] The act could thus be committed for any particular reason or motive as one Chamber put it,[122] such as punishment, revenge, or sheer sadism, or for no proven reasons at all.[123]

The suffering resulting from such conduct may be physical or mental, if sufficiently serious.[124] The precondition that the suffering be 'great' or the injury 'serious' 'merely require[s] a finding that a particular act of mistreatment, in order to fall within the ambit of this crime, must possess suffering or injury of the requisite level of seriousness'.[125] Such level will be determined on a case-by-case basis

---

dismissed'), concerning the substantive similarity between 'inhuman treatment' and 'cruel treatment'. Concerning the similarities between 'inhuman treatment' and 'inhumane acts' as a crime against humanity, see, for instance, *Čelebići* Trial Judgment, par 533; see also *Naletilić and Martinović* Trial Judgment, par 247; *Krnojelac* Trial Judgment, par 130.

[116] *Čelebići* Trial Judgment, par 442. See below, chapter 7.

[117] See generally M. Lippman, 'The Nazi Doctors Trial and the International Prohibition on Medical Involvement in Torture', 15 *Loyola L.A. International and Comparative Law Journal* 395 (1993). [118] *Naletilić and Martinović* Trial Judgment, par 340.

[119] *Čelebići* Appeal Judgment, par 424. See also, *inter alia, Naletilić and Martinović* Trial Judgment, par 339 and *Blaškić* Trial Judgment, par 156.

[120] Ibid.; *Čelebići* Trial Judgment, par 506.

[121] *Naletilić and Martinović* Trial Judgment, par 341; *Čelebići* Trial Judgment, pars 442, 508, 510–511; *Kordić and Čerkez* Trial Judgment, par 244; *Blaškić* Trial Judgment, par 156; *Čelebići* Trial Judgment, par 511: on the absence of purpose requirement, see also ICRC, *Commentary to Geneva Convention IV*, p 599. [122] *Naletilić and Martinović* Trial Judgment, par 340.

[123] Ibid., par 340. See also ICRC, *Commentary to Geneva Convention IV*, p 599.

[124] *Čelebići* Trial Judgment, par 509. See also ICRC, *Commentary to Geneva Convention IV*, p 599.

[125] *Kordić and Čerkez* Trial Judgment, par 244; *Čelebići* Trial Judgment, par 510; *Naletilić and Martinović* Trial Judgment, par 341.

taking into account all the circumstances at hand,[126] but not every infringement upon the victim's human dignity would necessarily meet that threshold.[127] As with the crimes of 'inhuman acts' and 'cruel treatment',[128] for instance, the seriousness assessment is necessarily a relative one, which must take into account all relevant circumstances, including the nature of the act or omission, the context in which the crime occurred, its duration and/or repetition, the physical, mental, and moral effects of the act on the victim and the personal circumstances of the victim, including age, sex, and health.[129] The seriousness of the act will be influenced, *inter alia*, by the lasting effect of the act upon the victim,[130] but the suffering or injury that has been inflicted need not be lasting 'so long as it is real and serious'.[131] When discussing the related underlying offence of 'serious bodily or mental harm', the *Krstić* Trial Chamber held that such harm or suffering 'need not cause permanent and irremediable harm, but it must involve harm that goes beyond temporary unhappiness, embarrassment or humiliation'.[132] The suffering inflicted need not in any case be such as to reach the threshold required by the offence of torture.

---

[126] *Naletilić and Martinović* Trial Judgment, par 343. See also *Krstić* Trial Judgment, par 513 (albeit in relation to a different underlying offence).

[127] *Kordić and Čerkez* Trial Judgment, par 245; *Naletilić and Martinović* Trial Judgment, par 341.

[128] Inhumane acts and cruel treatment, both of which require 'serious mental or physical suffering or injury' (*Krnojelac* Trial Judgment, par 130).

[129] *Krnojelac* Trial Judgment, par 131. See also *Čelebići* Trial Judgment, par 536; *Jelišić* Trial Judgment, par 57 in relation to outrages upon personal dignity.

[130] In *Naletilić and Martinović*, by reference to the ICRC Commentary, the Trial Chamber mentioned in particular 'the length of time the victim is incapacitated for work' (*Naletilić and Martinović* Trial Judgment, par 340). See also *Čelebići* Trial Judgment, par 510: 'the Commentary posits a possible criterion for judging the seriousness of the injury, being an incapacity to work. While this may well be the case in some situations, when ascertaining the meaning of the term "serious" in the absence of other interpretive material, the Trial Chamber must look to the plain ordinary meaning of the word. The *Oxford English Dictionary* defines this word as "not slight or negligible". Similarly, the term "great" is defined as "much above average in size, amount or intensity". The Trial Chamber therefore views these quantitative expressions as providing for the basic requirement that a particular act of mistreatment results in a requisite level of serious suffering or injury.'

[131] *Krnojelac* Trial Judgment, par 131. See, however, *Krstić* Trial Judgment, par 513, which claims (without support for its proposition, other than a cross-reference to the *Akayesu* Trial Judgment, par 502) that 'it must be harm that results in a grave and long-term disadvantage to a person's ability to lead a normal and constructive life'. If this sentence is read (in conjunction with the preceding sentence of the Judgment) as suggesting more than frivolous or momentary suffering, the conclusion seems to be correct. If, however, it suggests that the victim must bear the mark of the stigma of his or her suffering for a long period of time, such conclusion would find no support in the law and the practice of states as they exist at this time. It is noteworthy that the *Akayesu* Trial Chamber to which the *Krstić* Trial Chamber refers in support of its conclusion only suggests that 'serious bodily or mental harm [. . .] does not necessarily mean that the harm is permanent or irremediable' (*Akayesu* Trial Judgment, par 502). It does not suggest nor support the finding that it must result 'in a grave and long-term disadvantage to a person's ability to lead a normal and constructive life'.

[132] *Krstić* Trial Judgment, par 513, referred to in relation to the offence of 'willfully causing great suffering or serious injury to body or health' in *Naletilić and Martinović* Trial Judgment, par 342. See also *Akayesu* Trial Judgment, par 502. In *Čelebići*, the Trial Chamber held that the 'inhumane conditions' in which detainees where kept at the *Čelebići* prison camp did amount to 'wilfully causing great suffering or serious injury to body or health' pursuant to Article 2 of the Statute (*Čelebići* Trial Judgment, pars 554–558).

The act or omission must have been intentional, 'being an act which, judged objectively, is deliberate and not accidental, which causes serious mental or physical suffering or injury'.[133]

From a definitional point of view the offence of 'wilfully causing great suffering or serious injury to body or health' is related to and is in many respects essentially similar (but for the respective *chapeau* elements) to 'inhuman treatment' pursuant to Article 2 of the ICTY Statute, 'cruel treatment' pursuant to Article 3, and 'inhumane acts' pursuant to Article 5(i) of the ICTY Statute.[134]

Extensive destruction and appropriation of property, not justified by military necessity and carried out unlawfully and wantonly (Article 2(d) ICTY Statute)

A party to an armed conflict is prohibited from destroying property belonging to the enemy 'except where such destruction is made absolutely necessary by military operations'.[135] The scope of this prohibition will vary in depth depending on the context, notably whether there exists a state of occupation, but the general prohibition remains identical.[136] Article 147 of Geneva Convention IV lists extensive destruction and appropriation of property as a grave breach of the Conventions, whilst the ICRC *Commentary* to that provision sets out its intended scope:

The Fourth Convention forbids the destruction of civilian hospitals and their property or damage to ambulances or medical aircraft. Furthermore, the Occupying Power may not destroy in occupied territory real or personal property except where such destruction is rendered absolutely necessary by military operations. On the other hand, the destruction of property on enemy territory is not covered by the provision. In other words, if an air force bombs factories in an enemy country, such destruction is not covered either by Article 53 or by Article 147. On the other hand, if the enemy Power occupies the territory where the factories are situated, it may not destroy them unless military operations make it absolutely necessary.[137]

The Geneva Conventions identify (and the ICTY has taken notice of) particular types of property accorded general protection, such as civilian hospitals pursuant to Article 18 of Geneva Convention IV, which, but for 'exceptional circumstances' expressly provided for in the Conventions themselves, are 'presumptively immune from attack'.[138] The Geneva Conventions further provide for specific categories of protected properties which are protected if and when located in occupied territories. For instance, Article 53 of Geneva Convention IV protects all real and personal property, other than property accorded general protection

---

[133] Ibid., par 511.
[134] *Čelebići* Appeal Judgment, pars 424–426; *Kordić and Čerkez* Trial Judgment, par 245; *Čelebići* Trial Judgment, par 442; *Naletilić and Martinović* Trial Judgment, pars 25–246 and sources quoted therein.   [135] *Blaškić* Trial Judgment, par 157.
[136] See, in particular in relation to property in occupied territory, *Kordić and Čerkez* Trial Judgment, pars 336–337.   [137] ICRC, *Commentary to Geneva Convention IV*, p 601.
[138] See *Kordić and Čerkez* Trial Judgment, par 336.

under the Geneva Conventions, but it only applies in occupied territories.[139] 'Thus,' the *Kordić* Trial Chamber noted, 'the protective requirement set forth in Article 53 of Geneva Convention IV represents an additional duty that attaches only to an Occupying Power'.[140] Extensive destruction of property could therefore constitute a grave breach of the Geneva Conventions in essentially two sets of circumstances:[141]

(i) the property destroyed is of a type accorded general protection under the Geneva Conventions of 1949, regardless of whether or not it is situated in occupied territory; and the perpetrator acted with the intent to destroy the property in question or in reckless disregard of the likelihood of its destruction; or

(ii) the property destroyed is accorded protection under the Geneva Conventions, on account of its location in occupied territory; and the destruction occurs on a large scale; the same *mens rea* as above would seem to apply.

Regardless of whether properties fall within the first or the second of the above categories, the destruction of property must have been 'extensive, unlawful and wanton' to constitute a grave breach of the Geneva Conventions.[142] Such a requirement could possibly be met by a single act of destruction, such as in the case of the intentional bombing of a hospital.[143] In general, it would be difficult, however, to imagine many situations where an isolated act could in principle satisfy that requirement.[144] In addition, as noted above, to constitute a grave breach, the perpetrator must be shown to have acted 'with the intent to destroy the property in question or in reckless disregard of the likelihood of its destruction'.[145]

Such destruction or appropriation will not be regarded as a crime, however, if it was strictly justified by military necessity. Citing from the *Dictionary of International Law of Armed Conflict*, the *Galić* Trial Chamber noted that, in its broad sense, 'military necessity' means 'doing what is necessary to achieve a war aim'.[146] The principle of 'military necessity', the Trial Chamber continued, 'acknowledges the potential for unavoidable civilian death and injury ancillary to the conduct of legitimate military operations. However, this principle requires

---

[139] *Kordić and Čerkez* Trial Judgment, par 337; *Blaškić* Trial Judgment, par 148. Article 53 of Geneva Convention IV provides as follows: 'Any destruction by the Occupying Power of real or personal property belonging individually or collectively to private persons, or to the State, or to other public authorities, or to social or co-operative organizations, is prohibited, except where such destruction is rendered absolutely necessary by military operations.'

[140] *Kordić and Čerkez* Trial Judgment, par 337.

[141] Ibid., par 341; *Naletilić and Martinović* Trial Judgment, par 575.

[142] *Blaškić* Trial Judgment, par 157. See, generally, ICRC *Commentary to Geneva Convention IV* related to Article 147.

[143] *Blaškić* Trial Judgment, par 157; *Naletilić and Martinović* Trial Judgment, par 576.

[144] See ibid., n 1438, p 199 and ICRC, *Commentary to Geneva Convention IV*, p 601.

[145] *Kordić and Čerkez* Trial Judgment, par 341.

[146] *Galić* Trial Judgment, n 76, p 18.

that destroying a particular military objective will provide some type of advantage in weakening the enemy military forces.'[147]

This grave breach is closely related to other categories of criminal offences provided for in the Statute such as 'wanton destruction not justified by military necessity' in Article 3(b) of the ICTY Statute, and 'seizure, destruction, or wilfull damage done to institutions dedicated to religion', pursuant to Article 3(d) of the ICTY Statute.[148] The complementarity between those provisions is important in at least one respect. Certain types of properties are protected by the Geneva Conventions only if they are located in occupied territory, whilst others will not be protected by Article 2 if they are located in enemy territory. In the first scenario, the grave breach regime will provide added protection to that already provided under Article 3 of the ICTY Statute, whilst in the second case, the prohibition of Article 3 might bridge the gaps left by Article 2.[149]

The ICTY has not yet had to deal with the other subsumed offences of extensive 'appropriation of property' not justified by military necessity and carried out unlawfully and wantonly. It would appear that factual situations which would satisfy that description have instead been charged as 'plunder' pursuant to Article 3, rather than as a grave breach under Article 2(d).

Compelling a prisoner of war or a civilian to serve in the forces of a hostile power (Article 2(e) ICTY Statute)

No accused appearing before the ICTY has yet been charged with that particular crime.

Wilfully depriving a prisoner of war or a civilian of the rights of a fair and regular trial (Article 2(f) ICTY Statute)

Although the Tribunal has had plenty of opportunities to deal with the concept and scope of a fair trial insofar as it relates to the rights of an accused appearing before the *ad hoc* Tribunals, it has never done so as the subject-matter of a substantive crime, as this offence has yet to be charged by the prosecution. Instead of being

---

[147] Ibid. The Chamber cited with approval from the judgment of an American Military court in the *Hostages* case:

> Military necessity permits a belligerent, subject to the laws of war, to apply any amount and kind of force to compel the complete submission of the enemy with the least possible expenditure of time, life, and money. [. . .] It permits the destruction of life of armed enemies and other persons whose destruction is incidentally unavoidable by the armed conflicts of the war; it allows the capturing of armed enemies and others of peculiar danger, but does not permit the killing of innocent inhabitants for purposes of revenge or the satisfaction of a lust to kill. The destruction of property to be lawful must be imperatively demanded by the necessities of war. Destruction as an end in itself is a violation of international law. There must be some reasonable connection between the destruction of property and the overcoming of the enemy forces. (*Hostages* case, pp 1253–1254.)

[148] See, generally, *Naletilić and Martinović* Trial Judgment, pars 572 et seq. and *Kordić and Čerkez* Trial Judgment, pars 329 et seq. [149] See ibid., par 347.

charged under that sub-heading, conduct that could have qualified seems to have been subsumed in more general (and more serious) offences where the deprivation of the right to a fair and regular trial formed only one part of more extensive infringements upon the rights of prisoners of war or civilians such as the systematic illegal imprisonment of civilians accompanied by various forms of mistreatment.

Unlawful deportation or transfer or unlawful confinement of civilians (Article 2(g) ICTY Statute)

Unlawful deportation or transfer

Forced displacement under the laws of war   In the context of an armed conflict, the laws of war only permit displacement of civilians under limited circumstances.[150] Unless the displacement is grounded in one of those limited exceptions, the transfer from their place of residence is unlawful, whatever the reasons or purpose for it.

Article 147 of Geneva Convention IV, for instance, provides that unlawful deportation and unlawful transfer constitute a 'grave breach' of the Geneva Conventions. Article 49 of the same Convention in turn provides that '[i]ndividual or mass forcible transfers, as well as deportations of protected persons from occupied territory to the territory of the Occupying Power or that of any other country, occupied or not, are prohibited, regardless of their motive', thereby rendering illegal transfers from and within occupied territories.[151] Article 17 of Additional Protocol II provides that 'the displacement of the civilian population shall not be ordered for reasons related to the conflict unless the security of the population or imperative military reasons so demand.'

Deportation and transfer as criminal offences   Under certain circumstances, the forced displacement of civilians contrary to the laws of war, may constitute a criminal offence of 'deportation' or 'forcible transfer'.

Although they have been described in slightly different terms,[152] the two criminal offences, 'deportation' and '[forcible] transfer', protect a similar set of values, namely, 'the right of the victim to stay in his or her home and community and the right not to be deprived of his or her property by being forcibly displaced to another location'.[153] Deportation may be distinguished from 'forcible transfer',

---

[150]   The Tribunals have yet to address the legal grounds for displacement when the laws of war do not apply, because there was war at all relevant times.

[151]   See *Naletilić and Martinović* Trial Judgment, par 518.

[152]   'Deportation' has been described as 'the forced displacement of persons by expulsion or other coercive acts from the area in which they are lawfully present, across a national border, without lawful grounds' (*Milošević* Rule 98bis Decision, par 45; *Simić* Trial Judgment, par 122; *Naletilić and Martinović* Trial Judgment, par 670; *Krnojelac* Trial Judgment, par 476; *Krstić* Trial Judgment, pars 521, 531–532). 'Forcible transfer' has been described as 'a forced removal or displacement of people from one area to another which may take place within the same national borders' (*Milošević* Rule 98bis Decision, par 45; *Simić* Trial Judgment, par 122; *Krnojelac* Trial Judgment, pars 474 and 476 and sources quoted therein; *Krstić* Trial Judgment, par 521).

[153]   See, e.g. *Simić* Trial Judgment, par 130; *Milošević* Rule 98bis Decision, pars 45 and 69; *Krnojelac* Appeal Judgment, par 218: 'The prohibition against forcible displacements aims at

however, as the former requires movement *beyond* the home state borders, whilst the latter encompasses transfer *within* the victim's state, or even home region or town.[154] Transfer must, in any case, be distinguished from *mere* detention. In the former situation, the Prosecution must establish that the victims were indeed arrested or detained with the intention to expel or transfer them, and that the accused acted upon that intention by actually expelling or transferring them.[155]

There does not appear to be any requirement for either offences (deportation or forcible transfer) of any minimum distance between the place where the victim is living and the place whereto they are being transferred. In the *Naletilić* case, for instance, the victims were transferred from West Mostar to East Mostar, just across the front line dividing the Muslim from the Croatian side of town.[156]

As indicated above, not all transfers and deportation of civilians will constitute a criminal offence, let alone a grave breach. Geneva Convention IV, for instance, does not prohibit 'evacuations being transfers motivated by the security of the population or imperative military reasons'.[157] Nor does it preclude the transfer of individuals who *genuinely* wish to leave the area in question.[158] Consent will not

---

safeguarding the right and aspiration of individuals to live in their communities and homes without outside interference. The forced character of displacement and the forced uprooting of the inhabitants of a territory entail the criminal responsibility of the perpetrator, not the destination to which these inhabitants are sent.'

[154] See, e.g. *Krstić* Trial Judgment, pars 521, 531–532; *Krnojelac* Trial Judgment, par 474; *Simić* Trial Judgment, pars 122 and 129; *Milošević* Rule 98bis Decision, pars 47–69 and sources cited therein. See *Stakić* Trial Judgment which is the only judgment which suggests that a crossing of the border forms part of both offences (pars 679–680). As noted by the Trial Chamber in *Milošević*, 'there is no detriment to a victim if the crime of deportation is confirmed to transfer across borders, because if it is established that he has not been so transferred, then he is protected by the prohibition against forcible transfer, which applies to involuntary movements within national borders. In other words, the values so properly identified by the Trial Chamber in *Prosecutor v. Simić* of a right to remain in one's home and community are protected irrespective of whether deportation only takes place if there is transfer across borders.' (*Milošević* Rule 98bis Decision, par 69.)

[155] In *Naletilić and Martinović*, some of the victims were forced out of their homes and detained at the Heliodrom in Mostar (Southwestern Bosnia). The Trial Chamber was of the view that the Prosecution had failed to establish in relation to these victims that the perpetrators intended to transfer them, as opposed to merely detain them: 'The Chamber is not satisfied that these acts constitute unlawful transfer under Article 2(g) of the Statute, even though the persons, technically speaking, were moved from one place to another against their free will. They were apprehended and arrested in order to be detained and not in order to be transferred. Therefore, the requisite intent is not established' (*Naletilić and Martinović* Trial Judgment, par 537).

[156] See ibid., pars 538–542.   [157] Ibid., par 518.

[158] Ibid., par 519:

Transfers motivated by an individual's own genuine wish to leave, are lawful. In determining whether a transfer is based on an individual's 'own wish' the Chamber is assisted by Article 31 of the Geneva Convention IV. It provides for a general prohibition of physical and moral coercion covering pressure that is direct or indirect, obvious or hidden and further holds that this prohibition applies in so far as the other provisions of the Convention do not implicitly or explicitly authorize a resort to coercion. The jurisprudence of the Tribunal also supports that the term 'forcible' should not be restricted to physical coercion. [. . .] The determination as to whether a transferred person had a 'real choice' has to be made in the context of all relevant

be 'real' or 'genuine' when expressed in circumstances which deprive it of any value.[159] Political or military leaders may not, one Trial Chamber said, give that consent on behalf of those who are being transferred.[160] Likewise, according to the same Trial Chamber, *provisional* transfer would not in principle fall within the category of conduct prohibited by this provision.[161] Such a rule would have to be applied with great care, however, lest illegal acts of transfer and deportation be camouflaged into provisional measures by the perpetrators.

To decide whether the transfer of civilians was compulsory and illegal, the Court will have to consider all relevant factors, including the reasons and motivations that have presided over the transfer of individuals.[162] Absence of genuine consent to be moved, in view of the risk the deportees face if they try to resist, will be essential in determining the criminal character of the transfer.[163] Of great relevance to that determination is the use or threat of physical force which created a reasonable belief that failure to submit to the transfer would result in greater harm.[164]

circumstances on a case by case basis. Forcible transfer is the movement of individuals under duress from where they reside to a place that is not of their choosing (footnotes omitted).

See also references in nn 1357–1361 of the *Naletilić and Martinović* Trial Judgment in relation to the issue of genuine consent; *Milošević* Rule 98bis Decision, pars 70–76.

[159] *Krnojelac* Trial Judgment, par 229; *Simić* Trial Judgment, pars 125–126; *Milošević* Rule 98bis Decision, pars 70–76. Concerning factors that may be evidentially relevant to the Trial Chamber's finding in that respect, see *Milošević* Rule 98bis Decision, par 74: 'Whether a person would have wished to leave the area, absent circumstances of discrimination or persecution, may also be considered as indicative of a person's will. A lack of genuine choice may be inferred from, *inter alia*, threatening and intimidating acts that are calculated to deprive the civilian population of exercising its free will, such as shelling of civilian objects, the burning of civilian property, and the commission of – or the threat to commit – other crimes "calculated to terrify the population and make them flee the area with no hope of return" ' (footnote omitted).

[160] The *Naletilić and Martinović* Defence had argued that the transfer of Bosnian Muslims had been orchestrated with the assistance of one of their military leaders. The Trial Chamber rejected such a suggestion and added that, even if such assistance had been shown to exist, 'an agreement between two military commanders or other representatives of the parties in a conflict does not have any implications on the circumstances under which a transfer is lawful. Military commanders or political leaders cannot consent on behalf of the individual' (*Naletilić and Martinović* Trial Judgment, par 523). Although such a solution is meritorious from a human's point of view, its workability from a practical point of view and its accuracy from the legal standpoint is very doubtful, in particular when one deals with the transfer of large numbers of people which will necessarily involve the assistance of the authorities and their leaders. [161] See *Naletilić and Martinović* Trial Judgment, n 1362.

[162] In *Naletilić and Martinović*, for instance, the Trial Chamber noted that, once the hostilities were over, the displaced persons were not brought back, that no attempt to that end was made, and that, instead, many of their houses had been torched to prevent their return (*Naletilić and Martinović* Trial Judgment, par 526). The discriminatory nature of transfers (for instance, if only one ethnic or religious group is being transferred) is clearly a matter relevant to that assessment.

[163] For example, the Trial Chamber in *Nikolić* found the transfer was compulsory because: '[T]he detainees were transferred to Batkovi camp; they were forced to travel by bus with their heads down, their hands behind their heads. They were beaten and forced to sing "patriotic Serbian" songs. At Batković camp conditions were similar to those at Sušica camp, if not worse. [. . .] The Chamber, however, also considers that the same set of facts could be characterised as deportation and, accordingly, come under Article 5 of the Statute' (*Nikolić* Rule 61 Decision, par 23).

[164] The mere fear of discrimination against those being evacuated may not be sufficient to conclude that the transfer was indeed compulsory (see *Krstić* Trial Judgment, pars 528–530).

The limited circumstances under which a transfer is legitimate and authorized under the laws of war assume that proper facilities will be provided for that transfer. It is unclear, however, whether the conditions under which the displacement of people takes place – for example, long transfers on foot or the cramming of people into overcrowded buses and trains – could *in themselves* transform an otherwise legitimate transfer into a criminal offence of deportation.[165] In such circumstances, a transfer could amount to 'deportation' if the conditions of transfer cause a level of physical or mental suffering similar to that caused by the other offences listed in the Statutes. The matter has not been decided by either *ad hoc* Tribunal.

Finally, to be criminally liable for his part in such a transfer, an accused who has allegedly taken part in an illegal transfer must be shown to have intended the transfer of a person or group of persons.[166] According to one Trial Chamber, the accused must further be shown to have acted with the aim that the person being deported or transferred should not return.[167] As noted above, in such a case, the Chamber would have to look behind the stated intentions of the perpetrators (to *provisionally* remove people from a particular area, for instance), to consider the true nature of their actions.

Accordingly, 'unlawful deportation or transfer or unlawful confinement of civilians' has been said to consist of an intentional act or omission, not motivated by the security of the population or imperative military reasons, leading to the transfer of a person from occupied territory or within occupied territory.[168]

The grave breach of 'unlawful deportation or transfer or unlawful confinement of civilians' in many respects overlaps with the crimes against humanity of forcible transfer and deportation (as provided in Articles 5(d) and 3(d) of the ICTY and ICTR Statutes).[169] They differ only at the level of the *chapeau* elements required for each category of statutory offence. In addition, Articles 5(i) and 3(i) ('persecutions')[170] and Articles 5(i) and 3(i) of the ICTY and ICTR Statutes ('other inhumane acts') have also been interpreted as including cases of forcible transfer and displacement.[171]

---

[165] It has sometimes been argued that the criminal nature of 'deportation' lies in the 'arbitrary reasons' for moving those people, rather than with the manner in which the transfer took place. See, e.g. 1996 ILC Report, *supra* note, p 100.

[166] *Naletilić and Martinović* Trial Judgment, pars 520–521.

[167] Ibid., par 520. According to the Trial Chamber, 'deportation and forcible transfer are not by their nature provisional, which implies an intent that the transferred persons should not return' (*Naletilić and Martinović* Trial Judgment, n 1362). See also *Milošević* Rule 98bis Decision, par 78: 'in relation to forcible transfer or deportation there must be evidence of an intent to transfer the victim from his home or community; it must be established that the perpetrator either directly intended the victim would leave or that it was reasonably foreseeable that this would occur as a consequence of his action.' [168] *Naletilić and Martinović* Trial Judgment, par 521.

[169] See below, sub-section 12.4. See also *Krnojelac* Trial Judgment, pars 197 et seq;. *Krstić* Trial Judgment, pars 519 et seq;. *Stakić* Trial Judgment, pars 662 et seq. and 769 et seq.; *Milošević* Rule 98bis Decision, par 41.

[170] See, e.g. *Krnojelac* Trial Judgment, pars 472 et seq. and *Krnojelac* Appeal Judgment, pars 217 et seq.

[171] See *Milošević* Rule 98bis Decision, par 41; *Krstić* Trial Judgment, par 523; *Kupreškić* Trial Judgment, par 566.

Unlawful confinement of civilians

The protection of civilians from harm during armed conflict is 'a fundamental aim of international humanitarian law', but civilians do not possess, in armed conflicts, an absolute freedom of movement.[172] The freedom of movement during an armed conflict remains the principle, but civilians may be confined legally 'in limited cases', if a number of requirements are met.[173] In its relevant parts, Article 42 of Geneva Convention IV sets strict limitations upon the ability of a party to a conflict to confine civilians:

The internment or placing in assigned residence of protected persons may be ordered only if the security of the Detaining Power makes it absolutely necessary.

If any person, acting through the representatives of the Protecting Power, voluntarily demands internment, and if his situation renders this step necessary, he shall be interned by the Power in whose hands he may be.

The measure of internment must therefore be 'absolutely necessary' to the security of the detaining power and the measures least harmful to the rights of the person who is being confined must be adopted by the detaining authorities.[174] The measures can range widely in terms of their respective seriousness,[175] but they should be proportionate in every case to the actual security risk involved and should never affect the fundamental right of any person to be treated with humanity.[176] In addition, such measures are exceptional in character and they must be adopted on an individual basis, that is, in relation to each and every individual who is being detained.[177] The detaining power may not therefore decide to detain a population or groups of individuals on the basis that all of its members should be presumed to pose a security threat.

Article 5 of Geneva Convention IV also provides for the confinement of civilians in limited circumstances involving 'activities prejudicial or hostile to the security of the State'. This broadly worded concept appears to include, above all, as one Trial Chamber had noted, cases of espionage, sabotage, and intelligence activities for the enemy forces or enemy nationals.[178] The fact that a given individual is a national of the 'enemy' side, that he is opposed politically to the detaining power, or that he is of military age, is not sufficient in principle to detain him.[179]

---

[172] *Čelebići* Trial Judgment, par 565.

[173] See, e.g. ibid., pars 565–566; *Čelebići* Appeal Judgment, par 320.

[174] Ibid., pars 320, 330; *Čelebići* Trial Judgment, pars 571 and 576. In its assessment of the lawfulness of the confinement, the Appeals Chamber stated that recourse should also be made to Article 5 of Geneva Convention IV.

[175] As pointed out by the *Čelebići* Trial Chamber, the nature of the measure adopted depends a great deal upon the discretion of the State authorities (*Čelebići* Trial Judgment, par 574).

[176] Ibid., par 570. In relation to the rules on confinement applying in situations of occupation, see ibid., par 578.

[177] '[M]easure of internment for reasons of security is an exceptional one and can never be taken on a collective basis', ibid., par 583.

[178] Ibid., par 567; *Kordić and Čerkez* Trial Judgment, par 280.

[179] *Čelebići* Appeal Judgment, par 327 (footnote omitted): 'In the Appeals Chamber's view, there is no necessary inconsistency between the Trial Chamber's finding that the Bosnian Serbs were

There must be, in every case, 'serious and legitimate reason to think that [he is a member] of a subversive organization' or that he may otherwise 'seriously prejudice [the State's] security by means such as sabotage or espionage'.[180] It appears that the actions which may justify measures of confinement pursuant to that rule must be such as to engender penal consequences or, at least, be of a unlawful character or involve 'material, direct harm to the adversary, rather than merely granting support to the forces with which the civilian is aligned'.[181]

In all cases, the detaining power must have 'reasonable grounds to believe that the security of the State is at risk' and it must provide for the procedural safeguards required in Article 43 of Geneva Convention IV.[182] And as noted above, the situation of each and every individual who is being detained, and the *particular risk* to the security of the State that he or she is said to pose, must be assessed individually.[183]

Internment, which is initially lawful, may become unlawful (and possibly criminal) 'if the detaining party does not respect the basic procedural rights of the detained persons and does not establish an appropriate court or administrative board as prescribed in Article 43 of Geneva Convention IV', that is, in effect, if the conditions of both Articles 42 and 43 of the Geneva Convention IV are not

regarded by the Bosnian authorities as belonging to the opposing party in an armed conflict and the finding that some of them could not reasonably be regarded as presenting a threat to the detaining power's security. To hold the contrary would suggest that, whenever the armed forces of a State are engaged in armed conflict, the *entire* civilian population of that State is necessarily a threat to security and therefore may be detained.' See also *Čelebići* Trial Judgment, pars 567, 577, and 1134: 'the mere fact that a person is a national of, or aligned with, an enemy party cannot be considered as threatening the security of the opposing party where he is living, and is not, therefore, a valid reason for interning him', *Kordić and Čerkez* Trial Judgment, par 284.

180 Ibid., par 284; *Čelebići* Trial Judgment, par 576. See also ibid., par 577: 'To justify recourse to such measures, the party must have good reason to think that the person concerned, by his activities, knowledge or qualifications, represents a real threat to its present or future security.'

181 Ibid., par 568: 'While there is no requirement that the particular activity in question must be judged as criminal under national law before a State can derogate from the rights of protected civilians under article 5, it is almost certain that the condemned activity will in most cases be the subject of criminal punishment under national law. However, the instances of such action that might be deemed prejudicial or hostile to State security must be judged as such under international law, both for cases arising in occupied and unoccupied territory' (footnote omitted).

182 *Čelebići* Appeal Judgment, pars 320–322. Article 43 of Geneva Convention IV provides that:

Any protected person who has been interned or placed in assigned residence shall be entitled to have such action reconsidered as soon as possible by an appropriate court or administrative board designated by the Detaining Power for that purpose. If the internment or placing in assigned residence is maintained, the court or administrative board shall periodically, and at least twice yearly, give consideration to his or her case, with a view to the favourable amendment of the initial decision, if circumstances permit.

Unless the protected persons concerned object, the Detaining Power shall, as rapidly as possible, give the Protecting Power the names of any protected persons who have been interned or subjected to assigned residence, or have been released from internment or assigned residence. The decisions of the courts or boards mentioned in the first paragraph of the present Article shall also, subject to the same conditions, be notified as rapidly as possible to the Protecting Power.

See also *Kordić and Čerkez* Trial Judgment, pars 286–289.

183 *Čelebići* Appeal Judgment, par 327.

being complied with.[184] That requires, *inter alia*, that an appropriate court or administrative board[185] of the detaining power must review the legality of the detention as soon as possible and that the reviewing authority must treat the measures of internment as an exceptional measure:[186]

The judicial or administrative body reviewing the decision of a party to a conflict to detain an individual must bear in mind that such measures of detention should only be taken if absolutely necessary for reasons of security. Thus, if these measures were inspired by other considerations, the reviewing body would be bound to vacate them. Clearly, the procedures established in Geneva Convention IV itself are a minimum and the fundamental consideration must be that no civilian should be kept in assigned residence or in an internment camp for a longer time than the security of the detaining party absolutely demands.

Thus, an initially lawful measure of detention becomes unlawful where the detaining power does not respect the basic procedural rights of the detained persons or where it does not establish an appropriate court or administrative board as prescribed in Article 43 of Geneva Convention IV to review the legality of such measures.[187] The legality, and necessity of the measure, must be reviewed within 'reasonable time' and regularly.[188] As noted by the Appeals Chamber, the reasonableness of that period 'is *not* a matter solely to be assessed by the detaining power', and it must mean the shortest possible period of time required in view of the circumstances:[189]

The Appeals Chamber recalls that Article 43 of Geneva Convention IV provides that the decision to take measures of detention against civilians must be 'reconsidered *as soon as possible* by an appropriate court or administrative board.' Read in this light, the reasonable time which is to be afforded to a detaining power to ascertain whether detained civilians pose a security risk must be the *minimum* time necessary to make enquiries to determine whether a view that they pose a security risk has any objective foundation such that it would found a 'definite suspicion' of the nature referred to in Article 5 of Geneva Convention IV. Although the Trial Chamber made no express finding upon this issue, the Appeals Chamber is satisfied that the only reasonable finding upon the evidence is that the civilians detained in the Čelebići camp had been detained for longer than such a minimum time.

The effort by the authorities to determine the status of the detained person must be genuine and continued confinement may never depend on any lack of evidence that the individual in question does not present a threat to the security of the state.[190]

In many cases of armed conflicts, dozens if not hundreds of individuals might have been involved, at various stages and in various ways, in the unlawful detention and

---

[184] Ibid., pars 320 and 322. See also *Čelebići* Trial Judgment, par 580; *Kordić and Čerkez* Trial Judgment, pars 289, 291.

[185] *Čelebići* Trial Judgment, par 580. See also *Kordić and Čerkez* Trial Judgment, par 287.

[186] *Čelebići* Trial Judgment, par 581.   [187] Ibid., par 583.

[188] See, generally, *Čelebići* Appeal Judgment, par 328.   [189] Ibid.

[190] Ibid., par 329: 'It is upon the detaining power to establish that the particular civilian does pose such a risk to its security that he must be detained, and the obligation lies on it to release the civilian if there is inadequate foundation for such a view.'

confinement of civilians. But not every one of them may necessarily be found criminally liable for his or her part therein. In the words of the Appeals Chamber, 'something more must be proved than mere knowing "participation" in a general system or operation pursuant to which civilians are confined':[191]

In the Appeals Chamber's view, the fact alone of a role in some capacity, however junior, in maintaining a prison in which civilians are unlawfully detained is an inadequate basis on which to find primary criminal responsibility of the nature which is denoted by a finding that someone has *committed* a crime. Such responsibility is more properly allocated to those who are responsible for the detention in a more direct or complete sense, such as those who actually place an accused in detention without reasonable grounds to believe that he constitutes a security risk; or who, having some powers over the place of detention, accepts a civilian into detention without knowing that such grounds exist; or who, having power or authority to release detainees, fails to do so despite knowledge that no reasonable grounds for their detention exist, or that any such reasons have ceased to exist.

From a criminal liability perspective, the accused must therefore have been in a position to affect the continued detention of the civilians, in that he or she must have participated 'in some significant way in the continued detention of the civilians, whether to a degree which would establish primary responsibility, or to a degree necessary to establish liability as an accomplice or pursuant to a common plan'.[192] For instance, in the case of the accused Zdravko Mucić, who had been charged as a superior in relation to that crime, the Appeals Chamber held that, for him to be liable, he must have had the authority to release the civilian detainees and failed to exercise that power where (i) he has no reasonable grounds to believe that the detainees pose a real risk to the security of the state; or (ii) where he knows that they have not been afforded the requisite procedural guarantees (or is reckless as to whether those guarantees have been afforded or not).[193]

In sum, the confinement of civilians will be unlawful in either of these situations:[194]

(i) when a civilian or civilians have been detained in contravention of Article 42 of Geneva Convention IV, i.e. they are detained without reasonable grounds

---

[191] Ibid., par 342.

[192] Ibid., par 346. Accordingly, a mere guard would not be expected to take unauthorized steps to release prisoners for instance (ibid., par 342). During the *Kunarac* trial, it became clear that counsel for one of the accused had served as a camp guard at the KP Dom prison in Foča where numerous crimes had been committed (see *Krnojelac* Trial Judgment which dealt with those crimes). Witnesses testified, however, that he did not take any part in mistreatment that was carried out there, and that, instead, he attempted to use his position to help and assist many of the detainees. Such an individual, one would think, would fall outside of the scope of the crime of 'unlawful confinement'.

[193] *Čelebići* Appeal Judgment, par 378. The Appeals Chamber added the following (ibid., par 379): 'Where a person who has authority to release detainees knows that persons in continued detention have a right to review of their detention and that they have not been afforded that right, he has a duty to release them. Therefore, failure by a person with such authority to exercise the power to release detainees, whom he knows have not been afforded the procedural rights to which they are entitled, commits the offence of unlawful confinement of civilians, even if he is not responsible himself for the failure to have their procedural rights respected.'

[194] Ibid., par 322; *Kordić and Čerkez* Trial Judgment, par 291.

for believing that the security of the Detaining Power makes it absolutely necessary; or

(ii) where the procedural safeguards required by Article 43 of Geneva Convention IV are not complied with in respect of detained civilians, even where their initial detention may have been justified.

This grave breach of the Geneva Conventions overlaps in many respects with the crime against humanity of imprisonment (Article 5(e) ICTY Statute).

Taking civilians as hostages (Article 2(h) ICTY Statute)

The *Blaškić* Trial Chamber expressed the view that the concept of 'hostages' should be given a broad definition.[195] Civilian hostages, the Trial Chamber said, 'are persons unlawfully deprived of their freedom, often arbitrarily and sometimes under threat of death' where the act of detention is done 'in order to obtain a concession or gain an advantage' or 'to ensure that a belligerent, other person or other group of persons enter into some undertaking'.[196]

The crime of taking civilians hostage therefore consists of both an unlawful deprivation of liberty and the issuance of conditional threat, directed to the detainee or to other persons with a view to obtain a concession or to gain an advantage.[197]

---

[195] *Blaškić* Trial Judgment, par 187; *Kordić and Čerkez* Trial Judgment, par 319.

[196] *Blaškić* Trial Judgment, pars 158 and 187. The indictment charged the accused *Blaškić* with, *inter alia*, having taken hostage, from January 1993 until January 1994, Bosnian Muslim civilians and used them to bring a halt to Bosnian (Muslim) military operations against the Croatian forces. In its findings, the Trial Chamber found that a large number of Muslim civilians (and individuals placed *hors de combat*) had been unlawfully detained and that death threats had been made to them (*Blaškić* Trial Judgment, par 708). This, the Trial Chamber concluded, amounts to the taking of hostages (counts 17 and 18 of the indictment) and it went on to convict General Blaškić on that basis. This finding is somewhat astonishing as no mention is made of some advantage sought or obtained in doing so. Such a crime would have been more appropriately regarded as unlawful detention or imprisonment, unless the Trial Chamber implicitly accepted the suggestion of the prosecution that such detention were aimed at compelling Muslim forces to stop their counter-attack. The Trial Judgement referred to ICRC, *Commentary to Geneva Convention IV*, pp 600–601.

[197] See *Kordić and Čerkez* Trial Judgment, par 312–313. The *Kordić and Čerkez* Trial Chamber defined the crime in the following terms (par 314): 'an individual commits the offence of taking civilians as hostages when he threatens to subject civilians, who are unlawfully detained, to inhuman treatment or death as a means of achieving the fulfilment of a condition'. The Commentary to Article 3(b) of the Geneva Conventions defines hostage in the following terms: 'hostages are nationals of a belligerent State who of their own free will or through compulsion are in the hands of the enemy and are answerable with their freedom or their life for the execution of his orders and the security of his armed forces'. The ICRC Commentary goes on to say the following: '*The taking of hostages*: Hostages might be considered as persons illegally deprived of their liberty, a crime which most penal codes take cognizance of and punish. However, there is an additional feature, i.e. the threat either to prolong the hostage's detention or to put him to death. The taking of hostages should therefore be treated as a special offence. Certainly, the most serious crime would be to execute hostages which, as we have seen, constitutes wilful killing. However, the fact of taking hostages, by its arbitrary character, especially when accompanied by a threat of death, is in itself a very serious crime; it causes in the hostage and among his family a mortal anguish which nothing can justify.' ICRC, *Commentary to Geneva Convention IV*, pp 600–601.

Such threat, one Chamber said, must be 'intended as a coercive measure to achieve the fulfillment of a condition'[198] and the detention must be shown to have been undertaken with a view 'to obtain a concession or gain an advantage'[199] such as forcing a belligerent party or any particular individual to enter into some undertaking.[200]

The *mens rea* required for this offence has not been further elaborated in any of the Tribunals' judgments and decisions.[201]

The constitutive elements of the grave breach of 'taking civilians as hostages' are similar in substance to those required by violation of common Article 3 of the 'taking of hostages', but for the obvious difference that the former is limited to the taking of 'civilians' as hostages.[202]

---

[198] *Kordić and Čerkez* Trial Judgment, par 313.   [199] *Blaškić* Trial Judgment, par 158.

[200] Ibid., par 187.

[201] It is the position of the Prosecution that the civilians must have been 'willfully used for the purpose of obtaining some advantage or securing some commitment' (*Prosecutor v. Kordić and Čerkez*, IT-95-14/2-T, Prosecutor's Closing Brief, 13 December 2000). The *Blaškić* Trial Chamber stated, without supporting its conclusion, that 'the *mens rea* constituting all the violations of Article 2 of the Statute includes both guilty intent and recklessness which may be likened to serious criminal negligence' (*Blaškić* Trial Judgment, par 152).

[202] Ibid., pars 158, 187; *Kordić and Čerkez* Trial Judgment, pars 319–320.

8

Other Serious Violations of the Laws or Customs of War: Underlying Offences

The Statutes of the *ad hoc* Tribunals expressly stipulate a number of specific violations of the laws or customs of war which may form the basis of a conviction if the *chapeau* elements mentioned above, and the constitutive elements of the offence charged, are all proved. In addition, the *ad hoc* Tribunals have sanctioned the recognition of a number of war crimes which although not expressly mentioned in the Statutes were said to have been provided implicitly in the Statutes and to have been recognized as crimes under international law at the relevant time. It would appear that all of those underlying offences (listed or unlisted) could constitute war crimes whether committed in the context of an international armed conflict or in the context of an internal one. The Tribunals have not indicated that any of those underlying offences was limited in principle to one context while excluding the other.

8.1 Employment of poisonous weapons or other weapons calculated to cause unnecessary suffering (Article 3(a) ICTY Statute)

No charges have been brought in relation to this offence at either Tribunal, although there were allegations during the war in Bosnia that such weapons might have been used.[1] The only pronouncement relevant to this crime consists in an *obiter dictum* of the Appeals Chamber in the *Tadić* case where it said that the use of such weapons would be regarded as a violation of international law that would entail individual criminal responsibility, whether it took place in an internal or an international armed conflict.[2]

8.2 Wanton destruction of cities, towns, or villages, or devastation not justified by military necessity (Article 3(b) ICTY Statute)

'Even in destruction, there's a right way and a wrong way – and there are limits.'[3] The crime of 'wanton destruction of cities, towns or villages, or devastation not

---

[1] There were allegations (although, apparently, no evidence), for instance, that the Bosnian (Muslim) Army used chlorine-filled shells around Tuzla against Serb forces, and there were occasionally claims that Serb forces used some sort of chemical weapons on the column of Muslims escaping from the Srebrenica enclave. In the Final Report to the Prosecutor by the Committee Established to Review the NATO Bombing Campaign Against the Federal Republic of Yugoslavia, the Committee set up by the Prosecutor to draw up a report upon the legality of NATO's bombing campaign held that there was evidence of use of depleted uranium projectiles by NATO aircraft during the bombing campaign (par 26). The Committee concluded that 'it is possible that, in future, there will be a consensus view in international legal circles that use of such projectiles violate general principles of the law applicable to use of weapons in armed conflict [but no] such consensus exists at present' (ibid.). See generally, P. Benvenuti, 'The ICTY Prosecutor and the Review of the NATO Bombing Campaign against the Federal Republic of Yugoslavia', 12 European Journal of International Law (*EJIL*) 503 (2001).   [2] See *Tadić* Jurisdiction Decision, pars 119–124.

[3] A. Camus, 'The Just Assassins', in *Caligula and Three Other Plays*, trans. S. Gilbert (New York: Vintage Books, 1958) cited in M. Waltzer, *Just and Unjust Wars*, 3rd edn (New York: Basic Books, 1958), p 199.

justified by military necessity' sets a general framework around what is permitted. The definition of that offence has been said to consist of the following elements:[4]

(i)   destruction of properties occurring on a large scale;
(ii) such destruction is not justified by military necessity;
(iii) the perpetrator acted with intent to destroy the property in question or in reckless disregard of the likelihood of its destruction.

Within that general framework, two sets of conduct are criminalized pursuant to this provision: (i) wanton destruction of cities, towns, or villages, and (ii) devastation not justified by military necessity. The extent to which the two may be said to overlap is not fully elucidated, but it appears that the former would include the latter, whilst the reverse might not necessarily be true.[5] Concerning the first part of the prohibition ('Wanton destruction of cities, towns, or villages'), the destruction must be widespread enough and the effect of that destruction significant enough for it to be said to have been directed at 'cities, towns, or villages' as a whole, rather than simply at random dwellings or properties individually.[6] In addition, the destruction must have been 'wanton', that is, deliberate and without any justification ('sans motifs', in the French text).[7]

Concerning the second tier of this prohibition ('devastation not justified by military necessity'), the Tribunals have given no explicit definition of what may be said to constitute 'devastation' for the purpose of that rule. What is clear from the text of the Article, however, is that the devastation must not necessarily be directed at 'cities, towns, and villages' as in the case of 'wanton destruction', but that it could apparently be directed at properties falling short of an entire settlement.[8] Such devastation must, in addition, not have been justified by military

---

[4] *Kordić and Čerkez* Trial Judgment, par 346; *Naletilić and Martinović* Trial Judgment, par 579.

[5] The Trial Chamber in *Naletilić and Martinović* appears, however, to have merged the two into one (see *Naletilić and Martinović* Trial Judgment, par 597, for instance, where it talks of 'wanton destruction not justified by military necessity').

[6] In the *Naletilić and Martinović* case, the destruction which occurred in the village of Sovići was limited to Muslim, as opposed to Croatian houses, and the targeting of such dwellings was therefore, not all-encompassing, but discriminatory, based on the ethnic background of its inhabitants (see *Naletilić and Martinović* Trial Judgment, pars 583–585). See also *Kordić and Čerkez* Trial Judgment, pars 803 et seq., where the Trial Chamber talks of 'a pattern of destruction' (par 808). In such a case, it would be difficult to conclude that the village, as opposed to those Muslim properties in that village, were destroyed. The Tribunal has not specifically defined the phrase 'destruction' for the purpose of that prohibition. For a factual illustration of what one Trial Chamber has considered to come within the terms of that prohibition, see *Naletilić and Martinović* Trial Judgment, pars 581–597. For an illustration of what the Prosecution considers to qualify as 'wanton destruction of cities, towns and villages', see, for instance, *Rajić* Rule 61 Decision, pars 52 et seq.

[7] See, e.g. *Naletilić and Martinović* Trial Judgment, par 583. The manner in which the destruction takes place and the discriminatory character of the destruction are factors relevant to the determination of the wantonness of the destruction.

[8] It is indicative, for instance, that the Trial Chamber in *Naletilić and Martinović* directed its factual findings to the destruction of 'properties' rather than cities, towns, or villages (see, generally, *Naletilić and Martinović* Trial Judgment, pars 581 et seq.).

necessity, that is, that the destruction in question was not justified by 'an imperative necessity for the conduct of military operations'.[9]

The present crime has been said to cover or significantly overlap with certain prohibitions contained in Additional Protocol I: Articles 51 (Prohibition on Attacks on Civilians), Article 52 (General Protection of Civilian Objects), and Article 54 (Protection of Objects Indispensable to the Survival of the Civilian Population), as well as Article 23(g) of the Hague Regulations concerning unnecessary destruction of all enemy property in the territories at war 'unless such destruction [. . .] be imperatively demanded by the necessities of war'.[10] It would therefore apply in principle not only to property located in a territory under belligerent occupation (Article 53 of Geneva Convention IV) but also to property situated in enemy territory.[11]

In order to be held criminally responsible for this offence, the perpetrator of the relevant acts must apparently have acted with intent to destroy the property in question or in reckless disregard for the likelihood of its destruction.[12] It would be insufficient to establish that the destruction is accidental or the result of mere negligence.[13]

---

[9] *United States v. Krupp and others*, US Military Tribunal sitting at Nuremberg, Judgment of 30 July 1948, in *Law Reports of Trials of War Criminals*, IX ('*Krupp* case'), pp 136 et seq. The *Naletilić and Martinović* Trial Chamber said that it was satisfied that the destruction could not be justified by military necessity 'as it occurred [. . .] after the actual shelling had ceased', thereby suggesting that there must exist a temporal correlation between the destruction charged in the indictment and ongoing military operations (*Naletilić and Martinović* Trial Judgment, par 589 and n 1463, p 202). This seems a rather doubtful statement as there may be situations when destruction might be justified by military necessity although the fighting is over and the area has been, for the time being, momentarily secured by one party to the conflict.   [10] Ibid., n 1441, p 200.

[11] *Kordić and Čerkez* Trial Judgment, par 347: 'while property situated on enemy territory is not protected under the Geneva Conventions, and is therefore not included in the crime of extensive destruction of property listed as a grave breach of the Geneva Conventions, the destruction of such property is criminalized under Article 3 of the Statute'. Not abiding by such standards would therefore be 'a clear violation of the laws of war' (*Naletilić and Martinović* Trial Judgment, n 1441, p 200).

[12] Concerning the slight variations that exist between various Chambers on that point, see *Naletilić and Martinović* Trial Judgment, n 1440, p 199; *Blaškić* Trial Judgment, par 183; and *Kordić and Čerkez* Trial Judgment, par 346. Often, when determining the state of mind required for a particular criminal offence, Trial Chambers have failed to reveal the sources upon which they relied to come to their (distinct) conclusions concerning the *mens rea* required for this offence. In the *Kordić and Čerkez* case, for instance, the Trial Chamber merely pointed out that, according to the Prosecution, the *mens rea* for that offence consisted of a wilful act (whilst ordinary negligence would not suffice), and that the Defence did not appear to oppose the Prosecution's position on that matter. An agreement between the parties as to the elements of a criminal offence is, however, insufficient to determine whether that definition does indeed exist under customary international law. The determination of the required *mens rea* under customary law has often been a somewhat murky affair before the *ad hoc* Tribunals in relation to many offences, including this one. It is safe to suggest that many a definition of a state of mind which has been said by the Tribunals to form part of customary international law had much more to do with the view of the Chamber in question, than with the existence of sufficient state practice and *opinio juris* to support its finding.

[13] See, e.g. *Kordić and Čerkez* Trial Judgment, par 344 citing the Prosecution's Final Trial Brief in this case, Annex 5, par 82, in which the Prosecution conceded that point.

8.3   Attack, or bombardment, by whatever means, of undefended towns, villages, dwellings, or buildings (Article 3(c) ICTY Statute)

The *ad hoc* Tribunals have not had the occasion to consider this offence at the time of publication.

8.4   Seizure of, destruction or wilful damage done to institutions dedicated to religion, charity, education, the arts and sciences, historic monuments, and works of art and science (Article 3(d) ICTY Statute)

Wars have systematically been destructive of culture in all of its forms. German soldiers used Tolstoy's manuscripts as firewood,[14] whilst Bosnian Serb forces regarded the beautiful old National and University Library of Sarajevo as a target for shooting practice.[15] The recognition of such practices as criminal conduct is an important step forward. Institutions dedicated to religion, charity and education, the arts and sciences, historic monuments, and works of art and science are certainly at the forefront of institutions in need of particular protection during armed conflicts.

There is a great deal of overlap between the various categories of institutions protected under this provision as many of them will often serve more than one of the listed functions.[16] The fact that the protected institutions, monuments, or works are dedicated to charitable, artistic, or religious functions justifies the criminalization of their targeting and destruction, but to the extent that they are being used for military purposes, they are likely to lose their special status.[17]

Article 3(d) of the ICTY Statute criminalizes the 'seizure of', 'destruction', and 'wilful damage' done to such institutions to the extent only that such conduct was intentional.[18] The Tribunals have not specified the extent of destruction that must have been inflicted for it to be regarded as a war crime, nor has the court clearly

---

[14] J. Persico, *Nuremberg, Infamy on Trial* (London/New York: Penguin Books, 1994), p 257.

[15] See also *Final Report of Commission of Experts for the former Yugoslavia*, pars 285 et seq. ('Destruction of cultural property') dealing in particular with the 'battle of Dubrovnik' and the destruction of the old Mostar Bridge.

[16] This provision covers, in particular, educational institutions as they are 'undoubtedly immovable property of great importance to the cultural heritage of peoples in that they are without exception centres of learning, arts, and sciences, with their valuable collections of books and works of arts and science' (*Kordić and Čerkez* Trial Judgment, par 360).

[17] *Naletilić and Martinović* Trial Judgment, par 605. This conclusion, the Trial Chamber said, is based on Article 27 of the Hague Regulations (ibid., n 1484, p 206).

[18] *Blaškić* Trial Judgment, par 185; *Naletilić and Martinović* Trial Judgment, pars 603–604.

stated whether there is in fact any difference between 'destruction' and 'damage' for the purpose of this provision.[19] It would appear, however, that, because of the very nature of the institutions which are protected under the rule and in view of the object and purpose of the prohibition, the requirement of destruction should be a relatively low one.[20] Existing case law does not specify whether a criminal conviction might be entered under that heading for the destruction of or for damage done to a single protected entity or whether a number of such institutions must have been seized or damaged, i.e. whether the offence contains an element of scale. The plain objective of the provision would suggest that although the article uses the plural 'institutions', it is intended to prohibit any destruction of or damage to *any* institution, monument, or work.

Concerning the required *mens rea*, it is said that the destruction or damage must have been committed wilfully and that the accused must be shown to have intended by his acts or conduct to cause the destruction or damage of those institutions, works, or monuments.[21]

The protection afforded by the Statute to such institutions and monuments is not limited to Article 3(d) of the ICTY Statute and there is some degree of overlap between this provision and other statutory norms, in particular Article 2(d) of the ICTY Statute (extensive destruction and appropriation of property, not justified by military necessity and carried out unlawfully and wantonly), Article 3(b) of the ICTY Statute (wanton destruction of cities, towns, or villages, or devastation not justified by military necessity) and Articles 5(h)/3(h) of the ICTY/ICTR Statutes (persecutions on political, racial, and religious grounds).[22] Also, this prohibition

---

[19] It does not appear that charges of 'seizing' such an institution have ever been brought before the *ad hoc* Tribunals. The Trial Chamber in *Kordić and Čerkez* has stated that the protection of a given institution, monument, or work does not depend on its having acquired 'special protection' according to the Cultural Property Convention by having been registered in the International Register of Cultural Property under Special Protection (*Kordić and Čerkez* Trial Judgment, par 362).

[20] In the *Naletilić and Martinović* case, Mladen Naletilić was accused of having ordered the destruction of a single mosque (*Prosecutor v. Naletilić and Martinović*, IT-98-34-I, Second Amended Indictment, 16 October 2001, par 56). The Trial Chamber did not pronounce itself upon this matter as the accused was acquitted upon that count as there was no evidence of his implication in the destruction of this particular mosque (*Naletilić and Martinović* Trial Judgment, par 608). In order to determine the scope of that prohibition, recourse was made to relevant international instruments in particular Article 27 of the Hague Regulations, Article 53 of Additional Protocol I and Article 1 of the Convention for the Protection of Cultural Property in the Event of Armed Conflict (*Kordić and Čerkez* Trial Judgment, par 359). The *Naletilić and Martinović* Trial Chamber recognized the legitimacy of such recourse as, it said, the prohibition contained in Article 3(d) seems to be based on those very provisions (*Naletilić and Martinović* Trial Judgment, n 1483, p 206).

[21] Ibid., par 361; *Blaškić* Trial Judgment, par 185; *Kordić and Čerkez* Trial Judgment, par 361. It would appear from those three cases that negligent damage, even if gross or reckless, would not come within the realm of the prohibition. It should be noted, however, that none of these Trial Chambers offered any authority to support its conclusion that, under customary international law, the *mens rea* for that offence was so defined or so restricted.

[22] On the protection afforded to cultural property, under the ICTY Statute, and the overlap between statutory norms, see generally H. Abtahi, 'The Protection of Cultural Property in Times of Armed Conflict: The Practice of the International Criminal Tribunal for the Former Yugoslavia', 14 *Harvard Human Rights Journal* 1 (2001).

overlaps in part with the prohibition against attacks on civilian objects 'except that
the object of this offence [under Article 3(d) of the ICTY Statute] is more specific
[than the general prohibition on attacks against civilians]: the cultural heritage of
a certain population'.[23]

8.5   Plunder of public or private property (Article 3(e) ICTY Statute) and pillage (Article 4(f) ICTR Statute)

International humanitarian law 'not only proscribes certain conduct harmful to
the human person, but also contains rules aimed at protecting property rights in
times of armed conflict'.[24] 'Plunder' is one of those crimes which has long been
recognized as prohibited by both conventional and customary law.[25] It has been
defined in general terms by one Trial Chamber as 'the fraudulent appropriation of
public or private funds belonging to the enemy or the opposing party perpetrated
during an armed conflict and related thereto'[26] or simply as 'willful and unlawful
appropriation of property'.[27] The latter is a preferable definition in that there
appears to be no basis in customary law for limiting the subject matter of plunder
to 'funds' (as did the *Jelišić* Trial Chamber), as opposed to property. Plunder
covers the fraudulent appropriation of both public and private property, whether
movable or immovable.[28] It may be committed anywhere on the territory of
parties to the conflict.[29]

---

[23] *Kordić and Čerkez* Trial Judgment, par 361.

[24] *Čelebići* Trial Judgment, par 587: 'Thus, whereas historically enemy property was subject to
arbitrary appropriation during war, international law today imposes strict limitations on the
measures which a party to an armed conflict may lawfully take in relation to the private and
public property of an opposing party. The basic norms in this respect, which form part of
customary international law, are contained in the Hague Regulations, articles 46 to 56 which are
broadly aimed at preserving the inviolability of public and private property during military
occupation.'

[25] *Kordić and Čerkez* Trial Judgment, par 351 which mentions in the footnote the following
relevant instruments: see Hague Regulations, Article 46; the Charter of the International Military
Tribunal 1945, art. 6(b); *The Trial of German Major War Criminals* (Proceedings of the International
Military Tribunal sitting at Nuremberg, Germany), Part 22, IMT Judgment, p 457; *United States v.
Krauch and others*, US Military Tribunal sitting at Nuremberg, Judgment of 29 July 1948, in *Law
Reports of Trials of War Criminals*, VIII, 42–47 ('*I. G. Farben* trial'), which considers the term 'spolia-
tion' to be synonymous with that of 'plunder'.

[26] *Jelišić* Trial Judgment, par 48. See also *Čelebići* Trial Judgment, par 591, where the Chamber
held that plunder should be understood as encompassing 'all forms of unlawful appropriation of
property in armed conflict for which individual criminal responsibility attaches under international
law, including those acts traditionally described as "pillage" '. See also *Kordić and Čerkez* Trial
Judgment, par 352.   [27] *Naletilić and Martinović* Trial Judgment, par 612.

[28] *Čelebići* Trial Judgment, pars 587–588, 590–591; *Naletilić and Martinović* Trial Judgment,
par 612. Concerning the appropriation of 'private' property in particular, see *Čelebići* Trial Judgment,
pars 587–590.

[29] *Naletilić and Martinović* Trial Judgment, par 615; *Čelebići* Trial Judgment, par 588; in particular, plunder is not limited to fraudulent appropriation of goods in occupied territories (ibid.).

It is unclear from the jurisprudence of the Tribunals whether 'plunder' covers any sort of unlawful appropriation regardless of its scope and value or whether, as seems more likely, the prohibition is limited to such appropriation involving the systematic or large-scale appropriation of valuables. The Trial Chamber in *Kunarac* held the view that 'plunder' in its ordinary meaning was identical and synonymous to the concept of 'pillage' and that it suggests 'more than the theft of property from one person or even from a few persons in the one building is required':[30]

Plunder is synonymous with 'pillage', which more clearly emphasises that there must be theft involving a more extensive group of persons or a pattern of thefts over some identifiable area such as, for example, the Muslim section of a village or town or even a detention centre.

The word 'plunder' in Article 3(e) of the ICTY Statute, the *Kunarac* Trial Chamber added:[31]

refers to its ordinary meaning of involving unjustified appropriations of property either from more than a small group of persons or from persons over an identifiable area as already described. This interpretation is more consistent with plunder being a violation of the laws or customs of war. It is inappropriate to include within that term a theft from only one person or from only a few persons in the one building.

This position is not shared, however, by other Trial Chambers which have expressed the view that individual occurrences of misappropriation and dispossession could in principle qualify as 'plunder'.[32] It would appear that Chambers of

---

[30] *Kunarac* Rule 98bis Decision, par 15 (footnote omitted).

[31] Ibid., par 16. Dragoljub Kunarac, who had robbed a victim of gold and some money, was thus duly acquitted in relation to the plunder charges as there was no evidence in the present case which satisfies the interpretation adopted (ibid., par 16).

[32] See *Čelebići* Trial Judgment, par 590 ('the prohibition against the unjustified appropriation of public and private enemy property is general in scope, and extends both to acts of looting committed by individual soldiers for their private gain, and to the organized seizure of property undertaken within the framework of a systematic economic exploitation of occupied territory'); *Kordić and Čerkez* Trial Judgment, par 352; *Blaškić* Trial Judgment, par 184. See also ibid., par 424; *Jelišić* Trial Judgment, par 4; *Naletilić and Martinović* Trial Judgment, par 612 ('in international law, plunder does not require the appropriation to be extensive or to involve a large economic value. Dispossession of personal property, a common way individual soldiers gain illicit booty, is considered a war crime of the more traditional type'). As stated by the *Kunarac* Trial Chamber, '[n]either judgment [the *Čelebići* nor the *Blaškić* judgment] [. . .] found it necessary to consider whether plunder requires the thefts to be widespread' (*Kunarac* Rule 98bis Decision, par 15). The *Blaškić* Trial Chamber did not cite any authority in support of its position, limiting itself to referring back to the finding of the *Čelebići* Trial Chamber. Furthermore, the finding on that point is *obiter dicta* as the acts charged as plunder were said to have occurred on a widespread basis. See also *Jelišić* Trial Judgment, par 138, where a conviction for plunder was entered upon a guilty plea and where the Trial Chamber based its legal finding on a limited number of cases concerned with the law of *theft*, rather than plunder. Finally, it would appear that none of the authorities cited by these Chambers actually relates to the crime of 'plunder', but that all of them in fact refer to minor offences (generally, domestic ones) such as theft or robbery. The ICRC *Commentary to the Additional Protocols* says that the prohibition of 'pillage' is based on Article 33(2) of Geneva Convention IV and that it covers 'both organized pillage and pillage resulting

the Tribunals agree that the crime of 'plunder' as understood in Article 3(e) of the ICTY Statute is similar in substance to the crime of 'pillage' as provided in Article 4(f) of the ICTR Statute.[33]

Further, the qualification in Article 1 of the Statute that violations of international humanitarian law must be 'serious' may mean that single instances of plunder are unlikely to be successfully charged. Trial Chambers are in agreement to say that, to come within the jurisdiction of the Tribunal (because of the Article 1 'seriousness' requirement), such misappropriation must be of sufficient monetary value so as to involve grave consequences for the victims.[34]

And property must have been acquired 'unlawfully' in the sense that it must fall outside those exceptions provided for in the laws of war where property may be acquired without consent of its rightful owner.[35] The court might have to consider in that regard the ability of the owner who parted with his property to give proper and genuine consent at the time when ownership was being transferred or property taken from him.[36] The use of force or violence does not appear to be a requirement of the offence of 'plunder' and it could therefore be committed in principle where the perpetrator uses certain means of coercion falling short of violence.[37]

As for the requisite state of mind, it would appear that the perpetrator must have acted 'willfully', that is with '*intent* in the appropriation of property'.[38] Whether the perpetrator must also have known of the illegality of the appropriation is unclear, although it would seem well founded in principle to require him to have been aware of the illegality of his action before entering a conviction on that basis. The existence of particular motives of the perpetrator, such as for instance, 'private gain' or 'personal greed', is neither a requirement of the offence of plunder nor would the existence of such personalized motives negate the conclusion that his acts may qualify as the war crime of plunder.[39] It could, however, play a role in sentencing.

from isolated acts of indiscipline' (ICRC, *Commentary to Geneva Convention IV*, p 1376, par 4542). In turn, the ICRC *Commentary* to Article 33(2) provides that this prohibition against pillage is general in scope and that it concerns 'not only pillage through individual acts without the consent of the military authorities, but also organized pillage, the effects of which are recounted in the histories of former wars, when the booty allocated to each soldier was considered as part of his pay' (ibid., p 226).

[33] See, e.g. *Kunarac* Rule 98bis Decision, par 15. See also *Naletilić and Martinović* Trial Judgment, pars 613 and 615.

[34] *Čelebići* Trial Judgment, par 1154; *Naletilić and Martinović* Trial Judgment, par 613; *Kordić and Čerkez* Trial Judgment, par 352. See also *Blaškić* Appeal Judgment, par 148 ('There may be some doubt, however, as to whether acts of plunder, as and of themselves, may rise to the level of gravity required by crimes against humanity').

[35] See, e.g. *Naletilić and Martinović* Trial Judgment, par 616; *Čelebići* Trial Judgment, par 587.

[36] *Karadžić* and *Mladić* Rule 61 Decision, par 14.

[37] See, e.g. *Krupp* trial, p 1347, cited in *Čelebići* Trial Judgment, par 591, n 605.

[38] *Naletilić and Martinović* Trial Judgment, par 617 and n 1498; *Čelebići* Trial Judgment, par 590. See also *Blaškić* Trial Judgment, par 184 and *Jelišić* Trial Judgment, par 48.

[39] *Čelebići* Trial Judgment, par 590.

8.6 Violence to life and person (Article 4(a) ICTR Statute and Article 3 ICTY Statute generally)[40]

Common Article 3 of the 1949 Geneva Conventions lists 'violence to life and person' as one of the acts which must be prohibited at any time and in any place in the case of an armed conflict not of an international character. The *Blaškić* Trial Chamber defined it as 'a broad offence which, at first glance, encompasses murder, mutilation, cruel treatment and torture and which is accordingly defined by the cumulation of the elements of these specific offences'.[41] The Trial Chamber omitted, however, to identify the sources – in particular, relevant instances of state practice and *opinio juris* – upon which it had relied to provide this 'definition' of the elements of the crime.[42]

In a subsequent trial, Trial Chamber II took notice of the definition of the offence given in the *Blaškić* case and noted the absence of any support for that definition under customary international law.[43] The Trial Chamber said that, before it may enter a conviction in relation to a given offence, it must ensure that the act in question is indeed a crime under customary international law and that it was defined with sufficient clarity *under customary international law* for its general nature, its criminal character and its approximate gravity to have been sufficiently foreseeable and accessible.[44] The residual character of Article 3 of the ICTY Statute, the Chamber said, 'does not by itself provide for the criminalisation by analogy to any act which is even vaguely or potentially criminal'.[45] Nor does the fact that the offence appears in common Article 3 of the Geneva Conventions suffice to regard its breach as entailing individual criminal responsibility:[46]

The fact that an offence is listed in the Statute, or comes within Article 3 of the Statute through common article 3 of the Geneva Conventions, does not therefore create new law, and the Tribunal only has jurisdiction over any listed crime if it was recognised as such by customary international law at the time the crime is alleged to have been committed. Each Trial Chamber is thus obliged to ensure that the law which it applies to a given criminal offence is indeed customary. The Trial Chamber must further be satisfied that this offence was defined with sufficient clarity for it to have been foreseeable and accessible, taking into account the specificity of customary international law.

Having reviewed existing state practice, or, rather, having taken note of the absence thereof in relation to this provision, the Trial Chamber concluded that

---

[40] In full, Article 4(a) of the ICTR Statute provides for the criminalization of 'Violence to life, health and physical or mental well-being of persons, in particular murder as well as cruel treatment such as torture, mutilation or any form of corporal punishment.'
[41] *Blaškić* Trial Judgment, par 182.
[42] Colonel, later General, Blaškić was convicted upon that offence (*Prosecutor v. Blaškić*, IT-95-14-I, Second Amended Indictment, 25 April 1997, Count 9).
[43] *Vasiljević* Trial Judgment, par 194.   [44] Ibid., par 201; see also ibid., par 193.
[45] Ibid., par 195.   [46] Ibid., par 198.

there did not exist a sufficiently precise definition of 'violence to life and person' under customary law to warrant a conviction on that basis.[47] It therefore refrained from exercising its jurisdiction upon this charge.[48]

At this stage, it would therefore appear that 'violence to life and person' does not exist under customary international law as a discrete criminal offence.[49]

8.7 Collective punishment (Article 4(b) ICTR Statute)

The ICTR has not rendered any decision relevant to the definition or elements of that crime.

8.8 Taking of hostages (Article 4(c) ICTR Statute and Article 3 ICTY Statute generally)

Concerning this crime, see above the crime of 'taking civilians as hostages' under Article 2(h) of the ICTY Statute.[50] The substance, and elements of those two crimes, 'taking hostages' pursuant to Article 4(c) of the ICTR Statute, and 'taking civilians as hostages' under Article 2(h) of the ICTY Statute, are similar but for one aspect, obvious from the express terms of each provision namely, the fact that the latter offence is limited to 'civilians' having been taken as hostages, whereas the former applies to a broader category of potential victims (including prisoners of war).[51]

---

[47] On 1 February 2002, the parties had been requested by the Trial Chamber to provide assistance in respect of a number of issues, including the definition of 'violence to life and person' under customary international law (Notice addressed to the Parties, *Issues upon which the Assistance of the Parties is Sought*). It was subsequently made clear to the Prosecution that this request of assistance in relation to 'violence to life and person' was directed at the identification of relevant state practice which would support the definition of that crime under customary international law as given in the *Blaškić* Trial Judgment (see IT-95-14-T and T 4827–4829). As a result of the Trial Chamber's request, the Prosecution filed its 'Submission by the Prosecution on the Law with Respect to "Violence to Life and Person"' on 28 March 2002, and the Defence filed its 'Submission by the Defence on the Law with Respect to "Violence to Life and Person"' on 12 April 2002. In its Judgment, the Trial Chamber noted that the Prosecution failed to provide any assistance in the form of relevant state practice (*Vasiljević* Trial Judgment, par 194). See also *Ntakirutimana* Trial Judgment, par 860.

[48] See *Vasiljević* Trial Judgment, par 202, citing from *Hostages* case, p 1240). The Trial Chamber did not, however, make a finding as to whether that prohibition against violence to life and person was binding *upon states* (as opposed to individuals) *qua* customary law (*Vasiljević* Trial Judgment, n 549, p 78).

[49] One of the by-products of this decision has been the request by the Prosecution for withdrawal (at least on one occasion) of 'violence to life and person' counts. On 25 March 2003, in the *Hadžihasanović* case, the Prosecution filed a motion seeking leave to amend the indictment to replace 'violence to life and person' charges with 'cruel treatment' charges, arguing, somewhat disingenuously, that this amendment merely amount to 'retitling' of the charge (*Prosecutor v. Hadžihasanović et al.*, Motion for Leave to Amend the Amended Indictment, 25 March 2003, par 7).

[50] See above, Chapter 7, underlying offences.

[51] See *Prosecutor v. Blaškić*, IT-95-14-I, Decision on the Defence Motion to Dismiss the Indictment Based upon Defects in the Form Thereof (Vagueness/Lack of Adequate Notice of Charges), 4 April 1997, par 38. See also *Blaškić* Trial Judgment, par 187.

8.9   Acts of terrorism (Article 4(d) ICTR Statute)

The ICTR has not rendered any decision relevant to the definition or elements of this crime. The difficulty at arriving at a definition of what may be said to constitute 'terrorism' might explain that this underlying offence has never been charged before either Tribunal.

8.10   Outrages upon personal dignity (Article 4(e) ICTR Statute and Article 3 ICTY Statute generally)[52]

'Outrages upon personal dignity' pursuant to Article 3 of the ICTY Statute has been charged by reference to common Article 3(1)(c) of the Geneva Conventions which expressly prohibits 'outrages upon personal dignity, in particular humiliating and degrading treatment'.[53] This criminal offence has been said to constitute, 'a category of the broader proscription of inhuman treatment in common Article 3'.[54] Its elements are said to consist of the following:[55]

(i)   that the accused intentionally committed or participated in an act or omission which would be generally considered to cause serious humiliation, degradation, or otherwise be a serious attack on human dignity; and

(ii) that he knew that the act or omission could have that effect.

The gravity of the act may result from a single act or omission or from a combination of acts and/or omissions.[56] The humiliation or degradation engendered by such conduct need not be lasting, so long as it is 'real and serious'.[57] The measure of its

[52] In full, Article 4(e) of the ICTR Statute provides for the criminalization of 'Outrages upon personal dignity, in particular humilitating and degrading treatment, rape, enforced prostitution and any form of indecent assault.'

[53] The prohibition is also to be found in Art 75(2)(b) of Additional Protocol I and Art 4(2)(e) of Additional Protocol II.   [54] *Kunarac* Trial Judgment, par 501.

[55] Ibid., pars 507 and 514; *Kunarac* Appeal Judgment, pars 161 and 163. According to the *Aleksovski* Trial Chamber, '[a]n outrage upon personal dignity is an act which is animated by contempt for the human dignity of another person. The corollary is that the act must cause serious humilitation or degradation to the victim' (*Aleksovski* Trial Judgment, par 56).

[56] Ibid., par 57 (footnote omitted): 'Indeed, the seriousness of an act and its consequences may arise either from the nature of the act *per se* or from the repetition of an act or from a combination of different acts which, taken individually, would not constitute a crime within the meaning of Article 3 of the Statute. The form, severity and duration of the violence, the intensity and duration of the physical or mental suffering, shall serve as a basis for assessing whether crimes were committed. In other words, the determination to be made on the allegations presented by the victims or expressed by the Prosecution largely rest with the analysis of the facts of the case.'

[57] *Kunarac* Trial Judgment, pars 501 and 503: 'In the view of the Trial Chamber, it is not open to regard the fact that a victim has recovered or is overcoming the effects of such an offence as indicating of itself that the relevant acts did not constitute an outrage upon personal dignity. Obviously, if the humiliation and suffering caused is only fleeting in nature, it may be difficult to accept that it is real and serious. However this does not suggest that any sort of minimum temporal requirement of the effects of an outrage upon personal dignity is an *element* of the offence.'

impact is not, contrary to the suggestion of one Trial Chamber,[58] a purely subjective assessement of the victim's suffering *in casu*. The Court must consider, objectively, whether the act or omission in question 'would be generally considered to cause serious humiliation, degradation or otherwise be a serious attack on human dignity'.[59]

To be convicted for that crime, an accused must have known that his act or omission could cause serious humiliation, degradation, or affront to human dignity.[60] This is not the same as requiring that the accused knew of the *actual* consequences of the act, the Trial Chamber noted in *Kunarac*.[61] This crime only requires, in addition to the intention to commit the particular act or omission, 'knowledge of the "possible" consequences of the charged acts or omission'.[62] The perpetrator need not have acted pursuant to any discriminatory intent or motives,[63] nor is it necessary to prove any specific intent on his part to humiliate, ridicule or degrade the victim.[64]

The offence of outrage upon personal dignity has been used in relation to various forms of mistreatment, including sexual abuses,[65] and it subsumes, in particular, the offence of 'humiliating and degrading treatment' which has been said to consist of '[s]ubjecting victims to treatment designed to subvert their self-regard'.[66]

There is a high degree of overlap between the crime of 'outrages upon personal dignity' and the crimes of 'inhuman treatment' (as provided in Article 2(b) of the ICTY Statute), 'wilfully causing great suffering or serious injury to body or health' (Article 2(c) of the ICTY Statute), torture (as provided in Articles 3 and 5(f) of the ICTY Statute and Article 3(f) of the ICTR Statute), and rape (pursuant to Articles 3 and 5(g) of the ICTY Statute and Article 3(g) of the ICTR Statute).[67]

---

[58] *Aleksovski* Trial Judgment, par 56.

[59] *Kunarac* Trial Judgment, pars 504–507. See also *Aleksovski* Appeal Judgment, par 37 and *Čelebići* Trial Judgment, par 502.

[60] *Kunarac* Trial Judgment, par 512; *Kunarac* Appeal Judgment, par 165. See also *Aleksovski* Appeal Judgment, par 27. Rape and other sexual violence have, for instance, been regarded as amounting to outrages upon personal dignity (see, e.g. *Furundžija* Trial Judgment, pars 173 and 272; *Kunarac* Trial Judgment, pars 406 and 436).   [61] *Kunarac* Trial Judgment, par 512.

[62] Ibid., par 512: 'The Trial Chamber is of the view that the requirement of an intent to commit the specific act or omission which gives rise to criminal liability in this context involves a requirement that the perpetrator be aware of the objective character of the relevant act or omission. It is a necessary aspect of a true intention to undertake a particular action that there is an awareness of the nature of that act. As the relevant act or omission for an outrage upon personal dignity is an act or omission which would be generally considered to cause serious humiliation, degradation or otherwise be a serious attack on human dignity, an accused must know that his act or omission is of that character – ie, that it could cause serious humiliation, degradation or affront to human dignity. This is not the same as requiring that the accused knew of the *actual* consequences of the act.' On appeal, the Appeals Chamber rejected the appellants' argument that, to be convicted under that heading, the perpetrator needed to know that his acts or omission *would have* had such an effect (*Kunarac* Appeal Judgment, pars 164–166).   [63] *Aleksovski* Appeal Judgment, pars 18, 20, 23, and 28.

[64] *Kunarac* Trial Judgment, par 509; *Aleksovski* Appeal Judgment, par 27. In other words, although it may be the case evidentially, the perpetrator need not have 'aimed at humiliating and ridiculing' the victim (ibid).   [65] See, e.g. *Akayesu* Trial Judgment, par 688.

[66] *Musema* Trial Judgment, par 285.

[67] *Aleksovski* Trial Judgment, par 37; *Prosecutor v. Furundžija*, IT-95-17/1-I, First Amended Indictment, 2 June 1998, par 26; *Prosecutor v. Kunarac and Kovac*, IT-96-23-I, Third Amended Indictment, 1 December 1999, pars 9–11. See also, in relation to sexual offences: 'the forced

8.11 The passing of sentences and the carrying out of executions without previous judgment pronounced by a regularly constituted court, affording all the judicial guarantees which are recognized as indispensable by civilized peoples (Article 4(g) ICTR Statute)[68]

The ICTR has not rendered any decision relevant to the definition or elements of this crime.

8.12 Threats to commit statutory war crimes pursuant to Article 4(h) of the ICTR Statute

As noted above, no accused person has been charged with the offence of threats to commit war crimes before the ICTR and it is, in fact, quite unlikely that this ever will occur. In the event that the Tribunal was required to consider this offence, it would likely be necessary for the court to refer for assistance to the principles of law established in domestic criminal law systems of the world, as there are no obvious specifically international criminal law precedents on that point.

8.13 Other war crimes within the Tribunals' jurisdiction *ratione materiae*

The list of war crimes provided for in Article 3 of the ICTY Statute is, as its formulation makes clear, not exhaustive but illustrative.[69] As a result, a number of criminal offences that were not expressly provided for in the Statute have nevertheless been sanctioned as war crimes by the ICTY.[70] The list of war crimes which come within the ICTY's jurisdiction *ratione materiae* pursuant to Article 3 of the statute without their appearing expressly in that provision includes the following:

- murder
- rape
- torture

penetration of the mouth by the male sexual organ constitutes a most humiliating and degrading attack upon human dignity' (*Furundžija* Trial Judgment, par 183).

[68] Article 4(g) of the ICTR Statute.

[69] *Furundžija* Trial Judgment, par 133. It is unclear whether the ICTR also considers Article 4 of its Statute to be a residual clause or whether it regards the list of underlying offences provided for in that provision as being exhaustive.

[70] By contrast, it would not seem that any one accused who has appeared before the ICTR was ever charged (nor convicted) in relation to a war crime which was not *expressly* provided for in the Statute.

- cruel treatment
- enslavement
- attacks on civilians and civilian objects
- unlawful labour
- unlawful infliction of terror upon civilians or 'terror'.

8.13.1 Murder

'Murder is one of the offences which have been recognised as a criminal violation of the laws and customs of war ever since these violations were defined.'[71] It is both a domestic crime and an international offence and the law of murder under international law is essentially similar to that found in most domestic systems. The elements of the definition of that crime are as follows:[72]

(i) the victim is dead;

(ii) the death was caused by an act or omission of the accused, or of a person or persons for whose acts or omissions the accused bears criminal responsibility; and

(iii) that act was done, or that omission was made, by the accused, or a person or persons for whose acts or omissions he bears criminal responsibility, with an intention: to kill, or to inflict grievous bodily harm, or to inflict serious injury, in the reasonable knowledge that such act or omission was likely to cause death.

Concerning the death of the victim, a conviction for murder may be entered even though the body of the victim has not been recovered, as the fact of a victim's death can be proved circumstantially if the conclusion that the victim is indeed dead is the only reasonable inference to be drawn from the evidence.[73] Factors such as the following are relevant to the Chamber's conclusion in that regard: proof of incidents of mistreatment directed against the individual who is alleged to have been murdered; patterns of mistreatment and disappearances of other individuals detained or captured together with him or her; the general climate of lawlessness at the place where the acts were committed; the length of time which

---

[71] Trial of Susuki Motosuke, Amboina, Netherlands East Indies, Before the Netherlands Temporary Court Martial, January 1948 (reprinted in *Law Reports of Trials of War Criminals*, XIII, 126); and Friedman, *The Law of War*, vol. 2, p 1537).

[72] See, e.g. *Vasiljević* Trial Judgment, par 205; *Krnojelac* Trial Judgment, par 324; *Kvočka* Trial Judgment, par 132; *Krstić* Trial Judgment, par 485; *Stakić* Trial Judgment, pars 584 and 586–587; *Kordić and Čerkez* Trial Judgment, pars 235–236; *Kupreškić* Trial Judgment, pars 560–561; *Blaškić* Trial Judgment, par 217; *Jelišić* Trial Judgment, par 35; *Čelebići* Trial Judgment, pars 422 and 439; *Akayesu* Trial Judgment, pars 587–589; *Rutaganda* Trial Judgment, pars 79–80; *Naletilić and Martinović* Trial Judgment, par 248; *Musema* Trial Judgment, par 215; *Kayishema and Ruzindana* Trial Judgment, pars 150–151; *Stakić* Trial Judgment, par 584. The content of the offence of murder under Article 3 of the ICTY Statute is, the Tribunal said, the same as for wilful killing under Article 2 (see, e.g. *Blaškić* Trial Judgment, par 181; *Čelebići* Trial Judgment, pars 421–422; *Čelebići* Appeal Judgment, par 423).

[73] *Krnojelac* Trial Judgment, par 326: 'Proof beyond reasonable doubt that a person was murdered does not necessarily require proof that the dead body of that person has been recovered.' See also *Tadić* Trial Judgment, pars 240–241.

has elapsed since the person disappeared; and the fact that there has been no contact by that person with others whom he would have been expected to contact, such as his family.[74]

The death of the victim must have been caused by an act or omission of the accused, or of a person or persons for whose acts or omissions the accused bears criminal responsibility if he is charged pursuant to Articles 7(3)/6(3) of the ICTY/ICTR Statute.[75] The crucial issue here is that of 'causation and intent'.[76] In the *Krnojelac* case, the prosecution had charged the accused with murder, *inter alia*, for the death of a camp inmate who, the Prosecution alleged, was pushed to commit suicide by the mistreatment to which he had been subjected by subordinates of the accused.[77] The situation created by the mistreatment was such, the Prosecution argued, that it was reasonably foreseeable to the accused that the victim would kill himself as a result. The Trial Chamber held that to enter a murder conviction in such a situation, the accused (or his subordinates) must have caused the suicide of the victim and he, or those for whom he bore criminal responsibility, must have intended by that act or omission to cause the suicide of the victim, or he must have known that the suicide of the victim was a likely and foreseeable result of his act or omission:[78]

The Accused cannot be held criminally liable unless the acts or omissions for which he bears criminal responsibility induced the victim to take action which resulted in his death, and that his suicide was either intended, or was an action of a type which a reasonable person could have foreseen as a consequence of the conduct of the Accused, or of those for whom he bears criminal responsibility.

In this case, the Trial Chamber was not satisfied that such a case had been made as the evidence on that point was equivocal.[79] Milorad Krnojelac was accordingly acquitted upon this charge.[80]

---

[74] *Krnojelac* Trial Judgment, par 327. See also ibid., n 857, p 131, citing extensive – mostly human rights – authority supporting its approach.

[75] Concerning the possibility of murder by omission, see, e.g. *Čelebići* Trial Judgment, par 424. See also ICRC, *Commentary to Geneva Convention IV*, p 597.

[76] *Krnojelac* Trial Judgment, par 329.

[77] The acts and omissions alleged by the Prosecution to have caused the victim's suicide were the beating, the subsequent denial of medical treatment, and the confinement of the victim to an isolation cell (see *Krnojelac* Trial Judgment, par 328). [78] Ibid., par 329.

[79] Ibid., par 342: '[the victim] committed suicide in an isolation cell of the KP Dom after a severe beating. The evidence concerning his death was equivocal. Some witnesses gave evidence that he was depressed about his family situation and committed suicide for that reason. The Trial Chamber is not satisfied that the Prosecution has established beyond reasonable doubt that the beating inflicted on the victim at the KP Dom was the cause of the victim's suicide. This is the case to which the legal issue discussed above is directed' (footnotes omitted). It is worth noting also the Appeals Chamber's dissection, in the *Tadić* Appeal Judgment, of various cases from the Second World War concerned with instances of killing in common enterprise (pars 197–200).

[80] The issue of causation is particularly sensitive in situations where commanders have been charged with murders allegedly committed by subordinates as the causal link between the commander's failure to carry out his duties and the subsequent commission of crimes by his subordinates may be difficult to establish.

The Prosecution need not show that the accused personally killed anyone or inflicted a fatal injury to obtain a conviction for murder.[81] The Prosecution may, for instance, show that the accused was part of a joint criminal enterprise to murder – or commit another crime of physical violence, such as torture, against – an individual or a number of them, without his having physically taken part in the victim's murder. In such a case, the Prosecution must simply establish that each of the participants in the enterprise shared the intent that the victim or victims be murdered, or indeed simply mistreated, if it was reasonably foreseeable that the death of the victim would result therefrom.[82]

As far as the *mens rea* of murder is concerned, recklessness as well as intent would satisfy the required mental threshold.[83] In effect, the required state of mind may be divided as follows: the act must have been done, or an omission must have been made, by the accused, with an intention (a) to kill those victims; or (b) to inflict grievous bodily harm; or (c) to inflict serious injury, in the reasonable knowledge that such act or omission was *likely* to cause death.[84] Causing accidental – if not reckless – death would not therefore qualify as murder pursuant to Article 3 of the Statute.[85] Nor would negligence or even gross negligence be sufficient in principle, if it does not amount to recklessness of the sort described above.[86] The accused's *mens rea* may be inferred from all circumstances, but such an inference must be the only reasonable inference to be drawn from the evidence.[87]

---

[81] See, e.g. reference to *United Kingdom v. Feurstein and others*, British Military Court sitting at Hamburg, verdict of 24 August 1948, in Proceedings of a Military Court held at Curiohaus, Hamburg, original text in the Public Records Office, London, ('*Ponzano* case') in the *Tadić* Appeal Judgment, par 199: '[. . .] the requirement that an accused, before he can be found guilty, must have been concerned in the offence. [T]o be concerned in the commission of a criminal offence [. . .] does not only mean that you are the person who in fact inflicted the fatal injury and directly caused death, be it by shooting or by any other violent means; it also means an indirect degree of participation [. . .]. [I]n other words, he must be the cog in the wheel of events leading up to the result which in fact occurred. He can further that object not only by giving orders for a criminal offence to be committed, but he can further that object by a variety of other means [. . .].'

[82] *Vasiljević* Trial Judgment, par 207. In this case, the accused was convicted for the murder of five Muslim men although there was no evidence that he personally fired his gun at them (ibid., 209–211). See also *Tadić* Appeal Judgment, in particular pars 197 et seq.

[83] *Čelebići* Trial Judgment, pars 437–439.

[84] See, e.g. *Krnojelac* Trial Judgment, par 854; *Kordić and Čerkez* Trial Judgment, par 236. As pointed out by the *Krnojelac* Trial Chamber, that standard has been expressed in many different ways and with a different terminology, but it remains substantially the same (*Krnojelac* Trial Judgment, n 854, p 130 and references quoted therein). See also *Krnojelac* Appeal Judgment, pars 178–179 in relation to murders charged against a commander pursuant to Article 7(3) of the Statute.

[85] See, e.g. *Čelebići* Trial Judgment, pars 433 and 439.

[86] *Stakić* Trial Judgment, par 587. *Dolus directus* and *dolus eventualis* would satisfy the *mens rea* requirement for murder (ibid.).

[87] *Krnojelac* Trial Judgment, par 326; *Čelebići* Appeal Judgment, par 458; *Prosecuor v. Tadić*, IT-95-1-A-R77, Judgment on Allegations of Contempt against Prior Counsel, Milan Vujin, 31 January 2000, par 91; *Čelebići* Trial Judgment, par 437; *Stakić* Trial Judgment, par 616. See also *Čelebići* Trial Judgment, par 436: 'The Trial Chamber is mindful of the benefits of an approach which analyses the amount of risk taken by an accused that his actions will result in death and considers whether that risk

The definition of the crime of 'murder' pursuant to Article 3(a) of the ICTY Statute is identical to the definition of 'murder' pursuant to Article 5(a) of the ICTY Statute and Article 3(a) of the ICTR Statute ('crimes against humanity') and cumulative convictions pursuant to those two provisions under the same set of facts is possible insofar as the *chapeau* elements of each provision contain an element which the other does not possess.[88] It has also consistently been said that the elements of the crime of 'murder' are identical to those required for the offence of 'willful killing' pursuant to Article 2(a) of the ICTY Statute.[89] However, cumulative convictions for 'murder' pursuant to Article 3 and 'willful killing' pursuant to Article 2(a) in relation to the same facts are not permitted as the *chapeau* elements of each article do *not* contain an element which the other does not possess.[90] A conviction could only be entered in such a case based on the most specific of both provisions, namely, Article 2 of the ICTY Statute, which is more specific as it requires both that the armed conflict be international in character and that the victim be a 'protected person' (or 'protected property') as defined below.[91]

8.13.2   Rape

Although rape is not expressly identified in the Geneva Conventions as a grave breach, nor as a violation of common Article 3,[92] it is a clearly recognized international war crime.[93] It has been said to consist of the following:

[T]he sexual penetration, however slight: (a) of the vagina or anus of the victim by the penis of the perpetrator or any other object used by the perpetrator; or (b) of the mouth of the victim by the penis of the perpetrator; where such sexual penetration occurs without the consent of the victim. Consent for this purpose must be consent given voluntarily, as a result of the victim's free will, assessed in the context of the surrounding circumstances.[94]

might be deemed excessive. Under this approach, all of the circumstances surrounding the infliction of harm and the resulting death of the victim are examined and the relevant question is whether it is apparent from these circumstances that the accused's actions were committed in a manner "manifesting extreme indifference to the value of human life". Such an approach enables the adjudicative body to take into account factors such as the use of weapons or other instruments, and the position of the accused in relation to the victim.'

[88] See below, sub-section 24.

[89] See, e.g. *Čelebići* Trial Judgment, par 422; *Čelebići* Appeal Judgment, par 423.

[90] See below, sub-section 23.   [91] *Čelebići* Appeal Judgment, par 423.

[92] *Čelebići* Trial Judgment, par 475.

[93] Ibid., par 476; *Furundžija* Trial Judgment, pars 165–169. The Trial Chamber in the *Čelebići* case referred to a number of provisions which provide a clear indication of the existence of that prohibition under existing law (ibid., par 476): article 27 of Geneva Convention IV, Articles 4(1) and 4(2) of Additional Protocol II, Article 76(1) of Additional Protocol I, Article 46 of 1907 Hague Convention (IV), and Article 6(c) of the Nuremberg Charter.

[94] *Kunarac* Trial Judgment, par 460; *Kunarac* Appeal Judgment, pars 127–128. The penetration need not involve the penis or other parts of a human's body, but may involve the insertion of objects (*Akayesu* Trial Judgment, par 686). One Trial Chamber went as far as suggesting that rape may involve the use of orifices 'not considered to be intrinsically sexual' (*Akayesu* Trial Judgment, par 686). The Trial Chamber offered no authority in support of this conclusion. Concerning the criminalization of forced oral penetration as rape, see *Furundžija* Trial Judgment, pars 182–184. It is worth

The Trial Chamber in *Kunarac* held that a definition of rape given in earlier judgments focused too narrowly on the element of coercion, force, or threat of force, thus failing to recognize other factors which may render an act of sexual penetration non-consensual or non-voluntary,[95] and that it had therefore been defined more narrowly than was required by international law.[96] The essence of rape as an international crime was therefore said to consist in the non-consensual aspect of the act, rather than the use of force or constraint.[97] Such an approach was subsequently adopted by the ICTY Appeals Chamber. 'A narrow focus on force or threat of force could permit perpetrators to evade liability for sexual activity to which the other party had not consented by taking advantage of coercive circumstances without relying on physical force', the Appeals Chamber noted.[98]

---

noting that the definition of 'rape' given by the ICTY may not cover all the situations where it would be appropriate to enter a rape conviction. Thus, if two men were forced to have sexual intercourse with each other (a not uncommon occurrence during the Bosnian conflict), one of the victims would not, pursuant to the definition given above, in the absence of penetration of his body, be regarded as having been raped. This illogical discrepancy may call for a reassessment of the definition given by ICTY which would allow this incident to be regarded as rape with respect to the two victims.

[95] Ibid., par 438; *Kvočka* Trial Judgment, par 177, adopting the *Kunarac* definition. The *Furundžija* Trial Chamber had defined the elements of rape in the following manner:

(i) the sexual penetration, however slight:
  (a) of the vagina or anus of the victim by the penis of the perpetrator or any other object used by the perpetrator; or
  (b) of the mouth of the victim by the penis of the perpetrator;
(ii) by coercion or force or threat of force against the victim or a third person.

(*Furundžija* Trial Judgment, par 185). See also *Akayesu* Trial Judgment, pars 596–597, which first defined rape as an international offence in these terms:

The Tribunal defines rape as physical invasion of a sexual nature, committed on a person under circumstances which are coercive. The Tribunal considers sexual violence, which includes rape, as any act of a sexual nature which is committed on a person under circumstances which are coercive. Sexual violence is not limited to physical invasion of the human body and may include acts which do not involved penetration or even physical contact.

See also Trial Judgment, pars 478–479; *Musema* Trial Judgment, pars 220–229; *Niyitegeka* Trial Judgment, par 456.

[96] *Kunarac* Trial Judgment, par 438: 'In stating that the relevant act of sexual penetration will constitute rape only if accompanied by coercion or force or threat of force against the victim or a third person, the *Furundžija* definition does not refer to other factors which would render an act of sexual penetration *non-consensual or non-voluntary* on the part of the victim, which [. . .] is in the opinion of this Trial Chamber the accurate scope of this aspect of the definition of international law.' See also *Kamuhanda* Trial Judgment, pars 705–710.

[97] *Kunarac* Trial Judgment, par 457: 'The basic principle which is truly common to these [domestic] legal systems is that serious violations of sexual autonomy are to be penalised. Sexual autonomy is violated wherever the person subjected to the acts has not freely agreed to it or is otherwise not a voluntary participant.'

[98] *Kunarac* Appeal Judgment, par 129. In n 158, the Appeals Chamber in *Kunarac* noted that prior attention had focused on force as the defining characteristic of rape and that, under this line of reasoning, force or threat of force either nullifies the possibility of resistance through physical violence or renders the context so coercive that consent is impossible. See also *Furundžija* Trial Judgment, par 185.

The absence of genuine and freely given consent or voluntary participation on the part of the victim may be proven by the presence of various factors such as force or threats of force by the perpetrator, or the victim's inability to resist.[99] In other words, force is merely an *indicium* – among others – of the absence of consent on the part of the victim.[100] Another such *indicium* concerns the capacity, in view of the circumstances in which the victim found himself or herself at the time of giving (or not giving) it, in particular the existence of circumstances so coercive that he or she is not in a position, to give a true consent.[101] Detention, for instance, may vitiate consent in such a way that it may not be said to have been genuinely and freely given.[102] Contrary to the argument of defence counsel in one case, it is also not necessary, in order to establish the offence of rape, for the Prosecution to demonstrate that the victim had consistently and genuinely resisted.[103] It suffices to prove that he or she did not consent to the intercourse at the time when it took place.

Rule 96(ii) of the ICTY's Rules of Procedure and Evidence which provides that 'consent shall not be allowed as a defence if the victim (a) has been subjected to or threatened with or has reason to fear violence, duress, detention or psychological oppression, or (b) reasonably believed that if the victim did not submit another might be so subjected, threatened or put in fear' does not exclude the opportunity for the Defence to argue that the victim actually consented to sexual intercourse. Regardless of the nature of the charges, an accused person is always entitled to a full defence which in relation to this offence involves, *inter alia*, argument that the alleged victim consented to the intercourse. The apparent limitation contained in Rule 96(ii) is merely 'an indication of the understanding of the judges who adopted the rule of those matters which would be considered to *negate* any apparent consent'.[104]

The *mens rea* for rape consists of 'the intention to effect this sexual penetration, and the knowledge that it occurs without the consent of the victim'.[105] Such state of mind may be inferred from all the circumstances surrounding the events, including the coercive environment in which the act took place.

---

[99] *Kunarac* Trial Judgment, par 458. See also C. Chinkin, 'Rape and Sexual Abuse of Women in International Law', 5 EJIL 326 (1994); T. Meron, 'Rape as a Crime under International Humanitarian Law', 87 AJIL 424 (1993).

[100] *Kunarac* Appeal Judgment, par 130: 'Force or threat of force provides clear evidence of non-consent, but force is not an element *per se* of rape.' See also *Semanza* Trial Judgment, pars 344–346.

[101] In *Akayesu*, the Trial Chamber stated the following: 'coercive circumstances need not be evidenced by a show of physical force. Threats, intimidation, extortion and other forms of duress which prey on fear or desperation may constitute coercion, and coercion may be inherent in certain circumstances, such as armed conflict or the military presence of [enemy militias] among [refugees]' (*Akayesu* Trial Judgment, par 688). The question of true consent in the context of an armed conflict may prove a difficult one to deal with, but there may be no presumption that sexual intercourse between members of opposing parties is necessarily non-consensual.

[102] *Kunarac* Appeal Judgment, pars 130, 132–133.

[103] Ibid., par 125. There is no support under international law for such a proposition, the Appeals Chamber said (*Kunarac* Appeal Judgment, par 128: 'The Appellant's bald assertion that nothing short of continuous resistance provides adequate notice to the perpetrator that his attentions are unwanted is wrong on the law and absurd on the facts.') [104] *Kunarac* Trial Judgment, par 464.

[105] Ibid. See also *Kamuhanda* Trial Judgment, par 709.

Finally, as will be seen below, the conduct which may amount to a 'rape', pursuant to Article 3 of the ICTY Statute, may also constitute an act of torture if all other conditions of that latter offence are met.[106] And the definition of 'rape' as a war crime is identical (but for the *chapeau* elements) to the definition of 'rape' as a crime against humanity.

8.13.3   Torture

Torture constitutes one of the most serious attacks upon a person's mental or physical integrity.[107] Its importance under international law is revealed by a number of its characteristic features: the general prohibition against torture covers and sanctions even potential breaches,[108] it imposes obligations *erga omnes*,[109] and it has acquired *jus cogens* status under international law and it cannot therefore be derogated from.[110] The prohibition against torture applies at all times and in any context,[111] including in internal and international armed conflicts.[112]

---

[106] *Čelebići* Trial Judgment, pars 475 et seq.; *Furundžija* Trial Judgment, pars 163–164; *Kunarac* Appeal Judgment, pars 150–151; *Kunarac* Trial Judgment, par 545. See 'Torture' in the next sub-section.
[107] *Krnojelac* Trial Judgment, par 180.   [108] *Furundžija* Trial Judgment, pars 148–150.
[109] Ibid., par 151: 'the prohibition of torture imposes upon States obligations *erga omnes*, that is, obligations owed towards all the other members of the international community, each of which then has a correlative right. In addition, the violation of such an obligation simultaneously constitutes a breach of the correlative right of all members of the international community and gives rise to a claim for compliance accruing to each and every member, which then has the right to insist on fulfilment of the obligation or in any case to call for the breach to be discontinued.'
[110] Ibid., pars 153–157. That status as *jus cogens* does imply, the *Furundžija* Trial Chamber said, that the norm may not be derogated (par 153), it 'de-legitimise[s] any legislative, administrative or judicial act authorizing torture' (par 155), creates a universal jurisdiction over acts of torture (par 156) and excludes that such acts may ever be covered by a statute of limitation and must not be excluded from extradition under any political offence exemption (par 157). See also *Čelebići* Trial Judgment, par 454; *Kunarac* Trial Judgment, par 466; *Furundžija* Trial Judgment, pars 144, 153–157; and Report of the Special Rapporteur [on Torture], Mr P. Kooijmans, appointed pursuant to Commission on Human Rights, Security Council Resolution 1985/33, E/CN.4/1986/15, 19 February 1986, par 26.
[111] *Krnojelac* Trial Judgment, par 182; *Furundžija* Trial Judgment, par 139; *Čelebići* Trial Judgment, par 454 and sources quoted therein. The *Krnojelac* Trial Chamber cites the following authorities in support of its finding on that point: Articles 32 and 147 of Geneva Convention IV, Articles 12 and 50 of Geneva Convention I, Articles 12 and 51 of Geneva Convention II, Articles 13, 14, 17, and 130 of Geneva Convention III, common Article 3 to the four Geneva Conventions, Article 4 of Additional Protocol II and Article 75 of Additional Protocol I. Principle 6 of the *Body of Principles for the Protection of All Persons under Any Form Detention or Imprisonment*, 9 December 1988, provides that '[n]o person under any form of detention or imprisonment shall be subjected to torture or to cruel, inhuman or degrading treatment or punishment. No circumstance whatever may be invoked as a justification for torture or other cruel, inhuman or degrading treatment or punishment.' Those principles apply for the protection of *all persons* under any forms of detention or imprisonment.
[112] *Čelebići* Trial Judgment, par 446. See also ibid. par 454, where the Trial Chamber points out that the prohibition is 'absolute and non-derogable in any circumstances'. The Trial Chamber in that case pointed out that the prohibition against torture is specifically provided for in the Geneva Conventions as a grave breach as well as a violation of common Article 3 and other provisions of the Conventions and Additional Protocols (ibid.).

As a criminal offence, whether it is being charged as a war crime or as a crime against humanity,[113] 'torture' consists of the following elements:[114]

(i) the infliction, by act or omission, of severe pain or suffering, whether physical or mental;

(ii) the act or omission must be intentional;

(iii) the act or omission must aim at obtaining information or a confession, or at punishing, intimidating or coercing the victim or a third person, or at discriminating, on any ground, against the victim or a third person.

The crime of torture may, in principle, be committed by anyone, whether in a private or official capacity.[115] The official status of the perpetrator has been said not to constitute an element of the definition of torture as *an international crime* under customary international law,[116] although it may constitute an aggravating factor relevant to sentence.[117]

Torture may be committed either by an act or by an omission, provided all other conditions are met.[118] The act or omission which is said to amount to

---

[113] *Krnojelac* Trial Judgment, par 178 and decisions cited therein.

[114] *Kunarac* Trial Judgment, par 49 et seq.; *Kunarac* Appeal Judgment, pars 142–144.

[115] Ibid., par 148; *Kunarac* Trial Judgment, pars 488–496. As pointed out by the Trial Chamber in *Furundžija*, if the acts of torture are carried out by state officials, and if those acts are sufficiently widespread, the state may, in addition to the criminal responsibility of the perpetrators, engage its own – civil – responsibility (*Furundžija* Trial Judgment, par 142): 'Under current international humanitarian law, in addition to individual criminal liability, State responsibility may ensue as a result of State officials engaging in torture or failing to prevent torture or to punish torturers. If carried out as an extensive practice of State officials, torture amounts to a serious breach on a widespread scale of an international obligation of essential importance for safeguarding the human being, thus constituting a particularly grave wrongful act generating State responsibility.' See also ibid., par 146, on the complementarity of those two regimes: 'The existence of this corpus of general and treaty rules proscribing torture shows that the international community, aware of the importance of outlawing this heinous phenomenon, has decided to suppress any manifestation of torture by operating both at the interstate level and at the level of individuals. No legal loopholes have been left.'

[116] *Kunarac* Appeal Judgment, par 148: 'the public official requirement is not a requirement under customary international law in relation to the criminal responsibility of an individual for torture outside of the framework of the Torture Convention'. See also, *inter alia, Kunarac* Trial Judgment, par 496; *Naletilić and Martinović* Trial Judgment, par 338, and *Krnojelac* Trial Judgment, par 187. The Appeals Chamber explained that the requirement contained in the Torture Convention (and applied in the *Furundžija* case) pursuant to which the perpetrator must have acted in an official capacity was addressed to states and sought to regulate their conduct (*Kunarac* Appeal Judgment, par 146). Thus, in the words of the Appeals Chamber, 'the requirement set out by the Torture Convention that the crime of torture be committed by an individual acting in an official capacity may be considered as a limitation of the engagement of States', not an element of the crime of torture (ibid.; see also ibid., pars 147–148). See also, e.g. *Akayesu* Trial Judgment, pars 593–594 and *Čelebići* Trial Judgment, pars 473–474 which had erroneously applied the 'official status' requirement.

[117] See, e.g. *Čelebići* Trial Judgment, par 495.

[118] Ibid., par 468: 'From the foregoing discussion it can be seen that the most characteristic cases of torture involve positive acts. However, omissions may also provide the requisite material element, provided that the mental or physical suffering caused meets the required level of severity and that the act or omission was intentional, that is an act which, judged objectively, is deliberate and not accidental.' See also ibid., par 468; *Furundžija* Trial Judgment, par 162; *Kunarac* Trial Judgment, par 483; *Kvočka* Trial Judgment, par 157.

torture must be such as to cause 'severe pain or suffering, whether physical or mental'.[119] Suffering may be mental or physical, but it must, in all cases, be severe.[120] From the legal standpoint, it is difficult, if not impossible, to articulate with any degree of precision the exact threshold level of suffering at which other forms of mistreatment become torture.[121] But torture constitutes one of the gravest criminal offences existing under international law against a person's mental or physical integrity and care must be taken not to dilute its specificity by broadening its scope too far.[122]

As noted by one Chamber, the expression 'severe pain or suffering' conveys the idea that only acts of substantial gravity may be considered to be torture.[123] Less severe forms of mistreatment would therefore not in principle qualify as torture, although such acts may constitute other less serious offences, such as inhumane acts or cruel treatment.[124] In making that severity assessment, the court must consider all factors, objective and subjective,[125] that may be relevant to its finding on that point:[126]

When assessing the seriousness of the acts charged as torture, the Trial Chamber must take into account all the circumstances of the case, including the nature and context of the infliction of pain, the premeditation and institutionalisation of the ill-treatment, the physical condition of the victim, the manner and method used, and the position of inferiority of the victim. In particular, to the extent that an individual has been mistreated over a prolonged period of time, or that he or she has been subjected to repeated or various forms of mistreatment, the severity of the acts should be assessed as a whole to the extent that it can be shown that this lasting period or the repetition of acts are inter-related, follow a pattern or are directed towards the same prohibited goal.[127]

---

[119] *Kunarac* Appeal Judgment, par 149.   [120] See, *inter alia*, ibid.

[121] *Kvočka* Trial Judgment, par 161; *Kunarac* Appeal Judgment, par 149. See however the list of acts which the Special Rapporteur has regarded as *a priori* serious enough to qualify as torture (*Čelebići* Trial Judgment, par 467).   [122] *Krnojelac* Trial Judgment, par 181.

[123] *Čelebići* Trial Judgment, pars 468–469; *Krnojelac* Trial Judgment, par 181. The European Court of Human Rights held that 'torture' involves 'suffering of a particular intensity or cruelty' which accounts for the 'special stigma' attached to this offence (*Ireland v. United Kingdom*, 18 January 1978, Series A No. 25, par 167).   [124] *Krnojelac* Trial Judgment, par 181.

[125] Trial Chamber I in the *Kvočka* case held that, in making that assessment, the court should consider both objective factors concerning the severity of the acts inflicted and the subjective factors relating to the particular victim (par 143): 'In assessing the seriousness of any mistreatment, the Trial Chamber must first consider the objective severity of the harm inflicted. Subjective criteria, such as the physical or mental effect of the treatment upon the particular victim and, in some cases, factors such as the victim's age, sex, or state of health will also be relevant in assessing the gravity of the harm.'

[126] *Krnojelac* Trial Judgment, par 182.

[127] See *Kvočka* Trial Judgment, pars 143, 149, and 151 and sources quoted therein. See also *Keenan v. UK*, Judgment, 3 April 2001, Application No. 27229/95, par 112; *Selmouni v. France*, Judgment, Application No. 25803/94, 28 July 1999, par 104; *Ireland v. United Kingdom*, Judgment, 18 January 1978, Series A No. 25, pars 167 and 174; *Greek* case, Report of 5 November 1969 (1969) 12 Yearbook, vol. 2, pars 12, 18 of the Opinion of the Commission; *Aydin v. Turkey*, Judgment, 25 September 1997, Application No. 23178/94, par 84. On the effect of time on the court's assessment of the severity of the abuse, see for example *Soering v. United Kingdom*, Judgment, 7 July 1989, Series A No. 161, pars 106, 111.

Thus measures that might not at first sight appear sufficiently serious to amount to torture could, because of their intensity, their duration, or the manner in which they are being implemented, amount to torture, all circumstances having been taken into account.[128] One Trial Chamber suggested that when making that assessment the court could also take into consideration the social and cultural context in which the acts were committed, as some conduct may be rendered more serious (or its consequences more profound) depending on the context in which it occurs.[129] In any case, the consequences of the act need not be visible on the victim to amount to torture.[130] Nor does the victim need to bear the long-term – physical or mental – stigma of those acts.[131]

An exhaustive list of what acts or omissions may constitute torture is neither possible, nor desirable, as it could turn out to be, in the words of one author, 'a challenge to the ingenuity of the torturers', rather than a workable legal standard.[132] A number of actions have, however, been recognized as sufficiently serious to amount to torture, regardless of the context in which they are committed. This is the case, for instance, of the crime of rape, which *per se*, would be sufficiently serious to qualify as torture.[133] 'Severe pain or suffering, as required by the definition of the crime of torture, can thus be said to be established once rape has been proved, since the act of rape necessarily implies such pain or suffering', the Appeals Chamber noted.[134] However, in case of conviction for both torture and rape where the *actus reus* of torture consists of a rape, and under the test of permissible cumulative convictions, double conviction would be permissible as each offence contains a materially distinct element.[135] In other cases, in order to assess

---

[128] Concerning solitary confinement and the deliberate deprivation of food, see *Krnojelac* Trial Judgment, par 183 (footnote omitted): 'Solitary confinement is not, in and of itself, a form of torture. However, in view of its strictness, its duration, and the object pursued, solitary confinement could cause great physical or mental suffering of the sort envisaged by this offence. To the extent that the confinement of the victim can be shown to pursue one of the prohibited purposes of torture and to have caused the victim severe pain or suffering, the act of putting or keeping someone in solitary confinement may amount to torture. The same is true of the deliberate deprivation of sufficient food.' In *Furundžija*, the Appeals Chamber (and, no doubt, the Trial Chamber) took into account the particularly stressful and humiliating circumstances in which the mistreatment took place: 'It is difficult to ignore the intimidating and humiliating aspects of that scene and their devastating impact on the physical and mental state of Witness A.' See, generally, *Čelebići* Trial Judgment, pars 461 et seq.

[129] *Čelebići* Trial Judgment, par 495: 'The psychological suffering of persons upon whom rape is inflicted may be exacerbated by social and cultural conditions and can be particularly acute and long lasting.' This may be particularly pertinent in the context of sexual abuses (*Čelebići* Trial Judgment, par 486). [130] *Kunarac* Appeal Judgment, par 150.

[131] See, e.g. *Furundžija* Appeal Judgment, par 114.

[132] N. Rodley, *The Treatment of Prisoners under International Law*, 2nd edn (Oxford: Clarendon Press, 1998), cited in *Čelebići* Trial Judgment, par 469.

[133] *Kunarac* Appeal Judgment, par 150: 'Generally speaking, some acts establish *per se* the suffering of those upon whom they were inflicted. Rape is obviously such an act.'

[134] Ibid., par 151. See also *Furundžija* Trial Judgment, pars 163–164; *Akayesu* Trial Judgment, par 687; *Čelebići* Trial Judgment, pars 486 and 495.

[135] *Kunarac* Trial Judgment, par 557: 'a materially distinct element of rape *vis-à-vis* torture is the sexual penetration element. A materially distinct element of torture *vis-à-vis* rape is the severe

the gravity of the act in question, the court will take into account all relevant circumstances that may characterize it, such as the nature of the acts, their length, the means used, the method, the age and condition of the victims, the conditions (for instance, detention) in which the acts occurred, the long-term consequences of the acts upon the victim, the effect of the acts upon the community of which the victim is a member, and the systematic character of the acts.[136]

Mistreatment that does not rise to the threshold of severity necessary to be characterized as torture may constitute another, less serious, offence such as cruel treatment.[137] In case of doubt as to whether the act is sufficiently serious to amount to torture, this doubt should be interpreted in favour of the accused and he should be acquitted of torture and, if the conditions of that lesser offence are met, be convicted for it.[138]

But even more, perhaps, than the seriousness of the suffering that must be inflicted to amount to torture, it is the purpose that the torturer pursues that sets torture apart from other forms of mistreatment.[139] Thus:

[T]orture as a criminal offence is not a gratuitous act of violence; it aims, through the infliction of severe mental or physical pain, to attain a certain result or purpose. Thus, in the absence of such purpose or goal, even very severe infliction of pain would not qualify as torture pursuant to Article 3 or Article 5 of the Tribunal's Statute.[140]

It would appear that three alternative prohibited purposes are presently recognized under customary international law as satisfying the requirement that torture must have taken place in order to achieve a particular result:[141] (a) obtaining information or a confession; (b) punishing, intimidating, or coercing the victim or a third person; and (c) discriminating, on any ground, against the victim or a third person. Although there may be a tendency, particularly in the field of human rights, towards the enlargement of the list of prohibited purposes, it would appear that, at present, customary international criminal law would only recognize the above three purposes as satisfying the elements of the definition of torture as an international crime.[142]

infliction of pain or suffering aimed at obtaining information or a confession, punishing, intimidating, coercing or discriminating against the victim or a third person.'

[136] See, however, the list of acts which the Special Rapporteur has regarded as *a priori* serious enough to qualify as torture (*Čelebići* Trial Judgment, par 467).

[137] Ibid., par 468; see also *Krnojelac* Trial Judgment, par 181.   [138] Ibid., par 219.

[139] Ibid., par 180. See, for example, Article 1(2) of the Declaration on the Protection of All Persons from Being Subjected to Torture and Other Cruel, Inhuman or Degrading Treatment or Punishment, United Nations General Assembly Resolution 3452 (XXX) (9 December 1975) ('Torture Convention'): '[t]orture constitutes an aggravated and deliberate form of cruel, inhuman or degrading treatment or punishment'.   [140] *Krnojelac* Trial Judgment, par 180.

[141] See *Kunarac* Trial Judgment, par 485; *Čelebići* Trial Judgment, pars 470–472; *Akayesu* Trial Judgment, par 594; *Krnojelac* Trial Judgment, par 185.

[142] Although there are suggestions in the jurisprudence of the Tribunals that there may be other prohibited purposes recognized as such under international law or that torture could even be

The requirement that the act or omission constituting the crime of torture must have been committed in order to achieve one of the three above purposes does not necessarily mean that the purpose in question must be illegitimate, as in fact several of the listed purposes may legitimately be pursued on condition that appropriate methods are used to achieve them.[143] Nor does the act said to amount to torture need to have been committed exclusively for one of the prohibited purposes.[144] One of those prohibited purposes must simply be 'part of the motivation behind the conduct, and it need not be the predominant or sole purpose'.[145] The existence of one of the prohibited purposes may be inferred from the evidence, but, as with all evidentiary inferences in international criminal law, it must be the only reasonable inference to be drawn from it.[146] The fact that, in addition to one of those prohibited purposes, the perpetrator may have harboured motives or intentions unrelated to any of the prohibited purposes would not negate the fact (if established beyond reasonable doubt) that the perpetrator was indeed pursuing one such purpose. Thus, the fact that the perpetrator might have sexually abused his victim out of lust or out of cruelty does not (despite some submissions to that effect made by defence counsel in the *Kunarac* case) exclude that he might also

---

committed regardless of the aim sought to be attained, such proportions do not appear to be supported by enough state practice to conclude that, other than those three prohibited purposes, others have come to be recognized under customary law or that torture may be committed regardless of the aim of the perpetrator. This does not appear to reflect customary international law as it exists at this stage of its development. There is no requirement under customary international law that the conduct of the accused must be solely motivated by one of the prohibited purposes. As stated by the Trial Chamber in the *Čelebići* case, 'the prohibited purpose must simply be part of the motivation behind the conduct and need not be the predominating or sole purpose'. See also *Krnojelac* Trial Judgment, par 186 (footnotes omitted): 'The Trial Chamber is of the opinion that, although other purposes may come to be regarded as prohibited under the torture provision in due course, they have not as yet reached customary status. In particular, the purpose to "humiliate" the victim, mentioned in *Furundžija* and more recently in *Kvočka*, is not expressly mentioned in any of the principal international instruments prohibiting torture. Nor is there a clear jurisprudential disposition towards its recognition as an illegitimate purpose. There may be a tendency, particularly in the field of human rights, towards the enlargement of the list of prohibited purposes, but the Trial Chamber must apply customary international humanitarian law as it finds it to have been *at the time when the crimes charged were alleged to have been committed*. In light of the principle of legality, the proposition that "the primary purpose of [humanitarian law] is to safeguard human dignity" is not sufficient to permit the court to introduce, as part of the *mens rea*, a new and additional prohibited purpose, which would in effect enlarge the scope of the criminal prohibition against torture beyond what it was at the time relevant to the indictment under consideration.'

[143] *Krnojelac* Trial Judgment, par 184.

[144] Ibid.; *Kunarac* Appeal Judgment, par 155: 'If one prohibited purpose is fulfilled by the conduct, the fact that such conduct was also intended to achieve a non-listed purpose (even one of a sexual nature) is immaterial.'

[145] *Čelebići* Trial Judgment, par 470; *Kunarac* Trial Judgment, par 486; *Krnojelac* Trial Judgment, par 184.

[146] Ibid., par 269: 'As an evidentiary matter, the mere statement that the victim was "taken for interrogation" or "to give a statement" is an insufficient basis *by itself* for the Trial Chamber to conclude that the purpose behind the infliction of pain was to obtain information or a confession. The Prosecution must establish that the principal offender did in fact interrogate or try to obtain information or a confession from the victim or a third person.'

have intended, in so doing, to obtain information from her, which would bring his conduct within the definition of torture, all other conditions being met.[147]

Finally, the infliction of pain and suffering that is said to amount to torture must have been intentional, that is, it must have been done deliberately,[148] so that torture may not be committed negligently or recklessly.

8.13.4   Cruel treatment

In the most general terms, cruel treatment has been said to consist of 'treatment that is inhuman'[149] and has been described as 'a means to an end, the end being that of ensuring that persons taking no active part in hostilities shall in all circumstances be treated humanely'.[150] Cruel treatment, inhuman treatment, and inhumane acts basically require proof of the same elements, though the terminology may vary slightly between the three of them.[151] All three prohibitions function, under their respective statutory provisions, as residual clauses capturing all serious charges not otherwise enumerated under those Articles.[152] According to the Appeals Chamber, cruel treatment as a violation of the laws or customs of war requires proof of the following elements:[153]

(i)   an intentional act or omission which causes serious mental or physical suffering or injury or constitutes a serious attack on human dignity;

(ii) the act is committed against a person taking no active part in the hostilities.

The conduct that is said to amount to 'cruel treatment' must be of similar seriousness to the other enumerated crimes under Article 3 of the Statute.[154] As noted by one Trial Chamber, the assessment of the seriousness of an act or omission is, by its very nature, and as with torture, an essentially relative one:[155]

All the factual circumstances must be taken into account, including the nature of the act or omission, the context in which it occurs, its duration and/or repetition, the physical,

---

[147] See *Kunarac* Appeal Judgment, pars 153–155 concerning the sexual motivations behind the infliction of rape as torture (par 153: 'even if the perpetrator's motivation is entirely sexual, it does not follow that the perpetrator does not have the intent to commit an act of torture or that his conduct does not cause severe pain or suffering').

[148] *Krnojelac* Trial Judgment, par 184; *Furundžija* Trial Judgment, par 162; *Akayesu* Trial Judgment, par 594; *Kunarac* Trial Judgment, par 497.   [149] *Čelebići* Trial Judgment, par 550.

[150] *Tadić* Trial Judgment, par 723. See also *Ntegerura* Trial Judgment, par 765 and references cited therein.   [151] See, again, *Krnojelac* Trial Judgment, par 130 and references cited therein.

[152] See, generally, ibid. See also *Čelebići* Trial Judgment, par 552; *Naletilić and Martinović* Trial Judgment, par 246; *Blaškić* Trial Judgment, par 186; *Čelebići* Trial Judgment, pars 543–544, 551–552, and 533; *Kupreškić* Trial Judgment, par 711; *Krstić* Trial Judgment, par 516; *Kordić and Čerkez* Trial Judgment, par 265.

[153] *Čelebići* Appeal Judgment, par 424. See also, *Krstić* Trial Judgment, par 516; *Čelebići* Trial Judgment, pars 551–552; *Blaškić* Trial Judgment, par 186; *Jelišić* Trial Judgment, par 41.

[154] *Krnojelac* Trial Judgment, par 130.

[155] Ibid., par 131. See also *Kvočka* Trial Judgment, par 160: 'In assessing the degree of harm required for an offence to qualify as cruel treatment, consideration should be given to the object and purpose of Common Article 3, which attempts to delineate a minimum standard of treatment to be afforded to persons taking no active part in the hostilities.'

mental and moral effects of the act on the victim and the personal circumstances of the victim, including age, sex and health.[156] The suffering inflicted by the act upon the victim does not need to be lasting so long as it is real and serious.[157]

'Cruel treatment' has been charged in relation, *inter alia*, to acts such as beatings,[158] inhumane living conditions in a detention centre,[159] attempted murder,[160] use of human shields, or trench digging.[161]

The *mens rea* for this offence is met 'where the principal offender, at the time of the act or omission, had the intention to inflict serious physical or mental suffering or to commit a serious attack on the human dignity of the victim, or where he knew that his act or omission was likely to cause serious physical or mental suffering or a serious attack upon human dignity and was reckless as to whether such suffering or attack would result from his act or omission'.[162] The act must therefore be intentional, that is, deliberate and not accidental.[163]

Cruel treatment is also closely associated with the crime of torture so that cruel treatment includes the offence of torture, while also encompassing other conduct of less severe consequence.[164] Cruel treatment and torture may be distinguished, however, in at least two respects: (i) the degree of seriousness required for each offence; and (ii) the existence and requirement of a prohibited purpose for the offence of torture. First, whilst the act or omission that constitutes cruel treatment must be of similar seriousness to other enumerated crimes under Article 3 ICTY Statute,[165] it need not reach the higher level of gravity required for the crime of torture, so that offences which do not meet the gravity threshold required by torture could still qualify as cruel treatment.[166] As noted above, in case of doubt as to whether or not an act or omission is serious enough to amount to torture, the accused should have the benefit of that doubt, and the acts for which he is charged should be considered under the heading of the less serious offence, in that case, cruel treatment.[167] Secondly, unlike the case with torture, the Prosecution need

---

[156] *Čelebići* Trial Judgment, par 536; *Jelišić* Trial Judgment, par 57 referring to outrages upon personal dignity.

[157] This was recently held by the Trial Chamber with regard to the offence of outrages upon personal dignity in the *Kunarac* Trial Judgment, par 501.

[158] *Krnojelac* Trial Judgment, pars 176 et seq.; *Jelišić* Trial Judgment, pars 42–45.

[159] See, e.g. *Krnojelac* Trial Judgment, pars 128 et seq. See also *Čelebići* Trial Judgment, pars 554–558. In its Judgment, the Trial Chamber held, *inter alia*, that '[d]uring an armed conflict, persons should not be detained in conditions where this minimum standard cannot be met and maintained' (ibid., par 557). If they are kept in such conditions, and all other conditions being met, the acts of detaining them or keeping them in detention could amount to cruel treatment pursuant to Article 3 of the Statute.

[160] In the *Vasiljević* case, the accused was charged with two attempted murders as 'inhuman acts', the elements of which have been said to be similar to those required for 'cruel treatment' (see *Vasiljević* Trial Judgment, pars 234 and 238 et seq.).

[161] *Blaškić* Trial Judgment, pars 186, 735–738, and 742–743.

[162] *Krnojelac* Trial Judgment, par 132, citing *Kayishema and Ruzindana* Trial Judgment, par 153; *Aleksovski* Trial Judgment, par 56.   [163] *Čelebići* Trial Judgment, par 552.

[164] *Krstić* Trial Judgment, par 516. See, also, *Čelebići* Trial Judgment, pars 443 and 552.

[165] *Krnojelac* Trial Judgment, par 130.   [166] See, e.g. ibid., par 219.   [167] Ibid.

not prove, in relation to cruel treatment, that the perpetrator inflicted pain for the purpose of attaining a particular goal or purpose. Thus, an act or omission of sufficient gravity which has not been shown to have been committed for any particular reason or purpose, could still qualify as cruel treatment, all other conditions being met.[168] Because torture contains a materially distinct element (in fact, two of them: a particular purpose and a higher gravity threshold) which cruel treatment does not, and because the reverse is not true, in the case where an accused has been charged with both offences in relation to the same factual basis, and that the elements of both offences have been met, the torture charge would 'absorb' the lesser cruel treatment charge and conviction would be entered for torture only.[169]

8.13.5   Slavery

This violation of the laws or customs of war is closely related to the crime of enslavement (a crime against humanity) and the elements of both offences have in fact been regarded as identical in substance.[170] Enslavement under Article 5 of the ICTY Statute has been defined as the exercise of any or all of the powers attaching to the right of ownership over a person.[171] The *actus reus* of enslavement and slavery is therefore the exercise of those powers, and the required *mens rea* consists of the intentional exercise of such powers.[172]

Slavery is prohibited under customary international law, regardless of the context in which it occurs (international or internal armed conflict).[173] It may consist, for instance, in forcing individuals to work, but not all forms of labour, even if forced, qualify as slavery (or enslavement). International humanitarian law does not prohibit all forms of labour by protected persons in armed conflicts, even when forced.[174] The Prosecution must establish furthermore that the accused (or persons for whose actions he is criminally responsible) forced the detainees to work,[175] that he (or they) exercised any or all of the 'powers attaching to the right of ownership'

---

[168] *Krnojelac* Trial Judgment, pars 219 and 252.   [169] Ibid., par 314.

[170] Ibid., par 356. See also below sub-section 12.3. See also below sub-section 8.13.7 concerning the crime of 'unlawful labour' which covers much of the same ground.

[171] *Kunarac* Trial Judgment, par 539; *Krnojelac* Trial Judgment, par 350.

[172] *Kunarac* Trial Judgment, par 540; *Krnojelac* Trial Judgment, par 350.

[173] Ibid., pars 353–355. The *Krnojelac* Trial Chamber held in particular (par 353): 'the express prohibition of slavery in Additional Protocol II of 1977, which relates to internal armed conflicts, confirms the conclusion that slavery is prohibited by customary international humanitarian law outside the context of a crime against humanity. The Trial Chamber considers that the prohibition against slavery in situations of armed conflict is an inalienable, non-derogable and fundamental right, one of the core rules of general customary and conventional international law.' See also *Akayesu* Trial Judgment, par 610; *Rutaganda* Trial Judgment, par 87; *Musema* Trial Judgment, par 240.

[174] *Kunarac* Trial Judgment, par 542; *Krnojelac* Trial Judgment, par 359. See, e.g. Article 5(1) of Additional Protocol II.

[175] *Krnojelac* Trial Judgment, par 359. Involuntariness, as pointed out by the *Krnojelac* Trial Chamber, is the fundamental definitional feature of 'forced or compulsory labour' of the International Covenant on Civil and Political Rights (M. Bossuyt, *Guide to the 'Travaux Préparatoires' of the International Covenant on Civil and Political Rights* (Dordrecht/Boston: M. Nijhoff, 1987),

over them, and that he (or they) exercised those powers intentionally.[176] 'Slavery' or 'enslavement', as understood in the Statute, is not limited to instances of 'forced labour', where the victim is compelled to perform work for the accused. It also includes, for instance, forms of 'sexual enslavement' where the victim is deprived of his or her sexual autonomy and right to sexual self-determination by the accused for the purpose of obtaining sexual favours.[177]

Of relevance in that regard is, *inter alia*, the fact that the victims had *no real choice* as to whether they would work[178] and that the minimum procedural guarantees such as provided for in Articles 4 and 5 of Additional Protocol II, for instance, were violated by the accused or his subordinates.[179]

8.13.6 Attacks on civilians and civilian objects

The protection of civilians and civilian objects under the laws of war

The protection of civilians in times of armed conflicts, whether international or internal, is 'the bedrock of modern humanitarian law',[180] and civilians may not, under any circumstances, be the object of an attack.[181] Under no circumstances

---

p 167). 'In essence,' the Trial Chamber said, 'the determination of whether protected persons laboured involuntarily is a factual question which has to be considered in light of all the relevant circumstances on a case by case basis' (*Krnojelac* Trial Judgment, par 359).

[176] *Kunarac* Trial Judgment, pars 542–543 (where the Trial Chamber lists a number of *indicia* which may be taken into account to establish whether enslavement was committed); *Krnojelac* Trial Judgment, par 358.   [177] See, e.g. *Kunarac* Trial Judgment, pars 542–543 and 747–782.

[178] *Krnojelac* Trial Judgment, par 359 (emphasis added). The following circumstances are relevant to that determination: 'The consent or free will of the victim is absent. It is often rendered impossible or irrelevant by, for example, the threat or use of force or other forms of coercion; the fear of violence, deception or false promises; the abuse of power; the victim's position of vulnerability; detention or captivity, psychological oppression or socio-economic conditions' (*Kunarac* Trial Judgment, par 542; *Krnojelac* Trial Judgment, par 359).

[179] *Krnojelac* Trial Judgment, par 360. Concerning the extent to which those standards must be complied with, the Trial Chamber said the following: 'With respect to the interpretation to be attached to the provisions of Article 5, the Trial Chamber considers that the word "similar" means that the working conditions and safeguards need not be exactly the same as those enjoyed by the local civilian population. The terms "conditions" and "safeguards" mean that such persons need not necessarily be remunerated by wages for all work they are made to do. The absence of any explicit reference to "wages" in Article 5, in contrast to the explicit requirement that wages be paid in Geneva Convention IV Articles 40, 51 and 95, requires the Trial Chamber to determine on a case by case basis whether labour performed should have been compensated in some way' (ibid.).

[180] *Kupreškić* Trial Judgment, par 521.

[181] See *Blaškić* Appeal Judgment, par 157; *Kunarac* Trial Judgment, par 426; *Kordić and Čerkez* Articles 2 and 3 Jurisdiction Decision, par 31: 'It is indisputable that the general prohibition of attacks against the civilian population and the prohibition of indiscriminate attacks or attacks on civilian objects are generally accepted obligations. As a consequence, there is no possible doubt as to the customary status of these specific provisions [namely, Article 51(2) and 52(1) of Additional Protocol I and Article 13(2) of Additional Protocol II] as they reflect core principles of humanitarian law [. . .]' (footnote omitted). See also, for reference to material and state practice related to that prohibition, *Prosecutor v. Strugar*, IT-01-42-AR72, Prosecution's Response to Defence Brief on

would military necessity justify any encroachment upon that general prohibition against attacks on civilians and civilian objects.[182]

Civilians, for the purpose of this prohibition, are those who are not, or no longer, members of the fighting forces or of an organized military group belonging to a party to the conflict.[183] In case of doubt as to whether a given individual is or is not a civilian, he or she should be presumed to be a civilian.[184] The presence of individual combatants in the midst of the civilian population does not modify its civilian character, but combatants remain under the obligation to distinguish themselves at all times from the civilian population.[185] And although parties to a conflict are under an obligation to remove civilians to the maximum extent feasible from the vicinity of military objectives and to avoid locating military objectives within or near densely populated areas, their failure to abide by such a standard does not relieve the attacking side of its duty to abide by the principles of distinction and proportionality when launching an attack.[186] An accused could not therefore argue that his conduct may not constitute an attack on civilians merely because the other side failed to clearly separate its civilians and its combatants.

The protection of civilians and civilian objects provided by international law may cease entirely or be reduced or be suspended 'in three exceptional circumstances':[187] (i) when civilians abuse their rights, 'international rules operate to lift that protection which would otherwise be owed to them' under the laws of war;[188] (ii) when, although the object of a military attack consists of military objectives, belligerents cannot avoid causing so-called collateral damage to civilians; and (iii) at least according to some authorities, when civilians may legitimately be the object of reprisals.

Interlocutory Appeal on Jurisdiction, 22 August 2002. The unsupported assertion of the *Blaškić* Trial Chamber that '[t]argeting civilians or civilian property is an offence *when not justified by military necessity*' (emphasis added) appears to contradict existing state practice. Neither does it find any support in the literature and it has been shown to be wrong in law by the Appeals Chamber (*Blaškić* Trial Judgment, par 180). The Appeals Chamber pointed out the inaccuracy of the Trial Chamber's finding on that point ('The Appeals Chamber underscores that there is an absolute prohibition on the targeting of civilians in customary international law'; *Blaškić* Appeal Judgment, par 109). One author summarized it well when he said that the laws of war rest on a certain view of combatants which stipulates their battlefield equality, but 'it rests more deeply on certain view of noncombatants, which holds that they are men and women with rights and they cannot be used for some military purpose, even if it is a legitimate purpose' (M. Walzer, *Just and Unjust Wars*, 3rd edn (New York: Basic Books, 2000), p 137).

[182] *Galić* Trial Judgment, par 44. The prohibition against attacks on civilians and civilian objects is part of customary law (see, e.g. *Strugar* Jurisdiction Decision, par 10).

[183] A 'civilian population' consists of all persons who are civilians pursuant to this definition. See *Blaškić* Trial Judgment, par 180; *Galić* Trial Judgment, pars 47–49.

[184] *Kunarac* Trial Judgment, pars 426 and 435. As noted above, that presumption does not apply in the context of a criminal prosecution where the burden to establish the status of the alleged victims is always upon the Prosecution.   [185] *Galić* Trial Judgment, par 50.

[186] Ibid., par 61.   [187] *Kupreškić* Trial Judgment, par 522.   [188] Ibid., par 523.

The general prohibition against attacks on civilians may therefore be suspended, *inter alia*, if, when, and for such time as they directly participate in hostilities.[189] As noted by the *Galić* Trial Chamber, to take a 'direct' part in the hostilities means 'acts of war which by their nature or purpose are likely to cause actual harm to the personnel or matériel of the enemy armed forces'.[190] Combatants and other individuals directly engaged in hostilities are regarded as legitimate military targets deprived of the privileges normally guaranteed to civilians.[191]

The laws of war provide for a presumption of civilian status so that 'a person shall not be made the object of attack when it is not reasonable to believe, in the circumstances of the person contemplating the attack, including the information available to the latter, that the potential target is a combatant'.[192] This presumption of civilian status is limited to the 'expected conduct of a member of the military'.[193] When however, the latter's criminal responsibility is at issue, the burden of proof as to whether an alleged victim was a civilian rests on the Prosecution and no such presumption may apply in that context.[194] In a criminal case where the Prosecution has charged an accused with intentionally attacking civilians, for instance, the Prosecutor would therefore have to show that the accused could not reasonably have believed that the victim was a member of the armed forces.[195] In making that assessment, the Court must take into account all relevant factors, including the information at the disposal of the accused at the time in relation to the status of those caught in the middle of fightings.

The laws of war also provide that reasonable care must be taken when attacking military objectives 'so that civilians are not needlessly injured through carelessness'.[196] Although the attacking party possesses a margin of appreciation when carrying out the attack, that margin, the *Kupreškić* Trial Chamber said, must be construed as narrowly as possible.[197] As pointed out by Trial Chamber II in the *Kunarac* case:[198]

As a group, the civilian population shall never be attacked as such. Additionally, customary international law obliges parties to the conflict to distinguish at all times between the civilian population and combatants, and obliges them not to attack a military objective if the attack is likely to cause civilian casualties or damage which would be excessive in relation to the military advantage anticipated.

---

[189] *Galić* Trial Judgment, par 48. See also *Kupreškić* Trial Judgment, pars 522–523: 'the protection of civilian and civilian objects provided by modern international law may cease entirely or be reduced or suspended [. . .] if a group of civilians takes up arms [. . .] and engages in fighting against the enemy belligerent, they may be legitimately attacked by the enemy belligerent whether or not they meet the requirements laid down in Article 4(A)(2) of the Third Geneva Convention of 1949.'

[190] *Galić*, Trial Judgment par 48. See ICRC, *Commentary on the Additional Protocols*, par 1944.

[191] *Galić* Trial Judgment, par 48. According to the *Galić* Trial Chamber, 'Combatant status implies not only being considered a legitimate military objective, but also being able to kill or wound other combatants or individuals participating in hostilities, and being entitled to special treatment when hors-de-combat, *i.e.* when surrendered, captured or wounded (See Article 41(2) of Additional Protocol I)' (ibid., n 88).   [192] Ibid., par 50.

[193] *Blaškić* Appeal Judgment, par 111.   [194] Ibid.

[195] *Kunarac* Trial Judgment, par 435.   [196] *Kupreškić* Trial Judgment, par 524.

[197] Ibid., pars 524–525.   [198] Ibid., par 426 (footnotes omitted).

Attacks on civilians and civilian objects as criminal offences

Both the prohibition against attacks on civilians and that against attacks against civilian objects are now part of customary law and any serious violation thereof would constitute a war crime and entail the individual criminal responsibility of the violator.[199] As a criminal offence, 'attacks on civilians' has been said to consist of the following elements:[200]

(i) acts of violence directed against the civilian population or individual civilians not taking direct part in hostilities causing death or serious injury to body or health within the civilian population;

(ii) the offender wilfully made the civilian population or individual civilians not taking direct part in hostilities the object of those acts of violence.

To be regarded as criminal, such an attack must therefore have been committed wilfully, that is, 'intentionally in the knowledge, or when it was impossible not to know, that civilians [. . .] were being targeted not through military necessity'.[201] According to Trial Chamber I of the ICTY, 'the notion of "willfully" incorporates the concept of recklessness, whilst excluding mere negligence. The perpetrator who recklessly attacks civilians acts "willfully".'[202] The Prosecution must therefore demonstrate that the perpetrator was aware of the circumstances or should have been aware of the civilian status of the persons attacked. As noted above, the rule that 'in case of doubt' an individual should be presumed to be a civilian does not apply in the context of a criminal trial where the burden to establish that fact remains at all times upon the Prosecution.[203]

The acts of violence that may be said to constitute a criminal attack may be carried out either in offence or in defence.[204] A number of Trial Chambers have suggested that in order to be regarded as criminal, the attack must have caused death and/or serious injury within the civilian population so that the mere fact of

---

[199] See, e.g. *Prosecutor v. Strugar*, IT-01-42-AR72, Decision on Interlocutory Appeal, 22 November 2002, par 10: 'the principles prohibiting attacks on civilians and unlawful attacks on civilian objects stated in Articles 51 and 52 of Additional Protocol I and Article 13 of Additional Protocol II are principles of customary international law. Customary international law establishes that a violation of these principles entails individual criminal responsibility.' See also *Kordić and Čerkez* Articles 2 and 3 Jurisdiction Decision, par 31 (footnote omitted): 'It is indisputable that the general prohibition of attacks against the civilian population and the prohibition of indiscriminate attacks or attacks on civilian objects are generally accepted obligations. As a consequence, there is no possible doubt as to the customary status of these specific provisions as they reflect core principles of humanitarian law that can be considered as applying to all armed conflicts, whether intended to apply to international or non-international conflicts.' See also *Tadić* Jurisdiction Decision, par 125; *Kupreškić* Trial Judgment, par 521; *Rajić* Rule 61 Decision, pars 47–48; *Martić* Rule 61 Decision, par 10: 'As regards customary international law the rule that the civilian population as such, as well as individual civilians, shall not be the object of attack, is a fundamental rule of international humanitarian law applicable to all armed conflicts.'   [200] *Galić* Trial Judgment, par 56.
[201] *Blaškić* Trial Judgment, par 180; *Galić* Trial Judgment, par 42.
[202] Ibid., par 54.   [203] *Blaškić* Appeal Judgment, par 111.
[204] See also ibid., par 52.

attacking a civilian or a civilian population would not *per se* constitute a criminalized attack.[205] No authority was provided in support of such a conclusion and it might well be that such an attack could be regarded as criminal, regardless of any physical consequences upon the civilian population being targeted. As far as customary law is concerned, the question therefore remains very much an open one.

Disproportionate and indiscriminate attacks as war crimes

The general prohibition against attacks on civilians and civilian objects subsumes other categories of prohibited attacks, in particular 'disproportionate attacks' and 'indiscriminate attacks' the conduct of which may entail criminal consequences for those involved.

Concerning the second category of attacks ('indiscriminate attacks'), one Trial Chamber noted that the prohibition against attacking civilians stems 'from a fundamental principle of international humanitarian law, the principle of distinction, which obliges warring parties to distinguish *at all times* between the civilian population and combatants and between civilian objects and military objectives and accordingly to direct their operations only against military objectives'.[206] This prohibition on indiscriminate attacks also entails limitations on the sort of weaponry that an attacking force is allowed to use, in principle, and the manner in which it may be used.[207] If the attacking forces fail to discriminate between civilians or civilian objects on the one hand and military objectives on the other, their attack might qualify, all other conditions being met, as a direct attack against civilians which might be regarded as a war crime.[208]

---

[205] *Blaškić* Trial Judgment, par 180; *Kordić and Čerkez* Articles 2 and 3 Jurisdiction Decision, par 328; *Galić* Trial Judgment, par 42. No authority is provided in support of such a conclusion and it might well be that such attack could be regarded as criminal, regardless of any physical consequences upon the civilian population being targeted. The question is still very much an open one.

[206] *Galić* Trial Judgment, par 45 ; *Blaškić* Appeal Judgment, par 157.

[207] See *Martić* Rule 61 Decision, par 18. See also the Trial Chamber's statement that '[t]here exists no formal provision forbidding the use of cluster bombs in armed conflicts' (ibid., par 18).

[208] *Galić* Trial Judgment, par 57. Other Trial Chambers have found that attacks which employ certain means of combat which cannot discriminate between civilians and civilian objects and military objectives are tantamount to direct targeting of civilians. For example, the *Blaškić* Trial Chamber inferred from the arms used in an attack carried out against the town of Stari Vitez that the perpetrators of the attack had wanted to target Muslim civilians, since these arms were difficult to guide accurately, their trajectory was 'irregular' and non-linear, thus being likely to hit non-military targets (*Blaškić* Trial Judgment, pars 501 and 512). In the *Martić* Rule 61 proceedings, the Trial Chamber regarded the use of an Orkan rocket with a cluster bomb warhead as evidence of the intent of the accused to deliberately attack the civilian population. The Chamber concluded that 'in respect of its accuracy and striking force, the use of the Orkan rocket in this case was not designed to hit a military target but to terrorise the civilians of Zagreb. These attacks are therefore contrary to the rules of customary and conventional international law.' The Trial Chamber based this finding on the fact that the rocket was inaccurate, it landed in an area with no military objectives nearby, it was used as an antipersonnel weapon launched against the city of Zagreb and the accused indicated he intended to attack the city; *Martić* Rule 61 Decision, pars 23–31. On the limited precedential value of Rule 61 Decisions, see above, footnote 12, Chapter 5. It is relevant to note that the International Court of Justice

For the present purpose, military objectives must be understood as 'those objects which by their nature, location, purpose or use make an effective contribution to military action and whose total or partial destruction, capture or neutralization, in the circumstances ruling at the time, offers a definite military advantage' (Additional Protocol I, Article 52). In case of doubt as to whether an object which is normally dedicated to civilian purposes is being used to make an effective contribution to military action, one Trial Chamber held, it shall be presumed not to be so used.[209] The same Chamber added that 'such an object shall not be attacked when it is not reasonable to believe, in the circumstances of the person contemplating the attack, including the information available to the latter, that the object is being used to make an effective contribution to military action'.[210]

Also criminalized are so-called 'disproportionate attacks', that is, those attacks which violate the principle of proportionality.[211] The practical application of the principle of distinction requires that those who plan or launch an attack take 'all feasible precautions to verify that the objectives attacked are neither civilians nor civilian objects, so as to spare civilians as much as possible'.[212] Once the military character of a target has been ascertained, commanders must consider whether striking this target is 'expected to cause incidental loss of life, injury to civilians, damage to civilian objectives or a combination thereof, which would be excessive in relation to the concrete and direct military advantage anticipated':[213] 'If such casualties are expected to result, the attack should not be pursued. The basic obligation to spare civilians and civilian objects as much as possible must guide the attacking party when considering the proportionality of an attack.'

In determining whether an attack was proportionate or not, in the particular circumstances, the court will have to examine whether 'a reasonably well-informed person in the circumstances of the actual perpetrator, making reasonable use of the information available to him or her, could have expected excessive civilian casualties to result from the attack'.[214] An attack which, on its face, may appear to have been in compliance with the principle of proportionality may give rise to an inference that civilians were in fact being targeted as such (i) because of the manner in which it was carried out or (ii) because of the duration or intensity of the attack.[215] Also, although a single or limited number of attacks on military

has stated, with regard to the obligation of states not to make civilians the object of attack, that 'they must consequently never use weapons that are incapable of distinguishing between civilian and military targets' (*Legality of the Threat or Use of Nuclear Weapons*, Advisory Opinion, ICJ Reports 1996, par 78).

[209] *Galić* Trial Judgment, par 51, citing Article 52(3) of Additional Protocol I as authority for this proposition.   [210] Ibid., par 51.

[211] See, in particular, ibid., pars 58–60. Although Additional Protocol II, contrary to Additional Protocol I, does not explicitly incorporate the principle of proportionality, it appears that the Tribunal has regarded that principle as applying to all contexts, regardless of the nature of the armed conflict and that disproportionate attacks would therefore be regarded as criminal whether committed in the context of an international or internal armed conflict.

[212] Ibid., par 58 (footnotes omitted).   [213] Ibid.   [214] Ibid.   [215] Ibid., par 60.

objectives causing incidental damage to civilians would not amount in principle to 'attacks on civilians', the cumulative effect of such attacks on military objectives could under certain circumstances render it criminal:[216]

[I]t may happen that single attacks on military objectives causing incidental damage to civilians, although they may raise doubts as to their lawfulness, nevertheless do not appear on their face to fall foul *per se* of the loose prescriptions of Articles 57 and 58 (or of the corresponding customary rules). However, in case of repeated attacks, all or most of them falling within the grey area between indisputable legality and unlawfulness, it might be warranted to conclude that the cumulative effect of such acts entails that they may not be in keeping with international law. Indeed, this pattern of military conduct may turn out to jeopardise excessively the lives and assets of civilians, contrary to the demands of humanity.

As noted by the Prosecution itself, applying the principle of proportionality in concrete situations may prove very difficult and a finding as to whether this principle has been complied with in a particular case may depend a great deal on 'the background and values of the decision maker'.[217]

As with the general prohibition against attacks on civilians and civilian objects, the Prosecution would have to establish that the (allegedly disproportionate) attack was launched 'wilfully and in knowledge of circumstances giving rise to the expectation of excessive civilian casualties'.[218] The line has not clearly been drawn in the jurisprudence of the *ad hoc* Tribunals, however, between those attacks which would merely be regarded as having been conducted in breach of humanitarian law without entailing any criminal consequences and those which might entail the responsibility of those involved in preparing, ordering, or coming those out.

Reprisals

As for the use of reprisals by a warring party to enforce compliance with international humanitarian law, one Trial Chamber has held that they were now totally prohibited under customary international law or, if they were not, that they were subject to very strict limitations.[219] Whether, however, acts of reprisal would be

---

[216] *Kupreškić* Trial Judgment, par 526. See, however, a critic of that position in par 52 of its NATO Report, where the Prosecution suggests that the Trial Chamber's finding on that point constitutes a 'progressive statement of the applicable law with regard to the obligation to protect civilians' (Final Report to the Prosecutor by the Committee Established to Review the NATO Bombing Campaign against the Federal Republic of Yugoslavia, www.un.org/icty/pressreal/nato061300.htm).

[217] Ibid., pars 48–50. The Prosecution suggests that that determination must be that of the 'reasonable military commander' (ibid., par 50). [218] *Galić* Trial Judgment, par 59.

[219] *Kupreškić* Trial Judgment, pars 527–536. The decision of the Trial Chamber on that point has been strongly criticized as insufficiently supported in state practice (see, *inter alia*, F. Kalshoven, 'Reprisals and the Protection of Civilians: Two Recent Decisions of the Yugoslavia Tribunal', in L. C. Vohrah, F. Pocar, Y. Featherstone, O. Fourmy, C. Graham, J. Hocking, and N. Robson (eds.), *Man's Inhumanity to Man* (The Hague/London/New York: Kluwer Law International, 2003). See also *Martić* Rule 61 Decision, par 15: 'Might there be circumstances which would exclude the unlawfulness, in whole or in part [of attacks on civilians]? More specifically, does the fact that the attack was carried out as a reprisal reverse the illegality of the attack? The prohibition against attacking the civilian population as such as well as individual civilians must be respected in all circumstances regardless of the

regarded as *criminal* under customary international law has not yet been addressed by either Tribunal.

8.13.7   Unlawful labour

Not all labour required from enemy citizens is prohibited during an armed conflict and not all forced labour amounts to 'unlawful labour' pursuant to Article 3 of the ICTY Statute.[220] There are, however, strict limits as to the nature of work that can be required from enemy citizens and the conditions under which that work can take place.

The Trial Chamber in *Naletilić and Martinović* said that 'unlawful labour' may be defined as 'an intentional act or omission by which a prisoner of war is forced to perform labour prohibited under Articles 49, 50, 51 or 52 of Geneva Convention III'.[221] Prisoners of war may be required, pursuant to Geneva Convention III, to work 'provided this is done in their own interest, and those considerations relating to their age and sex, physical aptitude and rank are taken into account'.[222] The same Chamber further noted that, pursuant to Article 51 of Geneva Convention III, prisoners of war must work under 'suitable working conditions, especially as regards to accommodation, food and climatic conditions'.[223] Prisoners of war may not be required to perform labour connected with war operations, but they may be made to perform other sorts of labour: work connected with camp administration, installation and maintenance, work in relation to agriculture, commercial business, arts and crafts, and domestic services, regardless of whether the produce of such labour is intended for soldiers or the civilian population, work in industries other than metallurgical, machinery and chemical industries, public works and building operations, transport and handling of stores and public services provided that those forms of labour have no military character or purpose.[224] Other categories of labour, on the other hand, may not be expected from a prisoner of war, unless he or she genuinely consents to it. In particular, a prisoner of war may not be made to work in industries, public works and building operations, transport, handling of stores or public utility services where it has a military character or purpose, nor can he or she be employed in the metallurgical, machinery, or chemical industries unless he or she genuinely consents to it.[225]

---

behaviour of the other party. The opinion of the great majority of legal authorities permits the Trial Chamber to assert that no circumstances would legitimize an attack against civilians even if it were a response proportionate to a similar violation perpetrated by the other party. The exclusion of the application of the principle of reprisals in the case of such fundamental humanitarian norms is confirmed by Article 1 Common to all Geneva Conventions', pars 16 and 17, 'the rule which states that reprisals against the civilian population as such, or individual civilians, are prohibited in all circumstances, even when confronted by wrongful behaviour of the other party, is an integral part of customary international law and must be respected in all armed conflicts.' See also *Galić* Trial Judgment, n 77, p 18.

[220] *Naletilić and Martinović* Trial Judgment, par 252.   [221] Ibid., par 261.
[222] Ibid., par 254 (footnotes omitted).   [223] Ibid., par 254.
[224] Ibid., par 256.
[225] Ibid., par 257. According to the ICRC Commentary, the prohibition exists because, in time of war, 'these industries will always be turned over to armaments production' (ICRC, *Commentary to Geneva Convention III*, p 268).

In addition, a prisoner of war may not be required to perform unhealthy or dangerous work unless he or she volunteers to undertake such work, nor under any circumstances may he or she be obliged to perform work which would be considered humiliating for a member of the detaining forces.[226]

The *Naletilić* Trial Chamber also said, without much explanation, that the rules applying to work by prisoners of war could apply also to civilians to the extent that it would best protect them from any abuse.[227]

Concerning the consensual performance of such labour, heed must be paid to the genuine character of that consent and the ability of that person at the time to give it, i.e. that the prisoner had a 'real choice' to undertake labour in contravention of the law.[228] When determining whether his consent may be regarded as having been real and genuine, the court may take into account some of the following factors:[229] (i) the substantially uncompensated character of the labour performed; (ii) the vulnerable position in which the detainees or those forced to work found themselves at the time; (iii) the allegations that detainees or those forced to work who were unable or unwilling to work were either forced to do so or put in solitary confinement or otherwise mistreated; (iv) long-term physical consequences of the labour; (v) the fact and conditions of detention of those asked to perform certain labour; and (vi) the physical consequences of the work on their health.

The *mens rea* for the crime of 'unlawful labour' has been said to consist of an 'intent that the victim would be performing prohibited work'.[230] It would be more accurate, however, to define it as an intent that the victim performs certain labour, *in the knowledge that* such labour is prohibited.[231] In other words, it is not necessary that the perpetrator should intend the labour to be prohibited, but only that he should know about its unlawful character.

8.13.8 Unlawful infliction of terror upon civilians or 'terror'

Trial Chamber I of the ICTY found that a 'protracted campaign of shelling and sniping upon civilian areas of Sarajevo and upon the civilian population' carried out by Serb forces throughout the Bosnian conflict constituted a serious violation of the laws or customs of war which qualified, *inter alia*, as a crime of 'terror' as set

---

[226] *Naletilić and Martinović* Trial Judgment, par 257.

[227] The victims in this case were either civilians or prisoners of war. The Trial Chamber applied the regime provided for in Geneva Convention III to all of them, rather than Geneva Convention IV, as this regime is 'more favourable to the accused than the protection afforded to civilian detainees under Geneva Convention IV' (ibid., par 252). The propriety of applying a uniform regime to different categories of protected individuals (even for the laudable purpose of favouring a fair determination of the matter) without regard to their particulat status is somewhat questionable.

[228] Ibid., par 259.   [229] Ibid.; see also *Krnojelac* Trial Judgment, pars 372–378.

[230] *Naletilić and Martinović* Trial Judgment, par 260. The Trial Chamber did not reveal the authority upon which it based its conclusion as to the definition of the required *mens rea*.

[231] As provided by the Chamber, such an intent may be established 'by direct explicit evidence, or, in the absence of such evidence, can be inferred from the circumstances in which the labour was performed' (*Naletilić and Martinović* Trial Judgment, par 260).

forth in Article 51(2) of Additional Protocol I. The Trial Chamber ultimately held that the accused, Stanislav Galić, a Serbian Commander of the Sarajevo Romanija Corps who had taken part in this campaign, could be held responsible for 'terror' as a violation of the laws or customs of war. Relying upon Article 51(2) of Additional Protocol I, the Trial Chamber said that 'terror' as a violation of the laws or customs of war consisted of the following elements:[232]

(i) acts of violence directed against the civilian population or individual civilians not taking direct part in hostilities causing death or serious injury to body or health within the civilian population;

(ii) the offender wilfully made the civilian population or individual civilians not taking direct part in hostilities the object of those acts of violence;

(iii) the above acts were committed with the primary purpose of spreading terror among the civilian population.

The Trial Chamber held (but did not provide any authority in support of its suggestion) that the definition of terror contained no requirement that the intended result (the actual infliction of terror, in the lay sense of the word) must in fact have occurred,[233] and said (again, without much support) that there was no need for the Prosecution to demonstrate a causal connection between the unlawful acts of the accused (or his subordinates) and 'the production of terror'.[234] As for the phrase 'acts of violence', the Trial Chamber explained that these do not include legitimate attacks against combatants but only unlawful attacks against civilians.[235] Consistently with the offence of 'attacks upon civilians', 'the civilian population', is said to comprise 'all persons who are civilians'.[236]

As for the applicable *mens rea*, the *Galić* Trial Chamber said that the expression 'primary purpose' 'is to be understood as excluding *dolus eventualis* or recklessness from the intentional state specific to terror'.[237] Thus, the Trial Chamber said, the Prosecution is required 'to prove not only that the Accused accepted the likelihood that terror would result from the illegal acts – or, in other words, that he was aware of the possibility that terror would result – but that that was the result which he specifically intended. The crime of terror is a specific-intent crime'.[238]

---

[232] *Galić* Trial Judgment, pars 132–133.

[233] The Trial Chamber's assertion that 'the plain wording of Article 51(2), as well as the *travaux préparatoires* of the Diplomatic Conference exclude [the requirement of actual infliction of terror] from the definition of the offence' is open to serious questioning (*Galić* Trial Judgment, par 134). First, the wording of the provision certainly does not *exclude* this requirement, although it does not provide for it explicitly. Secondly, the *travaux préparatoires* to which the Trial Chamber refers in n 224, p 48 in no way support the Chamber's conclusion. During the negotiation, a number of states had indeed suggested substituting the intent requirement (to inflict terror) with the requirement that actual infliction of terror occurs. This suggestion was rejected and the intent requirement remained. But nothing in the *travaux* suggests that the 'actual infliction' requirement had thereby been abandoned.   [234] *Galić* Trial Judgment, par 134.

[235] Ibid., par 135.   [236] Ibid., pars 49 and 137.   [237] Ibid., par 136.   [238] Ibid.

While the Trial Chamber's findings as to the specific elements of such unlawful conduct may constitute a reasonable interpretation of the prohibition in Article 51(2) of Additional Protocol I, it must be underlined, however, that the reasoning of the Trial Chamber in relation to this offence appears flawed in that it seems to conflate the illegality of a conduct with its criminal character. As noted above, the Trial Chamber in this case relied upon treaty law alone, in the absence of accompanying customary law, to convict the accused, thereby going beyond the Tribunal's jurisdiction and infringing upon the principle of legality.

In view of the lack of state practice and *opinio juris*, the almost complete absence of relevant precedent and the fact that the Chamber relied upon a treaty to base its conviction, there are serious doubts as to whether 'terror' may in fact be said to have constituted a discrete criminal offence under intenational law that would entail individual criminal responsibility at the time relevant to the charges. In this respect it is noteworthy that 'terror' was not included as a war crime in the jurisdiction of the International Criminal Court.

9

War Crimes in Internal Armed Conflicts

9.1 Can war crimes be committed in internal armed conflicts?

Can a war crime be committed in the context of an internal armed conflict?[1] Although an affirmative answer to this question may appear to be self-evident today, from the point of view of customary international law, the response was not such a straightforward one when the question was first raised before the Yugoslav Tribunal. The Statute of the ICTY did not explicitly provide for, nor did it exclude, the criminalization of serious violations of the laws or customs of war if they were committed within the context of an internal armed conflict. But a number of commentators and observers, not least the International Committee of the Red Cross, had suggested that, back in 1993, the notion of war crimes was limited to situations of international armed conflict.[1a]

---

[1] Concerning the definition of what may be said to constitute on "internal armed conflict" for the purpose of, *inter alia*, common article 3, see above, pp 33–38.

[1a] Preliminary Remarks of the International Committee of the Red Cross upon the proposed Security Council Resolution 808, at 2, reproduced in Morris and Scharf, *The Yugoslav Tribunal*, vol. 2. See also ICRC, 'War Crimes', working paper prepared by the ICRC for the Preparatory Committee for the Establishment of an International Criminal Court, New York, 14 February 1997 and ICRC, Statement of the ICRC before the Preparatory Committee for the Establishment of an International Criminal Court, New York, 14 February 1997. See also D. Plattner, 'La Répression

The Tribunal did not follow a position which it regarded as essentially overtaken by policy imperatives. 'States have come to consider', the Appeals Chamber of the ICTY held, 'that they have a common interest in the observance of certain minimum standards of conduct in certain matters; this includes certain aspects of conduct in an internal armed conflict. To that extent, internal armed conflict is now the concern of international law without any question of reciprocity.'[2] In light of the fact that the majority of contemporary conflicts are internal, the Appeals Chamber said further, 'to maintain a distinction between the two legal regimes and their criminal consequences in respect of similarly egregious acts because of the difference in nature of the conflicts would ignore the very purpose of the Geneva Conventions, which is to protect the dignity of the human person'.[3] And the Statute of the Tribunal does provide for the punishment of war crimes, whether committed in an internal or an international armed conflict. The ICTY thereby ascertained its own jurisdiction over serious violations of the laws of war committed in the context of internal armed conflicts.

The matter was dealt with differently in relation to the ICTR insofar as the Statute itself recognizes that war crimes can be commited in the context of an internal armed conflict.[4]

All the rules applicable to international armed conflicts do not automatically apply to an internal armed conflict and what may constitute a war crime in the context of an international armed conflict does not necessarily constitute a war crime if committed in an internal conflict.[5] And the regulatory transfer that has taken place from the laws of war applying to international armed conflict into the body of rules regulating internal armed conflicts has indeed not been all-encompassing in that only some of its rules and principles have extended to the internal arena. The Appeals Chamber noted that this limited legal transplant – from international armed conflicts into internal ones – did not take place 'in the form of a full and mechanical transplant of those rules to internal conflicts [but instead] the general essence of those rules, and not the detailed regulation they may contain, has become applicable to internal conflicts'.[6]

pénale des violations du droit international humanitaire applicable aux conflits armés non internationaux', 1990 (IRRC) International Review of the Red Cross, vol. 72, issue 785, 443.

   [2] *Hadžihasanović* Command Responsibility Appeal Decision, par 19 (footnote omitted).
   [3] *Čelebići* Appeal Judgment, par 172 (footnote omitted). See also, generally, *Tadić* Jurisdiction Decision, pars 96 *et seq.*
   [4] See Secretary-General Report (ICTR), par 12, which provides that violations of common Article 3 of the Geneva Conventions had been criminalized for the first time in the ICTR Statute and the Appeals Chamber's statement that this assertion on the part of the Secretary-General did not mean that such violations had not been considered as criminal prior to that time, but that they had never been codified as such before (*Čelebići* Appeal Judgement, par 170).
   [5] *Hadžihasanović* Command Responsibility Appeal Decision, par 12.
   [6] *Tadić* Jurisdiction Decision, par 126. See also Swiss Federal Council to the Swiss Chambers on the ratification of the two 1977 Additional Protocols (38 *Annuaire Suisse de Droit International* (1982) 137, pp 145–149 (cited in *Tadić* Jurisdiction Decision, par 126). A good illustration of this is the application of the rules and principle of command responsibility in the context of an internal armed conflict (see, as a good illustration of that point, *Hadžihasanović* Command Responsibility Appeal Decision, pars 10 et seq.).

Thus, whereas the body of rules applicable to international armed conflict has been said to encompass the regime applicable to internal ones,[7] the reverse is not – yet – true. At times, however, the Tribunals have come very close to deducing the applicability of a prohibition (and the existence of a war crime) in the context of an internal armed conflict, based apparently on the sole existence of that prohibition in the regulatory regime applying to international armed conflicts.[8]

The acknowledgement by the *ad hoc* Tribunals that much of the law of international armed conflicts would apply in the context of internal armed conflicts may be one of their most significant jurisprudential achievements as far as war crimes are concerned.

Although the Tribunals have on occasion touched upon the law relating to the conduct of hostilities, thereby opening the door of internal armed conflicts to Hague law,[9] both the ICTR and the ICTY have focused their attention insofar as the law of internal armed conflicts is concerned, almost exclusively on those serious violations of common Article 3 and Additional Protocol II which are designed more directly to protect civilians or civilian objects from armed hostilities.

9.2   Serious violations of common Article 3 of the Geneva Conventions

9.2.1   Common Article 3 in the Statutes of the *ad hoc* Tribunals

As noted by one author, the traditional response of general international law to internal disorder has been one of neglect, and Article 3, common to all four Geneva Conventions, was the first real attempt to break through 'the wall of State sovereignty'.[10] This provision is present in all four Geneva Conventions with the same content and its substantive content has been said to be applicable, *qua* customary

---

[7] *Čelebići* Appeal Judgment, par 420.

[8] See, e.g. ibid., par 161: 'Following the appellants' argument, two different regimes of criminal responsibility would exist based on the different legal characterisation of an armed conflict. As a consequence, the same horrendous conduct committed in an internal conflict could not be punished. The Appeals Chamber finds that the arguments put forward by the appellants do not withstand scrutiny.'

[9] See *Tadić* Jurisdiction Decision, pars 96–127 and 53–68: protection of civilians, general duty to avoid unnecessary harm, certain limitations on the means and methods of warfare, including a ban on chemical weapons and perfidious means of warfare, and the protection of certain categories of objects and properties

[10] Gasser, *International Humanitarian Law*, p 3. For a brief history of common Article 3, see *Kayishema and Ruzindana* Trial Judgment, pars 159 et seq. See also Gasser, *Armed Conflict within the Territory of a State*, in pp 225–240.

law, to both internal and international conflicts alike.[11] The text of common Article 3 reads as follows:

In the case of armed conflict not of an international character occurring in the territory of one of the High Contracting Parties, each Party to the conflict shall be bound to apply, as a minimum, the following provisions:

(1) Persons taking no active part in the hostilities, including members of armed forces who have laid down their arms and those placed *hors de combat* by sickness, wounds, detention, or any other cause, shall in all circumstances be treated humanely, without any adverse distinction founded on race, colour, religion or faith, sex, birth or wealth, or any other similar criteria.

To this end, the following acts are and shall remain prohibited at any time and in any place whatsoever with respect to the above-mentioned persons:

(a) Violence to life and person, in particular murder of all kinds, mutilation, cruel treatment and torture;

(b) Taking of hostages;

(c) Outrages upon personal dignity, in particular humiliating and degrading treatment;

(d) The passing of sentences and the carrying out of executions without previous judgement pronounced by a regularly constituted court, affording all the judicial guarantees which are recognized as indispensable by civilised peoples.

(2) The wounded and the sick shall be collected and cared for.

Common Article 3 represents, the Appeals Chamber said, 'the quintessence of the humanitarian rules found in the Geneva Conventions as a whole'.[12] It is a sort

---

[11] *Čelebići* Appeal Judgment, pars 143 and 147 ('The rules contained in common Article 3 are considered as applicable to international conflicts because they constitute the core of the rules applicable to such conflicts'), par 150 ('It is both legally and morally untenable that the rules contained in common Article 3, which constitute mandatory minimum rules applicable to internal conflicts, in which rules are less developed than in respect of international conflicts, would not be applicable to conflicts of an international character. The rules of common Article 3 are encompassed and further developed in the body of rules applicable to international conflicts. It is logical that this minimum be applicable to international conflicts as the substance of these core rules is identical. In the Appeals Chamber's view, something which is prohibited in internal conflicts is necessarily outlawed in an international conflict where the scope of the rules is broader'), and par 420. In support of this finding (in n 651 at p 141 of the Judgment), the Appeals Chamber referred, *inter alia*, to the *Nicaragua* case, par 218: 'Article 3 which is common to all four Geneva Conventions of 12 August 1949 defines certain rules to be applied in the armed conflicts of a non-international character. There is no doubt that, in the event of international armed conflicts, these rules also constitute a minimum yardstick, in addition to the more elaborate rules which are also to apply to international conflicts; and they are rules which, in the Court's opinion, reflect what the Court in 1949 called elementary considerations of humanity'. See also *Akayesu* Trial Judgment, pars 608–609.

[12] *Čelebići* Appeal Judgment, par 143: 'It is indisputable that common Article 3, which sets forth a minimum core of mandatory rules, reflects the fundamental humanitarian principles which underlie international humanitarian law as a whole, and upon which the Geneva Conventions in their entirety are based. These principles, the object of which is the respect for the dignity of the human person, developed as a result of centuries of warfare and had already become customary law at the time of the adoption of the Geneva Conventions because they reflect the most universally recognized humanitarian principles. These principles were codified in common Article 3 to constitute the minimum core applicable to internal conflicts, but are so fundamental that they are regarded as governing both internal and international conflicts.

of '[Geneva] Convention in miniature',[13] a 'minimum yardstick',[14] the primary purpose of which is to extend the 'elementary considerations of humanity' to internal armed conflicts,[15] and 'to provide minimum guarantees of protection to persons who are in the middle of an armed conflict but are not taking any active part in the hostilities'.[16]

From a statutory point of view, the ICTR Statute explicitly provides for the Tribunal's jurisdiction over violations of common Article 3, whilst the ICTY Statute does so only implicitly through Article 3 of its Statute. The fact that no express mention of common Article 3 was made in the ICTY Statute was not, the Appeals Chamber has found, to be interpreted as an exclusion thereof from the jurisdiction of the Yugoslav Tribunal.[17] Instead, the Appeals Chamber held that serious violations of common Article 3 do, all other conditions being met, come within the ICTY's jurisdiction *ratione materiae* through the medium of the residual Article 3 of the Statute.[18]

9.2.2   The protection guaranteed by common Article 3

The protection afforded by common Article 3 is limited in two particular respects: first, it only applies to a certain category of internal hostilities and, secondly, it

In the words of the ICRC, the purpose of common Article 3 was to "ensur(e) respect for the few essential rules of humanity which all civilised nations consider as valid everywhere and under all circumstances and as being above and outside war itself". These rules may thus be considered as the "quintessence" of the humanitarian rules found in the Geneva Conventions as a whole' (footnotes omitted).

[13] *Kayishema and Ruzindana* Trial Judgment, par 165.

[14] *Čelebići* Appeal Judgment, par 147. Common Article 3 represents the 'compulsory minimum' of protection to be guaranteed in all contexts (see *Kayishema and Ruzindana* Trial Judgment, par 164; *Kordić and Čerkez* Articles 2 and 3 Jurisdiction Decision, pars 25–26). In *Čelebići*, the Appeals Chamber refers to common Article 3 variously as 'a mandatory minimum code to internal conflicts' (par 140), 'a minimum core of mandatory rules' (par 143), a 'minimum core applicable to internal conflicts' (par 143), 'fundamental standards of humanity applicable in *all* circumstances' (par 144), and a 'minimum yardstick [. . .] applicable to both internal and international conflicts' (par 147). See also ibid., par 143 (see n 12 above).   [15] *Čelebići* Trial Judgment, par 423.

[16] *Čelebići* Appeal Judgment, par 420. Another Trial Chamber said that common Article 3 constitutes a minimum level of protection which applies in any kind of armed conflict representing 'the fundamental principle underlying the four Geneva Conventions', that is, 'that of humane treatment' (*Blaškić* Trial Judgment, par 167). It continued: 'With Common Article 3 representing, as it does, the minimum which must be applied in the least determinate of conflicts, its terms must *a fortiori* be respected in the case of international conflicts proper, when all the provisions of the Convention are applicable.' see also the *Akayesu* Trial Judgment, par 601; *Tadić* Appeal Judgment, par 102; *Nicaragua* case, par 218.

[17] In their appeals against the Trial Chamber's Judgment, the appellants in the *Čelebići* case submitted that offences committed in violation of common Article 3 did not come within the realm of Article 3 of the ICTY Statute; see *Čelebići* Appeal Judgment, par 116 and reference to appellants' briefs in footnotes. The same argument was repeated by the appellants in *Kunarac* (e.g. *Prosecutor v. Kunarac*, IT-96-23 and IT-96-23/1-A, Appellant's Brief for the Acused [*sic*] Radomir Kovač against Judgment of 22 February 2001, 16 July 2001, pars 131–133, and *Prosecutor v. Kunarac*, IT-96-23 and IT-96-23/1-A, Prosecution's Consolidated Respondent Brief, 9 October 2001, par 2.2–2.4).

[18] See, in particular, *Tadić* Jurisdiction Decision, pars 128–133; see also *Čelebići* Appeal Judgment, pars 125–136 and 153–174.

only protects certain categories of victims of war. Concerning the first limitation, common Article 3 provides that it will apply 'in case of armed conflict not of an international character occurring on the territory of one of the High Contracting Parties'.[19] Prior to the adoption of Additional Protocol II unless the parties to an armed conflict had agreed otherwise, once common Article 3 was said to apply to a given armed conflict, no other part of the laws of war could superimpose itself and no other provisions in any of the Geneva Conventions applied to internal armed conflicts. Conversely, if any other provision of the Conventions applied, common Article 3 would not. That apparent restriction as to the sort of conflicts in which common Article 3 could be said to apply lost almost all constraining effect insofar as the *ad hoc* Tribunals are concerned when the Appeals Chamber of the ICTY declared that the principles and rules embodied in common Article 3 now apply to any sort of armed conflict, regardless of its characterization (internal or international), and gave the concept of 'armed conflict' the broadest of definitions.[20] Thus, once an armed conflict as defined by the Appeals Chamber has been shown to exist, regardless of its international or internal character, common Article 3 will apply, without a need for any recognition on the part of either party that the situation falls within the terms of that rule and regardless of any reciprocal abidance on their part.

The second limitation in that provision relates to the categories of people who come within its terms. To be afforded the protection of common Article 3, a victim must either be a civilian or someone who was 'taking no active part in the hostilities, including members of armed forces who have laid down their arms and those placed *hors de combat* by sickness, wounds, detention, or any other cause'.[21] Common Article 3 is therefore intended to apply to all those who found themselves on the territory of the state where the conflict was taking place, 'except combatants at the time engaged in fighting'.[22] The – negative – test to be applied to identify those protected under that regime is hence to ask whether, at the time of

---

[19] See, generally, *Akayesu* Trial Judgment, pars 601–602 and 619–625; *Rutaganda* Trial Judgment, pars 92–93; *Musema* Trial Judgment, pars 247–248.

[20] See above, Chapter 6, The definition of an 'armed conflict', international and internal.

[21] In the ICC Elements of Crimes, persons protected under common Article 3 are said to include those who were '*either hors de combat*, or were civilians, medical personnel, or religious personnel taking no active part in the hostilities' (see Elements of Crimes, Article 8(2) (c) *et seq.*).

[22] Final Record of the Diplomatic Conference of Geneva of 1949, Vol. II-B, at 84. See also *Tadić* Trial Judgment, pars 615–616. The *Tadić* Trial Chamber said that the protection of common Article 3 'embraces, at least, all of those protected persons covered by the grave breaches regime applicable to conflict of an international character: civilians, prisoners of war, wounded and sick members of the armed forces at sea' (ibid., par 615). Such statement is of limited assistance, however. The requirement that those protected under the grave breaches regime are protected on condition only that they find themselves 'in the hands of a party to the conflict or occupying power of which they are not nationals'. This requirement does not apply under common Article 3. Also, the protection guaranteed under common Article 3 is broader than that offered under the grave breaches system in that (i) it does not depend on the existence of an international armed conflict and (ii) is not limited to individuals who are not of the same nationality as the perpetrator.

the alleged offence, the victim was directly or actively taking part in hostilities.[23] If he or she was, that is, if that individual was actively or directly involved in the hostilities in the context of which the offence was committed, he or she will not be protected by common Article 3.[24] If, on the contrary, he or she was not so involved, common Article 3 will apply in principle.

In the jurisprudence, Article 3 has been said to protect civilians,[25] and to all those who are *hors de combat*, namely, all persons who are either unable or unwilling to fight.[26] Also, because of the humanitarian purpose of that provision,[27] the group of protected individuals coming within the terms of common Article 3 has been said to include detained persons who, prior to detention, were members of the armed forces or were engaged in armed hostilities.[28] It has also been said that, in case of doubt as to the status of the victim, that person should be presumed to be a civilian and should therefore be presumed to be protected by common Article 3.[29] Such a rule of thumb, however, only applies to the expected conduct of a member of the military.[30] Where the criminal responsibility of such an individual is at stake, however, the burden of proof to establish the civilian status of the victims remains at all times upon the Prosecution.[31] On the other hand, and as already noted above, common Article 3 would exclude, for instance, combatants until their capture and civilians who take a direct part in

---

[23] The *Akayesu* Trial Chamber stated that the phrases 'direct' and 'active' were synomymous (*Akayesu* Trial Judgment, par 629).

[24] *Tadić* Trial Judgment, par 615; *Blaškić* Trial Judgment, par 177.

[25] On the concept of civilians, see, *inter alia*, *Rutaganda* Trial Judgment, pars 100–101; *Kayishema and Ruzindana* Trial Judgment, pars 179–180.

[26] *Tadić* Jurisdiction Decision, par 175. The *Tadić* Trial Chamber held that it was 'unnecessary to define exactly the line dividing those taking an active part and those who are not so involved' (*Tadić* Trial Judgment, par 616). The Trial Chamber in *Stakić* said that this would 'automatically' include people kept in detention camps or those being forcibly displaced in convoys (*Stakić* Trial Judgment, par 580). See also *Naletilić and Martinović* Trial Judgment, par 229; *Čelebići* Appeal Judgment, par 420; *Semanza* Trial Judgment, par 365; *Bagilishema* Trial Judgment, pars 103–104; *Musema* Trial Judgment, par 280; *Rutaganda* Trial Judgment, par 101; *Tadić* Trial Judgment, pars 615–616.

[27] The influence of the views of the ICRC has been a factor of great importance in that respect. The number of references made to the ICRC Commentaries and the deference shown to those when ascertaining the meaning and scope of a provision whose roots are found in the Geneva Conventions or its Additional Protocols has simply been extraordinary. One telling illustration is the Appeals Judgment in *Čelebići* (see, e.g. pars 132, 143, 145, 146, and 166).

[28] See *Naletilić and Martinović* Trial Judgment, par 229; *Tadić* Trial Judgment, pars 615–616; *Blaškić* Trial Judgment, par 177; *Akayesu* Appeal Judgment, par 442: 'Protection of victims is [. . .] the core of common Article 3.' See also '[Common] Article 3 is humanitarian in purpose and content. It purports to benefit as wide a class of peoples as possible. It does not reach the persons engaged in the hostilities, but to those who are not, or who are no longer, so engaged. Further, the nature of humanitarian prohibitions is so fundamental in character, e.g. not to murder, mutilate or torture, that the weight of the article is against any narrow interpretation not demanded by clear language in the Article itself' (G. Draper, 'The Geneva Conventions of 1949', 114 (RCADI) Receuil des Cours de l' Académie de Droit International 63, 87 (1965).

[29] See, e.g. *Kunarac* Trial Judgment; *Galić* Trial Judgment.

[30] *Blaškić* Appeal Judgment, par 111. Such a presumption must in any case be applied most carefully and with regard to all the circumstances of the case.   [31] Ibid.

the hostilities and who thereby shed their privileges which they normally enjoy under that provision.[32]

When compared to the categories of persons protected by other relevant statutory provisions, common Article 3 may be said to protect, *inter alia*, all those protected under the grave breaches regime of the Geneva Conventions,[33] as well as those protected under Additional Protocol II.[34]

Whereas common Article 3 limits the scope of those who may enjoy the benefit of its protection, anyone – combatants and non-combatants alike – can in principle be held liable for a serious violation of that provision.[35] Common Article 3 indeed contains no restriction on the categories of potential violators.[36] In particular, there is no requirement that the perpetrator must in any way be related to one of the parties to the armed conflicts (although it is often the case in practice):[37]

This nexus [between the acts of the accused and the armed conflict] implies that, in most cases, the perpetrator of the crime will probably have a special relationship with one party to the conflict. However, such a special relationship is not a condition precedent to the application of common Article 3 and, hence of Article 4 of the [ICTR] Statute. In the opinion of the Appeals Chamber, the Trial Chamber erred in requiring that a special relationship should be a separate condition for triggering criminal responsibility for a violation of Article 4 of the Statute.

[32] *Kupreškić* Trial Judgment, par 523 ('In the case of clear abuse of their rights by civilians, international rules operate to lift that protection which would otherwise be owed to them.').

[33] *Tadić* Trial Judgment, par 615. The protective scope of common Article 3 is broader, however, than that of the grave breaches regime as provided under Article 2 of the ICTY Statute (*Čelebići* Appeal Judgment, par 420: 'Its coverage extends to *any* individual not taking part in hostilities and is therefore broader than that envisioned by Geneva Convention IV incorporated into Article 2 of the Statute, under which "protected person" status is accorded only in specially defined and limited circumstances, such as the presence of the individual in territory which is under the control of the Power in question, and the exclusion of wounded and sick members of the armed forces from protected person status; while protected person status under Article 2 therefore involves not taking an active part in hostilities, it also comprises further requirements. As a result, Article 2 of the Statute is more specific than common Article 3.').

[34] See *Akayesu* Trial Judgment, par 629: the same people are protected by both regimes and include those persons not taking an active part in the hostilities.

[35] See, generally, *Akayesu* Appeal Judgment, pars 443–445: 'the minimum protection provided for victims under common Article 3 implies necessarily effective punishment on persons who violate it. Now, such punishment must be applicable to everyone without discrimination. [. . .] [I]international law would be lessened and called into question if it were to be admitted that certain persons be exonerated from individual criminal responsibility for a violation of common Article 3 under the pretext that they did not belong to a specific category. [. . .] [I]n most cases, the perpetrator of the crime will probably have a special relationship with one party to the conflict. However, such a special relationship is not a condition precedent to the application of common Article 3 [of the Geneva Conventions]. [. . .] Accordingly, the Appeals Chamber finds that the Trial Chamber erred on a point of law in restricting the application of common Article 3 to a certain category of persons [. . .].'

[36] Ibid., par 443: 'international humanitarian law would be lessened and called into question if it were to be admitted that certain persons be exonerated from individual criminal responsibility for a violation of common Article 3 under the pretext that they did not belong to a specific category'. See also par 444 where the Appeals Chamber rejects the Defence's submission that a perpetrator of a violation of common Article 3 must somehow be linked to a party to the armed conflict.

[37] Ibid., par 444. See also *Rutaganda* Appeal Judgment, pars 569–570. See however *Akayesu* Trial Judgment, pars 630–634.

Once it is said to apply, common Article 3 would apply to all parties involved in an armed conflict and it represents the minimum standard with which they must comply during the conflict.[38] Not every breach of common Article 3, however, may be said to constitute a war crime pursuant to the Tribunals' Statutes. First, in addition to satisfying the general requirements applicable to all war crimes under the Statute,[39] the Tribunal must satisfy itself that the prohibition in question constituted a crime under customary international law at the relevant time.

Secondly, to come within the Tribunals' jurisdiction, the violation of common Article 3 must be a *serious* one.[40] A 'serious' violation, pursuant to that requirement, consists of 'a breach of a rule protecting important values [which] must involve grave consequences for the victim'.[41] Only a 'serious' violation of that provision entails individual criminal responsibility under the Statute of the Tribunals.[42] All violations of common Article 3 which fall below that standard would be outside of the Tribunals' jurisdiction although they may, and often will, constitute domestic crimes or disciplinary offences.

9.3   Serious violations of Additional Protocol II and the Statutes of the *ad hoc* Tribunals

9.3.1   Additional Protocol II in the Statutes of the *ad hoc* Tribunals

The Statute of the ICTY does not explicitly provide for the Tribunal's jurisdiction over serious violations of Additional Protocol II. Nor did the Secretary-General make any reference thereto in his Report to the Security Council. However, during the discussions that led to the adoption of the ICTY, proposals were made that serious violations of Additional Protocol II should come within the

---

[38] See *Semanza* Trial Judgment, par 358 ('Article 4 makes no mention of a possible delimitation of classes of persons likely to be prosecuted under this provision'), par 359 ('Common Article 3 and Additional Protocol II similarly do not specify classes of potential perpetrators, rather they indicate who is bound by the obligations imposed thereby'), and par 360 ('the protections of Common Article 3 imply effective punishment of perpetrators, whoever they may be'); *Akayesu* Appeal Judgment, pars 435 and 444–445.   [39] See above, '*Chapeau* elements of war crimes'.

[40] See, e.g. *Tadić* Jurisdiction Decision, pars 90–91 and 134; *Čelebići* Appeal Judgment, par 125; *Kunarac* Appeal Judgment, par 68; *Kunarac* Trial Judgment, par 408; *Akayesu* Trial Judgment, par 616; *Kayishema and Ruzindana* Trial Judgment, par 184; *Rutaganda* Trial Judgment, par 106; *Musema* Trial Judgment, pars 286–288; *Semanza* Trial Judgment, par 370.

[41] *Akayesu* Trial Judgment, par 616. According to the *Akayesu* Trial Chamber, all offences expressly listed in Article 4 of the ICTR Statute are *per se* 'serious' enough to satisfy the jurisdictional requirement of 'seriousness' (ibid.; see also *Semanza* Trial Judgment, pars 370–371).

[42] See, *inter alia*, *Tadić* Jurisdiction Decision, pars 98 and 134; *Čelebići* Appeal Judgment, par 143; *Kunarac* Trial Judgment, par 406; *Blaškić* Trial Judgment, par 166; *Kordić and Čerkez* Articles 2 and 3 Jurisdiction Decision, pars 26–29. See *Nicaragua* case on common Article 3 where the ICJ said that the rules contained in common Article 3 are an expression of the fundamental considerations of humanity (and is binding *qua jus cogens*).

Tribunal's jurisdiction.[43] The Yugoslav Tribunal accordingly recognized that serious violations of the Protocol had been intended to be and were indeed part of the Tribunal's jurisdiction *ratione materiae* and would come under the umbrella rule of Article 3 of the Statute all other jurisdictional requirements having been met.[44]

By contrast to what is the case at the ICTY, the ICTR Statute expressly mentions serious violations of Additional Protocol II as coming within the Tribunal's jurisdiction.[45] In fact, the ICTR's jurisdiction, insofar as Additional Protocol II is concerned, seems to be limited, if not completely, at least primarily, to serious violations of the 'fundamental guarantees' provided in Article 4 of Additional Protocol II.[46]

9.3.2 Status of Additional Protocol II under customary international law and relationship with common Article 3 of the Geneva Conventions

Customary status of Additional Protocol II

As a whole, Additional Protocol II may not yet be said to be part of customary international law, but many of its provisions are now considered to be customary in nature.[47] Additional Protocol II is, however, rarely used at the Tribunals as the sole, or even as a discrete basis, pursuant to which a crime is charged against an accused.

[43] In the discussions leading up to the adoption of the ICTY Statute by the Security Council, a number of states had proposed to recognize the Additional Protocols as applicable to the determination of individual criminal responsibility. See, e.g. American proposal '2.2 Subject matter jurisdiction. The International Tribunal shall have jurisdiction to try serious violations of international humanitarian law committed in the territory of the former Yugoslavia from January 1, 1991, including, but not limited to: (A) all humanitarian law agreements in force in the territory of the former Yugoslavia at the time the acts were committed, including the 1907 Hague Convention (IV) Respecting the Laws and Customs of War on Land and the Regulations annexed thereto, the 1949 Geneva Conventions, and the 1977 Additional Protocols to those conventions [. . .]' (reprinted in Morris and Scharf, *The Yugoslav Tribunal*, vol. 2, pp 509, 516) and the Russian proposal: '[Article 12. Crimes within the jurisdiction of the Tribunal] 1. The following crimes shall be within the jurisdiction of the Tribunal: (a) Military crimes such as serious violations of the Geneva Conventions for the protection of war victims of 12 August 1949 or the Protocols Additional thereto of 8 June 1977 [. . .]' (ibid., pp 439, 441).   [44] See, e.g. *Tadić* Jurisdiction Decision, par 89.

[45] See also Secretary-General Report (ICTR), pars 11–12.

[46] See ibid., pars 11–12 and *Akayesu* Trial Judgment, pars 616 (and 629). See also *Musema* Trial Judgment, pars 240–241, and references quoted therein. In addition, and as noted above, Article 4 of the ICTR has criminalized the mere 'threats to commit' any of the crimes listed in the Statute, including serious violations of Additional Protocol II.

[47] *Tadić* Jurisdiction Decision, par 117: 'many provisions of this [Additional Protocol II] can now be regarded as declaratory of existing rules or as having crystallized emerging rules of customary law or else as having been strongly instrumental in their evolution as general principles.' *Kordić and Čerkez* Articles 2 and 3 Jurisdiction Decision, par 30: 'While both Protocols have not yet achieved the near universal participation enjoyed by the Geneva Conventions, it is not controversial that major parts of both Protocols reflect customary law.' See also *Akayesu* Trial Judgment, par 609; Secretary-General Report (ICTR), pars 11–12: 'Additional Protocol II, which, as a whole, has not yet been universally recognized as part of customary international law.'

Because there are doubts as to which of its provisions are now part of customary international law, and because its fundamental guarantees largely overlap with common Article 3 (which is undoubtedly part of customary law), common Article 3 has almost systematically been preferred as a basis to bring criminal charges.[48] As a result, the importance of Additional Protocol II as a discrete basis for charging crimes and for conviction has been extremely modest at the *ad hoc* Tribunals.[49]

Relationship between Additional Protocol II and common Article 3

Until the adoption of Additional Protocol II, common Article 3 had been an island in the middle of regulations concerned almost exclusively international armed conflicts. Additional Protocol II purported mainly to improve and increase the protection of civilians during internal armed conflicts by developing and supplementing common Article 3 without modifying its existing conditions of applications.[50] The Protocol was not intended to diminish the autonomy of the regime established by common Article 3[51] and neither the conditions of application of common Article 3 nor the scope of its protection were modified by Additional Protocol II.[52] Common Article 3 and Additional Protocol II do not apply to the same categories of armed conflicts. Article 1(1) of the Protocol provides that the Protocol would only apply to those armed conflicts 'which take place in the territory of a High Contracting Party between its armed forces and dissident armed forces or other organized armed groups which, under responsible command, exercise such control over a part of its territory as to enable them to carry out sustained and concerted military operations and to implement this Protocol'. Common Article 3

---

[48] Sub-section 9.3.3, below. See, however, the indictment against Stanislav Galić (*Prosecutor v. Galić*, IT-98-29-I, Indictment, 26 March 1999) and indictment against Pavel Strugar, IT-01-42-I, Third Amended Indictment, 10 December 2003.

[49] See statement of M. J. Matheson, Deputy Legal Advisor of the US Department in 2 AUJILP (1987) 419, pp 430–431 (quoted in *Tadić* Jurisdiction Decision, par 117): '[T]he basic core of Protocol II is, of course, reflected in common Article 3 of the 1949 Geneva Conventions and therefore is, and should be, a part of generally accepted customary law. This specifically includes its prohibitions on violence towards persons taking no active part in hostilities, hostage taking, degrading treatment, and punishment without due process.' See also *Akayesu* Trial Judgment, par 610; *Blaškić* Trial Judgment, par 170.

[50] *Semanza* Trial Judgment, par 356; *Kayishema and Ruzindana* Trial Judgment, pars 166–168. In practice, Additional Protocol II 'elaborated and extended the protections of the Geneva Conventions' (*Galić* Trial Judgment, par 120).

[51] See Article 1 of Additional Protocol II which provides that the Protocol 'develops and supplements Article 3 common to the Geneva Conventions of 12 August 1949 without modifying its existing conditions of application'.

[52] It is important to note, for instance, that common Article 3 and Additional Protocol II may be said to apply, in part, to slightly different species of armed conflicts and that their scopes do not therefore perfectly cover each other's. See C. Greenwood, 'International Humanitarian Law (Laws of War): Revised Report for the Centennial Commemoration of the First Hague Peace Conference 1899', in F. Kalshoven (ed.), *The Centennial of the First International Peace Conference: Reports and Conclusions* (The Hague/Boston/London: Kluwer Law International, 2000) ('Greenwood, *International Humanitarian Law*').

applies 'in the case of armed conflict not of an international character occurring in the territory of one of the High Contracting Parties'.[53]

Categories of armed conflicts to which Additional Protocol II applies

In order to apply to internal hostilities, Additional Protocol II therefore requires that (i) one of the parties asserts its control over – part of – the territory of its enemy, and is limited to (ii) hostilities between government and insurgents whilst it does not apply to conflicts between groups of insurgents within a state.[54] Such limitations do not apply to those armed conflicts to which common Article 3 may apply. The requirement of territorial control contained in Additional Protocol II will exclude, from the realm of the Protocol, all sorts of internal hostilities which may fall short of full-scale civil wars, whilst the second limitation would exclude the application of Additional Protocol II in those conflicts between various warring factions within a state where none of the parties represents the governmental forces.[55] Furthermore, under the Protocol, the group or groups confronting the government forces must be under 'responsible command', which entails a certain degree of organization which would enable those groups to plan and carry out concerted military operations, to impose discipline within the ranks of the troops involved, and to ensure compliance with the Protocol.[56] As a result of those differences, there may be cases of internal armed conflict where common Article 3 would apply, whilst Additional Protocol II would not.[57] Whether the armed

---

[53] See, generally, *Kayishema and Ruzindana* Trial Judgment, pars 170–171. See S. Boelaert-Suominen, 'Grave Breaches, Universal Jurisdiction and Internal Armed Conflicts: Is Customary Law Moving towards a Uniform Enforcement Mechanism for All Armed Conflicts?', 5 *Journal of Conflict and Security Law* 63–103 (2000) and D. Schindler, 'The Different Types of Armed Conflicts according to the Geneva Conventions and Protocols', 163(II) *Recueil des Cours de l'Académie de droit international de La Haye*, 117 et seq. (1979), ('Schindler, *Armed Conflicts and the Geneva Conventions*').

[54] See *Rutaganda* Trial Judgment, par 95, which provides that the 'material requirements to be satisfied for the applicability of Additional Protocol II' are: (i) an armed conflict takes place in the territory of a High Contracting Party, between its armed forces and dissident armed forces or other organized armed groups; (ii) the dissident armed forces or other organized armed groups are under responsible command; (iii) the dissident armed forces or other organized armed groups are able to exercise such control over a part of their territory as to enable them to carry out sustained and concerted military operations; and (iv) the dissident armed forces or other organized armed groups are able to implement Additional Protocol II. See also *Musema* Trial Judgment, par 253. See also, generally, Schindler, *Armed Conflicts and the Geneva Conventions*, pp 148 et seq.

[55] The Trial Chamber in the *Akayesu* case said that the term 'armed forces' of a High Contracting Party 'is to be defined broadly, so as to cover all armed forces as described within national legislation' (par 625).

[56] Ibid., par 626; *Kayishema and Ruzindana* Trial Judgment, par 171; *Musema* Trial Judgment, par 257. The requirement of 'responsible command' does not mean, however, that there must be 'a hierarchical system of military organization similar to that of regular armed forces' (*Musema* Trial Judgment, par 257).

[57] *Akayesu* Trial Judgment, par 601. See also ibid., par 618: 'it will not suffice to establish that as the criteria of Common Article 3 have been met, the whole of Article 4 of the [ICTR] Statute, hence Additional Protocol II, will be applicable. Where alleged offences are charged under both Common Article 3 and Additional Protocol II, which has a higher threshold, the Prosecutor will need to prove that the criteria of applicability of, on the one hand, Common Article 3 and, on the other, Additional Protocol II have been met'; and par 607: 'Thus, if an offence [. . .] is charged under both Common

conflict under consideration is one that comes within the terms of common Article 3 and/or Additional Protocol II will depend on 'an analysis of the objective factors set out in the respective provisions'.[58] As noted by one author, '[t]he multiplication of armed conflicts can hardly be called the most fortunate of the achievements of the Geneva Conference of 1974–1977'.[59]

The question remains open, however, whether the general definition given by the *Tadić* Appeals Chamber of what may be said to constitute an 'internal armed conflict' for the purpose of the Tribunals' Statutes (and, therefore, for the purpose of charges brought under both common Article 3 and Additional Protocol II) has in fact neutralized the distinction between those different categories of armed conflict and whether it has bridged the gap between common Article 3 and Additional Protocol II concerning the categories of armed conflicts to which they both apply.[60]

In any case, situations of internal disturbances such as 'acts of banditry or short-lived insurrections', falling short of an armed conflict, are not regulated by international humanitarian law (whether common Article 3 or Additional Protocol II) and crimes committed in the context thereof would not fall within the Tribunals' jurisdiction over war crimes.[61] An armed conflict may be distinguished from such internal disturbances both by the intensity of the fighting and the degree of organization of the parties involved.[62]

Persons protected by Additional Protocol II and categories of perpetrators

Insofar as victims are concerned, common Article 3 protects 'persons taking no active part in the hostilities', whilst Additional Protocol II applies to 'all persons affected by an armed conflict' (art 2(1)) and guarantees the protection of 'all persons who do not take a direct part or who have ceased to take part in hostilities' (art 4(1)). According to the *Akayesu* Trial Chamber, despite slight terminological

Article 3 and Additional Protocol II, it will not suffice to apply Common Article 3 and take for granted that Article 4 of the [ICTR] Statute, hence Additional Protocol II, is therefore automatically applicable.' See also *Semanza* Trial Judgment, pars 356–357.

[58] *Semanza* Trial Judgment, par 357 and fn 595 attached to it. See also *Akayesu* Trial Judgment, par 619 (in relation to common Article 3) and par 623 (in relation to Additional Protocol II).

[59] Schindler, *Armed Conflicts and the Geneva Conventions*, p 153.

[60] The ICTR seems to have given a clear indication that, in cases where charges are brought pursuant to either common Article 3 and/or Additional Protocol II, the specific definitions of what constitute an armed conflict in each context had to be met (see, e.g. *Akayesu* Trial Judgment, par 618; *Rutaganda* Trial Judgment, pars 92–94).

[61] See *Akayesu* Trial Judgment, pars 601 and 620; *Kayishema and Ruzindana* Trial Judgment, par 171; *Rutaganda* Trial Judgment, par 92; *Musema* Trial Judgment, par 248. Crimes committed in the context thereof could still constitute acts of genocide or crimes against humanity, all other conditions being met.

[62] *Akayesu* Trial Judgment, par 625. According to the *Akayesu* Trial Chamber, the phrase 'armed conflict' 'in itself suggests the existence of hostilities between armed forces organized to a greater or lesser extent' (*Akayesu* Trial Judgment, par 620). See also *Musema* Trial Judgment, par 248: 'The expression "armed conflicts" involves a material criterion: the existence of open hostilities between armed forces which are organized to a greater or lesser degree. Internal disturbances and tensions, characterized by isolated or sporadic acts of violence, do not therefore constitute armed conflicts in a legal sense, even if the government is forced to resort to police forces or even armed units for the purpose of restoring law and order.' See above, subsection 6.2.12.

differences between the two provisions concerning their scope of protection, they may be regarded as identical as far as victims are concerned so that common Article 3 and Additional Protocol II may be said to protect the same categories of people, namely, any individual not taking an active part in the hostilities.[63]

Civilians will lose the benefit of the protection of Additional Protocol II (and common Article 3) when they take a direct part in the hostilities. For a civilian to be said to have taken a *direct* part in the hostilities he or she must have been involved in 'acts of war which by their nature or purpose are likely to cause actual harm to the personnel and equipment of the enemy armed forces'.[64] In its assessment as to whether a given individual may be said to have been a civilian for the purpose of Additional Protocol II (and common Article 3), the court is bound to consider 'the overall humanitarian purpose of the Geneva Conventions and their Protocols'. A civilian should therefore be considered to be 'any one who is not a member of the "armed forces" [. . .] or any one placed *hors de combat*'.[65] The same principles as described above in relation to common Article 3 with regard to the status of the victims will apply here.

Although, contrary to Additional Protocol I, Protocol II does not contain a definition of what constitutes a 'civilian population', the Tribunals have applied the same definition in both situations without any suggestion that the definition could be any different in the context of an internal armed conflict.[66]

There is no restriction as to the classes of individuals who may commit a serious violation of Additional Protocol II (or a serious violation of common Article 3) so that the perpetrator could be, for instance, a member of the warring forces or himself a civilian.[67] Contrary to what a number of Trial Chambers had suggested, the Appeals Chamber made it clear that the perpetrators need not (although they most often will) be connected or linked to one of the parties to the conflict.[68] In sum, once an internal armed conflict has been shown to exist, anyone may in principle commit a serious violation of common Article 3 or a serious violation of Additional Protocol II and may be held accountable.

---

[63] *Akayesu* Trial Judgment, par 629. See also *Kayishema and Ruzindana* Trial Judgment, pars 178–181 and *Semanza* Trial Judgment, par 365; *Bagilishema* Trial Judgment, pars 99 and 103–104; *Musema* Trial Judgment, par 280; *Rutaganda* Trial Judgment, par 101. See also *Čelebići* Appeal Judgment, par 420. According to the *Semanza* Trial Chamber, the question to be answered in that respect is whether, at the time of the alleged offence, the alleged victim was directly taking part in the hostilities: 'If the answer is negative, the alleged victim was a person protected by Common Article 3 and Additional Protocol II' (*Semanza* Trial Judgment, par 366).

[64] *Musema* Trial Judgment, par 279. See also *Semanza* Trial Judgment, par 366 and references quoted therein.

[65] See, e.g. *Bagilishema* Trial Judgment, par 104. The *ad hoc* Tribunals have not had an opportunity to state whether (i) crimes committed by a party to an armed conflict against members of its own side (civilians or combatants), (ii) crimes committed by government forces against its own forces (or supporters) or (iii) crimes committed by insurgents against its own members (or supporters), could qualify as serious violations of Additional Protocol II.

[66] See, e.g. *Kayishema and Ruzindana* Trial Judgment, pars 167 and 179.

[67] See, e.g. *Akayesu* Appeal Judgment, pars 443–445; *Akayesu* Trial Judgment, pars 630–633; *Kayishema and Ruzindana* Trial Judgment, par 176; *Semanza* Trial Judgment, pars 358–362.

[68] See, e.g. *Akayesu* Appeal Judgment, pars 443–445; *Musema* Trial Judgment, pars 264–275.

'Serious' violations of Additional Protocol II

From a jurisdictional point of view, as with common Article 3, only *serious* violations of the Protocol will come within the Tribunals' subject-matter jurisdiction.[69] The violation may be committed at any time during the armed conflict, as well as, *ratione loci*, in any part of the state where Additional Protocol II has been said to be applicable and, in particular, also outside the narrow geographical area where combat is taking place.[70]

9.3.3　Role of Additional Protocol II in the jurisprudence of the *ad hoc* Tribunals

The *ad hoc* Tribunals have produced very little jurisprudence related to Additional Protocol II of the Geneva Conventions and no accused has been convicted for a violation of the Protocol (or its customary reflection). The limited categories of armed conflicts to which Additional Protocol II may be said to apply and doubts as to the extent to which it is now part of customary international law have deterred the Prosecution (and Chambers) from entering the realm of Additional Protocol II with much enthusiasm, preferring instead to rely on common Article 3 of the Geneva Conventions. In the jurisprudence of the Tribunals, Additional Protocol II has been regarded mostly, not as an independent basis for conviction,[71] but as a relevant instance of state practice that might be pertinent to a determination that a rule or principle which it contains has become part of customary international law.[72] In that sense, recourse to the Protocol has been mostly evidentiary rather than substantive in kind.

The significance of the Tribunals' case law in relation to Additional Protocol II therefore appears to have been essentially twofold: first, it has been expressly acknowledged by an international tribunal that parts of Additional Protocol II (in particular, its fundamental guarantees contained in Article 4 of the Protocol) now form part of customary international law. Secondly, the *ad hoc* Tribunals have made it clear that serious violations of those standards and rules which are now part of custom would entail the individual criminal responsibility of those who infringe upon them.[73]

---

[69] See, e.g. *Kayishema and Ruzindana* Trial Judgment, par 184; *Akayesu* Trial Judgment, par 599; *Semanza* Trial Judgment, pars 370–371; *Bagilishema* Trial Judgment, par 102; *Musema* Trial Judgment, par 286; *Rutaganda* Trial Judgment, par 106. The test used to determine what infringements may be considered to be 'serious' for the purpose of Additional Protocol II is identical to that applied to common Article 3 (see above, sub-section 9.3.2.5).

[70] See *Akayesu* Trial Judgment, par 635; *Tadić* Jurisdiction Decision, par 69; *Semanza* Trial Judgment, par 367; *Bagilishema* Trial Judgment, par 101; *Musema* Trial Judgment, pars 283–284; *Rutaganda* Trial Judgment, pars 102–103; *Kayishema and Ruzindana* Trial Judgment, pars 182–183.

[71] See, however, *Galić* Trial Judgment in relation to attacks on civilians and terror.

[72] *Strugar* Jurisdiction Decision, pars 9–14.

[73] See *Akayesu* Trial Judgment, pars 611–615; *Kayishema and Ruzindana* Trial Judgment, pars 182–183.

PART III

CRIMES AGAINST HUMANITY[1]

[1] The author is grateful to the President and Fellows of Harvard College and the *Harvard International Law Journal* which granted permission to reprint parts of my article "Crimes against Humanity in the Jurisprudence of the International Tribunals for the Former Yugoslavia and for Rwanda", vol. 43, no. 1, Winter 2002.

10

Crimes against Humanity in the Statutes of the *ad hoc* Tribunals

The Tribunals have had an immense influence on the law of crimes against humanity, turning a set of abstract concepts into a fully fledged and well-defined body of law. In essence, the definition of crimes against humanity as identified by the *ad hoc* Tribunals consists of two superimposed layers. The first layer contains the *chapeau* elements or general requirements of the offence, which give a crime against humanity its specificity and its dimension, setting it apart from domestic crimes and distinguishing it from other international crimes such as war crimes or genocide. The *chapeau* which requires that the acts or conduct in question must have been part of a 'widespread or systematic attack against any civilian population' also sets out the context in which the acts of the accused must have been committed to constitute a crime against humanity. The second layer of the definition consists of one of the listed underlying offences, such as torture or murder, in the commission of which the accused is said to have partaken and which forms part of the above-mentioned attack.

The statutes of both Tribunals reflect this two-layered definition. Article 5 of the ICTY Statute defines 'crimes against humanity' as follows:

The International Tribunal shall have the power to prosecute persons responsible for the following crimes when committed in armed conflict, whether international or internal in character, and directed against any civilian population:

(a) murder;
(b) extermination;
(c) enslavement;
(d) deportation;
(e) imprisonment;
(f) torture;

(g) rape;
(h) persecutions on political, racial and religious grounds;
(i) other inhumane acts.[2]

The definition of crimes against humanity in Article 3 of the ICTR Statute is similarly layered:

The International Tribunal for Rwanda shall have the power to prosecute persons responsible for the following crimes when committed as part of a widespread or systematic attack against any civilian population on national, political, ethnic, racial or religious grounds:

(a) murder;
(b) extermination;
(c) enslavement;
(d) deportation;
(e) imprisonment;
(f) torture;
(g) rape;
(h) persecutions on political, racial and religious grounds;
(i) other inhumane acts.[3]

The list of underlying offences is identical in both Statutes, but their respective *chapeaux* are different in at least two respects: the Statute of the ICTY requires (whilst the Statute of the ICTR does not require) that crimes against humanity must be 'committed in armed conflict'; the Statute of the ICTR (but not the ICTY Statute) requires that crimes against humanity must have been committed on national, political, ethnic, racial, or religious grounds to come within the Tribunal's jurisdiction.

10.1   ICTY requirement: 'Committed in armed conflict'

Article 5 of the ICTY Statute requires that the crime which forms the basis of the charges against the accused must have been 'committed in armed conflict'. Though not found in customary international law, this requirement has a historical basis in the first prosecutions for crimes against humanity which took place in the aftermath of the Second World War.[4]

The requirement first appeared, albeit in a slightly different form, in Article 6(c) of the Nuremberg Charter in the form of a requirement that all crimes against

---

[2] ICTY Statute, Article 5.   [3] ICTR Statute, Article 3.

[4] For a historical perspective on the development of the concept of 'crimes against humanity,' see, *inter alia*, M. Lippman, 'Crimes against Humanity', 17 B.C. Third World Law Journal (*TWLJ*) 171 (1997); R. S. Clark, 'Crimes against Humanity at Nuremberg', in G. Ginsburgs and V. N. Kudriavtsev (eds.), *The Nuremberg Trial and International Law* (Leiden/Boston: M. Nijhoff, 1990), p 177; L. Mansfield, 'Crimes against Humanity: Reflections on the Fiftieth Anniversary of Nuremberg and a Forgotten Legacy', 64 *Netherlands Journal of International Law* 293 (1995). For a more personal account of the Nuremberg Trial, see D. A. Sprecher, *Inside the Nuremberg Trial: A Prosecutor's Comprehensive Account* (Lanham: University Press of America, 1999); T. Taylor, *The Anatomy of the Nuremberg Trials: A Personal Memoir* (Boston/New York/Toronto/London: Little, Brown & Co., 1992), pp 78–115.

humanity had to be committed 'in execution of or in connection with any crime within the jurisdiction of the Tribunal'.[5] In practice, this requirement meant that, under the Charter, crimes against humanity had to be committed in the context of an armed conflict or military occupation, since both war crimes and crimes against peace were *de facto* linked to the war.[6] By contrast, it could not have been committed in peacetime or without some sort of connection with the war.

This limitation had important implications for the Nuremberg Tribunal's ability to prosecute crimes committed *before* the outbreak of the Second World War. Thus, despite the court's mandate over crimes committed 'before and during the war', crimes committed prior to 1939 became almost unprosecutable under the Charter.[7] A telling illustration is the case of Julius Streicher, who was indicted for his 'twenty-five years of speaking, writing and preaching hatred of the Jews'.[8] Although the judgment referred to Streicher's propaganda activities before the war, the Tribunal convicted him only in relation to crimes committed during the war.[9]

Adopted in December 1945, Control Council Law No. 10 expanded the definition of crimes against humanity contained in the IMT's Charter,[10] but contained no requirement of a temporal relationship between the perpetrator's acts and the

---

[5] Charter of the International Military Tribunal, annexed to Agreement for the Prosecution and Punishment of the Major War Criminals of the European Axis, London, 8 August 1945, Art. 6(c), 59 Stat. 1544, 1547, 82 UNTS 279, 288 ('*Nuremberg Charter*'). On the role and interpretation of the war nexus at Nuremberg, see B. van Schaack, 'The Definition of Crimes against Humanity: Resolving the Incoherence', 37 Columbia Journal of Trans-national Law (*CJTL*) 787 (1999) ('van Schaack, *Crimes against Humanity*').

[6] See Q. Wright, 'The Law of the Nuremberg Trial', 41 *AJIL* 38, 61 (1947); H. Lauterpacht, 'The Subjects of the Law of Nations', 64 *LQR* 97, 103 (1948).

[7] The IMT held that '[t]o constitute Crimes against Humanity, the acts relied on before the outbreak of war must have been in execution of, or in connection with, any crime within the jurisdiction of the Tribunal. The Tribunal is of the opinion that revolting and horrible as many of these crimes were, it has not been satisfactorily proved that they were done in execution of, or in connection with, any such crime. The Tribunal therefore cannot make a general declaration that the acts before 1939 were Crimes against Humanity within the meaning of the Charter, but from the beginning of the war in 1939 War Crimes were committed on a vast scale, which were also Crimes against Humanity [. . .]' (*Trial of Major War Criminals Before the International Military Tribunal, Nuremberg 14 November 1945–1 October 1946* (Nuremberg, 1947) ('*Trial of the Major War Criminals*')). According to Quincy Wright, the IMT's refusal to convict any of the accused for war crimes or crimes against humanity committed before 1 September 1939 seemed to stem from its 'prevailing disposition to give the defendants the benefit of any doubt' (Wright, *supra* n 6, p 62). See also van Schaack, *Crimes against Humanity*, p 804, n 71. Goldstein has noted, however, a few instances where the IMT has taken into consideration acts committed before the war when they were committed in connection with a war crime or with a crime against peace (A. Goldstein, 'Crimes against Humanity: Some Jewish Aspects', 1948 Jewish Yearbook of International Law (*JYIL*) 206).

[8] See *Trial of the Major War Criminals*, p 34.   [9] Ibid.

[10] Article II 1(c) of Control Council Law No. 10 reads as follows: '*Crimes against Humanity.* Atrocities and offences, including but not limited to murder, extermination, enslavement, deportation, imprisonment, torture, rape, or other inhumane acts committed against any civilian population, or persecutions on political, racial or religious grounds whether or not in violation of the domestic laws of the country where perpetrated. . . .' (Control Council Law No. 10, Punishment of Persons Guilty of War Crimes Against Peace and Against Humanity, 20 December 1945, 3 *Official Gazette of the Control Council for Germany* 50–55 (1946) ('*Control Council Law No. 10*')). See also Y. Dinstein, 'Crimes against Humanity', in J. Makarczyk (ed.), *Theory of International Law at the Threshold of the 21st Century: Essays in Honour of Krzysztof Skubiszewski* (The Hague: Kluwer, 1996), p 891.

war. However, in later trials, many courts acting pursuant to Control Council Law No. 10 many continued to require a nexus between the war and the acts of the accused.[11]

Later international instruments differed over the inclusion of the nexus requirement. In 1946, the United Nations adopted the *Affirmation of the Principles of International Law Recognized by the Charter of the Nuremberg Trial*, including the requirement of a nexus between crimes against humanity and crimes against peace or war crimes.[12] In contrast, the International Law Commission's (ILC) *Draft Code of Offences against the Peace and Security of Mankind* omitted the nexus requirement,[13] and the requirement did not reappear in any other international instrument.[14]

---

[11] See, e.g. 14 Ann. Dig. 100 (Die Spruchgerichte, 1947) (Stade): 'Article 6 of the Charter does limit Law No. 10 in another respect: the Charter requires a connection with a crime within the jurisdiction of the International Military Tribunal [. . .] The requirement of a connection with the war, therefore, refers only to adjectival law [. . .] Therefore a person could commit a crime against humanity before as well as after 1939. Acts committed before September 1, 1939, are not subject to punishment. But they remain crimes against humanity. In an individual case they can be taken into account with reference to the question whether the accused had knowledge of the participation of his organisation in criminal acts.' See also *United States v. Flick and Others*, US Military Tribunal sitting at Nuremberg, judgment of 22 December 1947, in *Law Reports of Trials of War Criminals*, VI, 1187–223 ('*Flick* case'). Other decisions, however, followed the letter of the law and did not require a war nexus between the crimes and the armed conflict. See, e.g. *Einsatzgruppen* case, *United States v. Alstötter and others*, US Military Tribunal sitting at Nuremberg, Judgment of 4 December 1947, in *Law Reports of Trials of War Criminals*, III, at 954–1201 ('*Alstötter and others (Justice)* case'). For a thorough review and appraisal of the decisions rendered under Control Council Law No. 10, see H. Meyrowitz, *La Répression par les Tribunaux Allemands des Crimes Contre l'Humanité et de l'Appartenance à une Organisation Criminelle en Application de la Loi no. 10 du Conseil de Contrôle Allié* (Paris: Pichon et Durand-Auzias, 1960); and *Law Reports of Trials of War Criminals*, XV, 136–38 (1949).

[12] UN General Assembly Res. 95(I), UN GAOR, 1st Sess., part 2, UN Doc. A/64/Add.1 (1946), p 188. Principle VI(c) defined crimes against humanity as '[m]urder, extermination, enslavement, deportation and other inhuman acts done against any civilian population, or persecutions on political, racial or religious grounds, when such acts are done or such persecutions are carried on in execution of or in connection with any crime against peace or any war crime' (*Principles of International Law Recognized in the Charter and the Judgement of the Nürnberg Tribunal: Texts and Comments*, 2 Yearbook of International Law Commission (YILC) 191, UN Doc. A/CN.4/SER.A/1950/Add.1 (1950) ('*Nuremberg Principles*')).

[13] *Report of the International Law Commission to the General Assembly*, UN GAOR, 9th Sess., Supp. No. 9, UN Doc. A/2693 (1954) ('*1954 ILC Report*'). Article 2, par 11 of the Draft Code of Offences against the Peace and Security of Mankind defined crimes against humanity as: 'Inhuman acts such as murder, extermination, enslavement, deportation or persecutions, committed against any civilian population on social, political, racial, religious or cultural grounds by the authorities of a State or by private individuals acting at the instigation or with the toleration of such authorities' (ibid., at 50). The comment to this Article stated that the nexus with another crime had been removed. The International Law Commission considered, however, that 'in order not to characterize any inhuman act committed by a private individual as an international crime, it was found necessary to provide that such an act constitutes an international crime only if committed by the private individual at the instigation or with the toleration of the authorities of a State' (ibid.).

[14] See, e.g. Convention on the Non-Applicability of Statutory Limitation to War Crimes and Crimes Against Humanity, General Assembly Resolution 2391, UN GAOR, 23rd Sess., Agenda Item 64, UN Doc. A/7342 (1968) ('Statutory Non-Applicability Convention').

Against this backdrop, it might seem somewhat strange that Article 5 of the ICTY Statute would reintroduce the requirement that crimes against humanity be 'committed in armed conflict'.[15] In 1995, counsel for the accused Duško Tadić argued that this requirement implied a nexus between the act of the accused and another crime within the jurisdiction of the ICTY as had been the case in Nuremberg. Any different interpretation of Article 5, counsel contended, would constitute '*ex post facto* law violating the principle of *nullum crimen sine lege*'.[16] The Appeals Chamber disagreed, stating in response that the requirement of a nexus between crimes against humanity and another crime was 'peculiar to the jurisdiction of the Nuremberg Tribunal' and had long ago been abandoned.[17] The Appeals Chamber added that customary international law 'may not require a connection between crimes against humanity and any conflict at all' and that 'the Security Council may have defined the crime in Article 5 more narrowly than necessary under customary international law',[18] without however infringing upon the *nullum crimen sine lege* principle.[19] The drafters of the Statute thus intended to reintroduce this element of the definition for the purposes of the ICTY only, the Appeals Chamber concluded.[20] When providing for a definition of crimes against humanity in the ICTY Statute, the Security Council did not seek to give a general definition of that concept as would apply in every context, but tried to specify

[15] The expression 'when committed in armed conflict' is translated as 'lorsqu'ils ont été commis au cours d'un conflit armé' in the French text of the ICTY Statute.

[16] *Tadić* Jurisdiction Decision, par 139.

[17] Ibid., par 140: 'Although the nexus requirement in the Nuremberg Charter was carried over to the 1948 General Assembly resolution affirming the Nuremberg principles, there is no logical or legal basis for this requirement and it has been abandoned in subsequent State practice with respect to crimes against humanity.' See also *Dragan Nikolić* Rule 61 Decision, par 26; *Kayishema and Ruzindana* Trial Judgment, par 127; *Akayesu* Trial Judgment, par 582. See also *Trial of Eichmann*, Israel, District Court of Jerusalem, Judgment of 12 December 1961, English translation in 36 International Law Reports (ILR), par 28, holding that the requirement of a link to an armed conflict only reflected a jurisdictional, not a substantive, limitation which limited the jurisdiction of the Nuremberg Tribunal to try crimes of this kind which were bound up with 'war crimes' or 'crimes against peace'. This is consistent with the House of Lords' view in the *Pinochet* case that the requirement contained in the Nuremberg Charter that a crime against humanity had to be somehow connected to another crime within the jurisdiction of the Tribunal, was at most a jurisdictional requirement, not an element of the crime. See *Regina v. Bow Street Stipendiary Magistrate and others, ex parte Pinochet Ugarte*, United Kingdom, House of Lords, Judgment of 24 March 1999 in [1999] 2 All ER.

[18] *Tadić* Jurisdiction Decision, par 141. See also *Tadić* Trial Judgment, par 627, holding that the inclusion of this requirement deviated from the development of the doctrine after the Nuremberg Charter; *Kupreškić* Trial Judgment, pars 577 and 581, stating that the link between crimes against humanity and any other crimes has disappeared under customary international law.

[19] The Appeals Chamber specifically referred to two international conventions regarding genocide and apartheid, both of which prohibit certain forms of crimes against humanity regardless of any connection to another crime or, for that purpose, to an armed conflict. See Genocide Convention; International Convention on the Suppression and Punishment of the Crime of Apartheid, adopted 30 November 1973, Arts. I–II, 1015 UNTS 243 ('Apartheid Convention'); see also Statutory Non-Applicability Convention, *supra* n 14, Art. 1, providing that crimes against humanity can be committed 'in time of war or in time of peace'; Inter-American Convention on Forced Disappearance of Persons, adopted 9 June 1994, Arts. IX–X; ICC Statute, *infra* n 40, Art. 7.

[20] See *Tadić* Jurisdiction Decision, par 141. See also *Nikolić* Rule 61 Decision, par 26.

from a factual point of view the categories of crimes against humanity with which the Tribunal would be concerned whilst underlining the fact that such crimes could be committed in both international and internal armed conflicts.[21]

The limitation is therefore purely temporal in character and presumes the existence of an armed conflict at the time and place relevant to the indictment,[22] but it does not mean that the crimes have to occur in the heat of battle or that they must be materially connected to the armed conflict.[23] However, this requirement would preclude the prosecution from charging any of the accused with crimes that might have been committed prior to the commencement of the hostilities. Once the existence of an armed conflict has been established, international humanitarian law, including the law on crimes against humanity, continues to apply beyond the scene of actual fighting and after the cessation of hostilities.[24]

And the accused need not be shown to have intended to participate in the armed conflict. As such, a nexus between the acts of the accused and the armed conflict is not an element of the required *mens rea*.[25] Unlike in the case of war crimes, there need not be a substantive relationship between his acts or conduct and the armed conflict.[26] Rather, the armed conflict requirement is satisfied simply by proof that there *was* an armed conflict – international or internal[27] – at the time and place relevant to the indictment.[28]

---

[21] See L. D. Johnson, 'Ten Years Later: Reflections on the Drafting', 2(2) *Journal of International Criminal Justice* 368, 372 (June 2004). See also V. Morris and M. Scharf, *The International Criminal Tribunal for Rwanda* (Irvington-on-Hudson: Transnational Publishers, 1998, 2 vols.) ('Morris and Scharf, *The Rwanda Tribunal*'), pp 202–204.

[22] *Tadić* Appeal Judgment, par 249; *Kupreškić* Trial Judgment, par 546. Only the acts of the accused, as opposed to the attack as a whole, need to be temporally and geographically contemporaneous with the armed conflict.

[23] *Tadić* Trial Judgment, par 632; *Vasiljević* Trial Judgment: 'This jurisdictional requirement requires the existence of an armed conflict at the time and place relevant to the indictment, but it does not necessitate any material nexus between the acts of the accused and the armed conflict.' See also *Kunarac* Appeal Judgment, par 83; *Tadić* Appeal Judgment, pars 249 and 251; *Kunarac* Trial Judgment, par 413; *Kupreškić* Trial Judgment, par 71.

[24] The temporal and geographic scope of armed conflict extends beyond the exact time and place of hostilities. See *Tadić* Jurisdiction Decision, par 70 ('International humanitarian law applies from the initiation of such armed conflicts and extends beyond the cessation of hostilities until a general conclusion of peace is reached; or, in the case of internal conflicts, a peaceful settlement is achieved. Until that moment, international humanitarian law continues to apply in the whole territory of the warring States or, in the case of internal conflicts, the whole territory under the control of a party, whether or not actual combat takes place there'); and *Tadić* Trial Judgment, par 632.

[25] *Tadić* Appeal Judgment, par 272.

[26] Ibid., pars 249 and 272: holding that a nexus between the acts of the accused and the armed conflict is actually *not* required. See also *Blaškić* Trial Judgment, par 71.

[27] *Kupreškić* Trial Judgment, paragraph 545. See also *Tadić* Jurisdiction Decision, pars 141–142; *Report of the Secretary-General Pursuant to paragraph 2 of Security Council Resolution 808* (1993) ('UN Doc. S/25704'), par 47, stating that 'crimes against humanity are aimed at any civilian population and are prohibited regardless of whether they are committed in an armed conflict, international or internal in character'.

[28] *Tadić* Appeal Judgment, pars 249, 251. This reading of Article 5 is reinforced by the several interpretative declarations made by Security Council members in the process of adopting Security Council Resolution 827. UN SCOR, 48th Sess., 3217th mtg. UN Doc. S/PV.3217 (prov. ed 1993),

10.2 ICTR requirement: 'National, political, ethnic, racial, or religious discrimination'

Unlike the ICTY, the Statute of the ICTR limits the Tribunal's jurisdiction to crimes against humanity that have been committed 'on national, political, ethnic, racial, or religious grounds'.[29] It is not at all clear why the Security Council felt that such a limitation should be placed upon the Tribunal's jurisdiction in relation to crimes against humanity.

As with the requirement contained in Article 5 of the ICTY Statute that the acts be 'committed in armed conflict', this limitation is purely jurisdictional in nature and does not add any elements to the definition of crimes against humanity.[30] The ICTR Statute thus circumscribes crimes against humanity more narrowly than customary international law would allow and also more narrowly than the ICTY Statute.[31]

The Appeals Chamber has held that this additional requirement does not mean that a discriminatory *mens rea* must be established for each and every crime against humanity prosecuted at the ICTR.[32] The opposite interpretation would have blurred (if not cancelled out) the difference between persecution and other categories of crimes against humanity. The requirement means that the attack on the civilian population itself must be discriminatory in nature[33] and that the acts committed against persons outside these discriminatory categories may nevertheless form part of the discriminatory attack 'where the act against the

at 11 (Statement of France), 16 (Statement of the United States), 19 (Statement of Great Britain), 45 (Statement of the Russian Federation). See also *Kupreškić* Trial Judgment, par 545 ('It is . . . sufficient for the purposes of Article 5 that the act occurred in the course or duration of any armed conflict'); and *Kunarac* Trial Judgment, par 413 ('The requirement that there exists an armed conflict does not necessitate any substantive relationship between the acts of the accused and the armed conflict whereby the accused should have intended to participate in the armed conflict. The Appeals Chamber has held that a nexus between the acts of the accused and the armed conflict is not required. The armed conflict requirement is satisfied by proof that there was an armed conflict at the relevant time and place.')

[29] See *Rutaganda* Trial Judgment, par 73; *Akayesu* Appeal Judgment, pars 467, 469. It is interesting to note that a limitation similar to this one had been suggested by the United States in relation to the Statute of the ICTY (see Letter dated 12 April from the Permanent Representative of the United States of America to the United Nations Addressed to the Secretary-General, UN Doc S/25575 (1993), reprinted in Morris and Scharf, *The Yugoslav Tribunal*, 451, 454). The American suggestion was not adopted.   [30] See, e.g. *Akayesu* Appeal Judgment, par 465; *Kajelijeli* Trial Judgment, par 877.
[31] See, generally, Morris and Scharf, *The Rwanda Tribunal*, pp 196–197.
[32] *Akayesu* Trial Judgment, pars 464–469, 595; *Bagilishema* Trial Judgment, par 81. With that statement, the Appeals Chamber ensured that 'persecution' would keep its specificity vis-à-vis other listed crimes against humanity as it would remain the only underlying offence for which a discriminatory *mens rea* must be established.
[33] See, e.g. *Akayesu* Trial Judgment, pars 464–469, 595; *Bagilishema* Trial Judgment, par 81. Article 3 of the ICTR Statute thus limits the Tribunal's competence to crimes against humanity committed in the context of a widespread or systematic attack upon a civilian population when this attack is directed against this population because of one of the five listed discriminatory purposes.

outsider [*sic*] supports or furthers or is intended to support or further the attack on the group discriminated against on one of the enumerated grounds'.[34] In view of the nature of the events in Rwanda in 1994, proof of such a discriminatory attack has not been difficult to establish.

This requirement does not imply that the victim of the crime charged against the accused was himself or herself a member of the – nationally, politically, ethnically, racially, or religiously distinct – individuals targeted by the attack as long as the acts committed against him or her were based on discrimination against the targeted individuals.[35] Thus, the murder of a moderate Hutu who is protecting a Tutsi could qualify as a crime against humanity if it is shown that his killing was based on discriminatory grounds vis-à-vis the Tutsis. For the same reasons, with the exception perhaps of the crime of persecution, the fact that the perpetrator was mistaken as to the national, political, ethnic, racial, or religious characteristics of his victim – that he wrongly believed the victim was Tutsi when he was actually Hutu – would not in principle preclude criminal liability.[36]

---

[34] *Semanza* Trial Judgment, par 331; *Kamuhanda* Trial Judgment, par 673 ('acts committed against persons outside the discriminatory categories need not necessarily fall outside the jurisdiction of the Tribunal, if the perpetrator's intention in committing these acts is to support or further the attack on the group discriminated against on one of the enumerated grounds'). See also *Rutaganda* Trial Judgment, par 74; *Kajelijeli* Trial Judgment, par 878; *Musema* Trial Judgment, par 209.

[35] *Kayishema and Ruzindana* Trial Judgment, par 131. Note that this logic is analogous to the ICTY's treatment of crimes against victims who, while not members of the targeted civilian population, assist that population or are otherwise closely connected to it.

[36] *Kayishema and Ruzindana* Trial Judgment, par 132, noting that the Prosecutor would have to satisfy the court in such a case that the perpetrator's belief as to the characteristics of the victim was 'objectively reasonable – based upon real facts – rather than being mere speculation or perverted deduction'. Such a standard is highly disputable. It means that failing such an 'objective reasonableness' as to the true identity of the victim, that is when the perpetrator should have realized that his victim was not a member of the group he thought he or she was a member of, he should be acquitted thereof. Instead, one should only consider the objective consequences of his acts on the basis of his belief as to the identity of the victim. In the case *Re P.*, Appellate Court, Judgment of 20 May 1948, Criminal Chamber 3/48, the victim's true identity was held to be irrelevant for purposes of crimes against humanity: if the perpetrator knows that his deliberately offensive conduct is related to the conditions existing in the [Nazi] State and set forth in law and that these are conditions of arbitrary and violent rule, if the perpetrator knows what suffering awaits the victim and what this means for humanity, and if he also knows that he is doing something reprehensible but nevertheless acts out a decision freely taken, he is very much responsible for an inhumane act (ibid., at p 7). It is also irrelevant whether the content of the denunciation – the fact that the victim is a political opponent, for instance – is true or not. See Decision of the District Court (Landgericht) Hamburg, 11 November, 1948 (*Justiz und NS-Verbrechen* II, p 499).

11

Chapeau Elements of Crimes against Humanity

What distinguishes a crime against humanity from an ordinary crime (or from other international crimes) is the requirement that it must have been committed in the context of a 'widespread or systematic attack against a civilian population'.[1] This requirement, which constitutes the *chapeau* or general requirements of crimes against humanity, must be seen as a whole and it sets out the necessary context in which the acts of the accused must be inscribed. For the purpose of discussion, it may be divided, however, into five sub-elements:[2]

(i)   an 'attack';
(ii) a link or 'nexus' exists between the acts of the accused and the attack;
(iii) the attack is 'directed against any civilian population';
(iv) the attack is 'widespread or systematic'; and
(v)   the perpetrator has the appropriate *mens rea*.

---

[1] See, generally, *Naletilić and Martinović* Trial Judgment, par 232; *Tadić* Trial Judgment, pars 618 and 626; *Kupreškić* Trial Judgment, par 543; *Blaškić* Trial Judgment, pars 201–214; *Kordić and Čerkez* Trial Judgment, pars 172–187; *Jelisić* Trial Judgment, pars 50–57; *Kunarac* Trial Judgment, par 410; *Krstić* Trial Judgment, par 482; *Kvočka* Trial Judgment, par 127; *Krnojelac* Trial Judgment, par 53; *Tadić* Appeal Judgment, pars 247–272; *Kunarac* Appeal Judgment, pars 82–105. In the jurisprudence of the ICTR, see e.g. *Akayesu* Trial Judgment, pars 563–584; *Musema* Trial Judgment, pars 199–211; *Rutaganda* Trial Judgment, pars 34–35; *Kayishema and Ruzindana* Trial Judgment, pars 119–134; *Akayesu* Appeal Judgment, pars 460–469; *Semanza* Trial Judgment, par 326. Article 3 of the ICTR Statute expressly uses the expression 'crimes [. . .] committed as part of a widespread or systematic attack against any civilian population'.

[2] *Kunarac* Appeal Judgment, par 85 (and references given therein); *Kunarac* Trial Judgment, par 410; *Vasiljević* Trial Judgment, par 28 and references cited therein; *Ntagerura* Trial Judgment, par 698.

11.1   The 'attack'

An 'attack' for the purpose of crimes against humanity is a course of conduct involving the commission of acts of violence.[3] The acts committed in the course of the attack (and which actually constitute that attack) can vary extensively both in gravity and in nature. From an evidential point of view, but for the acts of the accused, the acts that form part of the attack need not be shown to amount to any of the crimes provided for in the Statute.[4]

The concepts of 'attack' and that of 'armed conflict' are distinct and independent, and an 'attack' does not even require the use of armed force on the part of the attacker although it generally does in practice.[5] As the Appeals Chamber stated, 'the two – the "attack on the civilian population" and the "armed conflict" – must be separate notions, although of course under Article 5 of the Statute the attack on "any civilian population" may be part of an "armed conflict"'.[6] This distinction is a logical consequence of the fact that under customary international law crimes against humanity may be committed independently of an armed conflict.[7] Even if it were to occur in the context of an armed conflict, the attack could precede, outlast, or run parallel to the armed conflict.[8]

---

[3] *Kunarac* Trial Judgment, par 415; *Vasiljević* Trial Judgment, par 29 and references cited therein. The acts which form part of the attack need not, strictly speaking, be crimes in the sense that they need not amount to any of the offences listed in the Statute; only those acts prosecuted as crimes against humanity have to meet the requirement of this offence (ibid.). The Trial Chamber in *Kayishema and Ruzindana* described the *attack* as 'the event in which the enumerated crimes must form part' (*Kayishema and Ruzindana* Trial Judgment, par 122). The Trial Chamber in *Akayesu* gave a slightly different definition of the 'attack': 'The concept of "attack" may be defined as an unlawful act of the kind enumerated in Article 3(a) to (i) of the Statute, like murder, extermination, enslavement, etc.' (*Akayesu* Trial Judgment, par 581); see also *Kajelijeli* Trial Judgment, par 867; *Musema* Trial Judgment, par 205; *Rutaganda* Trial Judgment, par 70. The *Akayesu* Trial Chamber further held (without providing any authority for its assertion) that an 'attack' may be non-violent in character – like imposing a system of apartheid (ibid.). The author does not agree with the view that the establishment and maintenance of such a system of apartheid can be regarded as 'non-violent' or that, for that matter, any 'attack' within the meaning of crimes against humanity could be non-violent in the broad sense of the word. See also Rome Statute of the International Criminal Court, 17 July 1998, Art. 7, par 2, UN Doc. A/CONF.183/9 (1998) ('ICC Statute'): ' "Attack directed against any civilian population" means a course of conduct involving the multiple commission of acts referred to in paragraph 1 against any civilian population, pursuant to or in furtherance of a State or organizational policy to commit such attack.'   [4] *Kayishema and Ruzindana* Trial Judgment, par 122.

[5] See, e.g. *Kunarac* Appeal Judgment, par 86; *Tadić* Appeal Judgment, par 251; *Vasiljević* Trial Judgment, pars 29–30; *Stakić* Trial Judgment, par 623; *Vasiljević* Trial Judgment, par 30; *Kajelijeli* Trial Judgment, par 868; *Semanza* Trial Judgment, par 327; *Musema* Trial Judgment, par 205; *Rutaganda* Trial Judgment, par 70; *Akayesu* Trial Judgment, par 581.

[6] *Tadić* Appeal Judgment, par 251; *Kunarac* Appeal Judgment, par 86.

[7] *Tadić* Jurisdiction Decision, pars 140–141. In any case, a nexus between the acts of the accused and the armed conflict is *not* required. *Tadić* Appeal Judgment, pars 248 and 251.

[8] See ibid., pars 248, 251, and 142; *Kunarac* Appeal Judgment, par 86: 'Under customary international law, the attack could precede, outlast, or continue during the armed conflict, but it need not be a part of it'; *Vasiljević* Trial Judgment, par 30; *Blaškić* Trial Judgment, par 71; *Kupreškić* Trial Judgment, par 546; *Tadić* Jurisdiction Decision, par 69; *Naletilić and Martinović* Trial

An 'attack' carries a different meaning in the context of a crime against humanity than in the context of the laws of war.[9] Unlike the case in the laws of war, an attack for the purpose of the definition of crimes against humanity is not limited to the conduct of hostilities, but also covers the mistreatment of persons taking no active part in hostilities.[10] In addition, the attack, pursuant to the definition of crimes against humanity, need not be directed at the enemy (the other side, militarily speaking); it may also be directed against any civilian population, including any part of the attacking state's own population. Also, whereas an attack is an independent violation of the laws of war, an attack pursuant to the definition of crimes against humanity is merely the vehicle for the commission of crimes against humanity. In other words, the attack is not in itself a crime against humanity.

The concept of 'attack' is based in both regimes on a similar assumption, however: that war should be a matter between armed forces or armed groups and that the civilian population cannot be a legitimate target.[11] But an attack against a civilian population pursuant to the law of crimes against humanity does not necessarily imply a breach of the laws of war, especially if the crime takes place in peacetime. The converse is also true. A military operation is not necessarily an 'attack against a civilian population' simply because breaches of the rules of warfare occur or because it leads to civilian casualties, even heavy ones. To the extent, however, that a military operation can be shown to be aimed at or directed against a civilian population, one of the prerequisites is established for the commission of crimes against humanity. In that respect, the laws of war become a reliable legal yardstick to assess the nature of the military enterprise that led to, or was allegedly

---

Judgment, par 233. In the *Kunarac* Trial Judgment (par 420), the Trial Chamber wrote that 'the attack *must* be part of the armed conflict' (emphasis added). Considering the sources cited in the footnote to that sentence – in particular the reference to the Appeals Chamber's decision on that point – and its 'Findings' later on in that Judgment, it seems that the sentence should have read 'the attack *may* be part of the armed conflict'.

[9] *Kunarac* Trial Judgment, par 416. See also Protocol Additional I to the Geneva Conventions of 12 August 1949, and Relating to the Protection of Victims of International Armed Conflicts, 8 June 1977, Art. 49(1) ('Additional Protocol I') defining 'attacks' as 'acts of violence against the adversary, whether in offense or in defense'.

[10] *Kunarac* Appeal Judgment, par 86 ('the attack in the context of a crime against humanity is not limited to the use of armed force; it encompasses any mistreatment of the civilian population [. . .]'); *Kunarac* Trial Judgment, par 416.

[11] The laws of war assume that a civilian or a civilian population should never be targeted as such. The protection of civilians in time of armed conflict indeed constitutes the 'bedrock of modern humanitarian law' (*Kupreškić* Trial Judgment, par 521). See, e.g. ibid.: 'It is now a universally recognised principle, recently restated by the International Court of Justice, that deliberate attacks on civilians or civilian objects are absolutely prohibited by international humanitarian law.' See also ICJ, *Advisory Opinion in Response to the United Nations General Assembly Request concerning Legality of the Threat or Use of Nuclear Weapons*, ICJ Reports 1996, 8 July 1996, [1996] ICJ 226, par 78, noting that the protection of civilians and civilian objects in time of war and the distinction to be made between them and combatants, respecting military objectives, is one of the 'cardinal principles contained in the texts constituting the fabric of humanitarian law'. Further, the ICJ added that these fundamental rules bind all states because they constitute 'intransgressible principles of international customary law' (ibid.).

accompanied by, an attack upon the civilian population and whether or not that attack may be said to have been directed at a civilian population.[12] To the extent that crimes against humanity are committed in the course of hostilities, the laws of war will thus set the framework as to the *attackability* of a target and help determine the circumstances under which an attack can be said to have been directed against a civilian population.

The mere fact that the military operation breached either or both principles of distinction and proportionality does not conclusively determine that there was an 'attack' within the meaning of Article 5/3 of the ICTY/ICTR Statute, or that the attack was indeed directed against a civilian population. Before reaching such a conclusion, the court must be satisfied that the attack was directed *primarily* against the civilian population, and was not simply the consequence of an overzealous use of military power. This does not mean that, alongside the 'attack against a civilian population', there could not be a military operation that might pursue some other, possibly legitimate, military purpose. The attack would thus still be regarded as being primarily directed toward the civilian population if the court were satisfied that, in pursuance of a given – possibly legitimate – military purpose, a party to the conflict has specifically or indiscriminately targeted the civilian population, civilian buildings, or other places over which it wanted to gain military control.[13] Similarly, the fact that the armed forces pursued one legitimate military purpose does not exclude the possibility that they also sought some less justifiable goals, such as ethnically cleansing a given area by targeting its civilian population.[14] When assessing the nature of the military operation under consideration, one should bear in mind the admonition of the *Kupreškić* Trial Chamber, that the law of targeting is 'an area where the "elementary considerations

---

[12] The *Abella* case before the Inter-American Commission on Human Rights offers an interesting insight into the way in which the laws of war may set the framework of any discussion upon the legality of acts committed in the context of an armed conflict even where it is not that body of law which is being applied. This case concerned events which took place at a military barrack in Buenos Aires in 1989. On 23 January 1989, forty-two armed persons launched an attack on the La Tablada military base. The attack led to combat which lasted approximately thirty hours between the attackers and the Argentine military personnel which resulted in several deaths on both sides. In their complaint, the petitioners alleged that, after the fighting had ceased, state agents summarily executed several of the attackers and tortured a number of them. Petitioners also claimed that the armed forces used excessive force and illegal means in their retaking of the base, thereby violating several rules of international humanitarian law. The Argentine State denied that the law of armed conflict was applicable in the present case but it conceded that the retaking of the base amounted to a 'military operation'. Having found that the situation was not merely an 'internal disturbance', but an 'internal armed conflict' pursuant to common Article 3 of the Geneva Conventions, the Inter-American Commission on Human Rights held that in order to assess the nature and legality of the alleged breaches, it should have recourse to humanitarian law, and in particular to Additional Protocol II (*Abella v. Argentina*, Case No. 11.137, IACHR 1997, 13 April 1998, par 161 ('*La Tablada* case')).

[13] See, e.g. *Blaškić* Trial Judgment, pars 425–428, 573–579, 623–634, 676–678.

[14] See *Kunarac* Trial Judgment, par 416: 'The Defence submitted that the aim of the Serb aggression was to gain supremacy over the Muslims in the region. It is irrelevant that the Serb aggression also pursued military goals and the objective of territorial gain, because the criteria of "armed conflict" and "attack upon a civilian population" are not synonymous'.

of humanity . . ." should be fully used when interpreting and applying loose international rules'.[15] The Trial Chamber in this case applied this logic when assessing the nature and legality of repeated attacks on military objectives:

[I]t may happen that single attacks on military objectives causing incidental damage to civilians, although they may raise doubts as to their lawfulness, nevertheless do not appear on their face to fall foul per se of the loose prescriptions of Articles 57 and 58 [of Additional Protocol I] (or of the corresponding customary rules). However, in case of repeated attacks, all or most of them falling within the grey area between indisputable legality and unlawfulness, it might be warranted to conclude that the cumulative effect of such acts entails that they may not be in keeping with international law. Indeed, this pattern of military conduct may turn out to jeopardise excessively the lives and assets of civilians, contrary to the demands of humanity.[16]

Even though civilians may not be targeted or made the tactical objective of a military attack, civilian casualties will not necessarily render the attack illegal.[17] Nor will the presence of civilians render a target immune from attack. Collateral damages are a part of almost every military operation and are regarded as acceptable to the extent that precautions are taken so that the civilian casualties are not disproportionate to the anticipated military advantage.[18] Furthermore, when determining whether an attack upon a given civilian population took place, it is irrelevant that the other side also committed similar crimes against the enemy's civilian population.[19] Neither the *tu quoque* defence nor the 'reprisals' justification would legitimize an attack against a civilian population:

[I]n international law there is no justification for attacks on civilians carried out either by virtue of the *tu quoque* principle (i.e., the argument whereby the fact that the adversary is committing similar crimes offers a valid defence to a belligerent's crimes) or on the strength

---

[15] *Kupreškić* Trial Judgment, par 524.   [16] Ibid., par 526.

[17] See Additional Protocol I, Art. 57 stating that precautions must be taken with a view to sparing civilians, both in planning and carrying out the attack, and providing commanders with a 'check list' to ensure that the provisions for the protection of the civilian population are observed; ibid. Art. 57(2) requiring that commanders deciding on an attack: '(i) Do everything feasible to verify that the objectives to be attacked are [. . .] military [. . .]; (ii) Take all feasible precautions in the choice of means and methods of attack with a view to avoiding, and in any event to minimizing, incidental loss of civilian life, injury to civilians, and damage to civilian objects; (iii) Refrain from deciding to launch any attack which may be expected to cause incidental loss of civilian life, injury to civilians, damage to civilian objects, or a combination thereof, which would be excessive in relation to the concrete and direct military advantage anticipated'. Paragraph 5 of the same Article reiterates that 'no provision of this Article may be construed as authorizing any attacks against the civilian population, civilians or civilian objects' (ibid., Arts. 57(5), 58).

[18] For an interesting discussion of this issue, compare the *Final Report to the Prosecutor by the Committee Established to Review the NATO Bombing Campaign Against the Federal Republic of Yugoslavia,* 8 June 2000, with *United States: Department of Defense Report to Congress on the Conduct of the Persian Gulf War: Appendix on the Role of the Law of War,* 10 April 1992, reprinted in 31 *ILM* 612 (1992).

[19] See *Kunarac* Trial Judgment, par 580 ('As the Defence was reminded many times during the trial, the fact that the Muslim side may have committed similar atrocities against Serb civilians, an argument brought up *mutatis mutandis* by almost every Serb accused and Defence counsel before the Tribunal, is irrelevant in the context of this case'); *Kunarac* Appeal Judgment, par 87 ('when establishing whether there was an attack upon a particular civilian population, it is not relevant that the other side also committed atrocities against its opponent's civilian population. The existence of an

of the principle of reprisals. Hence the accused cannot rely on the fact that allegedly there were also atrocities committed by Muslims against Croatian civilians.[20]

In such a scenario, each attack against the other side's civilian population 'would be equally illegitimate and crimes committed as part of this attack could, all other conditions being met, amount to crimes against humanity'.[21] And evidence of an attack by the other party on the accused's civilian population may not be put forth by the accused unless it tends 'to prove or disprove any of the allegations made in the indictment'.[22]

The laws of war are not, however, the sole resource available to the court in identifying the existence of an attack against a civilian population for the purpose of establishing whether a crime against humanity has been committed. In the *Dragan Nikolić* case, for example, the Trial Chamber identified six factors relevant in determining *post facto* whether an 'attack' against the civilian population had taken place:[23] (i) whether there has been an authoritarian takeover of the region where the crimes have been committed; (ii) whether a new authoritarian power structure has been established; (iii) whether discriminatory measures, such as restrictions on bank accounts held by one group of citizens, or *laissez-passer* requirements have been imposed; (iv) whether summary arrests, detention, torture, and other crimes have been committed; (v) whether massive transfers of civilians to camps have taken place; and (vi) whether the enemy population has been removed from the area.[24]

The intensity of the attack upon the civilian population will generally decrease over time as the attacking forces achieve their goals and the number of potential victims goes down accordingly. However, an 'attack' may be said to last for as long as the acts of violence that make it up can be shown to be directed against the civilian population as a whole, rather than against specifically identified members of that population.

---

attack from one side against the other side's civilian population would neither justify the attack by that other side against the civilian population of its opponent nor displace the conclusion that the other side's forces were in fact targeting a civilian population as such', footnotes omitted); *Vasiljević* Trial Judgment, par 31.

[20] *Kupreškić* Trial Judgment, par 765. Interestingly, the Trial Chamber in *Kupreškić* held that, although such evidence may not be introduced if it does not tend to prove or disprove any of the allegations made in the indictment, such evidence may be allowed in order to disprove or counter specific prosecution evidence, notably to rebut the prosecution's allegations that there is a widespread or systematic attack against a given civilian population or that a certain group of people was being persecuted. See *Prosecutor v. Kupreškić*, IT-95-16-T, Decision on Evidence of the Good Character of the Accused and the Defence of *Tu Quoque*, 17 February 1999.

[21] *Kunarac* Appeal Judgment, par 87.

[22] *Kunarac* Appeal Judgment, par 88. This would be the case, for instance, the Appeals Chamber said, where the accused seeks 'to refute the Prosecutor's contention that there was a widespread or systematic attack against a civilian population. A submission that the other side is responsible for starting the hostilities would not, for instance, disprove that there was an attack against a particular civilian population' (ibid.)   [23] *Dragan Nikolić* Rule 61 Decision, par 27.

[24] Ibid. For a thorough factual description of what constitutes an 'attack', a descriptive account of the elements taken into consideration, and the difficulties of separating the attack from the contingencies of war, see e.g. *Kunarac* Trial Judgment, pars 570–575; *Kupreškić* Trial Judgment, pars 761–764; *Blaškić* Trial Judgment, pars 402–428.

An attack against a civilian population need not be very large in scale to meet the *chapeau* requirement. In the *Tadić* case, for example, the geographical area under consideration was 20 km in diameter; in the *Kunarac* case, it consisted of three relatively small municipalities of Eastern Bosnia; in *Rutaganda*, it was two prefectures; and, in the *Musema* case, it was made up of two communes in the Kibuye Prefecture.[25] On the other hand, the fact that there are many victims does not in itself constitute a sufficient indication that a population is being attacked.

Ultimately, the scope of the attack is essentially determined by what the Tribunal has identified as the 'targeted civilian population'. The Court's identification of that population, in turn, depends greatly upon the Prosecution's position as to the geographical area covered by the indictment. However, and despite the geographical constraint set by the Prosecution in its indictment, the Court must be satisfied, as a minimum, that the attack is directed against a 'population' rather than against a loosely connected group of individuals. The Prosecutor could not therefore restrict the geographical scope of the indictment to an area so small, or geographically so insignificant, that the attack could not be said to be targeting a 'population' as defined below.

In essence, the attack requirement appears to be a descriptive device that captures in one word a pattern of criminal activity, in the context of which the acts of the accused must have taken place to be regarded as crimes against humanity. To the extent that the acts of the accused can be sufficiently linked to that attack, they acquire a greater criminal dimension which sets them apart from purely domestic crimes and differentiates them from ordinary war crimes.

11.2 Nexus between the acts of the accused and the attack

Not all crimes committed during the attack constitute crimes against humanity; to count as a crime against humanity, a crime must form *part of* that attack.[26] As the Appeals Chamber put it, the acts of the accused must be 'part of' a pattern of widespread and systematic crimes directed against a civilian population.[27] This nexus requirement between the acts of the accused and the attack may be subdivided into two elements:[28]

(i) the commission of an act which, by its nature or consequences, is liable to have the effect of furthering the attack;

(ii) knowledge on the part of the accused that there is an attack on the civilian population and that his act is part of the attack.[29]

---

[25] For the indictments in each of these cases, see the ICTY and ICTR websites, www.un.org/icty and www.ictr.org.

[26] See *Kunarac* Trial Judgment, par 417. See also *Tadić* Appeal Judgment, pars 248 and 255; *Mrkšić et al.* Rule 61 Decision, par 30; *Kayishema and Ruzindana* Trial Judgment, par 135.

[27] *Tadić* Appeal Judgment, pars 248 and 255; *Kunarac* Appeal Judgment, par 99 ('The acts of the accused must constitute part of the attack').

[28] Ibid. and references cited therein; *Vasiljević* Trial Judgment, par 32.

[29] *Kunarac* Trial Judgment, par 418.

The first condition is that the acts of the accused must be objectively part of the attack in that, by their nature or consequences, they are liable to have the effect of furthering the attack.[30] For example, the *Kunarac* Trial Chamber held that such a nexus existed between the acts of the accused – which consisted of various forms of sexual violence, acts of torture, and enslavement against Muslim women and girls – and the attack against the Muslim civilian population of the Foča region, as the three accused not only knew of the attack but also perpetuated it by taking advantage of the situation thereby created.[31]

The perpetrator need not have committed a series of crimes for his acts to be part of the attack; a single act is sufficient in principle.[32] Neither is it necessary that there be many victims involved.[33] As such, however, a so-called 'isolated' act – the killing of a Bosnian Muslim by Croat nationalists in Geneva in 1993, or the killing of a Jew by local fascists in Bolivia during the Second World War – would not qualify as a crime against humanity because the act would be too far removed from the core of the attack to be said to constitute a part thereof.[34] According to the Appeals Chamber, 'a crime would be regarded as an "isolated act" when it is so far removed from that attack that, having considered the context and circumstances in which it was committed, it cannot reasonably be said to have been part of the attack.'[35]

As already discussed, the underlying offence need not have been committed in the heat of the attack for it to be sufficiently connected to the attack and to

---

[30] *Kunarac* Trial Judgment, par 418. *Tadić* Appeal Judgment, pars 248, 251, 271; *Kupreškić* Trial Judgment, par 550. This assessment will depend on the nature and apparent purpose of the attack and also upon the court's view as to the adequacy and impact of the criminal act in question upon the attainment of that purpose. In the course of a campaign of ethnic cleansing, for example, killings, rapes, terrorization of the population, and burning of houses are the sort of acts which will have the effect of furthering the attack upon the civilian population.

[31] See *Kunarac* Trial Judgment, par 592.

[32] *Tadić* Trial Judgment, par 649: 'Clearly, a single act by a perpetrator taken within the context of a widespread or systematic attack against a civilian population entails individual criminal responsibility and an individual perpetrator need not commit numerous offenses to be held liable. Although it is correct that isolated, random acts should not be included in the definition of crimes against humanity, that is the purpose of requiring that the acts be directed against a civilian *population* [. . .].' See also *Mrkšić et al.* Rule 61 Decision, pars 29–30; *Blaškić* Appeal Judgment, par 101.

[33] *Tadić* Trial Judgment, par 649. See also *Mrkšić et al.* Rule 61 Decision, pars 29–30.

[34] See *Kupreškić* Trial Judgment, par 550; *Blaškić* Appeal Judgment, par 101; *Naletilić and Martinović* Trial Judgment, par 234 and sources quoted therein. See also *D. C. (T. A.), Attorney-General v. Enigster, Yehezkel Ben Alish*, Israel, District Court of Tel Aviv, Judgment of 4 January 1951, in 5 *Pesakim Mehoziim* (1951–2) (in Hebrew; summary in English in 18 *ILR* 1951, English translation on file with the author) ('*Enigster* case'), noting that on 30 May 1945, the legal committee of the United Nations War Crimes Commission stated that '[i]solated offences d[o] not fall within the notion of crimes against humanity. As a rule systematic mass action, particularly if it was authoritative, was necessary to transform a common crime, punishable only under municipal law, into a crime against humanity, which thus became the concern of international law. Only crimes which either by their magnitude and savagery or by their large number or by the fact that a similar pattern was applied at different times and places, endangered the international community or shattered the conscience of mankind, warranted intervention of states other than that on whose territory the crimes had been committed or whose subjects has become their victims.'   [35] *Kunarac* Appeal Judgment, par 100.

constitute a crime against humanity.[36] And a crime which is committed before or after the main attack against the civilian population or away from it could still, if sufficiently connected, be part of that attack.[37] Generally, however, the attack will decrease in intensity over time and the number of criminal offences committed during that attack may vary from one place to another. A crime committed several months after the main bulk of criminal acts has been committed can still in principle be part of the attack if it can be sufficiently connected to the attack.[38] Likewise, a criminal act taking place in an otherwise peaceful village could amount to a crime against humanity if it can be shown to be part of the attack taking place in the broader geographical area under consideration.

Ultimately, in determining whether a particular conduct forms sufficient part of the attack upon the civilian population, the court will consider all the circumstances of the case, including the 'characteristics, aims, nature, and consequence' of the acts of the accused.[39]

11.3 'Any civilian population' as the primary object of the attack

The third element of the *chapeau* requires that the attack be 'directed against any civilian population'. Taken as a whole, this phrase further emphasizes the element of scale already apparent in the 'attack' requirement discussed above. However, each part of the phrase ('directed against', 'any', and 'civilian population') serves distinct, if related, functions.

---

[36] Ibid.: 'The acts of the accused must be part of the "attack" against the civilian population, but they need not be committed in the midst of that attack. A crime which is committed before or after the main attack against the civilian population or away from it could still, if sufficiently connected, be part of that attack'; *Kupreškić* Trial Judgment, par 550.   [37] *Kunarac* Appeal Judgment, par 100.
[38] See, e.g. *Kunarac* Trial Judgment, par 717, noting the continued detention and continuous rape and enslavement of Muslim women over several months. This principle drives the interpretation of the so-called 'denunciation' cases several of which took place immediately after the Second World War. In these cases, the 'attack' was described by courts as the 'despotic rule of violence of the Nazis' or the 'National Socialist system of violence and arbitrary rule'. Although the intensity of the attack abated over time in certain areas, many of the crimes committed at that stage were still sufficiently linked to this attack to qualify as crimes against humanity. The arson of one synagogue or the denunciation of one man for his alleged anti-Nazism sufficed in the eyes of the court to regard it as being linked to the Nazi attack upon certain sections of the population. See *Entscheidungen des Obersten Gerichtshofes für die Britische Zone in Köln*, StS 78/48, 9 November 1948: '[Denunciation is] intimately linked to the National Socialists' regime of violence and arbitrariness because, from the very outset, it clearly fitted into the organised campaign of persecution against all Jews and everything Jewish in Germany which all humanity not under the sway of National Socialism perceived as an assault and, although directed against this one victim only, became part and parcel of all the mass crimes committed during the persecution of Jews'. See also *1 Entscheidungen des Obersten Gerichtshofes für die Britische Zone in Strafsachen* 19 (1949); *2 Entscheidungen des Obersten Gerichtshofes für die Britische Zone in Strafsachen* 321–343 (1949).
[39] *Kajelijeli* Trial Judgment, par 866; *Semanza* Trial Judgment, par 326.

First, the phrase 'directed against' requires that the civilian population be the primary object of the attack, not just an incidental victim of the attack.[40] This requirement further ensures that the alleged crime generally will not be one particular act but, instead, part of a course of criminal conduct.[41]

Under customary international law, it is the overall attack, not the perpetrator's individual act, that must be shown to be directed against the civilian population.[42] The jurisprudence of the ICTY confirms this interpretation; the *Tadić* Appeals Chamber stated that it may be inferred from the words 'directed against any civilian population' in Article 5 of the Statute that it is the attack – 'a pattern of widespread or systematic crimes' – which needs to be directed against a civilian population, not the acts of the accused.[43] In order to determine whether the attack may be said to have been so directed, the Trial Chamber will consider, *inter alia*:[44]

the means and method used in the course of the attack, the status of the victims, their number, the discriminatory nature of the attack, the nature of the crimes committed in its course, the resistance to the assailants at the time and the extent to which the attacking force may be said to have complied or attempted to comply with the precautionary requirements of the laws of war. To the extent that the alleged crimes against humanity were committed in the course of an armed conflict, the laws of war provide a benchmark against which the Chamber may assess the nature of the attack and the legality of the acts committed in its midst.

That being said, the perpetrator only needs to have *intended* to inflict injury upon the victim(s) of his crime while *knowing* about the context in which his acts occurred. He need not have intended to injure the civilian population as a whole, nor does he need to have intended to direct the attack against that group of civilians or to 'destroy' it as this expression is understood in the definition of genocide.

Secondly, the term 'any' means that crimes against humanity can be committed against members of *any* civilian population regardless of their nationality,

---

[40] *Kunarac* Appeal Judgment, par 91; *Naletilić and Martinović* Trial Judgment, par 235; *Kunarac* Trial Judgment, par 421; see also *Dragan Nikolić* Rule 61 Decision, par 26.

[41] *Prosecutor v. Tadić*, IT-94-1-T, Decision on the Form of the Indictment, 14 November 1995, par 11. It should be emphasized once again that a single act, if not 'isolated', may amount to a crime against humanity. The attack directed against a civilian population will, on the other hand, be composed of a relatively great number of acts of violence, although some authors have suggested that one massive criminal act could amount to such an attack. See also *Kunarac* Trial Judgment, par 422.

[42] Article 3 of the ICTR Statute, for instance, talks about an '*attack* directed against' the civilian population, not about the *acts* or state of mind of the accused being so directed. See also UN Doc. S/25704, par 48 (emphasis added) ('[C]rimes against humanity refer to inhumane acts of a very serious nature, such as willful killing, torture or rape, committed *as part of* a widespread or systematic attack against any civilian population [. . .]'); and Article 7 of the ICC Statute which deals with crimes against humanity and which talks about 'acts [. . .] committed as part of a widespread or systematic attack directed against any civilian population' (ICC Statute, Art. 7). See, however, *Blaškić* Trial Judgment, par 208 and fn 401.

[43] *Tadić* Appeal Judgment, par 248. The *Kunarac* Trial Chamber also adopted this approach: 'The expression "directed against" specifies that in the context of a crime against humanity the civilian population is the primary object of the attack' (*Kunarac* Trial Judgment, pars 410, 421–422).

[44] *Kunarac* Appeal Judgment, par 91.

ethnicity, or any other distinguishing feature, whether they are of the same nationality as the perpetrator or of a different nationality, or whether they are stateless;[45] a crime against humanity could therefore in principle be committed against a state's own population if that state participates in the attack.[46]

Originally, the inclusion of the state's own population within the scope of crimes against humanity was the very *raison d'être* of this category of crimes. At the time of the Nuremberg Prosecutions, the concept of war crimes did not permit the punishment of criminal acts committed against a state's own population. For example, it would not have covered the German Jews killed or mistreated by the German state during the Second World War.[47] Under the current law, it is unnecessary to demonstrate that victims of crimes against humanity are linked to any particular side of the conflict.[48]

Thirdly, the inclusion of the expression 'civilian population' resulted from the desire to exclude isolated or random acts from the scope of crimes against humanity.[49] However, the term 'population' does not mean that the *entire* population of the geographical entity in which the attack is taking place (a state, a municipality, or another circumscribed location) must be subject to the attack.[50] It is sufficient to establish that the scale, methods, or resources involved demonstrate that the attack was indeed directed at the civilian population generally or indiscriminately rather than at some selected members of that population.[51] For example, the killing of only a select group of civilians – a number of political opponents to the regime – could not be regarded, in principle, as a crime against humanity; in such a case, no 'population' can be said to have been attacked.[52] Numerically, a large number of victims may be indicative that the population itself was being attacked, and this number

---

[45] See *Tadić* Trial Judgment, par 635.

[46] *Vasiljević* Trial Judgment, par 33. See also *Kunarac* Trial Judgment, par 423; *Tadić* Trial Judgment, par 635. See also *Sivakumar v. Canada (Minister of Employment and Immigration)* [1994] FC 433, acknowledging that crimes against humanity can be committed against both enemy populations as well as against a country's own nationals.   [47] Lord Wright, Foreword to *UN War Crimes Commission*, at p 193.

[48] *Kunarac* Trial Judgment, par 423.

[49] See *Tadić* Trial Judgment, par 648; *Kunarac* Trial Judgment, par 422. See also *UN War Crimes Commission*, p 193: '[T]he word population appears to indicate that a larger body of victims is visualised, and that single or isolated acts against individuals may be considered to fall outside the scope of the concept'.

[50] See *Kunarac* Appeal Judgment, par 90; *Vasiljević* Trial Judgment, par 34; *Kunarac* Trial Judgment, par 424; *Tadić* Trial Judgment, par 644; *Stakić* Trial Judgment, par 624; *Kajelijeli* Trial Judgment, par 875; *Bagilishema* Trial Judgment, par 80. Interestingly, comment fourteen to Article 20 of Part III of the 1994 ILC *Draft Code for an International Criminal Court* defined 'crimes against humanity' as 'inhumane acts of a very serious character involving widespread or systematic violations aimed at the civilian population *in whole or in part*' (emphasis added), setting a numerical reference akin to that used in the Genocide Convention. *Report of the International Law Commission*, 2 May–22 July 1994, UN GAOR, 46th Sess., Supp. No. 10, UN Doc. A/49/10 (1994) ('1994 ILC Report').   [51] *Kunarac* Appeal Judgment, par 90.

[52] It could be argued that the systematic elimination of prominent personalities in a civilian population may support a conclusion that the attack was directed at the population rather than at some individual members. It should be emphasized that contrary to what is the case with respect to genocide, the definition of crimes against humanity does not imply that the attacking side must intend to destroy the population being targeted. It may, for instance, simply want to expel it from a certain geographical area.

will be evidentially relevant to determine whether the attack might be regarded as either 'widespread' or 'systematic' as defined below (recalling that international law does not set any minimum quantitative threshold starting with which a crime may become a crime against humanity).[53]

For the present purpose, a 'population' may be defined as a sizeable group of people who possess some distinctive features that mark them as targets of the attack.[54] The 'population' must form a somewhat self-contained group of individuals, either geographically or as a result of other common features. A group of individuals randomly or fortuitously assembled – such as a crowd at a football game – could not be regarded as a 'population' under this definition.

Identifying the relevant population that has allegedly been attacked serves several purposes. First, the concept of population operates as a minimum standard for determining which group of people may in principle be targeted by an attack. The size of a population must be considered within the context of the attack as a whole. Consequently, the few inhabitants of a tiny hamlet[55] or of a detention centre[56] may not in principle constitute a 'population,' unless, for instance, the crimes committed against that small group of individuals is part of a broader criminal campaign. In this sense, identifying a specific population is another reflection of the element of scale inherent in a crime against humanity.

Secondly, determining the targeted population is also important in assessing the *breadth* or *systematic nature* of the attack. The civilian population that is being targeted by the attack and is said by the Prosecution to constitute a 'civilian population' relevant to the charges might itself constitute only a small part of a broader group of – civilian – individuals. Thus, if two distinct ethnic groups, Group *A* and Group *B*, live together in a given town, the civilian population of that town is *AB*, but the targeted civilian population may consist of members of the *B* group only. The civilian members of the *B* group could form the civilian population referred

---

[53] *Blaškić* Trial Judgment, par 207.

[54] *Kunarac* Trial Judgment, par 423. See also *Naletilić and Martinović* Trial Judgment, par 235: 'The term "population" in the meaning of Article 5 of the Statute does not imply that the entire population of a geographical entity in which an attack is taking place must be subject to the attack. The element is fulfilled if it can be shown that a sufficient number of individuals were targeted in the course of an attack, or that they were targeted in such a way as to satisfy the Chamber that the attack was in fact directed against a civilian population, and not only against a limited number of individuals who were randomly selected' (footnote omitted).

[55] See *Kupreškić* Trial Judgment, noting that most of the victims were the inhabitants of a tiny village in Central Bosnia.

[56] But see the *Enigster* case, par 13(B)(5): '[T]he detainees at the Greiditz camps and the detainees at the Paulbrick camp consisted of a civilian population in the sense of the aforementioned definition'. In the alternative, the court might have found that the fate of those civilian detainees was closely related to that of other civilians, notably those living in the area where those people were captured, and that they therefore only constituted one part of a larger 'civilian population'. Under such circumstances, the prosecution could establish that the detention and mistreatment reserved to the civilian detainees was just one aspect of a broader criminal campaign which covered a given area and which, for example, saw the burning of houses, the killing and rape of civilians, and other violence generally attached with such campaigns.

to in the definition of crimes against humanity. It is only in the context of this subgroup (the defined civilian population) that the other elements (e.g. widespread or systematic nature) must be considered. If, on the contrary, one regarded Group *AB* as the targeted group (the defined civilian population), of which Group *B* is only a tiny minority, it could prove impossible to show that the attack is widespread or even systematic if only Group *B* was targeted during the attack.[57]

Thirdly, the Prosecution need not show that a particular victim was a member of a specifically targeted group, such as a particular ethnic or religious group; it need only show that he or she was a civilian and was targeted as part of an attack against a civilian population.[58] Thus, if the perpetrator detained and tortured a German citizen for hiding a Jewish friend during the Second World War, he could be convicted of a crime against humanity even though the German citizen was not part of the targeted Jewish population. As noted above, it is unnecessary in particular to show that the victims of a crime against humanity were linked – politically, ethnically, or otherwise – to any particular side of the conflict.[59]

The fact that the perpetrator is himself part of the targeted population, or even has been targeted, does not preclude a conviction for crimes against humanity.[60] And a criminal against humanity need not identify with the persecuting authorities or their persecutory project.

Fourthly, in all of these cases, it is the innocent character of the 'civilian' population that mandates its protection under international humanitarian law.[61] As such, the concept of 'civilian population' should be broadly defined.[62] To meet the *chapeau* requirements, the targeted population must be of a *predominantly* civilian nature.[63] The presence of non-civilians within the population does not change its

---

[57] If one considered Group *AB* to be the targeted civilian population, the complete elimination of Group *B* could amount to genocide, but not to a crime against humanity, if the attack is neither widespread nor systematic *vis-à-vis* the larger Group *AB*.

[58] See *Akayesu* Trial Judgment, par 584: 'Inhumane acts committed against persons not falling within any one of the discriminatory categories could constitute crimes against humanity if the perpetrator's intention was to further his attacks on the group discriminated against on one of the grounds mentioned in Article 3 of the Statute. The perpetrator must have the requisite intent for the commission of crimes against humanity'. See also *UN War Crimes Commission*, p 138.

[59] See *Kunarac* Trial Judgment, par 423.

[60] For example, in the *Enigster* case, the court held that a Jewish individual, who was imprisoned by the Nazis, could be found guilty of crimes against humanity for his acts against other Jewish inmates. See section 12.8 below.

[61] See, e.g. Y. Sandoz, C. Swinarski, and B. Zimmermann (eds.), *Commentary on the Additional Protocols of 8 June 1977 to the Geneva Conventions of 12 August 1949* (Geneva: ICRC and M. Nijhoff, 1986) ('ICTR, *Commentary to the Additional Protocols*'), Additional Protocol I, Art. 50: 'In protecting civilians against the dangers of war, the important aspect is not so much their nationality as the inoffensive character of the persons to be spared and the situation in which they find themselves'.

[62] *Tadić* Trial Judgment, par 643; *Kupreškić* Trial Judgment, par 547; *Akayesu* Trial Judgment, par 582; *Rutaganda* Trial Judgment, par 72; *Musema* Trial Judgment, par 207; *Kayishema and Ruzindana* Trial Judgment, pars 127–129.

[63] *Tadić* Trial Judgment, par 638; *Kordić and Čerkez* Trial Judgment, par 180; *Kayishema and Ruzindana* Trial Judgment, par 128; *Kunarac* Trial Judgment, par 425; *Bagilishema* Trial Judgment, par 80.

character – provided that the non-civilians are not regular units in fairly large numbers.[64] However, the presence of a large number of soldiers or combatants within that population may, under certain circumstances, deprive the population of its civilian character.[65] The same is true regardless of the existence of an armed conflict at the time and place of the act. Absent an armed conflict, the civilian population relevant to the definition of crimes against humanity shall include all persons *except* those who have the duty to maintain public order and have the legitimate means to exercise force, such as the police.[66] In the case of an armed conflict, the civilian population shall include all persons who are neither members of the armed forces nor other legitimate combatants.[67] The notion of civilian population is therefore broadly similar (in time of war) to the definition contained in the laws of war.[68]

It would appear that the requirement that the attack must be directed against a civilian population excludes in principle that combatants, in the traditional sense of the term, could ever be regarded as victims of a crime against humanity.[69] The Appeals Chamber pointed out that the specific situation of the victim at the time of the acts is not *per se* determinative of his civilian or non-civilian status, in the

[64] *Kupreškić* Trial Judgment, par 549; *Tadić* Trial Judgment, pars 638, 643; *Kunarac* Trial Judgment, par 425; *Akayesu* Trial Judgment, par 582; *Kayishema and Ruzindana* Trial Judgment, par 128; *Jelišić* Trial Judgment, par 54. See also *Minister of Citizenship and Immigration v. Sumaida* [2000] 3 FC 66 (Can.); Additional Protocol I, Art. 50(3); *Final Report of the Commission of Experts for the Former Yugoslavia*, pars 77–78.

[65] *Blaškić* Appeal Judgment, 115. The number of soldiers and whether they are on leave are factors to be considered in that regard, the Appeals Chamber said (ibid.).

[66] See *Kayishema and Ruzindana* Trial Judgment, par 127.

[67] See *Akayesu* Trial Judgment, par 582; *Kunarac* Trial Judgment, par 425; *Blaškić* Trial Judgment, par 214. Reliance on the laws of war for the purpose of defining what constitutes a 'civilian' population is limited to situations where crimes have been committed in the context of armed hostilities. Although the categories of people being protected by the law against crimes against humanity might be substantially similar during both warfare and peacetime, a judge could not, in peacetime, rely upon the laws of war to define what is to be understood by 'civilian' since, under the laws of war, the concept of 'civilian' is defined negatively, in opposition to the concept of 'combatants'. In wartime the court would have to give a broad definition of civilians, placing weight on the inoffensiveness of the group and particular individuals (*Kayishema amd Ruzindana* Trial Judgment, par 127). In cases of low-intensity conflicts that do not amount to armed conflicts, the court could probably still draw from the laws of war to determine what individuals are protected. See, e.g. *Blaškić* Appeal Judgment, par 110 (where the Appeals Chamber relied upon the definition of 'civilian population' contained in Additional Protocol I). See also ICRC, *Commentary to the Additional Protocols*, at pp 611, 1451–1452.

[68] See, e.g. *Akayesu* Trial Judgment, par 582; *Rutaganda* Trial Judgment, par 70; *Musema* Trial Judgment, par 282.

[69] See *Kunarac* Trial Judgment, par 435. *Compare UN War Crimes Commission*, p 193 ('The words "civilian population" appear to indicate that "crimes against humanity" are restricted to inhumane acts committed against civilians as opposed to members of the armed forces [. . .]') with Judgment of 20 December 1985, Cass. crim., 1986 J.C.P. II G, No. 20,655, 1986 JDI at 146–147 holding that members of the French *Résistance* were to be regarded as civilians for the purpose of crimes against humanity since they had opposed the Nazi hegemonic policy which constitutes the central element of the definition of this offence under French law. Peaceful Jewish civilians and *résistants* were therefore equally protected by this prohibition to the extent that they were systematically persecuted in the name of the 'Nazi hegemonic policy'. See also *Kupreškić* Trial Judgment, par 568, suggesting that, in the case of persecution as a crime against humanity, the victims need not necessarily be civilians *sensu stricto*, but may also include military personnel; and *Sumaida v. Canada (Minister of Citizenship and Immigration)* [1997] C. C. L. 37 (Fed. T. D.) raising, but not answering, the question of whether 'terrorists' could be regarded as members of the 'civilian population' for the purpose of crimes against humanity.

sense that the fact that he was not armed or was not otherwise engaged in combat at the time, would not necessarily entitle him to the status of civilian for the purpose of this regime.[70] But an individual's past acts of resistance would not necessarily rule him out of the scope of this provision if, at the time of the acts, he has become a civilian.[71]

Although crimes committed against combatants cannot in principle constitute crimes against humanity, such acts may form part of the attack against the civilian population when these acts are a consequence, direct or indirect, of the targeting of the civilian population. The presence of a handful of soldiers defending an otherwise civilian village would not prevent the court from concluding that the assault on the village was an attack upon its civilian population, but there may come a point where a large military presence could exclude the conclusion that the target of the attack was the civilian population itself rather than those among them who could legitimately be attacked.[72]

Under the laws of war, a person should be considered a civilian as long as there is a doubt as to his or her status;[73] and as a group, the civilian population should never be attacked.[74] The Appeals Chamber noted, however, that the presumption of civilian status mentioned above is limited to the expected conduct of a member of the military in the course of a military operation. By contrast, and as already noted, when the latter's criminal responsibility is at stake, as it would be before the *ad hoc*

---

[70] See *Blaškić* Appeal Judgment, par 114 ('If he is indeed a member of an armed organisation, the fact that he is not armed or in combat at the time of the commission of crimes, does not accord him civilian status').

[71] *Blaškić* Trial Judgment, par 214, adopting the approach of the French Cour de Cassation in *Barbie* and holding that crimes against humanity 'do not mean only acts committed against civilians in the strict sense of the term but include also crimes against two categories of people: those who were members of a resistance movement and former combatants – regardless of whether they wore wear [*sic*] uniform or not – but who were no longer taking part in hostilities when the crimes were perpetrated because they had either left the army or were no longer bearing arms or, ultimately, had been placed *hors de combat*, in particular, due to their wounds or their being detained'. See *Federation Nationale des Deportes et Internes Resistants et Patriotes and Others V. Barbie*, Judgment of 6 October 1983, re-printed in 78 *International Law Reports* (1985) Such a position is somewhat doubtful and does not appear to be supported by much state practice. See also *Mrkšić et al.* Rule 61 Decision, 32; *Tadić* Trial Judgment, par 643; *Kordić and Čerkez* Trial Judgment, par 180; *Final Report of the Commission of Experts for the Former Yugoslavia*, par 78. In *Kupreškić*, when the Trial Chamber held that 'those actively involved in a resistance movement can qualify as victims of crimes against humanity', it apparently meant to say that the fact that someone operated as a resistance fighter *at some stage* does not disqualify him or her (see *Kupreškić* Trial Judgment, par 549). However, if he or she is killed while undertaking some act of 'resistance', he or she is not a 'civilian'. See *Jelišić* Trial Judgment, par 54, adding that Article 5 also covered people placed *hors de combat* when the crime was perpetrated.

[72] See *Blaškić* Appeal Judgment, pars 114–115.

[73] *Kunarac* Trial Judgment, par 426.

[74] Ibid. Additionally, if the attack takes place in the context of an armed conflict, customary international law obliges parties to the conflict to distinguish, at all times, between the civilian population and combatants, and obliges them not to attack a military objective if the attack is likely to cause civilian casualties or damage which would be excessive in relation to the military advantage anticipated. See, e.g. Additional Protocol I, Arts. 43, 48, and 57. As is stated by the Commentary to the two Additional Protocols of 1977 to the Geneva Conventions of 1949, the entire system established in The Hague in 1899 and 1907 and in Geneva from 1864 to 1977 is founded on this rule of customary law. See ICRC, *Commentary to the Additional Protocols*.

Tribunals, 'the burden of proof as to whether a person is a civilian rests on the Prosecution'.[75] The status of the victim (as a civilian or a combatant) may not therefore be presumed.

To obtain a conviction, the Prosecutor must therefore show that the accused knew or considered the possibility that the victim of his crime was a civilian.[76] In effect, the Prosecutor must demonstrate that the accused could not reasonably have believed that the victim was a member of the armed forces in the particular circumstances of the case.[77]

11.4 'Widespread or systematic' character of the attack

The attack is not only characterized by its target (the civilian population) but also by its scale – the *widespread* nature of the attack – or by its systematicity – the *systematic nature* of the attack. These adjectives are in the alternative: the requirement can therefore be satisfied by an attack that is *either* widespread *or* systematic.[78] Once it is satisfied that either requirement has been met on the evidence, the court is not obliged to consider whether the 'alternative qualifier' is also satisfied.[79] The inclusion of the widespread or systematic prong excludes isolated and random acts from the scope of crimes against humanity.[80]

The adjective 'widespread' connotes the large-scale nature of the attack and the number of victims.[81] In the Commentary to its *Draft Code of Crimes Against Peace and Security of Mankind*, the International Legal Commission states:

Inhumane acts [must] be committed on a large scale meaning that the acts are directed against a multiplicity of victims. This requirement excludes an isolated inhumane act committed by a perpetrator acting on his own initiative and directed against a single victim.[82]

---

[75] *Blaškić* Appeal Judgment, par 111.

[76] *Kunarac* Trial Judgment, par 435, holding that in case of doubt, a person shall be considered to be a civilian.   [77] Ibid.

[78] *Kunarac* Appeal Judgment, par 93 and references given therein; *Blaškić* Appeal Judgment, par 101. See also *Mrškić et al.*, *Tadić*, *Akayesu*, and *Kayishema* cases and as it appears in the Report of the Secretary-General (ICTY), the Statute of the International Criminal Court and the work of the ILC, the conditions of scale and 'systematicity' are not necessarily cumulative. This means that for inhumane acts to be characterized as crimes against humanity it is sufficient that one of the conditions be met. See also *Blaškić* Trial Judgment, par 207; *Rutaganda* Trial Judgment, pars 67–68; *Jelišić* Trial Judgment, par 53; *Kunarac* Trial Judgment, par 427; *Kordić and Čerkez* Trial Judgment, par 178; *Kajelijeli* Trial Judgment, pars 869–870 and decisions cited therein; *Kamuhanda* Trial Judgment, par 664. See also International Law Commission, 1991 ILC Report and 1996 ILC Report.

[79] *Kunarac* Appeal Judgment, par 93.   [80] See *Tadić* Trial Judgment, par 648.

[81] *Kunarac* Appeal Judgment, par 94; *Tadić* Trial Judgment, par 648; *Blaškić* Trial Judgment, par 206; *Vasiljević* Trial Judgment, par 35; *Stakić* Trial Judgment, par 625; *Akayesu* Trial Judgment, par 580 ('The concept of "widespread" may be defined as massive, frequent, large scale action, carried out collectively with considerable seriousness and directed against a multiplicity of victims'). See also *Kajelijeli* Trial Judgment, par 871 (defining 'widespread' as 'large scale, involving many victims'); *Semanza* Trial Judgment, par 329; *Niyitegeka* Trial Judgment, par 439; *Ntakirutimana* Trial Judgment, par 804; *Bagilishema* Trial Judgment, par 33; *Musema* Trial Judgment, par 204; *Rutaganda* Trial Judgment, par 69; *Kayishema and Ruzindana* Trial Judgment, par 123.

[82] See 1996 ILC Draft Code, pp 94–95. See also 1991 ILC Draft Code, p 266.

The attack may be widespread due to the cumulative effect of a series of acts, or, it has been suggested, due to the effect of a single act of extraordinary magnitude.[83]

The adjective 'systematic' refers to the organized nature of the acts of violence and the improbability of their random occurrence.[84] Patterns of crimes – the non-accidental repetition of similar criminal conduct on a regular basis – are the natural expression of such systematic occurrences.[85]

In practice, these two criteria will often overlap. A widespread attack targeting a large number of victims generally reflects patterns of similar abuses and often relies on some form of planning or organization.[86] Likewise, a systematic attack frequently has the potential, purpose, or effect of reaching many people. The following factors might be considered, *inter alia*, when establishing whether the attack was indeed widespread or systematic:

  (i) the number of criminal acts;
 (ii) the existence of criminal patterns;
(iii) the logistics and financial resources involved;
 (iv) the number of victims;
  (v) the existence of public statements or political views underpinning the events;
 (vi) the existence of a plan or policy targeting a specific group of individuals;
(vii) the means and methods used in the attack;
(viii) the inescapability of the attack;
 (ix) the foreseeability of the criminal occurrences;
  (x) the involvement of political or military authorities;
 (xi) temporally and geographically repeated and coordinated military operations which all led to the same result or consequences;
(xii) alteration of the ethnic, religious, or racial composition of the population;
(xiii) the establishment and implementation of autonomous political or military structures at any level of authority in a given territory;
(xiv) adoption of various discriminatory measures.

All but one of the Trial Chambers have found that the attack said to be relevant to the charges was both widespread and systematic.[87]

---

[83] See 1996 ILC Draft Code, pp 94–95, quoted in *Blaškić* Trial Judgment, par 206.

[84] See *Kunarac* Trial Judgment, par 429 ('[the phrase "systematic" refers to] the organised nature of the acts of violence and the improbability of their random occurrence'); *Kunarac* Appeal Judgment, par 94; *Vasiljević* Trial Judgment, par 35; *Stakić* Trial Judgment, par 625; *Blaškić* Appeal Judgment, par 101. See also *Akayesu* Trial Judgment, par 580 ('[Systematic means] thoroughly organised and following a regular pattern on the basis of a common policy involving substantial public or private resources'); *Blaškić* Trial Judgment, par 203; *Tadić* Trial Judgment, par 648; *Semanza* Trial Judgment, par 329; *Kamuhanda* Trial Judgment, par 665. See also 1991 ILC Draft Code, p 266 ('The systematic element relates to a constant practice or to a methodical plan to carry out such violations'); 1996 ILC Report, pp 94–95.   [85] *Kunarac* Trial Judgment, par 429; *Kunarac* Appeal Judgment, par 94.

[86] *Blaškić* Trial Judgment, par 207. See also *Jelišić* Trial Judgment, par 53.

[87] See, e.g. *Tadić* Trial Judgment, par 660; *Akayesu* Trial Judgment, par 652; *Kayishema and Ruzindana* Trial Judgment, par 576; *Rutaganda* Trial Judgment, par 417; *Jelišić* Trial Judgment,

The 'widespread' and 'systematic' nature of the attack are relative notions which depend upon how the targeted population has been defined.[88] Therefore, the court must first identify the population that has allegedly been attacked and, in light of the means, methods, resources used, and the result of that attack, ascertain whether the attack might indeed be said to have been either widespread or systematic.[89] The Appeals Chamber said that the consequences of the attack upon the targeted population, the number of victims, the nature of the acts, the possible participation of officials or authorities or any identifiable patterns of crimes, could be taken into account to determine whether the attack satisfies either or both requirements of a 'widespread' or 'systematic' attack *vis-à-vis* this civilian population.[90]

Only the attack, not the individual acts of the accused, must be widespread or systematic.[91] A single act, unless isolated, could therefore in principle be regarded as a crime against humanity.[92]

And there is no requirement under customary international law (nor under the Statutes of the Tribunals) that the acts in question have been committed as a result or as part of a plan or policy to commit them.[93] At most, the existence of a policy or plan may be evidentially relevant (for instance, to determining the 'systematic' character of the attack), but it is not a legal element of the definition of crimes against humanity.[94]

pars 56–57. The *Kunarac* Trial Chamber found that the attack was systematic, but did not determine whether it was also widespread (*Kunarac* Trial Judgment, par 578). It is unclear what the finding of the Trial Chamber in *Kordić and Čerkez* was on that point, but it seems that the Trial Chamber concluded that the attack was at least of a systematic sort. See *Kordić and Čerkez* Trial Judgment, pars 800 and 806. See also *Krstić* Trial Judgment, par 482.

[88] See *Kunarac* Trial Judgment, par 430; *Kunarac* Appeal Judgment, par 95.

[89] *Kunarac* Trial Judgment, par 430; *Kunarac* Appeal Judgment, par 95.

[90] Ibid., par 95.

[91] See, e.g. *Kunarac* Trial Judgment, par 430; *Kunarac* Appeal Judgment, par 96; *Blaškić* Appeal Judgment, par 101.

[92] *Kunarac* Appeal Judgment, par 96. See also *Kupreškić* Trial Judgment, par 550: 'For example, the act of denouncing a Jewish neighbour to the Nazi authorities – if committed against a background of widespread persecution – has been regarded as amounting to a crime against humanity. An *isolated* act, however – i.e. an atrocity which did not occur within such a context – cannot.' See also *Tadić* Trial Judgment, par 649; *Mrkšić et al.* Rule 61 Decision, par 30.

[93] See, e.g. *Kunarac* Appeal Judgment, par 98 and references cited therein; *Vasiljević* Trial Judgment, par 36; *Naletilić and Martinović* Trial Judgment, par 234; *Blaškić* Appeal Judgment, pars 100, 120, and 126; *Krnojelac* Trial Judgment, par 58; *Vasiljević* Trial Judgment, par 36: 'The Appeals Chamber has stated that neither the attack nor the acts of the accused need to be supported by any form of "policy" or "plan". There is nothing under customary international law which requires the imposition of an additional requirement that the acts be connected to a policy or plan'. (footnotes omitted); *Semanza* Trial Judgment, par 329; *Kajelijeli* Trial Judgment, par 872. Until the *Kunarac* Trial and then Appeal Judgment, there had been some discussion as to whether a 'plan or policy' was a requirement for crimes against humanity (see, for an extensive discussion of existing state practice on that point prior to those two decisions, Mettraux, *Crimes against Humanity*, pp 270–282).

[94] *Blaškić* Appeal Judgment, par 130; *Vasiljević* Trial Judgment, par 36; *Kunarac* Appeal Judgment, par 98; see also *Krnojelac* Trial Judgment, par 58; *Kordić and Čerkez* Trial Judgment, par 182; *Kunarac* Trial Judgment, par 432; *Kajelijeli* Trial Judgment, par 872.

11.5   Requisite state of mind or *mens rea*

In addition to proving intent to commit the underlying offence, the perpetrator must know that there is an attack on the civilian population and that his acts comprise part of that attack; or he must at least take the risk that his acts are part of the attack.[95] It suffices that, through the function he willingly accepted, he knowingly took the risk of participating in the implementation of that attack.[96] The accused need not know the specific details of the attack,[97] nor does he need to know that his acts are directed against the targeted population: 'It is the attack, not the acts of the accused, which must be directed against the target population and the accused need only know that his acts are part thereof.'[98]

Knowledge of the attack and the perpetrator's awareness of his participation therein may be inferred from circumstantial evidence, examples of which include the accused's position in the military or civilian hierarchy; his voluntary assumption of an important role in the broader criminal campaign; his participation in the violent takeover of enemy villages; his acts of capture, detention, rape, brutalization, or murder; his presence at the scene of the crime; his membership in a group involved in the commission of such crimes; his utterances and references to the superiority of his group over the enemy group; the extent to which the crimes were reported in the media; the scale of the acts of violence, and the general historical and political environment in which the acts occurred; and the consistency and predictability of his criminal acts.[99] These *indicia* of knowledge must be assessed as a whole.

[95] See *Kunarac* Trial Judgment, par 434; *Kunarac* Appeal Judgment, par 102; *Blaškić* Appeal Judgment, pars 124–127. See also *Tadić* Appeal Judgment, par 248; *Blaškić* Trial Judgment, pars 247, 251; *Tadić* Trial Judgment, par 659; *Kupreškić* Trial Judgment, par 556; *Kordić and Čerkez* Trial Judgment, par 185; *Naletilić* and *Martinović* Trial Judgment, par 237; *Stakić* Trial Judgment, par 626; *Kayishema and Ruzindana* Trial Judgment, par 134; *Niyitegeka* Trial Judgment, par 442; *Kajelijeli* Trial Judgment, par 880 and references made therein to other cases. See also *Regina v. Finta* [1994] S.C.R. 701, 706 (Can.): 'The mental element of a crime against humanity must involve an awareness of the facts or circumstances which would bring the acts within the definition of a crime against humanity [. . .] the *mens* rea requirement of both crimes against humanity and war crimes would be met if it were established that the accused was wilfully blind to the facts of circumstances that would bring his or her actions within the provisions of these offences'.

[96] *Blaškić* Trial Judgment, par 251. See also *Vasiljević* Appeal Judgment, par 30.

[97] See *Kunarac* Trial Judgment, par 434; *Kunarac* Appeal Judgment, par 102.

[98] Ibid., par 103.

[99] See *Tadić* Trial Judgment, par 657 ('While knowledge is thus required, it is examined on an objective level and factually can be implied from the circumstances'); *Blaškić* Appeal Judgment, par 126 ('knowledge on the part of the accused depends on the facts of a particular case; as a result, the manner in which this legal element may be proved may vary from case to case'); *Kayishema and Ruzindana* Trial Judgment, pars 133–134; *Blaškić* Trial Judgment, par 259.

Where such knowledge is established beyond reasonable doubt, the accused's motive for participating in the attack is in principle legally irrelevant to the question of his guilt.[100] A crime against humanity may be committed for purely personal reasons or for no apparent reasons,[101] and the accused may therefore be convicted even if his personal motive differed from the purposes underscoring the attack.[102] Indeed, the perpetrator need not even approve of the attack, nor of the associated criminal acts.[103]

[100] *Kunarac* Appeal Judgment, par 103: 'At most', the Appeals Chamber said, 'evidence that he committed the acts for purely personal reasons could be indicative of a rebuttable assumption that he was not aware that his acts were part of that attack'. (*Kunarac* Appeal Judgment, par 103). See also *Tadić* Appeal Judgment, pars 248–252. See, however, *Tadić* Appeal Judgment, Separate Opinion of Judge Shahabuddeen, pars 33–38. See also *K and P* case, where it is said that 'the offender [who had been charged with a crime against humanity] must act with low, abominable and inhumane motives' Decision of the District Court (Landegericht) Hamburg, 11 May 1948 (*Justiz und NS-Verbrechen* II, pp 491–497).

[101] Ibid. See also *Kunarac* Trial Judgment, par 433; *Kordić and Čerkez* Trial Judgment, par 187; *In Re P.*, Appellate Court, Judgment of 20 May 1948, Criminal Chamber 3/48, 8 (on file with the author): holding that 'a crime against humanity may also be committed for a totally private reason'; *Bamlaku v. Canada* [1998] 2 F.C.D 24, 140; *Tutu v. Canada* [1994] 74 F.C.D. 39.

[102] See *Vasiljević* Trial Judgment, par 37: 'when it comes to his criminal liability, the motives of the accused for taking part in the attack are irrelevant, and a crime against humanity may be committed for purely personal reasons' (footnote omitted). See also the *Enigster* case.

[103] *Kunarac* Appeal Judgment, par 103; *Kordić and Čerkez* Trial Judgment, par 185. Neither indifference to the fate of the victim nor abhorrence of the criminal acts being committed bears relevance to the determination of the perpetrator's *mens rea*. It should be noted that in certain situations, the accused may raise the defence of duress – for example, where the defendant's acts, though reprehensible, were carried out to protect his victims from greater harm. See *Erdemović* Appeal Sentencing Judgment, par 17; *Erdemović* Sentencing Judgment II par 12. See also *Yang v. Canada* [1999] 15 F.C.D 5, par 10: 'It does not seem to me that the applicant's mens rea is disproved by the fact that he may secretly have harboured ethical reservations about some of the activities in which he was engaged as part of his responsibilities as village head, a position that he had willingly assumed in the knowledge of what it entailed'. The requirement contained in the ICTR Statute that the attack must be based on discriminatory grounds does not signify that the accused must have acted with discriminatory intent, unless he was charged with persecution; it is the attack itself that must be discriminatory in character (see, e.g. *Akayesu* Appeal Judgment, pars 447–469; *Semanza* Trial Judgment, par 332). See also H. Arendt, *Eichmann in Jerusalem: A Report on the Banality of Evil* (London/New York: Penguin Books, 1977), pp 276–277.

12

Underlying Offences

The *chapeau* elements discussed above represent the general requirements which any criminal act must meet before qualifying as a crime against humanity. In addition, the underlying offence which forms the basis of the charges against the accused must be one of the acts listed in Article 5 and Article 3, respectively, of the ICTY and ICTR Statutes of the *ad hoc* Tribunals, namely:

(a) murder;
(b) extermination;
(c) enslavement;
(d) deportation;
(e) imprisonment;
(f) torture;
(g) rape;
(h) persecutions on political, racial and religious grounds;
(i) other inhumane acts.

The perpetrator need not bear principal responsibility for any of these offences to be found guilty of a crime against humanity; it is enough that he participated in any manner specified in Article 7 and Article 6 of the ICTY and ICTR Statutes.

The Tribunal has not expressly stated whether the list of underlying criminal offences contained in Article 5/3 of the Statutes is exhaustive. It is open to question whether a category of crimes against humanity recognized as such by customary international law but not explicitly listed in the Statute – if such a crime exists – could nevertheless be sanctioned by a Trial Chamber without this offence further satisfying the conditions of one of the underlying offences listed such as 'persecution' or 'other inhumane acts'.[1] In any case, neither Tribunal has sanctioned as a crime against humanity any conduct that did not come within the terms of one of the listed offences.

12.1　Murder

The first offence mentioned in the Statute as a crime against humanity is 'murder', the definition of which is similar to the definition of murder given above when charged as a serious violation of the laws or customs of war (sub-section 8.13.1 above); elements of that definition are also similar in substance to those of 'willful killing' pursuant to Article 2(a) of the ICTY Statute.[2] The only difference between them as far as their definitions are concerned relates to their distinct *chapeau* elements as required by, respectively, Article 5 and Article 3 of the ICTY and ICTR Statutes (crimes against humanity), Article 3 and Article 4 of the ICTY and ICTR Statutes (war crimes), and Article 2 of the ICTY Statute (grave breaches of the Geneva Conventions).

12.2　Extermination

'Extermination' consists first and foremost of an act or combination of acts which contributes to the killing of a large number of individuals.[3] Criminal responsibility for extermination therefore only attaches to those individuals responsible for a large number of deaths, even if their part therein was remote or indirect.[4] By contrast,

---

[1] An indication of the drafters' intention in that respect may be drawn from par 48 of the Secretary-General Report (ICTY). There, the Secretary-General held that crimes against humanity refer to inhumane acts of a very serious nature 'such as' wilful killing, torture or rape, committed as part of a widespread or systematic attack upon a civilian population, thereby making it relatively clear that its list was exemplary, not exhaustive. This interpretation is reinforced by the Secretary-General's reference in the same paragraph to the crime of 'enforced prostitution', which is not expressly mentioned in Article 5 of the Statute. Several crimes have already been recognized as crimes against humanity under customary international law (though not by the *ad hoc* Tribunals) without their being expressly mentioned in that list, e.g. forced disappearance. See Inter-American Convention on Forced Disappearance of Persons, OEA/Ser.P AG/doc.3114/94 rev. 1 (9 June 1994); General Assembly Resolution 47/133, 47 UN GAOR Supp. (No. 49) at 207, UN Doc. A/47/49 (1992). See also *Forti v. Suarez-Mason*, 694 F. Supp. 707 (N.D. Cal., 1988) recognizing that 'disappearance' was a crime under international customary law. Other offences may be strong contenders for the status of crimes against humanity and could possibly come within the jurisdiction of the Tribunals if the Chambers were satisfied that they are recognized as international offences under customary international law. See, e.g. ICC Statute, Art. VII discussing the concept of 'enforced prostitution'.

[2] See, e.g. *Stakić* Trial Judgment, par 631.

[3] *Vasiljević* Trial Judgment, par 229; *Niyitegeka* Trial Judgment, par 450; *Nahimana* Trial Judgment, par 1061. Whereas the *Vasiljević* Trial Chamber appears to have undertaken an extensive review of state practice and other relevant precedents in relation to that offence, the definition of 'extermination' given in earlier cases often appears to be based on not much more than the Chamber's intuition as to the meaning of that expression (see, e.g. *Kayishema and Ruzindana* Trial Judgment, par 144; *Akayesu* Trial Judgment, pars 591–592; *Kayishema and Ruzindana* Trial Judgment, par 645, and the almost complete absence of authority in support of the Chambers' findings).

[4] *Vasiljević* Trial Judgment, par 227; *Ndindabahizi* Trial Judgment, par 479; *Kamuhanda* Trial Judgment, pars 691–692.

responsibility for one or for a limited number of such killings is insufficient in principle to constitute an act of extermination.[5] Acts of extermination must, therefore, be collective in nature rather than directed towards singled-out individuals.[6] Contrary to genocide, however, the offender need not have intended to destroy the *group* or part of the group to which the victims belong.[7] The large or massive scale of the factual basis that must underlie the crime of extermination is what differentiates it from murder.[8] Contrary to what might have been said in a number of unsupported decisions,[9] a single killing may not therefore qualify as extermination.[10]

In effect, based on this method of evaluation, any act or combination of acts could amount to extermination if it contributed, whether immediately or eventually, directly or indirectly, to the unlawful physical elimination of a large number of individuals.[11]

[5] *Vasiljević* Trial Judgment, par 227. The Trial Chamber in that case noted that the suggestion made by the *Kayishema and Ruzindana* Trial Chamber (par 147) that a limited number of killings or even one single killing could qualify as extermination if it forms part of a mass killing event was completely unsupported 'thereby very much weakening the value of its ruling as a precedent. No state practice has been found by this Trial Chamber which would support the finding of the *Kayishema and Ruzindana* Trial Chamber' (*Vasiljević* Trial Judgment, n 586).

[6] Ibid., par 227; *Kamuhanda* Trial Judgment, par 694. The Trial Chamber in *Vasiljević*, noted that it was not aware of cases which, prior to 1992, used the phrase 'extermination' to describe the killing of fewer than 733 persons (the same number of victims referred to as 'extermination' in existing case law). The Trial Chamber made it clear, however, that it did not thereby suggest that a lower number of victims would disqualify that act as 'extermination' as a crime against humanity, nor did it suggest that such a threshold must necessarily be met (*Vasiljević* Trial Judgment, n 587). See also *Ndindabahizi* Trial Judgment, par 479 (unsupported).

[7] *Vasiljević* Trial Judgment, par 227. See also *Krstić* Trial Judgement, par 49 ('In extermination, the killing may be indiscriminate'); *Musema* Appeal Judgment, pars 366–367. The perpetrator may not even have known the identity of any of the victims. In such a case, however, he must have known *generally* who his victims were, and that they were marked for elimination. The International Law Commission made it clear that the crime of 'extermination' was distinct from genocide. In particular, '[e]xtermination covers situations in which a group of individuals who do not share any common characteristics are killed' (1996 ILC Report, 97).

[8] *Akayesu* Trial Judgment, par 591: '[e]xtermination is a crime which by its very nature is directed against a group of individuals. Extermination differs from murder in that it requires an element of mass destruction which is not required for murder.' See also *Krstić* Trial Judgment, par 501; *Kajelijeli* Trial Judgment, pars 891–893; *Semanza* Trial Judgment, par 340; *Ntakirutimana* Trial Judgment, pars 813–814; *Nahimana* Trial Judgment, par 1061; *Niyitegeka* Trial Judgment, par 450; *Vasiljević* Trial Judgment, pars 216–229 which reviews extensively existing authority on that point. See also the unsubstantiated and unexplained suggestion of the *Nahimana* Trial Chamber whereby that distinction between murder and extermination would not merely be one concerned with the number of victims, but also with the manner in which they were targeted (*Nahimana* Trial Judgment, par 1062).

[9] See, e.g. *Kayishema and Ruzindana* Trial Judgment, par 645.

[10] See, e.g. *Kajelijeli* Trial Judgment, par 893: 'a single killing or a small number of killings do not constitute an extermination. In order to give practical meaning to the charge as distinct from murder, there must in fact be a large number of killings'; see also *Niyitegeka* Trial Judgment, par 450.

[11] *Kayishema and Ruzindana* Trial Judgment, pars 146–147, holding that '[t]he "creation of conditions of life that lead to mass killing" is the institution of circumstances that ultimately causes the mass death of others'. See also IMT Judgment pars 478, 480, 494–495; *Rutaganda* Trial Judgment, par 84 holding that an omission could also constitute extermination; and *Stakić* Trial Judgment, par 640, noting that an assessment of whether the element of 'massiveness' implicit in that crime is met depends on a case by case analysis of all relevant circumstances.

Furthermore, an act of extermination does not only include participation in mass killings, but also arguably participation in the planning of these killings.[12] Egon Schwelb suggested that the drafters of the Nuremberg Charter included the crime of extermination in order to 'bring the earlier stages in the organization of a policy of extermination under the action of the law'.[13] By focusing on the planning of the killing, the court may thus consider as extermination acts which would be too remote to constitute complicity to homicide.[14]

Despite an apparently unsupported suggestion by the *Krstić* Trial Chamber that an act of extermination must destroy a 'numerically significant part of the population',[15] there appears to be no requirement under customary international law that the murderous enterprise must impact or bring about the destruction of a specified proportion of a targeted population.[16] Indeed, there is no precedent nor any authority that supports the *Krstić* requirement.[17] It appears that the *Krstić* Trial Chamber mistakenly combined one element of the *chapeau* (a 'civilian population') with the definition of one underlying offence (extermination).[18] Such a requirement would blur the distinction between genocide and extermination, creating a dangerous gap in the protection afforded by international humanitarian law.[19]

Concerning the requisite *mens rea* for that offence, the Prosecution must establish that the offender intended to kill a large number of individuals, or to inflict grievous bodily harm, or to inflict serious injury, in the reasonable knowledge that such act or omission was likely to cause death as in the case of murder. In addition, the accused must also be shown to have known of the vast scheme of collective murders and have been willing to take part therein.[20] As

---

[12] *Kayishema and Ruzindana* Trial Judgment, par 146, holding that in such an event, the Prosecutor must establish a nexus between 'the planning and the actual killing'.

[13] E. Schwelb, 'Crimes against Humanity', (1946) *BYIL*, pp 178, 192.

[14] See, e.g. ibid., p 192.   [15] *Krstić* Trial Judgment, pars 502–503.

[16] *Blaškić* Trial Judgment, par 207, n 1148, quoting approvingly that 'neither international texts nor international and national case-law set any threshold starting with which a crime against humanity is constituted'.

[17] Ibid. The conclusions of the *Krstić* Trial Chamber in that respect seem to be *exclusively* based on the ICC definition of the offence. The ICC Statute, as already pointed out, although useful in determining the *opinio juris* of state parties *at the time when they adopted the Statute*, is not *per se* customary international law. See *Furundžija* Trial Judgment, par 227; *Kunarac* Trial Judgment, n 1210. It should also be noted that the ICC Statute was adopted *after* the facts which were the basis of the Judgment in the *Krstić* case, raising some question as to the law which was in force *at the time when the crimes were committed*.

[18] The reference in the *chapeau* to a 'civilian population' purports to underline the scale of the attack of which the crime of the accused – extermination, for instance – is only one, possibly little, part and it sets the context within which the acts of the accused take place. As stated above, the 'civilian population' is the object of the 'attack', not the victim of individualized crimes of the accused.

[19] See *Musema* Trial Judgment, par 366, noting the conceptual difference between extermination and genocide.

[20] *Vasiljević* Trial Judgment, pars 228–229, referring to the IMT Judgment in respect of Saukel, p 114 and in respect of Fritzsche, p 126; and par 229; *Semanza* Trial Judgment, par 341; *Stakić* Trial Judgment, par 641. The perpetrator must have acted intentionally. Recklessness or gross negligence is

opposed to persecution pursuant to Article 5(h) of the ICTY Statute and Article 3(h) of the ICTR Statute, however, the Prosecution need not demonstrate that the accused acted on any discriminatory grounds.[21] Also, Trial Chamber II of the ICTY noted that 'the ultimate reason or motives – political or ideological – for which the offender carried out the acts [of extermination] are not part of the required *mens rea* and are, therefore, legally irrelevant'.[22]

The Prosecution must only prove that the perpetrator intended to kill the individual victim, with knowledge of the larger murderous context. As such, the perpetrator's motive in selecting his victims is legally irrelevant.

12.3   Enslavement

Enslavement is defined as the 'exercise of any or all of the powers attaching to the right of ownership over a person'.[23] The *actus reus* of enslavement is the exercise of those powers, and the *mens rea* is the intentional exercise of such powers.[24] Under this definition, indicators of enslavement include control and ownership;[25] the restriction or control of an individual's autonomy, freedom of choice, or freedom of movement; and, often, the accruing of some gain to the perpetrator.[26] The consent or free will of the victim is absent.[27]

The offence of enslavement under Article 5 of the ICTY Statute and Article 3 of the ICTR Statute is the same substantively as the offence of slavery under Article 3 of the ICTY Statute.[28] Their respective *chapeau* elements differ, however.

---

therefore insufficient: *Kamuhanda* Trial Judgment, par 696; *Stakić* Trial Judgment, par 642; *Kajelijeli* Trial Judgment, par 894, noting that Trial Chambers had suggested otherwise in the previous cases and that they had failed to provide any authority in support of their position; and *Semanza* Trial Judgment, par 1098. See, also, *Krstić* Trial Judgment, par 495 which concludes (but does not support its conclusion) that the state of mind required for both murder and extermination is essentially similar.

[21] *Vasiljević* Trial Judgment, par 228.   [22] Ibid.

[23] *Kunarac* Trial Judgment, par 539; *Krnojelac* Trial Judgment, par 350.

[24] Ibid.; *Kunarac* Trial Judgment, par 540.

[25] See ibid., par 542.

[26] Evidence of 'enslavement' includes the control of someone's movement, control of physical environment, psychological control, measures taken to prevent or deter escape, use of force, threat of force or coercion, duration of the constraining measures, assertion of exclusivity subjection to cruel treatment and abuse, control of sexuality and forced labour. See *Kunarac* Trial Judgment, par 543; *Krnojelac* Trial Judgment, par 359.

[27] See *Kunarac* Trial Judgment, par 120: 'The "lack of resistance or the absence of a clear and constant lack of consent during the entire time of the detention" cannot be interpreted as a sign of consent. Lack of consent is not an element of the crime of enslavement.'

[28] According to the *Krnojelac* Trial Judgment: 'although not enumerated under Article 3, slavery may still be punishable under that Article if the four requirements specific to Article 3 [. . .] are met' (par 351). See also ibid., par 356; *Kunarac* Trial Judgment, par 523. See above sub-section 8.13.5.

12.4 Deportation and forcible transfer

The definition of that underlying offence is identical to the definition of the similarly named offences ('deportation' and 'forcible transfer') provided for under Article 2 of the ICTY Statute (and, arguably, under Article 4 ICTR Statute).[29]

12.5 Imprisonment

For the purposes of the Tribunals, imprisonment is defined as the arbitrary 'deprivation of liberty of the individual without due process of law'.[30] The crucial factors in the court's assessment of the arbitrariness of the deprivation of liberty are the existence of a valid legal justification for the deprivation of liberty, and the respect given to fundamental procedural rights of the detained person.[31] The *ad hoc* Tribunals have primarily used the laws of war to assess the arbitrary nature of wartime imprisonment,[32] but they also draw upon elements of human rights law, particularly in order to assess the existence of a proper legal justification for the deprivation of liberty, and the guarantee of the due process rights of the accused.[33]

But 'imprisonment' as a crime against humanity is not limited to situations which would otherwise amount to 'unlawful confinement' as understood under Article 2(g) of the ICTY Statute.[34] In fact, any form of arbitrary physical deprivation of liberty of an individual, if serious enough,[35] may in principle constitute

[29] See above, Chapter 7, Let (g) – unlawful deportation or transfer or unlawful confinement of civilians (Article 2 (g) ICTY Statute).

[30] *Kordić and Čerkez* Trial Judgment, par 302.

[31] Ibid. See also *Ntagerura* Trial Judgment, pars 702 and 728, where the Trial Chamber suggests that the Prosecution must establish that this detention is taking place against the will of the detained person and not, for instance, in order to protect him or her from harm.

[32] See *Kordić and Čerkez* Trial Judgment, par 303, referring in particular to the following elements: (i) civilians have been detained in contravention of Article 42 of Geneva Convention IV, they are detained without reasonable grounds to believe that the security of the detaining power makes it absolutely necessary, and (ii) the procedural safeguards required by Article 43 of Geneva Convention IV are not complied with in respect to detained civilians, even where initial detention may have been justified.

[33] Reliance upon human rights law for the purpose of defining international criminal offences is of limited and ambivalent assistance. See G. Mettraux, 'Using Human Rights Law for the Purpose of Defining International Criminal Offences: The Practice of the International Criminal Tribunal for the Former Yugoslavia', in R. Roth and M. Henzelin (eds.), *Le Droit pénal à l'épreuve de l'internationalisation* (Paris: LGDJ, Geneva: Georg, Brussels: Bruylant, 2002), 183 et seq.

[34] *Krnojelac* Trial Judgment, par 111.

[35] *Ntagerura* Trial Judgment, pars 702 ('It is not every minor infringement of liberty that forms the material element of imprisonement as a crime against humanity; the deprivation of liberty must be of similar gravity and seriousness as the other crimes enumerated as crimes against humanity [. . .] in Article 3(a) to (i) [of the ICTR Statute]') and 728.

imprisonment if they meet the following requirements:[36]

(i) an individual is deprived of his or her liberty;

(ii) the deprivation of liberty is imposed arbitrarily, that is, no legal basis can be invoked to justify the deprivation of liberty;[37]

(iii) the act or omission by which the individual is deprived of his or her physical liberty is performed by the accused or a person or persons for whom the accused bears criminal responsibility with the intent to deprive the individual arbitrarily of his or her physical liberty or in the reasonable knowledge that his act or omission is likely to cause arbitrary deprivation of physical liberty.

'For the purpose of Article 5(e) [ICTY Statute]', Trial Chamber II of the ICTY said, 'the deprivation of an individual's liberty is arbitrary if it is imposed without due process of law', that is, 'if no legal basis can be called upon to justify the initial deprivation of liberty'.[38] Furthermore, the legal basis for the initial deprivation of liberty must apply throughout the period of imprisonment:[39] 'If at any time the initial legal basis ceases to apply, the initially lawful deprivation of liberty may become unlawful at that time and be regarded as arbitrary imprisonment.'

As noted above, the requisite *mens rea* for that offence consists of an intent to deprive an individual arbitrarily of his or her physical liberty or in the reasonable knowledge that his act or omission is likely to cause arbitrary deprivation of physical liberty.

12.6   Torture

The definition of 'torture' as a crime against humanity is identical, but for the *chapeau* elements, to the definition of torture as a war crime (Article 3 and Article 4 of the ICTY and ICTR Statutes) as defined above (see sub-section 8.13.3).

---

[36] *Krnojelac* Trial Judgment, pars 112 and 115; *Kordić and Čerkez* Trial Judgment, par 303; *Naletilić and Martinović* Trial Judgment, par 642.   [37] *Krnojelac* Trial Judgment, par 115.

[38] Ibid., pars 113–114. The Trial Chamber in *Krnojelac* also noted that deprivation of liberty could be arbitrary because of the manner in which it was effectuated: 'The Trial Chamber notes that arbitrariness of imprisonment pursuant to Article 5(e) may further result from an otherwise justified deprivation of physical liberty if the deprivation is being administered under serious disregard of fundamental procedural rights of the person deprived of his or her liberty as provided for under international law. Basic procedural guarantees are, for instance, provided for in Articles 9 and 14 of the ICCPR. In addition, Article 43 of Geneva Convention IV, enshrines basic procedural rights of civilians who are detained on the legal basis of Article 42 of the same Convention. Article 43 entitles interned protected persons to have, *inter alia*, the internment reconsidered as soon as possible by an appropriate court or administrative board, and, in case that the internment is maintained, to have it periodically, re-considered. With regard to the case before it, however, the Trial Chamber sees no need to elaborate on this aspect, since the Prosecution and the Defence case focused on the allegation of the initial unlawfulness of the imprisonment of the non-Serbs' (*Krnojelac* Trial Judgment, par 115, n 347).

[39] Ibid., par 114; *Ntagerura* Trial Judgment, par 702.

12.7   Rape

The definition of 'rape' as a crime against humanity is identical in its elements to 'rape' charged as a war crime.[40] Only the *chapeau* elements will vary according to the provision pursuant to which it is being charged.

12.8   Persecutions on political, racial, or religious grounds

The *Kupreškić* Trial Chamber defined persecution as '[t]he gross or blatant denial, on discriminatory grounds, of a fundamental right, laid out in international customary or treaty law, reaching the same level of gravity as the other acts prohibited in Article 5.'[41] Fundamentally, the crime consists of three elements:

(i)   the occurrence of a discriminatory act or omission;[42]
(ii) a discriminatory basis for that act or omission on one of the listed grounds;[43] and
(iii) the intent to cause, and the resulting infringement of, an individual's enjoyment of a basic or fundamental right.[44]

Persecutory acts can take many forms and do not require any link to other crimes enumerated elsewhere in the Statute.[45] They can consist of acts enumerated in other sub-clauses of Article 5, of acts mentioned elsewhere in the Statute, or of acts not explicitly mentioned anywhere in the Statute.[46] According to the *Tadić*

---

[40] See above, sub-section 8.13.2.
[41] *Kupreškić* Trial Judgment, par 621. See also, e.g. *Tadić* Trial Judgment, pars 694 and 697; *Kvočka* Trial Judgment, pars 184–205; *Ruggiu* Trial Judgment, par 21.
[42] See, e.g. *Tadić* Trial Judgment, par 694; *Kupreškić* Trial Judgment, par 615; *Blaškić* Trial Judgment, par 218; *Kordić and Čerkez* Trial Judgment, par 195; *Krstić* Trial Judgment, par 535; *Kvočka* Trial Judgment, par 184; *Krnojelac* Trial Judgment, par 431; *Naletilić and Martinović* Trial Judgment, par 634.
[43] The act must be based on political, racial, or religious grounds and the perpetrator must have intended his acts to be based on one of these grounds.
[44] *Tadić* Trial Judgment, par 715. See also *Kordić and Čerkez* Trial Judgment, par 189; *Krstić* Trial Judgment, pars 533–538.
[45] See, e.g. *Tadić* Trial Judgment, par 709; *Kupreškić* Trial Judgment, par 614; *Blaškić* Trial Judgment, par 233; *Kordić and Čerkez* Trial Judgment, par 193; *Semanza* Trial Judgment, pars 347–350.
[46] See, e.g. *Kupreškić* Trial Judgment, pars 604–605 and 614–615, holding that persecution can involve 'a variety of other discriminatory acts, involving attacks on political, social, and economic rights' (*Naletilić and Martinović* Trial Judgment, par 635 and references cited therein). See also *Tadić* Trial Judgment, pars 699–710. For suggestions as to the acts which, though not enumerated anywhere in the Statute, could nevertheless qualify as persecutory acts within the meaning of Article 5 of the Statute, see, *inter alia*, 1991 ILC Report, p 268 and 1996 ILC Report, p 98. The Nuremberg Tribunal considered the following acts, among others, to amount to persecution: discriminatory laws limiting the offices and professions open to Jews, restrictions placed on their family life and their right to citizenship, the creation of ghettos, the plunder of their property and the imposition of collective fines (*Tadić* Trial Judgment, pars 704–706 quoting the IMT Judgment).

Trial Chamber, persecution encompasses a variety of acts, including, *inter alia*, those of a physical, economic, or judicial nature, which violate an individual's right to equal enjoyment of his or her basic rights.[47] The underlying conduct may consist in a series of acts or in a single act,[48] 'as long as this act or omission discriminates in fact and is carried out deliberately with the intention to discriminate on one of the listed grounds'.[49]

Due to the principle of *nullum crimen sine lege*, there must be some clearly defined limits on the scope of those persecutory acts that can amount to a crime against humanity.[50] In particular, the persecutory acts must be of the same gravity as the other offences listed in Articles 5/3 of the ICTY/ICTR Statutes.[51] 'It is not the case', the ICTY Appeals Chamber noted, 'that any type of act, if committed with the requisite discriminatory intent, amounts to persecutions as a crime against humanity.'[52] This test will only be met by 'gross or blatant denials of fundamental human rights'. An act that may not appear comparable in terms of gravity to the other acts enumerated in Article 5 might still reach the required level of gravity if it had or was likely to have had an effect similar to that of the other acts because of the context in which it was undertaken.[53] For example, the act of denouncing one's neighbour might not automatically seem as serious as an act of murder or torture unless the neighbour who was denounced to the authorities was a Jew hiding from the Nazis

---

[47] *Tadić* Trial Judgment, par 710. The *actus reus* of persecution may assume different forms and does not necessitate a physical element (*Kupreškić* Trial Judgment, par 568; *Krnojelac* Trial Judgment, par 433). Because of the principle of legality, however, the Prosecution must charge 'particular acts amounting to persecution rather than persecution in general' (*Krnojelac* Trial Judgment, par 433).

[48] See ibid.; *Kupreškić* Trial Judgment, par 624; *Blaškić* Appeal Judgment, par 135.

[49] *Vasiljević* Trial Judgment, par 113.

[50] *Kordić and Čerkez* Trial Judgment, pars 192 and 194: 'In order for the principle of legality not to be violated, acts in respect of which the accused are indicted under the heading of persecution must be found to constitute crimes under international law at the time of their commission.' See also *Kupreškić* Trial Judgment, par 618.

[51] See *Krnojelac* Appeal Judgment, pars 199 and 221; *Blaškić* Appeal Judgment, pars 135–141, 143–159; *Kordić and Čerkez* Trial Judgment, pars 195–196; *Kupreškić* Trial Judgment, pars 618–619, 621; *Krnojelac* Trial Judgment, par 434; *Stakić* Trial Judgment, par 736, noting that the gravity of the act in question should not be assessed in isolation, but in the overall context in which it occurred; *Deronjić* Sentencing Judgment, par 118. Acts or omissions listed under other sub-paragraphs of Article 5 of the ICTY Statute and Article 3 of the ICTR Statute are by definition serious enough (see *Krnojelac* Trial Judgment, par 434).

[52] *Blaškić* Appeal Judgment, par 139.

[53] See *Kordić and Čerkez* Trial Judgment, par 199, emphasizing the unique nature of the crime of persecution as a crime of cumulative effect; *Kupreškić* Trial Judgement, par 615. See also *Krnojelac* Trial Judgement, par 434: 'When invoking this test, acts should not be considered in isolation but rather should be examined in their context and with consideration of their cumulative effect. Separately or combined, the acts must amount to persecution, though it is not required that each alleged underlying act be regarded as a violation of international law. When invoking this test, acts should not be considered in isolation but rather should be examined in their context and with consideration of their cumulative effect. Separately or combined, the acts must amount to persecution, though it is not required that each alleged underlying act be regarded as a violation of international law' (footnotes omitted).

and knew what his fate once denounced was likely to be.[54] Acts of persecution cannot therefore be evaluated in isolation, but must be considered in their context by looking at their cumulative effect.[55]

A comprehensive list of persecutory acts has never been compiled, but the offence generally includes acts that cause physical and mental harm, infringe upon individual freedom,[56] or result in the seizure or destruction of property.[57] The Tribunals have identified, *inter alia*, the following acts as persecution: participation in attacks on civilians, including indiscriminate attacks on cities, towns, and villages, as well as the seizure, collection, segregation, and forced transfer of civilians to camps, calling-out of civilians, beatings, and killings; acts of torture or rape and other forms of sexual assault; murder, imprisonment, and such attacks on property as would constitute a destruction of the livelihood of a certain population; destruction or wilful damage to religious and cultural buildings; or the destruction and plunder of property where serious enough, either by reason of its magnitude or because of the value of the stolen property or the nature and extent of the destruction; unlawful detention of civilians, deportation or forcible transfer of civilians, and serious bodily and mental harm or other serious inhumane treatment of civilians.[58] In *Nahimana*, the Trial Chamber held that instances of 'hate speech' could under certain circumstances amount to persecution.[59] In the *Kupreškić* case, the Trial Chamber concluded that the 'deliberate and systematic killing of Bosnian Muslim civilians' as well as their 'organized detention' could constitute acts of persecution.[60] The Trial Chamber also found that the comprehensive destruction of Bosnian Muslim property could amount to persecution.[61] The court emphasized, however, that the destruction of certain types of property, such as a car, may not have a severe enough impact on the victim to qualify as a crime against humanity, even if the destruction is committed on discriminatory

---

[54] *Kupreškić* Trial Judgment, par 550: '[I]n certain circumstances, a single act has comprised a crime against humanity when it occurred within the necessary context.'

[55] Ibid., par 622.

[56] *Blaškić* Trial Judgment, par 233; *Kupreškić* Trial Judgment, par 615.

[57] *Blaškić* Trial Judgment, pars 218–234. See also *Kordić and Čerkez* Trial Judgment, par 198.

[58] Ibid.; *Stakić* Trial Judgment, pars 747–773; *Deronjić* Sentencing Judgment, pars 119–123; *Kvočka* Trial Judgment, pars 186–190; *Naletilić and Martinović* Trial Judgment, pars 633–715, considering whether the following conduct may constitute persecution: unlawful confinement and detention; conditions of detention; forcible transfer and deportation; torture, cruel treatment and wilfully causing great suffering; killings in the detention centres; murder; unlawful labour and human shields; plunder; destruction of property. See also *Blaškić* Appeal Judgment, pars 143–159; *Nikolić* Sentencing Judgment, par 104 (and footnote 148 of that judgment).

[59] *Nahimana* Trial Judgment, pars 1072–1084. The same Trial Chamber distinguished between the crime of 'incitement' ('which is defined in terms of intent') and the crime of 'persecution' ('[which] is defined also in terms of impact'). 'It is not provocation to cause harm. It is itself the harm. Accordingly, [in the case of persecution] there need not be a call to action in communications that constitute persecution. For the same reason, there need be no link between persecution and acts of violence' (ibid., par 1073). There may be a degree of overlap, however, between the crime of persecution and direct and public incitement to commit genocide where the underlying conduct consists in the expression or propagation of ethnic hatred (ibid., par 1077).

[60] *Kupreškić* Trial Judgment, par 629.   [61] Ibid., pars 630–631.

grounds.[62] In *Kordić and Čerkez*, the Trial Chamber held that attacking cities, towns, and villages, digging trenches, using hostages and human shields, committing wanton destruction and plundering, and destroying and damaging religious or educational institutions may also qualify.[63] Yet, the *Kordić and Čerkez* Trial Chamber also held that encouraging and promoting hatred, or the dismissal or removal of individuals from their place of employment, did not rise to the required level of gravity.[64]

There is no need for a discriminatory policy or plan to commit such crimes.[65] It would appear, furthermore, that the acts and conduct of the accused must not only be *intended* to discriminate, but that they must have 'discriminated in fact'.[66] If an accused acts with intent to discriminate against his victim on a particular ground but, for some reason (e.g. where he is mistaken as to the – political, racial, or religious – identity of the victim) he fails to actually act discriminatorily, his acts may not in principle amount to 'persecution'.

---

[62] Ibid., par 631.   [63] *Kordić and Čerkez* Trial Judgment, pars 202–207.

[64] Ibid., pars 208–210. The Trial Chamber reached this conclusion by pointing out first that the act of encouraging or promoting hatred did not appear anywhere in the Statute, did not reach the level of gravity generally required for a crime against humanity and, furthermore, had not acquired the status of a criminal offence under international criminal law. To convict the accused for such an act would violate the principle of legality (ibid., par 209). The Trial Chamber did not envisage the possibility of considering these acts in the broader context of, or together with, the other persecutory acts with which the accused was charged. But see the Trial Chamber's statement with respect to the act of dismissing and removing individuals from government on a vast scale (ibid., par 210).

[65] *Krnojelac* Trial Judgment, par 435 ('There is no requirement under persecution that a discriminatory policy exist or that, in the event that such a policy is shown to have existed, the accused has taken part in the formulation of such discriminatory policy or practice by a governmental authority'); *Vasiljević* Trial Judgment, par 248. The Trial Chamber in *Kupreškić* further held that even if the acts are part of a discriminatory policy, it is not necessary to show that the accused has taken part in the formulation of this policy or practice by a governmental authority (*Kupreškić* Trial Judgment, par 625). See, however, the unsupported assertion in *Kordić and Čerkez* Trial Judgment, par 220.

[66] *Krnojelac* Trial Judgment, pars 431–432; *Stakić* Trial Judgment, par 733. The *Krnojelac* Trial Chamber said that '[a]lthough the Statute [of the Tribunal] does not expressly require that the discrimination take place against a member of the targeted group, this is a necessary implication of the occurrence of an act or omission on a discriminatory basis' (ibid., par 432). See also *Vasiljević* Trial Judgment, par 249 ('The definition of persecution requires an act or omission that is in fact persecutory'); and *Krnojelac* Appeal Judgment, par 200, where the Appeals Chamber said that it had 'to determine whether the acts committed [by the accused] *were indeed discriminatory* and whether they were committed with discriminatory intent'; emphasis added). This requirement does not exclude the possibility that the victim not be a member of the group which the accused intends to discriminate against, if the victimization of that person is intentional (and that he or she is not mistaken as to the status of that person) and that his or her victimization does indeed result in – political, racial, or religious – discrimination (see *Naletilić and Martinović* Trial Judgment, par 636). Contrary to the suggestion of the *Naletilić and Martinović* Trial Chamber, this finding does not contradict the finding of the *Krnojelac* Trial Chamber concerning the mistaken victimization of an individual where he or she is mistaken for a member of a particular – political, racial, or religious – group (see *Naletilić and Martinović* Trial Judgment, n 1572). In the case of a mistaken belief as to the status of the victim, no discrimination results *in fact* and it may not constitute persecution; by contrast, where someone who may not be identifiable by reason of his – political, racial, or religious – status but whose killing or mistreatment may further the – political, racial, or religious – agenda of the accused, in such a case his or her victimization could very well amount to persecution (see, e.g. *Stakić* Trial Judgment, par 826).

The persecutory *mens rea*, consisting of a discriminatory intent based on political, racial, or religious grounds,[67] is the distinctive feature of the crime of persecution[68] and is 'an indispensable legal ingredient of [a crime against humanity] only with regard to those [underlying] crimes for which this is expressly required, that is, for Article 5(h), concerning various types of persecution'.[69]

This discriminatory intent might be inferred from the general discriminatory nature of an attack 'as long as, in view of the facts of the case, circumstances surrounding the commission of the alleged acts substantiate the existence of such intent'.[70] In other words, such a state of mind may never be presumed, not even where the acts take place in the context of a discriminatory attack on a given civilian population. In addition, it is not a requirement of the crime of persecution that it must be accompanied by a persecutory plan or policy.[71] Nor does the accused need to be shown to have possessed a 'persecutory', as opposed to 'discriminatory', intent.[72]

Any one of three discriminatory grounds – political, racial, or religious – may form a sufficient basis for persecution.[73] The fact that the accused might have intended to discriminate on more than one basis, or in relation to another non-listed basis in addition to one of those provided for, would not negate the fact that he possessed the required state of mind.[74] While the intent of the accused to discriminate against the victims need not even be the primary intent with respect to his conduct, 'it must be a significant one'.[75]

That special discriminatory state of mind will aggravate, all things being equal, the crime that forms the basis of the charges and make it a particularly reprehensible

---

[67] See, e.g. *Kupreškić* Trial Judgment, par 633; *Blaškić* Trial Judgment, par 235; *Kordić and Čerkez* Trial Judgment, par 211; *Kvočka* Trial Judgment, pars 194–198; *Nahimana* Trial Judgment, par 1073. There is no requirement that the acts be accompanied by a discriminatory policy.

[68] *Kordić and Čerkez* Trial Judgment, par 212; *Naletilić and Martinović* Trial Judgment, par 638 and references cited therein. If mere knowledge of the discriminatory grounds, as opposed to actual intent to discriminate, was a sufficient *mens rea* for persecution it would eviscerate the distinction between persecution and the other enumerated crimes against humanity and would dilute the gravity of persecution as a crime against humanity (ibid., par 217). Further, '[s]tretching notions of individual *mens rea* too thin may lead to the imposition of criminal liability on individuals for what is actually guilt by association, a result that is at odds with the driving principles behind the creation of this International Tribunal' (ibid., par 219).

[69] *Tadić* Appeal Judgment, par 305. The Trial Chamber in *Kordić and Čerkez* held that the discriminatory grounds comprised a special intent, a 'heightened' *mens rea* which consists of removing individuals from the society in which they live alongside the perpetrators, or eventually from humanity itself (*Kordić and Čerkez* Trial Judgment, pars 211–220).

[70] *Krnojelac* Appeal Judgment, par 184; *Blaškić* Appeal Judgment, par 164.

[71] Ibid., par 165.

[72] Ibid.: 'the Trial Chamber was correct when it held at paragraph 235 of the Trial Judgment that the *mens rea* for persecution "is the specific intent to cause injury to a human being because he belongs to a particular community or group" '.   [73] *Tadić* Trial Judgment, par 713.

[74] See, e.g. *Nahimana* Trial Judgment, par 1071 ('the group against which discriminatory attacks were perpetrated can be defined by its political component as well as its ethnic component.')

[75] *Krnojelac* Trial Judgment, par 435. Concerning the existence of personal motives and the fact that such motives would not exclude a finding that the acts were sufficiently connected to the attack on a civilian population, see *Tadić* Appeal Judgment, par 252. See also *1 Entscheidungen des Obersten Gerichtshofes für die Britische Zone in Strafsachen* 19 (1949): 'The law refers only to objective affiliation with the Nazi programme of persecution and not to a motive of the perpetrator.'

offence.[76] Where such a specifically persecutory mindset is established in relation to acts or conduct which have not been charged as 'persecutions', it could constitute an aggravating circumstance relevant to sentencing.[77]

It is not sufficient for the accused to be 'aware' that he is in fact acting in a discriminatory manner, nor would recklessness on his part suffice; he must 'consciously intend' to do so.[78] However, in the case, for instance, where an accused gives an order to another individual 'with the awareness of a substantial likelihood that persecutions as a crime against humanity will be committed in the order's execution', the individual who gave the order may be liable for 'ordering' the crime of persecutions as he would thereby be regarded as accepting that crime.[79] Finally, and in every case, the discriminatory intent of the accused must relate to his acts and conduct, not to the attack of which those acts are a part, and it is not sufficient for those acts and conduct to be part of a discriminatory attack, where established, to infer that the accused possessed the requisite *mens rea*.[80]

The specificity required for persecutory *mens rea* led the *Kupreškić* Trial Chamber to draw parallels between genocidal intent and the discriminatory intent required for persecution, as the victims of both crimes are targeted because of their belonging to a particular group. However, the Trial Chamber pointed out that, while in the case of persecution the discriminatory intent can take multifarious inhumane forms and manifest itself in a plurality of actions, including murder, in the case of genocide that intent to commit the underlying offence must be accompanied by an intention to destroy, in whole or in part, the group to which the victims of the genocide belong:

> Thus, it can be said that, from the viewpoint of *mens rea*, genocide is an extreme and most inhuman form of persecution. To put it differently, when persecution escalates to the extreme form of wilful and deliberate acts designed to destroy a group or part of a group, it can be held that such persecution amounts to genocide.[81]

---

[76] *Todorović* Sentencing Judgment, par 32, and *Stakić* Trial Judgment, par 907, holding that persecution is 'inherently very serious'; *Blaškić* Trial Judgment, par 785. Sentences imposed in relation to that crime (in particular following a guilty plea) have been relatively mild so that the general assertion that persecution will always attract a heavy sentence would be inaccurate.

[77] See, e.g. *Vasiljević* Trial Judgment, par 278; *Kunarac* Trial Judgment, par 867; *Nikolić* Sentencing Judgment, par 105 ('The Trial Chamber considers that the seriousness of the crime of persecutions cannot be emphasised enough: this is a crime that can be committed in different manners and incorporates manifold acts. It is the abhorrent discriminatory intent behind the commission of this crime against humanity that renders it particularly grave'; footnote omitted).

[78] *Krnojelac* Trial Judgment, par 435; *Vasiljević* Trial Judgment, par 248; *Kordić and Čerkez* Trial Judgment, par 217. [79] *Blaškić* Appeal Judgment, par 166.

[80] *Krnojelac* Trial Judgment, par 436; *Vasiljević* Trial Judgment, par 249; *Krnojelac* Appeal Judgment, par 235. See, however, *Stakić* Trial Judgment, pars 742–743, suggesting (without providing any authority for this suggestion) that 'proof of a discriminatory attack against a civilian population is a sufficient basis to infer the discriminatory intent of an accused for acts carried out as part of the attack'.

[81] *Kupreškić* Trial Judgment, par 636. In essence, genocide differs from persecution in that in the case of genocide, the perpetrator chooses his victims because they belong to a specific group *and* seeks to destroy this very group in whole or in part. See *Jelišić* Trial Judgment, par 79; *Krstić* Trial

In sum, persecution may be said to consist of 'an act or omission which discriminates in fact and which: denies or infringes upon a fundamental right laid down in international customary or treaty law (the *actus reus*); and was carried out deliberately with the intention to discriminate on one of the listed grounds, specifically race, religion or politics (the *mens rea*)'.[82]

12.9   Other inhumane acts

The last underlying offence enumerated in Article 5 of the ICTY Statute and Article 3 of the ICTR Statute is the broadly defined concept of 'other inhumane acts',[83] which is residual in character and therefore covers a relatively wide range of criminal activities.[84] Its elements consist of the following:[85]

 (i)   the occurrence of an act or omission of similar seriousness to the other enumerated acts under the Article;
 (ii) the act or omission caused serious mental or physical suffering or injury or constituted a serious attack on human dignity; and
 (iii) the act or omission was performed deliberately by the accused or a person or persons for whose acts and omissions he bears criminal responsibility.

Judgment, 684: 'The offences of genocide and persecutions both require proof of a special intent, respectively an intent to destroy a particular group (or part of that group) as such and an intent to discriminate against persons on political, racial or religious grounds. Clearly, genocide has a distinct, mutual element [*sic*] in the form of its requirement of an intent to destroy a group, altogether, in whole or in part, over and above any lesser persecutory objective. The offence of persecutions, on the other hand, contains no element of intent or implementation that would not be subsumed in the destruction requirement of genocide.'

[82] *Krnojelac* Appeal Judgment, par 185 (emphasis added). See also *Vasiljević* Appeal Judgment, par 113.

[83] *Blaškić* Trial Judgment, par 237 (' "[O]ther inhumane acts . . ." is a generic charge which encompasses a series of criminal activities not explicitly enumerated'; see also *Jelišić* Trial Judgment, par 52, holding that 'the notions of cruel treatment within the meaning of Article 3 and of inhumane treatment set out in Article 5 of the Statute have the same legal meaning'); 1996 ILC Report, p 103 ('other inhumane acts' cause 'severe damage to the physical or mental integrity, the health or the human dignity of the victim, such as mutilation and severe bodily harm [. . .] It should be noted that the notion of other inhumane acts is circumscribed by two requirements. First, this category of acts is intended to include only additional acts that are similar in gravity to those listed in the preceding subparagraphs. Second, the act must in fact cause injury to human being in terms of physical or mental integrity, health or human dignity.')

[84] See, e.g. *Kvočka* Trial Judgment, pars 206–208; *Vasiljević* Trial Judgment, par 2234; *Čelebići* Appeal Judgment, par 426; *Tadić* Trial Judgment, par 723; *Jelišić* Trial Judgment, par 52; *Čelebići* Trial Judgment, par 552; *Kordić and Čerkez* Trial Judgment, par 265; *Krnojelac* Trial Judgment, par 130; *Naletilić and Martinović* Trial Judgment, par 245, where the Trial Chamber held, for instance, that the use of detainees for certain forms of labour and as human shields may amount to inhumane act. The Trial Chamber in *Kupreškić* held that the phrase 'other inhumane acts' 'was deliberately designed as a residual category, as it was felt to be undesirable for this category to be exhaustively enumerated' (*Kupreškić* Trial Judgment, par 563). See also *Akayesu* Trial Judgment, par 585; *Naletilić and Martinović* Trial Judgment, par 247.

[85] *Vasiljević* Trial Judgment, par 234; *Krnojelac* Trial Judgment, par 130 and references cited therein.

As is apparent from the above, this particular offence basically requires proof of the same elements as the war crimes of cruel treatment and inhumane treatment.[86]

The underlying conduct that may constitute an inhumane act must be as serious as other underlying offences outlined in Articles 5/3 of the ICTY/ICTR Statutes,[87] even though the Trial Chamber in *Kupreškić* effectively widened the scope of the category by locating the notion of 'other inhumane acts' in the law of human rights.[88] 'Other inhumane acts' should be limited in any case to those acts of mistreatment or abuse which cause great suffering or serious injury to the physical or mental health of the victim,[89] and this crime should not serve as a mechanism to criminalize vaguely reprehensible conduct which does not satisfy the stricter requirement of other, better-defined criminal offences. To assess the seriousness of a particular conduct and its sufficient gravity, consideration must be given to all the factual circumstances, including the nature of the act or omission which forms the factual basis of the charges, the context in which it occurred, the personal circumstances of the victim including age, sex and health, as well as the physical, mental, and moral effects of the act upon the victim.[90] The *Rutaganda* Trial Chamber, which maintained a similarly wide scope for this crime,[91] implied that to qualify as a crime against humanity, an 'inhumane act' must have a direct

[86] The definitions adopted for each offence vary only by the expressions used (*Krnojelac* Trial Judgment, par 130). See also *Naletilić and Martinović* Trial Judgment, pars 246–247. See *Kayishema and Ruzindana* Trial Judgment, pars 148–151; *Niyitegeka* Trial Judgment, par 460; *Kajelijeli* Trial Judgment, pars 931–932. One Trial Chamber has suggested that once the legal parameters of this category have been identified with sufficient precision, courts may refer to the *ejusdem generis* principle to compare and assess the gravity of a prohibited act (see *Kupreškić* Trial Judgment, par 566). See also the *Enigster* case, par 11(B); *Attorney-General v. Elsa Ternek*, District Court of Tel Aviv, Judgment of 14 December 1951, in 5 *Pesakim Mehoziim* (1951–52), 142–52 (in Hebrew); summary in English in 18 ILR 1951, 539–40 (where it is wrongly mentioned as *Tarnek*). Both discuss the principle of *ejusdem generis*.

[87] *Kupreškić* Trial Judgment, par 566.

[88] Ibid. See *Stakić* Trial Judgment, par 721, noting the risk that relying upon human rights to define criminal offences may entail.

[89] See, e.g. *Tadić* Trial Judgment, pars 730, 736–738, 744, 754, and 764, holding that mutilation, severe bodily harm, beatings and other acts of violence were said to qualify as 'other inhumane acts'. However, 'the mere insertion of the hose into the mouth of that person without discharge of the contents of the fire extinguisher is not of a nature serious enough to amount to an inhumane act within the meaning of Article 5 of the Statute' (ibid., par 748). See also *Kupreškić* Trial Judgment, par 566, including within the concept of 'other inhumane acts' acts such as the forcible transfer of groups of civilians, enforced prostitution, and the enforced disappearance of persons.

[90] *Ćelebići* Trial Judgment, par 536; *Jelisić* Trial Judgment, par 57; *Kunarac* Trial Judgment, par 501; *Krnojelac* Trial Judgment, par 131; *Vasiljević* Trial Judgment, par 235.

[91] *Rutaganda* Trial Judgment, par 77. See also *Akayesu* Trial Judgment, par 578; *Musema* Trial Judgment, par 201; Secretary-General Report, par 48, noting that crimes against humanity refers to inhumane acts of a very serious nature. The report refers in particular to so-called 'ethnic cleansing' and widespread and systematic rape and other forms of sexual assault, including enforced prostitution. On this point, consider *Regina v. Finta* [1994] 1 SCR 701 (Can.). The Canadian Supreme Court first held that an element of inhumanity must be demonstrated to warrant a crimes against humanity conviction. It stated, however, that it would not be necessary to establish that the accused knew that his or her actions were inhumane. It is sufficient, the court said, that a reasonable person in

and seriously damaging effect upon the victim.[92] There is no requirement, however, that the suffering in question must have long-term effects on the victim. The fact that the conduct in question might have had such an effect is only relevant to the determination of the seriousness of the act.[93]

It is possible that a victim of an inhumane act could not be the physical target of the act; a third person, such as a mother forced to witness the torture of her son, could be considered an additional victim of this inhumane act.[94] In such a case, the Prosecution must prove that the perpetrator intended to inflict serious mental suffering on the mother, or was reckless as to whether such suffering might result.[95]

The *mens rea* for inhumane acts is satisfied where the offender, at the time of the act or omission that forms the basis of the charges, had 'the intention to inflict serious physical or mental suffering or to commit a serious attack on the human dignity of the victim, or where he knew that his act or omission was likely to cause serious physical or mental suffering or a serious attack upon human dignity and was reckless thereto'.[96]

the position of the accused would have realized that the acts were inhumane (ibid., at 706–707). However, later in the judgment, it becomes clear that the element of *inhumanity* is *not* an additional requirement of crimes against humanity but a restatement of the requirement that the acts be sufficiently serious to merit the qualification of crimes against humanity: in determining the *mens rea* of a war crime or a crime against humanity, the accused must have intended the factual quality of the offence. In almost if not every case, the domestic definition of the underlying offence will capture the requisite *mens rea* for the war crime or crime against humanity as well. Thus, the accused need not have known that his or her act, if it constitutes manslaughter or forcible confinement, amounted to an 'inhumane act' either in the legal or moral sense. One who intentionally or knowingly commits manslaughter or kidnapping would have demonstrated the mental culpability required for an inhumane act (ibid., at 713).

[92] See *Re P.*, Appellate Court, Judgment of 20 May 1948, Criminal Chamber 3/48: '[T]he act which was committed must affect the human being in the depths of his being. That is the physical and spiritual domain of being and acting which constitutes the value and dignity of the person according to the moral convictions of civilised humanity.' See also the *Enigster* case holding that, at a minimum, 'the action must be of a severe nature and one which would persecute a person, debase him, or cause severe anguish in body or in spirit'; see also *D.C. (T.A.), Attorney-General of the State of Israel v. Ternek*, par 3(B), 1951.

[93] *Kunarac* Trial Judgment, par 501; *Krnojelac* Trial Judgment, par 144; *Vasiljević* Trial Judgment, par 235.   [94] *Kayishema and Ruzindana* Trial Judgment, par 153.

[95] Ibid.

[96] *Vasiljević* Trial Judgment, par 236; *Krnojelac* Trial Judgment, par 132; *Kayishema and Ruzindana* Trial Judgment, par 153; *Aleksovski* Trial Judgment, par 56; *Krnojelac* Trial Judgment, par 132. See, however, *Kajelijeli* Trial Judgment, par 932 (unsupported) ('Inhumane acts are only those which deliberately cause suffering').

PART IV
GENOCIDE

13

Genocide and International Criminal Tribunals

13.1   The judgment of the International Military Tribunal in Nuremberg

The concepts of 'genocide' and 'crimes against humanity' essentially arose as a reaction to the crimes committed by Nazi Germany during the Second World War.[1] 'Never before in history ha[d] man's inhumanity to man reached such depths', one American Tribunal in Nuremberg remarked.[2] Had it not been for the horrors of the Second World War, the crimes of genocide and crimes against humanity may never have come to legal life. Because they were so intimately attached to these events, they remained for a long time almost indistinguishable from the historical circumstances that gave birth to them. And for many years, discussions and debates about the legal characterization of certain criminal acts as either genocide or crimes against humanity often led to fruitless comparison

---

[1] The pre-Nuremberg history of these two concepts is essentially one of incantation rather than one of legal norms. Earlier references to notions such as the 'laws of humanity' or to the 'principles of humanity' did not purport to constitute criminal offences, the breach of which would entail individual criminal liability. There is no doubt, however, that acts which would now be regarded as 'genocide' or as 'crimes against humanity' had been committed prior to the Second World War. The preamble of the Genocide Convention itself recognizes that 'at all periods of history genocide has inflicted great losses on humanity' (Convention on the Prevention and Punishment of the Crime of Genocide, UN General Assembly Resolution, 260 A (III) (9 December 1948) ('Genocide Convention'). See also R. Lemkin, *Axis Rule in Occupied Europe: Laws of Occupation – Analysis of Government – Proposals for Redress* (Washington, D.C.: Carnegie Endowment for International Peace, 1944).

[2] *United States v. Pohl*, US Military Tribunal sitting at Nuremberg, Judgment of 3 November 1947, *Law Reports of Trials of War Criminals*, V ('*Pohl* case'), pp 195, 974.

between the events under consideration and the crimes committed during the Second World War. As a result, genocide and crimes against humanity long remained legally impotent beyond the events of the Second World War.

Perhaps even more than crimes against humanity, genocide has continued to be associated in popular imagination with the Holocaust.[3] It is somewhat paradoxical therefore to observe that the events which came to best illustrate this crime were in fact so neglected in the Judgment of the International Military Tribunal in Nuremberg. Early on during the negotiations of the Charter of the International Military Tribunal, an American draft document had suggested that the jurisdiction of the Tribunal should include, *inter alia*, '*genocide* or destruction of racial minorities and subjugated populations by such means and methods as (1) underfeeding; (2) sterilization and castration; (3) depriving them of clothing, shelter, fuel, sanitation, medical care; (4) deporting them to forced labor; (5) working them in inhumane conditions.'[4] The phrase 'genocide' disappeared in later draft proposals and was never discussed by the Allied representatives, nor was it included in the Tribunal's Charter. Instead, the concept of 'persecution' was favoured and was eventually adopted as a form of crime against humanity in Article 6(c) of the Charter.[5]

Despite this omission in the text of the Charter, the indictment presented by the Prosecution to the Tribunal claimed that the defendants had 'conducted *deliberate and systematic genocide*, viz., the extermination of racial and national groups, against the civilian populations of certain occupied territories in order to destroy particular races and classes of people and national, racial or religious groups, particularly Jews, Poles and Gypsies and others'.[6] As pointed out by the United Nations War Crimes Commission, the reference made to 'genocide' in the indictment constituted a shorthand description to an attack upon the physical or biological existence of a given protected group of people, rather than an independent criminal offence:[7]

[. . .] the Prosecution, when preferring against the defendants the charge of genocide, adopted this term and conception in a restricted sense only, that is, in its direct and biological connotation. This is evident not only from the definition of genocide as stated in the Indictment and from the inclusion of this charge under the general count of murder

---

[3] *Jelišić* Trial Judgement, par 60.

[4] Article 9(a) of the *Planning Memorandum Distributed to Delegations at Beginning of London Conference*, June 1945 (reprinted in *Report of Robert H. Jackson, United States Representative to the International Conference on Military Trials* (London, 1945), p 37) (emphasis added).

[5] In a memorandum submitted to the United Nations General Assembly, the United Nations Secretary-General noted the similarity between persecution and genocide: 'This category of crimes against humanity [i.e. persecution] is apparently closely related to the crime of genocide.' Memorandum of the Secretary-General, 'The Charter and Judgment of the Nürnberg Tribunal, History and Analysis', UN Doc. A/CN.4/5 (1949) ('UN Doc. A/CN.4/5'), p 68.

[6] *Indictment Presented to the International Military Tribunal, the United States of America, the French Republic, the United Kingdom of Great Britain and Northern Ireland, and the Union of Soviet Socialist Republics against Hermann Wilhelm Göring et al.*, 18 October 1945, p 43 (emphasis added).

[7] *UN War Crimes Commission*, p 197.

and ill-treatment, but also from the fact that all other aspects and elements of the defendants' activities, aiming at the denationalization of the inhabitants of occupied territories, were made the subject of a separate charge [. . .].

In his closing speech on 26 and 27 July 1945, Sir Hartley Shawcross, Chief Prosecutor for the United Kingdom, once again made a few passing references to the concept of genocide.[8] He made it clear in particular that 'genocide' was not to be restricted to the extermination of Jews or Gypsies, but that it had occurred in different forms in Yugoslavia, in Alsace-Lorraine *vis-à-vis* non-Germans, in the Low Countries, and in Norway.[9] The technique varied from nation to nation, he said, from people to people, but '[t]he long-term aim was the same in all cases', namely, the annihilation of many.[10] Referring to the 'twelve million murders' committed by Nazi Germany, he reminded the Court that six million of them were European Jews killed in the most barbaric circumstances:[11] 'Murder conducted like some mass production industry in the gas chambers and the ovens of Auschwitz, Dachau, Treblinka, Buchenwald, Mauthausen, Maidanek and Oranienburg'.

None of the accused in Nuremberg was convicted for genocide however and the word 'genocide' does not even appear in the text of the judgment.[12] Instead, when dealing with the substance of the general charges which the Prosecution had depicted as genocidal, the Tribunal had recourse to expressions such as 'extermination', 'mass murders', and 'annihilation' of certain groups of individuals or 'populations' to describe the nature of the offence committed:[13]

The murder and ill-treatment of civilian populations reached its height in the treatment of the citizens of the Soviet Union and Poland. Some four weeks before the invasion of Russia began, special task forces of the SIPO and SD, called Einsatz Groups, were formed on the orders of Himmler for the purpose of following the German Armies into Russia, combating partisans and members of Resistance Groups, and exterminating the Jews and communist leaders and other sections of the population. [. . .] The foregoing crimes against the civilian population are sufficiently appalling, and yet the evidence shows that at any rate in the East, the mass murders and cruelties were not committed solely for the

---

[8] Sir Hartley Shawcross, in *Speeches of the Chief Prosecutors at the Close of the Case against the Individual Defendants* (London: His Majesty's Stationery Office, Cmd. 6964, 1946), pp 81–84 and 93.

[9] Ibid., pp 83–84.

[10] Ibid., p 84: 'The methods followed a similar pattern: first a deliberate programme of murder, of outright annihilation. This was the method applied to the Polish intelligentsia, to gypsies and to Jews. The killing of millions, even by the gas chambers and mass shootings employed, was no easy matter. The defendants and their confederates also used methods of protracted annihilation, the favourite being to work their victims to death [. . .].'

[11] Ibid, pp 33–34.

[12] The charge of genocide did not appear in the indictment against the major war criminals who appeared before the Tokyo Tribunal. Nor was there any reference to genocide in the body of the Judgment (see R. J. Pritchard and S. Magbanua Zaide (eds.), *The Tokyo War Crimes Trial* (The Complete Transcripts of the Proceedings of the International Military Tribunal for the Far East) (New York/London: Garland, 1981) ('International Military Tribunal for the Far East'), vol. 1).

[13] IMT Judgment, pp 219, 235–237.

purpose of stamping out opposition or resistance to the German occupying forces. In Poland and the Soviet Union these crimes were part of a plan to get rid of whole native populations by expulsion and annihilation, in order that their territory could be used for colonization by Germans.

The Tribunal did not make any attempt to define the concept of genocide, nor did it try to distinguish this notion from other crimes that were within the Tribunal's jurisdiction.[14]

One reason for the exclusion of genocide from the Tribunal's Charter appears to have been the Allies' reluctance to turn the Prosecution case into a patchwork composed of discrete, micro-, cases dealing with individualized victim groups.[15] In Nuremberg, victims were individuals, not groups of individuals or nations *per se*. If victims were distinguished at all in the judgment of the International Military Tribunal, they were distinguished primarily according to their country of origin, not according to their ethnicity or religion. The International Military Tribunal made it clear, however, that certain groups of individuals (including the Jews and the Gypsies) had suffered disproportionately at the hands of the Nazis or their proxies, but their suffering merely formed one aspect of the general factual basis laid out in the charges.[16] Another reason for the absence of genocide as a separate criminal offence might have been the real apprehension on the part of the Allies that certain groups of victims would attempt to use the trial as a way to avenge crimes committed against them, or at least that their close involvement in the trial might give the impression that such was the case.[17]

[14] While commenting upon the concept of genocide and the role of the International Military Tribunal, the United Nations War Crimes Commission recognized that much, but noted the pioneering work of Lemkin in this field and gave a few indications of its own understanding of the concept of 'genocide': 'Genocide is directed against a national group as an entity, and the actions involved are directed against individuals, not in their individual capacity, but as members of the national group. [. . .] [Genocide] is intended [. . .] to signify a co-ordinated plan of different actions aiming at the destruction of the essential foundations of the life of national groups, with the aim of annihilating the groups themselves' (*UN War Crimes Commission*, p 197).

[15] During the discussions of the United Nations War Crimes Commission, the question arose as to the Tribunal's responsibility *vis-à-vis* and mandate over crimes committed by the Nazis against Jews and stateless persons in Germany. In June 1944, the British Government, which was consulted on that point, took the view that the Commission should not undertake to consider this matter but that it might collect evidence on the policy of extermination carried out in the occupied territories (ibid., p 140).

[16] See IMT Judgment, pp 247 et seq. ('Persecution of the Jews').

[17] This resulted, *inter alia*, in the reluctance of the Allies to let Jews run parts of the Prosecution case (in particular, in relation to its Jewish aspects). Concerning that question, see D. Bloxham, *Genocide on Trial: War Crimes Trials and the Formation of History and Memory* (Oxford: Oxford University Press, 2001) ('Bloxham, *Genocide*'), pp 67, 68, and 75. During the discussion on the adoption of the 1950 Israeli *Law on the Doing of Justice to Nazis and their Collaborators*, one member of the Israeli Parliament recounted an incident which he said had taken place during the preparation of the Prosecution case in Nuremberg: 'When the war crime tribunal was established at Nuremberg, we appeared before the American prosecutor general and asking to call this journalist, who saw all the Nazi atrocities in all their forms at various concentration camps, over a period of eight years, to testify before the war crime tribunal at Nuremberg. The American prosecutor general told us: "yes, I agree, but on one condition: that this journalist should not appear as a Jew and should not appear in the name of the Jewish nation, but should speak only of the destruction of millions of human beings." At that moment we felt the pain of our nation, which had no spokesman even after the great disaster' (*Report of Discussions of the Knesset*, 25 March 1950; on file with the author).

Another explanation for the absence of 'genocide' from the International Military Tribunal's Judgment may have to do with a legitimate concern for the principle of legality. As stated in the *History of the United Nations War Crimes Commission*, '[b]y inclusion of this specific charge [i.e. genocide] the Prosecution attempted to introduce and to establish a new type of international crime'.[18] There was no way for the Allies to argue that this crime existed under international law prior to this time. It simply did not. And the Prosecution knew already that it had a challenging task in hand in proving the existence under international law of the crime of aggression and crimes against humanity, both of which were provided for in the Charter and charged in the indictment. The legacy of the International Military Tribunal's Judgment might have been gravely strained had the judges taken into account a crime for which there was no reliable precedent nor much (if any) supporting state practice establishing its existence under international law. Critics would have been quick to depict the recognition of such an offence as an act of revenge rather than as the unbiased application of existing law.

Although it did not discuss the legal meaning of genocide, the International Military Tribunal dealt with the facts which, had genocide charges been brought, would have been relevant to a determination and, possibly, a finding that a genocidal offence had been committed by some or all of the accused. The section of the Judgment devoted to the 'Persecution of the Jews', for instance, depicts in chilling fashion the murderous Nazi policy towards the Jews.[19] But the Tribunal's general approach to these events was somewhat unfortunate. The Holocaust was set by the Tribunal into the general matrix of Germany's aggressive war, that is, as merely one aspect of a broader policy of expansion and annexation, failing in so doing to recognize the specific criminal character of the 'Final Solution'.[20] In describing the destruction of the Jewish people as merely one aspect of the German aggressive

---

[18] *UN War Crimes Commission*, p 197.

[19] The description by the IMT of those events was to serve other tribunals in later cases. In the *Pohl* case, for instance, the US Military Tribunal was to open its finding on the 'Treatment of the Jews' with a reference to the depiction of these events given by the IMT in its Judgment: 'That disgraceful chapter in the history of Germany has been vividly portrayed in the judgment of the International Military Tribunal (pp 247–253 and 303, Official Edition). Nothing can be added to that comprehensive finding of facts, in which this Tribunal completely concurs. From it we see the unholy spectacle of six million human beings deliberately exterminated by a civilized state whose only indictment was that its victims had been born in the wrong part of the world of forebears whom the murderers detested.' *United States v. Oswald Pohl et al.*, United States Military Tribunal sitting at Nuremberg, judgment of 3 November 1947, in TWC, Vol. V, p 974.

[20] In his closing speech, Sir Hartley Shawcross laid down the view of the Prosecution in relation to the place of crimes committed against the Jews: 'So the crime against the Jews, in so far as it is a Crime Against Humanity and not a War Crime, is one which we indict because of its association with the Crime Against the Peace. That is, of course, a very important qualification, and is not always appreciated by those who have questioned the exercise of this jurisdiction. But subject to that qualification, we have thought it right to deal with matters which the Criminal Law of all countries would normally stigmatise as crimes' (Sir Hartley Shawcross, in *Speeches of the Chief Prosecutors at the Close of the Case against the Individual Defendants*, p 63). Such an interpretation of these events was correctly excluded by US Military Tribunal II in the *Einsatzgruppen* case, where it held that '[t]he annihilation of the Jews had nothing to do with the defense of Germany, the genocide program was in no way connected with the protection of the Vaterland, it was entirely foreign to the military issue' (*Einsatzgruppen* case, pp 411, 469–470).

war effort – rather than a criminal enterprise of mass extermination with no other purpose – the Tribunal apparently underestimated or misinterpreted the reality of this event, thereby undercutting its historical significance.[21] There is no question, however, that the treatment of the Holocaust by the Nuremberg Tribunal, and its meticulous documentation, contributed importantly to the public perception of those events and moulded much of the later historiography of the subject.[22]

Paradoxically, the very absence of any reference to 'genocide' in the Nuremberg Judgment may have prompted states to establish such a prohibition via an international treaty and may have facilitated the adoption of the Genocide Convention in its present form.[23] On 11 December 1946, less than two months after the Judgment of the International Military Tribunal had been rendered,[24] the General Assembly of the United Nations adopted a special resolution on genocide which provided that 'genocide is a denial of the right of existence of entire human groups, as homicide is the denial of the right to live of individual human beings',[25] and on 9 December 1948 the Convention on the Prevention and Punishment of the Crime of Genocide was adopted.[26] By contrast, the offence of 'crimes against

---

[21] Mettraux, *Crimes against Humanity*, p 245, n 35. See also W. Bosch, *Judgment on Nuremberg: American Attitudes towards the Major German War-Crime Trials*, (Chapel Hill: University of North Carolina Press, 1970) ('Bosch, *Judgment on Nuremberg*'), p 119. In the *Akayesu* case, the Trial Chamber was careful to distinguish between the armed conflict and the genocidal actions which occurred in its midst (*Akayesu* Trial Judgment, pars 127 and 128).

[22] Some authors have even talked of a 'Nuremberg historiography of the Holocaust'. See, generally, Bloxham, *Genocide* and sources quoted therein.

[23] The preamble of the Draft Convention prepared by the *ad hoc* Committee contained the following reference to the International Military Tribunal and to its Judgment: 'having taken note of the fact that the International Military Tribunal at Nuremberg in its Judgment of 30 September–1 October 1946 has punished under a different legal description certain persons who have committed acts similar to those which the present Convention aims at punishing'. This reference was eventually removed on the basis that the principles recognized in the Charter and in the Judgment of the Nuremberg Tribunal would, pursuant to Resolution 180(II) of the UN General Assembly, be subject to a separate convention (see N. Robinson, *The Genocide Convention: A Commentary* (New York: Institute of Jewish Affairs, 1960) ('Robinson, *Genocide Convention*'), pp 54–55). It was thought that this new crime, genocide, should not be equated to the concept of crimes against humanity which the IMT had to consider under its Charter. The Representative of Venezuela during the negotiation of the Genocide Convention said that: 'The acts prohibited by the Charter of the Nuremberg Tribunal did not correspond exactly to those which the United Nations intended to prevent and to make punishable through the convention on genocide; consequently there was no reason to include in the convention on genocide a reference to the judgment of the Tribunal' (see Official Record of the 3 Session of the General Assembly, Part I, Sixth Committee, Summary Records of the Meetings, 21 September–10 December 1948, UN Doc. A/C.6/SR.109, pp 489–490). The American Representative to the Sixth Committee, Mr. Maktos, agreed with this suggestion and said that such an omission would prevent confusion between the concept of crimes against humanity and that of genocide. He also pointed out that since the IMT had given no definition of genocide, its decision could not be regarded as a precedent in connection with genocide (ibid., p 490).

[24] The Judgment of the IMT was rendered over two days on 30 September 1946 and 1 October 1946.

[25] UN General Assembly Resolution. 96(I), UN GAOR, 1st Sess., UN Doc. A/RES/96(I) (1946), 11 December 1946 ('UN Doc. A/RES/96(I)').

[26] Approved and proposed for signature and ratification or accession by UN General Assembly Res. 260 A (III), UN GAOR, 3rd Sess., 179th Plenary mtg., UN Doc. A/810 (1948), 9 December 1948 ('UN Doc. A/810'). It entered into force on 12 January 1951.

humanity' which was regarded by the International Military Tribunal as being part of customary international law, was never codified in a similar convention.

13.2 The contribution of the *ad hoc* Tribunals for the former Yugoslavia and for Rwanda to the law of genocide

The contribution of the *ad hoc* Tribunals to the law of genocide has been primarily of two kinds. First, from a legal point of view, the jurisprudence of the two Tribunals has played a crucial role in giving some welcome precision and foreseeability to a body of law characterized by a high degree of uncertainty and generalization. Secondly, from a historical point of view, the application of the norm to different factual and political contexts has done a great deal to liberate genocide from the historical and sociological environment in which it was born.

The body of jurisprudence developed by the Tribunals has touched many facets of this small set of rules that constitutes the law of genocide. But the jurisprudential contribution of the *ad hoc* Tribunals has been case-specific and therefore necessarily patchy, as the Court's rulings were generally and appropriately limited to issues raised by the parties or otherwise stemming from the case itself.[27] As a consequence, some important aspects of the law of genocide have not yet been discussed by the *ad hoc* Tribunals or only superficially so.

In addition to defining and specifying the law of genocide, the Tribunals have also confirmed the special status of the genocidal prohibition under international law as the crime of all crimes, 'a crime against all of humankind',[28] and they have repeatedly emphasized the customary[29] and *jus cogens* nature of that prohibition.[30]

The second main contribution of the *ad hoc* Tribunals to the law of genocide has been a more subtle one. With their pronouncements on both the law and the facts relating to serious international crimes in both the former Yugoslavia and Rwanda, the Tribunals have turned much of international criminal law from paper into reality.[31] In particular, the very application of the law of genocide to

---

[27] The Tribunals' tendency for *obiter dicta* has been receding sharply with the increase in workload over the years. The Tribunals may also have realized that they were expected to act more as a traditional criminal court and less as some sort of supreme court for the development of international humanitarian law.

[28] *Krstić* Appeal Judgment, 19 April 2004, par 36.

[29] *Sikirica* Motion for Acquittal Decision, par 55; *Akayesu* Trial Judgment, par 495; *Musema* Trial Judgment, par 151; *Rutaganda* Trial Judgment, par 46. See Secretary-General Report (ICTY), par 45; *Stakić* Rule 98 bis Decision, par 20; *Jelišić* Trial Judgment, par 61.

[30] See *Reservations to the Convention on the Prevention and Punishment of Genocide*, Advisory Opinion, ICJ Reports (28 May 1951) ('ICJ, *Reservations to the Convention on the Prevention and Punishment of Genocide*'), p 23. See also *Jelišić* Trial Judgment, par 60; *Kayishema and Ruzindana* Trial Judgment, par 88; *Kupreškić* Trial Judgment, par 520; *Stakić* Rule 98 bis Decision, par 20.

[31] See *Report of the International Tribunal for the Prosecution of Persons Responsible for Serious Violations of International Humanitarian Law in the Territory of the Former Yugoslavia since 1991*, First Annual Report, UN Doc. A/49/342, S/1994/1007, 29 August 1994, par 196.

criminal acts which only remotely resemble the crimes of the Nazis against the Jews or Gypsies during the Second World War helped establishing genocide as a genuine legal norm of general application, rather than as a symbol of a unique historical phenomenon. The expression 'genocide' remains a potent cry for action, but it has now become one that can be tested against a clear legal definition. The Tribunals' patient consideration of the situations in which genocide or related offences were allegedly committed is rich in information as to both the nature of these crimes and the various factual circumstances in which it may be appropriate to charge an accused with and convict him or her for genocide. In the jurisprudence of the Tribunals, crimes are indeed assessed on their own facts against an existing legal definition, rather than being compared to or measured against Nazi atrocities.[32]

But the application of a norm to an increasing number of circumstances carries with it the risk of dilution of the original prohibition. In her partial dissent in the *Jelišić* Appeal Judgment, Judge Wald stressed the importance of resisting the temptation of enlarging a crime whose currency depends on its exceptional character.[33] The necessity for the Court to protect the integrity of legal norms is magnified, in the case of genocide, by the very history of that concept and the fact that it represents the pinnacle of evil in both its legal form and in the public perception of that crime. Ratner and Abrams have pointedly emphasized the necessity to 'rescue' genocide from linguistic dilution:[34]

And an opposite, yet equally disconcerting trend in contemporary discourse on genocide has also resulted – an abuse of the term that robs the concept of genocide of its definitional integrity. Such is the term's emotional and political potency that the label 'genocide' is used today in a more expansive sense than its legal definition might allow to refer to almost any instance of mass killing. In the words of Helen Fein: 'Since genocide is widely conceived as the most reprehensible of crimes, many people use genocide-labeling both to vent outrage and to describe situations in which they perceive themselves as threatened, regardless of how these situations have come about, the source of threat, the truth of accusation against putative perpetrator, and so on. Their reasoning seems to be: if this is awful, it must be genocide. [. . .] At times such labeling verges on the paranoid and incendiary, as when Westerners or Jews are accused of genocide by giving Africans or African-American AIDS' (Helen Fein, 'Genocide, terror, life integrity and war crimes: The case for discrimination',

---

[32] References to the events of the Second World War crop up from time to time in cases before the *ad hoc* Tribunals in relation to the crime of genocide. Thus, in the *Krstić* appeal, the Defence suggested that the Appeals Chamber should consider the gravity of the acts committed in light of other genocidal events of the past: 'while in no way justifying the events at Srebrenica, it cannot be ignored that its scale pales in comparison with the three *bona fide* genocides recognized in modern history: the Armenia [*sic*] genocide, the Holocaust, and the Rwanda genocide' (*Krstić* case, Defence Response to Prosecution Appeal Brief, 21 December 2001, par 58).

[33] *Jelišić* Appeal Judgment, Partial Dissenting Opinion of Judge Wald, p 66, par 1. See also *Stakić* Rule 98 bis Decision, par 22, which points out that Article 4 of the Statute needs to be interpreted 'restrictively and with caution' and stresses the 'exclusivity' of the crime of genocide.

[34] S. Ratner and J. Abrams, *Accountability for Human Rights Atrocities in International Law: Beyond the Nuremberg Legacy* (Oxford: Oxford University Press, 2001), pp 42–43.

in *Genocide: Conceptual and Historical Dimensions*, 95, G. Andreopoulos, ed. 1994). Rescuing genocide from this trend is part of the work which responsible decision-makers and commentators must vigilantly undertake.

The consideration of genocide as primarily a legal concept has allowed the two Tribunals, in most cases, to steer clear of any debate as to the political and historical merits and appropriateness of bringing genocide charges and convicting an accused upon that heading.[35] Genocide, as far as the *ad hoc* Tribunals are concerned, is a criminal offence, and discussions thereupon have mostly been limited to its *legal* meaning and its *legal* interpretation rather than upon any discussion as to its political significance.

Finally, the jurisprudence of the *ad hoc* Tribunals may also have contributed to some degree of closure for the victims of certain events, by putting these events into a legal and criminal framework, away from any political justification or ethnic 'explanation' of historical events, making it less likely that these events may later be reinterpreted or in any way 'justified'.[36] Many of the crimes committed in

[35] The political significance of any finding involving acts of genocide may be gauged from the reaction of the Supreme Court of Kosovo (Federal Republic of Yugoslavia) sitting in Plenary to a finding made by one of its chambers. On 31 August 2001, the Supreme Court of Kosovo sitting in a panel session of three judges, including one international judge, overruled a finding of a lower court which had found the accused, Miroslav Vucković, guilty of genocide. In the course of its Judgment, the panel made the following unsolicited finding: 'More generally, according to the Supreme Court, the exactions committed by the Milošević regime in 1999 cannot be qualified as criminal acts of genocide, since their purpose was not the destruction of the Albanian ethnic group in whole or in part, but its forceful departure from Kosovo as a result of a systematic campaign of terror including murders, rapes, arsons and severe maltreatments' (*In re Vucković*, Federal Republic of Yugoslavia (Serbia and Montegro), Supreme Court of Kosovo, decision of 31 August 2001, A.P.156/2001, 31 August 2001). Following that ruling, the Supreme Court sitting this time in plenary, strongly rebuffed its chamber and disowned the above-mentioned statement. On 11 September 2001, it issued a statement in relation to the above finding which provided as follows: 'It is the evaluation of the Plenary Session, of which the International Judge who drafted and signed the said Decision was himself a participant, that the observation quoted above falls beyond the scope of the present action and reflects the attitude of that particular panel only, which has exceeded the limits of its discretion since, through the handling of this case, it has offered assessments of a general nature regarding the policies that the regime of Milošević implemented during the year 1999 in Kosovo' (*Communiqué*, Supreme Court of Kosovo, Federal Republic of Yugoslavia, 11 September 2001; on file with the author). In September 2003, in an extraordinary report, the Republika Srpska Bureau for Cooperation with the Tribunal issued a statement suggesting that the mass murders which occurred in Srebrenica in 1995 had been committed by foreign secret services. This document may be found at: www.dcrs.org. A more *rational* 'Progress Report' was later published (www.ohr.int/ohr-dept/presso/pressr/default.asp?content_id=32405). The final report from the Republika Srpska Bureau for Cooperation with the Tribunal is expected on 15 October 2004 (www.ohr.int/ohr-dept/presso/pressr/default.asp?content_id=32969).

[36] From the victims' perspective, it is open to question whether a finding that the crimes committed against them constitute genocide as opposed to, say, crimes against humanity, is truly important to the sense of justice derived from a judicial decision. It is not the place here to offer a view on that point, but it is worth noting that the stigma of genocide has been regarded by many victims as the only one appropriate to characterize the horror of the crimes committed against them. It is a formidable question whether the fact that an accused person is convicted for, say, genocide rather than for crimes against humanity, would make any difference to the victim's perception of the criminal proceedings and the justice that he or she received from it. In certain cases, genocide as the ultimate crime has become the rallying cry for victims who consider that the seriousness and the horror of the

Rwanda or Srebrenica have now been said to amount to genocide and any challenges to the legal significance of these events is now to be tested against the Court's recounting of them.

13.3   Genocide and the International Criminal Court

Article VI of the Genocide Convention provides that persons charged with genocide shall be tried 'by a competent tribunal of the State in the territory of which the act was committed, *or by such international penal tribunal as may have jurisdiction*'.[37] At long last, more than fifty years on, such a permanent criminal court has finally arrived with great promises and enormous challenges ahead. The potential of such a court, in particular from a preventative point of view, is immense and its mere existence, let alone its jurisprudence, could play a pivotal role in the strengthening and refining of international criminal law and the law of genocide in particular.

Article 6 of the Statute of the International Criminal Court reproduces Article II of the Genocide Convention.[38] Contrary to the Statutes of the *ad hoc* Tribunals, however, it does not reproduce Article III of the Genocide Convention which lists the various forms of punishable criminal participation.[39] The ICC Statute provides separately for those forms of criminal participation which entail individual criminal liability under the Statute, including in relation to genocide.[40] A repetition of Article III, it was thought, would have been redundant and could have led to contradictions between discrete articles of the Statute. In at least one respect, however, the drafters of the Rome Statute have not gone as far as the Genocide Convention and, arguably, not as far as existing customary international law in other respects. Whereas, for instance, the Genocide Convention (and the *ad hoc* Tribunals[41]) suggest that 'conspiracy to commit genocide' may be punished

---

crimes committed against them and their families may only be reflected in law (and even then only imperfectly so) if they are labelled as genocide. The reactions (on the part of both Serbs and Bosnians) that greeted the Judgment of Trial Chamber I in the *Krstić* case where the accused were found guilty of genocide or the guilty pleas of Momir Nikolić and Dragan Obrenović (*Srebrenica* case) for persecution (rather than genocide, a crime with which both accused had also been charged but which was developed in both cases after the accused had agreed with the Office of the Prosecutor to plead guilty) are dramatic illustrations of the evident political and symbolic significance of that concept.

[37]   Emphasis added.

[38]   Article 6 of the ICC Statute provides as follows: 'For the purpose of this Statute, "genocide" means any of the following acts committed with intent to destroy, in whole or in part, a national, ethnical, racial or religious group, as such: (a) killing members of the group; (b) causing serious bodily or mental harm to members of the group; (c) deliberately inflicting on the group conditions of life calculated to bring about its physical destruction in whole or in part; (d) imposing measures intended to prevent births within the group; (e) forcibly transferring children of the group to another group.'

[39]   Article III of the Genocide Convention is as follows: 'The following acts are punishable: (a) genocide; (b) conspiracy to commit genocide; (c) direct and public incitement to commit genocide; (d) attempt to commit genocide; (e) complicity in genocide.'

[40]   See Article 25 of the ICC Statute.   [41]   See below, sub-section 16.2.2.

whether or not a genocidal act has in fact been committed as a result of this agreement or understanding, the Rome Statute opts for a more restrictive approach to this concept, requiring that the agreement which constitutes the conspiracy has led to the commission or attempted commission of such a crime.[42]

It has been suggested that the ICC Statute differs from customary law in yet another respect. Article 28 of the Statute provides that a commander may be held responsible for crimes (including genocide) committed by his subordinates if he 'knew or, owing to the circumstances at the time, should have known' that they were committing such crimes or were about to and failed to take the necessary and reasonable measures to punish or prevent them. A number of commentators have read in this a suggestion that a commander could be held responsible for genocide if it can be shown that he knew or should have known that his subordinates were committing or about to commit genocidal acts, but that he did not himself need to possess the genocidal intent.[43] It is submitted that the ICC Statute may be read in a way which may be more in conformity with customary law. As far as the commander's knowledge of the actions of his subordinates is concerned, the Statute should be read as that particular requirement of *mens rea* to the *underlying offences* only (killing, rape, torture, etc.) as opposed to the *chapeau* elements of genocide, including the specific genocidal intent. These *chapeau* elements must be met, the author argues, by each and every individual accused of genocidal actions (including commanders), just like all *chapeau* elements of crimes against humanity must be met by each and every person accused of having committed a crime against humanity. As far as genocide is concerned, these *chapeau* elements include a specific genocidal state of mind which the commander or superior in question must therefore possess personally.[44]

The fact that Article 6 of the ICC Statute does not provide for a list of specific forms of criminal liability specific to genocide may be a positive step towards the 'normalization' of genocide as a legal concept. It contains the implicit message that this crime may be committed in just the same manner and under the same conditions as any other crime within the Court's jurisdiction. Also, the fact that the Statute goes, in some respects, beyond the list of criminal forms of participation provided for in the Genocide Convention (and in the Tribunals' Statutes) marks the end of arguments as to whether or not genocide could be committed in any way other than those explicitly provided for in the Convention.[45] The organization of the ICC Statute also excludes potential contradictions between the genocide provision and the provision providing for individual criminal responsibility, as has been the case with the *ad hoc* Tribunals where Articles 4/2 and Articles 7/6 of the ICTY/ICTR Statutes overlap and may contradict each other in part.[46]

---

[42] According to one commentator, this discrepancy would appear to be inadvertent (W. A. Schabas, 'Genocide', in O. Triffterer (ed.), *Commentary on the Rome Statute of the International Criminal Court* (Baden-Baden: Nomos, 1999) ('Schabas, *Genocide in the Rome Statute*'), pp 107, 115–116).   [43] See, e.g., ibid., p 109.

[44] See below, sub-section 16.3.1.   [45] See below, sub-section16.3.

[46] For the ICTR Statute, these are, respectively, Article 2 and Article 6 of the Statute.

The ICC Statute is complemented by the 'Elements of Crimes' which were adopted, *inter alia*, for the purpose of assisting the Court in the interpretation and application of Article 6 (genocide), Article 7 (crimes against humanity), and Article 8 (war crimes) of the Statute.[47] Although Article 9(3) of the Statute provides that the *Elements of Crimes* shall be consistent with the Statute, it would appear that, as far as the definition of genocide is concerned, drafters of the *Elements of Crimes* have, in fact, introduced through this vehicle, restrictions upon the definition of that offence which do not appear in the Statute, in customary international law or in the Genocide Convention.

The most obvious departure from the definition contained in the Statute (and under existing customary law) is the requirement contained in the *Elements of Crimes* that the crimes must occur 'in the context of a manifest pattern of similar conduct directed against that group or was conduct that could itself effect such destruction'. Concern had been expressed during the drafting of the *Elements* about the risk of diluting the offence of genocide if it were to cover isolated crimes, and the phrase just quoted was added to quell such concerns.[48] In effect, the drafters were thereby adding to the definition of genocide a requirement similar in kind to the requirement that the act of a criminal against humanity must be part of a 'widespread and systematic attack' against a civilian population. This, no doubt, limits the *risk* that an individual might ever be charged with genocide in relation to isolated acts or events of limited criminal magnitude. Prosecutorial self-restraint, which had prevailed at the *ad hoc* Tribunals, is in effect replaced at the ICC by an express direction as to what, 'for the purposes of this Statute', may be regarded as genocidal actions. One problem with that solution is that customary law does not contain such a requirement.[49] Nor is there any indication that the drafters of the ICC Statute considered that such an element was part of the definition provided in the Statute. It would seem that the drafters of the *Elements of Crimes* have simply restricted their conception of what genocide *should be* beyond the customary definition.

As far as the *ad hoc* Tribunals are concerned, the ICC Statute has been of very limited assistance. The Tribunals' jurisdiction *ratione materiae* is indeed circumscribed and ultimately determined by customary international law (at least in the case of the ICTY) as it existed at the time of the crimes charged in the various indictments raised by the Tribunals' Prosecutors. Most of the crimes with which

---

[47] Article 9(1) of the ICC Statute provides that: 'Elements of Crimes shall assist the Court in the interpretation and application of articles 6, 7 and 8. They shall be adopted by a two-thirds majority of the members of the Assembly of States Parties.'

[48] See R. Lee (ed.), *The International Criminal Court: Elements of Crimes and Rules of Procedure and Evidence* (Ardsley: Transnational, 2001), pp 45–47.

[49] A. Cassese, 'Genocide', in A. Cassese, P. Gaeta, and J. Jones (eds.), *The Rome Statute of the International Criminal Court: A Commentary* (Oxford: Oxford University Press, 2002) ('Cassese, Gaeta, and Jones, *ICC Commentary*'), pp 335, 349. As will be pointed out below, it was in fact expressly rejected as an element of the definition of genocide under customary international law by the Appeals Chamber of the ICTY (*Jelišić* Appeal Judgment, par 48).

the ICTY might be concerned, and all of those with which the ICTR is concerned, were committed prior to adoption of the ICC Statute on 17 July 1998.[50] At most, the ICC Statute may provide some evidence of state *opinio juris* as to the relevant customary international law at the time at which the recommendations were adopted and has proved a useful instrument in confirming the content of customary international law, but it does not necessarily represent the present status of international customary law, let alone at the time relevant to the Yugoslav and Rwanda Tribunals.[51] The reverse influence, that is, the impact of the jurisprudence of the *ad hoc* Tribunals upon the making of the ICC Statute and the drafting of the *Elements of Crimes* has been very significant indeed, and many of the solutions and definitions laid down by the two Tribunals have been readily adopted by the ICC drafters, perhaps too rashly on occasions.[52]

[50] In practice, the temporal jurisdiction of the ICTY is ongoing and, if war crimes, crimes against humanity, or genocide were to be committed now in one of the constituent states of the former Yugoslavia, the Tribunal would still have jurisdiction over such crimes. The ICTY Statute merely provides that it has jurisdiction over such crimes committed 'since 1991'. By contrast, the ICTR Statute provides that it has jurisdiction over crimes committed 'between 1 January 1994 and 31 December 1994' (ICTR Statute, Article 1).

[51] *Kunarac* Trial Judgment, fn 1210, pp 169–170. See also *Furundžija* Trial Judgment, par 227; *Tadić* Appeal Judgment, par 223. Despite what has sometimes been quite brashly claimed, the solutions and definitions adopted in the ICC Statute were certainly not the complete reflection of existing customary international law at the time of their adoption. The whole body of law adopted in Rome is filled with too many political compromises, drafting infelicities, legal advances, and bold legal creations to merit the title of a codifying work. In the *Stakić* case, the Trial Chamber pointed out that 'the 1998 Rome Statute of the International Criminal Court is of limited assistance as an aid to the interpretation of the provisions on genocide under the ICTY Statute' (*Stakić* Rule 98 bis Decision, p 7, n 20).

[52] For illustrations of that point, see, e.g., The Hon. David A. Hunt, 'The International Criminal Court: High Hopes, "Creative Ambiguity" and an Unfortunate Mistrust in International Judges', 2(1) *Journal of International Criminal Justice* 56 (March 2004).

14

General or *Chapeau* Elements
of Genocide

14.1   General remarks

Article 4 of the ICTY Statute and Article 2 of the ICTR Statute are identical in both form and substance. They read as follows:

Genocide

1. The International Tribunal shall have the power to prosecute persons committing genocide as defined in paragraph 2 of this article or of committing any of the other acts enumerated in paragraph 3 of this article.

2. Genocide means any of the following acts committed with intent to destroy, in whole or in part, a national, ethnical, racial or religious group, as such:
   (a) killing members of the group;
   (b) causing serious bodily or mental harm to members of the group;
   (c) deliberately inflicting on the group conditions of life calculated to bring about its physical destruction in whole or in part;
   (d) imposing measures intended to prevent births within the group;
   (e) forcibly transferring children of the group to another group.

3. The following acts shall be punishable:
   (a) genocide;
   (b) conspiracy to commit genocide;
   (c) direct and public incitement to commit genocide;
   (d) attempt to commit genocide;
   (e) complicity in genocide.

This provision is intimately linked to the Genocide Convention which it simply reproduces in its relevant parts.[1] Consequently, both Tribunals have relied extensively upon the *Travaux Préparatoires* of the Convention to interpret the above article and to ascertain its scope.[2] It will be clear from what follows, however, that a great deal of the legal development which has taken place in The Hague and in Arusha concerning the law of genocide has more to do with judicial law-making than with the revelation of a legal or historical truth engraved somewhere in the *Travaux*.

The concept of genocide is historically loaded, which often leads commentators and laymen alike to equate the legal concept to the historical phenomenon which most closely came to illustrate it: the Holocaust. As a result, there are a lot of preconceptions about the exact legal meaning of that term. Thus, genocide, it is sometimes suggested, may only be committed by people holding high offices such as ministers or generals; genocide requires an overarching plan or policy to commit it, and only those who operate within that plan or policy may be said to commit genocide; genocide must be based on racist motives; the contribution of the *génocidaire* must clearly set him or her out in the hierarchy of crimes. None of those suggestions is fully accurate from a legal perspective.[3]

In fact, just as anyone may commit a crime against humanity,[4] all other conditions being met, anyone can commit a genocidal offence,[5] regardless of any hierarchical position,[6] regardless of the importance and form of his or her

---

[1] Paragraph 46 of the Secretary-General's Report of 3 May 1993 (ICTY) provides that the 'relevant provisions are reproduced in the corresponding article [4] of the statute' (UN Doc. S/25704).

[2] See, for instance, *Stakić* Rule 98bis Decision, par 21, where the Trial Chamber said that, when interpreting the crime of genocide as provided for in the Statute, it would rely, *inter alia*, on the Genocide Convention and its *Travaux Préparatoires*.

[3] For general works on genocide and the Genocide Convention, see in particular, Robinson, *Genocide Convention*; P. N. Drost, *The Crime of State: Penal Protection for Fundamental Freedoms of Persons and Peoples*, vol. 2, *Genocide: United Nations Legislation on International Criminal Law* (Leyden: A.W. Sythoff, 1959) ('Drost, *The Crime of State*, vol.2, *Genocide*'); W. A. Schabas, *Genocide in International Law* (Cambridge: Cambridge University Press, 2000) ('Schabas, *Genocide*').

[4] Article VI of the Genocide Convention provides that '[p]ersons committing genocide or any of the other acts enumerated in article III shall be punished, whether they are constitutionally responsible rulers, public officials or private individuals'. See also Mettraux, *Crimes against Humanity*, pp 306–312.

[5] *Kayishema and Ruzindana* Appeal Judgment, par 170. The sole existing restriction to be found in the case law on that point concerns the question of whether a member of the targeted group can himself or herself commit a genocidal offence. *A priori*, there does not appear to be any theoretical nor any practical reason why such a person could not be convicted of genocide. However, in the *Enigster* case, Justice Lem concluded that Enigster, a Jew, could not be convicted for (and had not been charged with) the crime against the Jewish people (equivalent to 'genocide' in the Israeli *Law on the Doing of Justice to Nazis and their Collaborators*) because of his membership of the Jewish people (see *Attorney-General v. Enigster, Yehezkel Ben Alish*, Israel, District Court of Tel Aviv, Judgment of 4 January 1951, in 5 *Pesakim Mehoziim* 1951–2) (in Hebrew, translation on file with the author); summary in English in 18 ILR 1951 ('*Enigster* case'). This decision on that point remains isolated however.

[6] See Article IV of the Genocide Convention: 'Persons committing genocide or any of the other acts enumerated in article III shall be punished, whether they are constitutionally responsible rulers, public officials or private individuals.'

contribution to the crime,[7] regardless of his or her membership of the victimized group,[8] regardless of his or her motives,[9] regardless of his or her civilian or military status, regardless of the fact that he or she may have been acting in a private or an official capacity,[10] regardless of the way in which the crime has been committed.[11]

There are essentially three elements that must be met before a genocidal offence may be said to have been committed:

(i) an individual possessed the required genocidal *mens rea* or, according to the Appeals Chamber and a number of Trial Chambers, where he knew of the principal's genocidal intent and that,

(ii) with that state of mind, he or she took part in the commission of one of the acts prohibited under Article 4 of the Statute, and that

(iii) he or she did so in one of the forms provided for in that Article, or in a capacity recognized as entailing individual criminal responsibility under customary international law.

The relevant state of mind for genocide is therefore composed of both the *mens rea* relating to the underlying offence (say, intending to kill members of the group or cause serious bodily or mental harm to members of the group) and the *mens rea* related to the *chapeau* elements of the crime (genocidal *mens rea* proper). Its *actus reus* is limited both as to the kind of underlying offences which may constitute genocide and in relation to the forms of participation which may entail individual criminal responsibility for participating in such an act.[12]

14.2   Elements of the genocidal *mens rea*

The perpetrator of a genocidal act must intend 'to destroy, in whole or in part, a national, ethnical, racial or religious group, as such'. He must therefore have had 'the intent to accomplish certain specified types of destruction', that is to say, that

---

[7] See below, sub-sections 16.2 and 16.3 concerning the various forms of criminal participation recognized by the *ad hoc* Tribunals in relation to genocidal actions.

[8] As noted below, it could well be the case that the perpetrator himself be part of the targeted group.   [9] See below, sub-section 14.2.1.

[10] Article 7(2) of the ICTY Statute provides that '[t]he official position of any accused person, whether as Head of State or Government or as a responsible Government official, shall not relieve such person of criminal responsibility nor mitigate punishment'. See also Article IV of the Genocide Convention.

[11] *Kayishema and Ruzindana* Appeal Judgment, par 169; *Krstić* Appeal Judgment, par 32.

[12] It should be noted that it has been the constant position of the Prosecution (e.g. in the *Ntakirutimana* appeal) that a distinction could be drawn between various forms of participation in a genocidal offence, not only by reason of the differing degree of contribution of each participant to the crime, but also by reason of distinct or differing *mens rea* whereby some participants (including an aider and abettor to genocide) could be held responsible even where they do not possess the specific genocidal intent. For the reasons laid down below, the author does not share such a view (see below, sub-section 14.2.1).

while committing one of the prohibited acts enumerated in the Statute, he must have sought (and intended) the destruction, in whole or in part, of a national, ethnical, racial, or religious group, as such.[13] The Appeals Chamber noted that, from an evidentiary point of view, the proof of the mental state with respect to the commission of the underlying offence charged against the accused may serve as evidence from which the Court may draw 'the further inference that the accused possessed the specific intent to destroy [one of the protected groups]'.[14] Although this requirement must be considered as a whole it may be divided, for the purpose of explanation, into five sub-elements:[15]

(i) an intent;
(ii) to destroy;
(iii) in whole or in part;
(iv) a national, ethnical, racial, or religious group;
(v) as such.

It is this peculiar mental state that primarily distinguishes genocide from other international crimes.[16] By contrast, the definition of crimes against humanity requires that the perpetrator knows of the wider context in which his acts occur ('a widespread or systematic attack against a civilian population') and that he knows that his acts are a part thereof.[17] The perpetrator of a crime against humanity need not have intended, nor does he even need to have known about, the consequences of his actions upon a given group of individuals or population. As for the perpetrator of a war crime, he must only be shown to have intended the underlying offence in which he participated (say, murder or torture) or be shown to have known of the intention of the principal if he is charged as an accomplice.[18] He need not be shown to have intended that his acts should have any impact upon the group of which the victim of his acts is a member. It is unclear, however, whether the nexus requirement for war crimes suggests that he must also be aware that his acts are somehow related to the armed conflict and, if so, what exactly he must have been aware of.

What matters for genocide is the intent of the accused to produce the specified result (that is, the destruction in whole or in part of a protected group as such), not some general intention to carry out such a criminal enterprise.[19] This state of

---

[13] *Jelišić* Appeal Judgment, pars 45–46.   [14] *Krstić* Appeal Judgment, par 20.

[15] The *mens rea* specific to underlying offences will be dealt with separately.

[16] *Akayesu* Trial Judgment, par 498: 'Genocide is distinct from other crimes inasmuch as it embodies a special intent or *dolus specialis*. Special intent of a crime is the specific intention, required as a constitutive element of the crime, which demands that the perpetrator clearly seeks to produce the act charged. Thus, the special intent in the crime of genocide lies in "the intent to destroy, in whole or in part, a national, ethnical, racial or religious group, as such".' It should be noted, however, that despite the above statement, the *Akayesu* Trial Chamber found that knowledge of the principal's genocidal intent would in fact be sufficient to enter a conviction for complicity to genocide (*Akayesu* Trial Judgment, pars 540 and 547). See also *Sikirica* Motion for Acquittal Decision, par 89; *Musema* Trial Judgment, par 164; *Jelišić* Trial Judgment, par 66.

[17] See *Kunarac* Appeal Judgment, pars 90–92.   [18] See below, sub-sections 20.4 and 20.5.

[19] See *Krstić* Trial Judgment, par 549.

mind at the time of the act must be established and it must be established beyond reasonable doubt. The five components of the genocidal *mens rea* referred to above will be dealt with in turn.

14.2.1 Intent

The requirement that the accused must have intended the destruction, in whole or in part, of a given group means that it is not sufficient for him to have envisaged such a result or regarded it as a possibility. He must be shown beyond reasonable doubt to have intended that result.[20] Mere negligence on his part would not satisfy this requirement.[21]

The required mental state must have been formed 'prior to the commission of the genocidal acts'[22] but genocide does not require the acts to have been premeditated, although this will generally be the case *in fact*.[23] There is no requirement either that the perpetrator's intent to destroy the group in whole or in part be the sole or even the primary force behind his desire to act against his victims. It is sufficient that it forms part of his overall *mens rea* at the time when he commits the acts in question.

The existence of a plan or policy to commit genocide is not a legal ingredient of that crime.[24] However, if established, such a plan or policy may have an important evidential value in determining the state of mind of the accused (and might facilitate proof of the crime itself) if he can be shown to have known of it and to have taken part therein.[25] Also, contrary to crimes against humanity which require that the perpetrator knows about the context in which his acts occur (namely, a

---

[20] 'Intent' requires both conscience (*Wissen*) and will (*Wollen*), in that the perpetrator must have considered his action, its result, and the causal relation between the two and, having done so, he must have decided consciously and willingly to proceed with his action. Article 30(2) of the ICC Statute says that a person has intent where '(a) In relation to conduct, that person means to engage in the conduct; (b) In relation to a consequence, that person means to cause that consequence or is aware that it will occur in the ordinary course of events.' In the *Einsatzgruppen* case, the following rule was laid down (*United States of America v. Otto Ohlendorf et al.*, (Case No. 9), Opinion and Judgment, in *Trials of War Criminals before the Nuremberg Military Tribunals under Control Council Law No. 10*, vol. 4 (Buffalo: William S. Hein, 1997), p 488):

Every man is presumed to intend the consequences of his acts.

Every man is responsible for those acts unless it be shown that he did not act of his own free will.

Deciding the question of free will, all the circumstances of the case must be considered because it is impossible to read what is in a man's heart. See *Stakić* Trial Judgment, par 520, which talks of a 'surplus of intent' to describe the genocidal intent.

[21] A voluntary omission may, however, suffice, as would be the case, for instance, if a camp commander purposefully declined to provide inmates with food, thereby condemning them to die, albeit slowly. See Schabas, *Genocide*, p 227.   [22] *Kayishema and Ruzindana* Trial Judgment, par 91.

[23] *Jelišić* Trial Judgment, par 100. Premeditation may, however, constitute an aggravating factor for sentencing (see Part VII 'Sentencing International Crimes'), and *Krstić* Trial Judgment, par 711; *Serushago* Trial Judgment, par 30; *Kambanda* Trial Judgment, par 61.

[24] *Jelišić* Appeal Judgment, par 48; *Krstić* Appeal Judgment, par 225. See also *Sikirica* Motion for Acquittal Decision, par 62.

[25] *Jelišić* Appeal Judgment, par 48. See also *Kayishema and Ruzindana* Trial Judgment, pars 91, 94, 276, and 528–545 and *Krstić* Trial Judgment, par 572; *Kambanda* Trial Judgment, par 16.

widespread or systematic attack against a civilian population), there is no such contextual requirement in relation to genocide.[26] Although it will generally be the case, a genocidal act need not therefore take place in the context of a vast criminal enterprise, nor does the perpetrator need to know that his or her criminal conduct fits in with the crimes of others or with a plan to commit such crimes.[27]

Intent should not be equated with motive. Only the former is a constitutive element of a genocidal offence, whilst the latter is in principle relevant to sentencing only if at all.[28] In some cases, however, motives, such as racist motivations or an extremist political agenda, may also be evidentially pertinent to a finding of the existence of a genocidal intent if it can be shown that these motivations are consistent with or indicative of a genocidal intent on the part of the accused.[29] But the fact that the accused may have had certain motives to commit a crime is not yet conclusive of his having had the required *mens rea*. Conversely, the fact that the accused may have had particular motives unrelated to a genocidal enterprise, such as a desire to avenge some old family feud, does not preclude the perpetrator from also having had the specific intent to commit genocide.[30] Nor does the fact that an accused has a mental disorder (falling short of disorders that would consistute the recognized defence of 'insanity') such as borderline personality disorder. Thus, the Appeals Chamber held in relation to Goran Jelišić, a lowly Bosnian Serb shift camp commander who liked to call himself 'Adolf', and whose mental fitness to stand trial had been questioned, that there was

no *per se* inconsistency between a diagnosis of immature, narcissistic, disturbed personality on which the Trial Chamber relied and the ability to form an intent to destroy a particular protected group. Indeed, as the prosecution points out, it is the borderline unbalanced personality who is more likely to be drawn to extreme racial and ethnical hatred than the more balanced modulated individual without personality defects.

It has been argued by some scholars that the required state of mind for genocide might have been receding, in relation to certain forms of criminal participation in genocidal actions, from a strict requirement of *intent* towards a more lenient 'knowledge' requirement.[31] In similar fashion, the Prosecutor of both *ad hoc*

---

[26] *Krstić* Appeal Judgment, par 223.

[27] See *Jelišić* Trial Judgment, pars 100–101; *Jelišić* Appeal Judgment, pars 66–68.

[28] Ibid., par 49 and *Kayishema and Ruzindana* Appeal Judgment, par 161. See also *Final Report of the Commission of Experts Established pursuant to Security Council Resolution 935* (1994), S/1994/1405 (3 December 1993) ('*Final Report of the Commission of Experts for Rwanda*'), par 159: 'the presence of political motive does not negate the intent to commit genocide if such [genocidal] intent is established in the first instance'.

[29] *Kayishema and Ruzindana* Appeal Judgment, par 160. The presence of odious or sadistic instincts does not exclude that the required *mens rea* has been met. For instance, the fact that an individual took pleasure in committing crimes does not preclude the finding that he intended to commit a genocidal crime (*Jelišić* Appeal Judgment, par 71).

[30] Ibid., par 49. See also *Krstić* Trial Judgment, par 597, concerning the impact of strategic or military ends to a finding that the accused possesses the genocidal *mens rea*.

[31] See A. K. A. Greenawalt, 'Rethinking Genocidal Intent: The Case for a Knowledge-Based Interpretation', 99 Columbia Law Review (*CLR*) 2259–2294 (1999).

Tribunals has repeatedly argued that not all forms of participation in a genocidal offence would necessarily require proof of a genocidal intent. It is said, for instance, that it would be sufficient for an accomplice to have known that the principal possessed a genocidal intent, but that he does not need to possess such an intent himself or even share it, in order to be convicted of complicity to genocide.[32] There is no doubt some support for that position in the case law of the *ad hoc* Tribunals, and the Appeals Chamber of the ICTY has indeed adopted such a view, in particular in relation to liability for aiding and abetting[33] and for joint criminal enterprise liability.[34] With all due respect, the author believes this position to be unsupported under existing customary international law. Genocide is unique by reason of its specific *mens rea* and it is debatable whether a crime which is characterized by this very element should be permitted to lose its specificity, its identity, as the ultimate crime, for the sake of expanding its criminalization and facilitating convictions.[35]

The only state of mind mentioned in the text of the Genocide Convention is that of intent and this *mens rea* is said to apply to all of those underlying offences which may constitute genocide. That principle is not qualified in any way in the text of the Convention, which does not provide for, nor even hint at, the possibility of a lower mental standard that would be applicable to any category of genocidal offence or participation therein. Nor does there seem to be any support in the *Travaux Préparatoires* for the possibility of a lower *mens rea*. In fact, until 1998, there seems to have been no support in state practice (nor any *opinio juris*) for the contention that knowledge as opposed to intent could ever suffice to enter a genocidal conviction (regardless of what form of participation is being considered).

The proposition that *knowledge*, as opposed to intent, is a sufficient degree of *mens rea* when it comes to certain forms of liability such as accomplice liability, is based on the following somewhat simplistic argument: because knowledge, as opposed to intent, is sufficient in a number of domestic legal systems to engage the criminal liability of accomplices, even in special-intent crimes such as murder, the same logic should necessarily hold true for genocide. Such a shortcut by analogy ignores a number of factors. First, a literal reading of Article 4 of the Statute (as well as Article 2 of the Genocide Convention) seems to suggest that the requirement of genocidal intent in sub-paragraph 2 applies across the board to all forms of criminal participation which are provided for in sub-paragraph 3. Such

---

[32] See, for instance, *Musema* Trial Judgment, par 181. This line of argument has systematically been pursued by the Prosecution: see, for instance, *Stakić* case, Prosecution's Final Trial Brief (Public Version), in *Stakić*, 30 May 2003, pars 293–296.

[33] See, e.g. *Krstić* Appeal Judgment, pars 140–143; *Stakić* Rule 98bis Decision, pars 63 et seq. See also, concerning complicity to genocide, *Akayesu* Trial Judgment, par 538.

[34] In *Krstić*, the Trial Chamber stated in relation to Article 7(3) of the Statute that the accused 'could not have failed to know' that a genocidal enterprise was under way (*Krstić* Trial Judgment, par 595). See also *Brdjanin* JCE III and Genocide Decision, pars 5–10.

[35] One Trial Chamber held that genocide was characterized by a 'surplus of intent' (*Stakić* Rule 98bis Decision, par 17).

an interpretation also finds support in the *Travaux Préparatoires* of the Genocide Convention.[36] Secondly, domestic crimes are not the same as international crimes and domestic forms of liability are not necessarily the same as those found in international law. International crimes are characterized by so-called *chapeau* elements which set them apart from mere domestic crimes: widespread or systematic attack against a civilian population for crimes against humanity, genocidal intent for genocide. These *chapeau* elements, be they the 'attack upon a given civilian population' in relation to crimes against humanity, or a genocidal intent in relation to genocide, set those crimes in a completely different criminal sphere than their domestic counterparts. And the jurisdictions of the *ad hoc* Tribunals are actually dependent upon those requirements having been met in relation to each and every accused person charged with a genocidal offence. In the case of crimes against humanity, this means that there must be a widespread or systematic attack against a civilian population, that the acts of the accused must objectively be part of that attack and that he knows that his acts are a part thereof.[37] In relation to genocide, which is a special-intent crime, it is suggested that each participant in a genocidal crime must likewise satisfy the *chapeau* elements of genocide, namely, its specific genocidal intent. Failing that, the acts of the accused would fall short of the requirements of genocide, and, arguably, would fall outside of the Tribunals' jurisdiction. As noted by the *Stakić* Trial Chamber, 'the application of a mode of liability can not replace a core element of a crime' such as the genocidal intent in relation to the crime of genocide.[38]

The analogy drawn between forms of liability at the national level and at the international level must also be considered carefully. Certain forms of liability, for instance, may not necessarily exist at the national level, or in a very different form than at the international level. Hence, 'joint criminal enterprise' or 'common purpose' liability is essentially a form of criminal responsibility known to common-law jurisdictions only. Conversely, the import of domestic concepts into the international context is not one of pure absorption, but one of selection and adaptation. The decision taken at the national level that certain acts or certain forms of participation are to be criminalized does not mean that the same decision has been taken at the international level, and vice versa. Many acts that are regarded as criminal at the domestic level are not international crimes.[39] Likewise, the fact that some domestic jurisdictions may provide that accomplice liability

---

[36] See, e.g. Summary Records of the Sixth Committee of the General Assembly (UN GAOR 49th Session, Plenary Meetings, 49 UN GAOR C.6, UN Doc A/C.6/49/SR.17–21 (1994)), p 109.

[37] *Kunarac* Appeal Judgment, par 99.   [38] *Stakić* Trial Judgment, par 530.

[39] See *Bagilishema* Appeal Judgment, par 36 ('Depending on the nature of the breach of duty (which must be a *gross* breach), and the gravity of the consequences thereof, breaches of duties imposed by the laws of war may entail a disciplinary rather than a criminal liability of a superior who is subject to military discipline. The line between those forms of responsibility which may engage the criminal responsibility of the superior under international law and those which may not can be drawn in the abstract only with difficulty, and the Appeals Chamber does not need to attempt to do so in the present Judgement.') See also Secretary-General Report (ICTY), par 36.

only requires knowledge of the principal's intent does not mean that such a principle is part of customary international law when applied to international crimes, let alone that it has been accepted in relation to international crimes characterized by a particular intent requirement. This must be established through clear and convincing state practice and *opinio juris*, and it has not been so established as far as genocide is concerned.[40]

There are other reasons still why it would seem genocidal intent must be established in relation to any accused charged with a genocidal offence regardless of the form of criminal participation under consideration. One such reason is a principle of justice which requires that, if faced with an uncertainty as to whether the definition of a crime (or the definition of a form of liability) requires a higher or lower mental threshold, the benefit of the doubt should accrue to the accused: *in dubio pro reo*.[41] In the case of genocide, this should mean that intent (rather than knowledge) should be required.[42] The law, including international law, should never be made at the expense of an accused person and if there is a doubt as to whether intent or knowledge is required for accomplice liability to genocide or command responsibility (and such a doubt clearly exists), for instance, the former should be favoured over the latter in light of that principle.

Another reason supporting the conclusion that intent, rather than knowledge, should be established is a purely policy decision about the function of a crime which is universally regarded as being located at the top of the hierarchy of international crimes.[43] Should the specificity of genocide be eroded by accepting that a conviction under that heading could be entered although the accused did not himself possess the required *mens rea*, but only knew that others possessed it? It is

---

[40] The Appeal Judgment in the *Krstić* case appears to fall far short of that standard (see *Krstić* Appeal Judgment, pars 143–144 and related footnotes).

[41] This principle was applied (although it was not expressly identified as such) by Trial Chamber II when assessing whether various instances of mistreatment were serious enough to amount to torture or whether they only amounted to the less serious offence of cruel treatment. In case of doubt as to whether the act is serious enough to amount to torture, the Trial Chamber gave the benefit of the doubt to the accused and regarded these acts as instances of cruel treatment which had been pleaded in the alternative: 'in case of doubt as to whether or not the act is serious enough to amount to torture, the Accused should have the benefit of that doubt, and the acts for which he is charged should be considered under the heading of the less serious offence, namely cruel treatment under Article 3 or inhumane acts under Article 5(i)' (*Krnojelac* Trial Judgment, par 219). See also *Tadić* case, Decision on Appellant's Motion for the Extension of the Time-Limit and Admission of Additional Evidence, 15 October 1998, par 73; *Čelebići* Trial Judgment, par 413; *Akayesu* Trial Judgment, par 319; *Kayishema and Ruzindana* Trial Judgment, par 103.

[42] See also *Stakić* Trial Judgment, par 502, which makes it clear that Article 4 ICTY Statute should be interpreted 'restrictively and with caution, always guided by the unique nature of the crime of genocide'.

[43] One Trial Chamber pointed at the risk of eroding the concept of genocide and creating a 'new crime' if the court were to lower the mental threshold in relation to joint criminal enterprise to one of knowledge, rather than intent: '[T]he legal construct of "joint criminal enterprise" can not create a new crime, which is not foreseen in the Statute and which might – if not carefully handled – tend to introduce a lower threshold with respect to the proof of the individual intent. This would indeed be a result that is not covered by the 1948 Genocide Convention and its verbatim incorporation in Article 4 of the Tribunal's Statute' (*Stakić* Rule 98bis Decision, par 93).

argued that the stigmatizing nature of this crime deserves to be guarded against the temptation of increased application and dilution.[44] It may be regrettable from a humanitarian point of view not to be able to convict for genocide someone, say, a Nazi camp guard, who went on with his duties in the full knowledge that those he was mistreating were bound for extermination because others intended their destruction as a group. It would be worse from the law's point of view, it is argued, if genocide merely became the common criminal crossroad at which each and every participant in a crime of scale were to meet. This norm, genocide, was adopted to sanction a very specific sort of criminal action. It would be regrettable to denature genocide for the sake of encompassing within its terms as many categories and degrees of criminal involvement as possible.

Finally, because the Tribunals are supposed to apply what is beyond any doubt part of customary international law, it must refrain from applying any such rule that falls short of that standard, in particular those rules which might have been evolving towards a different regime, but which have not yet hardened into customary law, or those for which state practice is inconclusive or *opinio juris* uncertain. There is very scant support in state practice, and negligible evidence of *opinio juris* (if any at all), to support the conclusion that knowledge may ever be a sufficient state of mind to enter a conviction in relation to any sort of participation in a genocidal offence. And the decisions, mentioned above, are unconvincing as they offer little persuasive reasoning and almost no authority in support of their finding, falling far short of the conclusion that their position may in fact truly reflect the state of customary international law at the time relevant to the counts of the indictment.

In sum, it is argued that, regardless of the form of participation with which an accused is charged (e.g. genocide, complicity to genocide, conspiracy to genocide, or criminal responsibility for genocide entailed as commander pursuant to Article 7(3)), he should be shown to have had the genocidal *intent* personally. If this mental state cannot be established by the Prosecution, it is the author's view that the accused should be acquitted of all genocide charges.

Whist this position had apparently been adopted by the Appeals Chamber in an earlier case,[45] it was later discarded at least in relation to 'aiding and abetting' genocide and 'joint criminal enterprise' for which, the Appeals Chamber said, knowledge was sufficient in principle to enter a genocide conviction.[46]

---

[44] The Appeals Chamber in the *Krstić* case recognized this: 'The gravity of genocide is reflected in the stringent requirements which must be satisfied before this conviction [of genocide] is imposed. These requirements – the demanding proof of specific intent and the showing that the group was targeted for destruction in its entirety or in substantial part – guard against a danger that convictions for this crime will be imposed lightly' (*Krstić* Appeal Judgment, par 37). Despite its statement on that point, the *Krstić* Appeals Chamber came to the conclusion that an accused could be held responsible for aiding and abetting genocide without himself possessing the genocidal intent, if he knows of the principal's intent to commit such a crime (*Krstić* Appeal Judgment, pars 140–143).

[45] *Rutaganda* Appeal Judgment, par 525.

[46] Concerning liability for 'aiding and abetting' genocide, see *Krstić* Appeal Judgment, pars 140–143; for 'joint criminal enterprise' and genocide, see *Brdjanin* JCE III and Genocide Decision, pars 5–10.

14.2.2   To destroy

The intention of the perpetrator must be *to destroy* the group, not merely to make it suffer or to discriminate against it. Destruction, pursuant to that definition, means *physical* destruction, as opposed to cultural destruction or geographical removal of the group from the area where they live.[47] An intent to 'destroy' a group therefore means that it would not be sufficient to establish that, short of destroying it, the perpetrator intended to expel the group from a given area or to deprive this group of some of its rights or privileges, although these considerations may be evidentially relevant to demonstrate the required intent.[48] What the perpetrator must intend to destroy is a group of individuals in its *physical* or *biological* existence.[49] It is not enough that the perpetrator intended to destroy (or to erase) those features – ethnic, racial, or religious – that characterize the group and qualify them for protection under that prohibition. The protected interest is indeed not the ethnicity, the religion, or the race of the group, but the physical group itself as identifiable by reason of one of these specific qualities.[50]

Contrary to popular belief, the crime of genocide does not require the actual extermination of a group of individuals.[51] Total or partial destruction of a group must merely be *intended* by the perpetrator when committing one of the prohibited

---

[47] *Krstić* Appeal Judgment, par 25. See, e.g. *Stakić* Rule 98bis Decision at p 9 which talks about the 'physical destruction of the group'; *Stakić* Trial Judgment, pars 518–519. See also *Semanza* Trial Judgment, par 315 which cites the Report of the International Law Commission on the Work of its 48th Session of 6 May–26 July 1996: 'As clearly shown by the preparatory work for the [Genocide] Convention, the destruction in question is the material destruction of a group either by physical or by biological means, not the destruction of the national, linguistic, religious, cultural or other entity of a particular group' (ILC Report 1996, p 10). See also *Krstić* Trial Judgment, pars 571 and 576; *Kajelijeli* Trial Judgment, par 808. See however, the ambiguous finding made without further discussion in the *Krstić* Trial Judgement that '[t]he physical destruction of a group is the most obvious method, but one may also conceive of destroying a group through purposeful eradication of its culture and identity resulting in the eventual extinction of the group as an entity distinct from the remainder of the community' (*Krstić* Trial Judgment, par 574). This proposition appears to mix up the protection of the group in its physical existence, as provided by the prohibition against genocide, with the protection of the attributes (national, ethnical, racial, or religious) which may distinguish such a group from one or several other groups. These attributes, as opposed to the group itself, are *not* protected by the prohibition against genocide.

[48] See, e.g. *Krstić* Appeal Judgment, pars 30–33, concerning the forcible transfer of individuals as indicative of a genocidal state of mind.

[49] A court making that determination is entitled to take into consideration, the Appeals Chamber of the ICTY said, the long-term impact of the crimes upon the survival of the group (*Krstić* Appeal Judgment, par 28).

[50] See *Milošević* Rule 98bis Decision, par 124 ('It is the material destruction of the group which must be intended and not the destruction of its identity'). Forced religious conversion, for instance, would therefore not qualify as genocide since the intention is not the physical annihilation of the group, but the erasing of its – in this case, religious – distinctiveness. That feature (religious, ethnic, or racial) is an identification tag to identify those groups protected by this norm.

[51] *Akayesu* Trial Judgment, par 497. The extent to which the group might in fact have been destroyed might, however, be a factor from which the inference may be drawn that the underlying acts were committed with genocidal intent (*Milošević* Rule 98bis Decision, par 125; *Ndindabahizi* Trial Judgment, par 454).

underlying offences, regardless of whether he was successful in carrying out his intentions.[52] Clearly, however, the fact that a large number of individuals were killed would be evidentially relevant to establishing the crime and the accused's *mens rea* if he can be shown to have known about the killing. And the accused need not be shown to have intended to achieve 'the complete annihilation of a group from every corner of the globe' but only of this group (or part thereof) which the Chamber has identified as being intended for destruction (and which may be geographically more limited in scope).[53]

A genocidal enterprise may be an evolving process. Acts or measures adopted against members of a particular group which originally may not have shown their true genocidal face, such as the adoption Laws of Nuremberg against the Jews, may later be seen as having been part of such a genocidal enterprise as they were one step towards the ultimate destruction of the group.[54] One should therefore refrain from deducing the genocidal *mens rea* solely from the immediacy which may or may not exist between the act of the accused and the consequences of his or her conduct (if any) upon the targeted group. Those consequences (the actual destruction of the group) may be far removed from the acts of the accused and, in fact, may never occur, but these acts may nevertheless contain the genocidal seeds which will permit the Court to conclude that the accused indeed possessed the requisite *mens rea*.[55] But when considering whether an accused was intent on destroying a particular group, one should equally guard against the temptation to reinterpret the significance of a particular conduct in order to fit it in with the genocidal picture in which it is placed *ex post facto*.

14.2.3 In whole or in part

In whole

As noted above, the *génocidaire* need not intend to achieve the complete annihilation of the group 'from every corner of the globe'.[56] It is enough that he intends to destroy the group (in whole or in part) identified by the Court as the protected group in the specific instance which relates to the charges brought against him. Nor must the accused be shown to have intended to kill or mistreat each and

---

[52] *Karadžić and Mladić* Rule 61 Decision, par 92: 'The degree to which the group was destroyed in whole or in part is not necessary to conclude that genocide has occurred.' See also *Krstić* Appeal Judgment, par 32. The fact that a group may indeed have suffered from the acts of the accused or from other people's actions in which he participated is not necessarily conclusive of the perpetrator's genocidal *mens rea* but it may be evidentially relevant insofar as it may allow the court to draw inferences as to the accused's mindset at the time when he committed the acts. See, for instance, *Krstić* Trial Judgement, par 584.   [53] *Kayishema and Ruzindana* Trial Judgment, par 95.

[54] See also *Krstić* Trial Judgment, par 547.

[55] R. Lemkin, *Axis Rule in Occupied Europe, Laws of Occupation: Analysis of Government: Proposals for Redress* (Washington, D.C.: Carnegie Endowment for International Peace, Division of International Law, 1944) ('Lemkin, *Axis Rule in Occupied Europe*'), pp 79, 87–89.

[56] *Jelišić* Trial Judgment, par 80; see also *Kayishema and Ruzindana* Trial Judgment, par 95.

every individual who is a member of the targeted group. The intent to destroy a multitude of individuals belonging to a particular group may amount to genocide even where these individuals constitute a geographically limited section of a larger group.[57] The *Krstić* Trial Chamber, for instance, stated as follows:[58] 'The intent to eradicate a group within a limited geographical area such as the region of a country or even a municipality may be characterized as genocide'.

It is unclear, however, how narrowly a protected group may be defined from a geographical point of view before this collectivity of individuals ceases to constitute a 'group' for the purpose of the Genocide Convention. The Prosecution should not be allowed to argue that such a 'group' may ever consist of the population of, say, a village, a camp, or a small county, lest the function of the prohibition against genocide be denatured and the intention of the Genocide Convention ignored. It is argued that the 'group' as understood in this definition must form a sizeable and sufficiently distinct and cohesive unit, although not necessarily an autarchic one, clearly distinguishable from those other groups with which it is associated (by reason of geography or history). A 'group' pursuant to that definition may not simply consist of a random collective of human beings and it must be sufficiently large in numbers to warrant the protection of the Genocide Convention.[59]

In situations where the group allegedly targeted is geographically circumscribed, the Court must ask itself whether the group (as opposed to any of its parts), as identified by the Prosecutor, is itself part of a broader unit characterized by one of the four attributes provided for in the Statute (national, ethnic, racial, or religious) and, if so, whether that smaller unit or group is distinguishable from the broader group only by reason of its geographical location or for other reasons too.[60] Once it has determined the geographical area to which the charges relate, the Court must determine whether that smaller group is sufficiently distinct or independent from the broader unit (for reasons of tradition, culture, mentality, geographical distance, for instance[61]) for it to be said to form an independent unit *vis-à-vis* that larger group and, thus, constitute a 'group' for the purpose of the Genocide Convention. This, no doubt, was the case, for instance, of the European Jewry

---

[57] *Sikirica* Motion for Acquittal Decision, par 68. In this case, the Trial Chamber therefore held that the group which had to be considered for the purpose of genocide was those Bosnian Muslims or Bosnian Croats from the Prijedor municipality considered as a whole, rather than those who had been detained in the Keraterm camp where the crimes for which the accused had been charged were committed. See also *Jelišić* Trial Judgment, par 83. See also *Krstić* Appeal Judgment, in relation to the Muslims of Srebrenica (pars 6 et seq.).   [58] *Krstić* Trial Judgment, par 589.

[59] Ibid. par 590; *Stakić* Trial Judgment, par 524.

[60] If, for instance, the Prosecution identifies the 'group' as a whole to consist of all members of religion *X*, from the municipality of *Y*, the Court must ask itself whether that 'group' is distinct from members of the religion *X* from, say, neighbouring municipalities *W* and *X*. See *Milošević* Rule 98bis Decision, pars 133–138.

[61] Also of relevance may be the scope of the whole geographical area within which genocidal activities could or are alleged to have taken place. If an armed conflict is taking place, for instance, this geographical area generally overlaps with the area within which the armed conflict is taking place, but not necessarily so.

vis-à-vis the whole of the world Jewish community during the 1930s and 1940s. It was culturally so different from the rest of the Jewish community and geographically so distant from other Jewish communities in different continents that it could easily have been regarded as a distinct 'group' for the purpose of the Genocide Convention, had the convention existed at that time.[62]

On the other hand, a collectivity of individuals which is geographically circumscribed (such as, say, Bosnian Muslims from Eastern Bosnia), but for whom this geographical circumscription signifies little or no boundary between it and the rest of its kin (Bosnian Muslims living in Bosnia, in this case) may not in principle be regarded as a 'group' for the purpose of the Genocide Convention, although it could constitute 'a part' thereof. In other words, the geographical circumscription may be a factor to take into account to determine whether the collectivity of individuals in question indeed forms an independent 'group' for the sake of the Convention, but this geographical location may not be the only trigger upon which the distinctiveness of that group may be based. In evidential terms, the Prosecution must establish that the geographically limited collectivity of individuals which it says constitutes a 'group' for the purpose of genocide is sufficiently distinct and independent from the rest of those who bear the same national, ethnic, racial, or religious features to have acquired an identity or individuality which differs in some significant fashion from the sum total of those who bear those features.[63]

The fact that, in the context of events described by the Prosecution as genocidal, there was only a limited number of victims (or, in fact, none at all) does not necessarily negate an inference on other evidence that the accused possessed an intent to destroy the group or its part.[64] Nor is the fact that the Prosecution was not able to establish the precise number of individuals killed or otherwise mistreated by the accused.[65] However, and as already pointed out above, the presence of a large number of victims considered in the context of other evidence may indeed point to the conclusion that such an intent was present:[66]

Although the perpetrators of genocide need not seek to destroy the entire group protected by the [Genocide] Convention, they must view the part of the group they wish to destroy as a distinct entity which must be eliminated as such. A campaign resulting in the killings, in different places spread over a broad geographical area, of a finite number of a protected group might not thus qualify as genocide, despite the high total number of casualties, because it would not show an intent by the perpetrators to target the very existence of the group as such. Conversely, the killing of all members of the part of a group located within a

---

[62] It is interesting to ponder whether the IMT, had it judged the Major War Criminals for genocide, would have regarded the European Jewry as a 'group' or only as a 'part of' a broader Jewish group.

[63] Because of the evidential difficulty in establishing genocide, the Prosecution has been tempted at times, to describe as 'groups' somewhat artificially circumscribed units of individuals. Thus, in the *Krstić* case, the Prosecution described the targeted groups alternatively as the Bosnian Muslims of Bosnia and Herzegovina and/or the Bosnian Muslims of Eastern Bosnia.

[64] *Sikirica* Motion for Acquittal Decision, par 75.   [65] *Jelišić* Trial Judgment, par 65.

[66] *Krstić* Trial Judgment, par 590. See also *Sikirica* Motion for Acquittal Decision, par 75.

small geographical area, although resulting in a lesser number of victims, would qualify as genocide if carried out with intent to destroy the part of the group as such located in this small geographical area. [. . .] In this regard, it is important to bear in mind the total context in which the physical destruction is carried out.

In part

If it cannot prove that the accused intended to destroy a group as a whole, the Prosecution may still obtain a conviction if it can establish that the perpetrator intended to destroy the group 'in part'. The United Nations Expert Study on Genocide defined the expression 'in part' as 'a reasonably significant number, relative to the total of the group as a whole, or else a significant section of a group such as its leadership'.[67] In the words of the Appeals Chamber, that part must be a 'substantial' one, in the sense of being significant enough that, if destroyed, its disappearance would have an impact on the group as a whole.[68] The number of individuals being targeted, in relative and absolute numbers by reference to the group as a whole, as well as the prominence of those targeted within the group, are important considerations to assess the likely consequence of the destruction of such a part on the group as a whole.[69] So is the 'area of the perpetrators' activity and control, as well as the possible extent of their reach', insofar as these may shed light on the relationship between the perpetrator's conduct and his state of mind.[70]

The first, numerical, alternative to the phrase 'in part' requires that the perpetrator intended to see that a 'considerable number of individuals who are part of the group' be destroyed.[71] As pointed out by one Trial Chamber, however, 'any mathematical calculation of the number of victims relative to the total

[67] M. Whitaker, Special Rapporteur, Revised and Updated Report on the Question of the Prevention and Punishment of the Crime of Genocide, 2 July 1985, UN Doc. E/CN.4/Sub.2/1985/6, par 29 (this passage is referred to in the *Sikirica* Motion for Acquittal Decision, par 65) (the report may be found at www.preventgenocide.org/prevent/Undocs/whitaker/section2.htm).

[68] *Krstić* Appeal Judgment, par 8; *Semanza* Trial Judgment, par 316. See also *Kajelijeli* Trial Judgment, par 809: 'the perpetrator must have intended to destroy more than an imperceptible number of the targeted group' and decisions cited therein. There is no minimum numerical threshold of victims to establish genocide.

[69] *Krstić* Appeal Judgment, par 12 ('The numeric size of the targeted part of the group is the necessary and important starting point, though not in all cases the ending point of the inquiry. The number of individuals targeted should be evaluated not only in absolute terms, but also in relation to the overall size of the entire group. In addition to the numeric size of the targeted portion, its prominence within the group can be a useful consideration. If a specific part of the group is emblematic of the overall group, or is essential to its survival, that may support a finding that the part qualifies as substantial within the meaning of Article 4 [of the ICTY Statute]'). See also *Kajelijeli* Trial Judgment, par 810 and *Kayishema and Ruzindana* Trial Judgment, par 93.

[70] *Krstić* Appeal Judgment, par 13 ('The intent to destroy former by a perpetrator of genocide will always be limited by the opportunity presented to him. While this factor alone will not indicate whether the targeted group is substantial, it can – in combination with other factors – inform the analysis').

[71] *Kayishema and Ruzindana* Trial Judgment, par 97. In *Bagilishema*, the Trial Chamber referred to a 'substantial part' of the group (*Bagilishema* Trial Judgment, par 64). In *Semanza*, the Trial Chamber held that the perpetrator must have intended to destroy a 'substantial' part of the group (*Semanza* Trial Judgment, par 316).

population of the group in this context [is] rather unhelpful'.[72] The court may consider both the number of victims relative to the size of the group as a whole as well as in absolute terms in view of the large number of individuals which have been targeted.[73]

If the quantitative criterion of a 'substantial' or 'considerable' number of victims has not been met, the intent to destroy the group 'in part' could also be established *qualitatively* if the targeted individuals constitute a 'significant' or 'emblematic' section of that group and that their elimination could in turn impact upon the group as a whole.[74] What needs to be considered again in such a case is the effect of the elimination (or intended elimination) of that 'significant' or 'substantial' section of the group upon 'the fate of the rest of the group'.[75] If the elimination of that section of the group may not impact upon the survival of the group as a whole, it may not be said to constitute 'a part' for the purpose of the Genocide Convention (nor the Tribunals' Statute).

It is somewhat unclear from the jurisprudence what sort of impact the intended destruction of 'a part' must have on the group as a whole to come within the terms of the prohibition. Clearly, it would not be sufficient to show that the destruction of that part would have some sort of effect upon the group as a whole, regardless of the nature or depth of that effect. If that were to be so, the killing or mistreatment

---

[72] *Stakić* Rule 98bis Decision, par 29.

[73] *Final Report of the Commission of Experts for the Former Yugoslavia*, par 94. See also *Krstić* Appeal Judgment, par 12.

[74] *Sikirica* Motion for Acquittal Decision, par 77. The *Sikirica* Trial Chamber also said that '[i]n examining the evidence to determine whether leaders were targeted, one is looking for Bosnian Muslims who, whether by reason of their official duties or by reason of their personality, had this special quality of directing the actions or opinions of the group in question, that is those who had a significant influence on its actions' (par 78). The Chamber went on to add that '[a] targeted part of a group would be classed as substantial either because the intent sought to harm a large majority of the group in question or the most representative members of the targeted community' (ibid.). See also *Krstić* Appeal Judgment, pars 12, 16, 21, and 37 and *Jelišić* Trial Judgment, par 82.

[75] *Milošević* Rule 98bis Decision, par 132: 'the operative requirement is that of substantiality, and the intention to destroy a significant section of the group such as its leadership is not an "independent consideration", but an element that may establish that requirement.' (*Krstić* Appeal Judgment, par 12). See also *Final Report of the Commission of Experts for the Former Yugoslavia*, par 94: 'If essentially the total leadership of a group is targeted, it could also amount to genocide. Such leadership includes political and administrative leaders, religious leaders, academics and intellectuals, business leaders and others – the totality per se may be a strong indication of genocide regardless of the actual numbers killed. A corroborating argument will be the fate of the rest of the group. The character of the attack on the leadership must be viewed in the context of the fact or what happened to the rest of the group. If a group has its leadership exterminated, and at the same time or in the wake of that, has a relatively large number of the members of the group killed or subjected to other heinous acts, for example deported on a large scale or forced to flee, the cluster of violations ought to be considered in its entirety in order to interpret the provisions of the Convention in a spirit consistent with its purpose. Similarly, the extermination of a group's law enforcement and military personnel may be a significant section of a group in that it renders the group at large defenceless against other abuses of a similar or other nature, particularly if the leadership is being eliminated as well. Thus, the intent to destroy the fabric of a society through the extermination of its leadership, when accompanied by other acts of elimination of a segment of society, can also be deemed genocide.' See also *Krstić* Appeal Judgment, par 8.

of a single individual could be said to impact upon the group as a whole, albeit in a very insignificant manner. The 'in part' requirement does not therefore mean that 'any part' of the group may be targeted for the purpose of this prohibition. A number of Chambers have said that to constitute a 'part', the destruction of the collectivity of individuals in question must have an impact (or be likely to impact) upon the *survival* of the group as a whole.[76] The Genocide Convention indeed primarily protects groups as such, and only those parts whose destruction would endanger the existence of the group as a whole.[77] Where the accused only intends to destroy a group 'in part', a conviction for genocide therefore depends on proof having been made that the destruction of that part, if carried out, would impact upon the survival of the group as a whole. And proof of that fact would in turn be met where the destruction of that part could impact upon the survival of the group either because that part is emblematic of the group as a whole or because it constitutes a sufficiently large part of that group.[78]

Does 'in part' cover a group of victims selected by kind (old or young, for instance) or by gender, rather than by number or geographical origin? Could, for instance, the intended killing of all the men of a group constitute a 'part' of that group? In *Krstić*, the Trial Chamber concluded that the killing of all able-bodied, military-aged Bosnian Muslim men of Srebrenica qualified as a group 'in part'.[79] The Trial Chamber was satisfied that the intent to kill all the Bosnian Muslim men of military age in Srebrenica constituted an intent to destroy in part the Bosnian Muslim group within the meaning of the definition of genocide. This finding of the Trial Chamber contained a triple qualification: based on the sex of the victim (men only), their age (only or mostly men of military age), and as to their geographical origin (Srebrenica and surrounding areas). On appeal, the Defence of Radislav Krstić challenged that finding by suggesting that the Trial Chamber had in fact considered the 'part of a part' of a protected group as the object of the

---

[76] See, e.g. *Sikirica* Motion for Acquittal Decision, par 77; *Jelišić* Trial Judgment, par 82.

[77] See e.g. United Nations General Assembly Resolution 96(I) describing genocide as 'a denial of the right of existence of entire human groups' (UN Doc. A/RES/96(I) (1946), 11 December 1946). See also *Reservations to the Convention on the Prevention and Punishment of Genocide, Advisory Opinion* [1951] *ICJ Reports* 14, p 23: '[the Genocide Convention seeks] to safeguard the very existence of certain human groups'. See *Krstić* Trial Judgment, pars 552–553; *Sikirica* Motion for Acquittal Decision, par 89; *Akayesu* Trial Judgment, par 521. See also R. Lemkin in *Executive Session of the Senate Foreign Relations Committee, Historical Series*, 1976, p 370; and implementing legislation proposed by the Nixon and Carter administrations where it was proposed that ' "substantial part" means a part of a group of such numerical significance that the destruction or loss of that part *would cause the destruction of the group as a viable entity*', S Exec. Rep. No. 23, 94th Cong., 2nd Sess. (1976), pp. 34–35 (emphasis added) (cited in fn 113 of *Jelišić* Trial Judgment).

[78] See, e.g., *Krstić* Appeal Judgment, pars 12, 16, 21, and 37.

[79] The *Krstić* Trial Chamber found that 'the military aged Bosnian Muslim men of Srebrenica do in fact constitute a substantial part of the Bosnian Muslim group, because the killing of these men inevitably and fundamentally would result in the annihilation of the entire Bosnian Muslim community at Srebrenica. In this respect, the intent to kill the men amounted to an intent to destroy a substantial part of the Bosnian Muslim group.' (*Krstić* Trial Judgment, par 634). The lives of women, children, and elderly men were generally spared by Bosnian Serb forces in Srebrenica.

accused's intent, thereby impermissibly expanding the application of the genocidal state of mind.[80] The Appeals Chamber rejected the Defence submissions saying that the intent to destroy a substantial part of a group (consisting of the Bosnian Muslims of Srebrenica) could be inferred from the intent to destroy a more limited group of individuals (in that case, the Srebrenica Muslim men of military age).[81] Such inference should be drawn with care, however, as the protection of this regime was clearly intended to cover certain groups and substantial parts thereof, not sub-entities or collectives of individuals falling short of a group or a substantial part thereof.[82]

The court possesses some discretion when determining whether a collectivity of individuals may be said to constitute 'a part' of a group.[83] It is the court's responsibility, however, not to allow the micro-description of an enterprise into small pieces (out of prosecutorial convenience) and to expect from such an infinitesimal breakdown a case true to the actual scope of the criminal enterprise to which an accused is said to have been a party.[84]

14.2.4 A protected group: a national, ethnic, racial, or religious group

The requirement that the targeted group which the perpetrator intends to destroy must be one of those groups – national, ethnic, racial, and religious – protected under the Genocide Convention contains two elements: an objective one and a subjective one.[85]

From the objective point of view, there must exist a group of individuals who may be identified by reason of a common national, ethnic, racial, or religious background. Such a group may not simply be imagined by the perpetrator; that group must have some sort of objective or tangible – national, ethnic, racial, or religious – existence.

---

[80] *Krstić* case Defence Appeal Brief, 10 January 2002, *infra* note 84, pars 35 et seq.

[81] *Krstić* Appeal Judgment, par 21 and 26 et seq.

[82] See *Stakić* Trial Judgment, par 523 ('In construing the phrase "destruction of a group in part", the Trial Chamber with some hesitancy follows the jurisprudence of the Yugoslavia and Rwanda Tribunals which permits a characterization of genocide even when the specific intent extends only to a limited geographical area, such as a municipality. The Trial Chamber is aware that this approach might distort the definition of genocide if it is not applied with caution', footnote omitted).

[83] *Krstić* Trial Judgment, par 590. The Trial Chamber in the *Krstić* case stated that discretionary power had to be exercised in a spirit consonant with the object and purpose of the Genocide Convention (ibid., par 590).

[84] Again, in *Krstić*, the Defence suggested that the scope given by the Trial Chamber to the definition of genocide would lead to a situation where killings carried out at the level of a village or neighbourhood would qualify as genocide (*Prosecutor v. Krstić*, IT-98-33-A, Defence Appeal Brief, 10 January 2002, par 39: 'By broadening the formula for genocide, the Trial Chamber has allowed for genocides to be found in small villages, or even neighborhoods').

[85] In *Semanza*, the Trial Chamber held that the protected group is to be identified on a case-by-case basis, 'consulting both objective and subjective criteria' (*Semanza* Trial Judgment, par 317). See also *Kamuhanda* Trial Judgment, par 630.

From a subjective perspective, however, the fact that the basis upon which the perpetrator relied to come to the conclusion that the group in question is nationally, ethnically, racially, or religiously distinct, is mistaken from a scientific or from a purely factual point of view, is irrelevant.[86] Thus, 'although membership of the targeted group must be an objective feature of the society in question, there is also a subjective dimension. A group may not have precisely defined boundaries and there may be occasions when it is difficult to give a definite answer as to whether or not a victim was a member of a protected group.'[87] In other words, what matters is the commonly shared perception of – national, ethnic, racial, or religious – specificity, not its scientific demonstrability.

The suggestion that the group must somehow have an objective existence (even one that cannot be established scientifically) is different from the question of the membership of a given individual (i.e. the victim of the underlying offence) to that group. In relation to the latter issue (that of membership), the subjective assessment of the perpetrator as to what renders such an individual different (by reason of nationality, ethnicity, race, or religion) does matter to the extent that it is relevant to the determination that he possessed the required genocidal intent, that is, to the establishment of what he intended to achieve:[88]

Although the objective determination of a religious group still remains possible, to attempt to define a national, ethnical or racial group today using objective and scientifically irreproachable criteria would be a perilous exercise whose result would not necessarily correspond to the perception of the persons concerned by such categorisation. Therefore, it is more appropriate to evaluate the status of a national, ethnical or racial group from the point of view of those persons who wish to single that group out from the rest of the community. The Trial Chamber consequently elects to evaluate membership in a national, ethnical or racial group using a subjective criterion. It is the stigmatisation of a group as a distinct national, ethnical or racial unit by the community which allows it to be determined whether a targeted population constitutes a national, ethnical or racial group in the eyes of the alleged perpetrators.[89] This position corresponds to that adopted by the Trial Chamber in its Review of the Indictment Pursuant to Article 61 filed in the Nikolić case.[90]

---

[86] *Final Report of the Commission of Experts for Rwanda*, par 159: 'to recognize that there exists discrimination on racial or ethnic grounds, it is not necessary to presume or posit the existence of race or ethnicity itself as a scientifically objective fact'. See also *Bagilishema* Trial Judgment, fn 63, pp 29–30.

[87] Ibid., par 65.

[88] *Jelišić* Trial Judgment, par 70. In *Bagilishema*, the Trial Chamber reached the same conclusion: 'If a victim is perceived by a perpetrator as belonging to a protected group, the victim could be considered by the Chamber as a member of the protected group, for the purposes of genocide.' (*Bagilishema* Trial Judgment, par 65). See also *Rutaganda* Trial Judgment, par 56. In his *Réflexions sur la question juive*, Sartre noted that 'le Juif est un homme que les autres hommes tiennent pour Juif' (J.-P. Sartre, *Réflexions sur la question juive* (Paris: Editions Gallimard, 1954), p 83).

[89] Here, the Trial Chamber follows in part the position taken by the ICTR which stated that 'an ethnic group is one whose members share a common language and culture; or a group which distinguishes itself, as such (self-identification); or, a group identified as such by others, including the perpetrators of the crimes (identification by others)' (*Kayishema and Ruzindana* Trial Judgment, par 98).

[90] *Nikolić* Rule 61 Decision, par 27, as part of the appraisal of the crime of 'persecution', the Trial Chamber stated as follows: 'the civilian population subjected to such discrimination was identified by *the perpetrators of the discriminatory measures*, principally by its religious characteristics' (emphasis added).

As far as the intent of the perpetrator is concerned, the question of the national, racial, religious, or ethnic distinctiveness of the group is not, therefore, one of scientific demonstration, but one, for lack of better expression, of social or societal perception of the identity of the group and its membership. This 'consciousness of otherness' both on the perpetrator's and the victim's part must however be sufficiently shared by the population to give the group at least a semblance of social or political (and, ultimately, legal) existence as a distinct national, racial, ethnic, or religious entity. That subjective stigmatization by the perpetrator of the victims can take both a negative or a positive form:[91]

A group may be stigmatised in this manner by way of positive or negative criteria. A 'positive approach' would consist of the perpetrators of the crime distinguishing a group by the characteristics which they deem to be particular to a national, ethnical, racial or religious group. A 'negative approach' would consist of identifying individuals as not being part of the group to which the perpetrators of the crime consider that they themselves belong and which to them displays specific national, ethnical, racial or religious characteristics. Thereby, all individuals thus rejected would, by exclusion, make up a distinct group. The Trial Chamber concurs here with the opinion already expressed by the Commission of Experts[92] and deems that it is consonant with the object and the purpose of the Convention to consider that its provisions also protect groups defined by exclusion where they have been stigmatised by the perpetrators of the act in this way.

The killing or mistreatment of a person who, though not himself or herself a member of the targeted group, but whose killing or mistreatment could further the attack against the protected group, could in principle be regarded as genocidal in character. Thus, the killing of a moderate Hutu who was opposed to the policy of the (Hutu) leaders, or married to a Tutsi, could be seen as genocidal to the extent that the removal of such an individual might arguably facilitate and contribute to the destruction of the Tutsi group by Hutu extremists.

A separate but related question relates to the potential circumstance of a victim being mistaken for a member of the group, or who was killed or mistreated as an unintentional result of a genocidal enterprise targeted at other individuals. On the one hand, it could be argued that the interest protected by the genocidal prohibition is the group as such and that the killing or mistreatment of a person who is neither a member of that group, nor closely associated therewith, did not and was not liable to impact upon that protected interest.[93] In other words, ultimately, the

---

[91] *Jelišić* Trial Judgment, pars 71. See also *Rutaganda* Trial Judgment, par 56.

[92] *Final Report of the Commission of Experts for the Former Yugoslavia*, par 96, p 25: 'If there are several or more than one victim groups, and each group as such is protected, it may be within the spirit and purpose of the Convention to consider all the victim groups as a larger entity. The case being, for example, that there is evidence that group A wants to destroy in whole or in part groups B, C and D, or rather everyone who does not belong to the national, ethnic, racial or religious group A. In a sense, group A has defined a pluralistic non-A group using national, ethnic, racial and religious criteria for the definition. It seems relevant to analyse the fate of the non-A group along similar lines as if the non-A group had been homogenous.'

[93] Only the membership in one of these groups, not the way in which one has become a member thereof (for instance, through marriage or adoption) matters for the purpose of this prohibition.

victim might have to be a member of that group (or someone closely associated therewith) as the prohibition against genocide is concerned with the protection of certain groups and their 'right to life', and not with the protection of individuals *per se*.[94] On the other hand, it could be said that the *discriminatory* aspect of the prohibition only needs to be intended by the accused and that conviction for certain genocidal offences (in particular, attempt to commit genocide and conspiracy to commit genocide) need not result in discrimination *in fact*. Alternatively, it might be said that the discrimination aspect will be satisfied by directing prohibited acts at individuals thought to be part of the group, because such acts will inevitably contribute to the overall sense of threat against the protected group.

It seems to the author that the first position should prevail. First; if the latter solution were to be adopted, the prohibition would be made to protect interests which it does not purport to protect (in the form of the life or physical or mental integrity of individuals who are neither members of a protected group, nor persons closely associated with any such group). More importantly still, reference in the text of the article to the protected 'group' is not limited to the perpetrator's *mens rea*, but is also inscribed in each and every underlying offence listed in Article 4/2 of the Statutes (and Article 2 of the Genocide Convention) which may constitute the basis of a genocidal conviction: killing, for the purpose of the Tribunals' Statutes and the Genocide Convention, is killing of *members of the group*, while causing serious bodily or mental harm is genocidal if committed against actual *members of the group*.[95] Finally, the application of the general principle of criminal law that where there is a doubt in the interpretation of the law, that doubt should always be interpreted in favour of the accused (*in dubio pro reo*), would lead to the same conclusion. This view seems to have been accepted in the jurisprudence of the Tribunals.[96]

---

[94] *Krstić* Trial Judgment, par 553. The United Nations General Assembly Resolution 96(I) described genocide as 'a denial of the right of existence of entire human groups' (UN Doc. A/RES/96(I) (1946), 11 December 1946). See also *Reservations to the Convention on the Prevention and Punishment of Genocide, Advisory Opinion* [1951] *ICJ Reports* 14, p 23: '[the Genocide Convention seeks] to safeguard the very existence of certain human groups and [. . .] to confirm and endorse the most elementary principles of morality' (cited in *Krstić* Trial Judgment, par 552). This fact may be said to render genocide particularly serious as a criminal offence (*Krstić* Trial Judgment, par 553). See also *Sikirica* Motion for Acquittal Decision, par 89: 'Whereas it is the individuals that constitute the victims of most crimes, the ultimate victim of genocide is the group, although its destruction necessarily requires the commission of crimes against its members.' The Trial Chamber in *Akayesu* clearly stated that, ultimately, 'the victim of the crime of genocide is the group itself and not only the individual' who is most directly victimized by the acts of the perpetrator (*Akayesu* Trial Judgment, par 521). A good illustration of this process relates to the sexual violence administered upon Tutsi women during the Rwandan conflict (see pars 732–733 of *Akayesu* Trial Judgment). See also *Rutaganda* Trial Judgment, par 60.   [95] See Schabas, *Genocide*, p 110.

[96] *Jelišić* Trial Judgment, par 66, stating that the victim must have 'belonged to an identified group' and *Akayesu* Trial Judgment, par 521 ('[. . .] for any of the acts charged under Article 2 (2) of the Statute to be a constitutive element of genocide, the act must have been committed against one or several individuals, *because such individual or individuals were members of a specific group, and specifically because they belonged to this group*') and par 712, finding that crimes committed by the – Hutu – accused against two Hutu victims may not constitute a genocidal offence.

The requirement that the crime must have resulted in discrimination *in fact* would not apply, however, to either attempt to commit genocide or to the inchoate offences of direct and public incitement to commit genocide and conspiracy to commit genocide, for which there is no requirement of *actual* victimization.

The Genocide Convention, and also the Statutes of the *ad hoc* Tribunals, identify four categories of protected groups: national, ethnical, racial, and religious. These four categories may overlap in part, but each one of them has a distinct core. The definitions which have been given by the Tribunals to these groups do not have any claim to scientific verifiability. These are 'legal' definitions and the boundaries set by those definitions upon what may constitute a national, ethnical, racial, or religious group for the purpose of the definition of genocide may be highly questionable from a sociological or scientific point of view. For the purpose of the Statute, the four categories of protected groups have been defined with varying degrees of specificity as follows:

1. A 'national' group has been said to consist of 'a collection of people who are perceived to share a legal bond based on common citizenship, coupled with reciprocity of rights and duties'.[97]

2. An 'ethnic' group has been defined as 'a group whose members share a common language or culture'.[98]

---

[97] *Akayesu* Trial Judgment, par 512. See also *Krstić* Trial Judgment, pars 558–559. According to Arendt, '[a] people becomes a nation when "it takes conscience of itself according to its history" ' (H. Arendt, *Essays in Understanding, 1930–1945* (New York: Harcourt Brace & Co., 1994), p 208). It is interesting in that context to consider the way in which the Appeals Chamber has defined the concept of nationality for the purpose of the Geneva Convention's grave breaches regime. For an individual to be protected under that regime, he or she must be 'in the hands of a Party to the conflict or Occupying Power of which he or she is *not a national*'. That requirement of a different nationality between the perpetrator and the victim has been interpreted quite liberally by the Appeals Chamber which held that nationality was not solely determined by the passport held by each one, but by their respective allegiance to a party to an armed conflict. (see *Tadić* Appeal Judgment, par 166: 'Th[e] legal approach, hinging on substantial relations more than on formal bonds, becomes all the more important in present-day international armed conflicts. While previously wars were primarily between well-established States, in modern inter-ethnic armed conflicts such as that in the former Yugoslavia, new States are often created during the conflict and ethnicity rather than nationality may become the grounds for allegiance. [T]he [Geneva] Convention's object and purpose suggest that allegiance to a Party to the conflict and, correspondingly, control by this Party over persons in a given territory, may be regarded as the crucial test.') Thus, the Appeals Chamber concluded, Bosnian Muslims and Bosnian Serbs, although they are all strictly speaking Bosnians, could be said to be of different nationality for the purpose of the grave breach regime, to the extent that they owed allegiance to different – national – fighting parties (Bosnia *sensu stricto* for the Muslims, Serbia, or greater Serbia for the Bosnian Serbs) (*Tadić* Appeal Judgment, pars 167–169). Whether the same reasoning could apply in relation to genocide is unclear, but there is no *a priori* reason why it could not or should not.

[98] *Akayesu* Trial Judgment, par 513. See also par 702 of the same decision where the Trial Chamber makes the finding that the Tutsis form an 'ethnic' group for the purpose of the prohibition against genocide. According to the *Kayishema and Ruzindana* Trial Chamber, an 'ethnic' group is 'one whose members share a common language and culture; or, a group which distinguishes itself, as such (self identification); or, a group identified as such by others, including perpetrators of the crimes (identification by others)' (*Kayishema and Ruzindana* Trial Judgment, par 98). This Trial Chamber was satisfied that the Tutsis formed an 'ethnic' group for the purpose of defining the scope of protected groups (*Kayishema and Ruzindana* Trial Judgment, par 523). The definition of what constitutes an 'ethnic' group for the purpose of genocide given by those various Chambers is, to say the least,

3. A 'racial' group 'is based on the hereditary physical traits often identified with a geographical region, irrespective of linguistic, cultural, national or religious factors'.[99] It has never been suggested that either Tutsis and Hutus on the one hand or Serbs, Croats, and Bosnians on the other constituted different races for the purpose of the Statutes. The concept of 'race' is, from a legal point of view, somewhat dated. It is also so politically charged that it may prove difficult to apply.

4. A 'religious' group is 'one whose members share the same religion, denomination or mode of worship'.[100]

At the Rwanda Tribunal, Hutus and Tutsis have been described as two different 'ethnic' groups for the purpose of the prohibition against genocide,[101] whilst the ICTY has not yet clearly laid down the existence of precise national, ethnical, racial or religious boundaries between Serbs, Croats, and Bosnian Muslims.[102]

---

extremely vague. The fact that individuals share a common language (as, for instance, many Nigerians and Australians do), or a common culture (as Bosnian Serbs and Bosnian Muslims do, in many respects) seems barely sufficient to suggest that they may, on that basis alone, be said to constitute a common 'ethnic' group for the purpose of the Genocide Convention. The concept of 'ethnicity' is no doubt an ambivalent concept and one of serious political significance. Criminal law (including the law of genocide) needs precision and the Tribunals should therefore attempt to give the law more certainty on that point, although it is perfectly acceptable, in light of the very purpose of the prohibition against genocide, that this concept should be given a relatively broad definition.

[99] *Akayesu* Trial Judgment, par 514. In *Krstić*, the Trial Chamber pointed out that the International Convention on the Elimination of All Forms of Racial Discrimination defines racial discrimination as 'any distinction, exclusion, restriction or preference based on race, colour, descent, or national or ethnic origin' (*Krstić* Trial Judgment, par 555). See also *Kayishema and Ruzindana* Trial Judgment, par 98.

[100] *Akayesu* Trial Judgment, par 515. This definition of 'religion' is strikingly circular as the attribute of the group (as a 'religious' group) is defined by the exercise of those features which makes the group a distinct religious group (for instance, its mode of worship). In most cases, it is true, the differences in religion between two or more groups of individuals will be self-evident, as for instance between Bosnian Muslims and Bosnian (Orthodox) Serbs. Sometimes, it may be less so. What, for instance, of two closely related sects within the same denomination? What of different degrees of commitment to a similar religion (say, non-practising Muslims versus fundamentalists)? What of religions or quasi-religious practices which are not officially recognized as religion (e.g., the Church of Scientology or Falun Gong)? Neither Tribunal may have to make such determinations, however, since in both cases (Rwanda and the former Yugoslavia) religious boundaries were quite clearly drawn between various groups.

[101] See, *inter alia*, *Akayesu* Trial Judgment, par 122; *Kayishema and Ruzindana* Trial Judgment, pars 522–526; *Kajelijeli* Trial Judgment, par 817. In *Akayesu*, the Trial Chamber said the following: 'The term ethnic group is, in general, used to refer to a group whose members speak the same language and/or have the same culture. Therefore, one can hardly talk of ethnic groups as regards Hutu and Tutsi, given that they share the same language and culture. However, in the context of the period in question, they were, in consonance with a distinction made by the colonizers, considered both by the authorities and themselves as belonging to two distinct ethnic groups; as such, their identity cards mentioned each holder's ethnic group' (*Akayesu* Trial Judgment, fn 56, p 62). See also *Preliminary Report of the Commission of Experts for Rwanda*, par 124, which considers Hutus and Tutsis to be different 'ethnic' groups.

[102] In *Krstić*, for instance, the Trial Chamber did not attempt to state what sort of protected group the Bosnian Muslims fell into (see *Krstić* Trial Judgment, pars 559–560). In *Stakić*, the Trial Chamber identified the Bosnian Muslims group as the targeted group (*Stakić* Trial Judgment, par 545). The Trial Chamber did not however, specify, the protected category into which that group of individuals would fall. The ICTY has had occasion, however, in relation to other offences (mainly torture and

In several decisions, Chambers of the Tribunals found that the victims were part of a particular protected group, but failed to specify the one category of group (national, ethnic, racial, or religious) within which they fell. In the *Krstić* case, for instance, the Trial Chamber took such a course simply concluding that the Bosnian Muslims of Srebrenica constituted a protected group pursuant to Article 4 of the ICTY Statute, whilst refraining from saying what sort of group it was or what characteristics made it a discrete 'group' for the purpose of this provision.[103] The Trial Chamber's approach seems to have been inspired by the *Interim Report of the Commission of Experts*, where they considered the situation of perpetrators of a Group *A* which intends to destroy not only Group *B* or Group *C*, but any non-*A* group.[104] While such an approach is an understandable reaction to the potentially controversial questions involved in consideration of the issues of nationality, ethnicity, race, and religion, it is open to question whether such a generic sort of finding on the part of a Trial Chamber would satisfy the Court's obligation to give reasoned opinions and whether such an approach is in fact supported in law.[105] What is certain, however, is that the targeted group may be distinguishable on more than one of the bases provided under that provision.[106]

It is clear, furthermore, that a group's characteristics 'must be identified within the socio-historic context which it inhabits' and 'by using as a criterion the stigmatization of the group, notably by the perpetrators of the crime, on the basis of its perceived national, ethnical, racial or religious characteristics'.[107] This context-specific assessment of the nature of the group may in turn influence the extent to which a certain conduct could be said to impact upon that group. Thus, certain forms of mistreatment might be regarded as having an impact (or a

persecution) to say that Bosnian Muslims and Bosnian Serbs could be distinguished (and discriminated against) on, *inter alia*, a religious or ethnic basis (see, for instance, *Krnojelac* Trial Judgment, par 438, where the Trial Chamber held that acts of persecution committed by Serb authorities against Muslim and other non-Serb male civilians could be said to be discriminating on 'religious or political grounds').

103 *Krstić* Trial Judgment, pars 559–560. See also *Stakić* Trial Judgment, par 512.

104 See *Final Report of the Commission of Experts for the Former Yugoslavia*, par 96: 'If there are several or more than one victim groups, and each group as such is protected, it may be within the spirit and purpose of the [Genocide] Convention to consider all the victim groups as a larger entity. [. . .] in one-against-everyone-else cases the question of a significant number or a significant section of the group must be answered with reference to all the target groups as a larger whole.'

105 According to the Appeals Chamber, '[a] Chamber is required to give reasons for its finding on the facts which led to its conclusion but this does not mean that it has a duty to give a detailed analysis of each such factor. In most applications for provisional release, it would be sufficient for a Chamber to state that the matters put forward by the applicant have not satisfied it that he will appear for trial, or that, if released, he will not pose a danger to any victim, witness or other person (as the case may be). In the particular case, one or more of the particular matters put forward by the applicant will be of such a nature that, in the discharge of its duty to give reasons, the Chamber will be obliged to explain why it has not accepted one or more of the various matters as being sufficient to establish the relevant fact. It is not possible to state in advance any specific test as when such an obligation will arise. Each case will depend upon its own circumstances' (*Prosecutor v. Milutinović et al.* Decision Refusing Milutinović Leave to Appeal, 3 July 2003, par 23).

106 *Stakić* Trial Judgment, par 512.   107 *Krstić* Trial Judgement, par 557.

particularly serious impact) upon the targeted group in question by reason of the context in which they occur:[108]

In patriarchal societies, where membership of a group is determined by the identity of the father, an example of a measure intended to prevent births within a group is the case where, during rape, a woman of the said group is deliberately impregnated by a man of another group, with the intent to have her give birth to a child who will consequently not belong to its mother's group.

Is the list of protected groups an exhaustive one or are there other groups, such as political, social, or sexual groups, which may be protected by the prohibition against genocide? The Genocide Convention and its *Travaux Préparatoires* suggest that, besides the groups expressly listed, no other group is protected by the international prohibition against genocide. In two successive Judgments,[109] however, Trial Chamber I of the ICTR (with the same judges sitting on both occasions) suggested that the prohibition may indeed extend beyond the four protected groups expressly mentioned in the Genocide Convention (and in the Tribunal's Statute) to include all stable or permanent groups.[110] Although the meritorious agenda behind such a position is obvious, this proposition would appear to be, unfortunately, unsupported in law and at the time of its exposition in fact constituted purely judicial law-making. The Genocide Convention and the Tribunals' Statutes only list four categories of protected groups, namely, national, ethnical, racial, and religious groups and there is not much indication that customary international law has evolved beyond those four groups to include other human collectivities.[111] This may be regrettable, but this is the way the law stands at present. It should be noted, however, that in most cases, if not all of them, crimes committed on a large scale against other groups of individuals would generally come within the definition of crimes against humanity or war crimes.[112]

14.2.5   As such

The requirement that the group must be targeted 'as such' is complementary and additional to the requirement that the perpetrator must have intended to destroy

---

[108] *Akayesu* Trial Judgment, par 507.

[109] Ibid., pars 511 and 516; *Rutaganda* Trial Judgment, pars 56–58. The Trial Chamber in *Akayesu* merely noted that a common feature of these groups is that membership thereto is generally of a permanent or at least of a stable sort in the sense that 'membership in such groups would seem to be normally not challengeable by its members, who belong to it automatically, by birth, in a continuous and often irremediable manner' (*Akayesu* Trial Judgment, par 511).

[110] In the *Rutaganda* Judgment, Trial Chamber I suggested that, on a case-by-case approach, other sufficiently stable groups could come under the protection of that norm (*Rutaganda* Trial Judgment, pars 57–58). See also *Akayesu* Trial Judgment, par 516, which also suggests that the list of protected groups is not necessarily exhaustive.

[111] *Jelišić* Trial Judgment, par 69. The fact, however, that a genocidal mindset might be related to (and may in fact be merging with) a particular political agenda would not negate the finding that the accused indeed possessed the required state of mind, and may in fact reinforce it (see *Nahimana* Trial Judgment, par 969).   [112] See generally below, sub-sections 25 and 26.

that group in whole or in part.[113] As pointed out above, 'the victim of the crime is the group itself and not only the individual' most directly concerned by the crime of the accused.[114] The crime in question 'must [therefore] be directed at their collectivity or at them in their collective character or capacity'.[115] In effect, a genocidal act consists of a dual victimization, of the individual who is killed or otherwise mistreated by the accused and, through him or her, of the group of which he or she is a member.[116]

What the phrase 'as such' means is that the physical victim of the crime must have been selected because he or she was a member of the targeted group and that, through his or her victimization, the perpetrator intended to inflict suffering (and ultimately destruction) upon this group.[117] The intention of the perpetrator must therefore be to destroy the group 'as a separate and distinct entity'.[118] By killing or mistreating a given individual, the perpetrator must in fact be intent on attacking the group of which the victim is a member.[119] Although the perpetrator must be

---

[113] *Sikirica* Motion for Acquittal Decision, par 90.

[114] See *Milošević* Rule 98bis Decision, par 123 ('Genocide is a discriminatory crime in that, for the crime to be established, the underlying acts must target individuals because of their membership of a group. The perpetrator of genocide selects and targets his victims because they are part of a group that he seeks to destroy. This means that the destruction of the group must have been sought as a separate and distinct entity. According to the International Law Commission, "the action taken against individual members of the group is the means used to achieve the ultimate objective with respect to the group", footnotes omitted); *Sikirica* Motion for Acquittal Decision, par 65 ('Whereas it is the individuals that constitute the victims of most crimes, the ultimate victim of genocide is the group, although its destruction necessarily requires the commission of crimes against members, that is, individuals belonging to that group') and par 87; *Jelišić* Appeal Judgment, par 67; *Akayesu* Trial Judgment, par 521; *Kayishema and Ruzindana* Trial Judgment, par 99; *Niyitegeka* Trial Judgment, par 410; *Nahimana* Trial Judgment, par 948.

[115] *Final Report of the Commission of Experts for the Former Yugoslavia*, par 97.

[116] See, e.g., *Bagilishema* Trial Judgment, par 61: 'the victim of the crime of genocide is singled out by the offender not by reason of his or her individual identity, but on account of his or her being a member of a national, ethnical, racial or religious group. This means that the victim of the crime of genocide is not only the individual but also the group to which he or she belongs.' See also *Akayesu* Trial Judgment, pars 521–522.

[117] See *Niyitegeka* Appeal Judgment, par 53 ('The words "as such," however, constitute an important element of genocide, the "crime of crimes." It was deliberately included by the authors of the Genocide Convention in order to reconcile the two diverging approaches in favour of and against including a motivational component as an additional element of the crime. The term "as such" has the *effet utile* of drawing a clear distinction between mass murder and crimes in which the perpetrator targets a specific group because of its nationality, race, ethnicity or religion. In other words, the term "as such" clarifies the specific intent requirement' footnotes omitted).

[118] *Stakić* Rule 98bis Decision, par 30; *Stakić* Trial Judgment, par 521.

[119] In other words, the commission of a genocidal act may be said to reach beyond the natural person who is a victim of the crime (*Akayesu* Trial Judgment, pars 521–522). 'The evidence must establish that it is the group that has been targeted, and not merely specific individuals within that group' (*Sikirica* Motion for Acquittal Decision, par 89). In *Jelišić*, the Trial Chamber said the following: 'By killing an individual member of the targeted group, the perpetrator does not thereby only manifest his hatred of the group to which his victim belongs but also knowingly commits this act as part of a wider-ranging intention to destroy the national, ethnical, racial or religious group of which the victim is a member' (*Jelišić* Trial Judgment, par 79). See also *Musema* Trial Judgment, par 165; *Jelišić* Trial Judgment, pars 66–67; *Rutaganda* Trial Judgment, par 399.

shown to have intended to destroy the group through the victims of his crimes, it is not required that the killing or mistreatment of that particular victim or victims has a direct impact upon the destruction of this group. This merely needs to have been intended by the accused.

From the perspective of the perpetrator, the victim must therefore have been selected not because of who he or she is, but (at least in part) because of his or her membership in a protected group.[120] Mere knowledge that the victim is a member of a targeted group is not therefore sufficient to establish an intent to destroy the group as such.[121] In addition, the perpetrator must be shown to have selected the victim for that reason, although it need not have been the only reason (and not even the primary reason) why he selected him or her.

As was pointed out above, if the perpetrator is mistaken about the victim's membership in a protected group, it would appear that he will in principle have committed no genocidal offence. In other words, genocide may not be committed putatively and the victim must *in fact* have been part of the protected group (or he or she must otherwise have been sufficiently related to that group) for the act to qualify as genocide.[122]

The display on the part of the perpetrator of a certain randomness in the selection of victims does not necessarily exclude an intention on his part to destroy in whole or in part the group of which those victims (and those who were not selected) were members.[123] A *génocidaire* is not necessarily a serial killer who systematically eliminates every single member of the targeted group he may encounter if given the chance. In almost every case of mass atrocities, and genocidal conduct in particular, there is an element of randomness or incoherence on the part of the killers, be it in the form of unexpected mercy on the part of an otherwise ruthless murderer or by reason of pure opportunism. A requirement that a *génocidaire* must have killed every single member of the targeted group whom he met would fail to account for the intricacies of the human mind. Thus, the Appeals Chamber said that the Trial Chamber should not have acquitted Goran Jelišić of genocide on the basis that his actions did not show an intent to destroy the group 'as such', simply because he spared a certain number of Muslim prisoners. The Trial Chamber should have 'discounted the few incidents where he showed mercy as aberrations in an otherwise relentless campaign against [Bosnian Muslims]', the Appeals Chamber held.[124]

---

[120] See, e.g. *Semanza* Trial Judgment, par 312.   [121] *Krstić* Trial Judgment, par 561.

[122] See above, sub-section 12.8. The same logic would seem to apply to the crime of persecution (see above, sub-section 14.2.4).   [123] *Jelišić* Appeal Judgment, par 71.

[124] Ibid. The Trial Chamber's reasoning in that respect is to be found at pars 106–108 of the Trial Chamber's Judgment. See also the decision of the Appeals Chamber (in *Kayishema and Ruzindana* Appeal Judgment, pars 147–149) where the Defence argued, unsuccessfully, that the fact that the Hutu accused Kayishema and Ruzindana may have saved 72 Tutsi children excluded that he may have had a genocidal *mens rea vis-à-vis* this ethnic group.

14.3   Establishing the genocidal *mens rea*

As Fuller once pointed out, 'if intention is a fact, it is a private fact inferred from outward manifestations'.[125] In the absence of explicit evidence of genocidal intent, the *mens rea* of the accused may be inferred from all the circumstances.[126] The Tribunals have listed a number of factors which may be relevant to the determination that the accused possessed the necessary genocidal intent: the general context in which the acts occurred; the perpetration of other culpable acts systematically directed against the same group; the scale of the atrocities; the systematic targeting of victims on account of their membership of a particular group; the repetition of destructive and discriminatory acts; the number of victims; the means and methods used to carry out the crimes; the area in which the perpetrator was active; and the perpetrator's demonstrated intent to kill his victims.[127] Other relevant factors have been mentioned such as the gravity of the act which is potentially indicative of a genocidal *mens rea*,[128] the scale of atrocities committed, their general occurrence in a region or a country, the fact that members of a particular group are being targeted, while the members of other groups are excluded,[129] the general political doctrine which gave rise to the acts,[130] or the fact that the crimes in question otherwise 'violate the very foundation of the group'.[131] Also, statements or utterances made by the accused relating to the fate of the group or the victims have been taken into account to establish his criminal state of mind.[132]

---

[125] L. L. Fuller, *The Morality of Law (Storr's Lectures on Jurisprudence)* (New Haven: Yale University Press, rev edn, 1977), p 72. See also *Akayesu* Trial Judgment, par 523 ('intent is a mental factor which is difficult, even impossible, to determine. This is the reason why, in the absence of a confession from the accused, his intent can be inferred from a certain number of presumptions of fact').

[126] '[E]xplicit manifestations of criminal intent are, for obvious reasons, often rare in the context of criminal trials. In order to prevent perpetrators from escaping convictions simply because such manifestations are absent, the requisite intent may normally be inferred from relevant facts and circumstances' (*Kayishema and Ruzindana* Appeal Judgment, par 159). See also *Rutaganda* Appeal Judgment, pars 525–530; *Karadžić and Mladić* Rule 61 Decision, pars 94–95; *Sikirica* Motion for Acquittal Decision, pars 61 and 46; *Stakić* Rule 98bis Decision, par 17; *Milošević* Rule 98bis Decision, par 120 ('While it is not impossible to have express evidence of the required intent, most usually the intent will have to be inferred from the evidence'); *Rutaganda* Trial Judgment, pars 63 and 399–400; *Kayishema and Ruzindana* Trial Judgment, pars 93 and 527; *Semanza* Trial Judgment, par 313. See also *Akayesu* Trial Judgment, par 478; *Bagilishema* Trial Judgment, par 63; *Kajelijeli* Trial Judgment, pars 804–807, 819–828; *Nahimana* Trial Judgment, pars 957–969; *Ndindabahizi* Trial Judgment, par 454. See also *Final Report of the Commission of Experts for the Former Yugoslavia*, par 97.

[127] See, *inter alia*, *Jelišić* Appeal Judgment, par 47; *Akayesu* Trial Judgment, par 523; *Jelišić* Trial Judgment, pars 73–77; *Karadžić and Mladić* Rule 61 Decision, pars 94–95; *Krstić* Appeal Judgment, pars 12–14 and 21; *Milošević* Rule 98bis Decision, pars 246 and 288; *Kayishema and Ruzindana* Trial Judgment, par 93; *Kajelijeli* Trial Judgment, par 806, and cases cited therein.

[128] *Nikolić* Rule 61 Decision, par 34.

[129] *Akayesu* Trial Judgment, par 523. See also, *Karadžić and Mladić* Rule 61 Decision, par 92.

[130] Ibid., par 94.

[131] Ibid. For an illustration as to how this intent is inferred in practice, see, for example, *Musema* Trial Judgment, pars 931–934.   [132] See, e.g. *Jelišić* Trial Judgment, par 73.

In a situation where the accused's *mens rea* is established circumstantially, however, the conclusion that he possessed the requisite genocidal intent must be the only reasonable conclusion available in light of the evidence. There may be situations where an inference as to the accused's intent could not be drawn from one or several evidential factors when considered individually, but 'when the evidence in relation to each is viewed as a whole, it would be perfectly proper to draw the inference'.[133] But if there is any other inference to be drawn from the evidence than that the accused possessed the requisite state of mind, that inference *must* be drawn.

The Tribunals' approach to this question highlights the close relationship which exists from an evidential point of view between the accused's *knowledge* of genocidal occurrences and the conclusion that he himself possessed the *intent* to commit such crime. In the *Stakić* or *Krstić* case, for instance, the Trial Chambers spent a great deal of time establishing that '*a* genocide' had been taking place in the relevant area in order to establish the accused's knowledge thereof and his part therein and, ultimately, his genocidal intent.[134] Often, the finding that the accused possessed the genocidal intent appears to be no more than a conclusion based on solid evidence of criminal participation with *knowledge* that members of a group are being killed or mistreated *en masse*. The reasoning goes as follows: having decided to take part in a criminal campaign whilst knowing what was happening (an enemy group was being destroyed or was marked for destruction), an accused who decides to participate therein must perforce himself have intended to destroy that group. As pointed out above, although knowledge on the part of the accused of other people's genocidal intentions may be evidentially relevant to the determination that he himself possessed the requisite genocidal state of mind, nevertheless the conclusion that he intended to commit genocide must be the only reasonable conclusion to be drawn from the evidence and it must be established beyond reasonable doubt.[135]

When making a finding as to the accused's *mens rea*, the Tribunals are expected to lay down in some detail the basis upon which its conclusion is based and to give detailed reasons why the evidence permits it to conclude that the accused indeed possessed the required intent. The right of an accused to a reasoned opinion is one of the elements of the fair trial requirement embodied in the Tribunal's Statute and it must be applied fairly strictly where the consequence of the court's finding may have such grave consequences for the accused.[136]

---

[133] *Sikirica* Motion for Acquittal Decision, par 65. Also, the nature of the armed conflict – if any – in which the crimes are being committed, the apparent geographical limits set by the perpetrator to their criminal enterprise or, in the case of a lower level perpetrator, the geographical area into which he and his group may be said to have operated, are relevant factors to consider when assessing the meaning of the 'in whole or in part' phrase. The temporal and geographical frame chosen by the Prosecutor for the indictment of the accused may therefore be crucial in that respect.

[134] *Stakić* Rule 98bis Decision, pars 31 et seq.; *Krstić* Trial Judgment, pars 544–549. See also *Akayesu* Trial Judgment, pars 112 et seq.

[135] See, *inter alia*, *Kayishema and Ruzindana* Trial Judgment, pars 531–545.

[136] *Furundžija* Trial Judgment, par 69.

15

Underlying Offences

Articles 4(2)/2(2) of the Statutes say that genocide means 'any of the following acts committed with intent to destroy in whole or in part, a national, ethnical, racial or religious group, as such', and then go on to list the following acts:

(a) Killing members of the group;
(b) Causing serious bodily or mental harm to members of the group;
(c) Deliberately inflicting on the group conditions of life calculated to bring about its physical destruction in whole or in part;
(d) Imposing measures intended to prevent births within the group; and
(e) Forcibly transferring children of the group to another group.

These acts are sometimes referred to as the *actus reus* of genocide.[1] The expression 'underlying crimes' or 'underlying offences' is preferred here for two reasons: first, it sets a distinction (applying to all crimes within the Tribunal's jurisdiction) between the so-called *chapeau* elements on the one hand and underlying offences on the other; secondly, these various underlying offences each are made up of both an *actus reus* and a *mens rea*. It may therefore be somewhat misleading to refer to them simply as '*actus reus*' since each one of them in fact contains its own individual *mens rea*.

These five categories of offences have at least two common features: a relatively high threshold of seriousness and the potential to contribute to the destruction of

---

[1] See, e.g. Schabas, *Genocide*, pp 151 et seq.

the group of which the victim is a member. Concerning their gravity, all five of them infringe upon fundamental protected values, human life and physical or mental integrity. Concerning the second characteristic, it is relevant here that the enumeration does not talk only of killing or of serious physical or mental harm, but of killing *members of the group*, or of causing serious bodily or mental harm *to members of the group*. The conduct of the accused must therefore in fact be directed at members of that group (or people closely related to it) and, according to the author, it should at least have the potential to contribute to the destruction of the targeted group.[2]

It is worth repeating that each one of these underlying offences must have been committed 'with intent to destroy, in whole or in part, a national, ethnical, racial or religious group, as such'. It is not sufficient, in other words, for the Prosecution to show that the accused committed such acts in the context of a genocidal campaign or that the accused harboured genocidal propensities: it must be established that the accused possessed a genocidal intent in relation to *that* crime for which he is charged and for which he could in turn be convicted.[3]

15.1   Killing members of the group

In the minds of many, genocide is murder on a massive scale. Although it may be accurate from a historical perspective that most genocides have involved the killing of many, the question as far as the *ad hoc* Tribunals are concerned is not whether many people have been killed as a result of a vast criminal enterprise referred to as 'a genocide', but whether an accused who has killed or mistreated one or more individuals may be found guilty of genocide.

From a numerical point of view, individual criminal responsibility for genocide covers a criminal range which goes – theoretically – from a situation where one person is killed to vast criminal enterprises where thousands are put to death. Where an accused has been specifically charged with 'killing members of the group', he must be shown to have killed or taken part in the killing of at least one person, or indeed, two or more, as the use of the plural ('killing members of the group') would suggest. Insofar as the perpetrator does so in one of the forms of criminal participation provided for in the Statute, the manner in which he kills his victim(s) is irrelevant to his guilt.[4]

The Appeals Chamber has made it clear that the expression 'killing' in that context was equivalent to that of '*meurtre*' in the French text (and not '*assassinat*', i.e. 'murder'), and that it therefore implies an intentional, although not necessarily

---

[2] This also explains why the killing or mistreatment of individuals who are mistaken for members of such groups would arguably not constitute a genocidal offence.

[3] For a similar reasoning in relation to persecution, see *Krnojelac* Trial Judgment, par 436.

[4] The killing or mistreatment need not have been carried out in any one particular way or by recourse to any particular method. See *Krstić* Appeal Judgment, par 32.

premeditated, conduct.[5] In other words, the victim must have been killed and death must have been caused intentionally.[6] Involuntary or negligent homicide therefore does not qualify as 'killing' for the purpose of this offence.[7] Nor, as was pointed out above, would the killing of an individual who was mistakenly believed to be part of the targeted group constitute a genocidal act.[8]

15.2 Causing serious bodily or mental harm to members of the group

The underlying offence of 'causing serious bodily or mental harm to members of the group' has been described more than defined by the *ad hoc* Tribunals. Its scope should be determined on a case-by-case basis, the Tribunals have said,[9] and it includes, *inter alia*, conduct that would amount to inhumane treatment, torture, rape, persecution, and deportation.[10] The *actus reus* of that offence may be realized by infliction of bodily harm ('which involves some type of physical injury'[11]) or mental harm ('which involves some type of impairment of mental faculties'[12]).

'Serious harm' does not mean that the consequences of the crime must be either irremediable or permanent.[13] The requirement that the harm be 'serious' entails more than 'minor impairment on mental or physical faculties',[14] and it should be applied strictly and, in case of doubt as to whether the act is sufficiently serious to qualify, the benefit of the doubt should accrue to the accused.[15] In *Kayishema and*

---

[5] *Kayishema and Ruzindana* Appeal Judgment, par 151. See also *Akayesu* Trial Judgment, pars 500–501; *Musema* Trial Judgment, par 155; *Rutaganda* Trial Judgment, par 50; *Kayishema and Ruzindana* Trial Judgment, pars 101–104; *Bagilishema* Trial Judgment, par 57; *Semanza* Trial Judgment, par 319; *Kajelijeli* Trial Judgment, par 813; *Kamuhanda* Trial Judgment, par 632; *Stakić* Trial Judgment, par 515.

[6] *Akayesu* Trial Judgment, par 500. The Trial Chamber referred in passing to the definition of murder in the Rwandan Penal Code which provides that 'homicide committed with intent to cause death shall be treated as murder' (ibid.).   [7] See, e.g. *Bagilishema* Trial Judgment, par 58.

[8] If, for instance, an accused were to rape a woman in the mistaken belief that she was a Muslim, although she was in fact a Serb, his act could not therefore qualify as genocide.

[9] See, e.g. *Kayishema and Ruzindana* Trial Judgment, par 110.

[10] *Karadžić and Mladić* Rule 61 Decision, par 93; *Akayesu* Trial Judgment, pars 503–504, 731; *Rutaganda* Trial Judgment, par 51; *Kayishema and Ruzindana* Trial Judgment, pars 105–113; *Stakić* Rule 98bis Decision, par 24. In the *Krstić* case, for instance, the Trial Chamber held that 'the ordeal inflicted on the men who survived the massacres [in Srebrenica] may appropriately be characterized as a genocidal act causing serious bodily and mental harm to members of the group' (*Krstić* Trial Judgment, par 635).

[11] *Kajelijeli* Trial Judgment, par 814. See also *Kamuhanda* Trial Judgment, par 634; *Ntagerura* Trial Judgment, par 664.   [12] Ibid.

[13] *Musema* Trial Judgment, par 156; *Akayesu* Trial Judgment, par 501–504; *Stakić* Rule 98bis Decision, par 24; *Kayishema and Ruzindana* Trial Judgment, pars 108–110; *Semanza* Trial Judgment, pars 320 and 322; *Kajelijeli* Trial Judgment, par 815.

[14] *Bagilishema* Trial Judgment, par 59; *Semanza* Trial Judgment, pars 320–322.

[15] This principle was applied by the Trial Chamber in *Krnojelac* in order, *inter alia*, to distinguish between acts sufficiently serious to amount to torture and those which would only amount to cruel treatment (e.g., *Krnojelac* Trial Judgment, par 219: 'in case of doubt as to whether or not the act is

Ruzindana, for instance, the Trial Chamber said that 'serious bodily harm' could be construed to include 'harm that seriously injures health, causes disfigurement or causes any serious injury to the external, internal organs or senses'.[16]

It is open to question whether *any* act or omission which causes serious bodily or mental harm could qualify as an underlying offence for genocide under that sub-heading or whether it must, in addition, be such as to be liable or have the potential to contribute in some way to the destruction of the group. Could, for instance, deportation unaccompanied by any other kind of mistreatment or forced labour or unlawful imprisonment ever be regarded as acts 'causing serious bodily or mental harm' and thus qualify as genocide all other conditions being met? Strictly speaking, the 'destruction' requirement for genocide is limited to the accused's *mens rea* so that no actual destruction needs to occur for relevant conduct to qualify as genocide. The answer would therefore appear, on its face, to be that any act that causes such harm could in principle qualify as genocide by causing serious bodily or mental harm to members of the group.[17] The International Law Commission has suggested, however, and the *Kajelijeli* Trial Chamber has quoted it with apparent approval, that the harm must be such as to threaten the destruction of the group in whole or in part.[18] This suggests, as noted above, that the acts of the accused must at the least have the potential to contribute to the destruction of the group, although they need not have had that effect.

15.3 Deliberately inflicting on the group conditions of life calculated to bring about its physical destruction in whole or in part

The Trial Chamber in *Akayesu* said that this phrase should be construed as a reference to 'the methods of destruction by which the perpetrator does not immediately kill the members of the group, but which, ultimately, seek their physical destruction'.[19] This offence has accordingly been described, quite

---

serious enough to amount to torture, the Accused should have the benefit of that doubt, and the acts for which he is charged should be considered under the heading of the less serious offence, namely cruel treatment under Article 3 or inhumane acts under Article 5(i)').

[16] *Kayishema and Ruzindana* Trial Judgment, par 109.

[17] In the course of discussing the definition of 'causing serious bodily or mental harm to members of a protected group', Drost noted that the purpose and *raison d'être* of the Genocide Convention was to protect the group, rather than its members: 'It must be remembered that the object of the Convention is the protection of the life of a human group as such. The crime to be prevented and punished must be directed against the continued existence of the protected group. The injury inflicted upon the individual members must be such as to endanger the continuation of normal life and the integrity or healthy existence of the group in whole or in part' (Drost, *The Crime of State*, vol. 2, *Genocide*, p 86).   [18] ILC Report 1996, p 91, cited in *Kajelijeli* Trial Judgment, par 814.

[19] *Akayesu* Trial Judgment, par 505; see also *Musema* Trial Judgment, par 157 and *Rutaganda* Trial Judgment, par 52.

broadly, as 'the denial to members of a certain group of the elementary means of existence enjoyed by other sections of the population'.[20] What distinguishes it from other underlying offences, such as killing members of the protected group, is the immediacy that must exist in the latter case between the act which forms the factual basis of the charge and the consequence upon the physical victims and the group itself. Whereas the act of killing has the immediate potential to contribute to the destruction of the group, such measures may have a much more remote capacity to contribute to the ultimate destruction of the group.[21]

The following measures have been said, for instance, to qualify as conditions of life calculated to bring about the group's physical destruction in whole or in part:[22] subjecting a group of people to a subsistence diet; systematic expulsion from homes; and reduction of essential medical services below minimum requirements.[23]

Perhaps the most obvious historical illustration of what would today be said to constitute 'conditions of life calculated to bring about its physical destruction in whole or in part' is the deportation of the Turkish Armenians at the hands of the Young Turk government during the First World War, although, at the time genocide (and the Genocide Convention) did not yet exist as a legal concept.[24] On 7 August 1919, a Turkish court martial in the trials of individuals accused of involvement in the deporation and massacres of Armenians in Yozgad (Turkey) chillingly described those events in the following terms:[25]

Impelled by their own personal ambition and greed, and [after] accepting the secret, illegal communications and instructions of a few evil individuals, they [Acting Lieutenant Governor of the provincial district of Yozgad, Kemal Bey, and Gendarmerie Commander

---

[20] *Stakić* Rule 98bis Decision, par 25.

[21] In *Krstić*, the Appeals Chamber made it clear that the court was legitimate in considering the long-term impact of the criminal acts on the likely survival of the group (*Krstić* Appeal Judgment, par 28). The mere geographical displacement of the group would not fall within the terms of that offence (*Stakić* Trial Judgment, par 519).

[22] *Akayesu* Trial Judgment, par 506. See also *Kayishema and Ruzindana* Trial Judgment, pars 115–116; *Stakić* Trial Judgment, par 517. Also included, according to the *Stakić* Trial Chamber, is the creation of circumstances that would lead to 'a slow death, such as lack of proper housing and hygiene or excessive work or physical exertion' (*Stakić* Trial Judgment, par 517). Such measures would have to be particularly serious, however, to allow the Chamber to draw an inference that such measures are imposed with a view to destroying the group if there is no more direct and clearer evidence of that intention.

[23] See list in *Kayishema and Ruzindana* Trial Judgment, pars 115–116; *Stakić* Rule 98bis Decision, par 25.

[24] For some literature on the subject, see, *inter alia*, V. Dadrian, 'Genocide as a Problem of National and International Law: The World War I Armenian Case and its Contemporary Legal Ramifications', 14(2)/1989 Yearbook of Jewish International Law (YJIL/221); R. Hovannisian (ed.), *The Armenian Genocide: History, Politics, Ethics* (London: Macmillan, 1992); V. Yeghiayan (ed.), *The Armenian Genocide and the Trials of the Young Turks* (LaVerne: American Armenian International College Press, 1990). See also www.umd.umich.edu/dept/armenian/facts/gen_bib1.html.

[25] *Takvîm-i Vekâyi'*, no. 3617, pp 1–2, *Yozgad Tehcîr ve Taktîli Muhâhemesi (Karâr Sûreti)*, rendered by the Extraordinary Court-Martial in the trials of those accused of involvement in the deportations and massacres in Yozgad. The verdict was read into the record on 8 April 1919 and published in the Supplement (*ilâve*) of *Takvîm-iVekâyi'* on 7 August 1919 (on file with the author).

for the provincial district of Yozgad, Major Tevfik Bey] [undertook the deportations] after taking all of the money and valuable possessions from these persons who made up the departing convoys, without any regard for their individual rights. Not only did they consciously and decisively fail to adopt the necessary measures to ensure [the fulfilment of] the order to protect the aforementioned [deportees], so that they might reach their destination point safely and without trouble, but instead, by binding the hands of the men in order to deny them the possibility of defending [themselves], [these defendants] deliberately caused all manner of slaughter, looting and pillaging, such as are entirely unacceptable to human and civilized sensibilities and which, in Islam's view [of the severity of these crimes], are considered among the greatest of offenses.

Although there remains serious doubt as to whether one may talk of 'genocide' in relation to crimes committed prior to the adoption of the Genocide Convention, it is certain that, had the Convention existed at the time of these acts, those death marches would have qualified as 'conditions of life calculated to bring about the group's physical destruction in whole or in part'.[26]

Adolf Eichmann's actions in organizing the deportation of millions of Jews to concentration camps, as recounted by the District Court of Jerusalem, are another major illustration of the sort of conduct which could come under that sub-heading.[27] Also, in the context of a review procedure pursuant to Rule 61 of the ICTY Rules of Procedure and Evidence,[28] Trial Chamber I held that this crime had been put into effect by the accused Radovan Karadžić and Ratko Mladić in the various Serb detention camps of Bosnia and through the siege and shelling of cities and protected areas.[29] Interestingly, the Amended Indictment against Radovan Karadžić contains the following factual basis in relation to that charge, which gives an indication of what the Prosecution regards as amounting to 'conditions calculated to bring about the physical destruction' of the group:[30]

CONDITIONS CALCULATED TO BRING ABOUT PHYSICAL DESTRUCTION

30. Conditions in the camps and detention facilities included inadequate food, often amounting to starvation rations, foul water, insufficient or non-existent medical care, inadequate hygiene conditions and lack of space.

31. Between 1 July 1991 and 30 November 1995, **Radovan KARADŽIĆ** knew or had reason to know that Bosnian Serb forces under his direction and control were committing

---

[26] See 'Verdict of the Tribunal', in The Permanent People's Tribunal, *A Crime of Silence: The Armenian Genocide* (1985) pp 211–227, reprinted in B. Weston, R. Falk and A. D'Amato (eds.), *International Law and World Order: A Problem-Oriented Coursebook* (St Paul: West Publishing Company, 1990) pp 1267 et seq. In his memoires as an American ambassador to Turkey during the First World War, Henry Morgenthau Sr. described in fascinating details the murderous policy of the Young Turks towards their Armenian citizens. On the true nature of the deportations, Morgenthau had no doubt that they were only meant to serve as an efficient way to kill and loot defenceless Armenians: 'The real purpose of the deportation was robbery and destruction; it really represented a new method of massacre' (H. Morgenthau, *Ambassador Morgenthau's Story* (Princeton: Gomidas Institute, 2000), p 205).   [27] See *Eichmann* District Court case, pars 199 and 204.
[28] Concerning the nature and scope of Rule 61 proceedings, see above footnote 12, Chapter 5.
[29] *Karadžić and Mladić* Rule 61 Decision, par 93.
[30] IT-95-5-I (24 July 1995). The indictment has since been amended.

the acts described in Paragraphs 17 through 30 above, or had done so. **Radovan KARADŽIĆ** failed to take the necessary and reasonable measures to prevent such acts or punish the perpetrators thereof.

32. In addition, between 1 December 1995 and 19 July 1996, **Radovan KARADŽIĆ** knew or had reason to know that Bosnian Serb forces under his direction and control had committed the acts described in Paragraphs 17 through 30 above. **Radovan KARADŽIĆ** failed to take the necessary and reasonable measures to punish the perpetrators thereof.

Because such a charge entails a somewhat less direct relationship between the conduct of the accused and its intended genocidal result, the evidence put forth to establish the perpetrator's genocidal *mens rea* must be particularly unambiguous.[31] The fact that such measures have had an effect upon a protected group is not sufficient in itself. This effect must also be shown to have been intended by the perpetrator. No Chamber has yet explicitly dealt with the *mens rea* required for this particular offence.[32]

Such criminal actions must be distinguished from measures adopted to rid a particular region of its population, a method which has been referred to above as 'ethnic cleansing'. In the latter situation, putting aside for a moment the killings and other mistreatments which may have occurred as a by-product of such a campain of ethnic cleansing, the ultimate purpose of ethnic cleansing is the geographical removal of a group from a particular area, not its physical destruction. Forcible physical displacement may, however, be evidentially relevant to the determination that the accused in fact intended to destroy a particular group.[33]

The crime of 'conditions of life calculated to bring about the group's physical destruction in whole or in part' must also be distinguished from mere casualties of war.[34] Military campaigns are systematically accompanied by their cortège of – civilian and military – deaths, and conditions of life during wars are always difficult. But the siege of a city, for instance, even as grim and unacceptable a siege as that of Sarajevo during the Bosnian conflict, or the blockading of a country or the systematic bombing of a town, does not *per se* qualify as a genocidal act unless those military measures are pushed to such a limit that they demonstrate beyond reasonable doubt that the warring party is seeking the annihilation of the other side, not just its military defeat.

Those measures imposed to bring about the physical destruction of a group do not need to be successful to qualify as genocide.[35] But if they are not successful,

---

[31] In the *Kayishema and Ruzindana* case, the Trial Chamber refused to consider the momentary deprivation of food, water, and adequate sanitary and medical facilities as amounting to such conditions of life intended to bring about the destruction of the group. The Trial Chamber essentially gave two reasons for its finding: first, the deprivation was relatively short-lived; and secondly, those people were in any case to be exterminated shortly thereafter (*Kayishema and Ruzindana* Trial Judgment, par 548).
[32] As to this issue, see Schabas, *Genocide*, pp 243–244.   [33] *Krstić* Appeal Judgment, pars 30–33.
[34] See *Legality of the Threat or Use of Nuclear Weapons, Advisory Opinion*, ICJ Reports 1996, 226, 240, par 26; *Case concerning Legality of Use of Force (Yugoslavia v. United Kingdom), Request for the Indication of Provisional Measures*, 2 June 1999, No. 113, par 35.
[35] See *Eichmann* District Court case, par 196.

the genocidal intent must be particularly clear from the perpetrator's conduct or words before a conviction may be entered on that basis. As with the crime of attempted genocide, it is very unlikely that an accused will ever be charged with such a crime before the *ad hoc* Tribunals if these measures are not at least in part successful in contributing to the destruction of the group.

15.4 Imposing measures intended to prevent births within the group

Such measures, which may have either physical or mental manifestations,[36] include, *inter alia*, sexual mutilations, sterilization, forced birth control, separation of the sexes, and prohibition of marriages.[37] The determination as to whether a given measure may be intended to have that effect depends in part on the place where or the context in which the measure in question is being implemented and, more specifically, on the cultural and social environment in which it is imposed. The *Akayesu* Trial Chamber, for instance, held that in patriarchal societies such as the Rwandan society, where membership of a group is determined by the identity of the father, an example of a measure intended to prevent births within a group is 'the case where, during rape, a woman of the said group is deliberately impregnated by a man of another group, with the intent to have her give birth to a child who will consequently not belong to its mother's group'.[38]

To be successful, a Prosecution based upon this underlying offence would need to establish that, through such action as rape, sexual mutilation, or sterilization of the victim, the perpetrator not only intended to abuse his victim sexually, but that in so doing he intended to prevent births within the group of his victim. The question as to whether violence against male victims – for instance, the infliction of sexual mutilations – could qualify under that heading has not been addressed by the Tribunals, but there does not appear to be any reason why such acts could not qualify as long as they can be shown to have been intended to prevent births within the group of the victim.

No accused has yet been charged with this crime in either Tribunal.[39] The main reason for it seems to be that acts which would qualify as 'measures intended to prevent births' would generally also qualify as 'causing serious bodily or mental

---

[36] *Akayesu* Trial Judgment, par 508.

[37] Ibid., par 507; *Musema* Trial Judgment, par 158; *Rutaganda* Trial Judgment, par 53; *Kayishema and Ruzindana* Trial Judgment, par 117. For domestic application of this prohibition, see also *Poland v. Hoess, Law Reports of Trials of War Criminals*, VII, 11, 25 (1948) and *United States v. Greifelt et al., Law Reports of Trials of War Criminals*, XIII, 1, 17 (1948) and *Eichmann* District Court case, par 244.

[38] See *Akayesu* Trial Judgment, par 507.

[39] While the definition of this offence was discussed in *Akayesu* in the context of sexual violence inflicted upon Tutsi women, the accused was in fact convicted for 'causing serious bodily and mental harm', not for 'imposing measures intended to prevent births within the group', in relation to these acts (see *Akayesu* Trial Judgment, pars 706–707, 731).

harm' which, from a prosecutor's point of view, is easier to establish since it need not be shown that the infliction of such harm is done for the purpose of preventing birth. The fact that harm has been inflicted with the required *mens rea* is sufficient.

15.5 Forcibly transferring children of the group to another group

According to the *Akayesu* Trial Chamber, the objective of this prohibition is 'not only to sanction a direct act of forcible physical transfer, but also to sanction acts of threats or trauma which would lead to the forcible transfer of children from one group to another'.[40] It should be noted that the accused in this case had not been charged with this particular crime, nor has there been evidence before the Tribunals that such genocidal transfers of children between groups ever took place in either Rwanda or in the former Yugoslavia during the relevant periods.[41]

15.6 Exhaustive character of the list of underlying crimes?

Is the list of crimes provided for in Articles 4(2)/2(2) of the Statutes exhaustive, or may other underlying offence qualify as genocide if the perpetrator bears the required *mens rea*? Could rape or torture, for instance, ever be recognized as discrete genocidal offences without also having to satisfy the definitional elements of one of the established offences expressly provided for in Articles 4/2 (for instance, that of causing serious bodily or mental harm to members of the group)? Authors have generally suggested that the list of five crimes enumerated in Article II of the Genocide Convention was indeed exhaustive or, as one author put it, 'limitative'.[42]

The text of the Article seems to be clear on that point: genocide, it says, means 'any of the following acts' committed with genocidal intent. It would appear, therefore, that to qualify as a genocidal offence, a criminal offence such as a rape or an act of torture would have to meet the requirements of, for instance, 'causing serious bodily or mental harm to members of the group' (which will no doubt almost invariably, if not always, be the case) or 'imposing measures intended to

---

[40] *Akayesu* Trial Judgment, par 509. See also *Musema* Trial Judgment, par 159; *Rutaganda* Trial Judgment, par 54; *Kayishema and Ruzindana* Trial Judgment, par 118.

[41] It should be pointed out here that it is not the responsibility of courts in principle to make law outside of the case before them. It is even less their responsibility to make law beyond the facts relevant to the case. In *The Cristina*, Lord Atkin had wisely suggested that, when it comes to questions of international law, the court 'should refrain from expressing opinions which are beside the question actually to be decided' (*Compania Naviera Vascongado v. SS Cristina* [1938] AC 485, [1938] 1 All ER 719, p 722).   [42] Robinson, *Genocide Convention*, pp 57, 64.

prevent births within the group'.[43] Other criminal conduct, 'forced disappearances', for instance, could probably be regarded as 'killing' or 'serious bodily or mental harm' (to the disappeared themselves or to their families) and qualify as genocidal offences through that conduit. It is possible, even likely, that certain crimes (torture, rape, and forced disappearances being obvious candidates) may in time come to be regarded under customary international law as discrete categories of underlying offences. As far as the *ad hoc* Tribunals are concerned, however, neither the Statutes, nor contemporary customary international law may be said to provide for underlying offences other than those expressly listed in the Statutes. It could even be argued that, even if customary international law provided for additional underlying offences, the Statutes of the Tribunals would set the outer limits of the Tribunals' jurisdiction *ratione materiae* in relation to genocide and that the Tribunals would not be allowed to convict an accused for any act not expressly (or implicitly) listed in their Statutes.[44]

---

[43] In the *Akayesu* case, for instance, the accused had been charged with genocide, *inter alia*, in relation to various sexual violence including rape (pars 12a and 12b of his indictment – ICTR96-4-I). Although he was convicted for these acts, Akayesu was not convicted for rape *qua* genocide proper, but for rape as 'causing serious bodily and mental harm' per Article 2(2)(b) of the ICTR Statute (*Akayesu* Trial Judgment, pars 706–707, 731).

[44] It is revealing that the Prosecutor of the *ad hoc* Tribunals has never charged an accused for an underlying offence which was not expressly provided in the Statute. Thus, conduct that might otherwise amount to 'rape' or 'torture', for instance, is systematically charged under one of the established underlying offences (see, e.g. *Akayesu* Trial Judgment, pars 706–707).

16

Genocide and other Forms of Criminal Involvement

16.1 General remarks

Any individual may in principle commit genocide:[1] 'Genocide is not a crime that can only be committed by certain categories of persons. As evidenced by history, it is a crime which has been committed by the low-level executioner and the high-level planner or instigator alike.'

A genocidal offence may be committed by act or omission,[2] and the perpetrator need not have been involved in any patterns of criminal behaviour.[3] A single criminal act could therefore theoretically constitute an act of genocide.[4] The list of punishable acts provided in the Statute (genocide, conspiracy to commit genocide, direct and public incitement to commit genocide, attempt to commit genocide, and complicity in genocide) indicates 'how far the crime needs to have advanced before it becomes punishable' and 'describes what kind of involvement in actual genocide may

---

[1] *Kayishema and Ruzindana* Appeal Judgment, par 170. See below, Chapter 19.

[2] See, e.g. *Kambanda* Trial Judgment, par 39(ix); *Bagilishema* Appeal Judgment, par 35. See below, sub-section 21.3.   [3] *Kayishema and Ruzindana* Appeal Judgment, par 163.

[4] Note, however, the use of the plural in the Statutes (e.g. 'killing members of the group', 'causing serious bodily or mental harm to members of the group').

result in penal responsibility'.[5] As with the other crimes within the jurisdiction of the *ad hoc* Tribunals, the official position of the accused may not relieve an accused of criminal responsibility for genocide, nor would it mitigate his punishment.[6]

The means and methods used to carry out the crimes are in principle irrelevant.[7] The *Krstić* Trial Chamber held, for instance, that one could conceive of destroying a group through purposeful eradication of its culture and identity resulting in the eventual extinction of the group as an entity distinct from the remainder of the community.[8] The Chamber noted, however, that the prohibition against genocide was limited to the physical or biological destruction of all or part of the group.[9] Its cultural or sociological disappearance would therefore not qualify as genocide *per se*, but attacks upon cultural and other characteristics of the group may be evidentially relevant to a finding that one of the protected groups was indeed being marked for physical or biological destruction.[10] The long-term impact of the perpetrator's conduct upon the group and its survival may be taken into account by the court to make such an assessment.[11]

16.2   The various listed forms of criminal participation (Articles 4/2 (a–e) of the Statutes of the Tribunals)

16.2.1   Genocide

Genocide, it has been said, 'is proven if it is established beyond reasonable doubt, firstly, that one of the acts listed under Article 2(2) of the ICTR Statute was

---

[5] *Final Report of the Commission of Experts for the Former Yugoslavia*, par 99.

[6] Article 7(2) of the Statute provides as follows: 'The official position of any accused person, whether as Head of State or Government or as a responsible Government official, shall not relieve such person of criminal responsibility nor mitigate punishment.' See also *Final Report of the Commission of Experts for the Former Yugoslavia*, par 100: 'To meet the aims of the Convention, people in the said categories must be treated equally irrespective of their de jure or de facto positions as decision-makers. As individuals, they are subject to Prosecution like any other individual violator. They cannot hide behind any shield of immunity. The legal and moral responsibilities are the same and the need to prevent genocide no less clear because of the position of the violator.' According to the International Court of Justice, such immunities and privileges could still be applicable, with some limitations, before domestic courts (*Case concerning the Arrest Warrant of 11 April 2000* (*Democratic Republic of Congo v. Belgium*), 14 February 2002, ICJ General List No. 121 ('*Yerodia* case')).

[7] In his appeal, Clément Ruzindana claimed that the Trial Chamber had omitted to conduct an analysis of the circumstances and means whereby he was alleged to have carried out his acts of genocide (*Kayishema and Ruzindana* Appeal Judgment, par 167). The Appeals Chamber held that there was no necessary relationship between the manner in which genocide is carried out and the personal circumstances of an accused; nor does genocide require proof that the accused possessed certain means to prepare or commit genocide (*Kayishema and Ruzindana* Appeal Judgment, par 169). See also *Krstić* Appeal Judgement, par 32: 'While this [genocidal] intent must be supported by the factual matrix, the offence of genocide does not require proof that the perpetrator chose the most efficient method to accomplish his objective of destroying the targeted part. Even where the method selected will not implement the perpetrator's intent to the fullest, leaving that destruction incomplete, this ineffectiveness alone does not preclude a finding of genocidal intent.'

[8] *Krstić* Trial Judgment, par 574.   [9] Ibid., par 580.   [10] Ibid., par 580.

[11] Ibid., par 28.

committed and, secondly, that this act was committed against a specifically targeted national, ethnical, racial or religious group, with the specific intent to destroy, in whole or in part, that group'.[12] It thus consists of a given criminal conduct – its *actus reus*[13] – coupled with a specific (genocidal) *mens rea*.[14] 'Genocide' as provided for in Articles 4(3)(a)/2(3)(a) is the most complete form of all genocidal offences provided for in the Statutes in that the conduct in question satisfies at once all the elements of the above-mentioned definition. It implies that the accused himself has committed one of the underlying offences *and* with the intent in so doing to destroy in whole or in part one of the protected groups as such.

Genocide as a criminal offence should be distinguished from a more recent concept commonly described as ethnic cleansing, which broadly describes a campaign of expulsion and violence against an ethnic group (generally, an ethnic minority) with the purpose of emptying a given geographic area of this group.[15] 'Ethnic cleansing' may, as pointed out in the *Karadžić and Mladić* Rule 61 Decision, reveal a genocidal intention,[16] but the two concepts should not be collapsed or equated for ethnic cleansing is, as far as customary law is concerned, not a crime in its own right and not all instances of ethnic cleansing are necessarily directed at the destruction of the group being ethnically cleansed. Often, they are directed at its mere *expulsion* from a given location or area,[17] and crimes committed in the context of a campaign of ethnic cleansing often fall short of genocidal actions and often more readily qualify as acts of persecution.[18] From an evidential point of

---

[12] *Bagilishema* Trial Judgment, par 55.   [13] See Chapter 15, 'Underlying Offences'.

[14] See *Krstić* Trial Judgment, par 542.

[15] *Stakić* Trial Judgment, pars 518–519. See, however, *Application of the Convention on the Prevention and Punishment of the Crime of Genocide, Provisional Measures, Order of 13 September 1993*, ICJ Reports 1993, 325, Separate Opinion of Judge Lauterpacht, pp 407, 431–432. The *Preliminary Report of the Commission of Experts for the Former Yugoslavia*, par 55, defined 'ethnic cleansing' as follows: 'The expression "ethnic cleansing" is relatively new. Considered in the context of the conflicts in the former Yugoslavia, "ethnic cleansing" means rendering an area ethnically homogeneous by using force or intimidation to remove persons of given groups from the area. "Ethnic cleansing" is contrary to international law.'

[16] *Karadžić and Mladić* Rule 61 Decision, par 94. See also *Nikolić* Rule 61 Decision, par 34 and *Krstić* Appeal Judgment, pars 30–33.

[17] See, for an example of the latter point, *Sikirica* Motion for Acquittal Decision, pars 92–94. The reverse policy of repopulation (one ethnic group taking over a geographical area inhabited by a different ethnic group) would likewise, in principle, not qualify as genocide, simply because what is destroyed is not the group in its *physical* existence, but either its attachment to a given location or its cohesion as a group.

[18] *Kupreškić* Trial Judgment, par 606 ('It should be added that if persecution was given a narrow interpretation, so as not to include the crimes found in the remaining sub-headings of Article 5, a *lacuna* would exist in the Statute of the Tribunal. There would be no means of conceptualising those crimes against humanity which are committed on discriminatory grounds, but which, for example, fall short of genocide, which requires a specific intent "to destroy, in whole or in part, a national, ethnical, racial, or religious group". An example of such a crime against humanity would be the so-called "ethnic cleansing", a notion which, although it is not a term of art, is particularly germane to the work of this Tribunal'); *Stakić* Trial Judgment, par 554 ('The intention to displace a population is not equivalent to the intention to destroy it'). It is revealing that the Report of the Secretary-General refers to 'ethnic cleansing' as one among other inhumane acts which may qualify as a crime against humanity, rather than genocide (Secretary-General Report (ICTY), par 48). Crimes committed in the context of a campaign of 'ethnic cleansing' could also qualify as 'persecutions', a crime against humanity.

view, however, instances of ethnic cleansing and in particular the method used to effect it may rise to the level of genocidal actions if it can be inferred therefrom that the perpetrator, not content to simply expel and displace individuals from a certain group, sought to destroy the group as such, including by way of forcible expulsion.[19]

The crime of genocide, as provided for in the Tribunals' Statutes and in the Genocide Convention, should also be distinguished from the socio-political or historical phenomenon referred to as 'genocide' or as 'a genocide'. The Court's mandate is limited, as far as genocide is concerned, to establishing whether or not the elements of this crime, as charged against an accused and as defined under customary international law, have been proved by the Prosecution beyond reasonable doubt. The events surrounding the actions of the accused, i.e. the context in which his acts may have been committed, are relevant only to the extent that they may shed light on and are evidentially relevant to one or several of the elements which must be established by the Prosecution to prove its case.[20] There are many reasons why the court should limit its finding to the accused's role and criminal liability and why it should not take upon itself the responsibility of writing history, be it that of extraordinary criminal events: first of all, judges of the *ad hoc* Tribunals do not have such a mandate. Nor do they generally have the expertise to take on such a task. Security Council Resolution 808[21] and the *First Annual Report* of the ICTY suggest that one of the Tribunal's objectives is the restoration and maintenance of peace.[22] Since then, however, the Tribunals have struggled to become as normal a criminal court as the oddity of their very existence would allow. This has meant, among other things, the need to try to shorten the length of trials, frequently at the cost of excluding from consideration matters not strictly related to the charges, or not strictly *necessary* to the determination of guilt or innocence on the crimes charged, including the general

---

[19] *Nikolić* Rule 61 Decision, par 34 ('In this instance, this policy of "ethnic cleansing" took the form of discriminatory acts of extreme seriousness which tend to show its genocidal character. [. . .] More specifically, the constitutive intent of the crime of genocide may be inferred from the very gravity of those discriminatory acts'); *Stakić* Trial Judgment, par 557 ('deporting a group or part of a group is insufficient [to establish the required genocide state of mind] if it is not accompanied by methods seeking the physical destruction of the group'). See also *Karadžić and Mladić* Rule 61 Decision, pars 94–95 and *Preliminary Report of the Commission of Experts for the Fromer Yugoslavia*, par 56: '[Ethnic cleansing] could also fall within the meaning of the Genocide Convention.' See also *Krstić* Appeal Judgment, pars 31–35, concerning the defence argument that the fact that the Bosnian Serb army decided to forcibly transfer, rather than kill, the women and children of Srebrenica undermines the Trial Chamber's finding of a genocidal intent on Krstić's part.

[20] The further one goes from the role and responsibility of the accused person, the less reliable the factual findings of the court may be said to become.

[21] UN Security Council Resolution 808, UN Doc. S/RES/808 (22 February 1993).

[22] *Report of the International Tribunal for the Prosecution of Persons Responsible for Serious Violations of International Humanitarian Law in the Territory of the Former Yugoslavia Since 1991, First Annual Report*, UN Doc. A/49/342, S/1994/1007 (29 August 1994), par 11.

historical background of the cases presented by the Prosecution.[23] Judges are lawyers by training, not historians. In general, they are not armed with the theoretical tools (or, for that matter, with adequate resources) to undertake the

---

[23] Systematically, in their final briefs and closing arguments, many ICTY defendants have included whole sections concerning the history of the region. As could be expected, the depiction thereby given is often a very subjective one. More importantly, it is generally irrelevant to the charges. For instance, revealingly, in the case against Mitar Vasiljević, a low-ranking Serb associated with a paramilitary group who was charged in relation to two localized incident of killings in the municipality of Višegrad (eastern Bosnia) in 1992, during his closing address, his counsel took the matter back to early Balkan history. Spurred by the obvious irrelevance, from a legal point of view, of this historical account, the Presiding Judge in this case, Judge David Hunt, took counsel to task by asking him to explain the relevance of its historical interlude (IT-98-32-T, Thursday, 14 March 2002, T 4932–4936):

Judge Hunt Now, what – to what issue do you say that the historical facts that you've referred to in great detail in your written submissions are relevant?

Mr. Domazet (counsel for Vasiljević) [Interpretation] Your Honour, I have dealt with them in detail because the Prosecution devoted a good deal of attention, including witness testimonies and other materials connected with this, although I personally do not feel that this is pertinent to Mitar Vasiljević, since he was neither a politician nor a leading figure, so he had no special role in what was happening in the time leading up to and during the conflict in Višegrad. I tried to draw attention to what was happening before the arrival of the Uzice Corps, when, according to the evidence I had at my disposal, it was the Serbs who were leaving Višegrad because of the situation that was prevalent then. This situation later changed and unfortunately, we know how and in what manner all this ended. It ended in a way that led to almost no Muslims being left in Višegrad. In my view, Mitar Vasiljević took no part in either political events or any other public events at the time, which would warrant the producing of more evidence, more than we actually have done during the trial.

Judge Hunt Leaving to one side what you told us had happened during the Second World War, let's come up to date a little bit. You gave us great detail through the witness of that – the evidence of a particular witness you called, about the Serbs being the victims of an attack upon them. Now, what is the relevance of that to anything we have to determine here? It's a matter which we raised in the Pre-Trial Conference and I still haven't got a sensible answer, I'm afraid, as to what its relevance is, other than the fact that it demonstrates that what the Serbs are alleged to have done to the Muslims was by way of retaliation, which hardly helps your client's case.

Mr. Domazet [Interpretation] Yes, Your Honour. I agree, in Mitar Vasiljević's case, this is not relevant.

Judge Hunt Why did you lead the evidence? It seems to be part of some overall instruction given to all Serb counsel to tell us what happened in 1285 or whenever it was, and to push as much of the history into the case as possible. I have never been given an answer which demonstrates how it is relevant.

Mr. Domazet [Interpretation] Your Honour, as far as I can remember, I did not go that far back into history. It's true that the witness I brought in did speak about World War II and was cautioned by you because of this. I was referring to the period in late 1990 and early 1991, the time of the first multi-party elections in Bosnia and Herzegovina, because that was the period when these disagreements among the ethnic groups began. I'm referring to the three ethnic groups in Bosnia and Herzegovina. But I still say that in Mitar Vasiljević's case, in my view, this really is not relevant. The reason I produced this evidence, and you may be right when you say that all Serb lawyers deal with this, I believe that if there are any future cases dealing with Višegrad and the surrounding area, we don't want it to appear that the Defence has taken no position on this and that in future cases, where this may be relevant, we don't want to be seen as having omitted to say this. If I may say, it always

task of writing the history of the events in the former Yugoslavia or in Rwanda.[24] The illusion that the law can somehow embody historical truths ignores the different texture of the 'truth' as pursued by the law on the one hand and that sought by history on the other. The judge may try to get as close as permits to the illusory pretence of historical truth, but he or she will never achieve such endeavour simply because his tools – the law – will not allow it.[25]

Secondly, although courts of law may have a privileged access to certain documents and to witnesses, the scope of their inquiry is limited (and, more, streamlined) by the Prosecution (and Defence) case which is presented to them; as a matter of principle, the Prosecution does not appear to regard it as one of its functions to establish historical truth. Only those events which set the acts of the accused into a relevant political, economic, or military context may be the subject of evidence to the extent that they might be relevant to the charges.[26] Also the witnesses who appear before the *ad hoc* Tribunals are, but for the rarest exceptions, the witnesses of the parties, rather than the witnesses of the court as would be the case generally in the civil-law system. The recounting of historical events is therefore naturally often a partial and often a very subjective one indeed.[27]

Finally, the proposition that the judges' acquaintance with the facts of the case would allow them to understand the historical or socio-political cause and effect of a particular incident of mass violence is illusory. Assessing facts and *understanding*

appeared that all the guilt was on one side, on the Serbian side, although I never myself measured the degree of guilt, but simply tried to produce some evidence which I was able to obtain, including written documents and witness testimonies, to show what had been happening in Višegrad for about two years before the outbreak of the tragic conflicts that have been our topic of discussion here.

Judge Hunt Well, let's assume for the purposes of this argument that it was the Muslims who erected the first roadblock and it was a Serb who was the first person who was killed and all of the other particular matters to which reference was made in that evidence. Is there any dispute in this case that there was an attack upon the non-Serb, civilian population, whether it happened at the same time, before or after those other events?

Mr. Domazet [Interpretation] No, Your Honour. There is no dispute in my view that this happened.

[24] 'Réduire l'historien au juge, c'est simplifier et appauvrir la connaissance historique; mais réduire le juge à l'historien, c'est pervertir irrémédiablement l'exercice de la justice' (C. Ginzburg, *Le Juge et l'historien: – Considérations en marge du procès Sofri* (Paris: Verdier, 1997), p 118.

[25] 'Il y a une consistance non juridique de la verité, telle qu'on ne pourra jamais rabattre la *quaestio facti* sur la *quaestio juris*' (G. Agamben, *Ce qui reste d'Auschwitz* (Paris: Rivage, 2003), pp 18–19).

[26] In that respect, the trial of Slobodan Milošević at the ICTY is a rare illustration of a prosecutorial attempt to retell historical and political events within the frame of a criminal trial. The scope of the indictment's geographical coverage, the time period under consideration, the nature of the witnesses being called, the issues being raised, the number of matters which are raised or discussed but which are only collateral to the indictment against the accused, the effort by the accused to reset these events into a specific political context, all highlight the fact that this trial is more than a criminal case where guilt and innocence are the sole matter to be fought over between the Prosecutor and the defendant or his counsel. In many ways, the *Milošević* trial has become, intentionally or not, a trial for history and a test case for international justice as a whole.

[27] If it does not call its own experts, the ability of a Trial Chamber to find out about 'the truth' between such competing versions of the events may therefore represent a further incentive for it to limit its findings to the matters *directly* at issue in the case.

their causes are two very different things, and judges are charged only with the former, not the latter. In *Le Chant des Morts*, Elie Wiesel recounts his meeting with one of the judges who sat on the trial of Adolf Eichmann in Jerusalem. Being asked by Wiesel whether, having dutifully and carefully gone through every piece of evidence on the trial record, having heard every testimony in the case, he understood this moment of history, the Judge trembled and answered softly: [28]

Not at all. I know all the facts and every incident; I know the unfolding of this tragedy minute by minute, but this knowledge as if coming from the outside does not have anything to do with understanding; there is a part of it which for ever will remain a mystery; a sort of restricted zone inaccessible to reason; fortunately so, I should say. Who knows, this might be a gift from God to human kind; He forbids him from understanding everything, thus saving him from madness and suicide.

Such considerations have not stopped a number of Chambers from entering the realm of history-writing. In the *Akayesu* trial, for instance, the Trial Chamber devoted a whole section of its Judgment to the question of whether there had been *a* genocide in Rwanda in 1994.[29] The answer to this question, the Trial Chamber said, 'would allow a better understanding of the context within which the crimes with which the accused is charged are alleged to have been committed'.[30] Having reviewed some evidence on that point, the Trial Chamber said that it was satisfied that the Tutsi ethnic group had indeed been targeted for total extermination by members of the Hutu ethnic group. The Trial Chamber had to concede, however, that its historical digression was beyond the scope of its judicial responsibility and that its 'sole task was to assess the individual responsibility of the accused for the crimes with which he is charged'.[31] Having made such a finding, the Chamber also had to disclaim any bias or prejudgment towards the accused.[32]

Rather than pre-empting historical revisionism, as some would have it,[33] such an exercise in history may instead facilitate such revisionism by allowing critics to challenge the court's finding by attacking the evidentiary basis (or potentially the lack thereof) upon which the finding has been made, including the evidence of witnesses upon whose evidence these findings were made.[34]

---

[28] E. Wiesel, *Le Chant des morts* (Paris: Le Seuil, 1966). Translation from French by the author.

[29] *Akayesu* Trial Judgment, pars 59–66.   [30] Ibid., par 112.   [31] Ibid., par 129.

[32] '[T]he fact that genocide was indeed committed in Rwanda in 1994 and more particularly in Taba, cannot influence it in its decision in the present case' (ibid., par 129). The Trial Chamber felt compelled to point out that 'the judges must examine the facts adduced in a most dispassionate manner, bearing in mind that the accused is presumed innocent' (ibid).

[33] At the Commonwealth Law Association Conference which took place in Melbourne in April 2003, Judge Williams, a Judge of the ICTR, suggested that the finding by the ICTR that there had been *a genocide* in Rwanda in 1994 would prevent historical revisionism of these events: 'And, importantly, the Tribunal [for Rwanda] held that genocide against Tutsis had occurred in Rwanda in 1994. This important finding was underscored by the former Primer Minister Kambanda who by pleading guilty to genocide counts acknowledged that genocide had indeed occurred in Rwanda in 1994 and that it was planned at the highest level. This acknowledgement forecloses future historical revisionism on this issue' (on file with the author).

[34] The finding of the Trial Chamber in *Akayesu* is essentially based on four witnesses (Alison Desforges, Dr Zachariah, Major-General Dallaire, and Simon Cox), all four of whom were Prosecution witnesses.

The legacy of the *ad hoc* Tribunals will be judged not by the breadth of their historical considerations, but by the quality of the justice which they deliver and by the fairness of their trials. Considering the short life expectancy of those institutions and their limited resources, focusing on its strictly judicial responsibility seems to be no luxury. No doubt, history may be based on the court's findings of facts, as was the case in Nuremberg, but the fact that the early tendency of some Chambers to consciously seek to make history out of their judgments and decisions has been curbed is a welcome one.[35]

16.2.2   Conspiracy to commit genocide

The concept of 'conspiracy' is one familiar to common-law lawyers, but less so to lawyers from the civil-law tradition. In Nuremberg, the introduction of the concept of conspiracy into the Charter of the International Military Tribunal was viewed with great suspicion by lawyers from the continental tradition,[36] and the International Military Tribunal did not make much of an effort to define this concept, stating merely that 'conspiracy must be clearly outlined in its criminal purpose' and suggesting that 'it must not be too far removed from the time of decision and of action'.[37]

A 'conspiracy' in criminal law is essentially an 'agreement between two or more persons to commit an unlawful act'.[38] The United Nations War Crimes Commission said that the doctrine of conspiracy was 'one under which it is a criminal offence to conspire or to take part in an allegiance to achieve an unlawful object, or to achieve a lawful object by unlawful means'.[39]

The crime of conspiracy to commit genocide may in turn be defined as an agreement between two or more individuals to commit the crime of genocide, with a

[35] For a contrary view see, *inter alia*, Mark Osiel's excellent book, *Mass Atrocity, Collective Memory and the Law* (New Brunswick: Transaction Publishers, 1999). See also P. Ricoeur, 'Les Rôles respectifs du juge et de l'historien', in D. Salas (ed.), *La Justice, une révolution démocratique* (Paris: Desclée de Brouwer, 2001), p 67.

[36] See T. Taylor, *Final Report to the Secretary of the Army on the Nuremberg War Crimes Trials under Control Council Law No. 10* (Buffalo: William S. Hein & Co., 1997), p 227. See also H. Donnedieu de Vabres, 'Le Procès de Nuremberg devant les Principes modernes du droit pénal international', 70 *Recueil des Cours de l'Académie de droit international de La Haye*, 477 et seq. (1947-I).

[37] IMT Judgment, p 225. The IMT also pointed out that there may have been several, partly overlapping, conspiracies (ibid.). In Tokyo, when discussing the charge of conspiracy to wage aggressive war, the International Military Tribunal for the Far East defined the concept of conspiracy in the following terms: 'A conspiracy to wage aggressive or unlawful war arises when two or more persons enter into an agreement to commit that crime. Thereafter, in furtherance of the conspiracy, follows planning and preparing for such war. Those who participate at this stage may be either original conspirators or later adherents. If the latter adopt the purpose of the conspiracy and plans and prepare for its fulfillment they become conspirators.' *Records of the Proceedings*, vol 146, pp 48, 448.

[38] *Musema* Trial Judgment, par 187, quoting from the Sixth Committee Report (see *Musema* Trial Judgment, fn 77, p 63); *Nahimana* Trial Judgment, par 1045.

[39] *War Crimes Commission*, p 196. In his Closing Speech before the IMT, Justice Robert Jackson stated that '[t]he forms of this grand type of conspiracy are amorphous, the means are opportunistic, and neither can divert the law from getting the substance of things' (Justice R. Jackson, in *Speeches of the Chief Prosecutors, Law Reports of Trials of War Criminals*, XX (1947)).

concerted intent to commit genocide, that is, with an intent to destroy, in whole or in part, a national, ethnic, racial, or religious group, as such.[40] The agreed contribution of each participant in the conspiracy need not be identical, but each one of them will be equally responsible for the acts of the other conspirators.[41] The existence of a such a conspiracy or agreement to commit genocide may be inferred from all the circumstances of the case.[42] The members of that conspiracy must have consciously interacted with each other and each one of them (if charged with conspiracy to commit genocide) must be shown to have possessed the required genocidal intent.[43] Their agreement may remain relatively informal so long as those operating within its framework are 'aware of its existence, their participation in it, and its role in furtherance of their common purpose [to commit genocide]'.[44]

Conspiracy is an inchoate offence. The mere agreement to commit genocide is, therefore, all other conditions being met, punishable in principle.[45] The rationale behind the criminalization under international law of an agreement to commit genocide lies in the very gravity of the crime which is the subject of the conspiracy and the necessity to prevent such crimes if possible. To be punishable, it is not necessary that any of the crimes which had been agreed upon by the conspirators were in fact carried out although the fact that they were may be relevant to establishing a conspiracy to commit them.[46] This distinguishes conspiracy from 'joint criminal enterprise' or 'common purpose' liability as it is sometimes called, which requires that in addition to an agreement to commit such crimes, crimes were actually committed pursuant to that agreement.[47] In other words, to prove a charge of conspiracy, it is enough to show that the participants had agreed to carry out the crime in question, whilst in the case of a joint criminal enterprise, the Prosecution must not only show that there was such an agreement, but also that crimes were committed 'in furtherance of [it]'.[48] The mere showing of a negotiation or discussions

---

[40] *Musema* Trial Judgment, par 191. See also *Ntakirutimana* Trial Judgment, pars 798–799.

[41] See *The Charter and Judgment of the Nürnberg Tribunal, History and Analysis*, Doc. A/CN.4/5, 3 March 1949, p 53: '[The conspirators'] contribution to the common plan need not be the same nor equally important. [. . .] one single man can even completely dominate the initiation and development of the plans without their ceasing to be common planning. The collaborators can have different spheres of activity.' [42] *Nahimana* Trial Judgment, par 1047.

[43] Ibid., pars 1042, 1047–1055; *Musema* Trial Judgment, par 192. The accidental 'meeting of mind' whereby a number of individuals would be acting in parallel but without agreement to achieve a common goal could not be said to be (co-)conspirators for the purpose of this provision (*Nahimana* Trial Judgment, pars 1048–1055). [44] Ibid., par 1047.

[45] See, e.g. *Musema* Trial Judgment, par 193; *Kajelijeli* Trial Judgment, par 788.

[46] See *Akayesu* Trial Judgment, par 479; *Musema* Trial Judgment, pars 184–198; *Ojdanić* Joint Criminal Enterprise Decision, par 23.

[47] See ibid., par 23. The terminology of the *ad hoc* Tribunals has varied on the point. It appears that, more recently, the phrase 'joint criminal enterprise' is favoured (*Ojdanić* Joint Criminal Enterprise Decision, par 36).

[48] Ibid., par 23. See also *Law Reports of Trials of War Criminals*, XV, pp 95 and 97–98: 'In conclusion, it may be repeated that the difference between a charge of conspiracy and one of acting in pursuance of a common design is that the first would claim that an agreement to commit offences had been made while the second would allege not only the making of an agreement but the performance of acts pursuant to it.'

to commit genocide will not in principle suffice, unless it is established that the commission of the crime was agreed upon by the conspirators.[49]

It should be noted, however, that it is very unlikely that conspiracy will be charged independently if the conspiracy did not in fact lead to the commission of some other genocidal crimes and it should therefore be no surprise that this crime has systematically been charged at the *ad hoc* Tribunals in conjunction with genocide 'proper'.[50]

The matter of cumulative conviction between genocide and conspiracy to commit genocide has arisen in several cases before the *ad hoc* Tribunals. In *Kambanda*, the Trial Chamber accepted a guilty plea by the accused on both counts and went on to convict him for both conspiracy to commit genocide and for genocide proper.[51] In *Niyitegeka* and in *Nahimana*, the Trial Chambers said that an accused could be convicted for both offences in relation to the same set of acts,[52] while in *Musema*, the Trial Chamber held that an accused cannot be convicted of both genocide and conspiracy to commit genocide, because, it said, its doing so would be contrary to the intention of the Genocide Convention, its *Travaux Préparatoires*, and a finding of guilt in relation to such conspiracy when a genocide conviction would have been entered would serve no purpose.[53] In view of the fact that each underlying crime (conspiracy to commit genocide and genocide) contains a least one element which the other does not possess, namely, an agreement for conspiracy and the actual carrying out of one of the listed underlying offences for genocide, the view of the *Kambanda, Niyitegeka*, and *Nahimana* Chambers seems to be the correct one. Consequently, pursuant to the test laid down by the Appeals Chamber an accused could be convicted for both genocide and conspiracy to commit genocide in relation to the same conduct.

16.2.3   Direct and public incitement to commit genocide

Direct and public incitement to commit genocide consists of 'directly provoking the perpetrator(s) to commit genocide, whether through speeches, shouting or threats uttered in public places or at public gatherings, or through the sale or dissemination, offer for sale or display of written material or printed matter in public places or at public gatherings, or through the public display of placards or posters, or through any other means of audiovisual communication'.[54]

The nature of what may be considered to be inciting for the purpose of that prohibition may depend on the context – political and cultural – and circumstances in which the impugned conduct occurs.[55] During both the Yugoslav and

---

[49] *Kajelijeli* Trial Judgment, par 787.
[50] See, e.g. *Kambanda* Trial Judgment. See also Schabas, *Genocide*, p 365.
[51] *Kambanda* Trial Judgment, par 27.
[52] *Niyitegeka* Trial Judgment, pars 429, 480, and 502; *Nahimana* Trial Judgment, par 1043.
[53] *Musema* Trial Judgment, par 198.   [54] *Akayesu* Trial Judgment, par 559.
[55] See ibid., pars 557–558.

the Rwandan conflicts, the media (mostly the television and the press in the case of Yugoslavia and the radio in the case of Rwanda) played a crucial role in the spreading of rumours of crimes allegedly committed by the enemy side, messages of ethnic hatred, and calls to violence.[56] In Rwanda in particular, various media outlets took a very direct part in the creation and the perpetuation of a criminal mindset and it had a clear legitimizing role in the carrying out of mass killings.[57] 'The power of the media to create and destroy fundamental human values', one Chamber noted, 'comes with great responsibility. Those who control such media are accountable for its consequences.'[58] The Chamber added that the fact that causation of killing or causation of other forms of mistreatment might have been effected by 'an immediately proximate cause in addition to the [media] communication itself' does not diminish the blame that might be attributed to the media, nor does it negate the criminal liability of those responsible for propagating inciteful messages by using those media.[59]

The line between 'legitimate' political propaganda and criminal incitement is a very difficult one to draw, particularly in times of war where all parties involved use the media to justify their actions and to shore up popular support for their cause, often by demonizing their enemies. As far as incitement to genocide is concerned, the Prosecution must establish that the perpetrator intended directly to prompt or provoke another to commit genocide by creating in that person a particular state of mind necessary to commit genocide.[60]

But not every sort of incitement has been criminalized under the Genocide Convention or, for that matter, under the Tribunals' Statutes: it must be both 'public' and 'direct'. The 'public' character of the incitement relates essentially to two elements: the place where the alleged incitement occurred (a public square or on television, for instance) and whether or not the attendance where the incitement allegedly took place had been preselected or not.[61] Private acts of incitement could, under certain circumstances, amount for instance to conspiracy to commit genocide, another punishable offence.[62] The means used to incite and to spread a

---

[56] See on this matter J.P. Chrétien (ed.), *Rwanda: Les Médias du génocide* (Paris: Karthala, 1995).

[57] See *Kambanda* Trial Judgment, par 39(ix). See also, *inter alia*, S. Majstorović, 'Ancient Hatreds or Elite Manipulation? Memory and Politics in the Former Yugoslavia' 159(4) *World Affairs* 170 et seq. (1997) and J.F. Metzl, 'Rwandan Genocide and the International Law of Radio Jamming' 91 *AJIL* 628 et seq. (1997).   [58] *Nahimana* Trial Judgment, par 945.

[59] Ibid., pars 952 and 1060.   [60] *Akayesu* Trial Judgment, par 560.

[61] Ibid., par 556; *Kajelijeli* Trial Judgment, par 851. The International Law Commission pointed out that such incitement was characterized by a 'call for criminal action to a number of individuals in a public place or to members of the general public at large'. See *Draft Code of Crimes Against Peace and Security of Mankind*, article 2(3)(f): 'The [. . .] element of public incitement requires communicating the call for criminal action to a number of individuals in person in a public place or by technical means of mass communication, such as by radio or television.' *Report of the International Law Commission to the General Assembly*, UN GOAR, 51st Sess., Supp. No.10, UN Doc. A/51/10 (1996) at 26, mentioned in *Akayesu* Trial Judgment, par 225, n 126.

[62] *Akayesu* Trial Judgment, par 556. See also *Akayesu* Appeal Judgment, par 480: 'the Statute makes clear that the act must be direct and public, which plainly excludes any other form of incitement to commit genocide, including private incitement to commit genocide'.

genocidal message, be it via television, print media, loudspeakers, or otherwise, is generally immaterial although the method used may reinforce a finding that the incitement was indeed 'public' in character.[63]

Incitement is 'direct' when it 'specifically provoke[s] another to engage in a criminal act, and that more than mere vague or indirect suggestion goes to constitute [it]'.[64] The incitement need not be explicit, however, but may instead be implicit or subdued, as long as the Prosecution can establish that the persons for whom the message was intended 'immediately grasped the implication thereof'.[65] The use of expressions such as 'cockroaches' in the context of the Rwandan conflict, for instance, to describe one particular ethnic group (the Tutsis) as targets for elimination could therefore be sufficient. What matters, ultimately, is whether the person to whom the message was intended could unambiguously understand its meaning and implication and that the message caused him or her to act.[66] It should be clear that the requirement that the incitement must have been 'direct' does not restrict the scope of responsibility to those who spoke or were the mouthpiece of a particular message, but also includes those who made the transmission or communication of that message possible, including editors of media outlets and their owners.[67]

'Direct and public incitement to commit genocide' is an inchoate offence and the Prosecution need not show, therefore, that anyone acted upon the act of incitement that forms the basis of the charges against the accused, nor that it produced any other result.[68] Evidence of causation may be relevant, however, to establish the 'direct' character of that alleged incitement.

Finally, concerning the *mens rea* applicable to that offence, the Prosecution must establish that the accused intended 'to create by his actions a particular state of mind necessary to commit such a crime in the minds of the person(s) he is so

---

[63] *Akayesu* Trial Judgment, par 556.

[64] Ibid., par 557. See also *Kajelijeli* Trial Judgment, par 852. In his *Commentary to the Genocide Convention*, Nehemia Robinson noted that the expression 'direct' in Article III(c) meant 'incitement which *calls* for the commission of acts of Genocide, not such which *may result* in such commission' (Robinson, *Genocide Convention*, p 67).

[65] *Akayesu* Trial Judgment, pars 557–558. See also *Mugesera et al. v. Minister of Citizenship and Immigration*, IMM-5946-98, 10 May 2001, Federal Court of Canada, Trial Division, pp 95–98.

[66] *Akayesu* Trial Judgment, par 558; *Nahimana* Trial Judgment, pars 1004–1006, 1008. See also *Kajelijeli* Trial Judgment, par 853, where the Trial Chamber indicates that the alleged incitement should be viewed 'in light of its cultural and linguistic content'.

[67] See, e.g. *Nahimana* Trial Judgment, pars 979 and 1001–1003, concerning the responsibility of editors or those responsible for the programming and owners of media outlets.

[68] *Akayesu* Trial Judgment, pars 561–562; *Musema* Trial Judgment, pars 193–194; *Kajelijeli* Trial Judgment, par 855. 'The Chamber holds that genocide clearly falls within the category of crimes so serious that direct and public incitement to commit such a crime must be punished as such, even where such incitement failed to produce the result expected by the perpetrator' (ibid., par 562). The concept of 'incitement' is known both in common law and civil law under different forms and definitions (see *Akayesu* Trial Judgment, par 555). The Prosecution need not, therefore, establish any causal relationship between the act of 'incitement' and the acts, if any, which it is said to have triggered; the Prosecution only needs to establish that, in view of all the circumstances, the conduct that consistutes 'incitement' for the purpose of the charges, had the 'potential' to cause genocide (*Nahimana* Trial Judgment, pars 1007–1017).

engaging, that is to say that the person who is inciting to commit genocide' and that he himself possessed the specific genocidal intent.[69]

16.2.4 Attempt to commit genocide

An 'attempt' is traditionally defined as an act carried out with intent to commit a certain crime which is more than merely preparatory to the commission of that crime but which has not been fully successful.[70] What can be attempted in relation to genocide is the underlying offence (killing, causing serious bodily or mental harm, etc.) that forms the basis of the charge of genocide. The genocidal *mens rea* must necessarily be met.

Considering the nature of this crime and the limited resources at the disposal of the Office of the Prosecutor, it is unlikely that the prosecutor of either *ad hoc* Tribunal will ever bring charges of 'attempt to commit genocide'. If ever charged, it would probably be charged cumulatively as a 'safety net' together with other categories of genocidal offences.

16.2.5 Complicity in genocide

The exact meaning of 'complicity' pursuant to Articles 4(3)(e)/2(3)(e) of the Statutes is still subject to much debate and it has given rise to contradictory definitions in the jurisprudence of the Tribunals.[71] The problem stems in part from the fact that Articles 4(3)(e)/2(3)(e) of the Statutes talk of 'complicity' in genocide, whilst Articles 7(1)/6(1) of the Statutes (which provide for forms of criminal liability in relation to *all* crimes within the Tribunals' jurisdiction, including genocide) talk of 'aiding and abetting'. The possible discrepancies and overlap between these two concepts may be due to the drafters overlooking possible inconsistencies between those two provisions, although the Appeals Chamber suggested that it was not so.[72] In the jurisprudence of the Tribunals, it has sometimes been suggested that 'complicity' pursuant to Articles 4(3)(e)/2(3)(e) was different from 'aiding and abetting' in Articles 7(1)/6(1) of the Statutes,[73] while in other cases, it was concluded that the elements of accomplice liability pursuant to Articles 4(3)(e)/ 2(3)(e) were in fact identical to those required under Articles 7(1)/6(1) for aiding and abetting.[74] Even if an accused were charged under both headings, it must be remembered that the

---

[69] *Kajelijeli* Trial Judgment, par 854; *Akayesu* Trial Judgment, par 560.

[70] Article 25(3)(f) of the ICC Statute provides that the 'attempt' to commit a crime means the commencement of its execution 'by means of a substantial step, but the crime does not occur because of circumstances independent of the person's intentions'.

[71] See, e.g. *Stakić* Rule 98bis Decision, pars 60–67.

[72] *Krstić* Appeal Judgment, pars 138–139. The Appeals Chamber held that the apparent discrepancy could be reconciled insofar as the concept of 'complicity' (as found in Article 4(3)(e) of the ICTY Statute) encompassed the narrower concept of 'aiding and abetting' (as provided in Article 7(1) of the ICTY Statute) (ibid., par 139).   [73] See, e.g. *Akayesu* Trial Judgment, pars 533–537, 547.

[74] *Stakić* Rule 98bis Decision, par 62; *Milošević* Rule 98bis Decision, pars 296–297. See also *Ntakirutimana* Trial Judgment, par 787.

jurisdiction of the ICTY – and, arguably, that of the ICTR – is ultimately circumscribed by customary international law and that the elements of each form of liability would have to be met as they are to be found in that body of law.[75]

Although the two notions, complicity and aiding and abetting, may cover slightly different (but also overlapping) forms of participation,[76] Chambers of the *ad hoc* Tribunals seem to be in agreement that, insofar as liability under Articles 4(3)(e)/2(3)(e) is concerned, the Prosecution must establish that the accomplice provided practical assistance, encouragement, or moral support which had a 'substantial effect on the perpetration of the crime'.[77] Encouragement or practical assistance for the purpose of Articles 4(3)(e)/2(3)(e) may be given, for instance, by transporting executioners to the killing site,[78] identifying the members of the enemy group and pointing at them,[79] providing forces and ammunition for the killing.[80]

More serious are the discrepancies which exist among various Chambers as to the required *mens rea* required for accomplice liability pursuant to Articles 4(3)(e)/2(3)(e). The Trial Chamber in *Akayesu* appeared at first to suggest that an accomplice must possess the special *mens rea*, although it later concluded that knowledge thereof was sufficient.[81] In *Jelišić*, the Trial Chamber held that an accomplice needed to possess the *dolus specialis* of genocide.[82] In other ICTR cases, knowledge of the principal's genocidal intent was considered to be sufficient for an accomplice to be held liable as an accomplice to genocide.[83] The ICTR made no secret of the fact that its interpretation of the concept of 'complicity' pursuant to Article 2(3)(e) of the ICTR Statute was defined 'per the Rwanda Penal Code'.[84] In *Stakić*, the Trial Chamber noted that certain Trial Chambers had been satisfied that knowledge, rather than intent, was sufficient for an accomplice to be held responsible for a genocidal offence.[85] It said, however, that this could constitute 'a departure from the strict pre-requisite of *dolus specialis* related to all forms

---

[75] See, generally, *Ojdanić* Joint Criminal Enterprise Decision, pars 9–10. See also *Vasiljević* Trial Judgment, pars 196–198.

[76] See, e.g. *Krnojelac* Appeal Judgment, par 70, and *Krstić* Appeal Judgment, par 139.

[77] See *Furundžija* Trial Judgment, par 249 and *Stakić* Rule 98bis Decision, par 62. See also *Musema* Trial Judgment, par 917; *Rutaganda* Trial Judgment, par 391.

[78] *Ntakirutimana* Trial Judgment, pars 789, 829.   [79] Ibid.

[80] Ibid., par 791; *Rutaganda* Trial Judgment, par 86.

[81] Compare *Akayesu* Trial Judgment, par 485 with pars 540 and 547 of the *same* judgment. In fact, it may be that the Trial Chamber did not consider aiding and abetting to be a form of accomplice liability or, more likely, it drew a distinction between these two modes of liability, but failed to specify clearly the nuances of each one of them and the respective requirements that must be met when they are charged in relation to genocidal offences (see *Stakić* Rule 98bis Decision, pars 60–67). See also *Bagilishema* Trial Judgment, par 71: 'The *mens rea* of complicity in genocide lies in the accomplice's knowledge of the commission of the crime of genocide by the principal perpetrator. Therefore, the accomplice in genocide need not possess the *dolus specialis* of genocide.'

[82] *Jelišić* Trial Judgment, par 86.

[83] See *Akayesu* Trial Judgment, pars 540, 544, 545, and 547; *Musema* Trial Judgment, par 181. According to those decisions, the required state of mind for accomplice liability implies that the accused must have knowingly aided or abetted one or more persons to commit the crime of genocide, but that he does not necessarily possessed the *dolus specialis* of genocide.   [84] *Akayesu* Trial Judgment, par 537.

[85] *Stakić* Rule 98bis Decision, par 66.

of committing and participation in genocide'.[86] This Chamber eventually refrained from expressly stating its own view on this matter. Finally, the Appeals Chamber in the *Krstić* case declared that, although there is authority to suggest that liability for complicity in genocide requires proof that the accomplice possessed the specific intent to destroy a protected group, no such requirement existed if the accomplice was charged with 'aiding and abetting' the principals.[87]

The Appeals Chamber's finding that aiding and abetting only requires knowledge of the principal's genocidal state of mind is rather unconvincing and finds only minuscule support in state practice.[88] The special genocidal intent does not form part of the *mens rea* specific to the mode of participation. Instead, it is an element of the *chapeau* of the offence which characterizes it as an international crime and which must be met (as with the requirement of a 'widespread or systematic attack on a civilian population' and knowledge thereof for crimes against humanity) in relation to each and every individual charged with such a crime.[89] Unless all *chapeau* elements are met by the accused individually, he or she is not participating in an international crime, but in something else and his acts do not come within the Tribunal's jurisdiction.[90] The Appeals Chamber's finding on that point appears to conflate the general or *chapeau* elements of the crime (genocidal *mens rea*) with the mental requirement of the mode of liability. It is all the more surprising that, having found that aiding and abetting constitutes a form of complicity, and having more than hinted at the fact that complicity in genocide would require genocidal intent on the part of the accomplice,[91] the Appeals Chamber failed to explain why aiding and abetting would not have to meet the requirements (including the apparent requirement of genocidal intent) that apply to the general form of liability from which it derives.

What is clear in any case is that complicity in genocide can only exist when there is a punishable principal act in which the accomplice was complicit.[92]

---

[86] Ibid., pars 48 and 67. The Trial Chamber in *Milošević* appears to consider that knowledge of the principal's genocidal intent is sufficient in principle for complicity as well as aiding and abetting genocide (*Milošević* Rule 98bis Decision, pars 297–298, 309; see also ibid., Dissenting Opinion of Judge O-Gon Kwon, par 3).   [87] *Krstić* Appeal Judgment, pars 142–143.

[88] The only state practice directly relevant to the issue which the Appeals Chamber could garner in support of its finding are two provisions of the French and German Criminal Codes (*Krstić* Appeal Judgment, par 141). All other authorities relate to accomplice liability in general, but do not provide any support for (or against) the contention that knowledge would suffice to be found responsible of aiding and abetting genocide or complicity in genocide (ibid.). Such state practice or rather the lack thereof would, in itself, fall far short of what could be regarded as sufficient to give rise to a rule of customary international law. In addition, it is worth noting that the Appeals Chamber has not provided any evidence of *opinio juris* on that matter, despite having found that 'to hold that a principle was part of customary international law, it has to be satisfied that State practice recognized the principle on the basis of supporting *opinio juris*' (*Hadžihasanović* Command Responsibility Appeal Decision, par 12).

[89] See *Brdjanin* JCE III and Genocide Decision, Separate Opinion of Judge Shahabuddeen, par 4.

[90] If the *chapeau* elements were not met in a specific case in the person of the accused, it would be open for the Defence to argue that the Tribunal does not have jurisdiction over his conduct as it falls short of any of the crimes provided for in the Statute.   [91] *Krstić* Appeal Judgment, par 142.

[92] *Akayesu* Trial Judgment, par 529; *Stakić* Trial Judgement, par 533 and references cited therein. See also *Musema* Trial Judgment, pars 173–174. The principal need not, however, have been prosecuted or even charged, or identified (*Stakić* Rule 98bis Decision, par 52).

Consequently, it must first be proven that the crime of genocide has indeed been committed before liability for complicity may attach to any other participant in this crime.[93] However, it has been said that a Chamber need not necessarily identify the specific individual who was the principal to the offence to convict an accused of aiding and abetting him.[94] Such a finding raises a number of evidential difficulties related to the specificity of genocide. The main difficulty perhaps has to do with the determination of the specific intent of the principal and the fact that, according to the Appeals Chamber, an aider and abettor may be found responsible for aiding and abetting genocide if he is shown to have known of the principal's genocidal intent. If, as the Appeals Chamber has concluded, a conviction for aiding and abetting genocide may be entered without the principal having been identified and that the establishment of the accused's *mens rea* depends on proof having been made of his knowledge of the principal's genocidal intent, how could he ever be said to have known of something that has not been established by the court? If the principal is not identified, how could the court make a finding beyond reasonable doubt that he possessed the specific genocidal mindset? In other words, how could the court satisfy itself that the accused shared the intent of a person (the principal) which it has not identified and whose *mens rea* has therefore not been established? This, again, militates in favour of the approach suggested above, namely, that any participant in a genocidal crime should be shown to have possessed the genocidal intent so that the establishment of his state of mind should not depend on establishing that of someone else.

A number of Trial Chambers have suggested that charges of complicity to genocide were limited to individuals who, from a hierarchical point of view, are lesser participants in a grander criminal scheme, whereas genocide would be reserved for high officials or military commanders, thereby creating a vertical divide between the 'planners' who would generally be principals to genocide while 'executioners' would generally be mere accomplices to such crimes.[95] This, with all due respect, is pure *lex praetoria*. It finds no support in the text of either the Statutes or the Genocide Convention, nor is it supported in existing state practice. Customary law does not support a suggestion that different forms of liability have been assigned (or should be assigned) depending on the hierarchical level of criminal participation. What matters for any form of liability is concerned is the nature of one's conduct and the extent to which that conduct partakes into the commission of the offence of the principal, not one's position in the hierarchy.

---

[93] *Akayesu* Trial Judgment, par 530. This requirement does not imply that the identity of the main perpetrator be determined (ibid., par 531).

[94] *Krstić* Appeal Judgment, pars 35, 134, and 137; *Krstić* Trial Judgment, pars 591–599; *Stakić* Trial Judgment, par 533.

[95] It has been suggested that the principal is '[the one] who devises the genocidal plan at the highest level and takes the major steps to put it into effect', 'the one who fulfills "a key co-ordinating role" and whose "participation is of an extremely significant nature and at the leadership level"' (*Stakić* Rule 98bis Decision, par 50; see also *Krstić* Trial Judgment, pars 642–644).

Finally, concerning the issue of cumulative convictions, if the requirements of both genocide and complicity in (or aiding and abetting) genocide were to be met in relation to a single-incident criminal conduct, the former would absorb the latter and conviction for genocide would exclude a conviction for complicity.[96]

16.3 Other forms of criminal participation?

Articles 4(3)/2(3) of the Statutes say that 'the following acts shall be punishable', and then goes on to list the acts mentioned above (genocide, conspiracy to commit genocide, etc.). This sentence has been interpreted by the *ad hoc* Tribunals as being illustrative, rather than exhaustive[97] so that other modes of participation included in Articles 7/6 of the Statutes must be read into Articles 4(3)/2(3), thereby adding to the categories of participation expressly mentioned in Articles 4/2 of the Statutes a number of other forms of criminal participation which could entail liability for a genocidal conduct.[98] Accused persons in both Tribunals have therefore been charged with and have been found guilty of genocide under heads of liability which are not expressly provided for in the statutory provision dealing specifically with genocide, in particular superior responsibility (pursuant to Articles 7(3)/6(3) of the Statutes) or for their part in a so-called 'joint criminal enterprise' to commit genocide pursuant to Articles 7(1)/6(1).[99]

16.3.1 Command responsibility and genocide

At the time of the adoption of the Genocide Convention, the possibility of a commander being held responsible for genocide had apparently not been considered by the drafters. This, clearly, does not mean that such a possibility has not later been recognized under international law and that the general principles recognized

---

[96] *Musema* Trial Judgment, par 175; *Bagilishema* Trial Judgment, par 67; *Akayesu* Trial Judgment, par 532; *Ntakirutimana* Trial Judgment, pars 796 and 837; *Nahimana* Trial Judgment, par 1056; *Stakić* Trial Judgment, par 534.

[97] See, e.g. *Akayesu* Trial Judgment, par 546; *Krstić* Appeal Judgment, pars 138–139.

[98] Ibid., pars 138–139. Article 7 of the ICTY Statute and Article 6 of the ICTR Statute ('Individual Criminal Responsibility') provide the general heads of responsibility upon which convictions may be based in relation to any crime within the Tribunal's jurisdiction, including genocide. Article 4(3), which is taken verbatim from Article III of the Genocide Convention, also provides for heads of responsibility, but it is limited to genocidal acts. As pointed out above, there is therefore a potential for overlap, but also for contradictions between these two provisions (see *Krstić* Trial Judgment, par 640).

[99] The structure of the Tribunals' Statutes indeed suggests that the Security Council intended the forms of individual criminal responsibility provided for in Article 7 of the Statute to apply to all crimes provided for in Articles 2–5, including genocide. See also par 54 of the Secretary-General Report (ICTY), which provides that: 'all persons who participate in the planning, preparation or execution of serious violations of international humanitarian law [. . .] contribute to the commission of the violation and are, therefore, individually responsible'.

in the Convention (or under customary law) may not apply to the acts of a commander if these acts may be said to reasonably fall within the application of these principles.[100] But a new factual situation does not change the terms of the principle itself. It is the principle that dictates the scope of its application and these rules and principles found in the Convention or under customary international law concerning the state of mind required for a genocide conviction would therefore apply to the case where a commander is implicated as they would in relation to other forms of participation.[101]

The principal difficulty that exists in respect of this form of criminal liability when applied to genocide concerns the mental state required for a commander to be held responsible for the acts of his subordinates. While knowledge (as defined below[102]) is sufficient in principle for a superior to be held responsible for the acts of his subordinates, genocide requires a specific intent to destroy in whole or in part a group as such. How can those two standards be reconciled? Is it sufficient for a commander to know or to have had reason to know that his subordinates were committing genocidal acts for him to be held responsible for genocide under Articles 7(3)/6(3) of the Statute or does he need to have possessed the genocidal intent himself?

In *Musema*, a Trial Chamber said that knowledge was sufficient for convicting an accused of genocide as a superior pursuant to Article 6(3) of the ICTR Statute because, as the test goes, 'he knew or, at least, had reason to know' that his subordinates were about to commit genocidal acts or had done so.[103] This, with respect, is unsatisfactory and appears to conflate forms of liability and elements of the crime. The requirement of knowledge exists so that a superior may not be held responsible for crimes of which he had no knowledge.[104] It does not mean,

---

[100] See generally *Hadžihasanović* Command Responsibility Appeal Decision, par 12, on the applicability of a principle to a new situation that falls reasonably within the principle itself.

[101] See Separate and Partially Dissenting Opinion of Judge David Hunt, par 40, in *Hadžihasanović* Command Responsibility Appeal Decision.   [102] See below, sub-section 21.3.

[103] *Musema* Trial Judgment, pars 894–895. See also *Kayishema and Ruzindana* Trial Judgment, pars 228, 555, and 559. The Trial Chamber in *Akayesu* which stated that knowledge was sufficient in relation to accomplice liability, stated that genocidal intent was required in respect of those other forms of criminal liability as set out in Article 6(1) of the ICTR Statute, thereby apparently distinguishing between complicity in genocide (for which knowledge is sufficient) and aiding and abetting (for which the special intent is required) (*Akayesu* Trial Judgment, pars 546–547). In *Krstić*, the accused was charged with genocide, *inter alia*, as a commander pursuant to Article 7(3). The Trial Chamber made no finding, however, upon this form of liability as it had already found that Krstić was guilty pursuant to Article 7(1) for his part in a joint criminal enterprise to commit genocide (*Krstić* Trial Judgment, par 652). In par 648 of its Judgment, when reviewing the requirements of Article 7(3), the Trial Chamber noted that Krstić had been 'aware of the genocidal objectives' of the operations in Srebrenica, thereby suggesting that such knowledge may have been enough for him to be guilty under that Article, would there have been a need to enter a conviction on that basis.

[104] The soundness of such a requirement can easily be grasped from the literature on the *Yamashita* trial, in which the United States Supreme Court found the accused responsible for criminal actions of which he seems to have had no knowledge (see, e.g. M. Stryszak, 'Command Responsibility: How Much Should a Commander Be Expected to Know?' 11 *Journal of Legal Studies* (2000/2001); M. Smidt, 'Yamashita, Medina, and Beyond: Command Responsibility in Contemporary Military Operations' 164 *Military Law Review* 155 (2000)).

however, that such knowledge is sufficient to establish his guilt, regardless of the crime charged against him.

As noted above, it is argued that the requirement of special genocidal intent must be met individually by each and every accused person changed with a genocidal offence and that it is not sufficient, regardless of the mode of participation, to establish that the accused knew of the genocidal intent of others to convict him or her of such an offence. This applies *inter alia* to the liability of a commander for the acts of his subordinates: to be held responsible for genocide as a commander, the accused must therefore be shown to have possessed the required genocidal intent himself. There is indeed no precedent which would support a finding that a commander could be held responsible where he merely knows of his subordinates' intent and, prior to 1998, there was simply no state practice (and no *opinio juris*) that such a state of mind could ever suffice to enter a genocide conviction, regardless of the form of participation under consideration.

To be liable for genocide as a superior, the accused need not know that his subordinates possessed the genocidal *mens rea*, and it may in fact happen that they do not possess it, though he could still be found guilty of genocide. What the commander must be shown to have known or have had reason to know, the author submits, is that his subordinates were committing or were about to commit any of the underlying genocidal offences (such as killing, causing serious mental or bodily harm, etc.), and to have had the genocidal intent *himself*.[105] The fact that he may have known of his subordinates' genocidal *mens rea* has evidential relevance to the extent that it may serve to establish *his own* genocidal state of mind.[106] But it is not sufficient to either deduce his own *mens rea* from the sole fact of his subordinates' genocidal *mens rea*, nor is it acceptable to conclude that his *knowledge* thereof renders him liable for genocide pursuant to Articles 7(3)/6(3).

This exigency of knowledge on the superior's part does not require that the superior must know the detail of his subordinates' actions, a requirement which would have rendered this form of liability almost meaningless.[107] What the superior must know, however, is the general nature and seriousness of the acts which his subordinates have committed or are about to commit so that he may take the measures which are reasonable and appropriate in relation to the relevant crimes and be held responsible if he fails to do so. Where the accused has been charged with failure to punish genocide, his *mens rea* must be established at the

---

[105] 'It follows from Article 4 [of the ICTY Statute] and the unique nature of genocide that the *dolus specialis* is required for responsibility under Article 7(3) as well' (*Stakić* Rule 98bis Decision, par 92). See also, *Krstić* Appeal Judgment, which provides that '[c]onvictions for genocide can be entered only where that [special genocidal] intent has been unequivocally established' (par 134). Note, however, that the statement of the Appeals Chamber in the *Krstić* case was made in relation to liability as a principal.

[106] It is therefore possible to imagine a situation where subordinates would commit crimes without genocidal intent and where their commander could nevertheless be held liable for genocide if *he* possessed such a genocidal state of mind and knew or had reason to know of his subordinates' crimes.

[107] See, e.g. *Bagilishema* Appeal Judgment, par 42; *Čelebići* Appeal Judgment, par 238.

time when he is said to have failed to fulfil his duty (to punish) his subordinates. His knowledge of those crimes coupled with his inaction may permit an inference, based on all the circumstances, that he possessed the requisite intent.

Finally, the reasonableness and appropriateness of the measures which the superior may be expected to adopt to prevent or punish crimes of his subordinates are dictated in part by the nature of the crimes that have been or are about to be committed.[108] Considering the seriousness of the underlying offences which may constitute acts of genocide, a superior who knows or has reason to know that such crimes have or are about to be committed is expected to take very effective measures to punish or prevent them and to implement them with some urgency.

16.3.2   Joint criminal enterprise or common purpose doctrine and genocide

Once again, the main issue concerning liability for participating in a joint criminal enterprise to commit genocide revolves around the state of mind that must be established to enter a conviction on that basis. What is the required *mens rea* for an accused charged for his part in a joint criminal enterprise, the purpose of which is to commit genocide or another crime of which genocide is said to be a natural and foreseeable consequence? Would knowledge of the fact that such crimes are envisioned be sufficient or would the accused have to share that intent personally?

When considering the relationship between Article 4(3) and Article 7(1) of the ICTY Statute, one Trial Chamber stated that Article 4(3) can be regarded as '*lex specialis* in relation to Article 7(1) (*lex generalis*)'.[109] It went on to add that, 'reading the modes of participation under Article 7(1) into Article 4(3), whilst maintaining the *dolus specialis* pre-requisite, would lead to the same result'.[110] Likewise, the Trial Chamber in the *Brdjanin* case found that liability for the third category of joint criminal enterprise required proof of a genocidal intent on the part of the accused.[111] Other Trial Chambers have, however, opted for a different view.[112] The Appeals Chamber in the *Brdjanin* case, in particular, said that as a mode of criminal liability, the third category of joint criminal enterprise is no different from other forms of criminal liability which do not require proof of intent to commit a crime on the part of the accused before criminal liability may attach.[113] The Appeals Chamber went on to find that the Trial Chamber had erred

---

[108] 'The measures required of the superior are limited to those which are feasible in all the circumstances and are "within his power". A superior is not obliged to perform the impossible. However, the superior has a duty to exercise the powers he has within the confines of those limitations.' (*Krnojelac* Trial Judgment, par 95). See also *Čelebići* Appeal Judgment, par 226.

[109] *Stakić* Rule 98bis Decision, par 48.   [110] Ibid.

[111] *Brdjanin* Rule 98bis Decision, pars 56–57.

[112] See *Krstić* Trial Judgment, pars 621–644, in particular par 644.

[113] *Brdjanin* JCE III and Genocide Decision, par 7. See also *Milošević* Rule 98bis Decision, par 291, citing with approval the *Brdjanin* Decision.

when suggesting that specific genocidal intent had to be shown and that an accused could therefore be held responsible where genocide is merely a natural and foreseeable consequence of his acts.[114] The Appeals Chamber's finding on that point is unconvincing. As with its finding re 'aiding and abetting' genocide in the *Krstić* case, the Appeals Chamber appears to be conflating modes of liability and *chapeau* elements of the offence and to ignore the specificity of that crime. Furthermore, the Appeals Chamber appears to have failed to provide any authority (let alone any state practice or *opinio juris*) which would support its finding under customary international law.[115] This question therefore remains a very debatable one.

[114] *Brdjanin* JCE III and Genocide Decision, par 10. See, however, *Stakić* Trial Judgment, pars 530 and 558, for a contrary view.
[115] See the Separate Opinion of Judge Shahabuddeen appended to the *Brdjanin* JCE III and Genocide Decision.

PART V

PARTICIPATION IN INTERNATIONAL CRIMES AND INDIVIDUAL CRIMINAL RESPONSIBILITY

17

General Remarks on Participation

'It is a feature of criminal responsibility that it can be distributed without being divided.'[1] The distribution of criminal responsibility takes different forms in different domestic legal systems and the scope and modes of criminal liability will be drawn more or less broadly in each one of those legal environments. Under the Tribunals' Statutes, one single statutory provision (Article 7 in the case of the ICTY Statute and Article 6 of the ICTR Statute) regulates those forms of participation for which individual criminal responsibility may be engaged under the Statute. This Article – which is identical in both Statutes – must be read into each and every one of the subject-matter Articles of the Statute so that any of the crimes listed in the Statute may, in principle, be committed in any of the forms provided for in Article 7 (Article 6).[2] The text of that article reads:

Individual criminal responsibility

1. A person who planned, instigated, ordered, committed or otherwise aided and abetted in the planning, preparation or execution of a crime referred to in articles 2 to 5 of the present Statute, shall be individually responsible for the crime.
[. . .]
3. The fact that any of the acts referred to in articles 2 to 5 of the present Statute was committed by a subordinate does not relieve his superior of criminal responsibility if he knew or had reason to know that the subordinate was about to commit such acts or had done so and the superior failed to take the necessary and reasonable measures to prevent such acts or to punish the perpetrators thereof.

Paragraph 1 contains a number of what may be called 'traditional' forms of criminal participation known under different nomenclature to most domestic systems: planning, instigating, ordering, committing, or otherwise aiding and abetting.[3] These forms of criminal liability are sometimes referred to as forms of 'direct' participation, by contrast to 'command responsibility' which is provided for in paragraph 3 and which may have the rare privilege of having been created and nurtured by international law rather than by domestic law.

---

[1] M. Walzer, *Just and Unjust Wars*, 3rd edn (New York: Basic Books, 2000), p 309.
[2] See, e.g., *Kajelijeli* Trial Judgment, par 756.
[3] The French text of Articles 7(1) and 6(1) of the Tribunals' Statutes provides as follows: 'Quiconque a planifié, incité à commettre, ordonné, commis ou de toute autre manière aide et encourage à planifier, préparer ou executer un crime visé aux articles 2 à 5 du présent statut est individuellement responsable du dit crime.'

18

Jurisdiction *ratione personae* and Applicable Law

The Statutes of the Tribunals do not explicitly specify the body of law according to which they are to determine the scope and definitions of those forms of liability which are provided for under their Statutes. At the ICTY, the Appeals Chamber has made it clear, however, that the Statute of the Tribunal only provides an *a priori* jurisdictional framework *ratione personae* and that, ultimately, the existence (and constitutive elements) of a particular form of criminal liability under international law as well as the Tribunal's jurisdiction over that particular form of liability (and scope thereof[1]) will be determined by customary international law.[2] The reach of the ICTY's jurisdiction *ratione personae* may therefore be said to be determined, as the Appeals Chamber put it, by 'both by the Statute [of the Tribunal], insofar as it sets out the jurisdictional framework of the International Tribunal, and by customary international law, insofar as the Tribunal's power to convict an accused of any crime listed in the Statute depends on its existence *qua* custom at the time this crime was allegedly committed'.[3] In practice, this means that, before an accused may be found guilty of any criminal involvement pursuant to one of the forms of criminal participation provided for in the Statute, Chambers of the ICTY must satisfy themselves that the form of liability with which he has been charged is indeed recognized by customary international law and that its elements have all been met in the particular case.[4] In addition, that form of liability must have been sufficiently accessible and foreseeable to attract penal consequences.

---

[1] See, e.g. *Hadžihasanović* Command Responsibility Appeal Decision, pars 37 et seq. ('Command responsibility for crimes committed before the superior–subordinate relationship exists').

[2] See ibid., par 44: 'it has always been the approach of this Tribunal not to rely merely on a construction of the Statute to establish the applicable law on criminal responsibility, but to ascertain the state of customary law in force at the time the crimes were committed.' See also *Ojdanić* Joint Criminal Enterprise Decision, par 9; *Čelebići* Appeal Judgment, par 178.

[3] *Ojdanić* Joint Criminal Enterprise Decision, par 9.

[4] Ibid., par 10: 'the principle of legality demands that the Tribunal shall apply the law which was binding upon individuals at the time of the acts charged. And, just as is the case in respect of the Tribunal's jurisdiction *ratione materiae*, that body of law must be reflected in customary international law.'

In sum, in order to come within the Tribunal's jurisdiction *ratione personae*, any form of liability must satisfy four preconditions:[5]

(i) it must be provided for in the Statute, explicitly or implicitly;
(ii) it must have existed under customary international law at the relevant time;
(iii) the law providing for that form of liability must have been sufficiently accessible at the relevant time to anyone who acted in such a way; and
(iv) such person must have been able to foresee that he could be held criminally liable for his actions if apprehended.

The issue of applicable law, *ratione personae*, has not yet been raised explicitly at the ICTR, but lest it would incur serious accusations of *ex post facto* law, it is more than probable that the Tribunal for Rwanda should also have recourse to customary international law to determine the scope of its jurisdiction *ratione personae*. It is unclear from its jurisprudence, however, whether it has indeed had recourse to that body of law and, if not, to what body of law it could otherwise have recourse.[6]

---

[5] Ibid., par 21.

[6] In fact, at the ICTR, the Appeals Chamber seems to have hinted that the ICTR should also have recourse to customary international law to determine the scope of its jurisdiction *ratione personae*. See *Bagilishema* Appeal Judgment, par 34 (emphasis added): 'The Statute does not provide for criminal liability other than those forms of participation stated therein, expressly or implicitly. In particular, it would be both unnecessary and unfair to hold an accused responsible under a head of responsibility *which has not clearly been defined in international criminal law*.'

19

The Person of the Perpetrator: Who Can Commit an International Crime?

In principle, anyone – civilian or military, high-ranking state official, or foot-soldier – can commit a war crime, a crime against humanity, or a genocidal offence.[1] There is no *domaine réservé* of international criminality as far as potential perpetrators are concerned and a look at the list of indictees at both *ad hoc* Tribunals reveals a diverse gallery of individuals, ranging from former heads of state and army generals to former bartenders and schoolteachers.[2]

Pursuant to Article 1 of both Statutes, read together with Articles 6/5 of the ICTY/ICTR Statutes, the Tribunals' jurisdiction *ratione personae* is also determined by the gravity of the alleged violation of international humanitarian law.[3] In principle, individuals may therefore be indicted (and held criminally responsible if found guilty) regardless of their exact role in the commission of the crime as long as their contribution to the crime meets the above jurisdictional requirement of gravity and that it falls within one of the forms of criminal participation

---

[1] See, generally, *Akayesu* Appeal Judgment, par 436 and pars 443–444. See also *Kayishema and Ruzindana* Appeal Judgment, par 170, in relation to the crime of genocide: 'Genocide is not a crime that can only be committed by certain categories of persons. As evidenced by history, it is a crime which has been committed by the low-level executioner and the high-level planner or instigator alike' *Tadić* Appeal Judgment, pars 248 and 252; *Kupreškić* Trial Judgment, par 555; *Kamuhanda* Trial Judgment, pars 725–729, concerning war crimes. See also Nuremberg Principles, Principles I and III affirming that 'any person' who commits a crime under international law is responsible and liable for it.

[2] The list of indictees appearing before both Tribunals is available on their respective websites (www.un.org/icty; www.ictr.org). For a journalistic portrayal of some of the accused who have appeared or are currently on trial before the ICTY, see S. Drakulić, *They Would Never Hurt a Fly* (London: Abacus, March 2004).

[3] The ICTY and ICTR Statutes provide that the Tribunal shall have the power to prosecute persons responsible for 'serious' violations of international humanitarian law (Article 1). The Trial Chamber in *Čelebići* held that the seriousness requirement did not limit the competence of the Tribunal to 'persons in positions of military or political authority'; *Čelebići* Trial Judgment, par 176; *Erdemović* Trial Judgement, par 83. It is the seriousness of the breach, as opposed to the position of the accused at the time of the act, which triggers the Tribunal's jurisdiction. See, e.g. *Prosecutor v. Kvočka et al.*, IT-98-30/1-PT, Decision on Preliminary Motions Filed by Mlado Radić and Miroslav Kvočka Challenging Jurisdiction, 1 April 1999, pars 9–11. Specifically with respect to Article 3 of the ICTY Statute, the *Tadić* Appeals Chamber held that a serious violation must 'constitute a breach of a rule protecting important values, and the breach must involve grave consequences for the victim' (*Tadić* Jurisdiction Decision, par 94(iii)).

provided for in the Statutes.[4] As the Secretary-General of the United Nations explained, all persons who participate in the commission of a statutory crime may, in principle, be prosecuted and may be found liable for their acts.[5] Within that framework, the selection of individuals to be indicted and prosecuted is first and foremost a matter for the Prosecutor to decide,[6] but the Prosecutor's discretion in that regard, though wide, is not unlimited.[7]

The Tribunals' jurisdiction *ratione personae* is limited to natural persons and it excludes juridical persons, such as political parties, paramilitary formations, or states.[8] In particular, unlike the situation in Nuremberg, criminal organizations cannot be declared criminal under the Statute, nor can their acts be sanctioned pursuant to the Statutes [9] and individuals cannot be held criminally liable merely

---

[4] See, e.g. *Tadić* Appeal Judgment, pars 248 and 252; Nuremberg Principles, Principles I and III (affirming that 'any person' who commits a crime under international law is responsible and liable for it); 1991 ILC Draft Code, pp 265–266; Convention on the Non-Applicability of Statutory Limitation to War Crimes and Crimes against Humanity, General Assembly Resolution 2391, UN GAOR, 23rd Sess., Agenda Item 64, UN Doc. A/7342 (1968) ('Statutory Non-Applicability Convention'), Art. II; International Convention on the Suppression and Punishment of the Crime of Apartheid, adopted 30 November 1973, 1015 UNTS 243 ('Apartheid Convention'), Art. III; Convention on the Prevention and Punishment of the Crime of Genocide, UN General Assembly Resolution 260 A (III) (9 December 1948) ('Genocide Convention'), Art. IV; Resolution of the First General Assembly of the United Nations of 13 December 1946; Draft Code of Offences against the Peace and Security of Mankind, *Yearbook of the International Law Commission*, Vol. II (1954), ('1954 ILC Draft Code'), at 149 (Art 2(11) providing that crimes against humanity could be committed 'by the authorities of a State or by private individuals acting at the instigation or with the toleration of such authorities'); ICC Statute, Art. 1, 27(1) providing that the court shall have jurisdiction over persons for the most serious crimes of international concern; and stating that the Statute shall apply 'equally to all persons without any distinction based on official capacity'.

[5] Secretary-General Report (ICTY), par 54. The Court must be satisfied that the accused participated in the commission of a crime within its jurisdiction *ratione materiae* in one of the ways provided for, expressly or implicitly, described in or implied in the Tribunals' Statutes (Articles 7(1) and 7(3) of the ICTY Statute, and Articles 6(1) and 6(3) of the ICTR Statute). One may wonder, however, whether the participation in a very indirect and unimportant manner may ever satisfy the requirement of 'seriousness' mentioned in Article 1 of both Statutes even where, strictly speaking, this participation might meet the requirements of Articles 7/6 of the Statutes. In other words, it is an open question whether anyone who participates in the commission of one of the statutory crimes in any of the forms of participation provided for in the Statute necessarily meets the seriousness threshold of Article 1.

[6] See, however, Article 28(A) of the ICTY Rules of Procedure and Evidence, as amended on 6 April 2004 (as discussed below in footnote 24 under sub-paragraph 19).

[7] See Articles 16 and 18 of the ICTY Statute and Articles 15 and 17 of the ICTR Statute. See also *Čelebići* Appeal Judgment, pars 602–605, noting that the Prosecutor has broad discretion in relation to the initiation of investigations and in the preparation of indictments, but the prosecutor may not exercise this discretion discriminatorily based on impermissible motives (such as, *inter alia*, race, colour, religion, opinion, national or ethnic origin). In order to show that his Prosecution is unlawful, the accused must demonstrate that the decision to prosecute him (i) was based on an unlawful or improper (including discriminatory) motive and that (ii) the Prosecution failed to prosecute similarly situated persons (ibid., pars 611–615).   [8] See, e.g. Secretary-General Report (ICTY), par 50.

[9] Ibid., par 51: 'The question arises, however, whether a juridical person, such as an association or organization, may be considered criminal as such and thus its members, for that reason alone, be made subject to the jurisdiction of the International Tribunal. The Secretary-General believes that this concept should not be retained in regard to the International Tribunal. The criminal acts set out in this Statute are carried out by natural persons; such persons would be subject to the jurisdiction of

because they belong to any such organization or group.[10] With respect to the Tribunals' jurisdiction, crimes are therefore committed, and liability incurred, *qua* the individual, and *qua* the individual only.[11]

Early on in the lives of the *ad hoc* Tribunals, it was generally accepted policy that 'the Tribunal was not intended to concern itself only with persons in positions of military or political authority', but that it would be dealing with both leaders and subordinate executioners alike.[12] Over the years, however, the Tribunals have turned their attention almost exclusively towards high-level perpetrators, those known colloquially as the 'big fish', and who played a prominent part in what one Trial Chamber called 'a system of criminality'.[13] That view of the ICTY's role and function was eventually supported by the Security Council and its President[14]

the International Tribunal irrespective of membership in groups.' See, by contrast, Article 9 of the Nuremberg Charter which provided that groups or organizations might be declared criminal. The Nuremberg Tribunal declared that four such organizations were criminal pursuant to Article 9: the Leadership Corps of the Nazi Party, the Gestapo, the SD, and the SS.

[10] See, generally, *Ojdanić* Joint Criminal Enterprise Decision, pars 24–26. See also Article 10 of the Nuremberg Charter which provided for this possibility: 'In cases where a group or organization is declared criminal by the Tribunal, the competent national authority of any Signatory shall have the right to bring individual [sic] to trial for membership therein before national, military or occupation courts. In any such case the criminal nature of the group or organization is considered proved and shall not be questioned.' Article 6(1) of the Nuremberg Charter states that '[t]he Tribunal [. . .] shall have the power to try and punish persons who, acting in the interest of the European Axis countries, whether as individuals or as members of organizations, committed any of the following crimes'. It is a fact, however, that most of the crimes which come within the Tribunals' jurisdiction have involved a relatively large number of participants. In *Tadić*, for instance, the Appeals Chamber noted that international crimes generally involved a collective of criminals: 'Most of the time these [international] crimes do not result from the criminal propensity of single individuals but constitute manifestations of collective criminality: the crimes are often carried out by groups of individuals acting in pursuance of a common criminal design. Although only some members of the group may physically perpetrate the criminal act (murder, extermination, wanton destruction of cities, towns or villages, etc), the participation and contribution of the other members of the group is often vital in facilitating the commission of the offence in question. It follows that the moral gravity of such participation is often no less – or indeed no different – from that of those actively carrying out the acts in question' (*Tadić* Appeal Judgment, par 191).

[11] As the Nuremberg Tribunal stated: 'Individuals have international duties which transcend the national obligations of obedience imposed by the individual state. He who violates the laws of war cannot obtain immunity while acting in pursuance of the authority of the state if the state in authorizing action moves outside its competence under international law' (IMT Judgment, p 223, cited in *Furundžija* Trial Judgment, par 155).

[12] *Čelebići* Trial Judgment, par 176. See also *Erdemović* Trial Judgment, par 83 (footnote omitted).

[13] See, for instance, *Martić* Rule 61 Decision, par 21.

[14] See Statement by the President of the Security Council, UN Doc. S/PRST/2002/21 (23 July 2002): 'the ICTY should concentrate its work on the Prosecution and trial of the civilian, military and paramilitary leaders suspected of being responsible for serious violations of international humanitarian law committed in the territory of the former Yugoslavia since 1991, rather than on minor actors'; Security Council Resolution 1503 (2003), UN Doc. S/RES/1503 (2003) (28 August 2003): 'Recalling and reaffirming in the strongest terms the statement of 23 July 2002 made by the President of the Security Council (S/PRST/2002/21), which endorsed the ICTY's strategy for completing investigations by the end of 2004, all trial activities at first instance by the end of 2008, and all of its work in 2010 (ICTY Completion Strategy) (S/2002/678), by concentrating on the Prosecution and trial of the most senior leaders suspected of being most responsible for crimes within the ICTY's

and made its way into the Rules of Procedure and Evidence of the ICTY which now acknowledges the power of the judges to refuse to confirm indictments that would be concerned with insufficiently senior individuals.[15]

The nationality of the perpetrator is generally immaterial to his or her individual criminal responsibility. A national of State *A* may therefore in principle equally commit a war crime, a crime against humanity, or an act of genocide against another national of State *A*, a national of State *B*, or even against a stateless individual. The victim and the perpetrator need not necessarily belong to enemy groups:[16] the perpetrator could in most cases himself be a member of the targeted group.[17] Nor is it necessary in general to demonstrate that the victims (or the perpetrator) were linked to any particular side of the conflict.[18] The only exception to that general rule concerns the requirement under the grave breaches regime that victims and perpetrators must be of different nationalities, as defined above. In any case, the jurisdiction of the Tribunals is not limited to nationals of the two countries under consideration (Rwanda and the former Yugoslavia[19]) so that anyone who has committed a serious violation of humanitarian law in the geographical area and during the period covered by the Statutes – including foreign mercenaries, NATO personnel, KFOR soldiers, or paramilitary groups of

---

jurisdiction and transferring cases involving those who may not bear this level of responsibility to competent national jurisdictions, as appropriate, as well as the strengthening of the capacity of such jurisdictions'; Security Council Resolution 1534, UN Doc. S/RES/1534 (2004) (26 March 2004): 'Calls on each [*ad hoc*] Tribunal, in reviewing and confirming any new indictments, to ensure that any such indictments concentrate on the most senior leaders suspected of being most responsible for crimes within the jurisdiction of the relevant Tribunal as set out in resolution 1503 (2003).'

[15] On 6 April 2004, Rule 28(A) of the Rules of Procedure and Evidence of the ICTY was amended, in effect, providing the judges (through the Bureau, a body composed of the President of the Tribunal, the Vice-President, and the Presiding Judges of the Trial Chambers) with a mechanism allowing them to filter out those potential indictees which they consider not sufficiently senior to appear before the International Tribunal. Article 28(A), as amended, reads as follows: 'On receipt of an indictment for review from the Prosecutor, the Registrar shall consult with the President. The President shall refer the matter to the Bureau which shall determine whether the indictment, *prima facie*, concentrates on one or more of the most senior leaders suspected of being most responsible for crimes within the jurisdiction of the Tribunal. If the Bureau determines that the indictment meets this standard, the President shall designate one of the permanent Trial Chamber Judges for the review under Rule 47 [of the Rules of Procedure and Evidence]. If the Bureau determines that the indictment does not meet this standard, the President shall return the indictment to the Registrar to communicate this finding to the Prosecutor.' See also Rule 11bis (Referral of the Indictment to Another Court), par (C) of the Rules of Procedure and Evidence, as amended on 30 September 2002: 'In determining whether to refer the case [to the authorities of a State] in accordance with paragraph (A) [of Rule 11bis], the Trial Chamber shall, in accordance with Security Council Presidential Statement S/PRST/2002/21, consider the gravity of the crimes charged and the level of responsibility of the accused.' [16] See *Enigster* case, par 5.

[17] See ibid. and Ternek Elsa, Israel, District Court of Tel Aviv, Judgment of 14 December 1951, in 5 *Pekasim Mehoziim* (1951–2), 142–52 (in Hebrew), par 8 (summary in English in 18 ILR 1951, 539–40; complete English translation on file with the author).

[18] *Kunarac* Trial Judgment, par 423.

[19] Article 1 of the ICTR Statute expressly refers to violations of international humanitarian law committed 'in the territory of neighbouring States'.

any ethnic affiliation – may in principle, and all other conditions being met, be found guilty under the Tribunals' Statutes.[20]

The ICTY and the ICTR Statutes also make it clear that the position of an accused as a head of state or the fact that he may have acted in an official capacity will neither relieve him from individual criminal responsibility, nor mitigate his punishment.[21] Before the *ad hoc* Tribunals, officials are therefore stripped of any privileges or immunities for the purpose of criminal liability, and may be prosecuted regardless of their position or role in the state apparatus and regardless too of any privilege or immunity that they may otherwise enjoy before domestic courts.[22] An international crime such as those provided for in the Statutes of the *ad hoc* Tribunals simply cannot constitute an 'act of criminal sovereignty' which could be excused away by reason of its having been committed by or on behalf of a state.[23] As one Trial Chamber put it:

[20] The ICTR has, for instance, convicted a Belgian citizen, Georges Ruggiu, for his part in the commission of mass crimes (see *Ruggiu* Trial Judgment). The Prosecutor of the ICTY has also indicated that it considered it was permitted to investigate crimes allegedly committed by NATO forces during the bombing campaign against the Federal Republic of Yugoslavia in 1999 (see *Final Report to the Prosecutor by the Committee Established to Review the NATO Bombing Campaign against the Federal Republic of Yugoslavia*).

[21] Articles 7(2) and 6(2) of the ICTY and ICTR Statutes provide: 'the official position of any accused person, whether as Head of State or Government or as a responsible Government official, shall not relieve such person of criminal responsibility nor mitigate punishment'. It is worth mentioning that virtually all of the written comments received by the Secretary-General before the adoption of the ICTY Statute pointed to the need for addressing this issue. The Secretary-General replied, drawing upon existing precedent, that the Statute should contain 'provisions which specify that a plea of head of State immunity or that an act was committed in the official capacity of the accused will not constitute a defence, nor will it mitigate punishment'. See also UN Doc. S/25704, par 55: 'The Statute should [. . .] contain provisions which specify that a plea of head of State immunity or that an act was committed in the official capacity of the accused will not constitute a defence, nor will it mitigate punishment.' One of the most spectacular illustration of this loss of official privilege before the *ad hoc* Tribunals took place during a fascinating exchange of views between former President Slobodan Milošević and Prosecution witness Mr Paddy Ashdown who recounted a meeting with Mr Milošević at a time when the latter was still in power and at which time Mr Ashdown forewarned Mr Milošević about the consequences of his acts and the possibility that he might once be asked to account for those: 'I said to you, in specific terms, that if you went on acting in this fashion, you would make it inevitable that the international community would have to act, and in the end they did have to act. And I warned you that if you took those steps and went on doing this, you would end up in this Court, and here you are.' See *Prosecutor v. Milošević*, IT-02-54-T, Transcript of hearing, T 2395, 15 March 2002 (www.un.org/icty/transe54/020315ED.htm).

[22] See Secretary-General Report (ICTY), par 55; Nuremberg Principles, Principle III: 'The fact that a person who committed an act which constitutes a crime under international law acted as Head of State or responsible Government official does not relieve him from responsibility under international law.' 1954 ILC Draft Code, (Draft Code of Offences against the Peace and Security of Mankind, art. 3); *Prosecutor v. Milošević*, IT-99-37, Decision on Review of Indictment and Application for Consequential Orders, 24 May 1999. In relation specifically to the crime of genocide, see the *Final Report of the Commission of Experts for the Former Yugoslavia*, par 100: 'To meet the aims of the Convention, people in the said categories must be treated equally irrespective of their de jure or de facto positions as decision-makers. As individuals, they are subject to Prosecution like any other individual violator. They cannot hide behind any shield of immunity. The legal and moral responsibilities are the same and the need to prevent genocide no less clear because of the position of the violator.'

[23] See *Blaškić* Trial Judgment, par 205. See also *Martić* Rule 61 Decision, par 27; *Nikolić* Rule 61 Decision, par 26; *Tadić* Trial Judgment, par 654.

[T]here is no privilege under international criminal law which would shield State representatives or agents from the reach of individual criminal responsibility. On the contrary, their acting in official capacity could constitute an aggravated circumstance when it comes to sentencing, because he or she illegitimately used and abused a power which was conferred upon him or her for different legitimate purposes.[24]

Therefore, there is no question today that international crimes can be committed by state or government officials as well as by private individuals.[25] With or without the involvement of the state or other organized entities, the crime committed remains the same and bears the same penal consequences for the perpetrator, because such involvement neither modifies nor limits, in principle, the guilt or responsibility of the perpetrator.[26]

Where an international crime is committed by a state official or by an agent of the state, his individual criminal liability does not preclude (nor does it depend on) the engagement of state responsibility,[27] but neither the ICTY nor ICTR are empowered to make a finding that the responsibility of a state is engaged by reason of the acts of one of its agents. The limitation of the Tribunals' jurisdiction in that respect simply means that a state's involvement in international crimes bears little or no relevance to the individual criminal responsibility of those who commit the acts.[28]

---

[24] *Kunarac* Trial Judgment, par 494. See also Principle III of the Nuremberg Principles, which provides that '[t]he fact that a person who committed an act which constitutes a crime under international law acted as Head of State or responsible Government official does not relieve him from responsibility under international law'.

[25] See, e.g. *Kupreškić* Trial Judgment, par 555; *Kunarac* Trial Judgment, par 493; *Tadić* Appeal Judgment, pars 248 and 252. See also *Sivakumar v. Minister of Employment and Immigration (Canada)* [1994] F.C. 433: '[I]t can no longer be said that individuals without any connection to the state, especially those involved in paramilitary or armed revolutionary movements, can be immune from the reach of international criminal law. On the contrary, they are now governed by it.' This principle had been hinted at when the Appeals Chamber held that crimes against humanity can be committed for purely personal motives. See generally Y. Dinstein, 'International Criminal Law', 20 Israeli Law Review (*IsrLR*) 206 (1985); A. Niang, 'Les Individus en tant que personnes privées', in H. Ascensio, E. Decaux, and A. Pellet (eds.), *Droit international pénal* (Paris: Editions Pedone, 2000), p 225.

[26] *Kunarac* Trial Judgment, par 493: 'A violation of one of the relevant articles of the Statute will engage the perpetrator's individual criminal responsibility. In this context, the participation of the state becomes secondary and, generally, peripheral. With or without the involvement of the state, the crime committed remains of the same nature and bears the same consequences. The involvement of the state in a criminal enterprise generally results in the availability of extensive resources to carry out the criminal activities in question and therefore greater risk for the potential victims. It may also trigger the application of a different set of rules, in the event that its involvement renders the armed conflict international. However, the involvement of the state does not modify or limit the guilt or responsibility of the individual who carried out the crimes in question.'

[27] As the *Furundžija* Trial Chamber stated, both forms of responsibility are indeed not exclusive of one another: 'Under current international humanitarian law, in addition to individual criminal liability, State responsibility may ensue as a result of State officials engaging in torture or failing to prevent torture or to punish torturers. If carried out as an extensive practice of State officials, torture amounts to a serious breach on a widespread scale of an international obligation of essential importance for safeguarding the human being, thus constituting a particularly grave wrongful act generating State responsibility' (*Furundžija* Trial Judgment, par 142). See also Article 29 of Geneva Convention IV and Art. 4 of *Draft Code of Crimes against the Peace and Security of Mankind*, in 1996 ILC Draft Code.

[28] *Kunarac* Trial Judgment, par 493, holding that, when it comes to individual criminal responsibility, the involvement of the state in the commission of the crime is peripheral, nay, irrelevant.

In particular, the commission of an international crime does not require any sort of policy or plan to commit such crimes.[29] Furthermore, the commission of a war crime, a crime against humanity, or a genocidal offence does not require, from a legal point of view, an organization or institution which would underlie or support the commission of such a crime.

Finally, concerning the conduct on which an international crime might be founded, it may, in principle, be committed by an act or omission,[30] and the perpetrator need not have been involved in any patterns of criminal behaviour to be found guilty.[31] A single criminal act may therefore, in principle, constitute a war crime, a crime against humanity, or an act of genocide. And the means and methods used to carry out that crime are generally irrelevant to the criminal responsibility of an accused although these may be highly relevant to sentencing.[32]

In sum, but for the matters referred to above, the only relevant consideration to assign individual criminal responsibility is whether the accused, private individual, or state official, took part in one of the crimes covered by the Statute, in one of the forms provided for in Articles 6(1) and 6(3) of the ICTR Statute or Articles 7(1) and 7(3) of the ICTY Statute.

---

[29] In the *Jelišić* case, the Trial Chamber stated the following: 'the drafters of the [Genocide] Convention did not deem the existence of an organisation or a system serving a genocidal objective as a legal ingredient of the crime. In so doing, they did not discount the possibility of a lone individual seeking to destroy a group as such'. The Trial Chamber pointed out, however, that it would be very difficult in such a case to establish that such a man possessed the required genocidal *mens rea* (*Jelišić* Trial Judgment, pars 100–101). See also *Jelišić* Appeal Judgment, par 48: 'The Appeals Chamber is of the opinion that the existence of a plan or policy is not a legal ingredient of the crime. However, in the context of proving specific intent, the existence of a plan or policy may become an important factor in most cases. The evidence may be consistent with the existence of a plan or policy, or may even show such existence, and the existence of a plan or policy may facilitate proof of the crime.' Concerning crimes against humanity, see *Kunarac* Appeal Judgment, par 98: 'Contrary to the Appellants' submissions, neither the attack nor the acts of the accused needs to be supported by any form of "policy" or "plan". There was nothing in the Statute or in customary international law at the time of the alleged acts which required proof of the existence of a plan or policy to commit these crimes' and n 114, p 32 of the Judgment.

[30] See, e.g. *Kambanda* Trial Judgment, par 39(ix); *Bagilishema* Appeal Judgment, par 35.

[31] *Kayishema and Ruzindana* Appeal Judgment, par 163.

[32] See, e.g. ibid., par 169.

20

Article 7(1) of the ICTY Statute and Article 6(1) of the ICTR Statute: 'Direct' Participation

20.1 Planning

'Planning', pursuant to Articles 7(1) and 6(1) of the Statutes, 'envisions one or more persons formulating a method of design or action, procedure, or arrangement for the accomplishment of a particular crime'.[1] The existence of such a plan may be established circumstantially, although it must be the only reasonable inference to be drawn from the evidence.[2]

The Trial Chamber in *Akayesu* has suggested that for the planning of a crime to be punishable under the Statute, the crime that had been planned must in fact have been committed.[3] The Trial Chamber did not provide any authority for its contention, but

---

[1] *Semanza* Trial Judgment, par 380. See also *Musema* Trial Judgment, par 119 ('planning of a crime implies that one or more persons contemplate the commission of a crime at both its preparatory and execution phase'); *Akayesu* Trial Judgment, par 480; *Rutaganda* Trial Judgment, par 37; *Kajelijeli* Trial Judgment, par 761; *Kamuhanda* Trial Judgment, par 592; *Blaškić* Trial Judgment, par 279; *Krstić* Trial Judgment, par 601; *Kordić and Čerkez* Trial Judgment, par 386; *Stakić* Trial Judgment, par 443. The *Akayesu* Trial Chamber noted that this form of criminal participation was, in some respect, similar to the notion of 'complicity' in civil law and 'conspiracy' under the common law, but that it differed in that 'planning' as understood in the Statute 'can be an act committed by one person' (*Akayesu* Trial Judgment, par 480). [2] See *Blaškić* Trial Judgment, par 279; *Kajelijeli* Trial Judgment, par 761. [3] *Akayesu* Trial Judgment, par 473.

explained that its view on that matter was based upon the fact that 'the principle of individual criminal responsibility for an attempt to commit a crime obtained only in case of genocide' and that with respect to any other crime, the perpetrator would only incur criminal responsibility if the offence planned was indeed completed.[4] The position of the *Akayesu* Trial Chamber (later reiterated by other Trial Chambers of the ICTR[5]) seems to be based on a misunderstanding as to the required degree of realization of the offence of 'planning'. 'Planning' constitutes, in most legal systems, an inchoate offence. It is therefore realized and complete, once all of its elements are met, without there being a need for the offence planned to have been committed. The commission of the offence that was planned constitutes a discrete criminal conduct and where the planner also committed this crime, conviction will generally be limited to the latter offence, not to its planning. It may be, however, that the Trial Chamber was just suggesting that, unless the offence that was planned is actually committed, it might be difficult from an evidentiary point of view to establish the sufficient gravity of the conduct of the accused pursuant to Article 1 of the Statute.

Where an accused has both planned and executed the crime that had been planned, he or she may only be found responsible for the commission of the crime and not, apparently, also for its planning.[6] The fact that the accused planned – as well as took part in the commission of – the crimes could, however, be considered an aggravating circumstance at the time of sentencing.

Apparently, the level of participation of the accused in the planning of the crime must have been 'substantial' enough to attract his individual criminal responsibility, 'such as formulating a criminal plan or endorsing a plan proposed by another'.[7] Secondary or minor involvement in such planning would therefore not necessarily suffice to bring that involvement within the jurisdiction of the *ad hoc* Tribunals.

In order to be held liable under the 'planning' head of responsibility, the accused must in addition be shown to have possessed the required criminal intent for the underlying offence in question, that is, that 'he [or she] directly or indirectly intended that the crime in question be committed'.[8]

20.2   Instigating

Someone who instigates – when understood as 'urging, encouraging or prompting'[9] – another to commit a crime listed in the Statute may be held responsible for his

[4] *Akayesu* Trial Judgment, par 473.
[5] See, e.g. *Kamuhanda* Trial Judgment, par 589 (unsupported).
[6] *Bagilishema* Trial Judgment, par 30; *Kordić and Čerkez* Trial Judgment, par 386.
[7] *Bagilishema* Trial Judgment, par 30; *Kajelijeli* Trial Judgment, par 761.
[8] *Blaškić* Trial Judgment, par 278. See also, e.g., *Kordić and Čerkez* Trial Judgment, par 386; *Bagilishema* Trial Judgment, par 31.
[9] *Semanza* Trial Judgment, par 381. See also *Krstić* Trial Judgment, par 601; *Blaškić* Trial Judgment, par 280; *Ndindabahizi* Trial Judgment, par 456. There could, therefore, be some degree of

acts, if his actions are shown to have been causal to the actual commission of the crime.[10] The causation requirement is not so stringent, however, as to require proof that 'but for' the acts of the accused the crime would not have been committed.[11] It would be met, for instance, where the conduct of the accused is shown to have been 'a clear contributing factor to the conduct of the other person(s)',[12] a test which perhaps does not significantly advance an understanding of the issue of the necessary degree of causation.

The act of instigation (or 'incitement', which has been said to be synonymous for the purpose of the Statutes[13]) need not have been made in 'public', nor does it need to have been 'direct' in the sense in which those adjectives are understood in relation to 'direct and public incitement to commit genocide' as discussed above.[14] Accordingly, instigation that took place in private (if it can be established beyond reasonable doubt), and instigation that might have been somewhat implicit or subdued, may in principle, be regarded as criminal pursuant to Articles 7(1) and 6(1) if it was causal – as defined above – to the commission of a crime by another. Both a positive act or an omission may constitute an act of 'instigation' for the purpose of this provision, if it can be established that the conduct of the accused was intended to cause the perpetrator to act and that it indeed had that result.[15]

Finally, a person charged with having instigated a crime must be shown to have possessed the required criminal intent, that is, that 'he [or she] directly or indirectly intended that the crime in question be committed'.[16] In addition, the accused must be shown to have 'intended to provoke or induce the commission of

---

overlap between 'instigating' and 'aiding and abetting' in the form of encouragement or moral support (see below).

[10] See *Bagilishema* Trial Judgment, par 30 ('An individual who instigates another person to commit a crime incurs responsibility for that crime. By urging or encouraging another person to commit a crime, the instigator may contribute substantially to the commission of the crime. Proof is required of a causal connection between the instigation and the *actus reus* of the crime'); *Semanza* Trial Judgment, par 381; *Rutaganda* Trial Judgment, par 38; *Akayesu* Trial Judgment, par 482; *Musema* Trial Judgment, par 120; *Kajelijeli* Trial Judgment, par 762; *Kamuhanda* Trial Judgment, par 593; *Blaškić* Trial Judgment, par 280. As noted above, such a requirement of causality does not exist in relation to the crime of 'direct and public incitement to commit genocide' (see, e.g. *Rutaganda* Trial Judgment, par 38; *Akayesu* Trial Judgment, par 562; *Musema* Trial Judgment, par 120).

[11] *Naletilić and Martinović* Trial Judgment, par 60; *Kvočka* Trial Judgment, par 252; *Kordić and Čerkez* Trial Judgment, par 387.

[12] *Kvočka* Trial Judgment, par 252. See also *Ndindabahizi* Trial Judgment, par 456: 'instigation does not arise unless it has directly and substantially contributed to the perpetration of the crime'.

[13] The Appeals Chamber has made it clear that these two expressions were synonymous, contrary to what a number of Trial Chambers had suggested (see, e.g. *Akayesu* Trial Judgment, pars 478, 481–482; see also *Rutaganda* Trial Judgment, par 38).

[14] *Akayesu* Appeal Judgment, pars 478–482; *Semanza* Trial Judgment, par 381; *Kajelijeli* Trial Judgment, par 762.

[15] *Blaškić* Trial Judgment, par 280; *Kordić and Čerkez* Trial Judgment, par 387; *Kajelijeli* Trial Judgment, par 762. See also *Semanza* Trial Judgment, par 381 and *Bagilishema* Trial Judgment, par 30.

[16] *Blaškić* Trial Judgment, par 278. See also *Kordić and Čerkez* Trial Judgment, par 386; *Bagilishema* Trial Judgment, par 31.

the crime, or was aware of the substantial likelihood that the commission of a crime would be a probable consequence of his acts'.[17]

20.3   Ordering

'Ordering' entails 'a person in a position of authority using that position to convince another to commit an offence'.[18] That position of authority need not have been formalized and may only last, in some cases, for as long as it takes for the order to be given and obeyed.[19] The order may have been given in any form and may have been implicit as well as explicit and the fact of its existence may be established circumstantially.[20] The order need not, in general, have been illegal on its face to engage the responsibility of the person who has issued it, nor does it need to have been given directly or personally to the individual who committed a crime pursuant to that order for the individual who issued it to be criminally responsible.[21] An individual who would pass such an illegal order down the chain of command could in certain circumstances himself be regarded as having 'ordered' a crime in the sense of 'reissuing [. . .] orders that were illegal in the circumstances'.[22] Depending on the nature of the order and how it would be understood by a person passing it on, the act of passing it on could also constitute aiding and abetting, discussed further below.

Insofar as the required state of mind is concerned, what matters is clearly the *mens rea* of the person giving the order, not that of the person who obeys it.[23] As previously discussed with respect to 'planning' and 'instigating', the accused must be shown to have possessed the required criminal intent in relation to the actual crime (as well, obviously, as the intention to give the order), that is, that 'he [or she] directly or indirectly intended that the crime in question be committed'.[24] According to the Appeals Chamber, a person who gives an order 'with the awareness of the substantial likelihood that a crime will be committed in the execution

---

[17] *Naletilić and Martinović* Trial Judgment, par 60. See also *Kordić and Čerkez* Trial Judgment, par 387 which appears slightly more restrictive on its face: '[I]t must be proved that the accused directly intended to provoke the commission of the crime'; *Kvočka* Trial Judgment, par 252.

[18] *Krstić* Trial Judgment, par 601. See also, e.g. *Stakić* Trial Judgment, par 445; *Bagilishema* Trial Judgment, par 31; *Rutaganda* Trial Judgment, par 39; *Kajelijeli* Trial Judgment, par 763; *Kamuhanda* Trial Judgment, par 594.

[19] There is some debate as to whether that position of authority need (see, e.g. *Akayesu* Trial Judgment, pars 483; *Blaškić* Trial Judgment, pars 280–281) or need not (see, e.g. *Kordić and Čerkez* Trial Judgment, par 388; *Kajelijeli* Trial Judgment, par 763; *Kamuhanda* Trial Judgment, pars 612) be equated to a superior–subordinate relationship as understood under Articles 7(3) and 6(3) of the Statutes. See, concerning this issue, G. Mettraux, 'Current Developments', 1 *International Criminal Law Review* 261 (2002) ('Mettraux, *Current Developments*').

[20] *Blaškić* Trial Judgment, par 281.   [21] Ibid., par 282.

[22] *Kupreškić* Trial Judgment, pars 827 and 862.   [23] *Blaškić* Trial Judgment, par 282.

[24] Ibid., par 278. See also *Kordić and Čerkez* Trial Judgment, par 386. See also *Bagilishema* Trial Judgment, par 31; *Stakić* Trial Judgment, par 445.

of that order', may be said to possess the requisite *mens rea* for 'ordering' insofar as he may be regarded as having accepted that crime.[25]

The Tribunals have not yet expressed a view as to whether an illegal order to commit a crime could be regarded as criminal under the Statute where that order has not been acted upon. Existing state practice suggests that, in certain circumstances, an order which is illegal 'on its face' may entail the individual criminal responsibility of the giver of that order regardless of the fact that it was never obeyed nor implemented.[26]

20.4   Committing

An individual may be said to have 'committed' a crime when 'he or she physically perpetrates the relevant criminal act or engenders a culpable omission in violation of a rule of criminal law'.[27] This form of liability covers 'first and foremost' personal physical involvement in the commission of the crime on the part of the accused.[28] The 'commission' of a crime under the Statutes may also take the form of co-perpetration in a joint criminal enterprise.[29]

To be held accountable for committing a statutory crime, the accused must have intended the relevant conduct or omission, and possessed the *mens rea* required for the particular offence with which he is charged or, at the least, one Trial Chamber suggested, he must have been aware of 'the substantial likelihood that a criminal act or omission would occur as a consequence of his conduct'.[30]

There can be several perpetrators who may be said to have 'committed' the same crime if 'the conduct of each one of them fulfills the requisite elements of the definition of the substantive offence'.[31] This does not mean, however, that the perpetrator must have contributed in equal terms to the offence that has been

---

[25] *Blaškić* Appeal Judgment, par 42.

[26] See *Court Martial of General Smith*, before a general court martial at Manila, 24 April–3 May 1902, in United States. Congress. Senate. *Trials of Court-Martial in the Philippines Islands in Consequence of Certain Instructions.* 57th Congress, 2nd Session. Senate Document 213. Washington: GPO, 1903; excerpts of General Smith's court-martial are reprinted in L. Friedman, *The Law of War: A Documentary History* (New York: Random House, 1972), vol. 1, pp 799 et seq. and the case is discussed in G. Mettraux, 'US Courts-Martial and the Armed Conflict in the Philippines (1899–1902): Their Contribution to National Case Law on War Crimes', 1(1) *Journal of International Criminal Justice*, April 2003, 135 et seq. See also *Law Reports of Trials of War Criminals*, XV, 133; and Case against Kurt Meyer, Canadian Military Court, Aurich in Germany, verdict of 28 December 1945, *Record of Proceedings (Revised)*, 2 vols. The summing-up of the Judge Advocate is in the first volume at pp 836–845 (on file with the author).

[27] *Kunarac* Trial Judgment, par 390. See also *Tadić* Appeal Judgment, par 188; *Vasiljević* Trial Judgment, par 62; *Krstić* Trial Judgment, par 601; *Kvočka* Trial Judgment par 251; *Krnojelac* Trial Judgment, par 73; *Stakić* Trial Judgment, par 439; *Kamuhanda* Trial Judgment, par 595.

[28] See, e.g., *Tadić* Appeal Judgment, par 188; *Vasiljević* Trial Judgment, par 62; *Kordić and Čerkez* Trial Judgment, par 376; *Kvočka* Trial Judgment par 251.

[29] See below, sub-section 20.6.   [30] *Kvočka* Trial Judgment, par 251.

[31] *Kunarac* Trial Judgment, par 390; *Kajelijeli* Trial Judgment, par 763.

committed. And in the case of co-perpetration in the context of a joint criminal enterprise, particular rules would apply which will be discussed below.

20.5 Aiding and abetting in the planning, preparation, or execution

'Aiding and abetting', well known to the field of common law, is a form of accessory liability to the 'commission' of a crime.[32] In such a case, the *actus reus* of the crime is performed, not by the accused himself, but by another person, the principal. 'Aiding' on the one hand and 'abetting' on the other have repeatedly been said in the jurisprudence of the *ad hoc* Tribunals to cover slightly distinct forms of participation. 'Aiding' has been described as meaning 'giving someone assistance', whilst 'abetting' stands for 'facilitating the commission of an act by being sympathetic thereto'.[33] The semantic distinction between those two forms of participation does not carry much weight, however, as they have systematically been charged together (as 'aiding and abetting' a particular crime) and the Prosecution has never been requested to specify in any of its indictments whether the accused had been charged in relation to one sort of assistance rather than the other.

An accused will incur individual criminal responsibility for aiding and abetting a crime where it is demonstrated that he or she carried out an act of practical assistance, encouragement, or moral support to the principal offender.[34] The act of assistance need not have caused the act of the principal, nor need it consist of one of the elements of the crime ultimately committed, but it must be shown to have had a 'substantial effect' on the commission of the crime by the principal offender.[35] The requirement that the contribution of the accused to the act of the principal must be 'substantial' is essentially conceived as a mechanism to exclude minor contributions from the realm of criminal liability. The crime which the accused is said to have aided or abetted must, the jurisprudence suggests, actually have been committed.[36]

---

[32] *Kunarac* Trial Judgment, par 391.

[33] See, e.g. *Kvočka* Trial Judgment, par 254; *Akayesu* Trial Judgment, par 484; *Ntakirutimana* Trial Judgment, par 787; *Semanza* Trial Judgment, par 384; *Kajelijeli* Trial Judgment, par 763.

[34] See, *inter alia, Kayishema and Ruzindana* Appeal Judgment, par 186; *Čelebići* Appeal Judgment, par 352; *Tadić* Appeal Judgment, par 229; *Blaškić* Appeal Judgment, par 46; *Furundžija* Trial Judgment, pars 235 and 249; *Vasiljević* Trial Judgment, par 70; *Kunarac* Trial Judgment, par 391; *Kajelijeli* Trial Judgment, par 763; *Kamuhanda* Trial Judgment, par 597.

[35] See *Furundžija* Trial Judgment, pars 223, 224 and 249; *Blaškić* Trial Judgment, par 285; *Blaškić* Appeal Judgment, par 48. See also *Aleksovski* Trial Judgment, par 61; *Kunarac* Trial Judgment, par 391; *Kordić and Čerkez* Trial Judgment, par 399; *Krstić* Trial Judgment, par 601: ' "Aiding and abetting" means rendering a substantial contribution to the commission of a crime'; *Krnojelac* Trial Judgment, par 88; *Vasiljević* Trial Judgment, par 70; *Vasiljević* Appeal Judgment, pars 134–135; *Rutaganda* Trial Judgment, par 43; *Musema* Trial Judgment, par 126; *Ntakirutimana* Trial Judgment, par 787; *Bagilishema* Trial Judgment, par 33; *Semanza* Trial Judgment, pars 33 and 386; *Kajelijeli* Trial Judgment, par 766. The responsibility of the aider and abettor is not negated by the fact that his assistance could have been obtained from another (see *Furundžija* Trial Judgment, par 224).

[36] *Akayesu* Trial Judgment, pars 473–475.

As the Statutes suggest, the contribution of the aider and abettor may be provided at any stage – planning, preparation, or execution – of the criminal process.[37] It may take the form of a positive act or an omission, and it may occur before, during, or after the act of the principal offender.[38] It can also take many different forms, such as providing weapons for the commission of a crime or otherwise providing the principal with practical assistance or encouragement. Mere presence at the scene of the crime could constitute aiding and abetting where 'it is demonstrated to have a significant encouraging effect on the principal offender'.[39] The fact that the individual standing by was the superior of the principal or was otherwise in a position of authority is relevant to that determination.[40] Where an accused is charged with having provided such assistance by reason of his presence in or near the scene of the crime, he must be shown furthermore to have known that his presence would indeed encourage or give moral support to the principal(s).[41] But other than for those who are alleged to have provided encouragement or

---

[37] Liability for aiding and abetting does not require the existence of an arrangement or plan between the aider and abettor and the principal (see *Tadić* Trial Judgment, par 677; *Čelebići* Trial Judgment, pars 327–328).

[38] See, e.g. *Aleksovski* Appeal Judgment, par 62: 'Participation may occur before, during or after the act is committed. It can, for example, consist of providing the means to commit the crime or promising to perform certain acts once the crime has been committed, that is, behavior which may in fact clearly constitute instigation or abetment of the perpetrators of the crime. For that reason, as stated by the Trial Chamber seized of the *Tadić* case, "the act contributing to the commission and the act of commission itself can be geographically and temporally distanced".'; *Blaškić* Appeal Judgment, pars 47–48; *Tadić* Trial Judgment, par 687; *Kunarac* Trial Judgment, par 391; *Krnojelac* Trial Judgment, par 88; *Vasiljević* Trial Judgment, par 70; *Blaškić* Trial Judgment, par 284; *Kajelijeli* Trial Judgment, par 186; *Semanza* Trial Judgment, par 386.

[39] *Vasiljević* Trial Judgment, par 70. See also *Furundžija* Trial Judgment, par 232; *Tadić* Trial Judgment, par 689; *Aleksovski* Trial Judgment, par 64; *Kunarac* Trial Judgment, par 393; *Krnojelac* Trial Judgment, par 88; *Kajelijeli* Trial Judgment, par 769 and decisions cited therein.

[40] *Aleksovski* Trial Judgment, par 65 ('the presence of an individual with authority will frequently be perceived by the perpetrators of the criminal act as a sign of encouragement likely to have a significant or even decisive effect on promoting its commission. The *mens rea* may be deduced from the circumstances, and the position of authority constitutes one of the circumstances which can be considered when establishing that the person against whom the claim is directed knew that his presence would be interpreted by the perpetrator of the wrongful act as a sign of support or encouragement. An individual's authority must therefore be considered to be a important indicia as establishing that his mere presence constitutes an act of intentional participation under Article 7(1) of the Statute. Nonetheless, responsibility is not automatic and merits consideration against the background of the factual circumstances'); *Blaškić* Trial Judgment, par 284; *Kayishema and Ruzindana* Trial Judgment, pars 200–201; *Bagilishema* Trial Judgment, par 34 ('presence, when combined with authority, may constitute assistance [. . .]. Insignificant status, may, however, put the "silent approval" below the threshold necessary for the *actus reus* [required for aiding and abetting]'). See also *Akayesu* Trial Judgment, par 693; *Bagilishema* Trial Judgment, par 386 (footnotes omitted) ('Criminal responsibility as an "approving spectator" does require actual presence during the commission of the crime or at least presence in the immediate vicinity of the scene of the crime, which is perceived by the actual perpetrator as approval of his conduct. The authority of an individual is frequently a strong indication that the principal perpetrators will perceive his presence as an act of encouragement. Responsibility, however, is not automatic, and the nature of the accused's presence must be considered against the background of the factual circumstances.')

[41] *Kayishema and Ruzindana* Trial Judgment, par 201. See also *Kamuhanda* Trial Judgment, par 600.

moral support by reason of their presence (and status),[42] presence at the scene of the crime is not a requirement of aiding and abetting and it may happen that the accused was far removed from the scene of the crime at the time when it was committed.[43]

To establish the *mens rea* for aiding and abetting, it must be demonstrated that the aider and abettor 'knew (in the sense that he was aware) that his own acts assisted in the commission of the specific crime in question by the principal offender'.[44] He need not have known the exact crime which the principal intended to commit,[45] nor is it necessary that he shared the intent of the principal offender.[46] But he must have been aware of 'the essential elements of the crime committed by the principal offender, including the principal offender's state of mind', and he must have taken the conscious decision to act in the knowledge that he would thereby support the commission of the crime.[47] The assistance itself can be a sufficient practical manifestation of that support and it is generally enough that the accomplice accepts that such assistance could be a possible consequence of his conduct.[48]

In sum, it is, in principle, sufficient that the aider and abettor had knowledge of the intent of the principal (to the extent mentioned above), that he knew that his acts or conduct would assist the principal in the commission of the crime and that, with that knowledge, he decided to provide substantial assistance to the principal. The Appeals Chamber in the *Krstić* Judgment has concluded that this general rule would also apply to the crime of genocide so that an aider and abettor to genocide

---

[42] See, e.g. *Bagilishema* Trial Judgment, par 385.

[43] See, e.g. *Tadić* Trial Judgment, par 691; *Akayesu* Trial Judgment, par 484; *Kayishema and Ruzindana* Trial Judgment, par 200; *Rutaganda* Trial Judgment, par 43; *Bagilishema* Trial Judgment, par 33.

[44] *Vasiljević* Trial Judgment, par 71. See also *Aleksovski* Appeal Judgment, par 162; *Tadić* Appeal Judgment, par 229; *Blaškić* Appeal Judgment, pars 46 and 49–50; *Kunarac* Trial Judgment, par 392.

[45] *Furundžija* Trial Judgment, par 246; *Kvočka* Trial Judgment, par 255; *Blaškić* Appeal Judgment, par 50. If the accused is aware that one of a number of crimes will probably be committed, and that one of those crimes is indeed committed, he may be said to have intended to facilitate the commission of that crime, and may be found guilty (all other conditions being met) as an aider and abettor (*Blaškić* Appeal Judgment, par 50; *Furundžija* Trial Judgment, par 246).

[46] *Aleksovski* Appeal Judgment, par 162; *Kunarac* Trial Judgment, par 392; *Furundžija* Trial Judgment, par 245. The suggestion made by one Trial Chamber that an aider and abettor may, in principle, be responsible for all that naturally results from his actions appears to have little support in international law, and does not seem to have been reaffirmed in any other decision of either Tribunals (see *Tadić* Trial Judgment, par 692).

[47] *Vasiljević* Trial Judgment, par 71. See also *Furundžija* Trial Judgment, par 245; *Kunarac* Trial Judgment, par 392; *Aleksovski* Appeal Judgment, pars 162–165; *Tadić* Appeal Judgment, par 229. See also *Blaškić* Trial Judgment, par 286 ('the aider and abettor needs to have intended to provide assistance, or as a minimum, accepted that such assistance would be a possible and foreseeable consequence of his conduct') and *Bagilishema* Trial Judgment, par 32 ('An accomplice must knowingly provide assistance to the perpetrator of the crime, that is, he or she must know that it will contribute to the criminal act of the principal. Additionally, the accomplice must have intended to provide assistance, or as a minimum, accepted that such assistance would be a possible and foreseeable consequence of his conduct'), which seem to go even one step further in suggesting that the resulting assistance might only have been foreseen, rather than intended.   [48] *Blaškić* Trial Judgment, par 286.

could be held responsible if it can be shown that, all other conditions being met, he knew of the genocidal intent of the principal(s), without the need for him to have possessed that specific intent.[49] As noted above, the appropriateness of this finding is open to serious doubt and there are strong reasons to argue that a conviction for aiding and abetting genocide – which for some purposes is in effect a conviction for 'genocide' itself – should require proof that the aider and abettor himself or herself possessed the required genocidal *mens rea*.[50]

Finally, concerning the issue of sentencing, the fact that an aider and abettor may not have shared the intent of the principal offender generally lessens his criminal culpability compared to that of a principal or compared to that of an accused acting pursuant to a joint criminal enterprise who does share the intent of the principal offender.[51] As a consequence, and all other conditions being equal, his or her sentence should, in principle, be lighter than that of either a principal or a co-perpetrator in a joint criminal enterprise. Ultimately, however, it is the gravity of the conduct which determines the appropriate sentence, not the legal label assigned to his actions.[52]

20.6   Joint criminal enterprise or common purpose

At Nuremberg, James Rowe, a member of the American Prosecution team, noted that 'conspiracy is one of those things that, the more you talk about it, the less clear it becomes'.[53] The same could be said today of 'joint criminal enterprise', a form of liability which has generally been described as 'an understanding or arrangement amounting to an agreement between two or more persons that they will commit a crime'.[54] After ten years of the *ad hoc* Tribunals, joint criminal enterprise still remains one of the most contentious issues in their jurisprudential

---

[49] *Krstić* Appeal Judgment, pars 140 and 143. See also *Akayesu* Trial Judgment, par 485. The same has been said in relation to the crime against humanity of 'persecution' (see *Krnojelac* Appeal Judgment, par 52; *Vasiljević* Appeal Judgment, par 142; *Krstić* Appeal Judgment, par 140; *Tadić* Appeal Judgment, par 229).   [50] See above, sub-sections 14.2.1 and 16.2.5.
[51] *Vasiljević* Trial Judgment, par 71. See also *Krstić* Appeal Judgment, par 268; *Vasiljević* Appeal Judgment, pars 181–182; *Kajelijeli* Trial Judgment, par 963.
[52] *Krstić* Appeal Judgment, par 268: 'aiding and abetting is a form of responsibility which generally warrants lower sentences than responsibility as a co-perpetrator'; *Vasiljević* Appeal Judgment, pars 181–182; *Vasiljević* Trial Judgment, par 272 and sources quoted therein.
[53] Interview with James Rowe, cited in B. F. Smith, *Reaching Judgment at Nuremberg* (New York: New American Library, 1977), p 114.
[54] *Krnojelac* Trial Judgment, par 80. The Trial Chamber in *Krnojelac* added the following: 'The understanding or arrangement need not be express, and its existence may be inferred from all the circumstances. It need not have been reached at any time before the crime is committed. The circumstances in which two or more persons are participating together in the commission of a particular crime may themselves establish an unspoken understanding or arrangement amounting to an agreement formed between them then and there to commit that crime' (ibid.). In *Tadić*, the Appeals Chamber used interchangeably the expressions 'joint criminal enterprise', 'common purpose', and 'criminal enterprise' (see *Vasiljević* Appeal Judgment, n 169, p 35).

life and its contours have fluctuated a great deal over the years.[55] What remains contentious is not that liability for co-perpetration exists under international law, but what form it should take and under what conditions liability would be entailed in such a case.

Joint criminal enterprise is not explicitly provided for as a discrete form of liability under the Statutes of the Tribunals. The ICTY Appeals Chamber has determined, however, that it may be said to constitute a form of 'commission' recognized under the Statute, and that its existence as a form of criminal liability as well as its constitutive elements are well founded under customary international law.[56] In view of the fact, however, that its elements are distinct from those required by other forms of 'committing' and that it raises particular issues in relation to the commission of international crimes, this form of liability must be dealt with separately.

The Tribunals may exercise their jurisdiction over three particular forms of joint criminal enterprise which the Appeals Chamber has identified as being part of customary international law:[57]

(i) The first category, known as the 'basic' form of joint criminal enterprise, includes cases where all participants, acting pursuant to a common purpose, share the same criminal intent and act to give effect to that intent;[58]

(ii) The second category is essentially similar to the first one, but is characterized by the 'systemic' nature of the crimes committed pursuant to the joint criminal enterprise, in the sense that it implies the existence of 'an organised system of ill-treatment';[59]

---

[55] See, for instance, *Kvočka* Trial Judgment, pars 265 et seq., and *Krnojelac* Trial Judgment, pars 78 et seq. See also Prosecution's appeal briefs in both cases.

[56] See *Vasiljević* Appeal Judgment, par 95; *Ojdanić* Joint Criminal Enterprise Decision, par 20; *Tadić* Appeal Judgment, pars 188 and 226; *Krnojelac* Appeal Judgment, par 29.

[57] See *Tadić* Appeal Judgment, pars 195–226; *Krnojelac* Appeal Judgment, par 30; *Vasiljević* Appeal Judgment, pars 96–99. The *Tadić* Appeals Chamber set the net very widely and left it to later Chambers to articulate the specific of that requirement (see *Tadić* Appeal Judgment, pars 185 et seq.). This Judgment was followed by others which narrowed down somewhat the scope of that form of criminal liability, although not always very coherently: *Krnojelac* Trial Judgment, pars 78 et seq.; *Prosecutor v. Brdjanin and Talić*, IT-99-36-PT, Decision on the Form of the Further Amended Indictment and Prosecution Application to Amend, 26 June 2001, pars 24 et seq.; *Kvočka* Trial Judgment, pars 265 et seq.; *Krstić* Trial Judgment, pars 621 et seq.

[58] *Vasiljević* Appeal Judgment, par 97: 'An example is a plan formulated by the participants in the joint criminal enterprise to kill where, although each of the participants may carry out a different role, each of them has the intent to kill'; *Tadić* Appeal Judgment, par 196; *Krnojelac* Appeal Judgment, pars 83–84.

[59] *Vasiljević* Appeal Judgment, par 98: 'An example is extermination or concentration camps, in which the prisoners are killed or mistreated pursuant to the joint criminal enterprise'; *Tadić* Appeal Judgment, pars 202–203. The *Krnojelac* Appeals Chamber made it clear that this 'systemic' category of joint criminal enterprise may come to apply to cases other than extermination and concentration camp cases of the sort that existed during the Second World War; in particular, the Appeals Chamber said, this category of joint criminal enterprise 'may be applied to other cases and especially to the serious violations of international humanitarian law committed in the territory of the former Yugoslavia since 1991' (*Krnojelac* Appeal Judgment, par 89).

(iii) The third category, known as the 'extended' form of joint criminal enterprise, concerns cases where all participants share a common intention to carry out particular criminal acts and where the principal offender commits an act which falls outside of the intended joint criminal enterprise but which was nevertheless a 'natural and foreseeable consequence' of effecting the agreed joint criminal enterprise.[60]

As far as *mens rea* is concerned, the first category of joint criminal enterprise requires that the Prosecution establish that the accused had an 'intent to perpetrate a certain crime (this being the shared intent on the part of all co-perpetrators)'.[61] The second, 'systemic', form of joint criminal enterprise requires 'personal knowledge of the system of ill-treatment' on the part of the accused 'as well as the intent to further this system of ill-treatment'.[62] Concerning the third type of joint criminal enterprise, the Prosecution must show that the accused possessed the '*intention* to participate in and further the criminal activity or the criminal purpose of a group and to contribute to the joint criminal enterprise or in any event to the commission of a crime by the group'.[63] Responsibility for a crime or crimes which had not been agreed upon, in this latter scenario, would be incurred only when (i) it was foreseeable that such a crime might be perpetrated by one or more members of the group; and (ii) the accused willingly took the risk that such a crime could be committed.[64] According to the Appeals Chamber, these general requirements would also apply to specific-intent crimes, in particular to genocide.[65] The author has already expressed his reservation about whether such a general finding is open.

All three forms of joint criminal enterprise require the existence of a criminal enterprise and the participation of the accused therein.[66] The required *actus reus* is

---

[60] *Tadić* Appeal Judgment, pars 204 et seq.; see also, *Prosecutor v. Brdjanin and Talić*, IT-99-36-PT, Decision on Form of Further Amended Indictment and Prosecution Application to Amend, 26 June 2001, pars 24–27; *Vasiljević* Appeal Judgment, par 99: 'An example is a common purpose or plan on the part of a group to forcibly remove at gun-point members of one ethnicity from their town, village or region (to effect "ethnic cleansing") with the consequence that, in the course of doing so, one or more of the victims is shot and killed. While murder may not have been explicitly acknowledged to be part of the common purpose, it was nevertheless foreseeable that the forcible removal of civilians at gunpoint might well result in the deaths of one or more of those civilians.'

[61] Ibid., par 101; *Krnojelac* Appeal Judgment, par 32. See, also *Krnojelac* Trial Judgment, par 83 and *Prosecutor v. Brdjanin and Talić*, IT-99-36-PT, Decision on Form of Second Amended Indictment, 11 May 2000, par 26. According to the Trial Chamber in *Krnojelac*, '[w]here the Prosecution relies upon proof of state of mind by inference, that inference must be the only reasonable inference available on the evidence' (*Krnojelac* Trial Judgment, par 83).

[62] *Vasiljević* Appeal Judgment, par 101 (and par 105); *Krnojelac* Appeal Judgment, par 32.

[63] *Tadić* Appeal Judgment, par 228. See also *Vasiljević* Appeal Judgment, par 101; *Krnojelac* Appeal Judgment, par 32.

[64] *Tadić* Appeal Judgment, par 228; *Vasiljević* Appeal Judgment, par 101.

[65] *Brdjanin* JCE III and Genocide Decision, pars 7–10.

[66] *Tadić* Appeal Judgment, par 227; *Krnojelac* Trial Judgment, par 79. These elements are in essence the same as those put forth by various Second World War courts. In its Report, the United Nations War Crimes Commission said that the following elements had to be established for 'common design' liability to attach: (i) there was a system in force to commit certain offences; (ii) the accused was aware of the system; and (iii) the accused participated in operating the system (*Law Reports of Trials of War Criminals*, XV, 95 and XI, 12–13).

therefore identical in all three cases and consists of three sub-requirements:[67] (i) a 'plurality of individuals',[68] (ii) a common criminal purpose 'which amounts to or involves the commission of a crime provided for in the Statute',[69] and (iii) the participation of the accused therein.[70] In turn, a person who participates in a joint criminal enterprise in any of the following ways may be found guilty for the crime ultimately committed, all other conditions being met:[71]

(i) by participating directly in the commission of the agreed crime itself (as a principal offender);

(ii) by being present at the time when the crime is committed, and (with knowledge that the crime is to be or is being committed) by intentionally assisting or encouraging another participant in the joint criminal enterprise to commit that crime; or

(iii) by acting in furtherance of a particular system in which the crime is committed by reason of the accused's position of authority or function, and with knowledge of the nature of that system and intent to further that system.

If the agreed crime is committed by one or another of the participants in that joint criminal enterprise, all of the participants in that enterprise may be guilty of the crime regardless of the part that was played by each one of them in its commission.[72]

Participation in a joint criminal enterprise as a form of 'commission' where the accused will be liable as a co-perpetrator must be distinguished from the liability of an aider and abettor who is an accessory to these co-perpetrators, and who is not a participant in the criminal enterprise.[73] An individual may aid and abet the (co-)perpetrators in a joint criminal enterprise without himself becoming a part thereof. In such a case, the (co-)perpetrators need not even know of the aider and abettor's contribution, but to be liable, the aider and abettor must meet all the

---

[67] See generally, *Krnojelac* Appeal Judgment, par 31, and *Vasiljević* Appeal Judgment, par 100.

[68] See ibid.: 'They need not be organized in a military, political or administrative structure.'

[69] Ibid. The Appeals Chamber made it clear that there is no necessity for this common criminal purpose to have been previously arranged or formulated: 'It may materialise extemporaneously and be inferred from the facts' (ibid.).

[70] As noted by the Appeals Chamber, this involves the commission of one of the statutory offences, but the participation of the accused in its commission does not require that he personally commits one of the listed offences, but may instead 'take the form of assistance in, or contribution to, the execution of the common purpose' (*Vasiljević* Appeal Judgment, par 100).

[71] *Krnojelac* Trial Judgment, par 81. The list is not necessarily an exhaustive one. See, e.g. *Vasiljević* Appeal Judgment, par 102 where the Appeals Chamber noted that it is generally sufficient for a participant in a joint criminal enterprise to perform acts that in some way are directed to the furtherance of the common design.

[72] *Krnojelac* Trial Judgment, par 82. See also *Prosecutor v. Brdjanin and Talić*, IT-99-36-PT, Decision on Form of Second Amended Indictment, 11 May 2000, par 15. Presence at the time a crime is committed is not necessary. A person can still be liable for criminal acts carried out by others without being present – all that is necessary is that the person forms an agreement with others that a crime will be carried out (see *Krnojelac* Trial Judgment, n 236, p 34).

[73] See *Vasiljević* Appeal Judgment, par 102. See also *Kunarac* Trial Judgment, par 391.

requirements laid down above for aiding and abetting, including the requirement that his acts must have made a substantial contribution to the commission of the crime.[74] As a result, the Appeals Chamber concluded, differences exist in both the *actus reus* and the *mens rea* between these two forms of criminal liability:[75]

(i) The aider and abettor carries out acts specifically directed to assist, encourage, or lend moral support to the perpetration of a certain specific crime (murder, extermination, rape, torture, wanton destruction of civilian property, etc.), and this support has a substantial effect upon the perpetration of the crime. By contrast, it is sufficient for a participant in a joint criminal enterprise to perform acts that in some way are directed to the furtherance of the common design.

(ii) In the case of aiding and abetting, the requisite mental element is knowledge that the acts performed by the aider and abettor assist the commission of the specific crime of the principal. By contrast, in the case of participation in a joint criminal enterprise, i.e. as a co-perpetrator, the requisite *mens rea* is intent to pursue a common purpose.

Liability for participation in a joint criminal enterprise must also be distinguished from membership of a criminal organization. This was criminalized as a separate offence in Nuremberg and in subsequent trials held under Control Council Law No. 10, where knowing and voluntary membership in one such organization was sufficient in some cases to entail individual criminal responsibility.[76] Criminal liability pursuant to a joint criminal enterprise is not liability for mere membership, but 'a form of liability concerned with the participation in the commission of a crime as part of a joint criminal enterprise, a different matter'.[77]

Finally, joint criminal enterprise is different from the crime of 'conspiracy'. As observed by the Appeals Chamber, '[w]hilst conspiracy requires a showing that several individuals have agreed to commit a certain crime or set of crimes, a joint criminal enterprise requires, in addition to such a showing, that the parties to that agreement took action in furtherance of that agreement'.[78] Thus, while mere agreement would, in principle, be sufficient in the case of conspiracy to engage criminal responsibility, the liability of a member of a joint criminal enterprise will depend upon the commission of a criminal act in furtherance of that enterprise.[79]

---

[74] Ibid.

[75] Ibid. See also *Krnojelac* Appeal Judgment, par 33 and *Tadić* Appeal Judgment, par 229.

[76] See *Ojdanić* Joint Criminal Enterprise Decision, par 25 and sources quoted therein. In Nuremberg, the discrete offence of membership in a criminal organization was essentially adopted to facilitate the later Prosecutions of minor offenders, it was actually interpreted quite strictly so as to avoid convictions based on mere membership to one of those organizations (see, *inter alia*, *Law Reports of Trials of War Criminals*, XV, 98–99).

[77] *Ojdanić* Joint Criminal Enterprise Decision, par 25.   [78] Ibid., par 23.

[79] Ibid. See also *Law Reports of Trials of War Criminals*, XV, 95 and 97. The United Nations War Crimes Commission stated that 'the difference between a charge of conspiracy and one of acting in pursuant of a common design is that the first would claim that an agreement to commit offences had been made while the second would allege not only the making of an agreement but the performance of acts pursuant to it' (ibid., pp 97–98).

The concept of joint criminal enterprise has been an important tool in describing crimes committed by individuals acting in concert to achieve their criminal objectives and has made a positive contribution to recognizing and establishing the reality of such joint actions. Since its use by the Appeals Chamber in the *Tadić* case, this form of liability has become a regular feature of indictments, particularly against the more senior political and military leaders.[80] In view of the extreme seriousness of the charges brought against accused persons appearing before the *ad hoc* Tribunals and the imprecision and continuous jurisprudential morphing of that concept, joint criminal enterprise has raised some serious and legitimate concerns.[81] There is indeed a real risk, for instance, that knowledge of the alleged criminal purpose of that enterprise be inferred mainly, if not solely, from the accused's association with members of that enterprise (even where loosely defined) and that rather secondary participants may be handed sentences disproportionate to their actual contribution to that enterprise by reason of the 'natural and foreseeable consequences' trigger embedded in that concept. In addition, the 'joint criminal enterprise' generally depicted by the Prosecution in its indictments is often no more than a general description of a set of factual events that forms the background to the charges (such as a campaign of ethnic cleansing) which may not itself be a crime within the Tribunals' Statutes and which may in fact consist of several joint criminal enterprises with different alleged objects, membership, and geographical scopes.

Equally problematic is the proliferation across indictments of various 'joint criminal enterprises' which – although relating to the same period and frequently many of the same incidents and facts, and sometimes many of the same principle participants – are however described inconsistently in different indictments issued at different times. The indictments against leadership figures before the ICTY are all characterized by heavy reliance on the joint criminal enterprise theory, but there appears to have been little thought about how the same interconnected events should be charged in different cases. It is instructive to compare, for instance, the *Milošević* indictment, which charged the former President with responsibility, *inter alia*, under a joint criminal enterprise involving members of the Serbian, Bosnian Serb and Croatian Serb leadership, for crimes across Bosnia, Croatia, and Kosovo, with the separate indictments against members of the joint criminal enterprise named in the *Milošević* indictment.[82] Although the indictments

---

[80] See, e.g. the following indictments: *Prosecutor v. Brdjanin*, IT-99-36-T, Sixth Amended Indictment, 9 December 2003; *Prosecutor v. Brdjanin and Talić*, IT-99-36-PT, Corrected Version of the Fourth Amended Indictment, 10 December 2001; *Prosecutor v. Milutinović et al.*, IT-99-37-PT, Third Amended Indictment (Kosovo), 5 September 2002; *Prosecutor v. Krajišnik and Plavšić*, IT-00-39&40-PT, Consolidated Amended Indictment, 7 March 2002; *Prosecutor v. Milošević*, IT-02-54-PT, Second Amended Indictment (Croatia), 23 October 2002; *Prosecutor v. Milošević*, IT-02-54-PT, Amended Indictment, (Bosnia) 21 April 2004.

[81] See, e.g., *Prosecutor v. Milutinović et al.*, IT-99-37-AR72, General Ojdanić's Appeal from Denial of Preliminary Motion to Dismiss for Lack of Jurisdiction: Joint Criminal Enterprise, 28 February 2003.

[82] Compare, e.g., *Prosecutor v. Milošević*, IT-02-54-PT, First Amended Indictment (Croatia), 23 October 2002 (pars 6–28); *Prosecutor v. Milošević*, IT-02-54-PT, Amended Indictment (Bosnia), 21 April 2004 (pars 7–26), *Prosecutor v. Milošević*, IT-02-54-PT, Second Amended Indictment

against Ms Plavšić, Mr Martić, and Mr Stanisić, for instance, relate to events and crimes alleged in the *Milošević* indictment, the joint criminal enterprises described therein – and of which Slobodan Milošević is said to be a member – are described differently to the alleged joint criminal enterprise in the *Milošević* indictment, including a different alleged membership. This variation and inconsistency in identifying the joint criminal enterprise relevant to any given event demonstrates the enormous elasticity of the joint criminal enterprise as used by the Prosecution at the ICTY, and gives an indication of the difficulty an accused may face in knowing exactly the case he must meet.

Unless narrowly construed, this form of liability could come dangerously close to assigning guilt for mere membership in a group (be it a political party, the main staff of an army, the crisis staff of a region, or a ministry) and *de facto* place the burden upon the accused to establish that, despite his belonging to such a group or despite his association with members of that group, he did not partake in a criminal purpose that was assisted or pursued by that group.

20.7   Attempt?

The Statutes of the *ad hoc* Tribunals expressly provide that attempt to commit genocide is an international crime which is *a priori* within the Court's jurisdiction *ratione materiae*. They do not specify, however, whether the Tribunals also have jurisdiction over attempted war crimes and attempted crimes against humanity. It would appear that they do not.

First, it must be noted that neither Statute explicity provides for it. Secondly, there seems to have been no suggestion on the part of the drafters of those Statutes that they ever intended to include this form of participation in the Tribunals' jurisdiction, other than with respect to genocide. Thirdly, it may be questionable in most cases whether the mere attempt to commit a war crime or a crime against humanity (regardless of its actual realization) could ever be serious enough (other than in the case of genocide) to pass the seriousness threshold of Article 1 of the Statutes and therefore come within the Tribunals' jurisdiction.

Finally, and even if there were indications that the drafters of the Statutes at least considered the possibility that attempt should be provided for in the Statutes in relation to war crimes and crimes against humanity, it is doubtful whether international law does in fact criminalize attempts to commit such crimes.[83] During the

(Kosovo), 29 October 2001 (pars 16–18) and *Prosecutor v. Krajišnik and Plavšić*, IT-00-39&40-PT, Consolidated Amended Indictment, 7 March 2002 (pars 3–9), *Prosecutor v. Šešelj*, IT-03-67-PT, Indictment, 14 February 2003 (pars 5–11), *Prosecutor v. Stanisić and Simatović*, IT-03-69-PT, Amended Indictment, 9 December 2003 (pars 8–14), *Prosecutor v. Babić*, IT-03-72-PT, Indictment, 17 November 2003 (pars 5–9), *Prosecutor v. Martić*, IT-95-11-PT, Second Amended Indictment, 9 September 2003 (pars 4–8).

[83] See, e.g., *Entscheidungen des Obersten Gerichtshofes für die Britische Zone in Strafsachen*, 11 (StS 5/48), Strafsenat (Criminal Senate), Judgment of 22 June 1948: 'Nor does the attempt to commit a crime against humanity come into question because, as stated in detail in [decision] StS 3/48, an

discussions on the scope and meaning of war crimes at the London International Assembly in 1942, for instance, the rapporteur M. de Baer had submitted that an 'attempt to commit a crime' should not be made a war crime, 'whatever may have been the reasons which caused the attempt to miscarry'.[84] Article II of Control Council Law No. 10 did not provide for attempt as a form of criminal liability in relation to any of the crimes, but it appears, however, that the list of forms of criminal participation found in this provision were not meant to be exhaustive, and that conviction could have been entered on the basis of 'analogy from almost all systems of domestic law'.[85] Also indicative of the position under international law is the 1968 Convention on Statutory Limitations which does not apply to attempted war crimes or attempted crimes against humanity but only to offences that have been fully realized.[86] In its *Commentary* to Additional Protocol I, the ICRC has expressed serious doubts as to whether the attempt to commit a grave breach or a similar crime should be regarded as criminal under international law.[87] There are only very few indications in international law that attempts to commit war crimes or crimes against humanity could be said to be criminalized.[88]

An indication that attempted war crimes and attempted crimes against humanity might be beyond the Tribunals' jurisdiction is the fact that, wherever the Prosecution of the *ad hoc* Tribunals could have brought such charges, it has systematically chosen to charge those attempted war crimes and crimes against humanity under the heading of some residual, albeit completed offences, such as 'inhumane acts' as provided under Articles 5(i)/3(i) of the Statutes. A good example of this

---

attempted crime of this nature is inconceivable.' And Appellate court criminal chamber, Judgment of 20 May 1948 against P., Criminal Chamber 3/48): 'the ingredients of the act cannot be realized by what the victim did not actually suffer but could easily have suffered. This clarification makes it possible to state that, in the German legal sense, in respect of a crime against humanity, attempt is conceptually impossible. Nonetheless, the attempt to commit harm may fulfil the definition of a crime against humanity even if the worst possible results did not occur.'

[84] *London International Assembly, Commission for the Trial of War Criminals*, 'Scope and Meaning of the Conception of War Crimes', p 6 (on file with the author).

[85] See T. Taylor, *Final Report to the Secretary of the Army on the Nuremberg War Crimes Trials under Control Council Law No. 10*, p 229. See also *Law Reports of Trials of War Criminals*, XV, 89.

[86] The only exception to that rule concerns the crime of conspiracy for which no statutory limitation will in principle apply (Article II).

[87] ICRC, *Commentary to Geneva Convention I*, pars 3414–3416, p 980: 'Humanitarian law does not specify whether the attempt of a grave breach is also punishable [. . .]. At the present stage of development of the law we find that under the relevant treaties the attempt to commit a grave breach or a similar crime is not always subject either to universal jurisdiction or to penal suppression. However, the attempt will be subject to penal or disciplinary sanctions under national legislation whenever this is felt to be desirable.'

[88] See, e.g., Article 3(3) of the 1995 ILC Draft Code, which provided for the criminalization of attempt in relation to what was known then as 'crimes against the peace of security of mankind'. International Law Commission, *Report of the International Law Commission on the work of its 47 Session*, 2 May–21 July 1995, UN GAOR, 47th Sess., Supp. No. 10 UN Doc. A/50/10 (1995), p 29: 'An individual who commits an act constituting an attempt to commit a crime against the peace or security of mankind [. . .] is responsible therefore and is liable to punishment. Attempt means any commencement of execution of a crime that failed or was halted only because of circumstances independent of the perpetrator's intention.' See also 1996 ILC Draft Code, par 2(3), which also provided for the criminalization of the mere attempt at committing such crimes.

preference may be found in the *Vasiljević* indictment in which Mitar Vasiljević was alleged to have killed five men and attempted to kill two others. The indictment alleged that, on or about 7 June 1992, the accused together with other individuals, led seven Bosnian Muslim men to the bank of the Drina River.[89] There, they were said to have forced the seven men to line up on the bank of the river, facing the river, and they opened fire at them. Five of the seven men were said to have died as a result of the shooting while the other two escaped without serious physical injury.[90] Instead of charging Vasiljević with attempted murder in relation to the two survivors, the Prosecution charged him with 'violence to life and person' pursuant to Article 3 of the ICTY Statute and 'inhumane acts' pursuant to Article 5.[91] The Prosecution did not explain why it had decided to do so, rather than charge the accused with the more serious, and perhaps more appropriate, offence of attempted murder.[92] Likewise, in the *Mrdja* case, the accused was charged with 'inhumane acts' in relation to twelve attempted murders.[93] Although not *per se* conclusive as to the state of international law on that point, the charging policy of the Prosecutor in relation to attempted war crimes and attempted crimes against humanity is at least indicative of the Prosecutor's understanding of what forms of liability might be provided for under the Statutes of the Tribunals.

In those circumstances, it is not surprising perhaps that those Chambers that have stated their views on the subject have expressed serious reservations as to the existence under customary international law – and under the Tribunals' Statutes – of a crime of attempted war crimes or attempted crimes against humanity.[94]

---

[89] See *Prosecutor v. Milan Lukić, Sredoje Lukić and Mitar Vasiljević*, IT-98-32-I, Amended Indictment, 12 July 2001. See also par 5 of the *Vasiljević* Trial Judgment (sub-section, 'Drina River incident') which contains a summary of the allegations contained in the indictment. On 12 July 2001, the Prosecution submitted a second amended indictment ('Indictment') to which the accused pleaded not guilty (see, IT-98-32-I, Decision to Vacate in full the Order for non-disclosure of 26 October 1998, 30 October 2000; IT-98-32-PT, Prosecution's Motion to Amend Indictment, 12 July 2001; the entering of a 'not guilty' plea is to be found in the Transcript of the trial at T 97 (28 January 2000)).

[90] *Vasiljević* Trial Judgment, pars 112–114.

[91] Vasiljević was acquitted for violence to life and person on the basis that this offence did not exist under customary international law, but he was convicted for inhumane acts in relation to both survivors. The Trial Chamber found as follows: 'The Trial Chamber is further satisfied that the attempted murder of VG-32 and VG-14 constitutes a serious attack on their human dignity, and that it caused VG-32 and VG-14 immeasurable mental suffering, and that the Accused, by his acts, intended to seriously attack the human dignity of VG-32 and VG-14 and to inflict serious physical and mental suffering upon them. The Trial Chamber is thus satisfied that the Accused incurred individual criminal responsibility for the attempted murder of these two Muslim men as inhumane acts pursuant to his participation in a joint criminal enterprise to murder them' (*Vasiljević* Trial Judgment, par 239).

[92] See IT-98-32-PT, Prosecution Revised Pre-Trial Brief pursuant to Rule 65ter, 24 July 2001 and IT-98-32-T, Prosecution Final Brief, 28 February 2002.

[93] *Prosecutor v. Mrdja*, IT-02-59-I, Indictment, 4 August 2003, Count 3, p 4.

[94] See, e.g. *Akayesu* Trial Judgment, par 473: 'the principle of individual criminal responsibility for an attempt to commit a crime obtained only in case of genocide. Conversely, this would mean that with respect to any other form of criminal participation and, in particular, those referred to in Article 6(1), the perpetrator would incur criminal responsibility only if the offence were completed'; *Krnojelac* Trial Judgment n 1292, p 181: 'The existence of a mistaken belief that the intended victim will be discriminated against, together with an intention to discriminate against that person because of that mistaken belief, may in some circumstances amount to the inchoate offence of attempted persecution, but no such crime falls within the jurisdiction of this Tribunal.'

21

Article 7(3) of the ICTY Statute and Article 6(3) of the ICTR Statute: Command or Superior Responsibility

21.1 Principle of command responsibility	296
21.2 Superior–subordinate relationship and 'effective control'	298
21.3 Knowledge requirement	301
21.4 Failure to prevent and punish	306

21.1 Principle of command responsibility

The principle of command responsibility provides that under certain circumstances a commander (or superior) may be held criminally responsible if he or she fails to prevent or punish the criminal acts of his or her subordinates of which he or she knew or had reason to know. According to the Appeals Chamber, '[c]ommand responsibility is the most effective method by which international criminal law can enforce responsible command'[1] and it applies, albeit not necessarily in exactly the same manner,[2] to both civilian and military superiors,[3] and whether the crimes charged have been committed in the context of an international or internal armed conflict.[4]

---

[1] *Hadžihasanović* Command Responsibility Appeal Decision, par 16. See also ibid., par 23: 'the duties comprised in responsible command are generally enforced through command responsibility. The latter flows from the former.'

[2] See *Bagilishema* Appeal Judgment, par 52, concerning the different way in which a civilian, as opposed to a military, superior, may be exercising 'effective control' over his subordinates.

[3] See, e.g. *Čelebići* Appeal Judgment, pars 195–197; *Bagilishema* Appeal Judgment, pars 35 and 51; *Čelebići* Trial Judgment, par 387; *Kayishema and Ruzindana* Trial Judgment, par 216; *Nahimana* Trial Judgment, pars 976–977, concerning the responsibility of the leader of a political party pursuant to Article 6(3) ICTR Statute.

[4] See generally *Hadžihasanović* Command Responsibility Appeal Decision, pars 11, 13, 18, and 31 (see also, ibid., par 20: 'The basis of the commander's responsibility lies in his obligations as commander of troops making up an organised military force under his command, and not in the particular theatre in which the act was committed by a member of that military force'). In relation more specifically to international armed conflicts, see also *Čelebići* Appeal Judgment, pars 222–241;

Command or superior responsibility pursuant to Articles 7(3) and 6(3) of the Statutes is not a form of vicarious responsibility, nor is it direct responsibility for the acts of subordinates.[5] Neither is it helpful to refer to it as a form of responsibility for 'negligence' as this is likely to lead to confusion of thought.[6] Command responsibility, pursuant to Articles 7(3) and 6(3) of the Statutes, is responsibility for the commander's own acts or omissions in failing to prevent or punish the crimes of his subordinates whom he knew or had reason to know were about to commit serious crimes or had already done so.[7] In the words of one Judge of the Appeals Chamber, 'command responsibility' as listed under the Statute 'mak[es] the commander guilty for failing in his supervisory capacity to take the necessary corrective action after he knows or has reason to know that his subordinate was about to commit the act or had done so. Reading the provision reasonably, it could not have been designed to make the commander a party to the particular crime committed by his subordinate.'[8]

Bagilishema Appeal Judgment, pars 35–37. Whether that principle (of command responsibility) applies to the same extent and to the same degree in both contexts has not been determined by the Appeals Chamber. In any case, the Appeals Chamber held that command responsibility was part of customary international law relating to international armed conflicts before the adoption of Additional Protocol I (*Hadžihasanović* Command Responsibility Appeal Decision, par 29). The Appeals Chamber did not make it clear when this form of liability became part of customary law insofar as it applies to internal armed conflict, nor whether the time at which it became customary in that context was different from the time at which it became customary in the context of international armed conflicts.

[5] *Čelebići* Appeal Judgment, par 239. See also *Bagilishema* Trial Judgment, pars 44–45; *Semanza* Trial Judgment, par 404. The Appeals Chamber for Rwanda has also warned against the use of the phrase 'negligence' to describe the true nature of 'command responsibility' as a form of criminal liability (*Bagilishema* Appeal Judgment, par 35: 'References to "negligence" in the context of superior responsibility are likely to lead to confusion of thought, as the Judgment of the Trial Chamber in the present case illustrates. The law imposes upon a superior a duty to prevent crimes which he knows or has reason to know were about to be committed, and to punish crimes which he knows or has reason to know have been committed, by subordinates over whom he has effective control. A military commander, or a civilian superior, may therefore be held responsible if he fails to discharge his duties as a superior by deliberately failing to perform them or by culpably or willfully disregarding them') See also *Blaškić* Appeal Judgment, par 63.

[6] *Bagilishema* Appeal Judgment, par 34; *Blaškić* Appeal Judgment, par 63 (endorsing that view).

[7] See Separate and Partially Dissenting Opinion of Judge David Hunt in *Hadžihasanović* Command Responsibility Appeal Decision, par 9 and references cited in n 130, p 52. See also *Kordić and Čerkez* Trial Judgment, par 447; *Čelebići* Appeal Judgment, par 239; *Bagilishema* Appeal Judgment, par 35; *Aleksovski* Trial Judgment, par 72. See also *Trial of General Tomoyuki Yamashita*, United States Military Commission, Manila, (8 October–7 December, 1945), and the Supreme Court of the United States (Judgments delivered on 4 February 1946) as reprinted in *Law Reports of the Trials of War Criminals*, IV, in particular pp 43–44: '[. . .] it is urged that the charge does not allege that petitioner has either committed or directed the commission of such acts, and consequently that no violation is charged against him. But this overlooks the fact that the gist of the charge is an unlawful breach of duty by petitioner as an army commander to control the operations of the members of his command by "permitting them to commit" the extensive and widespread atrocities specified.'

[8] See Judge Shahabuddeen's Partial Dissenting Opinion in *Hadžihasanović* Command Responsibility Appeal Decision, par 32. See also, ibid., par 33 (footnote omitted): 'Command responsibility imposes criminal responsibility on a commander for failure to take corrective action in respect of a crime committed by another; it does not make the commander a party to the crime committed by that other. The nature of the responsibility is pertinent to its extent.'

Customary international law provides that a superior or commander may be held criminally responsible for the acts of others if the following three conditions are met:[9]

(i) the existence of a superior–subordinate relationship between the commander or superior and the alleged principal offenders;

(ii) the superior knew or had reason to know that the subordinate was about to commit such acts or had done so; and

(iii) the superior failed to take the necessary and reasonable measures to prevent such acts or to punish the perpetrators thereof.

21.2 Superior–subordinate relationship and 'effective control'

The first requirement, namely, the existence of a superior–subordinate relationship, demands a hierarchical relationship, direct or indirect,[10] between the superior (the accused) and the subordinate who is alleged to have committed or to have been about to commit a crime within the Tribunal's jurisdiction.[11] A hierarchical relationship may exist by virtue of the accused's *de facto* authority over this subordinate or by virtue of his *de jure* position of superiority,[12] but that relationship need not have been formalized at any time prior to the commission of the crime.[13]

---

[9] See, *inter alia*, *Čelebići* Appeal Judgment, pars 189–198, 225–226, 238–239, 256, 263, and 346; *Aleksovski* Appeal Judgment, pars 72 and 76. See also, *inter alia*, *Bagilishema* Appeal Judgment, pars 24 et seq., *Kunarac* Trial Judgment, pars 394–399, *Krnojelac* Trial Judgment, par 92 with references to other cases quoted therein; *Kordić and Čerkez* Trial Judgment, par 401; *Blaškić* Trial Judgment, par 294; *Bagilishema* Trial Judgment, par 38; *Kajelijeli* Trial Judgment, par 772 and decisions cited therein.

[10] See *Čelebići* Appeal Judgment, pars 251–252; *Kajelijeli* Trial Judgment, par 771; *Semanza* Trial Judgment, par 400. In particular, a commander could be held responsible, not only for the acts of those who are his immediate subordinates, but also those who are subordinates of subordinates, as long as he may be shown to have had effective control over them, albeit through others.

[11] *Krnojelac* Trial Judgment, par 93. See also *Čelebići* Appeal Judgment, pars 205–206.

[12] See, e.g. ibid., pars 192–195, 266: '[193] The power or authority to prevent or to punish does not solely arise from *de jure* authority conferred through official appointment. In many contemporary conflicts, there may be only *de facto*, self-proclaimed governments and therefore *de facto* armies and paramilitary groups subordinate thereto. Command structure, organised hastily, may well be in disorder and primitive. To enforce the law in these circumstances requires a determination of accountability not only of individual offenders but of their commanders or other superiors who were, based on evidence, in control of them without, however, a formal commission or appointment. A tribunal could find itself powerless to enforce humanitarian law against *de facto* superiors if it only accepted as proof of command authority a formal letter of authority, despite the fact that the superiors acted at the relevant time with all the powers that would attach to an officially appointed superior or commander.' See also, e.g. *Bagilishema* Appeal Judgment, par 50; *Kordić and Čerkez* Trial Judgment, pars 405–406.

[13] See, e.g. *Krnojelac* Trial Judgment, par 93: 'The relationship need not have been formalised and it is not necessarily determined by formal status alone'; *Kunarac* Trial Judgment, par 397: 'The relationship between the commander and his subordinates need not have been formalized; a tacit or implicit understanding between them as to their positioning *vis-à-vis* one another is sufficient'; *Čelebići* Appeal Judgment, par 193: 'The power or authority to prevent or to punish does not solely

A military commander, regardless of rank,[14] or a civilian high official,[15] could be regarded as being in such a position of superiority by reason of their position in the military or state apparatus.[16]

But to be liable pursuant to Articles 7(3) and 6(3) of the Statutes, whether the accused has been formally appointed as leader or commander, he must, in addition, be shown to have exercised 'effective control' over those who are said to have been his or her subordinates and who are said to have committed crimes.[17] As noted by the Appeals Chamber, '[t]he *effective control* test applies to all superiors, whether *de jure* or *de facto*, military or civilian'.[18]

According to the jurisprudence of the *ad hoc* Tribunals, 'effective control' means 'the material ability to prevent offences or punish the principal offenders'.[19]

---

arise from de jure authority conferred through official appointment. In many contemporary conflicts, there may be only de facto, self-proclaimed governments and therefore de facto armies and paramilitary groups subordinate thereto. Command structure, organised hastily, may well be in disorder and primitive. To enforce the law in these circumstances requires a determination of accountability not only of individual offenders but of their commanders or other superiors who were, based on evidence, in control of them without, however, a formal commission or appointment. A tribunal could find itself powerless to enforce humanitarian law against de facto superiors if it only accepted as proof of command authority a formal letter of authority, despite the fact that the superiors acted at the relevant time with all the powers that would attach to an officially appointed superior or commander.' See also *Blaškić* Trial Judgment, par 301; *Kordić and Čerkez* Trial Judgment, par 424; *Semanza* Trial Judgment, par 401.

14 *Kunarac* Trial Judgment, par 398: 'Depending on the circumstances, a commander with superior responsibility under Article 7(3) may be a colonel commanding a brigade, a corporal commanding a platoon or even a rankless individual commanding a small group of men.'

15 See, e.g. *Čelebići* Appeal Judgment, pars 196–197; *Ntakirutimana* Trial Judgment, pars 819; *Kayishema and Ruzindana* Trial Judgment, pars 213–215; *Musema* Trial Judgment, par 148. The *degree of control* exercised by a civilian must be similar to that required for a military commander, although *the manner* in which that control is exercised may be different: 'the establishment of civilian superior responsibility requires proof beyond reasonable doubt that the accused exercised effective control over his subordinates, in the sense that he exercised a degree of control over them which is similar to the degree of control of military commanders. It is not suggested that "effective control" will necessarily be exercised by a civilian superior and by a military commander in the same way, or that it may necessarily be established in the same way in relation to both a civilian superior and a military commander' (*Bagilishema* Appeal Judgment, par 51, and pars 54–55). The Appeals Chamber added that: 'It is sufficient that, for one reason or another, the accused [a civilian] exercises the required "degree" of control over his subordinates, namely, that of effective control' (ibid., par 55). See also *Aleksovski* Appeal Judgment, par 76; *Čelebići* Trial Judgment, pars 377–378; *Aleksovski* Trial Judgment, par 78.

16 See *Čelebići* Appeal Judgment, par 197: 'In determining questions of responsibility it is necessary to look to effective exercise of power or control and not to formal titles.'

17 See, e.g. *Bagilishema* Appeal Judgment, par 50, and jurisprudence cited therein. In *Bagilishema*, the Appeals Chamber noted that it 'is not suggested that "effective control" will necessarily be exercised by a civilian superior and by a military commander in the same way, or that it may necessarily be established in the same way in relation to both a civilian superior and a military commander' (ibid., par 52; see also par 55).

18 Ibid., pars 50 and 56. See also *Aleksovski* Appeal Judgment, par 76; *Stakić* Trial Judgment, par 459.

19 See, *inter alia*, *Krnojelac* Trial Judgment, par 93; *Bagilishema* Appeal Judgment, pars 49–55; *Čelebići* Appeal Judgment, pars 196–198, 256; *Kayishema and Ruzindana* Appeal Judgment, par 294; *Blaškić* Trial Judgment, pars 300–302; *Kayishema and Ruzindana* Trial Judgment, par 229–231. This relationship of subordination need not have been formalized (*Kunarac* Trial Judgment, par 397).

The fact that the accused might, for instance, have been *de jure* superior to the perpetrator, or that he had the ability to give him orders, though evidentially relevant to the determination to be made by the Court as to whether they may be said to have been in a superior–subordinate relationship, is not by itself conclusive of whether that person indeed exercised 'effective control' over the perpetrator and that he may therefore be held responsible for failing to prevent or punish crimes committed by the perpetrator.[20]

What may be said to constitute 'effective control' for the purpose of Articles 7(3) and 6(3) must be distinguished from lower forms of influence or authority which will not suffice to attract criminal liability under Articles 7(3) and 6(3) of the Statutes. This is the case, for instance, where a certain individual, charismatic enough, respected, or otherwise persuasive enough to be followed, may be able to exercise some degree of influence over other individuals without their relationship being one of superior to subordinates and without this relationship reaching the threshold of 'effective control' required by Articles 7(3) and 6(3) of the Statutes.[21] Therefore, there may be cases where an individual had some authority and power over other individuals which allowed him to exercise even considerable influence over them but which fell short of effective control and therefore of imposing command responsibility:[22]

[S]ubstantial influence as a means of control in any sense which falls short of the possession of effective control over subordinates, which requires the possession of material abilities to prevent subordinate offences or to punish subordinate offenders, lacks sufficient support in State practice and judicial decisions.[23]

Where a superior has 'effective control' and fails to exercise his authority he could, in principle, be held responsible for the crimes committed by his subordinates.[24] That subordination and control need not have been permanent, however, and a commander could be held liable for crimes of subordinates who are only temporarily under his command if it can be shown that, at the time when the crimes were committed, he had effective control over them.[25] Two or more superiors may be held responsible for the same crime perpetrated by the same individual if it is established that the principal offender was under the command of both superiors at the relevant time.[26]

---

[20] See, generally, *Kordić and Čerkez* Trial Judgment, pars 416, 419–424; *Kunarac* Trial Judgment, pars 396–397; *Čelebići* Trial Judgment, par 736; *Čelebići* Appeal Judgment, pars 193 and 197; *Blaškić* Appeal Judgment, pars 68–69; *Kayishema and Ruzindana* Trial Judgment, par 222; *Bagilishema* Trial Judgment, par 39; *Kajelijeli* Trial Judgment, pars 773–774.

[21] *Čelebići* Appeal Judgment, pars 263 and 266.

[22] *Čelebići* Trial Judgment, par 658; *Kunarac* Trial Judgment, pars 863 and 628; *Kordić and Čerkez* Trial Judgment, pars 412–416, 838–841; *Čelebići* Appeal Judgment, par 266; *Stakić* Trial Judgment, par 459 (' "Substantial influence" over subordinates that does not meet the threshold of "effective control" is not sufficient under customary law to serve as a means of exercising command responsibility'); *Kayishema and Ruzindana* Trial Judgment, par 220.   [23] *Čelebići* Appeal Judgment, par 266.

[24] Ibid., pars 196–198 and *Krnojelac* Trial Judgment, par 93.

[25] *Kunarac* Trial Judgment, par 399.

[26] *Krnojelac* Trial Judgment, par 93; *Blaškić* Trial Judgment, par 303; *Aleksovski* Trial Judgment, par 106.

Somewhat controversially, the majority of the Appeals Chamber in the *Hadžhisanović* case held that there must be perfect temporal coincidence between the time when the crime that forms the basis of the charge against the accused is committed, and the existence of the superior–subordinate relationship between the accused and the perpetrator. Thus, crimes which, for instance, were committed prior to a commander's assumption of command could not, in principle, be charged against him under that heading even if he learns about them on assuming command and decides to do nothing about them.[27] The position of the majority of the Appeals Chamber in that case leaves, as one dissenting Judge observed, 'a gaping hole in the protection which international humanitarian law seeks to provide for the victims of the crimes committed contrary to that law' and the majority's view appears to be highly questionable from a legal and practical point of view.[28] As suggested by the Appeals Chamber, there must indeed be a temporal coincidence, but it is one between the time at which the commander had effective control over the perpetrator and the time at which the commander is said to have failed to exercise his powers (to prevent or punish), not the time at which the crimes were committed as the majority of the Appeals Chamber suggested.[29] Thus, for as long as a superior may be shown to have had effective control over subordinates, he may, in principle, be held responsible for their crimes if he fails to exercise such abilities of control.[30]

21.3   Knowledge requirement

Secondly, the superior must be shown to have known or, at least, have had reason to know that his subordinate was about to commit or had committed a crime within the Court's jurisdiction.[31] The requirements of knowledge come in the alternative: it must be proved either (i) that the superior had actual knowledge

---

[27] *Hadžihasanović* Command Responsibility Appeal Decision, pars 37 et seq., in particular, par 51.

[28] Judge David Hunt Separate and Partially Dissenting Opinion in *Hadžihasanović* Command Responsibility Appeal Decision, par 22. See generally the compelling arguments of Judge Shahabuddeen and Judge Hunt – Judge Shahabuddeen's Partial Dissenting Opinion in *Hadžihasanović* Command Responsibility Appeal Decision and Judge Hunt's Separate and Partially Dissenting Opinion in *Hadžihasanović* Command Responsibility Appeal Decision, 16 July 20.

[29] See *Kunarac* Trial Judgment, par 399. The Trial Chamber in that case pointed out that it must be shown that, 'at the time when the acts charged in the Indictment were committed, these [subordinates] were under the effective control of that particular individual'. See also Judge Shahabuddeen's Partial Dissenting Opinion (par 28) in *Hadžihasanović* Command Responsibility Appeal Decision: 'What, however, has to be simultaneous is the discovery by the commander and the existence of the superior/subordinate relationship.'   [30] *Čelebići* Appeal Judgment, par 198.

[31] This knowledge requirement applies to both civilian and military superiors (*Čelebići* Appeal Judgment, pars 196–197). In *Krnojelac*, the Trial Chamber said that: 'The Trial Chamber is [. . .] of the view that the same state of knowledge is required for both civilian and military commanders' (*Krnojelac* Trial Judgment, par 94). From an evidential point of view, however, it may be easier to establish that a military man 'considering that he will presumably be part of an organized structure with established reporting and monitoring systems', as opposed to a civilian, had acquired such knowledge (*Kordić and Čerkez* Trial Judgment, par 428). See also *Čelebići* Appeal Judgment, par 240, concerning the extent to which civilian, as opposed to military, commanders may have a duty to investigate information they have received concerning the commission of crimes by subordinates.

(he 'knew') that his subordinates were committing or about to commit crimes within the jurisdiction of the Tribunal, *or* (ii) that he had in his possession information which would at least put him on notice of the risk of such offences, such information alerting him to the need for additional investigation to determine whether such crimes were or were about to be committed by his subordinates (he 'had reason to know').[32]

Actual knowledge, which may be defined as the awareness that the relevant crimes were committed or were about to be committed,[33] may be established, either by direct evidence (e.g. by a signed report received at the command post relating to the commission of crimes by troops under this command) or circumstantially through evidence from which it may be inferred that the commander had indeed acquired such knowledge.[34] The form in which the information is received or knowledge is acquired is unimportant so long, presumably, as it is sufficient to make that person aware in the relevant sense.[35]

The second, imputed, form of knowledge requires that the commander possessed some general information which put him on notice of the likelihood of unlawful acts by his subordinates.[36] The mere awareness of a commander of the risk of a crime being committed by his subordinates would not suffice to engage his responsibility. The prosecution would have to show that he was aware of the substantial likelihood that a crime will be committed as a result of his failure to act and that, aware of that fact, he decided not to do anything about it

---

[32] *Čelebići* Appeal Judgment, pars 223–226; *Krnojelac* Trial Judgment, par 94; *Bagilishema* Appeal Judgment, pars 26–38. It should be noted that the 'had reason to know' standard applied at the *ad hoc* Tribunals apparently differs in substance from that provided in Article 86(2) of Additional Protocol I ('[. . .] knew, or had information which should have enabled [the commander] to conclude in the circumstances at the time [. . .]') (see ICRC, *Commentary to the Additional Protocols*, par 3545). See also Article 28, paragraphs (a)(i) and (b)(i) of the ICC Statute.

[33] *Kordić and Čerkez* Trial Judgment, par 427.

[34] See, e.g. *Blaškić* Trial Judgment, par 308; *Aleksovski* Trial Judgment, par 80; *Krnojelac* Trial Judgment, par 94. [35] *Čelebići* Appeal Judgment, par 238.

[36] See, e.g. ibid.; *Kordić and Čerkez* Trial Judgment, par 437. This requirement does not imply that the commander actually possessed such information, but only that he was provided with it or that it was available to him or was otherwise in his possession. Nor is it necessary for the Prosecution to establish that he actually acquainted himself with the content of the information as long as he had that information in his possession and that he was able in a position to acquaint himself with it (see *Čelebići* Appeal Judgment, par 239). This cannot be presumed and the circumstances under which a commander could be said to have been on notice of events which he was not acquainted with (but for which he had information in his possession) remain unclear. See also *Bagilishema* Appeal Judgment, par 28 ('The "had reason to know" standard does not require that actual knowledge, either explicit or circumstantial, be established. Nor does it require that the Chamber be satisfied that the accused actually knew that crimes had been committed or were about to be committed. It merely requires that the Chamber be satisfied that the accused had "some general information in his possession, which would put him on notice of possible unlawful acts by his subordinates" ') and, ibid., at par 42, where the Appeals Chamber distinguishes between information which the accused may have had about the general situation in the relevant area (and which is not sufficient for him to be held criminally responsible as a commander) and general information which put him on notice that his subordinates might commit crimes (which is, all other conditions being met, sufficient, in principle, for the commander to be found responsible for the acts of his subordinates).

('volitional element').[37] The information which the commander is shown to have received need not provide detail about unlawful acts committed or about to be committed, but the information in his possession must be sufficiently clear or alarming to indicate the likelihood of serious criminal offences having been or about to be committed and to trigger the commander's duty to investigate the matter further.[38] It must, furthermore, be established that the notice which the accused had received was notice of crimes of the sort with which he is now charged; in other words, the accused must be shown to have had information in his possession which put him on notice that crimes of similar gravity and similar nature as those with which he is charged had been or were about to be committed and not just some general information that some of his subordinates might be involved in criminal activities without more detail.[39] Therefore, it would not be sufficient for the Prosecution merely to show that the accused knew or had reason to know, in general terms, that crimes, regardless of their gravity and similarities to those being charged against him, were about to be committed, or had been committed, by his subordinates.

Nor can an accused be held responsible under the Tribunals' Statutes simply because he 'should have known' of such crimes, in the sense of being held responsible for failing to seek and obtain information which would have put him on notice that crimes had been committed or were about to be committed: only once he possesses sufficient general information putting him on notice may he in principle be held responsible.[40] It is not necessary, however, that the commander

[37] *Blaškić* Appeal Judgment, pars 41–42. Note that the finding of the Appeals Chamber on that point was limited, *sensu stricto*, to liability for 'ordering'. There would seem to be no reason, however, why a different solution should apply to a commander whose participation is even less significant in the alleged commission of a crime than one who is said to have ordered his subordinates to commit crimes. See, however, *Krnojelac* Trial Judgment, par 94.

[38] *Kordić and Čerkez* Trial Judgment, par 437; *Čelebići* Appeal Judgment, par 238; *Bagilishema* Appeal Judgment, par 42. The form in which the information is provided or received is in principle irrelevant (*Čelebići* Appeal Judgment, par 238).

[39] In particular, the commander could not be said to have known or have had reason to know that a given crime (say, torture) had been or was about to be committed because he may have known or have had reason to know that a less serious offence (e.g. cruel treatment) or one which does not contain all of the elements of the first one (e.g. other inhumane acts) had been or was about to be committed. See *Krnojelac* Appeal Judgment, par 155: 'using the above example of the crime of torture, in order to determine whether an accused "had reason to know" that his subordinates had committed or were about to commit acts of torture, the Court must ascertain whether he had sufficiently alarming information (bearing in mind that, as set out above, such information need not be specific) to alert him to the risk of acts of torture being committed, that is of beatings being inflicted not arbitrarily but for one of the prohibited purposes of torture. Thus, it is not enough that an accused has sufficient information about beatings inflicted by his subordinates; he must also have information – albeit general – which alerts him to the risk of beatings being inflicted for one of the purposes provided for in the prohibition against torture.' See also, ibid., pars 178–179.

[40] The Appeals Chamber in *Čelebići* explicitly rejected the Prosecution's submissions to the contrary (see *Čelebići* Appeal Judgment, pars 226, 232–238). See also *Kvočka* Trial Judgment, par 317 ('The Appeals Chamber in the *Čelebići* case found that Article 7(3) does not impose a duty upon a superior to go out of his way to obtain information about crimes committed by subordinates, unless he is in some way put on notice that criminal activity is afoot') and *Bagilishema* Appeal Judgment, par 37. As noted above, this standard differs from that provided in Article 86(2) of Additional Protocol I and Article 28 of the ICC Statute.

actually be shown to have acquainted himself with the information that has been provided to him if it is shown to have been both provided to him for that purpose and that it was readily available for consultation.[41]

As just pointed out, knowledge, actual or circumstantial, may not be presumed and superior responsibility (or 'liability as a superior') does not arise from failure to act in spite of knowledge.[42] His responsibility, therefore, will not be engaged merely because he neglected his duty to be informed of the behaviour of his subordinates.[43] The requirement that the superior or commander must know or have reason to know that his subordinates are committing crimes or are about to do so exists so that a superior may not be held responsible for crimes of which he had no knowledge.[44] An assessment of the mental element required under Articles 7(3) and 6(3) of the Statutes must therefore be conducted in the specific circumstances of each case, taking into account the actual and personal situation of the superior concerned at the time in question.[45] A number of *indicia* have been laid out which a Trial Chamber may take into account when determining whether a commander may be said to have known or have had reason to know that crimes had been committed or were about to be committed

---

[41] *Čelebići* Appeal Judgment, par 239: 'the relevant information only needs to have been provided or available to the superior, or in the Trial Chamber's words, "in the possession of". It is not required that he actually acquainted himself with the information.'

[42] Ibid., par 226: 'Neglect of a duty to acquire such knowledge, however, does not feature in the provision as a separate offence, and a superior is not therefore liable under the provision for such failures but only for failing to take necessary and reasonable measures to prevent or to punish.' See also *Čelebići* Trial Judgment, par 386; *Blaškić* Trial Judgment, par 307; *Kordić and Čerkez* Trial Judgment, par 427; *Semanza* Trial Judgment, par 405; *Bagilishema* Trial Judgment, par 46; *Kajelijeli* Trial Judgment, par 776: 'While an individual's hierarchical position may be a significant *indicium* that he or she knew or had reason to know about subordinates' criminal acts, knowledge will not be presumed from status alone' (footnote omitted); *Kamuhanda* Trial Judgment, par 607.

[43] *Blaškić* Appeal Judgment, pars 61–62; *Čelebići* Appeal Judgment, par 226.

[44] The soundness of such a requirement can easily be grasped from the literature on the *Yamashita* trial, in which the United States Supreme Court found the accused responsible for criminal actions of which he seems to have had no knowledge of (*In re Yamashita*, US Supreme Court, Judgment of 4 February 1946, 18 American International Law Cases (*AILC*), 1–23; 327 US 1; 66 S. Ct. 340; see, also for a critical appraisal of the *Yamashita* decision, M. Stryszak, 'Command Responsibility: How Much Should a Commander Be Expected to Know?', 11 Journal of Legal Studies (*JLS*) (2000/2001); M. Smidt, 'Yamashita, Medina, and Beyond: Command Responsibility in Contemporary Military Operations', 164 *Military Law Review* 155 (2000)).

[45] See, e.g. *Čelebići* Appeal Judgment, par 239; *Krnojelac* Appeal Judgment, par 156, ('an assessment of the mental element required by Article 7(3) of the Statute should, in any event, be conducted in the specific circumstances of each case, taking into account the specific situation of the superior concerned at the time in question'); *Kordić and Čerkez* Trial Judgment, par 428: 'Depending on the position of authority held by a superior, whether military or civilian, *de jure* or *de facto*, and his level of responsibility in the chain of command, the evidence required to demonstrate actual knowledge may be different. For instance, the actual knowledge of a military commander may be easier to prove considering the fact that he will presumably be part of an organised structure with established reporting and monitoring systems. In the case of *de facto* commanders of more informal military structures, or of civilian leaders holding *de facto* positions of authority, the standard of proof will be higher.'

by his subordinates, including the following:[46]

- the number, type and scope of illegal acts allegedly committed by his subordinates
- the length of time during which the illegal acts are said to have occurred
- the number and type of troops allegedly involved
- the logistics involved
- the geographical area in which the illegal acts were committed
- the widespread and systematic occurrence of the acts
- the tactical tempo of the operation, if any
- the *modus operandi* of similar illegal acts
- the officers and staff involved
- the location of the commander at the time when the acts were said to have been committed[47]
- the nature and scope of the accused's responsibility and his position in the hierarchy
- the character traits of the subordinates
- the fact that the events took place during any temporary absence of the commander
- the lack of instruction of subordinates
- the military, as opposed to civilian, nature of his command
- the existence of reports addressed to the superior
- the tactical situation at the time
- the level of training and instruction of the commander and his subordinates
- the geographical proximity between the crime committed and the place where the commander was located at the time
- the position of authority held by the superior and his level of responsibility.

These are only *indicia*, however, and in the absence of direct evidence of knowledge, the conclusion that the commander knew or had reason to know must be the only reasonable inference to be drawn from the evidence available and it must be established beyond reasonable doubt. It is not sufficient to simply demonstrate that the commander was aware that there was a risk that his subordinates could commit crimes. Because there is *always* a risk that such crimes

---

[46] See, generally, the *Final Report of the Commission of Experts for the Former Yugoslavia*, par 58; *Čelebići* Appeal Judgment, par 238; *Čelebići* Trial Judgment, par 386; *Kordić and Čerkez* Trial Judgment, pars 427–428 and 437; *Blaškić* Trial Judgment, pars 307–308; *Aleksovski* Trial Judgment par, 80; *Stakić* Trial Judgment, par 460. See also ICRC, *Commentary to Additional Protocol I* (art. 86), par 3545.

[47] See, in particular, *Naletilić and Martinović* Trial Judgment, par 72: 'the more physically distant the superior was from the commission of the crimes, the more additional *indicia* are necessary to prove that he knew of the crimes. On the other hand, if the crimes were committed next to the superior's duty-station this suffices as an important *indicium* that the superior had knowledge of the crimes, even more if the crimes were repeatedly committed.'

be committed, the Prosecution must at least establish 'an awareness [on his part] of a higher likelihood of risk and a volitional element'.[48]

Difficulties arise in respect of this form of criminal liability when applied to special intent crimes, such as genocide, persecution, or murder. While knowledge (as defined above) is sufficient in principle for a superior to be held responsible for the acts of his subordinates, genocide, for instance, requires a specific intent to destroy in whole or in part a group as such. As already explained, it is the view of the author that a commander may not be held responsible for genocide as a commander unless he himself possess the requisite genocidal intent.[49]

21.4   Failure to prevent and punish

Thirdly, and finally, the Prosecution must establish that the superior failed to take 'the necessary and reasonable measures to prevent or punish the crimes of his subordinates'.[50] What is 'necessary and reasonable' will depend primarily on the extent of the commander's *actual* and *proven* material ability to do anything (be it prevention or punishment) about the crimes that form the basis of the charges.[51] Deciding upon what measures would be appropriate in a particular case is an evidential matter, not a matter of substantive law, to be decided in light of all the circumstances of the case.[52] The urgency with which a commander may be

---

[48] *Blaškić* Appeal Judgment, par 41. Although that statement was made in relation in particular to 'ordering' pursuant to Article 7(1) ICTY Statute, it may also be said to apply to command responsibility pursuant to Articles 7(3) and 6(3) of the Statutes.

[49] See above, sub-sections 14.2.1 and 16.3.1. In a case where the commander possesses the genocidal intent, but where his subordinates have not been shown to have been aware of his assent to the commission of crimes, he should be held responsible for genocide pursuant to Articles 7(3)/6(3), rather than under Articles 7(1)/6(1) of the ICTY/ICTR Statutes. Where, however, his omission to act may be shown to have encouraged or assisted his subordinates in a substantial fashion in the commission of their crimes, the commander's responsibility would generally fall more appropriately within Articles 7(1)/6(1) of the Statutes (for instance, as aiding and abetting genocide).

[50] *Čelebići* Appeal Judgment, par 226; *Krnojelac* Trial Judgment, par 95.

[51] See, e.g. *Blaškić* Appeal Judgment, par 72 ('necessary and reasonable measures are such that can be taken within the competence of a commander as evidenced by the degree of effective control he wielded over his subordinates'); *Blaškić* Trial Judgment, pars 302 and 335 ('[335] it is a commander's degree of effective control, his material ability, which will guide the Trial Chamber in determining whether he reasonably took the measures required either to prevent the crime or to punish the perpetrator'); *Bagilishema* Trial Judgment, par 47 ('Article 6(3) [of the ICTR Statute] states that a superior is expected to take "necessary and reasonable measures" to prevent or punish crimes under the Statutes. The Chamber understands "necessary" to be those measures required to discharge the obligation to prevent or punish in the circumstances prevailing at the time; and, "reasonable" to be those measures which the commander was in a position to take in the circumstances'); *Bagilishema* Trial Judgment, par 48 ('it is the commander's degree of effective control – his or her material ability to control subordinates – which will guide the Chamber in determining whether he or she took reasonable measures to prevent, stop, or punish the subordinates' crimes. Such a material ability must not be considered abstractly, but must be evaluated on a case-by-case basis, considering all the circumstances'); *Aleksovksi* Trial Judgment, par 78; *Čelebići* Trial Judgment, pars 302, 394–395; *Kajelijeli* Trial Judgment, par 779 and authority cited therein; *Kamuhanda* Trial Judgment, par 630.

[52] *Blaškić* Appeal Judgment, par 72.

expected to act upon reports of criminal activity among his subordinates and the sort of responses that he may be expected to give to crimes allegedly committed (or about to be committed) by his subordinates will also be dictated, in part, by the nature and seriousness of the crimes.[53]

Considering the seriousness of most of the underlying offences which may constitute genocide, crimes against humanity, or war crimes, a superior may be expected to take prompt and effective measures to punish or prevent them and to implement them with some urgency.[54] But the measures required of the superior are limited to those which are 'feasible in all the circumstances and are "within his power" ':[55] 'A superior is not obliged to perform the impossible. However, the superior has a duty to exercise the powers he has within the confines of those limitations'.[56]

Those two duties, to prevent and to punish, are cumulative in the sense that the criminal liability of a commander may be engaged if he or she fails in carrying out either or both of those obligations.[57] As once pointed out, 'if the superior had reason to know in time to prevent, he commits an offence by failing to take steps to prevent, and he cannot make good that failure by subsequently punishing his subordinates who committed the offences'.[58]

The duty to prevent must be understood as resting on a superior at any stage before the commission of a crime by one of his subordinates if he or she acquires knowledge that such a crime is being prepared or planned, or when he has reasonable grounds to suspect that such crimes will be committed.[59]

The duty to punish, on the other hand, arises only after the crime has been committed. Depending on the circumstances, and in particular depending on the commander's proven ability to do so, his 'duty to punish' may entail investigating the alleged crimes to establish the facts or having them investigated, issuing appropriate orders to his subordinates, reporting crimes to the competent authorities, or taking

---

[53] *Krnojelac* Trial Judgment, par 95; *Čelebići* Appeal Judgment, par 226; *Aleksovski* Trial Judgment, par 81.

[54] See, generally, *Kvočka* Trial Judgment, par 317: 'Action is required on the part of the superior from the point at which he "knew or had reason to know" of the crimes committed or about to be committed by subordinates.' See also *Kordić and Čerkez* Trial Judgment, par 445 concerning the duty to prevent: 'The duty to prevent should be understood as resting on a superior at any stage before the commission of a subordinate crime if he acquires knowledge that such a crime is being prepared or planned, or when he has reasonable grounds to suspect subordinate crimes'; and par 446 concerning the duty to punish: 'The duty to punish naturally arises after a crime has been committed.'

[55] *Krnojelac* Trial Judgment, par 95. See also *Čelebići* Appeal Judgment, par 226; *Kordić and Čerkez* Trial Judgment, pars 441 and 445; *Bagilishema* Trial Judgment, par 48; *Čelebići* Trial Judgment, par 395.

[56] *Krnojelac* Trial Judgment, par 95. See also *Čelebići* Appeal Judgment, par 226; *Kayishema and Ruzindana* Appeal Judgment, par 302.

[57] See *Aleksovski* Appeal Judgment, pars 72, 76; *Čelebići* Appeal Judgment, at pars 192, 193, 198; *Blaškić* Trial Judgment, par 336; *Blaškić* Appeal Judgment, par 83; *Bagilishema* Trial Judgment, par 49.

[58] Judge Hunt's Separate and Partially Dissenting Opinion in *Hadžihasanović* Command Responsibility Appeal Decision, par 23. See also *Blaškić* Trial Judgment, par 336; *Kordić and Čerkez* Trial Judgment, pars 444–446.

[59] Ibid., par 445.

appropriate disciplinary measures against the perpetrators.[60] The superior does not have to be the person who dispenses the punishment and the fact that he has failed to take particular steps following reports of crimes having been committed by his subordinates (such as reporting the acts to his superiors) are not *per se* conclusive of his failure to abide by his duties, although it may be relevant to the Chamber's determination that he had the material ability to do so and that he should have taken such measures in the circumstances of the case.[61]

It must be emphasized that, although the commander must make a genuine attempt to prevent or punish the crimes of his subordinates, he may have been unsuccessful in doing so without being responsible for it. In other words, and from an evidential point of view, the commander's failure to carry out his duty (to prevent and punish) may not be inferred solely from the fact that his subordinates did commit crimes or that they remained unpunished for those crimes. Thus, when determining whether a commander may be said to have adopted all necessary and reasonable measures, the Chamber will have to take into account all circumstances that could have prevented him from doing more than he did (such as insufficient time to take particular measures or achieve a certain result or lack of resources to investigate, or obstructions from superior officers).

In addition, not every breach of a commander's duties (to prevent or to punish) would necessarily entail his criminal responsibility pursuant to Articles 7(3) and 6(3) of the Statutes. First, a military commander, or a civilian superior, may only be held responsible where he consciously fails to discharge his duties as a superior 'either by deliberately failing to perform them or by culpably or wilfully disregarding them'.[62] A commander who, despite his best efforts, was unable to prevent or punish crimes could not therefore be regarded as criminally liable. In addition, as noted by the Appeals Chamber, the breach of duty must have been 'gross', failing which his disciplinary, rather than his criminal, responsibility might be engaged.[63] Thus, minor violations of his duties or the violation of relatively unconsequential duties would not be such as to engage his or her command

---

[60] See, *inter alia*, *Kordić and Čerkez* Trial Judgment, par 446; *Kvočka* Trial Judgment, par 315; *Stakić* Trial Judgment, par 461. The *Kordić and Čerkez* Trial Chamber held that, '[t]his duty [to punish] includes at least an obligation to investigate the crimes to establish the facts and to report them to the competent authorities, if the superior does not have the power to sanction himself' (*Kordić and Čerkez* Trial Judgment, par 446). One Trial Chamber has suggested, without providing much authority in support, however, that a failure to punish crimes could be established where the commander has failed to 'create or sustain among the persons under his or her control, an environment of discipline and respect for the law' (*Bagilishema* Trial Judgment, par 50). 'It follows', the Chamber continued, 'that command responsibility for failure to punish may be triggered by a broadly based pattern of conduct by a superior, which in effect encourages the commission of atrocities by his or her subordinates' (ibid.). The validity of this pronouncement and the conditions under which the responsibility of a commander could be engaged in such circumstances is open to a wide range of questions.

[61] See, e.g. *Blaškić* Appeal Judgment, pars 68, 69, and 72; *Blaškić* Trial Judgment, par 302; *Kvočka* Trial Judgment, par 316.   [62] *Bagilishema* Appeal Judgment, par 35.

[63] Ibid., par 36. Other, less serious, violations of his duties could engage his disciplinary, as opposed to criminal, responsibility (ibid.).

responsibility pursuant to Articles 7(3) and 6(3) of the Statutes. Finally, command responsibility is triggered by a failure to prevent or punish crimes of subordinates and only where he had information that put him on notice of their actions. The mere neglect on the part of the commander to acquire such knowledge would not in itself engage his responsibility under Articles 7(3) and 6(3) of the Tribunals' Statutes.[64]

Does the Prosecution have to establish a causal link between the failure of the commander to fulfil his obligations and the commission of crimes by his subordinates? In the *Čelebići* case, the Trial Chamber held that it had found no support for the existence of such a requirement of causation as a separate element of superior responsibility and therefore concluded that 'causation has not traditionally been postulated as a *conditio sine qua non* for the imposition of criminal liability on superiors for their failure to prevent or punish offences committed by their subordinates'.[65] Likewise, in *Blaškić*, the Appeals Chamber stated that it had not been convinced by the appellant's submission in that case that causation was required and the Appeals Chamber added somewhat cryptically that this matter was more a question of fact than a question of law in general.[66] The position of those two Chambers seems doubtful enough. In fact, insofar as precedent and literature exist on that matter, they seem to point to the opposite conclusion, namely, that there must indeed exist a causal relationship between the failure of the commander to fulfil his duties and the crimes that have been committed by his subordinates.[67] Insofar as the superior's obligation to prevent is concerned, as acknowledged by the *Čelebići* Trial Chamber itself, 'a necessary causal nexus may be considered to be inherent in the requirement of crimes committed by

---

[64] *Čelebići* Trial Judgment, par 226; *Blaškić* Appeal Judgment, par 72.

[65] *Čelebići* Trial Judgment, par. 398. See also, ibid., pars 399–400 and *Kordić and Čerkez* Trial Judgment, par. 447. See also Judge Shahabuddeen's position in Judge Shahabuddeen's Partial Dissenting Opinion in *Hadžihasanović* Command Responsibility Appeal Decision, par 16: 'The submission assumes that there is need for proof of a causal connection between the commander's failure to exercise his powers and the commission of the particular crime by the subordinate. There is no such requirement, certainly not where the charge is for failure to punish for a crime already committed. In the latter case, there is not, because there cannot be, a causal connection between the commander's failure to exercise his power to punish and the already committed crime.'

[66] *Blaškić* Appeal Judgment, par 77.

[67] In the *Hostages* case, for instance, the Tribunal acquitted Foertsch of command responsibility as the evidence 'fail[ed] to show the commission of an unlawful act which *was the result of* any action, affirmative or passive, on the part of this defendant' (see *Hostages* case in relation to the accused Foertsch, quoted in *Law Reports of Trials of War Criminals*, XV, pp 76–77, emphasis added). In all other reviewed cases, when a causal relation was not explicitly required, the Court systematically underlined that the commander's failure to act had an impact on the commission of the crimes. Also, as acknowledged by the *Čelebići* Trial Chamber, causation has a 'central place' in criminal law (*Čelebići* Trial Judgment, par 398). To the extent that it has expressed a view on the matter, the doctrine also appears to support the conclusion that causality is an element of command responsibility: see, e.g. O. Triffterer, 'Causality, a Separate Element of the Doctrine of Superior Responsibility as Expressed in Article 28 Rome Statute?', 15 *Leiden Journal of International Law*, 179–205 (2002); O. Triffterer, 'Command Responsibility', in C. Prittwitz *et al.* (eds.), *Festschrift für Klaus Lüdersen – Zum 70. Geburtstag* (Baden-Baden: Nomos, 2002), pp 437–462.

subordinates and the superior's failure to take the measures within his powers to prevent them'.[68] As far as failure to prevent is concerned, causation would therefore have to be established between the commander's failure and the crime or crimes by his subordinates, whilst in the case of a failure to punish the causal relation is one between the commander's failure to act and the resulting impunity of the perpetrators generated (at least in part) by his inaction. Complete dissociation between the superior's failure to act and the crimes committed by his subordinates would render command responsibility dangerously close to an objective form of strict liability whereby a commander could be held responsible for *any* crimes committed by his subordinates.

The law of command responsibility is not indifferent to the result of the superior's failure. For one thing, the sentence which will be imposed upon a superior will obviously depend in part on the seriousness of the superior's failure, but also on the nature of the crimes which the commander's omission has failed to prevent or to punish.[69] This, in turn, means that, when determining the gravity of the acts of an accused and upon deciding on an appropriate sentence for those acts (or omissions), a Chamber must determine the extent to which the commander's failure might have contributed to the commission of that crime, as with any other form of criminal participation under the Statute. Also, if no causal relation were required between the commander's failure and the crimes of his subordinates, this could in fact create a disincentive for commanders to comply with their duties: knowing that they could be held responsible regardless of any relationship between their alleged failure to prevent or punish and the crimes, they may prefer to stay clear of any attempt to prevent or punish such crimes where such failed attempt may later serve to establish their guilt.[70]

In sum, it would appear that a showing on the part of the Prosecution of a causal relation between the failure to the commander to fulfil his obligations and the commission of crimes by his subordinates should be established in every case where that commander is charged with command responsibility.

---

[68] *Čelebići* Trial Judgment, par 399.

[69] *Čelebići* Appeal Judgment, par 732: 'As a practical matter, the seriousness of a superior's conduct in failing to prevent or punish crimes must be measured to some degree by the nature of the crimes to which this failure relates. A failure to prevent or punish murder or torture committed by a subordinate must be regarded as being of greater gravity than a failure to prevent or punish an act of plunder, for example.'

[70] For instance, in a situation when crimes have been committed by subordinates, a commander might be tempted to cover them up even if he had no part in it rather than bring them to light by punishing the perpetrators because his responsibility for failing to prevent the crimes would not be dependent on his having played a role therein.

22

Convictions Under Articles 7(1) and 7(3) of the ICTY Statute and Articles 6(1) and 6(3) of the ICTR Statute

If the conditions of liability required by both Articles 7(1)/6(1) and 7(3)/6(3) of the Statutes are met, could the accused then be found responsible for taking part in the commission of this crime as well as failing in his duty to prevent or punish it? Some case law had suggested that he probably could, whilst other cases pointed to the opposite conclusion.[1] The jurisprudence of the *ad hoc* Tribunals reveals two main streams of jurisprudence upon this issue. One, best illustrated by the *Blaškić* Trial Judgment, suggests that it would be illogical to hold a commander criminally responsible for planning, instigating, or ordering the commission of a crime whilst, at the same time, reproaching him for not preventing or punishing that same crime.[2] The other line of reasoning suggests that each article – Articles 7(1)/6(1)) or Articles 7(3)/6(3) – criminalizes a different aspect of the accused's criminal actions, that is, that each article protects different values or interests.[3] While Articles 7(1)/6(1) sanction an individual's involvement in the commission of a crime, Articles 7(3)/6(3) punish the superior's failure to fulfil his obligations as a commander which are specifically placed upon any superior or commander. According to that latter view, responsibility under Article 7(3) (or 6(3)) is an added sanction for failure to abide by a specific standard which a superior is bound to uphold, rather than merely to prevent or punish the acts of his subordinates. A variant of that argument is that an accused may be convicted

---

[1] Mario Čerkez, for instance, was apparently convicted under both articles for the same acts under both Article 7(1) – for his direct involvement in the commission of the crimes – and Article 7(3) of the Statute for his responsibility as a superior (*Kordić and Čerkez* Trial Judgment, par 842). *Musema* Trial Judgment and *Kayishema and Ruzindana* Trial Judgment, par 210. There is no doubt in any case that an individual could be charged under both Article 7(1) and 7(3) of the Statute (see, e.g. *Blaškić*, IT-95-14-PT, Decision on the Defence Motion to Dismiss the Indictment Based upon Defects in the Form Thereof (Vagueness/Lack of Adequate Notice of Charges), 4 April 1997, par 32; *Čelebići* Trial Judgment, pars 1221–1222. [2] *Blaškić* Trial Judgment, par 337.
[3] The Appeals Chamber seems to have accepted the possibility that, in principle, an accused may be convicted under both articles under a single count; it is unclear, however, whether the acts for which the accused Mucić was convicted under both heads of responsibility may be said to be identical (see *Čelebići* Appeal Judgment, pars 743 et seq.).

under both headings if, by doing so, the Court's finding may fully reflect the totality of the criminal conduct of the accused.

The Appeals Chamber adopted the first, and fairer, approach to this question. The Appeals Chamber noted that Article 7(1) and Article 7(3) of the ICTY Statute connote distinct categories of criminal responsibility. It added, however, that where an accused has been charged pursuant to both provisions based on the same conduct, it would 'not [be] appropriate' to convict him under both headings.[4] Instead, in order to show the totality of his guilt while not convicting him twice for the same acts, the Appeals Chamber said that an accused who meets the requirements of both Article 7(1) and Article 7(3) of the Statute should be convicted pursuant to Article 7(1) whilst his position as a superior should be regarded as an aggravating factor for sentencing.[5]

---

[4] *Blaškić* Appeal Judgment, par 91.

[5] Ibid. See also *Furundžija* Trial Judgment, par 230; *Todorović* Sentencing Judgment; *Krnojelac* Trial Judgment, par 173; *Naletilić and Martinović* Trial Judgment, par 81. It is debatable whether a Chamber should always and invariably convict an accused under Article 7(1) in those circumstances, or whether it should have the discretion to opt for an Article 7(3) conviction if more appropriate in that specific case (see *Krnojelac* Trial Judgment, par 173; *Kupreškić* Appeal Judgment, par 451; *Kamuhanda* Trial Judgment, par 623). Considering that Article 7(3) has not been made subject to Article 7(1) by the Statute and that there is no *a priori* hierarchy between those two provisions and that there may indeed be situations where the conduct of the accused would be best characterized as command responsibility (as where his 'aiding and abetting' a crime would be strictly limited to his failure to abide by his obligations as a commander), it is suggested that Trial Chambers should have the discretion to opt for one rather than the other, depending on the circumstances of the case. See, however, *Stakić* Trial Judgment, par 465, which asserts (but does not support the assertion) that Article 7(3) ICTY Statute is 'an omnibus clause' which only becomes applicable 'where the primary basis of responsibility [i.e., Article 7(1)] can not be applied'.

PART VI

DISTINGUISHING GENOCIDE, WAR CRIMES, AND CRIMES AGAINST HUMANITY: CUMULATIVE CHARGING AND CUMULATIVE CONVICTIONS

23

Cumulative Charging and Cumulative Convictions

As described in the preceding chapters, war crimes, crimes against humanity, and genocide have very different histories. The last two are essentially the penal legacy of the Second World War, whilst war crimes have a much older pedigree. Despite their differences in origin, and under the pressure, in part, of the human rights movement, all three categories have grown ever closer and much criminal conduct would now satisfy the requirements of more than one of them.

When deciding to indict an individual for serious violations of humanitarian law, the Prosecutors of the *ad hoc* Tribunals enjoy a great deal of discretion in the choice of charges that they may bring against a particular accused. Regrettably, the charging policy of the Office of the Prosecutor in both Tribunals has remained completely obscure to most observers and practically beyond the reach of the Tribunals' supervision.[1] Clearly, the charging policy of the Prosecutor *ratione materiae* and the characterization of the conduct under the different categories of crimes will be dictated primarily by the evidence that has been collected in the course of its investigation: is there any evidence to establish that the victims were civilians? Is there evidence that the suspect possessed a genocidal state of mind? Is there any evidence that there was a widespread or systematic attack upon a civilian population at the relevant time? But the choice of the Prosecutor when charging an accused is also dictated by particular policy choices. The fact that all individuals accused in relation to the massacre in Srebrenica have been charged with genocide may reveal as much about the nature of the events as it does about the political pressure which is upon the Prosecutor to describe these events in no other than in genocidal terms, though the propriety of genocidal charges in relation to some of those involved (and prosecuted before the ICTY) may be open to question. Likewise, the fact that, for instance, no genocidal charges have ever been brought in relation to the events of Kosovo or in relation to the Croatian war may have more to do with policy considerations than with a purely legal assessment of the evidence available to the Prosecution. In the context of the Tribunals, which

---

[1] See, however, Rule 28(A) of the Rules of Procedure and Evidence (ICTY) which allows the Bureau of the ICTY to refuse to confirm an indictment where it considers that the individual concerned is not senior enough.

were established in intensely political and divisive circumstances and which continue to evoke strong and divided reactions, it is regrettable, but perhaps inevitable, that prosecutorial choices have apparently been guided not solely by objective choices made according to the available evidence, but also by considerations of what public messages particular types of charges will convey. Charging a head of state or a particular political leader with murder as a war crime sends a very different message than does the addition of a charge of genocide.

Once the Prosecution has decided what charges to bring against an accused, it is permitted, in principle, to charge him or her cumulatively with various criminal offences in light of the fact that, prior to the presentation of the evidence at trial, it is not always possible to determine with any certainty which of the charges brought against an accused will be proven.[2] It appears, however, that the Prosecution established early on an unfortunate practice of simply charging all possible crimes (and forms of liability for them), without any attempt to ascertain the most appropriate ones based on the evidence.[3] A more recent tendency has been to bring very extensive series of charges against an accused person, apparently with a view to a possible plea agreement where certain charges (generally the most serious among them) would be withdrawn in exchange for a guilty plea to the lesser charges.[4] Such practice, and the appearance that it creates, has been rightfully criticized by Trial Chamber I of the ICTY in two cases where the Prosecution apparently used genocide charges as a bargaining chip to obtain a plea agreement in exchange for the withdrawal of those charges.[5] It would indeed be wrong to suggest that crimes against humanity could somehow replace the stigmatizing effect of genocide and that genocide charges should be dropped in order to expedite the proceedings.[6] In the mind of the lay person, or even in the minds of lawyers, genocide remains the ultimate crime which alone can express the true gravity of a particular kind of criminal conduct. A Judge of the ICTY Appeals Chamber in the *Jelišić* case acknowledged that much when she argued convincingly that, where genocide charges have been brought together and charged

---

[2] *Čelebići* Appeal Judgment, par 400. According to the Appeals Chamber, the Trial Chamber which will hear the case at trial is better placed, after the parties' presentation of the evidence, to evaluate which of the charges may be retained, based upon the sufficiency of the evidence (ibid.). See also for ICTR, *Musema* Appeal Judgment, pars 346–370; *Nahimana* Trial Judgment, par 1089. See also *Čelebići* Appeal Judgment, Separate and Dissenting Opinion of Judge David Hunt and Judge Mohamed Bennouna, par 12.

[3] In some instances, the Prosecution has charged an accused pursuant to Article 7(1) generally, that is, without specifying the particular form of participation which was relevant to the charges against that accused. Such pleadings are likely to cause serious ambiguities (see *Aleksovski* Appeal Judgment, par 171; *Čelebići* Appeal Judgment, par 351) and might allow the Prosecution to remodel its case in light of the evidence that comes through during trial. See, generally, *Prosecutor v. Brdjanin and Talić*, IT-99-36-PT, Decision on Objections by Momir Talić to the Form of the Amended Indictment, 20 February 2001, par 10.

[4] See *Momir Nikolić* Sentencing Judgment, pars 63 and 65: 'Once a charge of genocide has been confirmed, it should not simply be bargained away.'

[5] See, in particular, ibid., pars 61–65.   [6] Ibid., par 65.

cumulatively with crimes against humanity charges, there still remains a public interest to make findings upon the former set of charges even where the accused has already been found guilty of the latter charges.[7] Likewise, where the Prosecution has brought genocide charges against a particular accused and has therefore established a *prima facie* case for it, there is a fundamental public interest that those charges be proved if they can.

Distinguishing between these three categories of offences is not, however, purely a matter of historiography nor solely one of prosecutorial policy. Where an accused person has been charged with several offences in relation to the same set of facts, the Court will eventually have to determine whether cumulative conviction is possible in relation to the various offences charged against the accused. The test for cumulative conviction and the extent to which cumulative conviction is permissible was established by the Appeals Chamber in the *Čelebići* case and later adopted by the ICTR:[8]

412. [. . .] [R]easons of fairness to the accused and the consideration that only distinct crimes may justify multiple convictions, lead to the conclusion that multiple criminal convictions entered under different statutory provisions but based on the same conduct are permissible only if each statutory provision involved has a materially distinct element not contained in the other. An element is materially distinct from another if it requires proof of a fact not required by the other.

413. Where this test is not met, the Chamber must decide in relation to which offence it will enter a conviction. This should be done on the basis of the principle that the conviction under the more specific provision should be upheld. Thus, if a set of facts is regulated by two provisions, one of which contains an additional materially distinct element, then a conviction should be entered only under that provision.[9]

Under this test, the Court must first determine whether an accused is charged with more than one offence based upon the same conduct. Then, if the evidence establishes both offences, but based on the same underlying conduct, the Trial Chamber must determine whether *each* relevant statutory provision has a materially distinct element not contained in the other. This involves comparing the legal elements of the relevant statutory provisions; the specific facts of the case play no role in this

---

[7] *Jelišić* Appeal Judgment, Partial Dissenting Opinion of Judge Wald, par 13: 'the view that there is no additional public interest in determining a genocide charge simply because the underlying killings have already been dealt with as crimes against humanity and violations of the laws or customs of war may be problematic in the development of international criminal law.' In that case, the majority of the Appeals Chamber found that the Trial Chamber had erred when acquitting the accused of genocide. Instead of ordering a retrial upon this charge, however, and in view *inter alia* of the fact that he had already been convicted and sentenced to forty-years' imprisonment for crimes against humanity, the majority of the Appeals Chamber, Judge Wald dissenting, declined to reverse the acquittal on genocide and declined to remit the case for further proceedings (see *Jelišić* Appeal Judgment, pars 73–77). See also *Momir Nikolić* Sentencing Judgment, par 65; *Krstić* Appeal Judgment, pars 36 and 275.

[8] The *Čelebići* test for cumulative convictions was adopted by the ICTR (see *Musema* Appeal Judgment, pars 346–370).

[9] See ibid., Separate and Dissenting Opinion of Judges Hunt and Bennouna, Part XVI, pars 32–38.

determination.[10] Finally, if the relevant provisions do not each have a materially distinct element, the Trial Chamber should select the more specific provision.

This test is applied first to the *chapeau* elements of the crimes charged, and then, where several offences have been charged infra-article, the test is also applied to the *actus reus* and *mens rea* of the underlying offences charged within that one statutory provision. As will be seen below, the test adopted by the majority of the Appeals Chamber is somewhat unsatisfactory, and has incurred judicial criticism as such.[11] This is principally because the test permits cumulative convictions based on the same conduct to be entered under potentially many different headings in relation to all but one combination of articles.[12] For instance, an individual who is charged pursuant to Articles 3, 4, and 5 of the ICTY Statute for a rape could be charged and convicted cumulatively with, for instance, rape as a war crime, rape as a crime against humanity, and causing serious bodily and mental harm as a genocidal offence, the first two differing only in relation to the different contextual elements of the offences as required by the *chapeau*, and not by reference to any act or intention of the accused. In addition, there is potential for the same act of rape, depending on the specific facts, also to be characterized as torture as a war crime, torture as a crime against humanity, an outrage upon personal dignity (a crime against humanity), and persecution.

As noted by the majority of the Appeals Chamber itself, 'reasons of fairness to the accused' would dictate that only genuinely distinct crimes may justify multiple convictions and that cumulative convictions for offences which are not genuinely distinct should not be permitted in respect of the same conduct.[13] In their dissent, Judge Hunt and Judge Bennouna pointed out that accumulating convictions is not innocuous and may in fact truly prejudice the convicted person.[14] In view of the

[10] *Kunarac* Trial Judgment, par 550.

[11] See *Čelebići* Appeal Judgment, Separate and Dissenting Opinion of Judge David Hunt and Judge Mohamed Bennouna.

[12] The only exception being the case where charges were brought cumulatively based on Article 2 and Article 3 of the ICTY Statute in relation to the same conduct, where a conviction based on Article 2 would exclude cumulative conviction based on Article 3.

[13] *Čelebići* Appeal Judgment, par 412; Separate and Dissenting Opinion of Judge David Hunt and Judge Mohamed Bennouna, par 22.

[14] See ibid., par 23: 'Prejudice to the rights of the accused – or the very real risk of such prejudice – lies in allowing cumulative convictions. The Prosecution suggests that cumulative convictions "do not cause any substantive injustice to the accused" as long as the fact that such convictions are based on the same conduct is taken into account in sentencing. This does not take into account the punishment and social stigmatisation inherent in being *convicted* of a crime. Furthermore, the number of crimes for which a person is convicted may have some impact on the sentence ultimately to be served when national laws as to, for example, early release of various kinds are applied. The risk may therefore be that, under the law of the State enforcing the sentence, the eligibility of a convicted person for early release will depend not only on the sentence passed but also on the number and/or nature of convictions. This may prejudice the convicted person notwithstanding that, under the Statute, the Rules and the various enforcement treaties, the President has the final say in determining whether a convicted person should be released early. By the time national laws trigger early release proceedings, and a State request for early release reaches the President, the prejudice may already have been incurred. Finally, cumulative convictions may also expose the convicted person to the risk of increased sentences and/or to the application of "habitual offender" laws in case of subsequent convictions in another jurisdiction.'

fact that the fundamental consideration arising from charges relating to the same conduct is that an accused should not be penalized more than once for the same *conduct*, it would have been preferable, as suggested by Judge Hunt and Judge Bennouna, to exclude from consideration legal prerequisites or contextual elements contained in the definition of crimes which do not have a bearing on the accused's actual conduct (such as the requirement of an 'international' conflict or 'protected' status of the victims in relation to charges under Article 2 of the ICTY Statute or the limitation of offences charged under common Article 3 to 'persons taking no active part in hostilities' under Article 3 of the ICTY Statute), and to focus instead on 'the substantive elements which relate to an accused's conduct, including his mental state'.[15] Only if those elements are different are the crimes *genuinely* different in the relevant sense. As noted by the two dissenting judges, '[t]he fundamental function of the criminal law is to punish the accused for his criminal conduct, and only for his criminal conduct'.[16] Taking into account definitional elements which have no bearing on the nature or gravity of the criminal conduct that must be sanctioned, as the majority of the Appeals Chamber has done, could be gravely unfair to the accused as he or she may ultimately be punished for more (by reason of the cumulation of convictions) than he or she actually did. The purely legal (and unnecessary) artifice relied upon by the Appeals Chamber to allow (and exclude) cumulative convictions also makes it extremely difficult to determine the true nature of the crimes of the accused from the convictions which have been entered.

It is clear, however, that, where the accused has been convicted cumulatively in relation to the same conduct, and because the fact of cumulative conviction may in itself constitute a form of punishment,[17] the Court must take the fact of cumulative conviction into account so that the final or aggregate sentence reflects the totality of the criminal conduct and overall culpability of the offender so that he is not prejudiced by reason of the multiple convictions entered against him on the basis of the same facts.[18]

---

[15] Ibid., pars 26 et seq.   [16] Ibid., par 27.

[17] The Appeals Chamber has accepted that cumulative convictions, in and of themselves, involve an additional punishment – not only by reason of the social stigmatization inherent in being convicted of that additional crime, but also because of the risk that, under the law of the State enforcing the sentence, the eligibility of a convicted person for early release will depend to some extent upon the number or nature of the convictions entered. See, *inter alia, Mucić* Appeal Judgment, par 25.

[18] *Kunarac* Trial Judgment, par 551 ('The prejudice that an offender will or may suffer because of cumulative convictions based on the same conduct has to be taken into account when imposing the sentence'); *Čelebići* Appeal Judgment, pars 429–430; *Vasiljević* Trial Judgment, par 266.

24

War Crimes and Crimes against Humanity

At Nuremberg, where crimes against humanity were first prosecuted, it was necessary to prove a connection between the conduct that was said to constitute a crime against humanity and another crime within the Tribunal's jurisdiction, namely war crimes or crimes against peace.[1] The main justification for this was the concern expressed by many of those involved in the setting up of the International Military Tribunal that crimes against humanity might in fact constitute a new category of crimes which did not exist under international law at the relevant time. By linking crimes against humanity to other categories of crimes, which were considered to be better established under international law, it was thought that accusations of *ex post facto* law in relation to crimes against humanity would be severely weakened, if not completely laid to rest. In practice, this nexus requirement blurred the distinction between war crimes and crimes against humanity, and the two categories of crimes were often indiscriminately charged together.[2] Neither the International Military Tribunal in Nuremberg, nor the domestic Courts subsequently operating under Control Council Law No. 10 attempted a conceptual distinction between these two categories of crimes and therefore provided precious little guidance as to which acts should be labelled war crimes and which should constitute crimes against humanity and which ones might fall into both categories. The concept of crimes against humanity only began a life of its own when the nexus requirement disappeared.[3] Today, four elements in the

---

[1] See Chapter 1.

[2] The United Nations War Crimes Commission essentially described crimes against humanity in Nuremberg as *subsidiary* crimes. See *United Nations War Crimes Commission*, pp 201–02.

[3] See M. Lippman, 'Crimes against Humanity', 17 Boston College Third World Law Journal (*BCTWLJ*) 2 (1997); See also B. Jia, 'The Differing Concepts of War Crimes and Crimes against

respective definitions of war crimes and crimes against humanity distinguish the two categories of crimes.

24.1   Existence of an armed conflict and the nexus between the acts of the accused and the armed conflict

War crimes may only be committed during an armed conflict; crimes against humanity, on the other hand, can be committed both in times of war and of peace. As noted above, the specific requirement in the ICTY Statute that crimes against humanity be committed 'in armed conflict' is not an element of that crime in customary law, but merely a jurisdictional requirement specific to the ICTY.[4]

Also, whereas a war crime requires a material link (a 'nexus') between the criminal act of the accused and the armed conflict, it is not the case for a crime against humanity.[5] The ICTY's jurisdictional limitation pursuant to which crimes against humanity must be committed in armed conflict does not require any substantive nexus between the armed conflict and the act of the accused, but merely a temporal and geographical coincidence.[6] And what is more, such a jurisdictional requirement exists under neither customary international law, nor in the ICTR Statute. Accordingly, whilst a crime which is completely unrelated to the armed conflict could constitute a crime against humanity, it could not amount to a war crime.

24.2   Persons protected under each regime

Originally, war crimes could only be committed against enemy nationals, neutrals, or nationals of an occupied territory – not against a state's own nationals. For crimes against humanity, however, there has never been such a restriction. A crime against humanity may be committed against nationals of any state, including that state's own nationals, if the state takes part in the attack.[7] The fact that the Allied

---

Humanity in International Criminal Law' in G. Goodwin-Gill *et al.* (eds.), *The Reality of International Law: Essays in Honour of Ian Brownlie* (Oxford: Clarendon Press, 1999), p 243.

[4] See Chapter 1.

[5] In order to amount to a war crime, the acts of the accused need to be 'closely related' to the armed conflict. In practice, this means that the acts must either be made possible by the armed conflict, or committed as part of or in pursuance of this very armed conflict. *Kunarac* Trial Judgment, par 568. See also *Tadić* Jurisdiction Decision, par 70; *Blaškić* Trial Judgment, pars 63–65; *Čelebići* Trial Judgment, pars 182–85, 193–95. See also above, sub-section 6.2.2   [6] See *Tadić* Appeal Judgment, par 205.

[7] The *Law Reports of the Trials of War Criminals* further illustrates this traditional distinction: '[T]he possible victims of crimes against humanity form a wider group than the possible victims of war crimes. The latter category comprises broadly speaking the nationals of armed forces of belligerent countries or inhabitants of territories occupied after conquest (other than enemy nationals) against whom offences are committed by enemy nationals as long as peace has not been declared. Crimes against humanity on the other hand could have included also offences committed by German nationals against other German nationals or any stateless person, and apparently also against nationals of Hungary and Rumania.' See *United Nations War Crimes Commission*, p 135.

Powers intended to punish the crimes of Nazi Germany against its own nationals is probably the main reason why it was decided to include crimes against humanity alongside traditional war crimes in the indictments against the Nazi leadership.

Historically, the requirement that the perpetrator of a war crime and his victims be of different nationalities quietly receded with the development of the laws of war applicable to internal armed conflicts, and the recognition of individual criminal responsibility for atrocities committed in the context of an internal armed conflict.[8] The *Tadić* Appeals Chamber probably gave this requirement the *coup de grâce* when interpreting the prerequisite for protection under the grave breaches regime of Geneva Conventions that the victims must find themselves 'in the hands of a Party to the conflict or Occupying Power *of which they are not nationals*'[9] (emphasis added). The Appeals Chamber said that formal bonds – a passport, for example – matter less than actual allegiance and ethnicity, which may therefore become determinative of 'nationality' for the purpose of this regime.[10] Thus, while Bosnian Muslims and Bosnian Serbs formally share the same nationality (Bosnian), they may be considered as being of different nationalities for the purpose of the grave breaches regime of the Geneva Conventions, and were so considered by the ICTY in various cases.[11]

Additionally, whereas crimes against humanity may only be committed against *civilians*,[12] most war crimes may be committed against both civilians and enemy combatants.[13]

24.3   Widespread or systematic attack upon a civilian population

A crime against humanity must be committed as part of a 'widespread or systematic attack upon a civilian population'. There is no such requirement for a war crime. An isolated act could therefore qualify as a war crime, but not as a crime against humanity.[14]

24.4   Underlying offences

A war crime consists of a particular violation of the laws or customs of war which entail individual criminal responsibility. By convention or by custom, the laws of

---

[8] According to the *Tadić* Appeals Chamber, there is no requirement under Article 3 of the ICTY Statute that victims and perpetrators be of different nationality. See also *Tadić* Jurisdiction Decision, pars 94, 103–105, 116, and 131–137.   [9] *Tadić* Appeal Judgment, pars 164–166.

[10] See ibid., par 166.

[11] See, e.g. *Čelebići* Trial Judgment, par 262; *Čelebići* Appeal Judgment, pars 95–98; *Tadić* Appeal Judgment, pars 167–169 and *Aleksovski* Appeal Judgment, pars 137–152.

[12] See above sub-section 11.3

[13] For example, the use of unlawful weapons against combatants could under certain circumstances give rise to a war crime.

[14] See above, Chapter 6, Role and function of the nexus requirement and Chapter 11, 'Any civilian population' as the primary object of the attack.

war provide a relatively large number of prohibitions which, if breached, could entail individual criminal responsibility.[15] The range of underlying offences which could constitute crimes against humanity on the other hand appears more limited in scope than those underlying offences which could amount to war crimes, as the underlying offences for crimes against humanity share a relatively high level of gravity (not always met by certain categories of war crimes) and protect a more limited set of fundamental interests than may be the case under the laws of war.[16] Nearly all of the underlying offences which could qualify as crimes against humanity would also amount, all other conditions being met, to war crimes,[17] but the converse is not necessarily true. Yet this difference does not suggest that crimes against humanity are more serious than war crimes. In fact, all other conditions being equal, the two crimes have been said by the Tribunals to be *a priori* of equal gravity.[18] Thus, a rape or a murder as a crime against humanity is no more, and no less serious than the same rape or murder if charged as a war crime.[19]

Where an accused has been charged cumulatively for crimes against humanity and war crimes (whether it is pursuant to Article 2 and/or Article 3 in the case of the ICTY Statute) in relation to the same acts, the Trial Chamber will have to decide upon the possibility of a cumulative conviction between the various statutory provisions. As noted above, under the test developed by the majority of the Appeals Chamber, a Trial Chamber must first determine whether an accused is charged with more than one offence based upon the same conduct. Then, if there is evidence to establish both offences, and the underlying conduct is the same, the

---

[15] Not all breaches of the laws or customs of war amount to war crimes, and not all breaches of the laws or customs of war entail individual criminal responsibility. Some of those breaches, for instance, are simply not serious enough to rise to the level of an international offence. They may entail disciplinary measures, or possibly criminal responsibility before a national court that may know of a lower gravity threshold, but a 'war crime' entailing individual criminal responsibility before the Tribunals must necessarily pass the 'seriousness' test of Article 1 of the Statute and satisfy the *ejusdem generis* principle implicit in Article 3 of the ICTY Statute and Article 4 of the ICTR Statute.

[16] See Part I. above, sub-section 12.

[17] It could be argued, however, that acts of 'persecution' can only be committed as a crime against humanity, but not as a war crime. See J. Rikhof, 'Access, Asylum and Atrocities, An Unholy Alliance', 19 *Refuge* 4 (February 2001), pp 100, 105. It should be noted, however, that in practice the *actus reus* of many violations of the laws or customs of war could constitute the *actus reus* of persecution and may constitute a crime against humanity to the extent that they satisfy the other general requirements of this crime – in particular, the special intent attached to persecution.

[18] See, e.g. *Tadić* Sentencing Judgment on Appeal, par 69; *Furundžija* Appeal Judgment, pars 243 and 247; *Vasiljević* Trial Judgment, par 275 and reference cited therein. See, however, *Fédération Nationale des Déportés et Internés Résistants et Patriotes and Others v. Barbie*, 20 December 1985, reprinted in 78 *ILR* 125, 143 (Submissions by the Advocate-General).

[19] See ibid. See also *Erdemović* Trial Sentencing Judgment, pars 27–28. On the difficulty of explaining the difference between the nature of a war crime and a crime against humanity to an accused person, in particular with respect to their gravity, see *Prosecutor v. Kunarac*, IT-96-23 and IT-96-23/1 Transcript, pp 35–46 (13 March 1998). The similarities in nature and gravity between war crimes and crimes against humanity have prompted some authors to suggest that the two categories of crimes might come to fuse at some point. See generally W. J. Fenrick, 'Should Crimes Against Humanity Replace War Crimes?', 37 *CJTL* 767 (1999).

Trial Chamber must determine whether *each* relevant statutory provision has a materially distinct element not contained in the other. This involves comparing the *chapeau* elements of the relevant statutory provisions; the specific facts of the case play no role in this determination.[20] Since war crimes and crimes against humanity each have at least one distinctive definitional element (in fact, they may have four of them – see above), cumulative conviction is *always* possible between these two crimes.[21] However, as noted previously, the sentence imposed should reflect the totality of the criminal conduct and the culpability of the offender, and should take into account the prejudice that an offender may suffer because of cumulative convictions based on the same conduct.[22]

---

[20] *Kunarac* Trial Judgment, par 550. See also the dissent of Judge Hunt and Judge Bennouna on that point (*Čelebići* Appeal Judgment, Separate and Dissenting Opinion of Judge David Hunt and Judge Mohamed Bennouna).

[21] *Vasiljević* Appeal Judgment, par 145; *Jelisić* Appeal Judgment, para. 82. See also *Kunarac* Appeal Judgment, par 176 ; *Kunarac* Trial Judgment, pars 687, 704, and 782. See also *Kordić and Čerkez* Trial Judgment, pars 834 and 836. The same conclusion would most likely be reached if both Article 2 (*Grave breaches of Geneva Conventions IV*) and Article 5 of the ICTY Statute were charged cumulatively.

[22] See *Čelebići* Appeal Judgment, pars 429–30; *Kunarac* Trial Judgment, par 551.

25

War Crimes and Genocide

25.1   Common features

Both genocide and war crimes are regarded as serious violations of international humanitarian law. Just as with genocide, war crimes may, in principle, be committed by and against civilians and military alike.[1] Also, neither of these two categories of crimes limit responsibility to high-level officials (or, for that matter, to low-level perpetrators or any other particular categories of individuals).

The law of genocide, on the one hand, and the laws of war, on the other, have very different origins however. Whereas genocide was essentially born out of the events of the Second World War and has little to do with the regulation of warfare, the laws or customs of war go back to ancient times and were first and foremost a code of military conduct between fighting parties.[2] Over the years, however, the laws of war have grown away from their essentially military preoccupations to become an increasingly humanitarian-oriented body of rules and have therefore come to criminalize certain conduct which may also be regarded as genocidal.[3]

25.2   Different protected interests

But both categories of crime cover essentially different protected interests. While genocide protects a limited set of interests (primarily, defined protected groups

---

[1] Some war crimes are such, however, that it is difficult to imagine that civilians in the narrow sense of the term could commit them (e.g. attacks on undefended towns and villages or wanton destruction of cities).

[2] See, generally, L. C. Green, *The Contemporary Law of Armed Conflict* (Manchester/New York: Manchester University Press, 2000).   [3] Ibid.

and, through them, the life and the physical and mental integrity of the groups' members), war crimes safeguard a much broader set of values, interests, and objects ranging from the protection of cultural properties to the protection of private and public properties from plundering, and criminalizing for instance certain means and methods of warfare and the use of certain weapons. As a result, although most genocidal acts would also constitute war crimes, the reverse is not necessarily true. Furthermore, the laws of war do not protect groups as such, but only their constituent entities, individuals, be they civilians or combatants (or indeed certain objects).

25.3　Distinct material elements

Both categories of crimes, war crimes and genocide, contain a number of elements which are not required by the other, the most obvious being that while war crimes, of their nature, may only be committed in times of war, genocide may be committed during war or peace.[4] Although it is not a legal ingredient of the offence of genocide, an armed conflict generally provides the opportunity or 'cover' to commit crimes on a wide scale. This is demonstrated by several past examples of genocidal actions – during the First World War in Turkey against the Armenians, during the Second World War against the Jews and Gypsies, among others, and in Rwanda more recently.[5] It is important in that context to note that even mass deaths resulting from military operations will not necessarily constitute genocide.[6] Equally, as mentioned above in relation to the finding of the International Military Tribunal in Nuremberg, a failure to distinguish a military operation in the course of which war crimes might have been committed and a genocidal campaign occurring in the course of that operation could lead to a distorted understanding of these criminal events. The facts of a particular situation may be such that both genocidal crimes

---

[4] See, *inter alia*, the Secretary-General Report (ICTY) which provides that 'genocide, whether committed in time of peace or in time of war, is a crime under international law' reflecting Article I of the Genocide Convention which provides that 'genocide, whether committed in time of peace or in time of war, is a crime under international law'. As already pointed out above, the Tribunal has repeatedly pointed out, however, that the laws of war 'apply and continue to apply to the whole of the territory under the control of one of the parties to the conflict, whether or not actual combat takes place there, until a general conclusion of peace or a peaceful settlement is achieved' (Secretary-General Report (ICTY), par 45). See also *Tadić* Jurisdiction Decision, par 70; *Kunarac* Appeal Judgment, par 57.

[5] See *Akayesu* Trial Judgment: 'genocide did indeed take place against the Tutsi group, alongside the conflict. The execution of this genocide was probably facilitated by the conflict, in the sense that the fighting against the RPF forces was used as a pretext for the propaganda inciting genocide against the Tutsi. [. . .] 128. [. . .] although the genocide against the Tutsi occurred concomitantly with the above-mentioned conflict, it was, evidently, fundamentally different from the conflict' (pars 127 and 128).

[6] *Hostages* case, pp 1230, 1309: 'War at its best is a business but under no circumstances can cold-blooded mass murder such as these two cases establish be considered as related remotely even to the exigencies of war.'

and war crimes might have been committed in the course of a particular conflict and it will be appropriate to recognize these as distinct criminal events.[7]

Secondly, whereas genocidal offences require a special or genocidal *mens rea* to destroy a protected group in whole or in part as such, war crimes do not contain such a requirement. The perpetrator of a war crime must simply intend that the underlying offence (say, murder) be committed or, if he is an accomplice to that crime, know of the relevant intention of the principal.[8]

Thirdly, while a genocidal offence may only be committed against certain categories of victim (i.e. members of a protected group or an individual closely associated to one such group), war crimes may for the most part be committed against anyone, regardless of any membership in any given group.[9] Some war crimes do not even need to be committed against persons. Some of them may be directed at buildings of cultural significance, undefended towns, or civilian objects, for instance.[10] The prohibition against genocide by contrast only protects groups (and through them their members), not things or objects.

Fourthly, and more subtly, not all offences that are sufficiently serious to qualify as a war crime would be serious enough to amount to a genocidal offence. In terms of seriousness, war crimes cover a much broader spectrum of offences than genocide, ranging from the relatively minor (say, plunder of public property) to the very serious (say, murder or employment of poisonous weapons). As pointed out above, by reason of the fact that genocide protects only the most fundamental human values (the existence of a human group and indirectly the life and physical or mental integrity of their members), every genocidal action will *per se* be very serious. On the other hand, as is obvious when comparing the list of underlying offences provided in the Statutes in relation to each category of crimes, war

---

[7] As with crimes against humanity, the laws of war may provide the court with a useful standard against which to judge actions and conduct committed in the context of a conflict and to decide upon their criminal character. 'To the extent that the alleged crimes against humanity were committed in the course of an armed conflict, the laws of war provide a benchmark against which the Chamber may assess the nature of the attack [against a civilian population] and the legality of the acts committed in its midst' (*Kunarac* Appeal Judgment, par 91).

[8] It is unclear, however, whether, pursuant to the definition of war crimes given by the *ad hoc* Tribunals, the perpetrator must know of the existence of an armed conflict and that he must know that he acts 'in furtherance of, or at least under the guise of, the situation created by the fighting' or whether his acts merely need to be objectively part of the armed conflict. Generally, it will be hard for an accused to deny knowledge of the existence of an armed conflict (none has done so so far at the *ad hoc* Tribunals), but an accused could reasonably claim to have been unaware that his acts were carried out in pursuance or under the guise of the armed conflict, if indeed there is a requirement that it be so in the definition of war crimes. See, for instance, *Kunarac* Trial Judgment, pars 567 et seq.

[9] Certain war crimes may only be committed against certain categories of individuals, such as civilians (e.g., indiscriminate attacks against civilians or civilian objects) or against combatants (e.g. killing of combatants who are *hors de combat* or giving no quarter to surrendering enemy soldiers).

[10] Article 3 of the ICTY Statute provides, *inter alia*, for the protection cities, towns, and villages against wanton destruction (Article 3(b)), undefended towns, villages, dwellings, and buildings against attack or bombardment (Article 3(c)) and institutions dedicated to religion, charity and education, the arts and sciences, historic monuments and works of art and science, against seizure, destruction, or wilful damage (Article 3(d)).

crimes protect a much broader sets of interests, some of which may not be as fundamental. This is the result, in part, of the fact that, as noted above, crimes that may qualify as genocide must at least have the potential to contribute to the destruction of the targeted group. Thus, while certain crimes such as plunder or the taking of hostages may be serious enough to qualify as war crimes, they will not necessarily be serious enough to be regarded as genocidal acts.[11]

Under the prevailing test of cumulative convictions developed by a majority of the Appeals Chamber,[12] an individual who has been charged with both war crimes and genocide for the same criminal conduct could be convicted for both categories of crimes as both of them have elements which the other one does not possess (in particular, the existence of an armed conflict and nexus therewith in relation to war crimes and a genocidal state of mind in relation to genocide).[13]

[11] Such act could be evidentially relevant to a finding that genocide has (or has not) been committed, but they could not constitute discrete underlying – genocidal – offences.

[12] *Čelebići* Appeal Judgment, pars 429–430. A different result would ensue from the dissenting Opinion (*Čelebići* Appeal Judgement, Separate and Dissenting Opinion of Judge David Hunt and Judge Mohamed Bennouna, pars 46 et seq.).

[13] See, e.g. *Krstić* Trial Judgment, par 681, in relation to an accused who was charged with 'murder' both as genocide and as a violation of the laws or customs of war: 'The relationship between genocide and murder as a war crime can be characterised as follows. The offence of genocide requires a special intent to destroy a national, ethnical, racial or religious group (or part thereof). Murder as a war crime requires a close nexus between the acts of the accused and an armed conflict, which is not required by genocide. The test for separate convictions is satisfied. Accordingly, convictions must be entered on both charges in respect of the same criminal conduct because genocide and murder under Article 3 each contain an additional element not required by the other.'

26

Genocide and Crimes against Humanity

26.1 Common features and distinctions

It is often suggested that genocide is the ultimate crime against humanity.[1] Whilst the historical and sociological treatment of these two crimes may support such an assertion, particularly because the fact patterns generally supporting these two crimes tend to be quite similar,[2] they remain legally distinct. Qualifying genocide as a species of crime against humanity is neither helpful nor completely accurate from the legal standpoint. It is not helpful because it does not tell us anything about the specificities of either crime, and it is inaccurate from a legal point of view in that the definition of each crime is in fact markedly distinct.[3]

First, crimes against humanity and genocide have a different *mens rea*. The perpetrator of a genocidal offence must intend to destroy all or part of a protected

---

[1] Several international instruments and court decisions have described genocide as a form of crime against humanity. See, e.g. Convention on the Non-Applicability of Statutory Limitation to War Crimes and Crimes Against Humanity, General Assembly Resolution 2391, UN GAOR, 23rd Sess., Agenda Item 64, UN Doc. A/7342 (1968) ('Statutory Non-Applicability Convention'); *Jelišić* Trial Judgment, par 68; *Kayishema and Ruzindana* Trial Judgment, pars 577–578; *Trial of Eichmann*, Israel, district Court of Jerusalem, Judgment of 12 December 1961, English translation in 36 *ILR*, 5–276 ('*Eichmann* District Court case'). Recently, a Trial Chamber of the ICTY held that genocide is 'a species of crimes against humanity' (*Stakić* Rule 98bis Decision, par 26).

[2] In several cases before the ICTY and the ICTR, the same set of facts form the basis of genocide and crimes against humanity charges. See *Prosecutor v. Jelišić*, IT-95-10-I, Initial Indictment, 21 July 1995; *Prosecutor v. Brdjanin and Talić*, IT-99-36-PT, Third Amended Indictment, 16 July 2001; *Prosecutor v. Krstić*, IT-98-33-I, Initial Indictment, 2 November 1998.

[3] See Mettraux, *Crimes against Humanity*, pp 302–306.

group,[4] whilst the perpetrator of a crime against humanity need only be aware of an attack against a civilian population and of his part therein.[5]

Secondly, the range of underlying offences which may qualify as genocidal is more restricted in scope than those that may qualify as crimes against humanity. It has been argued above that all underlying genocidal offences must at least have the potential, even if remotely, to contribute to the complete or partial destruction of the victim's group.[6] Crimes against humanity do not require such a potential, nor do they need to affect the group of which the victim is a member, which explains that crimes of somewhat lesser gravity such as imprisonment or deportation may constitute crimes against humanity, but not in principle genocide. To that extent and as is apparent from a simple comparison of the crimes listed in each article of the Statutes, a wider range of underlying offences may qualify as crimes against humanity than as genocide.

---

[4] *Jelišić* Appeal Judgment, pars 45–46, holding that genocidal intent should be understood as 'the intent to accomplish certain specified types of destruction'; in other words, by committing one of the acts enumerated in Article 4 of the ICTY Statute, the perpetrator seeks to achieve the destruction, 'in whole or in part, of a national, ethnical, racial or religious group, as such'.

[5] The *mens rea* for genocide supposes that the perpetrator intended 'to destroy, in whole or in part, a national, ethnical, racial, or religious group, as such' (*Akayesu* Trial Judgment, par 521). A criminal against humanity, on the other hand, merely needs to know that there is an attack against a civilian population and that his acts are part of that attack, but he does not need to intend the destruction of the group (or population) of which his victim is a member. See above, sub-section 11.5. The distinction thins out with respect to 'persecution', a crime against humanity, with genocidal connotations. The Trial Chamber in *Kupreškić* held that persecution – one type of crime against humanity – had a lot in common with genocide: '[I]t can be said that, from the viewpoint of *mens rea*, genocide is an extreme and most inhuman form of persecution. To put it differently, when persecution escalates to the extreme form of willful and deliberate acts designed to destroy a group or part of a group, it can be held that such persecution amounts to genocide' (*Kupreškić* Trial Judgment, par 636). For the crime of genocide, the criminal intent is to destroy the group or its members; for the crime of persecution, the criminal intent is instead to discriminate against members of a particular group by grossly and systematically violating their fundamental rights. See *Tadić* Appeal Judgment, par 305; *Jelišić* Trial Judgment, pars 67–68.

[6] This is evident already from the type of acts listed in the Genocide Convention – as well as in the Tribunals' Statutes – as criminal offences which could qualify as genocide. The imposition of 'measures intended to prevent births within the group,' for instance, constitute a genocidal act to the extent only that those measures are directed at the destruction of the group. In *Akayesu*, the Trial Chamber thus held that: 'In patriarchal societies, where membership of a group is determined by the identity of the father, an example of a measure intended to prevent births within a group is the case where, during rape, a woman of the said group is deliberately impregnated by a man of another group, with the intent to have her give birth to a child who will consequently not belong to its mother's group. Furthermore, the Chamber notes that measures intended to prevent births within the group may be physical, but can also be mental. For instance, rape can be a measure intended to prevent births when the person raped refuses subsequently to bear children, in the same way that members of a group can be led, through threats or trauma, not to bear children.' See *Akayesu* Trial Judgment, pars 507–508. Hence, the list of underlying offences which could form the basis of a genocide charge as opposed to a charge of crime against humanity is more limited both in kind and in gravity. See also C. Bassiouni and P. Manikas, *The Law of the International Criminal Tribunal for the Former Yugoslavia* (Irvington-on-Hudson: Transnational Publishers, 1996). Professor Schabas points out, however that the Prosecution need not demonstrate a cause and effect relationship between the acts of violence and the destruction of the group (Schabas, *Genocide in the Rome Statute*, p 164).

Thirdly, whilst the ICTY Statute requires that crimes against humanity must be committed in the context of an armed conflict,[7] there is no such requirement for genocide.[8] Genocide may be committed in time of peace as well as in time of war.

Fourthly, the definition of genocide unlike that of crimes against humanity does not require that the acts of the accused occur in the context of a 'widespread or systematic attack against a civilian population'.[9] An act of genocide could take place on a large scale or with significant systematicity, but it could also, theoretically at least, occur as an individual undertaking.[10] In other words, and contrary to crimes against humanity, the definition of genocide does not require that the acts of the accused take place in the context of an attack defined as a 'course of conduct involving the commission of acts of violence', let alone a widespread or systematic one.[11] And the perpetrator of a genocidal offence need not, therefore, know of any relationship between his acts and a widespread or systematic attack.[12] From an evidential point of view, however, it may be exceedingly difficult, if not impossible, to establish a genocidal mindset in the absence of a situation resembling at least an attack on a civilian population and the accused's part therein.

Fifthly, whereas a crime against humanity may only be committed against 'civilians', genocide can be committed against any member of the targeted group, whether combatants or civilians.[13] Also, whereas crimes against humanity may, in principle, be committed against any member of a civilian population regardless of his nationality, ethnicity, race, or religion, genocidal offences can only be committed against individuals who belong to specifically protected groups characterized by their national, ethnical, racial, or religious identity, or those who are otherwise intimately connected to such groups.[14] The scope of those protected under the genocide prohibition is therefore more narrowly circumscribed than under the prohibition against crimes against humanity.

One Trial Chamber suggested that the requirement contained in Article 5 of the ICTY Statute that crimes against humanity must be 'part of a widespread or systematic attack on a civilian population' is comprised within the genocide requirement that there be an intent on the part of the perpetrator 'to destroy in

---

[7] The ICTR Statute does not contain such a requirement.

[8] As noted, above, sub-section 10.1, the requirement of an armed conflict in Article 5 of the ICTY Statute is not a substantive requirement of the definition of crimes against humanity under customary international law. See also *Krstić* Trial Judgment, par 682.

[9] *Krstić* Appeal Judgment, par 223. Both genocide and crimes against humanity contain an intrinsic element of scale. See, generally, *supra* sub-paragraph 26.1. However, whereas the scale of crimes against humanity is assessed on the basis of the widespread or systematic nature of the attack, the scale of genocide is assessed on the basis of its intended effect upon the group the destruction of which is being pursued. [10] *Jelišić* Trial Judgment, pars 98 and 100.

[11] *Jelišić* Appeal Judgment, pars 45–46, 100. [12] *Krstić* Appeal Judgment, par 223.

[13] In *Krstić*, for instance, the Trial Chamber made no distinction between those victims who were civilians or those who could have been regarded as combatants.

[14] When convicting the relationship between crimes against humanity and genocide, the United Nations War Crimes Commission noted that with respect to crimes against humanity 'it is not necessary that the wronged person belong to an organised or well-defined group.' See *War Crimes Commission*, p 138.

whole or in part a specific protected group as such'.[15] There are at least five reasons which militate against the blending of these two legal requirements:[16]

(i) A protected 'group' under the genocide regime differs from a 'population' for the purpose of crimes against humanity.[17] A population may contain several protected groups, and a widespread and systematic attack upon a civilian population may have no discriminatory effect upon any particular protected group that forms part thereof.[18] The attack could, for instance, have been directed against a certain civilian population which is not distinguishable on national, ethnic, racial or religious grounds from the attacking side.

(ii) With respect to crimes against humanity, although the acts of the accused must be *part of* the attack, it is the 'attack' itself, not the acts of the accused, which must be shown to have been directed at the civilian population. In the case of genocide, *the acts of the accused themselves* must be shown to have been directed at the destruction, in whole or in part, of one of the protected groups (albeit possibly indirectly).

(iii) There is no requirement in the elements of crimes against humanity that the attack, as defined above, have the effect or purpose of destroying a population, let alone a group. The perpetrator must only act *with the knowledge that* his acts form part of a widespread or systematic attack against a civilian population. In the case of genocide, on the other hand, the prosecutor must establish that the perpetrator *intended* the complete or partial destruction of one of the protected groups.

(iv) The attack requirement for a crime against humanity relates to both the context of the acts and the perpetrator's *mens rea*; the destruction requirement for genocide on the other hand relates only to the perpetrator's *mens rea*, so that the prosecutor need not prove that any part of the group was actually destroyed. Thus, whereas a crime against humanity may not be committed in the absence of an attack upon the civilian population, an act of genocide could be committed by a single individual regardless of the context in which he committed his crimes.[19]

(v) Both the attack and the destruction requirements do indeed have the effect of excluding consideration of random or isolated acts. This common consequence does not, however, permit the logical conclusion that these

---

[15] *Krstić* Trial Judgment, par 682. See also *Musema* Appeal Judgment, par 366 adopting, without reference to the *Krstić* Trial Chamber, the opposite position.

[16] See also Mettraux, *Crimes against Humanity*, pp 305–306.

[17] *Krstić* Trial Judgment, par 682.

[18] This would be the case, for instance, when the attack discriminates on a political basis.

[19] Hence, the *Jelišić* Trial Chamber said – and the Appeals Chamber apparently accepted – that a single individual may be charged with genocide if he has the required genocidal *mens rea*. An attack upon a civilian population, let alone a widespread or systematic one, is therefore not a requirement of genocide; although individual genocidal acts usually occur in the midst of massive atrocities, they may also arise in other contexts. See *Jelišić* Trial Judgment, par 100; *Jelišić* Appeal Judgment, pars 45–46, 66, referring also to a 'one-man genocide mission'.

requirements are similar.[20] Furthermore, when it comes to cumulative conviction, the Chamber must assess whether each offence has materially different legal elements, and not what the impact of this element may entail *in practice*.[21]

Accordingly, the concept of 'widespread or systematic attack against any civilian population' and the genocidal *mens rea* may be considered completely different legal requirements.

Pursuant to the test in relation to cumulative convictions adopted by the Appeals Chamber, if crimes against humanity and genocide are charged cumulatively in relation to the same criminal conduct, conviction may be entered under both headings.[22] Because each crime has at least one distinct element (and, in fact, they have several of them as noted above), a cumulative conviction would *always* be possible where an accused has been charged with both genocide and crimes against humanity in relation to the same conduct, regardless of the underlying offence which has been charged under both headings.[23]

26.2   Genocide and persecution[24]

Persecution, a crime against humanity pursuant to Article 5(h) of the ICTY Statute and Article 3(h) of the ICTR Statute, has been described as '[t]he gross or blatant denial, on discriminatory grounds, of a fundamental right, laid out in international customary or treaty law, reaching the same level of gravity as the other acts prohibited in [Articles 5/3 of the ICTY/ICTR Statutes]'.[25] In addition to the *chapeau* elements of crimes against humanity, persecution requires proof of three additional elements:

 (i) a discriminatory act or omission;
 (ii) a discriminatory basis for that act or omission on one of the listed grounds;[26]
 (iii) the intent to cause, and the resulting infringement of, an individual's enjoyment of a basic or fundamental right.[27]

[20] If this argument were adopted, it could equally be said that the requirements for war crimes are the same as those for genocidal acts, since so many people, including those groups protected under a genocide regime, are usually killed in any armed conflict, so that it might be argued that the knowledge of participation in an armed conflict is identical to the intent to destroy, in whole or in part, a protected group. Clearly, such an argument would be inaccurate.
[21] *Čelebići* Appeal Judgment, par 412.   [22] See, e.g. *Musema* Appeal Judgment, par 366.
[23] See ibid., pars 366–367, comparing extinction as a crime against humanity and genocide.
[24] On the law of persecution, see, generally, K. Roberts, 'The Law of Persecution Before the International Criminal Tribunal for the Former Yugoslavia', 15 *Leiden Journal of International Law* 623 (2002) ('Roberts, *Persecution*'); J. de Hemptinne, 'Controverses Relatives à la Définition du Crime de Persécution', 53 *Revue Trimestrielle des Droits de l'Homme* 15 (2003); Mettraux, *Crimes against Humanity*, pp 294–298.
[25] *Kupreškić* Trial Judgment, par 621. See also *Tadić* Trial Judgment, pars 694 and 697 and *Kvočka* Trial Judgment, pars 184–205.
[26] The act must be based on political, racial, or religious grounds and the perpetrator must have intended his acts to be based on one of these grounds.
[27] *Tadić* Trial Judgment, par 715. See also *Kordić and Cerkez* Trial Judgment, pars 195–196 and 198, and *Krstić* Trial Judgment, pars 533–538.

In both persecution and genocide, the victim may be targeted, at least in part, because of his or her membership in a group.[28] And in both cases, the acts must in fact be directed against a member of that group.[29] Persecution is, it may be said, an offence of the same genus as genocide,[30] but its discriminatory *mens rea* stops short of the genocidal intent to destroy a particular group:[31]

Both persecution and genocide are crimes perpetrated against persons that belong to a particular group and who are targeted because of such belonging. In both categories what matters is the intent to discriminate: to attack persons on account of their ethnic, racial, or religious characteristics (as well as, in the case of persecution, on account of their political affiliation). While in the case of persecution the discriminatory intent can take multifarious inhumane forms and manifest itself in a plurality of actions including murder, in the case of genocide that intent must be accompanied by the intention to destroy, in whole or in part, the group to which the victims of the genocide belong. Thus, it can be said that, from the viewpoint of *mens rea*, genocide is an extreme and most inhuman form of persecution. To put it differently, when persecution escalates to the extreme form of wilful and deliberate acts designed to destroy a group or part of a group, it can be held that such persecution amounts to genocide.

It is therefore the relation of the crimes to the targeted group that first and foremost distinguishes genocide from persecution.[32] Whereas a genocidal act targets the group as such, persecution does not: it stops with the victim.[33] Persecution only relates to a group of individuals insofar as the selection of the victim must have been dictated, at least in part, by his or her membership in a particular political, racial, or religious group. But the perpetrator of an act of persecution need not be shown to have intended the destruction of the group of which the victim is a member, unlike the case where an accused is charged with genocide.[34]

---

[28] See, eg, *Blaškić* Trial Judgment, par 235: 'the perpetrator of the acts of persecution does not initially target the individual but rather membership in a specific racial, religious or political group'.
[29] See Roberts, *Persecution*, pp 628–629.　　　[30] *Kupreškić* Trial Judgment, par 636.
[31] Ibid., See also *Sikirica* Motion for Acquittal Decision, par 58 and *Jelišić* Trial Judgment, par 68.
[32] '[I]t is the mental element of the crime of genocide that distinguishes it from other crimes that encompass acts similar to those that constitute genocide. The evidence must establish that it is the group that has been targeted, and not merely specific individuals within that group. That is the significance of the phrase "as such" in the *chapeau*. Whereas it is the individuals that constitute the victims of most crimes, the ultimate victim of genocide is the group, although its destruction necessarily requires the commission of crimes against its members, that is, against individuals belonging to that group. This is what differentiates genocide from the crime against humanity of persecution' (*Sikirica* Motion for Acquittal Decision, par 89). In *Krstić*, the Trial Chamber stated the following: 'The offences of genocide and persecution both require proof of a special intent, respectively an intent to destroy a particular type of group (or part of that group) as such and an intent to discriminate against persons on political, racial or religious grounds. Clearly, genocide has a distinct, mutual element in the form of its requirement of an intent to destroy a group, altogether, in whole or in part, over and above any lesser persecutory objective' (*Krstić* Trial Judgment, par 684).
[33] Persecution does not protect the group as such, but its members in their (political, racial, or religious) differences. Whereas in the case of persecution the intent can take 'multifarious inhumane forms and manifest itself in a plurality of actions including murder, in the case of genocide that intent must be accompanied by the intention to destroy, in whole or in part, the group to which the victims of the genocide belong' (*Kupreškić* Trial Judgment, par 636). See also *Krstić* Trial Judgment, par 553.　　　[34] *Jelišić* Trial Judgment, par 79.

As an evidentiary matter, then, proof that there was a plan to persecute a particular group of individuals, even a general or widespread plan, would not necessarily permit an inference to be drawn to the effect that the perpetrator (or those with whom he may have acted) intended to destroy such a group.[35] The policy of discrimination set in place by the South African apartheid regime, for instance, was clearly intended to discriminate against a specific racial group, but there is no indication that it intended thereby to destroy it in whole, or even in part.[36]

The respective *mens rea* for each type of offence differs for yet another reason. Although both *mens rea* are discriminatory in nature, they only overlap in part. Whereas a persecutor may discriminate on 'political, racial, or religious' grounds, the perpetrator of a genocidal act must have done so on 'national, ethnical, racial, or religious' grounds. Political grounds are thus limited to persecution charges and national and ethnic grounds to genocide charges.[37]

Genocide and persecution also differ at the *actus reus* level, both in relation to the range of protected interests covered by each prohibition and in relation to the respective gravity of the relevant underlying conduct. Whereas the protection afforded by the genocidal prohibition is limited to the protection of the group as such and, through those, to the protection of the life, physical, and mental integrity of its members, persecution protects all 'elementary and inalienable rights of man'.[38] Persecution generally includes, for instance, acts that cause physical and mental harm, infringe upon individual freedom,[39] or result in the seizure or destruction of property.[40] This represents a much broader scope of protected interests than those covered by the prohibition against genocide, which, for instance, does not protect property or material objects.

Persecution also covers acts of a much greater variety in terms of their severity than genocide.[41] It has been noted that 'not every denial of human rights may constitute [persecution]',[42] and that acts of persecution must be of equal gravity or seriousness

---

[35] *Sikirica* Motion for Acquittal Decision, par 94. See also *Krstić* Trial Judgment, par 568: 'a purposeful decision was taken by the Bosnian Serb forces to target the Bosnian Muslim population in Srebrenica, by reason of their membership in the Bosnian Muslim group. It remains to determine whether this discriminatory attack sought to destroy the group, in whole or in part, within the meaning of Article 4 of the [ICTY] Statute.'

[36] See, *Kupreškić* Trial Judgment, par 636: 'Thus, it can be said that, from the viewpoint of *mens rea*, genocide is an extreme and most inhuman form of persecution. To put it differently, when persecution escalates to the extreme form of wilful and deliberate acts designed to destroy a group or part of a group, it can be held that such persecution amounts to genocide.'

[37] The suggestion made in the *Akayesu* Trial Judgment to the effect that the Genocide Convention's intention was to protect 'any stable and permanent group' is simply unsupported in law (*Akayesu* Trial Judgment, par 516). The scope of the crime of genocide was clearly circumscribed and the protected group strictly limited to national, ethnical, racial, or religious groups (see Schabas, *Genocide in the Rome Statute*, pp 130–133). [38] *Blaškić* Trial Judgment, par 220.

[39] Ibid., par 233; *Kupreškić* Trial Judgment, par 615.

[40] *Blaškić* Trial Judgment, pars 218–234; *Kordić and Cerkez* Trial Judgment, par 198.

[41] *Tadić* Trial Judgment, par 704. Due to its discriminatory nature, persecution is generally considered to be a particularly serious crime against humanity (see, e.g. *Todorović* Sentencing Judgment, par 32; *Blaškić* Trial Judgment, par 785). [42] *Kupreškić* Trial Judgment, par 618.

to the other acts enumerated in Articles 5/3 of the Statutes.[43] But the seriousness of the offences listed in Articles 5/3 varies greatly, from extermination to imprisonment or other inhumane acts. All acts listed in Article 4/2 of the Statutes, on the other hand, reach a minimum level of seriousness which is not necessarily (and often is not) met by acts of persecution even where the denial of a fundamental right is 'gross or blatant'.[44]

Although they are different *legally*, both categories of crimes are often intertwined as far as factual (and evidential) bases are concerned. *A genocide*, seen from a sociological point of view, is an evolving process, often starting with relatively minor discriminatory measures, which will increase both in scope and in seriousness with time and sometimes end in massacre. In his opening speech before the International Military Tribunal, Justice Robert Jackson had carefully described the incremental nature of the attack on the European Jewry:[45]

The persecution policy against the Jews commenced with non-violent measures, such as disfranchisement and discriminations against their religion, and the placing of impediments in the way of success in economic life. It moved rapidly to organised mass violence against them, physical isolation in ghettos, deportation, forced labour, mass starvation, and extermination. [. . .] The conspiracy or common plan to exterminate the Jew was so methodically thoroughly pursued, that despite the German defeat and Nazi prostration this Nazi aim largely succeeded. Only remnants of the European Jewish population remain in Germany, in the countries which Germany occupied, and in those which were her satellites or collaborators.

Persecution may, therefore, be a first step in a genocidal enterprise and it may serve from a prosecutorial point of view as a gap-filling criminal prohibition between other crimes against humanity which are not otherwise motivated by a persecutory agenda, and genocide, the *mens rea* of which may be difficult to prove. In practice, 'persecution' charges appear to have been favoured by the Prosecution, over and instead of genocide charges, in relation to lower-level perpetrators or those whose acts are, in the big criminal picture, of lesser magnitude or severity.[46]

---

[43] *Kupreškić* Trial Judgment, par 619.

[44] Ibid., par 621. The seriousness of persecutory acts should not, however, be considered individually or in isolation, but they should be assessed for their cumulative effect. An act which, in itself, may not appear to be particularly serious, may, because of the context in which it is committed, be particularly grave (*Kupreškić* Trial Judgment, pars 615 and 622; *Krnojelac* Trial Judgment par 434). Acts of 'denunciation' are obvious examples (see, e.g. *Entscheidungen des Obersten Gerichtshofes für die Britische Zone in Strafsachen* 19 (1949); 2 *Entscheidungen des Obersten Gerichtshofes für die Britische Zone in Strafsachen* 321–343 (1949)).

[45] *Opening Speeches of the Chief Prosecutors*, The Trial of German Major War Criminals by the International Military Tribunal Sitting at Nuremberg, Germany, 20 November 1945, pp 14 and 18.

[46] Consider, for instance, the nature of the charges brought against Dragan Nikolić, Milan Martić, Milan and Sredoje Lukić, Mitar Vasiljević, Zoran Kupreškić, Mirjan Kupreškić, Vlatko Kupreškić, Drago Josipović, Dragan Papić, Vladimir Santić, Stevan Todorović, Miroslav Kvočka, Dragoljub Prcać, Milojica Kos, Mlado Radić, and Zoran Žigić. The case against Goran Jelišić, a low-level, but particularly murderous individual, and that against Milorad Stakić, a mid-ranking regional politician, are abnormalities from a prosecutorial point of view and their prosecutions for genocide may have had a lot to do with an attempt by the Prosecution to test the law on genocide before charging more significant individuals with this crime.

As a result of the different elements required for each crime (both in respect of the distinct *chapeau* elements of genocide and crimes against humanity, and in respect of the respective definitions of genocide and persecution), and pursuant to the test for cumulative conviction laid down by the Appeals Chamber,[47] an accused could therefore be convicted for both genocide and persecution (a crime against humanity) in relation to the same conduct.[48]

26.3 Genocide and extermination

Extermination is often associated with genocide as a crime of a collective nature, in that it must be directed towards a collectivity of individuals.[49] However, contrary to genocide, the perpetrator of an act of extermination may but need not have intended to destroy the *group* or part of the *group* to which the victims belonged.[50] The Prosecution must only establish that he intended to kill a large number of individuals, or to inflict grievous bodily harm, or to inflict serious injury, in the reasonable knowledge that such act or omission was likely to cause death. And as opposed to both persecution and genocide, extermination does not require a discriminatory *mens rea*.[51]

These two categories of crimes also differ in the context in which each sort of crime must take place and in relation to the categories of people to which they respectively apply. In addition, as with all other crimes against humanity, the perpetrator's acts must have been part of a widespread or systematic attack against a civilian population,[52] and he must have known of the vast scheme of collective

---

[47] *Čelebići* Appeal Judgment, pars 412–413; *Musema* Appeal Judgment, pars 346–370. Cumulative convictions (i.e. convictions for different crimes based on the same conduct) are permissible only if each crime involved has a 'materially distinct element not contained in the other'; an element is materially distinct 'if it requires proof of a fact not required by the other'.

[48] See *Krstić* Appeal Judgment, par 229 (Appeals Chamber overturning the Trial Chamber's finding on that point).

[49] As pointed out by the Trial Chamber, most cases from the Second World War address thousands of deaths when using the term 'extermination'; in one case, a court used the expression 'extermination' when referring to the killing of 733 civilians (e.g. the *Einsatzgruppen* case). The Trial Chamber in *Vasiljević* said that it was not aware of cases which, prior to 1992, used the phrase 'extermination' to describe the killing of fewer than 733 persons. The Trial Chamber made it clear, however, that it did not suggest that a lower number of victims would disqualify that act as 'extermination' as a crime against humanity, nor does it suggest that such a threshold must necessarily be met. See *Vasiljević* Trial Judgment, par 227.

[50] Ibid. See also *Krstić* Appeal Judgment, par 222; *Musema* Appeal Judgment, par 363.

[51] *Vasiljević* Trial Judgment, par 228. The Trial Chamber in *Vasiljević* added that 'the ultimate reason or motives – political or ideological – for which the offender carried out the acts are not part of the required *mens rea* and are, therefore, legally irrelevant' (ibid., par 228). In a footnote attached to this statement, the Trial Chamber pointed out that in Nuremberg, the IMT had made reference to 'extermination', *inter alia*, in relation to mass murders committed for ideological reasons (Jews), political reasons (political opponents, communists and intelligentsia in occupied territories), economic reasons (creation of a *lebensraum*), military reasons (resistance members) (ibid., n 589).

[52] *Musema* Appeal Judgment, par 363; *Kajelijeli* Trial Judgment, par 751.

murder, and have been willing to take part therein.[53] Such a contextual requirement, it has been pointed out, does not apply to genocide. Contrary to genocide, which may be directed against civilians and military alike, extermination (as with any other crime against humanity) may be committed against civilians only.[54]

Counter-intuitively, extermination is, from a purely legal sense, more of a crime of scale than even genocide. While, as pointed out above, a conviction for genocide may occur even without the accused having killed or taken part in the killing of any one individual,[55] extermination requires that the accused contributed to the killing of a large number of individuals.[56]

Also, whilst genocide may be attempted, it appears that at least in the law of the *ad hoc* Tribunals, extermination only exists if and when a large number of individuals have in fact been killed.[57] Before that time, the killing of only a few may, for instance, amount to murder (as a crime against humanity, or, if an armed conflict takes place, a war crime), but it would be unlikely to constitute extermination. Also, there is generally a more direct link between the acts of the exterminator and the result which he intended to achieve than there may be with genocide: whereas the exterminator intends to kill many, and must, by his acts or omission cause death, the relationship between the acts of the *génocidaire* and the result sought to be attained (the destruction of the group in whole or in part) is often much more indirect and difficult to establish. How, for instance can one establish that the transfer of a number of children to another ethnic group was intended to annihilate a group in the longer term, rather than, for example, to have been carried out for medical, social, or economic reasons (even if such reasons would not in themselves be legitimate or even lawful)? This ambiguity between means and ends stems from the fact that whilst extermination is exclusively a crime of the 'murderous' genre, genocide is a more complex sort of crime, for which the route between the acts of the accused and the result intended by him is generally much more difficult to trace.

From the above, a difference may be identified as to the necessary extent of the accused's criminal conduct. Whereas an individual may be convicted for genocide even where his victims (actual or potential) are few, the exterminator must, either by reason of his position of authority or because of the *de facto* context in which he acted (for instance, if he was the governor of a concentration camp), have had control over a vast number of people whom he killed or took a sufficiently substantial part in killing or mistreating. As pointed out by the *Vasiljević* Trial

---

[53] See, e.g. the IMT Judgment, in respect of Saukel, p 114, and in respect of Fritzsche, p 126.

[54] See *Krstić* Appeal Judgment, par 226.

[55] As already pointed out, if charged with 'killing members of the group' the killing of one, or possibly two, members of such group would be sufficient to qualify as genocide.

[56] *Vasiljević* Trial Judgment, par 227.

[57] See below, sub-paragraph 20.7.

Chamber, historically, extermination charges seem to have been limited to those individuals who could decide upon the fate of many:[58]

> Those who were charged with that criminal offence did in fact exercise authority or power over many other individuals or did otherwise have the capacity to be instrumental in the killing of a large number of individuals. Those, such as executioners, who were not in such position but who had participated in the killing of one or a number of individuals were generally charged with murder or related offences whilst the charge of 'extermination' seems to have been limited to individuals who, by reason of either their position or authority, could decide upon the fate or had control over a large number of individuals.

Criminal responsibility for extermination is therefore limited to those individuals responsible for a large number of deaths, even if their part therein has been relatively remote or indirect,[59] whilst responsibility for one or a limited number of deaths would be insufficient to guarantee a conviction.[60] Such a limitation does not apply in the context of genocidal charges where a single murder could, for instance, constitute genocide, all other conditions being met.

As with persecution, and as a result of the different elements required for each crime (both in respect of the distinct *chapeau* elements of genocide and crimes against humanity, and in view of the respective definitions of genocide and extermination),

---

[58] *Vasiljević* Trial Judgment, par 222. See also IMT Judgment, in respect of Goering (p 83); Ribbentrop (pp 87–88); Kaltenbrunner (p 91); Frank (p 95); Julius Streicher (p 99). See also *Einsatzgruppen* case.

[59] The Trial Chamber noted that the definition of 'extermination' in the 'elements of crimes' which supplement the Statute of the ICC does not contain such a requirement. It noted furthermore that it was thought during the discussions of these 'elements' that such a requirement would be overburdensome for the Prosecution, and that it was therefore undesirable (see, e.g. R. Lee (ed.), *The International Criminal Court: Elements of Crimes and Rules of Procedure and Evidence* (Ardsley: Transnational Publishers, 2001), p 83). Such concern, the Trial Chamber made clear, had to remain, for the purpose of the *ad hoc* Tribunal, beyond the scope of its consideration, particularly when the adoption of a more lenient definition would be prejudicial to the accused. The International Tribunal must apply the law as it finds it, not as it would wish it to be, the Chamber concluded. The definition eventually adopted in the elements of crimes for the ICC is directly inspired by the definition of 'extermination' given in the *Kayishema and Ruzindana* Trial Judgment, where it is stated that a limited number of killings or even one single killing could qualify as extermination if it forms part of a mass killing event (*Kayishema and Ruzindana* Trial Judgment, par 147). The *Vasiljević* Trial Chamber noted that the *Kayishema and Ruzindana* Trial Chamber omitted to provide *any* state practice in support of its ruling on that point, thereby greatly weakening the value of its ruling as a precedent. Although the *Kayishema and Ruzindana* Trial Judgment went on to appeal, the definition of 'extermination' which it had adopted was not the subject of an appeal nor was it dealt with by the Appeals Chamber in any way (*Kayishema and Ruzindana* Appeal Judgment).

[60] *Vasiljević* Trial Judgment, par 227. The Trial Chamber did not suggest a minimum threshold number of killings. It noted, however, that cases from the Second World War involving extermination charges were generally concerned with thousands of deaths and that one court used the expression 'extermination' when referring to the killing of 733 civilians (*Einsatzgruppen* case, p 421). The Trial Chamber did not exclude, however, that a lower number of victims would disqualify that act as 'extermination', nor that this threshold must necessarily be met (ibid., n 587).

an accused could be convicted for both genocide and extermination (a crime against humanity) in relation to the same criminal conduct.[61]

Concerning the possibility to convict an individual for both extermination and persecution in relation to the same conduct, where persecution takes the form of killings, it has been suggested in one case that persecution would constitute a lesser offence and that conviction could, therefore, be entered in relation to extermination only.[62] Conversely, it has been suggested that, because of its particular discriminatory state of mind, persecution will always be the most specific of all crimes against humanity and that it would rule out a cumulative conviction for any other underlying offence (including extermination) based on the same facts. Both statements appear equally misguided as the test for cumulative conviction developed by the majority of the *Čelebići* Appeals Chamber only takes into account the *legal* elements pertaining to each offence, not the facts underlying each one of them. In situations where an accused has been charged with persecution and extermination in relation to the same facts, and even where the facts in question consist of multiple killings, it remains that both underlying offences contain a *legal* element that is not required by the other (a discriminatory mindset in relation to persecution and involvement in a large number of deaths – and awareness thereof – in the case of extermination) and that cumulative conviction between the two is, therefore, always permissible under that test.

---

[61] See, e.g. *Musema* Appeal Judgment, pars 364–367; *Krstić* Appeal Judgment, pars 223–227.
[62] *Nahimana* Trial Judgment, par 1080.

PART VII

SENTENCING INTERNATIONAL CRIMES

27

Applicable Law and Purposes of Sentencing

It would be hard to identify crimes more difficult to sentence than those provided for in the Statutes of the *ad hoc* Tribunals. The political significance of phrases such as 'genocide' or 'crimes against humanity', the greatness of the harm which the judges of both Tribunals are generally expected to punish, the immense suffering of the many victims involved, and the public expectation that sentences will match the abhorrence of the crimes, all coalesce as a heavy burden on the shoulders of judges who are to decide upon a sentence appropriate to the crimes of the accused they must sentence. The difficulty of their task is made no easier by the fact that neither the Statutes of the Tribunals, nor applicable precedents, offer much guidance in respect of sentencing international crimes. As far as penalties go, the Statutes of the Tribunals are limited to the following general directions:[1]

Penalties

1. The penalty imposed by the Trial Chamber shall be limited to imprisonment. In determining the terms of imprisonment, the Trial Chambers shall have recourse to the general practice regarding prison sentences in the courts of the former Yugoslavia [respectively, Rwanda].

2. In imposing the sentences, the Trial Chambers should take into account such factors as the gravity of the offence and the individual circumstances of the convicted person.

3. In addition to imprisonment, the Trial Chambers may order the return of any property and proceeds acquired by criminal conduct, including by means of duress, to their rightful owners.

The provision that penalties are limited to imprisonment contains three implicit restrictions upon the Court's power to punish those whom they find guilty: (i) the Tribunal is not empowered to impose the death penalty;[2] and prison sentences are limited to imprisonment for a term of up to and including the remainder of the convicted person's life;[3] (ii) non-custodial sentences are not

---

[1] Article 24 of the ICTY Statute and Article 22 of the ICTR Statute, respectively.

[2] Secretary-General Report (ICTY), par 112. By contrast to those tried before the ICTR, individuals who are prosecuted in local courts in Rwanda still incur the death penalty if found guilty.

[3] Rule 101(A) of the ICTY Rules of Procedure and Evidence. The substance of Rule 101(A) of the ICTR Rules of Procedure and Evidence is identical. See also *Blaškić* Appeal Judgment, par 678.

provided for under the Statute;[4] and (iii) the Statute does not allow for physical punishment or fines.[5]

As for the requirement that, in determining sentences, Trial Chambers should have recourse to the general practice regarding prison sentences in the courts of, respectively, the former Yugoslavia and Rwanda (Articles 24 and 22, par 1 of the Statutes), both Tribunals have made it clear that the sentencing practice of those two countries was merely 'an aid in determining the sentence to be imposed', one that was not binding upon them.[6] The ICTY could, therefore, impose a sentence in excess of the maximum sentence provided under the law of the former Yugoslavia and the Appeals Chamber explained somewhat circularly that this would not violate the principle *nullum crimen sine lege* 'because an accused must have been aware that the crimes for which he is indicted are the most serious violations of international humanitarian law, punishable by the most severe penalties'.[7] In most cases, Chambers of both Tribunals appear to have paid lip service to the sentencing practice of the two countries and their recitation of applicable provisions have generally been more *pro forma* than in any way determinative of sentences.[8]

---

[4] It is interesting to note in that regard the ambiguity of Article 23(1) of the ICTY Statute (and, respectively, Article 22(1) of the ICTR Statute) which talks about 'sentences and penalties' ('peines et sanctions' in the French text), whilst Article 24(1) (and, respectively, Article 23(1) of the ICTR Statute) is limited to terms of 'imprisonment' ('peines d'emprisonnement'), thereby suggesting that penalties other than sentences could in principle be provided for.

[5] See, e.g. *Kambanda* Trial Judgment, par 10: 'the only penalties the Tribunal can impose on an accused who pleads guilty or is convicted as such are prison terms up to and including life imprisonment [. . .]. The Statute of the Tribunal excludes other forms of punishment such as the death sentence, penal servitude or a fine.' See also *Serushago* Trial Judgment, par 12; *Rutaganda* Trial Judgment, par 448.

[6] See, e.g. *Tadić* Sentencing Judgment on Appeal, par 21; *Čelebići* Appeal Judgment, par 813; *Jelišić* Appeal Judgment, pars 116–117; *Blaškić* Appeal Judgment, par 681: *Blaškić* Trial Judgment, pars 759–760. In *Kunarac*, the Trial Chamber made it clear that the differences that existed between crimes provided for in these domestic jurisdictions and those before the *ad hoc* Tribunals justified the limited relevance of national sentencing patterns: 'The Trial Chamber notes that, because very important underlying differences often exist between national prosecutions and prosecutions in this jurisdiction, the nature, scope and the scale of the offences tried before the International Tribunal do not allow for an automatic application of the sentencing practices of the former Yugoslavia.' In relation to the ICTR, this has allowed the Tribunal to conclude that the death sentence could not be imposed (*Kambanda* Trial Judgment, pars 22–23). See also *Rutaganda* Trial Judgment, par 454; *Serushago* Appeal Judgment, par 30; *Ruggiu* Trial Judgment, par 31.

[7] *Blaškić* Appeal Judgment, par 681. The ICTR may not impose the death sentence despite the fact that Rwandan law provides for it.

[8] See, e.g. *Mrdja* Sentencing Judgment, pars 119–121; *Ndindabahizi* Trial Judgment, par 501; *Kajelijeli* Trial Judgment, par 964. See, however, *Kunarac* Trial Judgment, par 829 ('Clearly, recourse must be had to the sentencing practice of the former Yugoslavia as an aid in determining the sentence to be imposed. Although the Trial Chamber is not bound to apply the sentencing practice of the former Yugoslavia, what is required certainly goes beyond merely reciting the relevant criminal code provisions of the former Yugoslavia. Should they diverge, care should be taken to explain the sentence to be imposed with reference to the sentencing practice of the former Yugoslavia, especially where international law provides no guidance for a particular sentencing practice. The Trial Chamber notes that, because very important underlying differences often exist between national prosecutions and prosecutions in this jurisdiction, the nature, scope and the scale of the offences tried before the International Tribunal do not allow for an automatic application of the sentencing practices of the former Yugoslavia'); *Krstić* Appeal Judgment, par 260; *Deronjić* Sentencing Judgment, pars 158–159 and 160–170.

Concerning the purpose of sentencing, it is generally accepted in the jurisprudence of the two Tribunals that sentencing shall serve primarily the following two purposes: (i) *retribution*,[9] described as punishment of an offender for his specific criminal conduct;[10] and (ii) *general deterrence*, understood as deterrence of future violations of international humanitarian law.[11] In addition to the two principal purposes of sentencing mentioned above, a number of Chambers of the Tribunals have insisted that a sentence should also serve other purposes such as 'individual and affirmative prosecution aimed at influencing the legal awareness of the accused, the victims, the relatives, the witnesses, and the general public in order to reassure them that the legal system is being implemented and enforced',[12] the

---

[9] See, *inter alia*, *Blaškić* Appeal Judgment, par 678; *Tadić* Sentencing Judgment on Appeal, par 7; *Furundžija* Trial Judgment, par 288; *Todorović* Sentencing Judgment, pars 29–30; *Krnojelac* Trial Judgment, par 508; *Aleksovski* Appeal Judgment, par 185; *Čelebići* Appeal Judgment, par 806; *Kunarac* Appeal Judgment, pars 840–841; *Vasiljević* Trial Judgment, par 273; *Simić* Trial Judgment, par 33; *Nikolić* Sentencing Judgment, pars 86–87; *Obrenović* Sentencing Judgment, pars 50–51; *Naletilić and Martinović* Trial Judgment, par 739; *Stakić* Trial Judgment, par 900; *Banović* Sentencing Judgment, par 34; *Deronjić* Sentencing Judgment, par 150; *Babić* Sentencing Judgment, par 44 and sources quoted therein ('As a form of retribution, punishment expresses society's condemnation of the criminal act and of the person who committed it. It should be proportional to the seriousness of the crime. The Tribunal's punishment thus conveys the indignation of humanity for the serious violations of international humanitarian law of which a person is found guilty. Punishment may in this way reduce the anger and sense of injustice caused by the commission of the crimes among the victims and in their wider community. In considering retribution as an objective of punishment, the Trial Chamber focuses on the seriousness of the crimes to which Babić has pleaded guilty' footnotes omitted); *Kambanda* Trial Judgment, par 28; *Rutaganda* Trial Judgment, par 456; *Musema* Trial Judgment, par 986; *Niyitegeka* Trial Judgment, par 484; *Ruggiu* Trial Judgment, par 33; *Plavšić* Sentencing Judgment, pars 22–23. [10] *Vasiljević* Trial Judgment, par 273.

[11] *Tadić* Sentencing Judgment on Appeal, par 48; *Todorović* Sentencing Judgment, pars 29–30; *Krnojelac* Trial Judgment, par 508; *Aleksovski* Appeal Judgment, par 185 ('An equally important factor is retribution. This is not to be understood as fulfilling a desire for revenge but as duly expressing the outrage of the international community at these crimes.'); *Čelebići* Appeal Judgment, pars 801–802, 806; *Kunarac* Trial Judgment, pars 839–841; *Vasiljević* Trial Judgment, par 273; *Obrenović* Sentencing Judgment, pars 51–52 (par 52: 'One may ask whether the individuals who are called before this Tribunal as accused are simply an instrument through which to achieve the goal of the establishment of the rule of law. The answer is no. Indeed, the Appeals Chamber has held that deterrence should not be given undue prominence in the overall assessment of a sentence.'); *Stakić* Trial Judgment, pars 901–902; *Naletilić and Martinović* Trial Judgment, par 739; *Deronjić* Sentencing Judgment, pars 144–149; *Babić* Trial Judgment, par 45; *Blaškić* Appeal Judgment, par 678; *Kambanda* Trial Judgment, par 28; *Plavšić* Sentencing Judgment, pars 22 and 24; *Ntakirutimana* Trial Judgment, par 882; *Niyitegeka* Trial Judgment, par 484. According to the *Rutaganda* Trial Chamber, 'deterrence' means an attempt 'to dissuade for ever, others who may be tempted in the future to perpetrate such atrocities by showing them that the international community shall not tolerate the serious violations of international humanitarian law and human rights' (*Rutaganda* Trial Judgment, par 456). At the ICTY, the Appeals Chamber has had occasion to point out that this purpose should not be given undue weight in sentencing (*Aleksovski* Appeal Judgment, par 185; *Čelebići* Appeal Judgment, par 801). See also *Erdemović* Trial Sentencing Judgment, par 64; *Čelebići* Trial Judgment, par 1234; *Furundžija* Trial Judgment, par 288; *Kambanda* Trial Judgment, par 28; *Akayesu* Trial Judgment, par 19; *Serushago* Trial Judgment. par 20; *Rutaganda* Trial Judgment, par 456; *Musema* Trial Judgment, par 986. *Individual*, as opposed to *general* deterrence has been mentioned at times as a relevant purpose for sentencing (see, e.g. *Blaškić* Appeal Judgment, par 678 and references cited in n 1420 of that Judgment). [12] Ibid., par 678.

'protection of society, stigmatisation and public reprobation of international crimes',[13] the 'rehabilitation' of the perpetrator,[14] or even 'reconciliation'.[15] The Appeals Chamber said that in all cases, 'a sentence of the International Tribunal should make plain the condemnation of the international community of the behaviour in question and show "the international community was not ready to tolerate serious violations of international humanitarian law and human rights" '.[16]

---

[13] See, e.g., *Ntakirutimana* Trial Judgment, pars 881–882; *Blaškić* Appeal Judgment, par 678. See also *Erdemović* Trial Sentencing Judgment, par 65: 'the International Tribunal sees public reprobation and stigmatisation by the international community, which would thereby express its indignation over heinous crimes and denounce the perpetrators, as one of the essential functions of a prison sentence for a crime against humanity'; *Blaškić* Trial Judgment, par 763; *Ndindabahizi* Trial Judgment, par 498.

[14] See, e.g. *Blaškić* Appeal Judgment, par 678; *Čelebići* Trial Judgment, par 1233; *Blaškić* Trial Judgment, par 761; *Kunarac* Trial Judgment, par 836; *Nikolić* Sentencing Judgment, par 93; *Obrenović* Sentencing Judgment, par 53; *Serushago* Trial Judgment, par 39; *Kayishema and Ruzindana* Trial Judgment; *Kayishema and Ruzindana* Appeal Judgment, pars 389–390. This factor should not be given undue weight in sentencing, the Appeals Chamber made explicit (*Čelebići* Appeal Judgment, par 806: 'although rehabilitation (in accordance with international human rights standards) should be considered as a relevant factor, it is not one which should be given undue weight'). See also *Babić* Sentencing Judgment, par 46: 'Punishment is also understood as having a rehabilitative purpose. The loss of freedom, which is the form of punishment imposed by the Tribunal, provides the context for the convicted person's reflection on the wrongfulness of his acts and may give rise to an awareness of harm and suffering these acts have caused to others. This process contributes to the reintegration of the convicted person into society. The Trial Chamber is of the opinion that when an accused pleads guilty, he takes an important step in this process.' (footnote omitted); *Banović* Sentencing Judgment, par 76.

[15] *Kamuhanda* Trial Judgment, par 754; *Nikolić* Sentencing Judgment, par 93: 'Particularly in cases where the crime was committed on a discriminatory basis, like this case, the process of coming face-to-face with the statements of victims, if not the victims themselves, can inspire – if not reawaken – tolerance and understanding of "the other", thereby making it less likely that if given an opportunity to act in a discriminatory manner again, an accused would do so. Reconciliation and peace would thereby be promoted.'

[16] *Aleksovski* Appeal Judgment, par 185 (footnotes omitted); *Nikolić* Sentencing Judgment, par 82. See also *Erdemović* Trial Sentencing Judgment, pars 64–65; *Kambanda* Trial Judgment, par 28.

28

Relevant Factors in Sentencing

In addition to the general sentencing practice in the Courts of the former Yugoslavia and Rwanda, the Trial Chamber will take into account the gravity of the offence which it must punish and all other relevant circumstances pertaining to the conduct in question (whether mitigating or aggravating). Also, the Court will give due regard to the time which the individual might already have spent in detention (pending transfer to the International Tribunal, trial or appeal) and the extent to which any penalty imposed upon him by another court for the same act has already been served.[1] Within that general framework, the Trial Chamber possesses a large amount of discretion to decide upon a sentence appropriate to the crimes and the individual being sentenced.[2]

28.1 Gravity of the acts of the accused

The primary consideration in sentencing crimes within the jurisdiction of the *ad hoc* Tribunals, both Tribunals have pointed out, is the gravity of the criminal

---

[1] See, generally, *Blaškić* Appeal Judgment, par 679 and references cited therein and par 709: 'Any time spent in custody for the purpose of this case must necessarily be taken into account.' Credit will be given for time in detention pending trial (see Rule 101(C) Rules of Procedure and Evidence, of both Tribunals; see also *Tadić* Sentencing Judgment on Appeal, pars 38 and 75) and Chambers have sometimes recommended a minimum sentence (*Stakić* Trial Judgment, Disposition, p 253; see also *Kordić and Čerkez* Trial Judgment, par 850).

[2] See *Deronjić* Sentencing Judgment, pars 138 and 155; *Čelebići* Appeal Judgment, par 777, concerning the Chamber's discretion in relation to the weight to be given to mitigating and aggravating factors. The *Deronjić* Trial Chamber also underlined the importance of what it called the 'fundamental principle of proportionality' that must exist between the conduct and its punishment (*Deronjić* Sentencing Judgment, pars 138 and 155).

conduct of the accused, in particular the form and degree of his participation in the crime or crimes in question, and the circumstances of the case.[3] The legal labelling attached to that conduct will, in principle, only be a secondary consideration.[4] It is true, however, that by reason of its peculiar *mens rea*, genocide is generally regarded as more serious than either war crimes or crimes against humanity,[5] whilst crimes against humanity and war crimes have been regarded as equally

---

[3] See, e.g. *Čelebići* Appeal Judgment, par 731; *Blaškić* Appeal Judgment, par 683: 'Factors to be considered include the discriminatory nature of the crimes where this is not considered as an element of a conviction, and the vulnerability of the victims. The consequences of the crime upon the victim directly injured is always relevant to sentencing, that is, "the extent of the long-term physical, psychological and emotional suffering of the immediate victims is relevant to the gravity of the offences". Furthermore, the effects of the crime on relatives of the immediate victims may be considered as relevant to the culpability of the offender and in determining a sentence.'; *Čelebići* Trial Judgment, par 1225; *Kupreškić* Trial Judgment, par 852; *Kvočka* Trial Judgment, par 701; *Aleksovski* Appeal Judgment, par 182; *Stakić* Trial Judgment, pars 903 and 910; *Naletilić and Martinović* Trial Judgment, par 718; *Plavšić* Sentencing Judgment, par 25: 'The cardinal feature in sentencing is the gravity of the crime'; *Krnojelac* Trial Judgment, par 522: 'the sentence to be imposed must reflect the inherent gravity of the criminal conduct of the accused, and the determination of that issue requires a consideration of the particular circumstances of the case, as well as of the form and degree of the participation of the accused in the crime. The nature of the actions of others for which the accused is found to be responsible is therefore relevant, but those actions are considered principally by reference to the nature of the accused's responsibility for them' footnote omitted); *Banović* Sentencing Judgment, pars 36 and 38 et seq.; *Jokić* Sentencing Judgment, par 41–58; *Deronjić* Sentencing Judgment, par 154; Mrdja Trial Judgment, pars 20–21 (par 21: 'In determining the gravity of the crimes, the Trial Chamber will give consideration to the legal nature of the offences committed, their scale, the role of Darko Mrdja played in their commission and the impact upon the victims and their families'); *Babić* Sentencing Judgment, par 47; *Obrenović* Sentencing Judgment, pars 61 et seq.; *Kambanda* Trial Judgment, par 42; *Ntakirutimana* Trial Judgment, par 883; *Kajelijeli* Trial Judgment, pars 946 and 963. The Trial Chamber in the *Mrđja* case also said that the impact that the crimes had on the victims and their family could, in principle, be taken into consideration to assess the gravity of the criminal conduct (*Mrdja* Sentencing Judgment, par 39). The Trial Chamber added that, where the suffering of the victims and their families, significantly exceeds 'what is usually suffered by the victims and their families', this fact may be regarded as an aggravating circumstance for the purpose of sentencing (*Mrdja* Sentencing Judgment, par 41).

[4] See, e.g. *Krstić* Trial Judgment, par 700: 'Assessing the seriousness of the crimes is not a mere matter of comparing and ranking the crimes in the abstract.' Several Chambers have underlined, however, the *per se* gravity of genocide as a starting point for sentencing. See also, *Ntakirutimana* Trial Chamber, par 881: 'Both Accused have been found guilty of genocide and crimes against humanity. These crimes are of an utmost gravity; they are shocking to the conscience of mankind, in view of the fundamental human values deliberately negated by their perpetrators and the sufferings inflicted. These crimes threaten not only the foundations of the society in which they are perpetrated but also those of the international community as a whole.' See also *Musema* Trial Judgment, par 1001; *Rutaganda* Trial Judgment, pars 451–452, 468; *Kayishema and Ruzindana* Trial Judgment, par 9; *Sikirica* Sentencing Judgment, par 267; *Čelebići* Appeal Judgment, par 731; *Todorović* Sentencing Judgment, par 31.

[5] *Kambanda* Trial Judgment, par 16. 'Indisputably, genocide is at the apex of this hierarchy' (*Jelišić* Appeal Judgment, par 13); see also *Musema* Trial Judgment, par 981; *Rutaganda* Trial Judgment, par 451; *Kayishema and Ruzindana* Trial Judgment, par 9; *Kambanda* Trial Judgment, pars 14 and 16; *Krstić* Trial Judgment, par 700; *Krstić* Appeal Judgment, pars 36 and 275, confirming the particular status of genocide as a crime of extreme gravity.

serious in principle.[6] For sentencing purposes, the specific genocidal *mens rea* operates as a weighty aggravating factor:[7]

It can also be argued, however, that genocide is the most serious crime because of its requirement of the intent to destroy, in whole or in part, a national, ethnic, racial or religious group, as such. In this sense, even though the criminal acts themselves involved in a genocide may not vary from those in a crime against humanity or a crime against the laws and customs of war, the convicted person is, because of his specific intent, deemed to be more blameworthy. However, this does not rule out the Trial Chamber's duty to decide on the appropriate punishment according to the facts of each case.

Thus, a murder carried out with a genocidal intent would, in principle, carry a heavier sentence than one committed absent that mindset, whilst if charged as a war crime or as a crime against humanity it would, all things being equal, be regarded as equally serious (and carry the same sentence).[8] It would be inaccurate to suggest, however, that the mere qualification of an act as genocidal would *per se* warrant a heavy sentence. An appropriate punishment depends not on 'comparing and ranking the crimes in the abstract', but on the facts of each case:[9]

Genocide embodies a horrendous concept, indeed, but a close look at the myriad of situations that can come within its boundaries cautions against prescribing a monolithic punishment for one and all genocides or similarly for one and all crimes against humanity or war crimes.

Concerning the gravity of grave breaches of the Geneva Conventions (Article 2 of the ICTY Statute) as opposed to any other serious violations of the laws or customs of war (Article 3 of the ICTY Statute), it must be noted that a serious violation of the laws or customs of war is not considered to be more serious due to the fact that it amounts to a 'grave breach' of the Geneva Conventions. In other

---

[6] See, *inter alia*, *Tadić* Sentencing Judgment on Appeal, par 69; *Furundžija* Appeal Judgment, pars 243, 247; *Kunarac* Trial Judgment, par 851; *Krnojelac* Trial Judgment, par 511; *Mrdja* Sentencing Judgment, par 24. For a contrary view at the Trial Chamber level, see *Tadić* Sentencing Judgment, par 73; *Erdemović* Trial Sentencing Judgment, pars 27–28; *Krnojelac* Trial Judgment, par 511.

[7] *Krstić* Trial Judgment, par 700. A discriminatory mindset has systematically been regarded as an aggravating factor in sentencing. See *Vasiljević* Trial Judgment, par 278: 'A discriminatory state of mind may [. . .] be regarded as an aggravating factor in relation to offences for which such a state of mind is not an element.' See also, *Kunarac* Trial Judgment, pars 867 and 879. Sentencing patterns in relation to genocidal offences primarily reflect the gravity of the factual basis upon which convictions and sentences have been based, rather than the nature of the offence charged: genocide charges are generally reserved for those suspected of having committed or taken part in particularly atrocious or large-scale crimes. When conviction is entered upon such charges, the factual basis upon which sentence is based is therefore particularly serious, involving many victims or very serious crimes. Not surprisingly, therefore, those individuals charged but acquitted for genocide and convicted on alternatives charges (such as crimes against humanity) have received very heavy sentences. Goran Jelišić was charged with genocide, violations of the laws or customs of war, and crimes against humanity. He was acquitted of genocide all together, but he was sentenced to forty-years' imprisonment based on the remaining charges (*Jelišić* Trial Judgment).

[8] See, e.g. *Krstić* Appeal Judgment, par 268 where Krstić's sentence was reduced from forty-six years to thirty-five years in part because the Appeals Chamber was not satisfied that he possessed the required intent ('the finding that [*Krstić*] lacked genocidal intent significantly diminishes his responsibility').   [9] *Krstić* Trial Judgment, par 700.

words, none of the general requirements of the grave breaches regime aggravates the underlying conduct so that a war crime would not be regarded all else being equal, as more serious when charged as a grave breach than it would when charged as a general violation of the laws or customs of war. Thus, for instance, the murder of a civilian would lead to the same sentence whether it is charged pursuant to Article 2 or Article 3 of the ICTY Statute.

28.2   Mitigating and aggravating factors

The intrinsic seriousness of the crimes listed in the Statute does not exclude the possibility that they may be aggravated by other circumstances which may relate to both the accused and his crimes. The following factors, for instance, have been regarded as aggravating circumstances by the *ad hoc* Tribunals:

- the abuse of a position of authority[10]
- the personal or direct involvement of the accused in the commission of the crimes[11]
- the discriminatory state of mind with which the acts were committed[12]
- reprehensible motives[13]

---

[10] See, e.g. *Krnojelac* Trial Judgment, par 512; *Krstić* Trial Judgment, par 709; *Sikirica* Sentencing Judgment, par 172; *Čelebići* Appeal Judgment, par 736: 'proof of active participation by a superior in the criminal acts of subordinates adds to the gravity of the superior's failure to prevent or punish those acts and may therefore aggravate the sentence'; *Aleksovski* Appeal Judgment, par 183; *Plavšić* Sentencing Judgment, par 57; *Simić* Trial Judgment, par 67; *Stakić* Trial Judgment, par 912; *Nikolić* Sentencing Judgment, par 135; *Obrenović* Sentencing Judgment, par 99; *Banović* Sentencing Judgment, par 55; *Jokić* Sentencing Judgment, par 61; *Mrdja* Sentencing Judgment, pars 51–54; *Babić* Sentencing Judgment, pars 54–62 (in particular, par 59).

[11] See, e.g. *Blaškić* Trial Judgment, pars 790 ('Active and direct participation in the crime means that the accused committed by his own hand all or some of the crimes with which he is charged. Direct participation in the crime is accordingly an aggravating circumstance which will more often than not be held against the actual perpetrators rather than against the commanders.'); *Krstić* Trial Judgment, par 708; *Blaškić* Appeal Judgment, par 686. In some cases, however, the gravity of the acts committed by an accused who is somewhat remote from the crimes might be greater than the acts of the physical perpetrator (see *Stakić* Trial Judgment, par 918).

[12] See *Blaškić* Appeal Judgment, par 686 and references cited therein. But when an otherwise aggravating factor is at the same time an element of the offence (as is a discriminatory mindset for the crime of persecution), it cannot also constitute an aggravating factor for the purpose of sentencing (*Blaškić* Appeal Judgment, pars 693 and 695; *Vasiljević* Trial Judgment par 278: 'A discriminatory state of mind may however be regarded as an aggravating factor in relation to offences for which such a state of mind is not an element'; *Kunarac* Trial Judgment, par 867).

[13] *Krstić* Trial Judgment, par 711; *Blaškić* Trial Judgment, par 785; *Blaškić* Appeal Judgment, pars 686 and 694 (on the distinction between motives and intent). See also *Vasiljević* Trial Judgment, par 278: 'During the Bosnian conflict, ethnicity has variedly been exploited to gain political prominence or to retain power, to justify criminal deeds, or for the purpose of obtaining moral absolution for any act coloured by the ethnic cause. No such absolution is to be expected from this Tribunal. The Trial Chamber considers that crimes based upon ethnic grounds are particularly reprehensible, and the existence of such a state of mind is relevant to the sentence to be imposed either as an ingredient of that crime or as a matter of aggravation where it is not such an ingredient.'; *Vasiljević* Appeal Judgment, pars 168 et seq.

- premeditated or enthusiastic participation in the commission of the crimes[14]
- the number of victims, their age, status and vulnerability and effects of the crimes on them[15]
- the brutal or vicious manner or circumstances in which the crimes were committed[16]
- the length of time over which the crimes were committed and repetition thereof.[17]

But before any such factor may be taken into account in aggravation of sentence, it must have been established by the Prosecution beyond reasonable doubt.[18]

Likewise, any such crime may, in principle, be subject to mitigation, either by reason of circumstances attendant to the accused or by taking into account the prevailing circumstances at the time of the acts.[19] Factors such as:

- the nature of the accused's relatively minor or remote participation[20]
- duress[21]

---

[14] See, *Krstić* Trial Judgment, par 711: 'Premeditated or enthusiastic participation in a criminal act necessarily reveals a higher level of criminality on the part of the participant. In determining the appropriate sentence, a distinction is to be made between the individuals who allowed themselves to be drawn into a maelstrom of violence, even reluctantly, and those who initiated or aggravated it and thereby more substantially contributed to the overall harm. Indeed, reluctant participation in the crimes may in some instances be considered as a mitigating circumstance.' See also, *Blaškić* Appeal Judgment, par 686; *Jelišić* Trial Judgment, pars 130–131. Concerning the willing and enthusiastic participation of the accused in the commission of the crimes as a relevant sentencing factor, see, *inter alia, Tadić* Sentencing Judgment, par 57 and *Tadić* Sentencing Judgment II, par 20; *Blaškić* Trial Judgment, par 792–793; *Vasiljević* Trial Judgment, par 305; *Ntakirutimana* Trial Judgment, par 884.

[15] See, e.g. *Kunarac* Trial Judgment, pars 352 and 864–867, 874–875; *Furundžija* Trial Judgment, pars 282–283; *Blaškić* Trial Judgment, pars 783–787; *Nikolić* Sentencing Judgment, par 137; *Banović* Sentencing Judgment, par 50; *Jokić* Sentencing Judgment, pars 64–65; *Deronjić* Sentencing Judgment, pars 186 and 207–209; *Mrdja* Sentencing Judgment, pars 46 and 55–56; *Blaškić* Appeal Judgment, par 686. The 'civilian' status of the victims may not be regarded as an aggravating factor where such a status is in fact an element of the crime charged (*Mrdja* Sentencing Judgment, par 46).

[16] See, e.g. *Kunarac* Trial Judgment, par 874; *Krstić* Trial Judgment, par 703; *Blaškić* Trial Judgment, par 783; *Furundžija* Trial Judgment, pars 282–283; *Obrenović* Sentencing Judgment, par 102; *Blaškić* Appeal Judgment, par 686.

[17] See, e.g. *Kunarac* Trial Judgment, par 865; *Plavšić* Sentencing Judgment, par 52; *Erdemović* Appeal Sentencing Judgment, par 15; *Blaškić* Appeal Judgment, par 686.

[18] See *Vasiljević* Trial Judgment, par 272; *Čelebići* Appeal Judgment, par 763; *Kunarac* Trial Judgment, par 847; *Babić* Sentencing Judgment, par 48; *Blaškić* Appeal Judgment, par 686.

[19] Whereas aggravating factors must be established beyond reasonable doubt (see, e.g. *Čelebići* Appeal Judgment, par 763), mitigating factors must be established by the accused on a balance of probabilities only: *Kunarac* Trial Judgment, par 847; *Vasiljević* Trial Judgment, par 272; *Sikirica* Sentencing Judgment, par 110. The absence of any mitigating factors may never be regarded as an aggravating factor (*Blaškić* Appeal Judgment, par 687; *Plavšić* Sentencing Judgment, par 64). The Trial Chamber in *Banović* suggested that a Chamber has the discretion to consider any factor which it considers to be mitigating (*Banović* Sentencing Judgment, par 62).

[20] See, e.g. *Furundžija* Trial Judgment, par 282; *Krstić* Trial Judgment, par 714: 'Indirect participation is one circumstance that may go to mitigating a sentence.'

[21] See Joint Separate Opinion of Judge McDonald and Judge Vohrah, pars 59 et seq. and Separate and Dissenting Opinion of Judge Cassese, par 11 in *Erdemović* Appeal Judgment; *Krstić* Trial Judgment, par 714; *Mrdja* Sentencing Judgment, pars 65–66.

- superior orders pursuant to Articles 7(4) and 6(4) of the Statutes[22]
- his or her diminished mental responsibility[23]
- personal circumstances of the accused, such as his family situation, his/her health, or his/her age[24]
- the good character of the accused[25]
- his or her substantial cooperation with the Prosecutor[26]
- an admission of guilt[27]

[22] See, e.g. *Mrdja* Sentencing Judgment, pars 65 and 67. The Trial Chamber in *Mrdja* made it clear that 'superior orders may be pleaded in mitigation independently of duress, and vice versa' (*Mrdja* Sentencing Judgment, par 65; see also *Erdemović* Appeal Judgment, Joint Separate Opinion of Judge McDonald and Judge Vohrah, par 34).

[23] See, e.g. *Čelebići* Appeal Judgment, par 590; *Vasiljević* Trial Judgment pars 282–283 (par 283: 'an accused suffers from a diminished mental responsibility where there is an impairment to his capacity to appreciate the unlawfulness of or the nature of his conduct or to control his conduct so as to conform to the requirements of the law.')

[24] See, for instance, *Kunarac* Appeal Judgment, par 362; *Blaškić* Appeal Judgment, par 708; *Krstić* Trial Judgment par 714; *Vasiljević* Trial Judgment, par 300. Concerning the relevance of the age of the accused, see *Plavšić* Sentencing Judgment, pars 103–105; *Blaškić* Trial Judgment, par 779; *Simić* Trial Judgment, par 98. Concerning the issue of age, young age (*Erdemović* Appeal Sentencing Judgment par 16; *Blaškić* Trial Judgment, par 778) as well as old age could be considered a mitigating factor (*Plavšić* Sentencing Judgment, pars 95 et seq.; *Krnojelac* Trial Judgment, par 533; *Stakić* Trial Judgment, par 923; *Serushago* Trial Judgment, pars 36–37; *Rutaganda* Trial Judgment, par 472; *Mrdja* Sentencing Judgment, par 91: 'the Tribunal has taken into consideration various personal circumstances as mitigating factors in sentencing, such as the young age of an accused, his good behaviour whilst at the United Nations Detention Unit [. . .], his family situation, his efforts to reintegrate into society, and the fact that he has no criminal record' (footnotes omitted); *Babić* Sentencing Judgment, pars 87–89; *Serushago* Trial Judgment, pars 36–37; *Rutaganda* Trial Judgment, par 472. The Tribunals have generally attached limited weight to such circumstances (see, e.g. *Mrdja* Sentencing Judgment, pars 92–94; *Banović* Sentencing Judgment, par 75).

[25] *Erdemović* Appeal Sentencing Judgment, par 16(i); *Čelebići* Appeal Judgment, par 788; *Blaškić* Appeal Judgment, par 706; *Krstić* Trial Judgment, par 714; *Krnojelac* Trial Judgment, par 519; *Babić* Sentencing Judgment, par 91; *Blaškić* Trial Judgment, par 780; *Nikolić* Sentencing Judgment, par 164; *Ntakirutimana* Trial Judgment, pars 895–898, 908–909; *Semanza* Trial Judgment, par 577.

[26] *Blaškić* Trial Judgment, par 774; *Plavšić* Sentencing Judgment, pars 63–64; *Todorović* Sentencing Judgment, pars 83–88; *Erdemović* Trial Sentencing Judgment, pars 99–101; *Simić* Trial Judgment, par 112; *Nikolić* Sentencing Judgment, par 156; *Jokić* Sentencing Judgment, pars 93–96; *Deronjić* Sentencing Judgment, pars 244–255; *Mrdja* Sentencing Judgment, pars 71–74; *Babić* Sentencing Judgment, par 72–75; *Kambanda* Trial Judgment, pars 47 and 61–62; *Serushago* Trial Judgment, par 31–33. The determination as to whether the accused's cooperation with the Prosecution has been 'substantial' 'depends on the extent and quality of the information he or she provides' (*Plavšić* Sentencing Judgment, par 63; *Todorović* Sentencing Judgment, par 86).

[27] See, e.g. *Jelišić* Appeal Judgment, pars 119–123; *Blaškić* Appeal Judgment, par 714; *Nikolić* Sentencing Judgment, pars 46–78 on the conditions of acceptance of a guilty plea, the Trial Chamber's role in case of a guilty plea and propriety of plea agreements in cases involving serious violations of international humanitarian law; and pars 142 et seq.; *Sikirica* Sentencing Judgment, pars 149–151, 193, and 227–228; *Todorović* Sentencing Judgment, pars 75–82; *Plavšić* Sentencing Judgment, pars 66 et seq. (see, in particular, par 80: 'The Trial Chamber accepts that acknowledgement and full disclosure of serious crimes are very important when establishing the truth in relation to such crimes. This, together with acceptance of responsibility for the committed wrongs, will promote reconciliation.'); *Obrenović* Sentencing Judgment, pars 111 and 115–116; *Simić* Trial Judgment, pars 84–85; *Jokić* Sentencing Judgment, pars 74–78; *Deronjić* Sentencing Judgment, pars 229–241; *Mrdja* Sentencing Judgment, par 78 ('a guilty plea may demonstrate honesty, helps to

- expression of remorse[28]
- benevolent actions towards some of the victims[29]
- voluntary surrender to the Tribunal[30]
- comportment in detention[31]

have all been taken into account in mitigation of sentences when established by the Defence on the balance of probability.[32] The mere fact that a war was going on at the time, and that a degree of chaos might have ensued therefrom, is not a factor to be considered in mitigation.[33] As with aggravating factors, Trial Chambers possess a great deal of discretion as to the weight to be attributed to any of those factors.[34]

The relative significance of the accused in the context of the conflict may also play a role at the sentencing stage, both in his favour and against him.[35] An individual will not be sentenced more harshly simply because he finds himself

---

establish the truth, may contribute to peace-building and reconciliation and saves the Tribunal the time and resources of a lengthy trial. Moreover, victims and witnesses are relieved from the possible stress of testifying at trial', footnotes omitted); *Babić* Sentencing Judgment, pars 65–71; *Banović* Sentencing Judgment, pars 65 and 66–69; *Kambanda* Trial Judgment, pars 50–54 and 61; *Serushago* Trial Judgment, par 35. The Tribunal has made it clear that plea bargain agreements reached between the Defence and the Prosecution are not binding upon the Chamber (see, e.g. *Todorović* Sentencing Judgment, par 79). It also said that a guilty plea made at the commencement of the trial could justify a greater mitigation than one entered at a later stage 'considering the additional savings to the International Tribunal on account of his more timely guilty plea' (*Sikirica* Sentencing Judgment, par 228). Concerning the relationship between a guilty plea and the process of civil reconciliation as a factor relevant to sentencing, see again, *Plavšić* Sentencing Judgment, pars 66 et seq.

[28] See, for instance, ibid.; *Todorović* Sentencing Judgment, pars 89–92 and references quoted therein; *Sikirica* Sentencing Judgment, pars 152, 194, and 230; *Simić* Trial Judgment, par 92. The Trial Chamber must satisfy itself that the expression of remorse is sincere (see, e.g. *Todorović* Sentencing Judgment, par 89; *Erdemović* Appeal Sentencing Judgment, par 16(iii); *Jelišić* Trial Judgment, par 127); *Nikolić* Sentencing Judgment, par 161; *Obrenović* Sentencing Judgment, par 121; *Jokić* Sentencing Judgment, pars 89–92; *Banović* Sentencing Judgment, pars 65 and 70 et seq.; *Deronjić* Sentencing Judgment, pars 263–264; *Mrdja* Sentencing Judgment, pars 85–87; *Babić* Sentencing Judgment, pars 81–84; *Serushago* Trial Judgment, pars 40–41; *Musema* Trial Judgment, pars 1005–1006. To constitute a mitigating factor, the expression of remorse must be 'real and sincere' (*Blaškić* Appeal Judgment, par 705; *Simić* Trial Judgment, par 1066).

[29] See, e.g. *Blaškić* Appeal Judgment, par 696; *Sikirica* Trial Judgment pars 195 and 229; *Serushago* Trial Judgment, par 38; *Rutaganda* Trial Judgment, par 471; *Niyitegeka* Trial Judgment, par 494.

[30] See, e.g. *Plavšić* Sentencing Judgment, pars 82–84; *Blaškić* Trial Judgment, par 776; *Jokić* Sentencing Judgment, pars 70–73; *Babić* Trial Judgment, pars 85–86; *Serushago* Trial Judgment, par 34.

[31] *Blaškić* Appeal Judgment, par 696; *Jokić* Sentencing Judgment, par 100; *Nikolić* Sentencing Judgment, par 168.

[32] See *Vasiljević* Trial Judgment, pars 272, 282, 295, and 300; *Kunarac* Trial Judgment, par 847; *Sikirica* Sentencing Judgment, par 110; *Simić* Trial Judgment, par 40; *Čelebići* Appeal Judgment, par 590; *Babić* Sentencing Judgment, par 48.   [33] *Blaškić* Appeal Judgment, par 711.

[34] See e.g. *Naletilić and Martinović* Trial Judgment, par 742; *Niyitigeka* Appeal Judgment, par 268.

[35] See, for instance, *Tadić* Sentencing Judgment on Appeal, par 55; *Blaškić* Appeal Judgment, par 686; *Naletilić and Martinović* Trial Judgment, par 744: 'It has been held that the sentence imposed should reflect the relative significance of the role of the accused in the context of the conflict in the former Yugoslavia. However, this has been interpreted to mean that even if the position of an accused in the overall hierarchy in the conflict in the former Yugoslavia was low, it does not follow that

higher up in the hierarchy,[36] but his sentence may be aggravated if he has abused or wrongly exercised the powers and responsibilities placed upon him for the purpose of committing or facilitating crimes.[37] More controversial is the sentence to be imposed upon low-level perpetrators, whose role might have been relatively minor in the broader picture, but whose conduct might have been very significant at a more localized level. It has long been agreed that lower-level perpetrators may not hide behind the relatively modest contribution they may have made to the global criminal picture in order to mitigate their responsibility. As far back as October 1865, the Judge-Advocate in the trial of Henri Wirz, commander of the Andersonville prison during the American Civil War, had set out this principle in no uncertain terms:[38]

And notwithstanding his earnest appeal, made to you in his final statement, begging that, he poor subaltern, acting only in obedience to his superior, should not bear the odium and the punishment deserved, with whatever force these cries of a desperate man, in a desperate and terrible strait may come to you, there is no law, no sympathy, no code of morals, that can warrant you in refusing to let him have justice, because the lesser and not the greater criminal is on trial.

On occasion, both Tribunals have been relatively lenient with some low-level perpetrators,[39] but mostly they have not.[40] In the *Kunarac* case, for instance, the

---

a low sentence is to be automatically imposed' (footnote omitted); *Krnojelac* Trial Judgment, par 509; *Čelebići* Appeal Judgment, par 847.

[36] *Krstić* Trial Judgment, par 709: 'A high rank in the military or political field does not, in itself, lead to a harsher sentence.' See, however, *Ndindabahizi* Trial Judgment, par 500, concerning the suggestion that there should exist a 'graduation of sentences, according to which the highest penalties are to be imposed upon those who planned or ordered atrocities, or those who committed crimes with particular zeal or sadism'. See also *Stakić* Trial Judgment, pars 928–933, concerning the relevancy and interpretation of 'patterns' in sentencing.

[37] *Krstić* Trial Judgment, par 709. See also *Rutaganda* Trial Judgment, par 469; *Kambanda* Trial Judgment, par 44; *Sikirica* Sentencing Judgment, par 210; *Plavšić* Sentencing Judgment, pars 54, 57, and 127.

[38] House Executive Documents, Vol. 8, No. 23 No. 1381, 40th Cong. 2nd Sess. (1868), p 778. In a strange echo to this statement, the Trial Chamber in *Jelišić* made the same point: 'One of the missions of the International Criminal Tribunal is to contribute to the restoration of peace in the former Yugoslavia. To do so, it must identify, prosecute and punish the principal political and military officials responsible for the atrocities committed since 1991 in the territories concerned. However, where need be, it must also recall that although the crimes perpetrated during armed conflicts may be more specifically ascribed to one or other of these officials, they could not achieve their ends without the enthusiastic help or contribution, direct or indirect, of individuals like Goran Jelišić.' (*Jelišić* Trial Judgment, par 133).

[39] For instance, Stevan Todorović, Dragan Kolundžija, and Damir Došen, who all pleaded guilty received, respectively, ten-year, three-year, and five-year sentences. Miroslav Kvočka was convicted for persecution (a crime against humanity) and murder and torture (as violations of the laws or customs of war) and was sentenced to seven-years' imprisonment.

[40] For instance, Mitar Vasiljević was sentenced to twenty years, Dusko Tadić and Radomir Kovač also received twenty-year sentences, Zoran Žigić was sentenced to twenty-five years, Dragoljub Kunarac received a twenty-eight year sentence, Mlado Radić received a twenty-year sentence, and Goran Jelišić was sentenced to forty years' imprisonment. As pointed out in *Krstić*, 'current case law of the Tribunal does not evidence a discernible pattern of the Tribunal imposing sentences on subordinates that differ greatly from those imposed on their superiors' (*Krstić* Trial Judgment, par 709).

Trial Chamber clearly stated that a low position in the hierarchy was no shield against severe punishment when the crimes warranted it:[41]

The three accused are certainly not in the category of the political or military masterminds behind the conflicts and atrocities. However, the Trial Chamber wishes to make it perfectly clear that, although in these cases before this Tribunal it is generally desirable to prosecute and try those in the higher echelons of power, the Trial Chamber will not accept low rank or a subordinate function as an escape from criminal prosecution.

The Appeals Chamber also made it very clear that the establishment of a gradation in sentencing, as may indeed be desirable, 'does not entail a low sentence for all those in a low level of the overall command structure'.[42] 'In certain circumstances', the Appeals Chamber noted, 'the gravity of the crime may be so great that even following consideration of any mitigating factors, and despite the fact that the accused was not senior in the so-called overall command structure, a very severe penalty is nevertheless justified.'[43]

28.3 Totality principle and individualization of sentences

Although Trial Chambers have the discretion to impose sentences that are either global, concurrent, or consecutive, or a mixture of concurrent and consecutive,[44] they must make sure in every case that the sentence imposed reflects the totality of the culpable conduct of the accused ('totality' principle). That is, the sentence must reflect both the gravity of the offences and the culpability of the accused.[45] The sentence must also be individualized so as to take into account the individual

---

[41] See the summary of the Judgment read out in court on 22 February 2001 by the Presiding Judge of Trial Chamber II in this case (www.un.org/icty/latest/index.htm). See also, *Čelebići* Appeal Judgment, par 847: 'That Judgment did not purport to require that, in every case before it, an accused's level in the overall hierarchy in the conflict in the former Yugoslavia should be compared with those at the highest level, such that if the accused's place was by comparison low, a low sentence should automatically be imposed. Establishing a gradation does not entail a low sentence for all those in a low level of the overall command structure. On the contrary, a sentence must always reflect the inherent level of gravity of a crime [. . .].' See also *Vasiljević* Trial Judgment, pars 301–303. See, however, *Tadić* Appeal Judgment, pars 55–57.

[42] *Čelebići* Appeal Judgment, par 847: 'On the contrary, a sentence must always reflect the inherent level of gravity of a crime which requires consideration of the particular circumstances of the cases, as well as the form and degrees of the participation of the accused in the crime.' See also *Vasiljević* Trial Judgment, pars 301–304 (par 304: 'The fact that he was a low-level offender in terms of the overall conflict in the former Yugoslavia cannot alter the seriousness of the offences for which he has been convicted or the circumstances in which he committed them').   [43] *Čelebići* Appeal Judgment, par 847.

[44] Ibid., par 429; *Blaškić* Appeal Judgment, par 717. See also *Musema* Trial Judgment, par 989; *Kambanda* Trial Judgment, pars 101–102; *Ntakirutimana* Trial Judgment, par 917; *Ndindabahizi* Trial Judgment, par 497 (suggesting that a single sentence would usually be appropriate where the offences may be said to form part of a single criminal transaction); *Nahimana* Trial Judgment, par 1104.

[45] *Čelebići* Appeal Judgment, par 429. See also ibid., par 430: 'the overarching goal in sentencing must be to ensure that the final or aggregate sentence reflects the totality of the criminal conduct and overall culpability of the offender. This can be achieved through either the imposition of one sentence in respect of all offences, or several sentences ordered to run concurrently, consecutively or both.

circumstances of the accused and to avoid unjustified disparities between accused persons appearing before different Chambers when their respective conduct is comparable in relevant ways.[46] In that context, the discretion of the Tribunals is almost unfettered and Chambers of the Tribunals have taken into account all those factors which they considered relevant to the determination of an appropriate sentence, whether or not these factors are mentioned in the Statutes of the Tribunals.[47]

As noted by the Appeals Chamber of the ICTY, 'it is thus premature to speak of an emerging "penal regime" and the coherence in sentencing practice that this denotes'.[48] The degree of pre-visibility of sentences handed down by both *ad hoc* Tribunals is indeed still at a very low level and many of their sentences appear to be coloured as much by the national sentencing practices of the judges sitting on any particular bench as by any rules and principles specific to international criminal tribunals.

In a domestic legal system, such a situation would raise serious questions of legality. On the international plane, however, the maxim *nulla poena sine lege* has had an almost ethereal existence. During the trials that followed the Second World War, this fundamental principle of criminal law was barely acknowledged, and when it was, it was generally explained away on the basis that it was a principle that did not apply to international law or that it could be set aside by reason of the nature and gravity of the crimes under consideration.[49] The jurisprudence of the

The decision as to how this should be achieved lies within the discretion of the Trial Chamber.' See also *Mucić* Appeal Judgment, par 46: 'sentencing in relation to more than one offence involves more than just an assessment of the appropriate period of imprisonment for each offence and the addition of all such periods so assessed as a simple mathematical exercise. The total single sentence, or the effective total sentence where several sentences are imposed, must reflect the totality of the offender's criminal conduct but it must not exceed that totality. Where several sentences are imposed, the result is that the individual sentences must either be less than they would have been had they stood alone or they must be ordered to be served either concurrently or partly concurrently.'

[46] *Čelebići* Appeal Judgment, pars 721, 756–757; *Jelišić* Appeal Judgment, pars 96 and 101; *Furundžija* Appeal Judgment, pars 237, 249–250; *Krnojelac* Trial Judgment, pars 526–532; *Akayesu* Appeal Judgment, par 416; *Semanza* Trial Judgment, par 560; *Kambanda* Trial Judgment, par 29; *Kayishema and Ruzindana* Trial Judgment, pars 10–12; *Ntakirutimana* Trial Judgment, par 883. On the importance of consistency in the punishments and application thereof, see *Krnojelac* Trial Judgment, par 526–532.

[47] See, generally, *Rutaganda* Trial Judgment, par 458; *Kayishema and Ruzindana* Trial Judgment, par 4; *Kambanda* Trial Judgment, pars 29–31; *Ruggiu* Trial Judgment, par 34: '[the Judges'] unfettered discretion to evaluate the facts and attendant circumstances should enable them to take into account any other factor that they deem pertinent [in determining sentence].'

[48] *Furundžija* Appeal Judgment, par 237: 'It is true that certain issues relating to sentencing have now been dealt with in some depth; however, still others have not yet been addressed. The Chamber finds that, at this stage, it is not possible to identify an established "penal regime". Instead, due regard must be given to the relevant provisions in the Statute and the Rules which govern sentencing, as well as the relevant jurisprudence of this Tribunal and the ICTR, and of course to the circumstances of each case.'

[49] See, e.g. Principle II of the Nuremberg principles which would sanction such an approach: 'The fact that international law does not impose a penalty for an act which constitutes a crime under international law does not relieve the person who committed the act from responsibility under

ad hoc Tribunals is consistent with that somewhat unfortunate tradition and the Judges have thus far refrained from adopting sentencing guidelines which would have provided some needed predictability in sentencing and would have somewhat constrained the almost absolute discretion which Judges have in regard to this matter.[50] Equally unfortunate is the failure of the Appeals Chamber to bring some order into the relatively uncharted territory of sentencing.[51] In those circumstances, it is left to the almost unconstrained discretion of each Trial Chamber to find its own compass and to determine the extent of punishment appropriate in view of the circumstances pertaining to each case and each accused.[52]

As time passes, however, sentences will lose some of their significance and much of their potency as an expression of the gravity of the crimes that have been punished. Who today can remember the sentences handed down to the various accused in Nuremberg? What seems to matter most is the ability of the court to explain the sentence handed down to those who expect it to reflect their suffering or the suffering of others. It might be the case that those who were mistreated or who lost their loved ones in Srebrenica or in the Kibuye prefecture may never be able to measure their pain against the sentence handed down to some of those responsible for what happened in those places. But they may find some degree of solace in the knowledge that those who punished those crimes understood their demand for justice and were able to express it on their behalf.

---

international law.' See also summing-up in the *Peleus* trial, the Judge-Advocate advised the court that the maxim *nulla poena sine lege* was essentially a principle applying to domestic crimes, not the sort of crimes under consideration (see *Law Reports of Trials of War Criminals*, XV, 167) or the *Rauter* case, where a Dutch court was even blunter in its rejection of the principle (*Law Reports of Trials of War Criminals*, Vol XV, 169).

[50] See *Blaškić* Appeal Judgment, par 680: 'it is inappropriate to set down a definitive list of sentencing guidelines'; *Krstić* Appeal Judgment, par 242.

[51] The Appeals Chamber will only intervene with regard to sentence where there is a 'discernible error in the Trial Chamber's exercise of discretion in imposing sentence', a tall order (*Aleksovski* Appeal Judgment, par 187).

[52] The Appeals Chamber made it clear, however, that Trial Chambers have a duty to render a reasoned opinion on sentence and that their failure to do so might 'undermin[e] the objectives of sentencing by failing to state what conduct is being punished and why' (*Blaškić* Appeal Judgment, par 722; *Simić* Trial Judgment, par 761).

29

Other Available Penalty: Return of Property

Articles 24 and 23, paragraph 3, of the Tribunals' Statutes (ICTY and ICTR, respectively) provide that, in addition to imprisonment, a Trial Chamber may order the return of any property and proceeds acquired by criminal conduct to their rightful owners.[1] Rule 105 (Restitution of Property) further provides that a Trial Chamber which finds an accused guilty of a crime and concludes from the evidence that unlawful taking of property by the accused was associated with it, shall make a specific finding to that effect in its judgment and shall order restitution of that property to its rightful owner.[2]

The practical difficulties involved in such a process (including the problems involved in the actual recovery of stolen property and the identification of the rightful owner of the property) appear to have deterred all Trial Chambers from any attempt to apply that provision. There is no known case in the jurisprudence of either Tribunal where a Chamber has ordered an individual which it had convicted to return any stolen property criminal proceeds, despite the fact that several Trial Chambers have had ample opportunity to do so.[3]

---

[1] See also Secretary-General Report (ICTY), par 114, which provides that: 'In addition to imprisonment, property and proceeds acquired by criminal conduct should be confiscated and returned to their rightful owners. This would include the return of property wrongfully acquired by means of duress. In this connection the Secretary-General recalls that in Resolution 779 (1992) of 6 October 1992, the Security Council endorsed the principle that all statements or commitments made under duress, particularly those relating to land and property, are wholly null and void.' See also *Ntakirutimana* Trial Judgment, par 880; *Kambanda* Trial Judgment, par 22.

[2] See, in particular, Rules 105(A) and (D) of the Rules of Procedure and Evidence of both Tribunals. See also Rule 98ter(B) of the ICTY Rules of Procedure and Evidence: 'If the Trial Chamber finds the accused guilty of a crime and concludes from the evidence that unlawful taking of property by the accused was associated with it, it shall make a specific finding to that effect in its judgment. The Trial Chamber may order restitution as provided in Rule 105.'

[3] In the *Kunarac* case, for instance, there was ample evidence that two of the accused persons had stolen money and valuables from some of their victims (mainly women taken for the purpose of rape and/or enslavement). The Trial Chamber did not avail itself of the opportunity to use Article 24(3) ICTY Statute to try to recover that property, despite the express wish of a number of victims that the Chamber should do so.

30

Enforcement of Sentences

Once an accused has been sentenced and has exhausted all possibility of appeal, he will serve his sentence in one of the countries that have signed an agreement to that effect with the Tribunals.[1] Pursuant to Article 27 of the ICTY Statute (Enforcement of sentences), '[i]mprisonment shall be served in a State designated by the International Tribunal from a list of States which have indicated to the Security Council their willingness to accept convicted persons'. Article 26 of the ICTR Statute provides for a similar system although it also provides for the possibility of the sentence being served in Rwanda itself.[2]

The fact that a convicted person might have to serve his or her sentence in a country not his or her own may not be regarded in principle as a mitigating factor for sentencing.[3] But when deciding in what state the convicted person must serve his or her sentence, the President of the Tribunal will take into consideration that person's personal circumstances, and, *inter alia*, the proximity to the convicted person's relations.[4]

The Statutes of both Tribunals further provide that 'imprisonment shall be in accordance with the applicable law of the State concerned, subject to the supervision of the International Tribunal'. Although such a provision may be a sensible one from a practical and jurisdictional point of view, it may lead to some rather unfortunate results. In particular, two individuals who have been handed similar sentences by the International Tribunals may be sent to two different countries to serve their sentence in which their entitlement to parole or early release may vary greatly due to the local applicable law, and they may therefore end up serving, *in fact*, two very different sentences.[5]

[1] For those agreements, see www.ictr.org/ENGLISH/agreements/index.htm (ICTY) and www.un.org/icty/legaldoc/index.htm (ICTR).

[2] That possibility was expressly rejected in relation to the ICTY 'given the nature of the crimes in question and the international character of the tribunal' (Secretary-General Report (ICTY), par 121).

[3] *Mrdja* Sentencing Judgment, pars 107–109. The Trial Chamber pointed out, however, that it would take that factor into account when deciding upon an appropriate sentence, albeit not as a mitigating factor (ibid., par 109).

[4] See generally 'Practice Direction on the Procedure for the International Tribunal's Designation of the State in which a Convicted Person is to Serve his/her Sentence' concerning some of the factors relevant to the President's decision in that regard. See also *Mrdja* Sentencing Judgment, pars 107–109.

[5] Another accused, Goran Jelišić, who had been convicted and sentenced by the ICTY to forty-years' imprisonment was sent to serve his sentence in Italy. Once there, his sentence was reduced by an Italian court to thirty years' imprisonment, the maximum sentence available in Italy at the time (without prior consultation with the President of the ICTY contrary to the Statute and the Rules of the Tribunal which provide for consultation of and supervision by the President over such matters). See Corte di Cassazione Sez. I, 5/12/02, dep. 14/01/03, n 3785.

PART VIII
CONCLUSIONS

31

Concluding Remarks

In the wake of the Nuremberg Trial, an American Military Tribunal remarked that '[i]f the laws of war are to have any beneficent effect, they must be enforced'.[1] The same could have been said of the law of genocide or the law of crimes against humanity, then and now.

Several years into their existence, there was not much enforcement to talk about in The Hague or in Arusha. In some ways, the very existence of the two *ad hoc* Tribunals had even come to symbolize the failure of their powerful creators to do more than to promise and forget and for months and years, gross violations of humanitarian law continued unabated in the former Yugoslavia, the Tribunals barely noticeable.

The existence of *ad hoc* Tribunals did not stop crimes from being committed, as became apparent, most tragically perhaps, in Srebrenica in the summer of 1995, months after the adoption of the Statute of the ICTY by the Security Council. When asked about the relevance of the Geneva Conventions to his actions at the time, one of the participants in that massacre could not hide his surprise at such a question and expressed the profound irrelevance into which the law had fallen:[2]

Do you really think that in an operation where 7,000 people were set aside, captured, and killed that somebody was adhering to the Geneva Conventions? Do you really believe that somebody adhered to the law, rules and regulations in an operation where so many were killed? First of all, they were captured, killed and then buried, exhumed once again, buried again. Can you conceive of that, that somebody in an operation of that kind adhered to the Geneva Conventions? Nobody [. . .] adhered to the Geneva Conventions or the rules and regulations. Because had they, then the consequences of that particular operation would not have been the total of 7,000 people dead.

But nowhere are courts of law expected to make crimes impossible. As Sir Hartley Shawcross, the British Chief Prosecutor at Nuremberg, noted, the law should not be blamed for its weaknesses: '[I]t may be that the policemen did not

---

[1] *United States v. List and others*, United States Military Tribunal sitting at Nuremberg, judgment of 19 February 1948, *Law Reports of Trials of War Criminals*, XI (1950) ('*Hostages* case'), 1230, 1253–1254.

[2] *Blagojević* Trial, Trial Proceedings – Transcript of hearing, 25 September 2003, T 1959–1960, cited in *Nikolić* Sentencing Judgment, par 88.

act as effectively as one could have wished them to act', he remarked, '[b]ut that was a failure of the policemen, not of the law.'[3]

Slowly, almost imperceptibly, however, through a combination of perseverance and good fortune, the Tribunals found a place for themselves, somewhere between international politics and a stubborn commitment to the rule of law.

With the jurisprudence of the Tribunals, a trickle at first, and an overwhelming volume of case law today, the laws of genocide, crimes against humanity, and war crimes have ceased to be a monument to the dead of the Second World War living only in textbooks and treaties, and have entered into the world of enforceable norms.

The application of humanitarian law by the *ad hoc* Tribunals showed that law does not cease to exist because it is repeatedly violated in wartime, so outrageously that it makes one doubt the law's relevance. Even at the worst of times during the conflicts in the former Yugoslavia and in Rwanda, none of the parties ever suggested that humanitarian law did not apply to them or that they could disregard it.

If nothing else, the existence and jurisprudence of the Tribunals is a formidable victory for international law. This time, and in distinction to what might have been said about Nuremberg, there is no suggestion to be made that the accused who appear before them could reasonably have been in doubt that most of those crimes provided for in the Statutes were indeed criminal under international law at the time. Certainly, the *ad hoc* Tribunals have not of themselves created a culture of law abidance in the international sphere as may be understood in most domestic systems. But the law's pertinence is not reflected only (and perhaps not even primarily) by the degree of compliance which it is able to guarantee, but also by the extent to which particular conduct is assessed and judged in light of it and the extent to which those accused of breaching that law want to distance their conduct from it. In that respect, the findings of the *ad hoc* Tribunals as to many different aspects of international humanitarian law provide clear benchmarks against which allegations of violations (or assertions of compliance) may now be tested.

In that regard, the first major jurisprudential achievement of the *ad hoc* Tribunals is to have identified a whole body of rules whose existence under international law had until then been almost mythical. Between the two of them, the Tribunals have uncovered literally dozens of rules, principles, criminal offences, and forms of liability which they said are now part of customary international law and therefore of potentially universal application. In so doing, the Tribunals have not just uncovered a body of law that had been hidden since the end of the Second World War. Rather, taking advantage of the agreeable plasticity of customary international law, the Tribunals have taken stock of the numerous developments that have taken place in the field over the past sixty years and have promoted

---

[3] Trial of German Major War Criminals by the International Military Tribunal sitting at Nuremberg, Germany, *Speeches of the Chief Prosecutors at the Close of the Case against the Individual Defendants*, p 55.

a more human-oriented reading of international humanitarian law, hardening in passing many quasi-legal norms standards into clear legal prohibitions.[4]

Whilst Nuremberg might have been the cradle of the law of international crimes as we know it today, the *ad hoc* Tribunals may be lauded for getting it out of the Museum of International Law. And if the Nuremberg Judgment is remembered among other things for acknowledging that individuals not only have rights under international law but also obligations, the Hague and Arusha Tribunals may be remembered ultimately, through some trial and error in the development of its jurisprudence, for bringing precision to international criminal law, for spelling out many of its aspects, and for extending the realm of its application. Many of these developments have been discussed above and they will not be reiterated here, but to highlight perhaps some of the most significant among them: the Tribunals have defined, for instance, what constitutes 'an armed conflict' for the purpose of war crimes and have specified what nexus needs to exist between a particular conduct and the armed conflict for it to constitute a war crime; they have spelled out the elements (*mens rea* and *actus reus*) of dozens of international crimes such as rape, persecution, or extermination, which until then had only had a most hazy existence under international law; they have explained and detailed almost every aspect of the *chapeau* elements and general requirements of all three great categories of crimes; they have specified which individuals could be considered victims under each of those categories and set out the conditions under which an individual may be held criminally responsible for his involvement in the commission of any such crime; and they have provided some general guiding principles concerning the sentencing of international crimes.

Many of those developments have now made their way into the Statute of the ICC or the *Elements of Crimes* that accompany the Statute, while some of the Tribunals' holdings have been adopted and furthered by domestic courts and tribunals.[5] The body of jurisprudence which the Tribunals for the former Yugoslavia and for Rwanda have produced over the years might thus become a *trait d'union* between Nuremberg and that incredible project of a permanent international criminal court which is now taking roots in the Dutch city of The Hague.

---

[4] *Kupreškić* Trial Judgment, pars 515, 518 and 529.

[5] Thus far, domestic tribunals have proved extremely deferential towards the two Tribunals and have at times shown a submissiveness in matters of international humanitarian law not very different from that of a local district court *vis-à-vis* its national supreme court. See, for instance, *People v. Trajković*, P Nr 68/2000, District Court of Gjilan, Kosovo, Federal Republic of Yugoslavia (Mar. 6, 2001); *In re Bouterse*, Hof, Amsterdam, 20 November 2000 (The Netherlands); and *In re Jorgić*, Docket No. 2 BvR 1290/99, Decision of 12 December 2000 – available at the website of the German Constitutional Court under <www.bundesverfassungsgericht.de>. Compare, also, 2 BvR 1290/99, Decision of 12 December 2000, 32 and 33, and *Jelišić* Trial Judgment, pars 66 and 98. Pursuant to Article 9 of the ICTY (Article 8 of the ICTR Statute), the International Tribunal and national courts in the former Yugoslavia (respectively, in Rwanda) shall have concurrent jurisdiction to prosecute persons for serious violations of international humanitarian law. The International Tribunal shall, however, have primacy over national courts (par 2).

Ultimately, however, the 'gravitational force'[6] of the Tribunals' jurisprudence will depend, not on the fact that a statement of law has originated in an international tribunal (although that may somewhat increase its authority), but upon the persuasiveness of the statement itself and on the 'quality' of the justice delivered in those institutions.[7] A finding by either of the Tribunals that a particular rule is now part of customary international law will not carry much weight in the long term where, for instance, the Chamber making that finding failed to support it with adequate evidence of state practice and *opinio juris*.[8]

As noted above, the jurisprudence of the *ad hoc* Tribunals is not just the unthinking application of existing precedents. Instead, the Tribunals have generously extended the boundaries of international humanitarian law by giving, for instance, the concept of 'armed conflict' a very broad definition, by applying most (if not all) of the law of international armed conflicts to internal ones, by giving a very liberal interpretation of the concept of 'protected persons' under the grave breaches regime, by loosening the war nexus demanded for all war crimes, or by severing at once the war nexus requirement for all crimes against humanity.

But despite the sometimes quasi-legislative activity of those two courts, international criminal law remains to a large extent incomplete and fragmentary. The law of the *ad hoc* Tribunals should not, therefore, be looked at as a fully matured body of law nor as an end in itself, but should serve as an incentive for further development.

Whatever judgment is passed upon the merits and failings of the *ad hoc* Tribunal once the dust settles, their legacy will not disappear with the Tribunals themselves as they eventually close down. The value of such an International Tribunal to the world does not depend on 'living like a tree a thousand years', Lord Wright pointed out more than half a century ago; it was enough, for instance, that the Nuremberg Tribunal took its place in history and was recorded.[9] And so is it for the *ad hoc* Tribunals, whose jurisprudence will survive them.

The judicial activity of the *ad hoc* Tribunals has been more than the occasion for developing international law and punishing the guilty. The King in Lewis Carroll's *Through the Looking-Glass* swore that '[t]he horror of that moment I shall never, *never* forget!' 'You will, though', his Queen retorted, 'if you don't make a memorandum of it.'[10] The *ad hoc* Tribunals are not in the business of writing history; they are writing criminal law judgments. But their jurisprudence is full of those little memoranda which record the crimes of particular individuals, the suffering of their victims and the context in which such events occurred. As they do so, the Tribunals contribute to removing the obstacle to belief that the sheer horror of some of those crimes might raise and they leave for future generations some record of those events free of the burden of collective guilt. The existence

---

6 R. Dworkin, *Taking Rights Seriously*, revd edn (Cambridge: Harvard University Press, 1978), p 111.
7 See *Nikolić* Sentencing Judgment, par 67.   8 See *Vasiljević* Trial Judgment, fn 586, p 86.
9 Lord Wright, '*Foreword*' to *UN War Crimes Commission*, p vi.
10 L. Carroll, *Through the Looking-Glass* (London: Allan Wingate, 1954), p 142.

and the work of the Tribunals also demonstrate the commitment of the international community at large to the rule of international law, with the hope of achieving, by these small inroads on impunity a real, not just theoretical deterrent to international criminal conduct.

At the very least, the prosecution and punishment of crimes committed in the former Yugoslavia and in Rwanda made us realize that 'law and justice play a far more essential part in the life of the people than we [had] hitherto realized'.[11] It might also have made us less cynical about our ability to do something about such atrocities, and thus a little bit more responsible when we fail to act.

[11] Citation attributed to Monsieur Terge Wold, Norwegian Minister of Justice, International Commission for Penal Reconstruction and Development, Proceedings of the Conference Held in Cambridge on 14 November 1941, between Representatives of Nine Allied Countries and of the Department of Criminal Science in the University of Cambridge, L. Radzinowicz and J.W. Cecil Turner (eds.), p 44.

Select Bibliography

DOCUMENTS AND INTERNATIONAL INSTRUMENTS
RELATING TO THE *AD HOC* TRIBUNALS

Tribunals' Statutes and Rules of Procedure and Evidence

Statute of the International Criminal Tribunal for the Former Yugoslavia, Security Council Resolution 808, UN SCOR, 48th Session, 3217th meeting, Annex, UN Doc. S/RES/808 (1993) ('ICTY Statute') (as last amended on 19 May 2003)

Statute of the International Criminal Tribunal for Rwanda, Security Council Resolution 955, UN SCOR, 49th Session, 3453rd meeting, Annex, UN Doc. S/RES/955 (1994) ('ICTR Statute') (as last amended on 27 October 2003)

Rules of Procedure and Evidence (ICTY) (as last amended on 12 August 2004) (IT/32/Rev. 32)

Rules of Procedure and Evidence (ICTR) (as last amended on 24 April 2004)

The most relevant texts, regulations and instruments applicable to both Tribunals are available on their respective websites (see below).

Security Council Resolutions and the establishment of the *ad hoc* Tribunals

Security Council Resolution 808 (1993), UN Doc. S/RES/808 (22 February 1993)

Security Council Resolution 827 (1993), UN Doc. S/RES/827 (25 May 1993)

Security Council Resolution 955 (1994), UN Doc. S/RES/955 (8 November 1994)

There are other Security Council resolutions which deal generally with the events in the former Yugoslavia (prior to and after to the establishment of the ICTY) and Rwanda. Some of those deal with different matters relating to the work and functioning of the Tribunals. Those resolutions (as well as those mentioned above) are available on the Tribunals' respective websites or on the website of the United Nations (www.un.org).

Other important documents

Preliminary Report of the Commission of Experts Established pursuant to Security Council Resolution 780 (1992), UN Doc. S/25274 (10 February 1993) ('Preliminary Report of the Commission of Experts for the Former Yugoslavia')

Report of the Secretary-General pursuant to Para 2 of Security Council Resolution 808 (1993), UN Doc. S/25704 (3 May 1993) ('Secretary-General Report (ICTY)')

Final Report of the Commission of Experts Established pursuant to Security Council Resolution 935 (1994), UN Doc. S/1994/1405 (3 December 1993) ('Final Report of the Commission of Experts for Rwanda')

Final Report of the Commission of Experts for the Former Yugoslavia Established pursuant to Security Council Resolution 780 (1992), UN Doc. S/1994/674 (5 May 1994) ('Final Report of the Commission of Experts for the Former Yugoslavia')

Preliminary Report of the Independent Commission of Experts Established in accordance with Security Council Resolution 935 (1994), UNSCOR, UN Doc. S/1994/1125 (1 October 1994) ('Preliminary Report of the Commission of Experts for Rwanda')

Report of the Secretary-General Pursuant to Paragraph 5 of the Security Council Resolution 955 (1994), UN Doc. S/1995/134 (13 February 1995) ('Secretary-General Report (ICTR)')

Further Report of the Secretary-General Pursuant to Paragraph 5 of the Security Council 955 (1994), UN Doc. S/1995/533 (30 June 1995)

Third Report of the Secretary-General Pursuant to Paragraph 5 of the Security Council 955 (1994), UN Doc. S/1995/741 (25 August 1995)

See also the Tribunals' *Annuals Reports* submitted by the Presidents of the Tribunals to the United Nations General Assembly and Security Council, which contain much important information about the work and functioning of the *ad hoc* Tribunals since their inception (as available on their respective websites, see below)

ICTY AND ICTR PUBLICATIONS

The Press and Information Section of the ICTY publishes a number of useful documents related to the Tribunal and its jurisprudence, including the following:

- *The Path to The Hague: Selected Documents on the Origins of the ICTY* is a short publication which contains some important and less-known documents relating to the coming to life of the ICTY and contains a number of important texts by the actors of the establishment of the Tribunal (The Hague: United Nations Publications, 2001)

- *Weekly update* contains a brief weekly overview of the main judicial activity of the Tribunal – available on the Tribunal's website

- *Judicial Supplements* is a monthly publication containing summaries of the most significant decisions, orders and judgments of the past month – available on the Tribunal's website

- *Basic Documents* containing the most important texts and instruments applicable to the ICTY, published in 1995, 1998, and 2001 (The Hague: United Nations Publications, 1995, 1998, and 2001)

- *Yearbook of the ICTY* is a collection of official documents issued in a given calendar year either by the Tribunal itself or in relation to the Tribunal; it also features biographies and a bibliography. Thus far, the ICTY has published *Yearbooks* for the period 1994–1999 (The Hague: United Nations Publications)

- *Judicial Reports* comprise all public indictments, as well as Decisions and Judgments issued in a given year, in English and French. Thus far, *Judicial Reports* covering the period 1994–1997 have been published (The Hague: Martinus Nihjoff/Brill Publishers for 1994–1996, The Hague: Brill Publishers for 1997)

The ICTR also publishes a number of useful documents, some of which may be found on its website:

- *ICTR Bulletin* provides an overview of the activity and main court decisions rendered by the ICTR – available on the Tribunal's website
- *ICTR Newsletter* available on the Tribunal's website
- *Reports of Orders, Decisions and Judgments* comprise all Judgments, Decisions and Orders issued in a given year by the court as well as all public indictments (in English and French); reports for 1995–1998 have already been published (Brussels: Bruylant Publishers)
- *Basic Documents and Caselaw*, 1995–2000 and 2001–2002 (CDs containing the most important texts applicable to the ICTR and the most important judgments, orders and decisions of the Tribunal) (Arusha: United Nations Publications); the ICTR also publishes a printed version of its basic documents (last amended and published 27 May 2003)

BOOKS AND MONOGRAPHS

J. E. Ackerman and E. O'Sullivan, *Practice and Procedure of the International Criminal Tribunal for the Former Yugoslavia* (The Hague/London/Boston: Kluwer Law International, 2000)

Y. Aksar, *Implementing International Humanitarian Law: From the* ad hoc *Tribunals to a Permanent International Criminal Court* (New York: Frank Cass Publishers, 2004)

H. Ascensio, E. Decaux, and A. Pellet, *Droit international pénal* (Paris: Pedone, 2000)

K. D. Askin, *War Crimes Against Women: Prosecution in International War Crimes Tribunals* (The Hague/Boston/London: Martinus Nijhoff Publishers, 1997)

H. Ball, *Prosecuting War Crimes and Genocide: The Twentieth Century Experience* (Kansas: University of Kansas Press, 1999)

J. P. Baselain and T. Cretin, *La Justice pénale internationale: Son evolution, son avenir de Nuremberg à La Haye* (Paris: Presses Universitaires de France, 2000)

G. J. Bass, *Stay the Hand of Vengeance: The Politics of War Crimes Tribunals* (Princeton: Princeton University Press, 2002)

M. C. Bassiouni, *Crimes Against Humanity in International Criminal Law*, 2nd revd edn (The Hague/Boston/London: Martinus Nijhoff Publishers, 1999)

M. C. Bassiouni and P. Manikas, *The Law of the International Criminal Tribunal for the Former Yugoslavia* (Irvington-on-Hudson: Transnational Publishers, 1996)

Y. Beigbeder, *Judging Criminal Leaders: The Slow Erosion of Impunity* (The Hague/Boston/London: Martinus Nijhoff Publishers, 2002)

G. Boas and W. A. Schabas (eds.), *International Criminal Law Developments in the Case Law of the ICTY* (The Hague/Boston/London: Martinus Nijhoff Publishers, 2003)

M. Boot, *Genocide, Crimes Against Humanity, War Crimes*: Nullum Crimen Sine Lege *and the Subject Matter Jurisdiction of the International Criminal Court* (Antwerp/Oxford/New York: Intersentia, 2002)

M. Bothe, K. Partsch, and W. Solf, *New Rules for Victims of Armed Conflicts: Commentary on the Two 1977 Protocols Additional to the Geneva Conventions of 1949* (The Hague: Martinus Nijhoff, 1982)

B. Broomhall, *International Justice and the International Criminal Court: Between Sovereignty and the Rule of Law* (Oxford: Oxford University Press, 2003)

P. Calvocoressi, *Nuremberg: The Facts, the Law and the Consequences* (London: Chatto and Windus, 1947)

J. Carey and R. Pritchard (eds.), *International Humanitarian Law: Origins, Challenges and Prospects* (Lampeter, UK: Edwin Mellen Press, 2000)

A. Cassese, *International Criminal Law* (Oxford: Oxford University Press, 2003)

A. Cassese and M. Delmas-Marty (eds.), *Crimes internationaux et juridictions internationales* (Paris: Presses Universitaires de France, 2002)

G. Creel, *War Criminals and Punishment* (New York: Hutchinson & Co., 1945)

E. David, *Précis de droit des conflits armés* (Bruxelles: Bruylant, 1994)

Y. Dinstein and M. Tabory (eds.), *War Crimes in International Law* (The Hague/Boston/London: Martinus Nijhoff, 1996)

R. Dixon and K. Khan, *Archbold International Criminal Courts Practice, Procedure and Evidence* (London: Sweet & Maxwell, 2003)

K. Dörmann, *Elements of War Crimes under the Rome Statute of the International Criminal Court: Sources and Commentary*, (Geneva: ICRC/Cambridge: Cambridge University Press, 2003)

G. Draper, *The Red Cross Conventions* (New York: Draeper, 1958)

P. N. Drost, *The Crime of State: Penal Protection for Fundamental Freedoms of Persons and Peoples*, vol. 2 *Genocide: United Nations Legislation on International Criminal Law* (Leyden: A. W. Sythoff, 1959) ('Drost, *The Crime of State*')

J. Dugard and C. van den Wyngaert, *International Criminal Law and Procedure* (Aldershot/Brookfield/Singapore/Sydney: Dartmouth, 1996)

H. Fischer, C. Kress, and S. R. Lüder (eds.), *International and National Prosecution of Crimes under International Law* (Berlin: Berlin Verlag, 2001)

D. Fleck (ed.), *The Handbook of Humanitarian Law in Armed Conflicts* (Oxford: Oxford University Press, 1995)

L. Friedman, *The Law of War: A Documentary History* (New York: Random House, 1972) ('Friedman, *The Law of War*')

H. P. Gasser, *International Humanitarian Law: An Introduction*, Henry Dunant Institute (Bern: Paul Haupt, 1993) ('Gasser, *International Humanitarian Law*')

S. Glueck, *War Criminals: Their Prosecution and Punishment* (New York: A. Knopf, 1944)

L. C. Green, *The Contemporary Law of Armed Conflict* (Manchester: Manchester University Press, 2000)

J. Hagan, *Justice in the Balkans: Prosecuting War Crimes in The Hague* (Chicago: Chicago University Press, 2003)

R. Haveman, O. Kavran, and J. Nicholls (eds.), *Supranational Criminal Law: a System* Sui Generis (Antwerp/Oxford/New York: Intersentia, 2003)

P. Hazan, *Justice in Time of War: The True Story behind the International Criminal Tribunal for the Former Yugoslavia* (Texas: A&M University Press, College Station, Texas 2004)

M. Henzelin and R. Roth (eds.), *Le Droit pénal à l'épreuve de l'internationalisation* (Paris: LGDJ/Geneva: Georg/Brussels: Bruylant, 2002)

M. Hudson, *International Tribunals: Past and Future* (Clark, New Jersey: The Lawbook Exchange, Ltd., 2003)

Human Rights Watch, *Genocide, War Crimes, and Crimes Against Humanity: Topical Digest of the Case Law of the International Criminal Tribunal for Rwanda and the International Criminal Tribunal for the Former Yugoslavia* (2004) (this valuable document may be downloaded from Human Rights Watch's website: www.hrw.org)

J. R. W. D. Jones and S. Powles, *International Criminal Practice* (Ardsley: Transnational Publishers, 2003)

F. Kalshoven and Y. Sandoz (eds.), *Implementation of International Humanitarian Law: Mise en oeuvre du droit international humanitaire* (Dordrecht/Boston/London: Martinus Nijhoff, 1989)

F. Kalshoven and L. Zegveld, *Constraints on the Waging of War* (Geneva: ICRC, 2001)

R. Kerr, *The International Criminal Tribunal for the Former Yugoslavia: An Exercise in Law, Politics, and Diplomacy* (Oxford: Oxford University Press, 2004)

K. Kittichaisaree, *International Criminal Law* (Oxford: Oxford University Press, 2001)

A. Klip and G. Sluiter, *Annotated Leading Cases of International Criminal Tribunals for the Former Yugoslavia and for Rwanda*, vols. 1 to 6 (covering 1993–2001) (Antwerp/Oxford/New York: Intersentia, 2003)

G. J. A. Knoops, *An Introduction to the Law of International Criminal Tribunals* (Ardsley: Transnational Publishers, 2003)

F. Lattanzi and E. Sciso (eds.), *Dai Tribunali Penali Internazionali Ad Hoc a Una Corte Permanente* (Naples: Editoriale Scientifica, 1996)

R. Lemkin, *Axis Rule in Occupied Europe: Laws of Occupation – Analysis of Government – Proposals for Redress* (Washington, D.C.: Carnegie Endowment for International Peace, 1944) ('Lemkin, *Axis Rule in Occupied Europe*')

K. Lescure and F. Trintignac, *International Justice for Former Yugoslavia: The Working of the International Criminal Tribunal of the Hague* (The Hague/London/Boston: Kluwer Law International, 1996)

R. May *et al.* (eds.), *Essays on ICTY Procedure and Evidence in Honour of Gabrielle Kirk McDonald* (The Hague/London/Boston: Kluwer Law International, 2001)

T. L. H. McCormack and G. J. Simpson (eds.), *The Law of War Crimes* (The Hague/London/Boston: Kluwer Law International, 1997)

G. K. McDonald and O. Swaak-Goldman (eds.), *Substantive and Procedural Aspects of International Criminal Law I* (The Hague/London/Boston: Kluwer Law International, 2000)

F. Mégret, *Le Tribunal Pénal International pour le Rwanda* (Paris: Pedone, 2002)

T. Meron, *War Crimes Law Comes of Age: Essays* (Oxford: Oxford University Press, 1999)

H. Meyrowitz, *La Répression par les Tribunaux Allemands des Crimes Contre l'Humanité et de l' Appartenance à une Organisation Criminelle en Application de la Loi no. 10 du Conseil de Contrôle Allié* (Paris: Pichon et Durand-Auzias, 1960)

V. Morris and M. Scharf, *An Insider's Guide to the International Criminal Tribunal for the Former Yugoslavia*, vol. 2 (Ardsley: Transnational Publishers, 1995) ('Morris and Scharf, *The Yugoslav Tribunal*)

V. Morris and M. Scharf, *The International Criminal Tribunal for Rwanda* (Irvington-on-Hudson: Transnational Publishers, 1998, 2 vols) ('Morris and Scharf, *The Rwanda Tribunal*')

N. Passas, *International Crimes* (Aldershot: Ashgate/Burlington: Dartmouth, 2003)

J. J. Paust, M.C. Bassiouni, M. Scharf, J. Gurulé, L. Sadat, B. Zagaris, and S.A. Williams, *International Criminal Law: Cases and Materials* (Durham: Carolina Academic Press, 2000)

V. Pella, *La Guerre-Crime et les criminels de guerre: Réflexions sur la justice pénale internationale* (Neuchâtel: Editions de la Baconnière, 1949)

J. Pictet (gen. ed.) *Commentary, Geneva Convention for the Amelioration of the Condition of the Wounded and Sick in Armed Forces in the Field,* Convention I (Geneva: ICRC, 1960) ('ICRC, *Commentary to Geneva Convention I*')

J. Pictet (gen. ed.) *Commentary, Geneva Convention for the Amelioration of the Condition of the Wounded, Sick and Shipwrecked Members of Armed Forces at Sea,* Convention II (Geneva: ICRC, 1960) ('ICRC, *Commentary to Geneva Convention II*')

J. Pictet (gen. ed.) *Commentary, Geneva Convention Relative to the Treatment of Prisoners of War,* Convention III (Geneva: ICRC, 1960) ('ICRC, *Commentary to Geneva Convention III*')

J. Pictet (gen. ed.) *Commentary, Geneva Convention Relative to the Protection of Civilian Persons,* Convention IV (Geneva: ICRC, 1960) ('ICRC, *Commentary to Geneva Convention IV*')

C. Pilloud, Y. Sandoz, C. Swinarski, and B. Zimmermann (eds.), *Commentary on the Additional Protocols of 8 June 1977 to the Geneva Conventions of 12 August 1949* (Geneva: ICRC/The Hague: Martinus Nijhoff Publishers, 1987) ('ICRC, *Commentary to the Additional Protocols*')

S. Ratner and J. Abrams, *Accountability for Human Rights Atrocities in International Law: Beyond the Nuremberg Legacy* (Oxford: Oxford University Press, 2001)

A. Roberts and R. Guelff (eds.), *Documents on the Laws of War*, 3rd edn (Oxford: Oxford University Press, 2000)

G. Robertson, *Crimes against Humanity: The Struggle for Global Justice* (London: Penguin Books, 1999)

N. Robinson, *The Genocide Convention: A Commentary* (New York: Institute of Jewish Affairs, 1960) ('Robinson, *Genocide Convention – A Commentary*')

P. Sands (ed.), *From Nuremberg to The Hague: The Future of International Criminal Justice* (Cambridge: Cambridge University Press, 2003)

M. Sassòli and A. Bouvier, *How Does Law Protect in War? Cases, Documents and Teaching Materials on Contemporary Practice in International Humanitarian Law* (Geneva: ICRC, 1999)

W. A. Schabas, *Genocide in International Law* (Cambridge: Cambridge University Press, 2000) ('Schabas, *Genocide*')

C. Scheltema and W. van der Wolf, *The International Tribunal for Rwanda: Facts, Cases, Documents* (Nijmegen: Global Law Association, The Netherlands 1999)

D. Schindler and J. Toman (eds.), *The Law of Armed Conflicts: A Collection of Conventions, Resolutions and Other Documents*, 3rd edn (Alphen a/d Rijn/Geneva: Stijhoff & Noordhoff/Henri Dunant Institute, 1988) ('Schindler and Toman, *The Law of Armed Conflicts*')

E. van Sliedregt, *The Criminal Responsibility of Individuals for Violations of International Humanitarian Law* (Cambridge: Cambridge University Press, 2003)

L. S. Sunga, *The Emerging System of International Criminal Law: Developments in Codification and Implementation* (The Hague/London/Boston: Kluwer Law International, 1997)

T. Taylor, *The Anatomy of the Nuremberg Trials* (Boston: Little, Brown & Co., 1993)

N. Tutorow, *War Crimes, War Criminals, and War Crimes Trials: An Annotated Bibliography and Source Book* (New York: Greenwood Press, 1986)

L. C. Vohrah, F. Pocar, Y. Featherstone, O. Fourmy, C. Graham, J. Hocking, and N. Robson (eds.), *Man's Inuhumanity to Man* (The Hague/London/Boston: Kluwer Law International, 2003)

R. Woetzel, *The Nuremberg Trials in International Law* (New York: Stevens & Praeger, 1960)

S. Zappalà, *Human Rights in International Criminal Proceedings* (Oxford: Oxford University Press, 2003)

LAW REVIEW ARTICLES

H. Abtahi, 'The Protection of Cultural Property in Times of Armed Conflict: The Practice of the International Criminal Tribunal for the Former Yugoslavia', 14 *Harvard Human Rights Journal (HHRL)* 1 (2001)

P. Akhavan, 'Punishing War Crimes in the Former Yugoslavia: A Critical Juncture for the New World Order', 15 *Human Rights Quarterly* 262 (1993)

P. Akhavan, 'The International Criminal Tribunal for Rwanda: The Politics and Pragmatics of Punishment', 90 *American Journal of International Law (AJIL)* 501–510 (1996)

P. Akhavan, 'Beyond Impunity: Can International Criminal Justice Prevent Future Atrocities?', 95(1) *American Journal of International Law (AJIL)* 7–31 (2001)

P. Akhavan, R. Goldman, T. Meron, and H.W. Parks, 'War Crimes Tribunals: the Record and the Prospects: the Contribution of the *Ad Hoc* Tribunals to International Humanitarian Law', 13 *American University International Law Review* 1509–1531 (1998)

G. Aldrich, 'Jurisdiction of the International Criminal Tribunal for the Former Yugoslavia' 90 *American Journal of International Law (AJIL)* 64 (1996)

J. Alvarez, 'Nuremberg Revisited: The Tadić Case', 7 *European Journal of International Law (EJIL)* 245 (1996)

J. Alvarez, 'Crimes of States/Crimes of Hate: Lessons from Rwanda', 24 *Yale Journal of International Law* 365–483 (1999)

C. Aptel, 'The Intent to Commit Genocide in the Case Law of the International Criminal Tribunal for Rwanda', 13(3) *Criminal Law Forum* 273–291 (2002)

L. Arbour, 'The International Tribunals for Serious Violations of International Humanitarian Law in the Former Yugoslavia and Rwanda', 46(1) *McGill Law Journal* 195–201 (2000)

L. Arbour and A. Neier, 'History and Future of the International Criminal Tribunals for the Former Yugoslavia and Rwanda', 13(6) *American University International Law Review* 13, 1495–1508 (1998)

K. Askin, 'Sexual Violence in Decisions and Indictments of the Yugoslav and Rwandan Tribunals: Current Status', 93 *American Journal of International Law (AJIL)* 97 (1999)

K. Askin, 'Reflections on Some of the Most Significant Achievements of the ICTY ', 37 *New England Law Review* 903–914 (2003)

M. C. Bassiouni, 'The United Nations *ad hoc* Tribunal for the Former Yugoslavia', *Proceedings of the American Society of International Law* 20 (1993)

P. Benvenuti, 'The ICTY Prosecutor and the Review of the NATO Bombing Campaign against the Federal Republic of Yugoslavia', 12 *European Journal International Law (EJIL)* 503 (2001)

S. Beresford, 'Unshackling the Paper Tiger: The Sentencing Practices of the ad hoc Tribunals for the Former Yugoslavia and Rwanda', 1(1–2) *International Criminal Law Review* 33–90 (2001)

G. Boas, 'Comparing the ICTY and the ICC: Some Procedural and Substantive Issues', 47(3) *Netherlands International Law Review* 267 (2000)

R. Boed, 'Individual Criminal Responsibility for Violations of Articles 3 Common to the Geneva Conventions of 1949 and of Additional Protocol II thereto in the Case Law of the International Criminal Tribunal for Rwanda', 13(3) *Criminal Law Forum* 292–322 (2002)

S. Boelaert-Suominen, 'Grave Breaches, Universal Jurisdiction and Internal Armed Conflicts: Is Customary Law Moving towards a Uniform Enforcement Mechanism for All Armed Conflicts?', 5 *Journal of Conflict and Security Law (JCSL)* 63–103 (2000)

A. Cassese, 'On the Current Trends Towards Criminal Prosecution and Punishment of Breaches of International Humanitarian Law', 9(1) *European Journal of International Law (EJIL)* 2 (1998)

A. Cassese, 'Black Letter Lawyering v. Constructive Interpretation: The *Vasiljević* Case', 2(1) *Journal of International Criminal Justice* 265–274 (2004)

A. Cassese, 'The ICTY: A Living and Vital Reality', 2(2) *Journal of International Criminal Justice* 585 (2004)

M. Castillo, 'La Competence du tribunal pour l'ex-Yougoslavie', 98 *Revue générale de droit international public* 61 (1994)

S. Chesterman, 'An Altogether Different Order: Defining the Elements of Crimes Against Humanity', 10(2) *Duke Journal of Comparative and International Law* 307 (2000)

C. Cisse, 'The International Tribunals for the Former Yugoslavia and Rwanda: Some Elements of Comparison', 7 *Transnational Law and Contemporary Problems* 103–118 (1997)

C. Cisse, 'The End of a Culture of Impunity in Rwanda', 1 *Yearbook of International Humanitarian Law (YIHL)* 161 (1998)

R. S. Clark, 'Crimes against Humanity at Nuremberg', in G. Ginsburg and V. N. Kudriavtsev (eds.), *The Nuremberg Trial and International Law* (Dordrecht: Martinus Nijhoff, 1990), pp 177–199

M. Damaška, 'Shadow Side of Command Responsibility', 49 *American Journal of Comparative Law* 455 (2001)

E. David, 'Le Tribunal Pénal pour l'ex-Yougoslavie', 1992 *Revue Belge de droit international* 574

Y. Dinstein, 'Crimes Against Humanity', in J. Makarczyk (ed.), *Theory of International Law at the Threshold of the 21st Century: Essays in Honour of Krzysztof Skubiszewski* (The Hague: Kluwer Law International, 1996), pp 891–908

H. Donnedieu de Vabres, 'Le Procès de Nuremberg devant les principes modernes du Droit Pénal International', 70 *Recueil des Cours de l'Académie de droit international de La Haye* 477 et seq. (1947)

K. Dörmann, 'Contributions by the Ad Hoc Tribunals for the Former Yugoslavia and Rwanda to the Ongoing Work on Elements of Crimes in the Context of the ICC', 94 *Proceedings of the Annual Meeting of the ASIL* 284 (2000)

G. Draper, 'The Geneva Conventions of 1949', 114 *Recueil des Cours de l' Académie de droit international (RCADI)* 63, 87 (1965)

C. Edwards and P. Rowe, 'The International Criminal Tribunal for the Former Yugoslavia: The Decision of the Appeals Chamber on the Interlocutory Appeal on Jurisdiction in the Tadić Case', 45 *International and Comparative Law Quarterly* 691 (1996)

W. J. Fenrick, 'International Humanitarian Law and Criminal Trials', 7 *Transnational Law and Contemporary Problems* 23 (1997)

W. J. Fenrick, 'Should Crimes against Humanity Replace War Crimes?', 37 *CJTL* 767 (1999)

D. Forsythe, 'Politics and the International Tribunal for the Former Yugoslavia', 5 *Criminal Law Review* 401 (1994)

H. Fujita, 'Les Crimes contre l'humanité dans les procès de Nuremberg et Tokyo', 34 *Kobe University Law Review* 1–15 (2000)

H. P. Gasser, 'Armed Conflict within the Territory of a State', in W. Haller *et al.* (eds.) *Im Dienst and der Gemeinschaft* (Basel/Bern/Frankfurt: Helbing & Lichtenhann, 1989), pp 225–240, ('Gasser, *Armed Conflict within the Territory of a State*')

R. Goldstone, 'The International Tribunal for the Former Yugoslavia: A Case Study of Security Council Action', 6 *Duke Journal of Comparative and International Law* 7 (1995)

T. Graditzky, 'Individual Criminal Responsibility for Violations of International Humanitarian Law Committed in Non-International Armed Conflicts', 322 *International Review of the Red Cross* 29 (1998)

J. Graven, 'La Définition et la répression des crimes contre l'humanité', 1 *Revue de droit international de sciences diplomatiques et politiques* 1 (1948)

J. Graven, 'Les Crimes contre l'humanité', 76 *Recueil des Cours de l'Académie de droit international de La Haye* 427 et seq. (1950)

A. K. A. Greenawalt, 'Rethinking Genocidal Intent: The Case for a Knowledge-Based Interpretation', 99 *Columbia Law Review* 2259–2294 (1999)

C. Greenwood, 'The International Tribunal for the Former Yugoslavia' 69 *International Affairs* 641, 161–259 (1993)

C. Greenwood, 'International Humanitarian Law and the Tadić case', 7 *European Journal of International Law (EJIL)* 265–283 (1996)

C. Greenwood, 'International Humanitarian Law (Laws of War): Revised Report for the Centennial Commemoration of the First Hague Peace Conference 1899', in F. Kalshoven (ed), *The Centennial of the First International Peace Conference: Reports and Conclusions* (The Hague/Boston/London: Kluwer Law International, 2000), pp 265–283

O. Gross, 'The Grave Breaches System and the Armed Conflict in the Former Yugoslavia', 16 *Michigan Journal of International Law* 783 (1995)

F. Harhoff, 'Consonance or Rivalry? Calibrating the Efforts to Prosecute War Crimes in National and International Tribunals', 7 *Duke Journal of Comparative and International Law* 571–596 (1997)

C. Harris, 'Precedent in the Practice of the ICTY', in R. May *et al.* (eds.), *Essays on ICTY Procedure and Evidence in Honour of Gabrielle Kirk McDonald* (The Hague/London/Boston: Kluwer Law International, 2001), pp 341–356

J. de Hemptinne, 'Controverses relatives à la définition du crime de persécution', 53 *Revue trimestrielle des droits de l'homme* 15 (2003)

R. Henham, 'The Philosophical Foundations of International Sentencing', *Journal of International Criminal Justice* 64–85 (2003)

Hon. David A. Hunt, 'The International Criminal Court: High Hopes, "Creative Ambiguity" and an Unfortunate Mistrust in International Judges', 2(1) *Journal of International Criminal Justice* 56 (2004)

B. B. Jia, 'The Differing Concepts of War Crimes and Crimes against Humanity in International Criminal Law', in G. Goodwin-Gill *et al.* (eds.), *The Reality of International Law: Essays in Honour of Ian Brownlie* (Oxford: Clarendon Press, 1999), pp 243–271.

L. D. Johnson, 'Ten Years Later: Reflections on the Drafting', 2(2) *Journal of International Criminal Justice* 368 (2004)

M. Klarin, 'The Tribunal's Four Battles', 2(2) *Journal of International Criminal Justice* 546 (2004)

R. Kolb, 'The Jurisprudence of the Yugoslav and Rwandan Criminal Tribunals on their Jurisdiction and on International Crimes', 71 *British Yearbook of International Law (BYIL)* 259–315 (2000)

R. Lee, 'The Rwanda Tribunal', 9 *Leiden Journal of International Law* 42 (1996)

R. Lemkin, 'Genocide as Crime under International Law', 41 *American Journal of International Law (AJIL)* 145 (1947)

H. Levie, 'The Statute of the International Tribunal for the Former Yugoslavia: A Comparison with the Past and a Look at the Future', 21 *Syracuse Journal of International and Comparative Law* 1 (1995)

M. Lippman, 'The Drafting of the 1948 Genocide Convention on the Prevention and Punishment of the Crime of Genocide: Forty-Five Years Later', 3 *Boston University International Law Journal* 1 (1985)

M. Lippman, 'Crimes against Humanity', 17 *British Columbia Third World Law Journal* 171 (1997)

M. Lippman, 'The Convention on the Prevention and Punishment of the Crime of Genocide: Fifty Years Later', 15 *Arizona Journal of International and Comparative Law* 415 (1998)

S. Majstorović, 'Ancient Hatreds or Elite Manipulation? Memory and Politics in the Former Yugoslavia', 159(4) *World Affairs* 170 (1997)

L. Mansfield, 'Crimes against Humanity: Reflections on the Fiftieth Anniversary of Nuremberg and a Forgotten Legacy', 64 *Netherlands Journal of International Law* 293 (1995)

G. K. McDonald, 'The International Criminal Tribunals: Crime and Punishment in the International Arena', 7(3) *ILSA Journal of International and Comparative Law* 667–686 (2001)

J. Meernik, 'Proving and Punishing Genocide at the International Criminal Tribunal for Rwanda', 4(1) *International Criminal Law Review* 65–81 (2004)

T. Meron, 'Rape as a Crime under International Humanitarian Law', 87 *American Journal of International Law (AJIL)* 424 (1993)

T. Meron, 'The Case for War Crimes Trials in Yugoslavia', 72 *Foreign Affairs* 122 (1993)

T. Meron, 'International Criminalization of Internal Atrocities', 89 *American Journal of International Law (AJIL)* 237–316 (July 1995)

T. Meron, 'The Continuing Role of Custom in the Formation of International Humanitarian Law', 90 *American Journal of International Law (AJIL)* 238, 247 (1996)

T. Meron, 'Is International Law Moving Towards Criminalization?', 9 *European Journal of International Law (EJIL)* 18–31 (1998)

T. Meron, 'The Humanization of Humanitarian Law', 95(2) *American Journal of International Law (AJIL)* 239–278 (2000)

G. Mettraux, 'Crimes against Humanity in the Jurisprudence of the International Criminal Tribunals for the Former Yugoslavia and for Rwanda', 43 *Harvard Journal of International Law* 237 et seq. (2002) ('Mettraux, *Crimes Against Humanity*')

G. Mettraux, 'Using Human Rights Law for the Purpose of Defining International Criminal Offences: The Practice of the International Criminal Tribunal for the Former Yugoslavia', in M. Henzelin and R. Roth (eds.), *Le Droit pénal à l'épreuve de l'internationalisation* (Paris: LGDJ/Geneva: Georg/Brussels: Bruylant, 2002), pp 183 et seq.

J. F. Metzl, 'Rwandan Genocide and the International Law of Radio Jamming', 91 *American Journal of International Law (AJIL)* 628 et seq. (1997)

B. Muna, N. Pillay, and T. Rudasingwa, 'The Rwanda Tribunal and its Relationship to National Trials in Rwanda', 13(6) *American University International Law Review*, 1469–1493 (1998)

D. Mundis, 'Improving the Operation and Functioning of the International Criminal Tribunals', 94(4) *American Journal of International Law (AJIL)* 759–773 (2000)

S. Murphy, 'Progress and Jurisprudence of the International Criminal Tribunal for the former Yugoslavia,' 93 *American Journal of International Law (AJIL)* 57 (1999)

A. Obote-Odora, 'Complicity in Genocide as Understood through the ICTR Experience', 2(4) *International Criminal Law Review* 375–408 (2002)

J. Paust, 'Applicability of International Criminal Laws to Events in the Former Yugoslavia', 9 *American University Journal of International Law* 499 (1994)

A. Pellet, 'Le Tribunal criminal international pour l'ex-Yougoslavie: Poudre aux yeux ou avancée décisive?', 98(1) *Revue generale de droit international public* 7–60 (1994)

D. Plattner, 'La Répression pénale des violations du droit international humanitaire applicable aux conflits armés non internationaux', 72 *International Review of the Red Cross* 785,443–455 (1990)

S. Powles, 'Joint Criminal Enterprise: Criminal Liability by Prosecutorial Ingenuity and Judicial Creativity', 2(2) *Journal of International Criminal Justice* 606–619 (2004)

M.-C. Roberge, 'Jurisdiction of the Ad Hoc Tribunals for the Former Yugoslavia and Rwanda over Crimes against Humanity and Genocide', 321 *International Review of the Red Cross* 651 (1997)

K. Roberts, 'The Law of Persecution Before the International Criminal Tribunal for the Former Yugoslavia', 15 *Leiden Journal of International Law* 623 (2002) ('Roberts, *Persecution*')

W. A. Schabas, '*Genocide*', in O. Triffterer (ed.), *Commentary on the Rome Statute of the International Criminal Court* (Baden-Baden: Nomos, 1999), pp 107–116 ('Schabas, *Genocide in the Rome Statute*')

W. A. Schabas, 'Groups Protected by the Genocide Convention: Conflicting Interpretations form the International Criminal Tribunal for Rwanda', 6(2) *ILSA Journal of International and Comparative Law* 375 (2000)

W. A. Schabas, 'Perverse Effects of the *Nulla poena* Principle: National Practice and the Ad Hoc Tribunals', 11(3) *European Journal of International Law (EJIL)* 521 (2000)

M. Scharf, 'The Tools for Enforcing International Criminal Justice in the New Millenium: Lessons for the Yugoslavia Tribunal', 49(4) *DePaul Law Review* 925 (2000)

D. Schindler, 'The Different Types of Armed Conflicts According to the Geneva Conventions and Protocols', 163(II) *Recueil des Cours de l'Académie de droit international de La Haye* 117 et seq. (1979) ('Schindler, *Armed Conflicts and the Geneva Conventions*')

E. Schwelb, 'Crimes Against Humanity', *British Yearbook of International Law (BYIL)* 178–226 (1946)

D. Shraga, 'International Criminal Tribunal for Rwanda', 7 *European Journal of International Law (EJIL)* 501 (1996)

D. Shraga and R. Zacklin, 'The International Criminal Tribunal for Rwanda', 7(4) *European Journal of International Law (EJIL)* 501–518 (1996)

I. Simonovic, 'The Role of the ICTY in the Development of International Criminal Adjudication', 23 *Fordham International Journal of Law* 440 (1999)

M. Smidt, 'Yamashita, Medina, and Beyond: Command Responsibility in Contemporary Military Operations', 164 *Military Law Review* 155 (2000)

L. B. Sohn, 'From Nazi Germany and Japan to Yugoslavia and Rwanda: similarities and differences', 12(2) *Connecticut Journal of International Law* 209 (1997)

P. Tavernier, 'The Experience of the International Criminal Tribunals for the Former Yugoslavia and for Rwanda', 321 *International Review of the Red Cross* 605 (1997)

V. Tochilovsky, 'Proceedings in the International Criminal Court: Some Lessons to Learn from ICTY Experience', 10(4) *European Journal of Crime, Criminal Law and Criminal Justice* 268–275 (2002)

C. Tournaye, 'Genocidal Intent before the ICTY', 52(2) *International and Comparative Law Quarterly* 447–462 (2003)

B. van Schaack, 'The Definition of Crimes Against Humanity: Resolving the Incoherence', 37 *Columbia Journal of Transnational Law* 787 (1999)

G. Verdirame, 'The Genocide Definition in the Jurisprudence of the *ad hoc* Tribunals', 49 *International and Comparative Law Quarterly* 578 (2000)

L. Vierucci, 'The First Steps of the International Criminal Tribunal for the Former Yugoslavia', 6(1) *European Journal International Law (EJIL)* 134 (1995)

P. Wald, 'Judging War Criminals', 1 *Chicago Journal of International Law* 189 (2000)

P. Wald, 'ICTY Judicial Proceedings: An Appraisal from Within', 2(2) *Journal of International Criminal Justice* 466 (2004)

P. Weckel, 'L'Institution d'un tribunal international pour la repression des crimes de droit humanitaire en Yougoslavie', 39 *Annuaire français de droit international* 232 (1993)

M. Wierda, 'What Lessons Can Be Learned from the Ad Hoc Criminal Tribunals?', 9 *University of California Davis Journal of International Law and Policy* 13 (2002)

Q. Wright, 'The Law of the Nuremberg Trial', 41 *American Journal of International Law (AJIL)* 38–72 (1947)

R. Zacklin, 'Some Major Problems in the Drafting of the ICTY Statute', 2(2) *Journal of International Criminal Justice* 361 (2004)

R. Zacklin, 'The Failings of Ad Hoc International Tribunals', 2(2) *Journal of International Criminal Justice* 541 (2004)

Many generic international law journals have published papers related to some particular aspects of the work of the *ad hoc* Tribunals. There are also a number of specialized publications which regularly published articles related to the issues of international crimes. See in particular *International Criminal Law Review, Journal of International Criminal Justice, Criminal Law Forum, Leiden Journal of International Law*, and *Netherlands Journal of International Law*.

Volume 2(2) (June 2004) of the *Journal of International Criminal Justice* contains a special issue on the 10th anniversary of the ICTY, with many papers relating to issues dealt with in this book. In 2005, the *Journal of International Criminal Justice* will publish a similar special issue to mark the tenth anniversary of the establishment of the ICTR.

WEBSITES

ICTY official website: www.un.org/icty.

ICTR official website: www.ictr.org.

Some other websites contain useful material, articles or resources relating, *inter alia*, to the *ad hoc* Tribunals:

Utrecht University (search engine for ICTR caselaw): www.law.uu.nl\sim and http:// sim.law.uu.nl/sim/Dochome.nsf

Avocats sans frontières: www.asf.be

Diplomatie Judiciaire-Judicial Diplomacy: www.diplomatiejudiciaire.com

Fondation Hirondelle: www.hirondelle.org

Institute for Peace and War Reporting: www.iwpr.net

Domovina (www.domovina.net) and courttv.com (www.courttv.com) provide live access to ICTY courtrooms

International Humanitarian Law Research Initiative: www.ihlresearch.org

Coalition for International Justice: www.cij.org

Crimes of War Project: www.crimesof war.org

International Criminal Court: www.icc.int

International Committee of the Red Cross: www.icrc.org

Nizkor project: www.nizkor.org

Avalon Project at Yale University: www.yale.edu/lawweb/avalon

Project on International Courts and Tribunals: www.pict-pcti.org/news/archvie.html

War Crimes and War Criminals: www.ess.uwe.ac.uk/genocide/war_criminals.htm

UC Berkeley War Crimes Studies Center: http://socrates.berkeley.edu/~warcrime/

International and Comparative Criminal Trial Project: www.nls.ntu.ac.uk/CLR/ICTP/ Project%20Aim/ProjectAim.htm

Annexes

I ICTY

RESOLUTION 808 (1993),
(ADOPTED 22 FEBRUARY 1993)
(S/RES/808 (808))

The Security Council,

Reaffirming its resolution 713 (1991) of 25 September 1991 and all subsequent relevant resolutions,

Recalling paragraph 10 of its resolution 764 (1992) of 13 July 1992, in which it reaffirmed that all parties are bound to comply with the obligations under international humanitarian law and in particular the Geneva Conventions of 12 August 1949, and that persons who commit or order the commission of grave breaches of the Conventions are individually responsible in respect of such breaches,

Recalling also its resolution 771 (1992) of 13 August 1992, in which, *inter alia*, it demanded that all parties and others concerned in the former Yugoslavia, and all military forces in Bosnia and Herzegovina, immediately cease and desist from all breaches of international humanitarian law,

Recalling further its resolution 780 (1992) of 6 October 1992, in which it requested the Secretary-General to establish, as a matter of urgency, an impartial Commission of Experts to examine and analyse the information submitted pursuant to resolutions 771 (1992) and 780 (1992), together with such further information as the Commission of Experts may obtain, with a view to providing the Secretary-General with its conclusions on the evidence of grave breaches of the Geneva Conventions and other violations of international humanitarian law committed in the territory of the former Yugoslavia,

Having considered the interim report of the Commission of Experts established by resolution 780 (1992) (S/25274), in which the Commission observed that a decision to establish an ad hoc international tribunal in relation to events in the territory of the former Yugoslavia would be consistent with the direction of its work,

Expressing once again its grave alarm at continuing reports of widespread violations of international humanitarian law occurring within the territory of the former Yugoslavia, including reports of mass killings and the continuance of the practice of "ethnic cleansing",

Determining that this situation constitutes a threat to international peace and security,

Determined to put an end to such crimes and to take effective measures to bring to justice the persons who are responsible for them,

Convinced that in the particular circumstances of the former Yugoslavia the establishment of an international tribunal would enable this aim to be achieved and would contribute to the restoration and maintenance of peace,

Noting in this regard the recommendation by the Co-Chairmen of the Steering Committee in the International Conference on the Former Yugoslavia for the establishment of such a tribunal (S/25221),

Noting also with grave concern the "report of the European Community investigative mission into the treatment of Muslim women in the former Yugoslavia" (S/25240, Annex 1),

Noting further the report of the committee of jurists submitted by France (S/25266), the report of the commission of jurists submitted by Italy (S/25300), and the report transmitted by the Permanent Representatives of Sweden on behalf of the Chairman-in-Office of the Conference on Security and Cooperation in Europe (CSCE) (S/25307),

1. *Decides* that an international tribunal shall be established for the prosecution of persons responsible for serious violations of international humanitarian law committed in the territory of the former Yugoslavia since 1991;

2. *Requests* the Secretary-General to submit for consideration by the Council at the earliest possible date, and if possible no later than 60 days after the adoption of the present resolution, a report on all the aspects of this matter, including specific proposals and where appropriate options for the effective and expeditious implementation of the decision contained in paragraph 1 above, taking into account suggestions put forward in this regard by Member States;

3. *Decides* to remain actively seized of the matter.

RESOLUTION 827 (1993),
(ADOPTED 25 MAY 1993)
(S/RES/827 (1993))

The Security Council,

Reaffirming its resolution 713 (1991) of 25 September 1991 and all subsequent relevant resolutions,

Having considered the report of the Secretary-General (S/25704 and Add.1) pursuant to paragraph 2 of resolution 808 (1993),

Expressing once again its grave alarm at continuing reports of widespread and flagrant violations of international humanitarian law occurring within the territory of the former Yugoslavia, and especially in the Republic of Bosnia and Herzegovina, including reports of mass killings, massive, organized and systematic detention and rape of women, and the continuance of the practice of "ethnic cleansing", including for the acquisition and the holding of territory,

Determining that this situation continues to constitute a threat to international peace and security,

Determined to put an end to such crimes and to take effective measures to bring to justice the persons who are responsible for them,

Convinced that in the particular circumstances of the former Yugoslavia the establishment as an ad hoc measure by the Council of an international tribunal and the prosecution of persons responsible for serious violations of international humanitarian law would enable this aim to be achieved and would contribute to the restoration and maintenance of peace,

Believing that the establishment of an international tribunal and the prosecution of persons responsible for the above-mentioned violations of international humanitarian law will contribute to ensuring that such violations are halted and effectively redressed,

Noting in this regard the recommendation by the Co-Chairmen of the Steering Committee of the International Conference on the Former Yugoslavia for the establishment of such a tribunal (S/25221),

Reaffirming in this regard its decision in resolution 808 (1993) that an international tribunal shall be established for the prosecution of persons responsible for serious violations of international humanitarian law committed in the territory of the former Yugoslavia since 1991,

Considering that, pending the appointment of the Prosecutor of the International Tribunal, the Commission of Experts established pursuant to resolution 780 (1992) should continue on an urgent basis the collection of information relating to evidence of grave breaches of the Geneva Conventions and other violations of international humanitarian law as proposed in its interim report (S/25274),

Acting under Chapter VII of the Charter of the United Nations,

1. *Approves* the report of the Secretary-General;

2. *Decides* hereby to establish an international tribunal for the sole purpose of prosecuting persons responsible for serious violations of international humanitarian law committed in the territory of the former Yugoslavia between 1 January 1991 and a date to be determined by the Security Council upon the restoration of peace and to this end to adopt the Statute of the International Tribunal annexed to the above-mentioned report;

3. *Requests* the Secretary-General to submit to the judges of the International Tribunal, upon their election, any suggestions received from States for the rules of procedure and evidence called for in Article 15 of the Statute of the International Tribunal;

4. *Decides* that all States shall cooperate fully with the International Tribunal and its organs in accordance with the present resolution and the Statute of the International Tribunal and that consequently all States shall take any measures necessary under their domestic law to implement the provisions of the present resolution and the Statute, including the obligation of States to comply with requests for assistance or orders issued by a Trial Chamber under Article 29 of the Statute;

5. *Urges* States and intergovernmental and non-governmental organizations to contribute funds, equipment and services to the International Tribunal, including the offer of expert personnel;

6. *Decides* that the determination of the seat of the International Tribunal is subject to the conclusion of appropriate arrangements between the United Nations and the Netherlands acceptable to the Council, and that the International Tribunal may sit elsewhere when it considers it necessary for the efficient exercise of its functions;

7. *Decides also* that the work of the International Tribunal shall be carried out without prejudice to the right of the victims to seek, through appropriate means, compensation for damages incurred as a result of violations of international humanitarian law;

8. *Requests* the Secretary-General to implement urgently the present resolution and in particular to make practical arrangements for the effective functioning of the International Tribunal at the earliest time and to report periodically to the Council;

9. *Decides* to remain actively seized of the matter.

REPORT OF THE SECRETARY-GENERAL
PURSUANT TO PARAGRAPH 2 OF SECURITY COUNCIL
RESOLUTION 808 (1993) (*excerpts*)

PRESENTED 3 MAY 1993
(S/25704)

Introduction

1. By paragraph 1 of resolution 808 (1993) of 22 February 1993, the Security Council decided "that an international tribunal shall be established for the prosecution of persons responsible for serious violations of international humanitarian law committed in the territory of the former Yugoslavia since 1991".

2. By paragraph 2 of the resolution, the Secretary-General was requested "to submit for consideration by the Council at the earliest possible date, and if possible no later than 60 days after the adoption of the present resolution, a report on all aspects of this matter, including specific proposals and where appropriate options for the effective and expeditious implementation of the decision [to establish an international tribunal], taking into account suggestions put forward in this regard by Member States."

3. The present report is presented pursuant to that request.[1]

A

4. Resolution 808 (1993) represents a further step taken by the Security Council in a series of resolutions concerning serious violations of international humanitarian law occurring in the territory of the former Yugoslavia.

5. In resolution 764 (1992) of 13 July 1992, the Security Council reaffirmed that all parties to the conflict are bound to comply with their obligations under international humanitarian law and in particular the Geneva Conventions of 12 August 1949, and that persons who commit or order the commission of grave breaches of the Conventions are individually responsible in respect of such breaches.

6. In resolution 771 (1992) of 13 August 1992, the Security Council expressed grave alarm at continuing reports of widespread violations of international humanitarian law occurring within the territory of the former Yugoslavia and especially in Bosnia and Herzegovina, including reports of mass forcible expulsion and deportation of civilians, imprisonment and abuse of civilians in detention centres, deliberate attacks on non-combatants, hospitals and ambulances, impeding the delivery of food and medical supplies to the civilian population, and wanton devastation and destruction of property. The Council strongly condemned any violations of international humanitarian law, including those involved in the practice of "ethnic cleansing", and demanded that all parties to the conflict in the former Yugoslavia cease and desist from all breaches of international humanitarian law. It called upon States and international humanitarian organizations to collate substantiated information relating to the violations of humanitarian law, including grave breaches of the Geneva

---

[1] On 19 April 1993, the Secretary-General addressed a letter to the President of the Security Council informing him that the report would be made available to the Security Council no later than 6 May 1993.

Conventions, being committed in the territory of the former Yugoslavia and to make this information available to the Council. Furthermore, the Council decided, acting under Chapter VII of the Charter of the United Nations, that all parties and others concerned in the former Yugoslavia, and all military forces in Bosnia and Herzegovina, should comply with the provisions of that resolution, failing which the Council would need to take further measures under the Charter.

7. In resolution 780 (1992) of 6 October 1992, the Security Council requested the Secretary-General to establish an impartial Commission of Experts to examine and analyse the information as requested by resolution 771 (1992), together with such further information as the Commission may obtain through its own investigations or efforts, of other persons or bodies pursuant to resolution 771 (1992), with a view to providing the Secretary-General with its conclusions on the evidence of grave breaches of the Geneva Conventions and other violations of international humanitarian law committed in the territory of the former Yugoslavia.

8. On 14 October 1992 the Secretary-General submitted a report to the Security Council pursuant to paragraph 3 of resolution 780 (1992) in which he outlined his decision to establish a five-member Commission of Experts (S/24657). On 26 October 1992, the Secretary-General announced the appointment of the Chairman and members of the Commission of Experts.

9. By a letter dated 9 February 1993, the Secretary-General submitted to the President of the Security Council an interim report of the Commission of Experts (S/25274), which concluded that grave breaches and other violations of international humanitarian law had been committed in the territory of the former Yugoslavia, including wilful killing, "ethnic cleansing", mass killings, torture, rape, pillage and destruction of civilian property, destruction of cultural and religious property and arbitrary arrests. In its report, the Commission noted that should the Security Council or another competent organ of the United Nations decide to establish an ad hoc international tribunal, such a decision would be consistent with the direction of its work.

10. It was against this background that the Security Council considered and adopted resolution 808 (1993). After recalling the provisions of resolutions 764 (1992), 771 (1992) and 780 (1992) and, taking into consideration the interim report of the Commission of Experts, the Security Council expressed once again its grave alarm at continuing reports of widespread violations of international humanitarian law occurring within the territory of the former Yugoslavia, including reports of mass killings and the continuation of the practice of "ethnic cleansing". The Council determined that this situation constituted a threat to international peace and security, and stated that it was determined to put an end to such crimes and to take effective measures to bring to justice the persons who are responsible for them. The Security Council stated its conviction that in the particular circumstances of the former Yugoslavia the establishment of an international tribunal would enable this aim to be achieved and would contribute to the restoration and maintenance of peace.

11. The Secretary-General wishes to recall that in resolution 820 (1993) of 17 April 1993, the Security Council condemned once again all violations of international humanitarian law, including in particular, the practice of "ethnic cleansing" and the massive, organized and systematic detention and rape of women, and reaffirmed that those who commit or have committed or order or have ordered the commission of such acts will be held individually responsible in respect of such acts.

B

12. The Security Council's decision in resolution 808 (1993) to establish an international tribunal is circumscribed in scope and purpose: the prosecution of persons responsible for serious violations of international humanitarian law committed in the territory of the former Yugoslavia since 1991. The decision does not relate to the establishment of an international criminal jurisdiction in general nor to the creation of an international criminal court of a permanent nature, issues which are and remain under active consideration by the International Law Commission and the General Assembly.

C

13. In accordance with the request of the Security Council, the Secretary-General has taken into account in the preparation of the present report the suggestions put forward by Member States, in particular those reflected in the following Security Council documents submitted by Member States and noted by the Council in its resolution 808 (1993): the report of the committee of jurists submitted by France (S/25266), the report of the commission of jurists submitted by Italy (S/25300), and the report submitted by the Permanent Representative of Sweden on behalf of the Chairman-in-Office of the Conference on Security and Cooperation in Europe (CSCE) (S/25307). The Secretary-General has also sought the views of the Commission of Experts established pursuant to Security Council resolution 780 (1992) and has made use of the information gathered by that Commission. In addition, the Secretary-General has taken into account suggestions or comments put forward formally or informally by the following Member States since the adoption of resolution 808 (1993): Australia, Austria, Belgium, Brazil, Canada, Chile, China, Denmark, Egypt,* Germany, Iran (Islamic Republic of),* Ireland, Italy, Malaysia,* Mexico, Netherlands, New Zealand, Pakistan,* Portugal, Russian Federation, Saudi Arabia,* Senegal,* Slovenia, Spain, Sweden, Turkey,* United Kingdom of Great Britain and Northern Ireland, United States of America and Yugoslavia. He has also received suggestions or comments from a non-member State (Switzerland).

14. The Secretary-General has also received comments from the International Committee of the Red Cross (ICRC), the International Criminal Police Organization and from the following non-governmental organizations: Amnesty International, Association Internationale des Jeunes Avocats, Ethnic Minorities Barristers' Association, Fédération internationale des femmes des carrières juridiques, Jacob Blaustein Institution for the Advancement of Human Rights, Lawyers Committee for Human Rights, National Alliance of Women's Organisations (NAWO), and Parliamentarians for Global Action. Observations have also been received from international meetings and individual experts in relevant fields.

15. The Secretary-General wishes to place on record his appreciation for the interest shown by all the Governments, organizations and individuals who have offered valuable suggestions and comments.

* On behalf of the members of the Organization of the Islamic Conference (OIC) and as members of the Contact Group of OIC on Bosnia and Herzegovina.

D

16. In the main body of the report which follows, the Secretary-General first examines the legal basis for the establishment of the International Tribunal foreseen in resolution 808 (1993). The Secretary-General then sets out in detail the competence of the International Tribunal as regards the law it will apply, the persons to whom the law will be applied, including considerations as to the principle of individual criminal responsibility, its territorial and temporal reach and the relation of its work to that of national courts. In succeeding chapters, the Secretary-General sets out detailed views on the organization of the international tribunal, the investigation and pre-trial proceedings, trial and post-trial proceedings, and cooperation and judicial assistance. A concluding chapter deals with a number of general and organizational issues such as privileges and immunities, the seat of the international tribunal, working languages and financial arrangements.

17. In response to the Security Council's request to include in the report specific proposals, the Secretary-General has decided to incorporate into the report specific language for inclusion in a statute of the International Tribunal. The formulations are based upon provisions found in existing international instruments, particularly with regard to competence *ratione materiae* of the International Tribunal. Suggestions and comments, including suggested draft articles, received from States, organizations and individuals as noted in paragraphs 13 and 14 above, also formed the basis upon which the Secretary-General prepared the statute. Texts prepared in the past by United Nations or other bodies for the establishment of international criminal courts were consulted by the Secretary-General, including texts prepared by the United Nations Committee on International Criminal Jurisdiction,[2] the International Law Commission, and the International Law Association. Proposals regarding individual articles are, therefore, made throughout the body of the report; the full text of the statute of the International Tribunal is contained in the annex to the present report.

I. THE LEGAL BASIS FOR THE ESTABLISHMENT OF THE INTERNATIONAL TRIBUNAL

18. Security Council resolution 808 (1993) states that an international tribunal shall be established for the prosecution of persons responsible for serious violations of international humanitarian law committed in the territory of the former Yugoslavia since 1991. It does not, however, indicate how such an international tribunal is to be established or on what legal basis.

19. The approach which, in the normal course of events, would be followed in establishing an international tribunal would be the conclusion of a treaty by which the States parties would establish a tribunal and approve its statute. This treaty would be drawn up and adopted by an appropriate international body (e.g. the General Assembly or a specially convened conference), following which it would be opened for signature and ratification. Such an approach would have the advantage of allowing for a detailed examination and elaboration of all the issues pertaining to the establishment of the international tribunal. It

---

[2] The 1953 Committee on International Criminal Jurisdiction was established by General Assembly Resolution 687 (VII) of 5 December 1952.

also would allow the States participating in the negotiation and conclusion of the treaty fully to exercise their sovereign will, in particular whether they wish to become parties to the treaty or not.

20. As has been pointed out in many of the comments received, the treaty approach incurs the disadvantage of requiring considerable time to establish an instrument and then to achieve the required number of ratifications for entry into force. Even then, there could be no guarantee that ratifications will be received from those States which should be parties to the treaty if it is to be truly effective.

21. A number of suggestions have been put forward to the effect that the General Assembly, as the most representative organ of the United Nations, should have a role in the establishment of the international tribunal in addition to its role in the administrative and budgetary aspects of the question. The involvement of the General Assembly in the draft- ing or the review of the statute of the International Tribunal would not be reconcilable with the urgency expressed by the Security Council in resolution 808 (1993). The Secretary-General believes that there are other ways of involving the authority and prestige of the General Assembly in the establishment of the International Tribunal.

22. In the light of the disadvantages of the treaty approach in this particular case and of the need indicated in resolution 808 (1993) for an effective and expeditious implementation of the decision to establish an international tribunal, the Secretary-General believes that the International Tribunal should be established by a decision of the Security Council on the basis of Chapter VII of the Charter of the United Nations. Such a decision would constitute a measure to maintain or restore international peace and security, following the requisite determination of the existence of a threat to the peace, breach of the peace or act of aggression.

23. This approach would have the advantage of being expeditious and of being immedi- ately effective as all States would be under a binding obligation to take whatever action is required to carry out a decision taken as an enforcement measure under Chapter VII.

24. In the particular case of the former Yugoslavia, the Secretary-General believes that the establishment of the International Tribunal by means of a Chapter VII decision would be legally justified, both in terms of the object and purpose of the decision, as indicated in the preceding paragraphs, and of past Security Council practice.

25. As indicated in paragraph 10 above, the Security Council has already determined that the situation posed by continuing reports of widespread violations of international humani- tarian law occurring in the former Yugoslavia constitutes a threat to international peace and security. The Council has also decided under Chapter VII of the Charter that all parties and others concerned in the former Yugoslavia, and all military forces in Bosnia and Herzegovina, shall comply with the provisions of resolution 771 (1992), failing which it would need to take further measures under the Charter. Furthermore, the Council has repeatedly reaffirmed that all parties in the former Yugoslavia are bound to comply with the obligations under international humanitarian law and in particular the Geneva Conventions of 12 August 1949, and that persons who commit or order the commission of grave breaches of the Conventions are individually responsible in respect of such breaches.

26. Finally, the Security Council stated in resolution 808 (1993) that it was convinced that in the particular circumstances of the former Yugoslavia, the establishment of an international tribunal would bring about the achievement of the aim of putting an end to

such crimes and of taking effective measures to bring to justice the persons responsible for them, and would contribute to the restoration and maintenance of peace.

27. The Security Council has on various occasions adopted decisions under Chapter VII aimed at restoring and maintaining international peace and security, which have involved the establishment of subsidiary organs for a variety of purposes. Reference may be made in this regard to Security Council resolution 687 (1991) and subsequent resolutions relating to the situation between Iraq and Kuwait.

28. In this particular case, the Security Council would be establishing, as an enforcement measure under Chapter VII, a subsidiary organ within the terms of Article 29 of the Charter, but one of a judicial nature. This organ would, of course, have to perform its functions independently of political considerations; it would not be subject to the authority or control of the Security Council with regard to the performance of its judicial functions. As an enforcement measure under Chapter VII, however, the life span of the international tribunal would be linked to the restoration and maintenance of international peace and security in the territory of the former Yugoslavia, and Security Council decisions related thereto.

29. It should be pointed out that, in assigning to the International Tribunal the task of prosecuting persons responsible for serious violations of international humanitarian law, the Security Council would not be creating or purporting to "legislate" that law. Rather, the International Tribunal would have the task of applying existing international humanitarian law.

30. On the basis of the foregoing considerations, the Secretary-General proposes that the Security Council, acting under Chapter VII of the Charter, establish the International Tribunal. The resolution so adopted would have annexed to it a statute the opening passage of which would read as follows:

Having been established by the Security Council acting under Chapter VII of the Charter of the United Nations, the International Tribunal for the Prosecution of Persons Responsible for Serious Violations of International Humanitarian Law Committed in the Territory of the Former Yugoslavia since 1991 (hereinafter referred to as "the International Tribunal") shall function in accordance with the provisions of the present Statute.

II. COMPETENCE OF THE INTERNATIONAL TRIBUNAL

31. The competence of the International Tribunal derives from the mandate set out in paragraph 1 of resolution 808 (1993). This part of the report will examine and make proposals regarding these fundamental elements of its competence: *ratione materiae* (subject-matter jurisdiction), *ratione personae* (personal jurisdiction), *ratione loci* (territorial jurisdiction) and *ratione temporis* (temporal jurisdiction), as well as the question of the concurrent jurisdiction of the International Tribunal and national courts.

32. The statute should begin with a general article on the competence of the International Tribunal which would read as follows:

Article 1
Competence of the International Tribunal

The International Tribunal shall have the power to prosecute persons responsible for serious violations of international humanitarian law committed in the territory of the former Yugoslavia since 1991 in accordance with the provisions of the present Statute.

A. *Competence ratione materiae (subject-matter jurisdiction)*

33. According to paragraph 1 of resolution 808 (1993), the international tribunal shall prosecute persons responsible for serious violations of international humanitarian law committed in the territory of the former Yugoslavia since 1991. This body of law exists in the form of both conventional law and customary law. While there is international customary law which is not laid down in conventions, some of the major conventional humanitarian law has become part of customary international law.

34. In the view of the Secretary-General, the application of the principle nullum crimen sine lege requires that the international tribunal should apply rules of international humanitarian law which are beyond any doubt part of customary law so that the problem of adherence of some but not all States to specific conventions does not arise. This would appear to be particularly important in the context of an international tribunal prosecuting persons responsible for serious violations of international humanitarian law.

35. The part of conventional international humanitarian law which has beyond doubt become part of international customary law is the law applicable in armed conflict as embodied in: the Geneva Conventions of 12 August 1949 for the Protection of War Victims;[3] the Hague Convention (IV) Respecting the Laws and Customs of War on Land and the Regulations annexed thereto of 18 October 1907;[4] the Convention on the Prevention and Punishment of the Crime of Genocide of 9 December 1948;[5] and the Charter of the International Military Tribunal of 8 August 1945.[6]

36. Suggestions have been made that the international tribunal should apply domestic law in so far as it incorporates customary international humanitarian law. While international humanitarian law as outlined above provides a sufficient basis for subject-matter jurisdiction, there is one related issue which would require reference to domestic practice, namely, penalties (see para. 111).

Grave breaches of the 1949 Geneva Conventions

37. The Geneva Conventions constitute rules of international humanitarian law and provide the core of the customary law applicable in international armed conflicts. These Conventions regulate the conduct of war from the humanitarian perspective by protecting certain categories of persons: namely, wounded and sick members of armed forces in the

---

[3] Convention for the Amelioration of the Condition of the Wounded and Sick in Armed Forces in the Field of 12 August 1949, Convention for the Amelioration of the Condition of the Wounded, Sick and Shipwrecked Members of Armed Forces at Sea of 12 August 1949, Convention relative to the Treatment of Prisoners of War of 12 August 1949, Convention relative to the Protection of Civilian Persons in Time of War of 12 August 1949 (United Nations, *Treaty Series*, vol. 75, No. 970–973).

[4] Carnegie Endowment for International Peace, *The Hague Conventions and Declarations of 1899 and 1907* (New York: Oxford University Press, 1915), p. 100.

[5] United Nations, *Treaty Series*, vol. 78, No. 1021.

[6] The Agreement for the Prosecution and Punishment of the Major War Criminals of the European Axis, signed at London on 8 August 1945 (United Nations, *Treaty Series*, vol. 82, No. 251); see also Judgment of the International Military Tribunal for the Prosecution and Punishment of the Major War Criminals of the European Axis (United States Government Printing Office, *Nazi Conspiracy and Aggression, Opinion and Judgement*) and General Assembly Resolution 95 (I) of 11 December 1946 on the Affirmation of the Principles of International Law Recognized by the Charter of the Nürnberg Tribunal.

field; wounded, sick and shipwrecked members of armed forces at sea; prisoners of war, and civilians in time of war.

38. Each Convention contains a provision listing the particularly serious violations that qualify as "grave breaches" or war crimes. Persons committing or ordering grave breaches are subject to trial and punishment. The lists of grave breaches contained in the Geneva Conventions are reproduced in the article which follows.

39. The Security Council has reaffirmed on several occasions that persons who commit or order the commission of grave breaches of the 1949 Geneva Conventions in the territory of the former Yugoslavia are individually responsible for such breaches as serious violations of international humanitarian law.

40. The corresponding article of the statute would read:

Article 2
Grave breaches of the Geneva Conventions of 1949

The International Tribunal shall have the power to prosecute persons committing or ordering to be committed grave breaches of the Geneva Conventions of 12 August 1949, namely the following acts against persons or property protected under the provisions of the relevant Geneva Convention:

    (a) wilful killing;

    (b) torture or inhuman treatment, including biological experiments;

    (c) wilfully causing great suffering or serious injury to body or health;

    (d) extensive destruction and appropriation of property, not justified by military necessity and carried out unlawfully and wantonly;

    (e) compelling a prisoner of war or a civilian to serve in the forces of a hostile power;

    (f) wilfully depriving a prisoner of war or a civilian of the rights of fair and regular trial;

    (g) unlawful deportation or transfer or unlawful confinement of a civilian;

    (h) taking civilians as hostages.

Violations of the laws or customs of war

41. The 1907 Hague Convention (IV) Respecting the Laws and Customs of War on Land and the Regulations annexed thereto comprise a second important area of conventional humanitarian international law which has become part of the body of international customary law.

42. The Nürnberg Tribunal recognized that many of the provisions contained in the Hague Regulations, although innovative at the time of their adoption were, by 1939, recognized by all civilized nations and were regarded as being declaratory of the laws and customs of war. The Nürnberg Tribunal also recognized that war crimes defined in article 6(b) of the Nürnberg Charter were already recognized as war crimes under international law, and covered in the Hague Regulations, for which guilty individuals were punishable.

43. The Hague Regulations cover aspects of international humanitarian law which are also covered by the 1949 Geneva Conventions. However, the Hague Regulations also recognize that the right of belligerents to conduct warfare is not unlimited and that resort to certain methods of waging war is prohibited under the rules of land warfare.

44. These rules of customary law, as interpreted and applied by the Nürnberg Tribunal, provide the basis for the corresponding article of the statute which would read as follows:

Article 3
Violations of the laws or customs of war

The International Tribunal shall have the power to prosecute persons violating the laws or customs of war. Such violations shall include, but not be limited to:

(a) employment of poisonous weapons or other weapons calculated to cause unnecessary suffering;

(b) wanton destruction of cities, towns or villages, or devastation not justified by military necessity;

(c) attack, or bombardment, by whatever means, of undefended towns, villages, dwellings, or buildings;

(d) seizure of, destruction or wilful damage done to institutions dedicated to religion, charity and education, the arts and sciences, historic monuments and works of art and science;

(e) plunder of public or private property.

Genocide

45. The 1948 Convention on the Prevention and Punishment of the Crime of Genocide confirms that genocide, whether committed in time of peace or in time of war, is a crime under international law for which individuals shall be tried and punished. The Convention is today considered part of international customary law as evidenced by the International Court of Justice in its Advisory Opinion on Reservations to the Convention on the Prevention and Punishment of the Crime of Genocide, 1951.[7]

46. The relevant provisions of the Genocide Convention are reproduced in the corresponding article of the statute, which would read as follows:

Article 4
Genocide

1. The International Tribunal shall have the power to prosecute persons committing genocide as defined in paragraph 2 of this article or of committing any of the other acts enumerated in paragraph 3 of this article.

2. Genocide means any of the following acts committed with intent to destroy, in whole or in part, a national, ethnical, racial or religious group, as such:

(a) killing members of the group;

(b) causing serious bodily or mental harm to members of the group;

(c) deliberately inflicting on the group conditions of life calculated to bring about its physical destruction in whole or in part;

(d) imposing measures intended to prevent births within the group;

(e) forcibly transferring children of the group to another group.

---

[7] Reservations to the Convention on the Prevention and Punishment of the Crime of Genocide: Advisory Opinion of 28 May 1951, International Court of Justice Reports, 1951, p. 23.

3. The following acts shall be punishable:

(a) genocide;
(b) conspiracy to commit genocide;
(c) direct and public incitement to commit genocide;
(d) attempt to commit genocide;
(e) complicity in genocide.

Crimes against humanity

47. Crimes against humanity were first recognized in the Charter and Judgement of the Nürnberg Tribunal, as well as in Law No. 10 of the Control Council for Germany.[8] Crimes against humanity are aimed at any civilian population and are prohibited regardless of whether they are committed in an armed conflict, international or internal in character.[9]

48. Crimes against humanity refer to inhumane acts of a very serious nature, such as wilful killing, torture or rape, committed as part of a widespread or systematic attack against any civilian population on national, political, ethnic, racial or religious grounds. In the conflict in the territory of the former Yugoslavia, such inhumane acts have taken the form of so-called "ethnic cleansing" and widespread and systematic rape and other forms of sexual assault, including enforced prostitution.

49. The corresponding article of the statute would read as follows:

Article 5
Crimes against humanity

The International Tribunal shall have the power to prosecute persons responsible for the following crimes when committed in armed conflict, whether international or internal in character, and directed against any civilian population:

(a) murder;
(b) extermination;
(c) enslavement;
(d) deportation;
(e) imprisonment;
(f) torture;
(g) rape;
(h) persecutions on political, racial and religious grounds;
(i) other inhumane acts.

---

[8] *Official Gazette of the Control Council for Germany*, No. 3, p. 22, *Military Government Gazette, Germany, British Zone of Control*, No. 5, p. 46, *Journal Officiel du Commandement en Chef Français en Allemagne*, No. 12 of 11 January 1946.

[9] In this context, it is to be noted that the International Court of Justice has recognized that the prohibitions contained in common Article 3 of the 1949 Geneva Conventions are based on "elementary considerations of humanity" and cannot be breached in an armed conflict, regardless of whether it is international or internal in character. Case concerning Military and Paramilitary Activities in and against Nicaragua (*Nicaragua v. United States of America*), Judgment of 27 June 1986, ICJ Reports 1986, p. 114.

B. Competence *ratione personae* (personal jurisdiction) and individual criminal responsibility

50. By paragraph 1 of resolution 808 (1993), the Security Council decided that the International Tribunal shall be established for the prosecution of persons responsible for serious violations of international humanitarian law committed in the territory of the former Yugoslavia since 1991. In the light of the complex of resolutions leading up to resolution 808 (1993) (see paras. 5–7 above), the ordinary meaning of the term "persons responsible for serious violations of international humanitarian law" would be natural persons to the exclusion of juridical persons.

51. The question arises, however, whether a juridical person, such as an association or organization, may be considered criminal as such and thus its members, for that reason alone, be made subject to the jurisdiction of the International Tribunal. The Secretary-General believes that this concept should not be retained in regard to the International Tribunal. The criminal acts set out in this statute are carried out by natural persons; such persons would be subject to the jurisdiction of the International Tribunal irrespective of membership in groups.

52. The corresponding article of the statute would read:

Article 6
Personal jurisdiction

The International Tribunal shall have jurisdiction over natural persons pursuant to the provisions of the present Statute.

Individual criminal responsibility

53. An important element in relation to the competence *ratione personae* (personal jurisdiction) of the International Tribunal is the principle of individual criminal responsibility. As noted above, the Security Council has reaffirmed in a number of resolutions that persons committing serious violations of international humanitarian law in the former Yugoslavia are individually responsible for such violations.

54. The Secretary-General believes that all persons who participate in the planning, preparation or execution of serious violations of international humanitarian law in the former Yugoslavia contribute to the commission of the violation and are, therefore, individually responsible.

55. Virtually all of the written comments received by the Secretary-General have suggested that the statute of the International Tribunal should contain provisions with regard to the individual criminal responsibility of heads of State, government officials and persons acting in an official capacity. These suggestions draw upon the precedents following the Second World War. The Statute should, therefore, contain provisions which specify that a plea of head of State immunity or that an act was committed in the official capacity of the accused will not constitute a defence, nor will it mitigate punishment.

56. A person in a position of superior authority should, therefore, be held individually responsible for giving the unlawful order to commit a crime under the present statute. But he should also be held responsible for failure to prevent a crime or to deter the unlawful behaviour of his subordinates. This imputed responsibility or criminal negligence

is engaged if the person in superior authority knew or had reason to know that his subordinates were about to commit or had committed crimes and yet failed to take the necessary and reasonable steps to prevent or repress the commission of such crimes or to punish those who had committed them.

57. Acting upon an order of a Government or a superior cannot relieve the perpetrator of the crime of his criminal responsibility and should not be a defence. Obedience to superior orders may, however, be considered a mitigating factor, should the International Tribunal determine that justice so requires. For example, the International Tribunal may consider the factor of superior orders in connection with other defences such as coercion or lack of moral choice.

58. The International Tribunal itself will have to decide on various personal defences which may relieve a person of individual criminal responsibility, such as minimum age or mental incapacity, drawing upon general principles of law recognized by all nations.

59. The corresponding article of the statute would read:

Article 7
Individual criminal responsibility

1. A person who planned, instigated, ordered, committed or otherwise aided and abetted in the planning, preparation or execution of a crime referred to in articles 2 to 5 of the present Statute, shall be individually responsible for the crime.

2. The official position of any accused person, whether as Head of State or Government or as a responsible Government official, shall not relieve such person of criminal responsibility nor mitigate punishment.

3. The fact that any of the acts referred to in articles 2 to 5 of the present Statute was committed by a subordinate does not relieve his superior of criminal responsibility if he knew or had reason to know that the subordinate was about to commit such acts or had done so and the superior failed to take the necessary and reasonable measures to prevent such acts or to punish the perpetrators thereof.

4. The fact that an accused person acted pursuant to an order of a Government or of a superior shall not relieve him of criminal responsibility, but may be considered in mitigation of punishment if the International Tribunal determines that justice so requires.

C. Competence *ratione loci* (territorial jurisdiction) and *ratione temporis* (temporal jurisdiction)

60. Pursuant to paragraph 1 of resolution 808 (1993), the territorial and temporal jurisdiction of the International Tribunal extends to serious violations of international humanitarian law to the extent that they have been "committed in the territory of the former Yugoslavia since 1991".

61. As far as the territorial jurisdiction of the International Tribunal is concerned, the territory of the former Yugoslavia means the territory of the former Socialist Federal Republic of Yugoslavia, including its land surface, airspace and territorial waters.

62. With regard to temporal jurisdiction, Security Council resolution 808 (1993) extends the jurisdiction of the International Tribunal to violations committed "since 1991". The Secretary-General understands this to mean anytime on or after 1 January 1991. This is a neutral date which is not tied to any specific event and is clearly intended to convey the

notion that no judgement as to the international or internal character of the conflict is being exercised.

63. The corresponding article of the statute would read:

Article 8
Territorial and temporal jurisdiction

The territorial jurisdiction of the International Tribunal shall extend to the territory of the former Socialist Federal Republic of Yugoslavia, including its land surface, airspace and territorial waters. The temporal jurisdiction of the International Tribunal shall extend to a period beginning on 1 January 1991.

D. Concurrent jurisdiction and the principle of
non-bis-in-idem

64. In establishing an international tribunal for the prosecution of persons responsible for serious violations committed in the territory of the former Yugoslavia since 1991, it was not the intention of the Security Council to preclude or prevent the exercise of jurisdiction by national courts with respect to such acts. Indeed national courts should be encouraged to exercise their jurisdiction in accordance with their relevant national laws and procedures.

65. It follows therefore that there is concurrent jurisdiction of the International Tribunal and national courts. This concurrent jurisdiction, however, should be subject to the primacy of the International Tribunal. At any stage of the procedure, the International Tribunal may formally request the national courts to defer to the competence of the International Tribunal. The details of how the primacy will be asserted shall be set out in the rules of procedure and evidence of the International Tribunal.

66. According to the principle of *non-bis-in-idem*, a person shall not be tried twice for the same crime. In the present context, given the primacy of the International Tribunal, the principle of *non-bis-in-idem* would preclude subsequent trial before a national court. However, the principle of *non-bis-in idem* should not preclude a subsequent trial before the International Tribunal in the following two circumstances:

(a) the characterization of the act by the national court did not correspond to its characterization under the statute; or

(b) conditions of impartiality, independence or effective means of adjudication were not guaranteed in the proceedings before the national courts.

67. Should the International Tribunal decide to assume jurisdiction over a person who has already been convicted by a national court, it should take into consideration the extent to which any penalty imposed by the national court has already been served.

68. The corresponding articles of the statute would read:

Article 9
Concurrent jurisdiction

1. The International Tribunal and national courts shall have concurrent jurisdiction to prosecute persons for serious violations of international humanitarian law committed in the territory of the former Yugoslavia since 1 January 1991.

2. The International Tribunal shall have primacy over national courts. At any stage of the procedure, the International Tribunal may formally request national courts to defer to the competence of the International Tribunal in accordance with the present Statute and the Rules of Procedure and Evidence of the International Tribunal.

Article 10
Non-bis-in-idem

1. No person shall be tried before a national court for acts constituting serious violations of international humanitarian law under the present Statute, for which he or she has already been tried by the International Tribunal.

2. A person who has been tried by a national court for acts constituting serious violations of international humanitarian law may be subsequently tried by the International Tribunal only if:

(a) the act for which he or she was tried was characterized as an ordinary crime; or

(b) the national court proceedings were not impartial or independent, were designed to shield the accused from international criminal responsibility, or the case was not diligently prosecuted.

3. In considering the penalty to be imposed on a person convicted of a crime under the present Statute, the International Tribunal shall take into account the extent to which any penalty imposed by a national court on the same person for the same act has already been served.

II ICTR

RESOLUTION 955 (1994)
(Adopted 8 November 1994)
S/RES/955 (1994)

Adopted by the Security Council at its 3453rd meeting, on 8 November 1994

The Security Council,

Reaffirming all its previous resolutions on the situation in Rwanda,

Having considered the reports of the Secretary-General pursuant to paragraph 3 of resolution 935 (1994) of 1 July 1994 (S/1994/879 and S/1994/906), and *having taken note* of the reports of the Special Rapporteur for Rwanda of the United Nations Commission on Human Rights (S/1994/1157, annex I and annex II),

Expressing appreciation for the work of the Commission of Experts established pursuant to resolution 935 (1994), in particular its preliminary report on violations of international humanitarian law in Rwanda transmitted by the Secretary-General's letter of 1 October 1994 (S/1994/1125),

Expressing once again its grave concern at the reports indicating that genocide and other systematic, widespread and flagrant violations of international humanitarian law have been committed in Rwanda,

Determining that this situation continues to constitute a threat to international peace and security,

Determined to put an end to such crimes and to take effective measures to bring to justice the persons who are responsible for them,

Convinced that in the particular circumstances of Rwanda, the prosecution of persons responsible for serious violations of international humanitarian law would enable this aim to be achieved and would contribute to the process of national reconciliation and to the restoration and maintenance of peace,

Believing that the establishment of an international tribunal for the prosecution of persons responsible for genocide and the other above-mentioned violations of international humanitarian law will contribute to ensuring that such violations are halted and effectively redressed,

Stressing also the need for international cooperation to strengthen the courts and judicial system of Rwanda, having regard in particular to the necessity for those courts to deal with large numbers of suspects,

Considering that the Commission of Experts established pursuant to resolution 935 (1994) should continue on an urgent basis the collection of information relating to evidence of grave violations of international humanitarian law committed in the territory of Rwanda and should submit its final report to the Secretary-General by 30 November 1994,

Acting under Chapter VII of the Charter of the United Nations,

1. *Decides* hereby, having received the request of the Government of Rwanda (S/1994/1115), to establish an international tribunal for the sole purpose of prosecuting persons responsible for genocide and other serious violations of international humanitarian law committed in the territory of Rwanda and Rwandan citizens responsible for genocide and other such violations committed in the territory of neighbouring States, between 1 January 1994

and 31 December 1994 and to this end to adopt the Statute of the International Criminal Tribunal for Rwanda annexed hereto;

2. *Decides* that all States shall cooperate fully with the International Tribunal and its organs in accordance with the present resolution and the Statute of the International Tribunal and that consequently all States shall take any measures necessary under their domestic law to implement the provisions of the present resolution and the Statute, including the obligation of States to comply with requests for assistance or orders issued by a Trial Chamber under Article 28 of the Statute, and *requests* States to keep the Secretary-General informed of such measures;

3. *Considers* that the Government of Rwanda should be notified prior to the taking of decisions under articles 26 and 27 of the Statute;

4. *Urges* States and intergovernmental and non-governmental organizations to contribute funds, equipment and services to the International Tribunal, including the offer of expert personnel;

5. *Requests* the Secretary-General to implement this resolution urgently and in particular to make practical arrangements for the effective functioning of the International Tribunal, including recommendations to the Council as to possible locations for the seat of the International Tribunal at the earliest time and to report periodically to the Council;

6. *Decides* that the seat of the International Tribunal shall be determined by the Council having regard to considerations of justice and fairness as well as administrative efficiency, including access to witnesses, and economy, and subject to the conclusion of appropriate arrangements between the United Nations and the State of the seat, acceptable to the Council, having regard to the fact that the International Tribunal may meet away from its seat when it considers it necessary for the efficient exercise of its functions; and *decides* that an office will be established and proceedings will be conducted in Rwanda, where feasible and appropriate, subject to the conclusion of similar appropriate arrangements;

7. *Decides* to consider increasing the number of judges and Trial Chambers of the International Tribunal if it becomes necessary;

8. *Decides* to remain actively seized of the matter.

Annex

Statute of the International Tribunal for Rwanda

REPORT OF THE SECRETARY-GENERAL
PURSUANT TO PARAGRAPH 5
OF THE SECURITY COUNCIL RESOLUTION 955 (1994) (*excerpts*)

PRESENTED 13 FEBRUARY 1995
(S/1995/134)

I.

1. Resolution 955 (1994) of 8 November 1994, by which the Security Council established an international tribunal for the sole purpose of prosecuting persons responsible for genocide and other serious violations of international humanitarian law committed in the territory

of Rwanda and Rwandese citizens responsible for genocide and other such violations committed in the territory of neighbouring States, represented the culmination of a series of resolutions in which the Council had condemned the systematic and widespread violations of international humanitarian law in Rwanda and, in particular, the mass killing of tens of thousands of civilians with impunity.

2. In resolution 918 (1994) of 17 May 1994, the Secretary-General was requested to present a report on the investigation of serious violations of international humanitarian law committed in Rwanda. In my report to the Council of 31 May 1994 (S/1994/640), I noted that massacres and killings had continued in a systematic manner throughout Rwanda and that only a proper investigation could establish the facts in order to determine responsibility.

3. By resolution 935 (1994) of 1 July 1994, the Secretary-General was requested to establish an impartial commission of experts. In its interim report (S/1994/1125), the Commission submitted its preliminary conclusions on serious breaches of international humanitarian law and acts of genocide committed in Rwanda, and recommended that the individuals responsible for those acts be brought to justice before an independent and impartial international criminal tribunal. In its final report (S/1994/1405), the Commission concluded that there existed overwhelming evidence to prove that acts of genocide against the Tutsi ethnic group had been committed by Hutu elements in a concerted, planned, systematic and methodical way, in violation of article II of the Convention on the Prevention and Punishment of the Crime of Genocide, 1948[1] (hereinafter "the Genocide Convention"); that crimes against humanity and serious violations of international humanitarian law were committed by individuals on both sides of the conflict, but there was no evidence to suggest that acts committed by Tutsi elements were perpetrated with an intent to destroy the Hutu ethnic group as such, within the meaning of the Genocide Convention.

4. The present report is submitted pursuant to paragraph 5 of resolution 955 (1994), by which the Security Council requested the Secretary-General to implement the resolution urgently and to make practical arrangements for the effective functioning of the Tribunal, including recommendations to the Council as to possible locations for the seat of the Tribunal, and to report periodically to the Council.

5. While the Council has been periodically informed of the implementation of resolution 955 (1994), through letters from the Secretary-General, oral briefings and recently through the progress report on the United Nations Assistance Mission for Rwanda (UNAMIR) (S/1995/107, paras. 19–22), this is the first time that the Secretary-General is submitting a formal report on the Tribunal. Accordingly, I have decided that it would be useful to provide the Council with a comprehensive report. The first section analyses the legal basis for the establishment of the International Tribunal for Rwanda (hereinafter also referred to as "the Rwanda Tribunal") and its legal status. The second contains a succinct review of the main provisions of the statute of the Rwanda Tribunal where they differ from the provisions of the statute of the International Tribunal for the Prosecution of Persons Responsible for Serious Violations of International Humanitarian Law Committed in the Territory of the Former Yugoslavia (hereinafter "the Yugoslav Tribunal") (see S/25704). The third section of the report outlines the two-stage approach to the establishment of the Rwanda Tribunal and the practical arrangements made thus far for its functioning. Finally,

---

[1] General Assembly Resolution 260 (A) (III).

in the fourth section of the report, the Secretary-General examines the various options for the location of the seat of the Tribunal in the light of the criteria set out in paragraph 6 of resolution 955 (1994) and makes his recommendation for the location of the seat of the Tribunal.

II. LEGAL BASIS FOR THE ESTABLISHMENT OF THE INTERNATIONAL TRIBUNAL FOR RWANDA

6. Having determined on two previous occasions that the situation in Rwanda constituted a threat to peace and security in the region,[2] the Council, in its resolution 955 (1994), determined that the situation in Rwanda continued to constitute a threat to international peace and security and, accordingly, decided to establish the International Tribunal for Rwanda under Chapter VII of the Charter of the United Nations. The establishment of the International Tribunal under Chapter VII, notwithstanding the request received from the Government of Rwanda,[3] was necessary to ensure not only the cooperation of Rwanda throughout the life-span of the Tribunal, but the cooperation of all States in whose territory persons alleged to have committed serious violations of international humanitarian law and acts of genocide in Rwanda might be situated. A Tribunal based on a Chapter VII resolution was also necessary to ensure a speedy and expeditious method of establishing the Tribunal.

7. Unlike the establishment of the Yugoslav Tribunal, which was done in a two-stage process of two Security Council resolutions (resolutions 808 (1993) and 827 (1993)) and gained in the Yugoslav Tribunal, a one-step process and a single resolution would suffice to establish the International Tribunal for Rwanda.

8. The International Tribunal for Rwanda is a subsidiary organ of the Security Council within the meaning of Article 29 of the Charter. As such, it is dependent in administrative and financial matters on various United Nations organs; as a judicial body, however, it is independent of any one particular State or group of States, including its parent body, the Security Council.

9. The establishment of the Rwanda Tribunal at a time when the Yugoslav Tribunal was already in existence, dictated a similar legal approach to the establishment of the Tribunal. It also mandated that certain organizational and institutional links be established between the two Tribunals to ensure a unity of legal approach, as well as economy and efficiency of resources. The statute of the Rwanda Tribunal, which was an adaptation of the statute of the Yugoslav Tribunal to the circumstances of Rwanda, was drafted by the original sponsors of

---

[2] In Resolution 918 (1994), the Council decided to impose sanctions against Rwanda and, in resolution 929 (1994), it authorized a temporary humanitarian operation under the command and control of a Member State ("Operation Turquoise").

[3] In its letter to the Secretary-General of 6 August 1994, the Government of Rwanda stated that an international tribunal, along the lines of the Yugoslav Tribunal, would help to promote peace and reconciliation among the parties and remove destabilizing elements from Rwanda and neighbouring States. The Government undertook to prevent summary executions and to hold in custody persons alleged to have committed acts of genocide pending prosecution by the International Tribunal. In addition, in a statement dated 28 September 1994 on the question of refugees and security in Rwanda (S/1994/1115, annex), the Government of Rwanda called for the setting up, as soon as possible, of an international tribunal to try persons alleged to have committed genocide.

Security Council resolution 955 (1994) and discussed among members of the Council. Rwanda, as a member of the Security Council at the time that resolution 955 (1994) was adopted, thus participated fully in the deliberations on the statute and the negotiations leading to the adoption of the resolution.

III. MAIN PROVISIONS OF THE STATUTE OF THE INTERNATIONAL TRIBUNAL FOR RWANDA

A. Competence of the International Tribunal

10. The competence of the International Tribunal for Rwanda is circumscribed in time, place and subject-matter jurisdiction. Article 1 of the statute provides that the International Tribunal shall have the power to prosecute persons responsible for serious violations of international humanitarian law committed in the territory of Rwanda and Rwandese citizens responsible for such violations committed in the territory of neighbouring States, between 1 January 1994 and 31 December 1994. The crimes in respect of which the Tribunal is competent are set out in articles 2 to 4 of the Statute.

1. Subject-matter jurisdiction

11. Given the nature of the conflict as non-international in character, the Council has incorporated within the subject-matter jurisdiction of the Tribunal violations of international humanitarian law which may either be committed in both international and internal armed conflicts, such as the crime of genocide[4] and crimes against humanity,[5] or may be committed only in internal armed conflict, such as violations of article 3 common to the four Geneva Conventions,[6] as more fully elaborated in article 4 of Additional Protocol II.[7]

12. In that latter respect, the Security Council has elected to take a more expansive approach to the choice of the applicable law than the one underlying the statute of the Yugoslav Tribunal, and included within the subject-matter jurisdiction of the Rwanda Tribunal international instruments whether they were considered part of customary international law or whether they have customarily entailed the individual criminal responsibility of the perpetrator of the crime. Article 4 of the statute, accordingly, includes violations of Additional Protocol II, which, as a whole, has not yet been universally recognized as part

---

[4] Genocide, According to Article I of the Genocide Convention, is a crime under international law whether committed in time of peace or in time of war.

[5] Crimes against humanity were described in Article 5 of the statute of the Yugoslav Tribunal as those enumerated in the article, 'when committed in armed conflict, whether international or internal in character'. Article 3 of the Rwanda statute makes no reference to the temporal scope of the crime; there is, therefore, no reason to limit its application in that respect.

[6] Convention for the Amelioration of the Condition of the Wounded and Sick in Armed Forces in the Field, of 12 August 1949, Convention for the Amelioration of the Condition of the Wounded, Sick and Shipwrecked Members of Armed Forces at Sea, of 12 August 1949, Convention relative to the Treatment of Prisoners-of-War of 12 August 1949, Convention relative to the Protection of Civilian Persons in Time of War, of 12 August 1949 (United Nations, *Treaty Series*, Vol. 75, Nos. 970–973).

[7] Protocol Additional to the Geneva Conventions of 12 August 1949 and relating to the Protection of Victims of Non-International Armed Conflicts (Protocol II) of 8 June 1977, (United Nations, *Treaty Series*, Vol. 1125, No. 17513).

of customary international law, and for the first time criminalizes common article 3 of the four Geneva Conventions.[8]

2. Territorial and temporal jurisdiction

13. The territorial jurisdiction of the International Tribunal extends beyond the territory of Rwanda to that of neighbouring States, in respect of serious violations of international humanitarian law committed by Rwandan citizens. In extending the territorial jurisdiction of the Tribunal beyond the territorial bounds of Rwanda, the Council envisaged mainly the refugee camps in Zaire and other neighbouring countries in which serious violations of international humanitarian law are alleged to have been committed in connection with the conflict in Rwanda.

14. The temporal jurisdiction of the Tribunal is limited to one year, beginning on 1 January 1994 and ending on 31 December 1994. Although the crash of the aircraft carrying the Presidents of Rwanda and Burundi on 6 April 1994 is considered to be the event that triggered the civil war and the acts of genocide that followed, the Council decided that the temporal jurisdiction of the Tribunal would commence on 1 January 1994, in order to capture the planning stage of the crimes.

B. Organization and structure of the International Tribunal

15. The International Tribunal for Rwanda consists of three organs:

(a) The chambers, comprising two trial chambers and an appeals chamber; each Trial Chamber is composed of three judges and the Appeals Chamber is composed of five;
(b) A Prosecutor; and
(c) A Registry.

16. Under article 12, paragraph 2, of the statute, the members of the Appeals Chamber of the International Tribunal for the Former Yugoslavia shall also serve as the members of the Appeals Chamber of the International Tribunal for Rwanda. In providing for a common Appeals Chamber for the two Tribunals, the Council was aware of the fact that, if no restrictions are put on the nationalities of nominees for judges, there could be a situation where more than one judge of the Rwanda Tribunal will have the same nationality. In order to prevent such an eventuality, article 12, paragraph 3 (b), of the Rwanda statute provides in its relevant part that:

". . . each State may nominate up to two candidates meeting the qualifications set out in paragraph 1 above, no two of whom shall be of the same nationality and neither of whom shall be of the same nationality as any judge of the Appeals Chamber".

17. Article 15, paragraph 3 of the Statute of the Rwanda Tribunal provides that the Prosecutor of the International Tribunal for the Former Yugoslavia shall also serve as the Prosecutor of the International Tribunal for Rwanda, with such additional staff, including an additional Deputy Prosecutor, to assist with prosecutions before the International

---

[8] Although the question of whether common Article 3 entails the individual responsibility of the perpetrator of the crime is still debatable, some of the crimes included therein, when committed against the civilian population, also constitute crimes against humanity and as such are customarily recognized as entailing the criminal responsibility of the individual.

Tribunal for Rwanda. The statute thus envisages commonality not only in the person of the Prosecutor, but also in the staff of the Prosecutor's Office.

C. Other statutory provisions

18. Article 14 of the statute of the Rwanda Tribunal provides that the judges of the International Tribunal shall adopt the rules of procedure and evidence for the conduct of the pretrial phase of the proceedings, trials and appeals, the admission of evidence, the protection of victims and witnesses and other appropriate matters of the International Tribunal for the Former Yugoslavia, with such changes as they deem necessary. It was thus the intention of the Council that, although the rules of procedure and evidence of the Yugoslav Tribunal should not be made expressly applicable to the Rwanda Tribunal, they should nevertheless serve as a model from which deviations will be made when the particular circumstances of Rwanda so warrant.

19. Imprisonment shall, according to article 26 of the statute, be served in Rwanda, or in any of the States on a list of States that have indicated to the Security Council their willingness to accept convicted persons. Unlike the former Yugoslavia, Rwanda is not excluded from the list of States where prison sentences pronounced by the International Tribunal for Rwanda may be served.

20. Article 30 of the statute provides that the expenses of the Tribunal shall be the expenses of the Organization in accordance with Article 17 of the Charter. In clearly distinguishing between the competence of the Security Council to establish the International Tribunal and the budgetary authority of the General Assembly to decide on its financing, the Security Council did not pronounce itself on the mode of financing, i.e., regular budget or a special account.

[. . .]

STATUTE OF THE INTERNATIONAL TRIBUNAL FOR RWANDA

(As amended)

As amended by the Security Council acting under Chapter VII of the Charter of the United Nations, the International Criminal Tribunal for the Prosecution of Persons Responsible for Genocide and Other Serious Violations of International Humanitarian Law Committed in the Territory of Rwanda and Rwandan Citizens responsible for genocide and other such violations committed in the territory of neighbouring States, between 1 January 1994 and 31 December 1994 (hereinafter referred to as "The International Tribunal for Rwanda") shall function in accordance with the provisions of the present Statute.

Article 1: Competence of the International Tribunal for Rwanda

The International Tribunal for Rwanda shall have the power to prosecute persons responsible for serious violations of international humanitarian law committed in the territory of Rwanda and Rwandan citizens responsible for such violations committed in the territory of neighbouring States between 1 January 1994 and 31 December 1994, in accordance with the provisions of the present Statute.

Article 2: Genocide

1. The International Tribunal for Rwanda shall have the power to prosecute persons committing genocide as defined in paragraph 2 of this Article or of committing any of the other acts enumerated in paragraph 3 of this Article.

2. Genocide means any of the following acts committed with intent to destroy, in whole or in part, a national, ethnical, racial or religious group, as such:

    (a) Killing members of the group;
    (b) Causing serious bodily or mental harm to members of the group;
    (c) Deliberately inflicting on the group conditions of life calculated to bring about its physical destruction in whole or in part;
    (d) Imposing measures intended to prevent births within the group;
    (e) Forcibly transferring children of the group to another group.

3. The following acts shall be punishable:

    (a) Genocide;
    (b) Conspiracy to commit genocide;
    (c) Direct and public incitement to commit genocide;
    (d) Attempt to commit genocide;
    (e) Complicity in genocide.

Article 3: Crimes against Humanity

The International Tribunal for Rwanda shall have the power to prosecute persons responsible for the following crimes when committed as part of a widespread or systematic attack against any civilian population on national, political, ethnic, racial or religious grounds:

    (a) Murder;
    (b) Extermination;
    (c) Enslavement;
    (d) Deportation;
    (e) Imprisonment;
    (f) Torture;
    (g) Rape;
    (h) Persecutions on political, racial and religious grounds;
    (i) Other inhumane acts.

Article 4: Violations of Article 3 Common to the Geneva Conventions and of Additional Protocol II

The International Tribunal for Rwanda shall have the power to prosecute persons committing or ordering to be committed serious violations of Article 3 common to the Geneva Conventions of 12 August 1949 for the Protection of War Victims, and of Additional Protocol II thereto of 8 June 1977. These violations shall include, but shall not be limited to:

    (a) Violence to life, health and physical or mental well-being of persons, in particular murder as well as cruel treatment such as torture, mutilation or any form of corporal punishment;
    (b) Collective punishments;
    (c) Taking of hostages;

(d) Acts of terrorism;

(e) Outrages upon personal dignity, in particular humiliating and degrading treatment, rape, enforced prostitution and any form of indecent assault;

(f) Pillage;

(g) The passing of sentences and the carrying out of executions without previous judgement pronounced by a regularly constituted court, affording all the judicial guarantees which are recognized as indispensable by civilised peoples;

(h) Threats to commit any of the foregoing acts.

Article 5: Personal Jurisdiction

The International Tribunal for Rwanda shall have jurisdiction over natural persons pursuant to the provisions of the present Statute.

Article 6: Individual Criminal Responsibility

1. A person who planned, instigated, ordered, committed or otherwise aided and abetted in the planning, preparation or execution of a crime referred to in Articles 2 to 4 of the present Statute, shall be individually responsible for the crime.

2. The official position of any accused person, whether as Head of state or government or as a responsible government official, shall not relieve such person of criminal responsibility nor mitigate punishment.

3. The fact that any of the acts referred to in Articles 2 to 4 of the present Statute was committed by a subordinate does not relieve his or her superior of criminal responsibility if he or she knew or had reason to know that the subordinate was about to commit such acts or had done so and the superior failed to take the necessary and reasonable measures to prevent such acts or to punish the perpetrators thereof.

4. The fact that an accused person acted pursuant to an order of a government or of a superior shall not relieve him or her of criminal responsibility, but may be considered in mitigation of punishment if the International Tribunal for Rwanda determines that justice so requires.

Article 7: Territorial and Temporal Jurisdiction

The territorial jurisdiction of the International Tribunal for Rwanda shall extend to the territory of Rwanda including its land surface and airspace as well as to the territory of neighbouring States in respect of serious violations of international humanitarian law committed by Rwandan citizens. The temporal jurisdiction of the International Tribunal for Rwanda shall extend to a period beginning on 1 January 1994 and ending on 31 December 1994.

Article 8: Concurrent Jurisdiction

1. The International Tribunal for Rwanda and national courts shall have concurrent jurisdiction to prosecute persons for serious violations of international humanitarian law committed in the territory of Rwanda and Rwandan citizens for such violations committed in the territory of the neighbouring States, between 1 January 1994 and 31 December 1994.

2. The International Tribunal for Rwanda shall have the primacy over the national courts of all States. At any stage of the procedure, the International Tribunal for Rwanda may formally request national courts to defer to its competence in accordance with the present Statute and the Rules of Procedure and Evidence of the International Tribunal for Rwanda.

Article 9: *Non Bis in Idem*

1. No person shall be tried before a national court for acts constituting serious violations of international humanitarian law under the present Statute, for which he or she has already been tried by the International Tribunal for Rwanda.

2. A person who has been tried before a national court for acts constituting serious violations of international humanitarian law may be subsequently tried by the International Tribunal for Rwanda only if:

    (a) The act for which he or she was tried was characterised as an ordinary crime; or

    (b) The national court proceedings were not impartial or independent, were designed to shield the accused from international criminal responsibility, or the case was not diligently prosecuted.

3. In considering the penalty to be imposed on a person convicted of a crime under the present Statute, the International Tribunal for Rwanda shall take into account the extent to which any penalty imposed by a national court on the same person for the same act has already been served.

Article 10: Organisation of the International Tribunal for Rwanda

The International Tribunal for Rwanda shall consist of the following organs:

    (a) The Chambers, comprising three Trial Chambers and an Appeals Chamber;
    (b) The Prosecutor;
    (c) A Registry.

Article 11: Composition of the Chambers

1. The Chambers shall be composed of 16 permanent independent judges, no two of whom may be nationals of the same State, and a maximum at any one time of four *ad litem* independent judges appointed in accordance with article 12 *ter*, paragraph 2, of the present Statute, no two of whom may be nationals of the same State.

2. Three permanent judges and a maximum at any one time of four *ad litem* judges shall be members of each Trial Chamber. Each Trial Chamber to which *ad litem* judges are assigned may be divided into sections of three judges each, composed of both permanent and *ad litem* judges. A section of a Trial Chamber shall have the same powers and responsibilities as a Trial Chamber under the present Statute and shall render judgement in accordance with the same rules.

3. Seven of the permanent judges shall be members of the Appeals Chamber. The Appeals Chamber shall, for each appeal, be composed of five of its members.

4. A person who for the purposes of membership of the Chambers of the International Tribunal for Rwanda could be regarded as a national of more than one State shall be deemed to be a national of the State in which that person ordinarily exercises civil and political rights.

Article 12: Qualification and Election of Judges

The permanent and *ad litem* judges shall be persons of high moral character, impartiality and integrity who possess the qualifications required in their respective countries for appointment to the highest judicial offices. In the overall composition of the Chambers and sections of the Trial Chambers, due account shall be taken of the experience of the judges in criminal law, international law, including international humanitarian law and human rights law.

Article 12 *bis*: Election of Permanent Judges

1. Eleven of the permanent judges of the International Tribunal for Rwanda shall be elected by the General Assembly from a list submitted by the Security Council, in the following manner:

    (a) The Secretary-General shall invite nominations for permanent judges of the International Tribunal for Rwanda from States Members of the United Nations and non-member States maintaining permanent observer missions at United Nations Headquarters;

    (b) Within sixty days of the date of the invitation of the Secretary-General, each State may nominate up to two candidates meeting the qualifications set out in article 12 of the present Statute, no two of whom shall be of the same nationality and neither of whom shall be of the same nationality as any judge who is a member of the Appeals Chamber and who was elected or appointed a permanent judge of the International Tribunal for the Prosecution of Persons Responsible for Serious Violations of International Humanitarian Law Committed in the Territory of the Former Yugoslavia since 1991 (hereinafter referred to as 'the International Tribunal for the Former Yugoslavia') in accordance with article 13 *bis* of the Statute of that Tribunal;

    (c) The Secretary-General shall forward the nominations received to the Security Council. From the nominations received the Security Council shall establish a list of not less than twenty-two and not more than thirty-three candidates, taking due account of the adequate representation on the International Tribunal for Rwanda of the principal legal systems of the world;

    (d) The President of the Security Council shall transmit the list of candidates to the President of the General Assembly. From that list the General Assembly shall elect eleven permanent judges of the International Tribunal for Rwanda. The candidates who receive an absolute majority of the votes of the States Members of the United Nations and of the non-member States maintaining permanent observer missions at United Nations Headquarters, shall be declared elected. Should two candidates of the same nationality obtain the required majority vote, the one who received the higher number of votes shall be considered elected.

2. In the event of a vacancy in the Chambers amongst the permanent judges elected or appointed in accordance with this article, after consultation with the Presidents of the Security Council and of the General Assembly, the Secretary-General shall appoint a person meeting the qualifications of article 12 of the present Statute, for the remainder of the term of office concerned.

3. The permanent judges elected in accordance with this article shall be elected for a term of four years. The terms and conditions of service shall be those of the permanent judges of the International Tribunal for the Former Yugoslavia. They shall be eligible for re-election.

Article 12 *ter*: Election and Appointment of *Ad Litem* Judges

1. The *ad litem* judges of the International Tribunal for Rwanda shall be elected by the General Assembly from a list submitted by the Security Council, in the following manner:

(a) The Secretary-General shall invite nominations for *ad litem* judges of the International Tribunal for Rwanda from States Members of the United Nations and non-member States maintaining permanent observer missions at United Nations Headquarters;

(b) Within sixty days of the date of the invitation of the Secretary-General, each State may nominate up to four candidates meeting the qualifications set out in article 12 of the present Statute, taking into account the importance of a fair representation of female and male candidates;

(c) The Secretary-General shall forward the nominations received to the Security Council. From the nominations received the Security Council shall establish a list of not less than thirty-six candidates, taking due account of the adequate representation of the principal legal systems of the world and bearing in mind the importance of equitable geographical distribution;

(d) The President of the Security Council shall transmit the list of candidates to the President of the General Assembly. From that list the General Assembly shall elect the eighteen *ad litem* judges of the International Tribunal for Rwanda. The candidates who receive an absolute majority of the votes of the States Members of the United Nations and of the non-member States maintaining permanent observer missions at United Nations Headquarters shall be declared elected;

(e) The *ad litem* judges shall be elected for a term of four years. They shall not be eligible for re-election.

2. During their term, *ad litem* judges will be appointed by the Secretary-General, upon request of the President of the International Tribunal for Rwanda, to serve in the Trial Chambers for one or more trials, for a cumulative period of up to, but not including, three years. When requesting the appointment of any particular *ad litem* judge, the President of the International Tribunal for Rwanda shall bear in mind the criteria set out in article 12 of the present Statute regarding the composition of the Chambers and sections of the Trial Chambers, the considerations set out in paragraphs 1 (b) and (c) above and the number of votes the *ad litem* judge received in the General Assembly.

Article 12 *quater*: Status of *Ad Litem* Judges

1. During the period in which they are appointed to serve in the International Tribunal for Rwanda, *ad litem* judges shall:

(a) Benefit from the same terms and conditions of service *mutatis mutandis* as the permanent judges of the International Tribunal for Rwanda;

(b) Enjoy, subject to paragraph 2 below, the same powers as the permanent judges of the International Tribunal for Rwanda;

(c) Enjoy the privileges and immunities, exemptions and facilities of a judge of the International Tribunal for Rwanda.

2. During the period in which they are appointed to serve in the International Tribunal for Rwanda, *ad litem* judges shall not:

(a) Be eligible for election as, or to vote in the election of, the President of the International Tribunal for Rwanda or the Presiding Judge of a Trial Chamber pursuant to article 13 of the present Statute;

(b) Have power:

    (i) To adopt rules of procedure and evidence pursuant to article 14 of the present Statute. They shall, however, be consulted before the adoption of those rules;

    (ii) To review an indictment pursuant to article 18 of the present Statute;

    (iii) To consult with the President of the International Tribunal for Rwanda in relation to the assignment of judges pursuant to article 13 of the present Statute or in relation to a pardon or commutation of sentence pursuant to article 27 of the present Statute;

    (iv) To adjudicate in pre-trial proceedings.

Article 13: Officers and Members of the Chambers

1. The permanent judges of the International Tribunal for Rwanda shall elect a President from amongst their number.

2. The President of the International Tribunal for Rwanda shall be a member of one of its Trial Chambers.

3. After consultation with the permanent judges of the International Tribunal for Rwanda, the President shall assign two of the permanent judges elected or appointed in accordance with article 12 *bis* of the present Statute to be members of the Appeals Chamber of the International Tribunal for the Former Yugoslavia and eight to the Trial Chambers of the International Tribunal for Rwanda.

4. The members of the Appeals Chamber of the International Tribunal for the Former Yugoslavia shall also serve as the members of the Appeals Chamber of the International Tribunal for Rwanda.

5. After consultation with the permanent judges of the International Tribunal for Rwanda, the President shall assign such *ad litem* judges as may from time to time be appointed to serve in the International Tribunal for Rwanda to the Trial Chambers.

6. A judge shall serve only in the Chamber to which he or she was assigned.

7. The permanent judges of each Trial Chamber shall elect a Presiding Judge from amongst their number, who shall oversee the work of that Trial Chamber as a whole.

Article 14: Rules of Procedure and Evidence

The Judges of the International Tribunal for Rwanda shall adopt, for the purpose of proceedings before the International Tribunal for Rwanda, the Rules of Procedure and Evidence for the conduct of the pre-trial phase of the proceedings, trials and appeals, the admission of evidence, the protection of victims and witnesses and other appropriate matters of the International Tribunal for the former Yugoslavia with such changes as they deem necessary.

Article 15: The Prosecutor

1. The Prosecutor shall be responsible for the investigation and prosecution of persons responsible for serious violations of international humanitarian law committed in the territory of Rwanda and Rwandan citizens responsible for such violations committed in the territory of neighbouring States, between 1 January 1994 and 31 December 1994.

2. The Prosecutor shall act independently as a separate organ of the International Tribunal for Rwanda. He or she shall not seek or receive instructions from any government or from any other source.

3. The Prosecutor of the International Tribunal for the Former Yugoslavia shall also serve as the Prosecutor of the International Tribunal for Rwanda. He or she shall have additional staff, including an additional Deputy Prosecutor, to assist with prosecutions before the International Tribunal for Rwanda. Such staff shall be appointed by the Secretary-General on the recommendation of the Prosecutor.

Article 16: The Registry

1. The Registry shall be responsible for the administration and servicing of the International Tribunal for Rwanda.

2. The Registry shall consist of a Registrar and such other staff as may be required.

3. The Registrar shall be appointed by the Secretary-General after consultation with the President of the International Tribunal for Rwanda. He or she shall serve for a four-year term and be eligible for re-appointment. The terms and conditions of service of the Registrar shall be those of an Assistant Secretary-General of the United Nations.

4. The Staff of the Registry shall be appointed by the Secretary-General on the recommendation of the Registrar.

Article 17: Investigation and Preparation of Indictment

1. The Prosecutor shall initiate investigations ex-officio or on the basis of information obtained from any source, particularly from governments, United Nations organs, intergovernmental and non-governmental organizations. The Prosecutor shall assess the information received or obtained and decide whether there is sufficient basis to proceed.

2. The Prosecutor shall have the power to question suspects, victims and witnesses, to collect evidence and to conduct on-site investigations. In carrying out these tasks, the Prosecutor may, as appropriate, seek the assistance of the State authorities concerned.

3. If questioned, the suspect shall be entitled to be assisted by Counsel of his or her own choice, including the right to have legal assistance assigned to the suspect without payment by him or her in any such case if he or she does not have sufficient means to pay for it, as well as necessary translation into and from a language he or she speaks and understands.

4. Upon a determination that a *prima facie* case exists, the Prosecutor shall prepare an indictment containing a concise statement of the facts and the crime or crimes with which

the accused is charged under the Statute. The indictment shall be transmitted to a judge of the Trial Chamber.

Article 18: Review of the Indictment

1. The judge of the Trial Chamber to whom the indictment has been transmitted shall review it. If satisfied that a *prima facie* case has been established by the Prosecutor, he or she shall confirm the indictment. If not so satisfied, the indictment shall be dismissed.

2. Upon confirmation of an indictment, the judge may, at the request of the Prosecutor, issue such orders and warrants for the arrest, detention, surrender or transfer of persons, and any other orders as may be required for the conduct of the trial.

Article 19: Commencement and Conduct of Trial Proceedings

1. The Trial Chambers shall ensure that a trial is fair and expeditious and that proceedings are conducted in accordance with the Rules of Procedure and Evidence, with full respect for the rights of the accused and due regard for the protection of victims and witnesses.

2. A person against whom an indictment has been confirmed shall, pursuant to an order or an arrest warrant of the International Tribunal for Rwanda, be taken into custody, immediately informed of the charges against him or her and transferred to the International Tribunal for Rwanda.

3. The Trial Chamber shall read the indictment, satisfy itself that the rights of the accused are respected, confirm that the accused understands the indictment, and instruct the accused to enter a plea. The Trial Chamber shall then set the date for trial.

4. The hearings shall be public unless the Trial Chamber decides to close the proceedings in accordance with its Rules of Procedure and Evidence.

Article 20: Rights of the Accused

1. All persons shall be equal before the International Tribunal for Rwanda.

2. In the determination of charges against him or her, the accused shall be entitled to a fair and public hearing, subject to Article 21 of the Statute.

3. The accused shall be presumed innocent until proven guilty according to the provisions of the present Statute.

4. In the determination of any charge against the accused pursuant to the present Statute, the accused shall be entitled to the following minimum guarantees, in full equality:

    (a) To be informed promptly and in detail in a language which he or she understands of the nature and cause of the charge against him or her;

    (b) To have adequate time and facilities for the preparation of his or her defence and to communicate with counsel of his or her own choosing;

    (c) To be tried without undue delay;

    (d) To be tried in his or her presence, and to defend himself or herself in person or through legal assistance of his or her own choosing; to be informed, if he or she does not have legal assistance, of this right; and to have legal assistance assigned to him or her, in any case where the interests of justice so require, and without payment by him or her in any such case if he or she does not have sufficient means to pay for it;

(e) To examine, or have examined, the witnesses against him or her and to obtain the attendance and examination of witnesses on his or her behalf under the same conditions as witnesses against him or her;

(f) To have the free assistance of an interpreter if he or she cannot understand or speak the language used in the International Tribunal for Rwanda;

(g) Not to be compelled to testify against himself or herself or to confess guilt.

Article 21: Protection of Victims and Witnesses

The International Tribunal for Rwanda shall provide in its Rules of Procedure and Evidence for the protection of victims and witnesses. Such protection measures shall include, but shall not be limited to, the conduct of in camera proceedings and the protection of the victim's identity.

Article 22: Judgement

1. The Trial Chambers shall pronounce judgements and impose sentences and penalties on persons convicted of serious violations of international humanitarian law.

2. The judgement shall be rendered by a majority of the judges of the Trial Chamber, and shall be delivered by the Trial Chamber in public. It shall be accompanied by a reasoned opinion in writing, to which separate or dissenting opinions may be appended.

Article 23: Penalties

1. The penalty imposed by the Trial Chamber shall be limited to imprisonment. In determining the terms of imprisonment, the Trial Chambers shall have recourse to the general practice regarding prison sentences in the courts of Rwanda.

2. In imposing the sentences, the Trial Chambers should take into account such factors as the gravity of the offence and the individual circumstances of the convicted person.

3. In addition to imprisonment, the Trial Chambers may order the return of any property and proceeds acquired by criminal conduct, including by means of duress, to their rightful owners.

Article 24: Appellate Proceedings

1. The Appeals Chamber shall hear appeals from persons convicted by the Trial Chambers or from the Prosecutor on the following grounds:

(a) An error on a question of law invalidating the decision; or
(b) An error of fact which has occasioned a miscarriage of justice.

2. The Appeals Chamber may affirm, reverse or revise the decisions taken by the Trial Chambers.

Article 25: Review Proceedings

Where a new fact has been discovered which was not known at the time of the proceedings before the Trial Chambers or the Appeals Chamber and which could have been a decisive factor in reaching the decision, the convicted person or the Prosecutor may submit to the International Tribunal for Rwanda an application for review of the judgement.

Article 26: Enforcement of Sentences

Imprisonment shall be served in Rwanda or any of the States on a list of States which have indicated to the Security Council their willingness to accept convicted persons, as designated by the International Tribunal for Rwanda. Such imprisonment shall be in accordance with the applicable law of the State concerned, subject to the supervision of the International Tribunal for Rwanda.

Article 27: Pardon or Commutation of Sentences

If, pursuant to the applicable law of the State in which the convicted person is imprisoned, he or she is eligible for pardon or commutation of sentence, the State concerned shall notify the International Tribunal for Rwanda accordingly. There shall only be pardon or commutation of sentence if the President of the International Tribunal for Rwanda, in consultation with the judges, so decides on the basis of the interests of justice and the general principles of law.

Article 28: Cooperation and Judicial Assistance

1. States shall cooperate with the International Tribunal for Rwanda in the investigation and prosecution of persons accused of committing serious violations of international humanitarian law.

2. States shall comply without undue delay with any request for assistance or an order issued by a Trial Chamber, including but not limited to:

    (a) The identification and location of persons;
    (b) The taking of testimony and the production of evidence;
    (c) The service of documents;
    (d) The arrest or detention of persons;
    (e) The surrender or the transfer of the accused to the International Tribunal for Rwanda.

Article 29: The Status, Privileges and Immunities of the International Tribunal for Rwanda

1. The Convention on the Privileges and Immunities of the United Nations of 13 February 1946 shall apply to the International Tribunal for Rwanda, the judges, the Prosecutor and his or her staff, and the Registrar and his or her staff.

2. The judges, the Prosecutor and the Registrar shall enjoy the privileges and immunities, exemptions and facilities accorded to diplomatic envoys, in accordance with international law.

3. The staff of the Prosecutor and of the Registrar shall enjoy the privileges and immunities accorded to officials of the United Nations under Articles V and VII of the Convention referred to in paragraph 1 of this article.

4. Other persons, including the accused, required at the seat or meeting place of the International Tribunal for Rwanda shall be accorded such treatment as is necessary for the proper functioning of the International Tribunal for Rwanda.

Article 30: Expenses of the International Tribunal for Rwanda

The expenses of the International Tribunal for Rwanda shall be expenses of the Organisation in accordance with Article 17 of the Charter of the United Nations.

Article 31: Working Languages

The working languages of the International Tribunal for Rwanda shall be English and French.

Article 32: Annual Report

The President of the International Tribunal for Rwanda shall submit an annual report of the International Tribunal for Rwanda to the Security Council and to the General Assembly.

STATUTE OF THE INTERNATIONAL CRIMINAL TRIBUNAL FOR THE FORMER YUGOSLAVIA

(Adopted on 25 May 1993 by Resolution 827)
(As last amended on 19 May 2003 by Resolution 1481)

Having been established by the Security Council acting under Chapter VII of the Charter of the United Nations, the International Tribunal for the Prosecution of Persons Responsible for Serious Violations of International Humanitarian Law Committed in the Territory of the Former Yugoslavia since 1991 (hereinafter referred to as "the International Tribunal") shall function in accordance with the provisions of the present Statute.

Article 1
Competence of the International Tribunal

The International Tribunal shall have the power to prosecute persons responsible for serious violations of international humanitarian law committed in the territory of the former Yugoslavia since 1991 in accordance with the provisions of the present Statute.

Article 2
Grave breaches of the Geneva Conventions of 1949

The International Tribunal shall have the power to prosecute persons committing or ordering to be committed grave breaches of the Geneva Conventions of 12 August 1949, namely the following acts against persons or property protected under the provisions of the relevant Geneva Convention:

(a) wilful killing;
(b) torture or inhuman treatment, including biological experiments;
(c) wilfully causing great suffering or serious injury to body or health;
(d) extensive destruction and appropriation of property, not justified by military necessity and carried out unlawfully and wantonly;
(e) compelling a prisoner of war or a civilian to serve in the forces of a hostile power;
(f) wilfully depriving a prisoner of war or a civilian of the rights of fair and regular trial;
(g) unlawful deportation or transfer or unlawful confinement of a civilian;
(h) taking civilians as hostages.

Article 3
Violations of the laws or customs of war

The International Tribunal shall have the power to prosecute persons violating the laws or customs of war. Such violations shall include, but not be limited to:

(a) employment of poisonous weapons or other weapons calculated to cause unnecessary suffering;

(b) wanton destruction of cities, towns or villages, or devastation not justified by military necessity;

(c) attack, or bombardment, by whatever means, of undefended towns, villages, dwellings, or buildings;

(d) seizure of, destruction or wilful damage done to institutions dedicated to religion, charity and education, the arts and sciences, historic monuments and works of art and science;

(e) plunder of public or private property.

Article 4
Genocide

1. The International Tribunal shall have the power to prosecute persons committing genocide as defined in paragraph 2 of this article or of committing any of the other acts enumerated in paragraph 3 of this article.

2. Genocide means any of the following acts committed with intent to destroy, in whole or in part, a national, ethnical, racial or religious group, as such:

(a) killing members of the group;

(b) causing serious bodily or mental harm to members of the group;

(c) deliberately inflicting on the group conditions of life calculated to bring about its physical destruction in whole or in part;

(d) imposing measures intended to prevent births within the group;

(e) forcibly transferring children of the group to another group.

3. The following acts shall be punishable:

(a) genocide;

(b) conspiracy to commit genocide;

(c) direct and public incitement to commit genocide;

(d) attempt to commit genocide;

(e) complicity in genocide.

Article 5
Crimes against humanity

The International Tribunal shall have the power to prosecute persons responsible for the following crimes when committed in armed conflict, whether international or internal in character, and directed against any civilian population:

(a) murder;

(b) extermination;

(c) enslavement;

(d) deportation;

(e) imprisonment;
(f) torture;
(g) rape;
(h) persecutions on political, racial and religious grounds;
(i) other inhumane acts.

Article 6
Personal jurisdiction

The International Tribunal shall have jurisdiction over natural persons pursuant to the provisions of the present Statute.

Article 7
Individual criminal responsibility

1. A person who planned, instigated, ordered, committed or otherwise aided and abetted in the planning, preparation or execution of a crime referred to in articles 2 to 5 of the present Statute, shall be individually responsible for the crime.

2. The official position of any accused person, whether as Head of State or Government or as a responsible Government official, shall not relieve such person of criminal responsibility nor mitigate punishment.

3. The fact that any of the acts referred to in articles 2 to 5 of the present Statute was committed by a subordinate does not relieve his superior of criminal responsibility if he knew or had reason to know that the subordinate was about to commit such acts or had done so and the superior failed to take the necessary and reasonable measures to prevent such acts or to punish the perpetrators thereof.

4. The fact that an accused person acted pursuant to an order of a Government or of a superior shall not relieve him of criminal responsibility, but may be considered in mitigation of punishment if the International Tribunal determines that justice so requires.

Article 8
Territorial and temporal jurisdiction

The territorial jurisdiction of the International Tribunal shall extend to the territory of the former Socialist Federal Republic of Yugoslavia, including its land surface, airspace and territorial waters. The temporal jurisdiction of the International Tribunal shall extend to a period beginning on 1 January 1991.

Article 9
Concurrent jurisdiction

1. The International Tribunal and national courts shall have concurrent jurisdiction to prosecute persons for serious violations of international humanitarian law committed in the territory of the former Yugoslavia since 1 January 1991.

2. The International Tribunal shall have primacy over national courts. At any stage of the procedure, the International Tribunal may formally request national courts to defer to the competence of the International Tribunal in accordance with the present Statute and the Rules of Procedure and Evidence of the International Tribunal.

Article 10
Non-bis-in-idem

1. No person shall be tried before a national court for acts constituting serious violations of international humanitarian law under the present Statute, for which he or she has already been tried by the International Tribunal.

2. A person who has been tried by a national court for acts constituting serious violations of international humanitarian law may be subsequently tried by the International Tribunal only if:

   (a) the act for which he or she was tried was characterized as an ordinary crime; or

   (b) the national court proceedings were not impartial or independent, were designed to shield the accused from international criminal responsibility, or the case was not diligently prosecuted.

3. In considering the penalty to be imposed on a person convicted of a crime under the present Statute, the International Tribunal shall take into account the extent to which any penalty imposed by a national court on the same person for the same act has already been served.

Article 11
Organization of the International Tribunal

The International Tribunal shall consist of the following organs:

   (a) the Chambers, comprising three Trial Chambers and an Appeals Chamber;
   (b) the Prosecutor; and
   (c) a Registry, servicing both the Chambers and the Prosecutor.

Article 12
Composition of the Chambers

1. The Chambers shall be composed of sixteen permanent independent judges, no two of whom may be nationals of the same State, and a maximum at any one time of nine *ad litem* independent judges appointed in accordance with article 13 *ter*, paragraph 2, of the Statute, no two of whom may be nationals of the same State.

2. Three permanent judges and a maximum at any one time of six *ad litem* judges shall be members of each Trial Chamber. Each Trial Chamber to which *ad litem* judges are assigned may be divided into sections of three judges each, composed of both permanent and *ad litem* judges. A section of a Trial Chamber shall have the same powers and responsibilities as a Trial Chamber under the Statute and shall render judgement in accordance with the same rules.

3. Seven of the permanent judges shall be members of the Appeals Chamber. The Appeals Chamber shall, for each appeal, be composed of five of its members.

4. A person who for the purposes of membership of the Chambers of the International Tribunal could be regarded as a national of more than one State shall be deemed to be a national of the State in which that person ordinarily exercises civil and political rights.

Article 13
Qualifications of judges

The permanent and *ad litem* judges shall be persons of high moral character, impartiality and integrity who possess the qualifications required in their respective countries for appointment to the highest judicial offices. In the overall composition of the Chambers and sections of the Trial Chambers, due account shall be taken of the experience of the judges in criminal law, international law, including international humanitarian law and human rights law.

Article 13 *bis*
Election of permanent judges

1. Fourteen of the permanent judges of the International Tribunal shall be elected by the General Assembly from a list submitted by the Security Council, in the following manner:

(a) The Secretary-General shall invite nominations for judges of the International Tribunal from States Members of the United Nations and non-member States maintaining permanent observer missions at United Nations Headquarters;

(b) Within sixty days of the date of the invitation of the Secretary-General, each State may nominate up to two candidates meeting the qualifications set out in article 13 of the Statute, no two of whom shall be of the same nationality and neither of whom shall be of the same nationality as any judge who is a member of the Appeals Chamber and who was elected or appointed a permanent judge of the International Criminal Tribunal for the Prosecution of Persons Responsible for Genocide and Other Serious Violations of International Humanitarian Law Committed in the Territory of Rwanda and Rwandan Citizens Responsible for Genocide and Other Such Violations Committed in the Territory of Neighbouring States, between 1 January 1994 and 31 December 1994 (hereinafter referred to as "The International Tribunal for Rwanda") in accordance with article 12 *bis* of the Statute of that Tribunal;

(c) The Secretary-General shall forward the nominations received to the Security Council. From the nominations received the Security Council shall establish a list of not less than twenty-eight and not more than forty-two candidates, taking due account of the adequate representation of the principal legal systems of the world;

(d) The President of the Security Council shall transmit the list of candidates to the President of the General Assembly. From that list the General Assembly shall elect fourteen permanent judges of the International Tribunal. The candidates who receive an absolute majority of the votes of the States Members of the United Nations and of the non-member States maintaining permanent observer missions at United Nations Headquarters, shall be declared elected. Should two candidates of the same nationality obtain the required majority vote, the one who received the higher number of votes shall be considered elected.

2. In the event of a vacancy in the Chambers amongst the permanent judges elected or appointed in accordance with this article, after consultation with the Presidents of the Security Council and of the General Assembly, the Secretary-General shall appoint a person meeting the qualifications of article 13 of the Statute, for the remainder of the term of office concerned.

3. The permanent judges elected in accordance with this article shall be elected for a term of four years. The terms and conditions of service shall be those of the judges of the International Court of Justice. They shall be eligible for re-election.

Article 13 *ter*
Election and appointment of *ad litem* judges

1. The *ad litem* judges of the International Tribunal shall be elected by the General Assembly from a list submitted by the Security Council, in the following manner:

    (a) The Secretary-General shall invite nominations for *ad litem* judges of the International Tribunal from States Members of the United Nations and non-member States maintaining permanent observer missions at United Nations Headquarters.

    (b) Within sixty days of the date of the invitation of the Secretary-General, each State may nominate up to four candidates meeting the qualifications set out in article 13 of the Statute, taking into account the importance of a fair representation of female and male candidates.

    (c) The Secretary-General shall forward the nominations received to the Security Council. From the nominations received the Security Council shall establish a list of not less than fifty-four candidates, taking due account of the adequate representation of the principal legal systems of the world and bearing in mind the importance of equitable geographical distribution.

    (d) The President of the Security Council shall transmit the list of candidates to the President of the General Assembly. From that list the General Assembly shall elect the twenty-seven *ad litem* judges of the International Tribunal. The candidates who receive an absolute majority of the votes of the States Members of the United Nations and of the non-member States maintaining permanent observer missions at United Nations Headquarters shall be declared elected.

    (e) The *ad litem* judges shall be elected for a term of four years. They shall not be eligible for re-election.

2. During their term, *ad litem* judges will be appointed by the Secretary-General, upon request of the President of the International Tribunal, to serve in the Trial Chambers for one or more trials, for a cumulative period of up to, but not including, three years. When requesting the appointment of any particular *ad litem* judge, the President of the International Tribunal shall bear in mind the criteria set out in article 13 of the Statute regarding the composition of the Chambers and sections of the Trial Chambers, the considerations set out in paragraphs 1 (b) and (c) above and the number of votes the *ad litem* judge received in the General Assembly.

Article 13 *quater*
Status of *ad litem* judges

1. During the period in which they are appointed to serve in the International Tribunal, *ad litem* judges shall:

    (a) Benefit from the same terms and conditions of service mutatis mutandis as the permanent judges of the International Tribunal;

    (b) Enjoy, subject to paragraph 2 below, the same powers as the permanent judges of the International Tribunal;

    (c) Enjoy the privileges and immunities, exemptions and facilities of a judge of the International Tribunal;

    (d) Enjoy the power to adjudicate in pre-trial proceedings in cases other than those that they have been appointed to try.

2. During the period in which they are appointed to serve in the International Tribunal, *ad litem* judges shall not:

(a) Be eligible for election as, or to vote in the election of, the President of the Tribunal or the Presiding Judge of a Trial Chamber pursuant to article 14 of the Statute;

(b) Have power:

    (i) To adopt rules of procedure and evidence pursuant to article 15 of the Statute. They shall, however, be consulted before the adoption of those rules;

    (ii) To review an indictment pursuant to article 19 of the Statute;

    (iii) To consult with the President in relation to the assignment of judges pursuant to article 14 of the Statute or in relation to a pardon or commutation of sentence pursuant to article 28 of the Statute.

Article 14
Officers and members of the Chambers

1. The permanent judges of the International Tribunal shall elect a President from amongst their number.

2. The President of the International Tribunal shall be a member of the Appeals Chamber and shall preside over its proceedings.

3. After consultation with the permanent judges of the International Tribunal, the President shall assign four of the permanent judges elected or appointed in accordance with article 13 *bis* of the Statute to the Appeals Chamber and nine to the Trial Chambers.

4. Two of the permanent judges of the International Tribunal for Rwanda elected or appointed in accordance with article 12 *bis* of the Statute of that Tribunal shall be assigned by the President of that Tribunal, in consultation with the President of the International Tribunal, to be members of the Appeals Chamber and permanent judges of the International Tribunal.

5. After consultation with the permanent judges of the International Tribunal, the President shall assign such *ad litem* judges as may from time to time be appointed to serve in the International Tribunal to the Trial Chambers.

6. A judge shall serve only in the Chamber to which he or she was assigned.

7. The permanent judges of each Trial Chamber shall elect a Presiding Judge from amongst their number, who shall oversee the work of the Trial Chamber as a whole.

Article 15
Rules of procedure and evidence

The judges of the International Tribunal shall adopt rules of procedure and evidence for the conduct of the pre-trial phase of the proceedings, trials and appeals, the admission of evidence, the protection of victims and witnesses and other appropriate matters.

Article 16
The Prosecutor

1. The Prosecutor shall be responsible for the investigation and prosecution of persons responsible for serious violations of international humanitarian law committed in the territory of the former Yugoslavia since 1 January 1991.

2. The Prosecutor shall act independently as a separate organ of the International Tribunal. He or she shall not seek or receive instructions from any Government or from any other source.

3. The Office of the Prosecutor shall be composed of a Prosecutor and such other qualified staff as may be required.

4. The Prosecutor shall be appointed by the Security Council on nomination by the Secretary-General. He or she shall be of high moral character and possess the highest level of competence and experience in the conduct of investigations and prosecutions of criminal cases. The Prosecutor shall serve for a four-year term and be eligible for reappointment. The terms and conditions of service of the Prosecutor shall be those of an Under-Secretary-General of the United Nations.

5. The staff of the Office of the Prosecutor shall be appointed by the Secretary-General on the recommendation of the Prosecutor.

Article 17
The Registry

1. The Registry shall be responsible for the administration and servicing of the International Tribunal.

2. The Registry shall consist of a Registrar and such other staff as may be required.

3. The Registrar shall be appointed by the Secretary-General after consultation with the President of the International Tribunal. He or she shall serve for a four-year term and be eligible for reappointment. The terms and conditions of service of the Registrar shall be those of an Assistant Secretary-General of the United Nations.

4. The staff of the Registry shall be appointed by the Secretary-General on the recommendation of the Registrar.

Article 18
Investigation and preparation of indictment

1. The Prosecutor shall initiate investigations *ex-officio* or on the basis of information obtained from any source, particularly from Governments, United Nations organs, inter-governmental and non-governmental organisations. The Prosecutor shall assess the information received or obtained and decide whether there is sufficient basis to proceed.

2. The Prosecutor shall have the power to question suspects, victims and witnesses, to collect evidence and to conduct on-site investigations. In carrying out these tasks, the Prosecutor may, as appropriate, seek the assistance of the State authorities concerned.

3. If questioned, the suspect shall be entitled to be assisted by counsel of his own choice, including the right to have legal assistance assigned to him without payment by him in any such case if he does not have sufficient means to pay for it, as well as to necessary translation into and from a language he speaks and understands.

4. Upon a determination that a *prima facie* case exists, the Prosecutor shall prepare an indictment containing a concise statement of the facts and the crime or crimes with which the accused is charged under the Statute. The indictment shall be transmitted to a judge of the Trial Chamber.

Article 19
Review of the indictment

1. The judge of the Trial Chamber to whom the indictment has been transmitted shall review it. If satisfied that a *prima facie* case has been established by the Prosecutor, he shall confirm the indictment. If not so satisfied, the indictment shall be dismissed.

2. Upon confirmation of an indictment, the judge may, at the request of the Prosecutor, issue such orders and warrants for the arrest, detention, surrender or transfer of persons, and any other orders as may be required for the conduct of the trial.

Article 20
Commencement and conduct of trial proceedings

1. The Trial Chambers shall ensure that a trial is fair and expeditious and that proceedings are conducted in accordance with the rules of procedure and evidence, with full respect for the rights of the accused and due regard for the protection of victims and witnesses.

2. A person against whom an indictment has been confirmed shall, pursuant to an order or an arrest warrant of the International Tribunal, be taken into custody, immediately informed of the charges against him and transferred to the International Tribunal.

3. The Trial Chamber shall read the indictment, satisfy itself that the rights of the accused are respected, confirm that the accused understands the indictment, and instruct the accused to enter a plea. The Trial Chamber shall then set the date for trial.

4. The hearings shall be public unless the Trial Chamber decides to close the proceedings in accordance with its rules of procedure and evidence.

Article 21
Rights of the accused

1. All persons shall be equal before the International Tribunal.

2. In the determination of charges against him, the accused shall be entitled to a fair and public hearing, subject to article 22 of the Statute.

3. The accused shall be presumed innocent until proved guilty according to the provisions of the present Statute.

4. In the determination of any charge against the accused pursuant to the present Statute, the accused shall be entitled to the following minimum guarantees, in full equality:

  (a) to be informed promptly and in detail in a language which he understands of the nature and cause of the charge against him;

  (b) to have adequate time and facilities for the preparation of his defence and to communicate with counsel of his own choosing;

  (c) to be tried without undue delay;

  (d) to be tried in his presence, and to defend himself in person or through legal assistance of his own choosing; to be informed, if he does not have legal assistance, of this right; and to have legal assistance assigned to him, in any case where the interests of justice so require, and without payment by him in any such case if he does not have sufficient means to pay for it;

(e) to examine, or have examined, the witnesses against him and to obtain the attend-
    ance and examination of witnesses on his behalf under the same conditions as
    witnesses against him;

(f) to have the free assistance of an interpreter if he cannot understand or speak the
    language used in the International Tribunal;

(g) not to be compelled to testify against himself or to confess guilt.

Article 22
Protection of victims and witnesses

The International Tribunal shall provide in its rules of procedure and evidence for the
protection of victims and witnesses. Such protection measures shall include, but shall not be
limited to, the conduct of in camera proceedings and the protection of the victim's identity.

Article 23
Judgement

1. The Trial Chambers shall pronounce judgements and impose sentences and penalties on
persons convicted of serious violations of international humanitarian law.

2. The judgement shall be rendered by a majority of the judges of the Trial Chamber, and
shall be delivered by the Trial Chamber in public. It shall be accompanied by a reasoned
opinion in writing, to which separate or dissenting opinions may be appended.

Article 24
Penalties

1. The penalty imposed by the Trial Chamber shall be limited to imprisonment. In determining the terms of imprisonment, the Trial Chambers shall have recourse to the general
practice regarding prison sentences in the courts of the former Yugoslavia.

2. In imposing the sentences, the Trial Chambers should take into account such factors as
the gravity of the offence and the individual circumstances of the convicted person.

3. In addition to imprisonment, the Trial Chambers may order the return of any property and
proceeds acquired by criminal conduct, including by means of duress, to their rightful owners.

Article 25
Appellate proceedings

1. The Appeals Chamber shall hear appeals from persons convicted by the Trial Chambers
or from the Prosecutor on the following grounds:

(a) an error on a question of law invalidating the decision; or
(b) an error of fact which has occasioned a miscarriage of justice.

2. The Appeals Chamber may affirm, reverse or revise the decisions taken by the Trial
Chambers.

Article 26
Review proceedings

Where a new fact has been discovered which was not known at the time of the proceedings
before the Trial Chambers or the Appeals Chamber and which could have been a decisive

factor in reaching the decision, the convicted person or the Prosecutor may submit to the International Tribunal an application for review of the judgement.

Article 27
Enforcement of sentences

Imprisonment shall be served in a State designated by the International Tribunal from a list of States which have indicated to the Security Council their willingness to accept convicted persons. Such imprisonment shall be in accordance with the applicable law of the State concerned, subject to the supervision of the International Tribunal.

Article 28
Pardon or commutation of sentences

If, pursuant to the applicable law of the State in which the convicted person is imprisoned, he or she is eligible for pardon or commutation of sentence, the State concerned shall notify the International Tribunal accordingly. The President of the International Tribunal, in consultation with the judges, shall decide the matter on the basis of the interests of justice and the general principles of law.

Article 29
Co-operation and judicial assistance

1. States shall co-operate with the International Tribunal in the investigation and prosecution of persons accused of committing serious violations of international humanitarian law.

2. States shall comply without undue delay with any request for assistance or an order issued by a Trial Chamber, including, but not limited to:

    (a) the identification and location of persons;
    (b) the taking of testimony and the production of evidence;
    (c) the service of documents;
    (d) the arrest or detention of persons;
    (e) the surrender or the transfer of the accused to the International Tribunal.

Article 30
The status, privileges and immunities of the International Tribunal

1. The Convention on the Privileges and Immunities of the United Nations of 13 February 1946 shall apply to the International Tribunal, the judges, the Prosecutor and his staff, and the Registrar and his staff.

2. The judges, the Prosecutor and the Registrar shall enjoy the privileges and immunities, exemptions and facilities accorded to diplomatic envoys, in accordance with international law.

3. The staff of the Prosecutor and of the Registrar shall enjoy the privileges and immunities accorded to officials of the United Nations under articles V and VII of the Convention referred to in paragraph 1 of this article.

4. Other persons, including the accused, required at the seat of the International Tribunal shall be accorded such treatment as is necessary for the proper functioning of the International Tribunal.

Article 31
Seat of the International Tribunal

The International Tribunal shall have its seat at The Hague.

Article 32
Expenses of the International Tribunal

The expenses of the International Tribunal shall be borne by the regular budget of the United Nations in accordance with Article 17 of the Charter of the United Nations.

Article 33
Working languages

The working languages of the International Tribunal shall be English and French.

Article 34
Annual report

The President of the International Tribunal shall submit an annual report of the International Tribunal to the Security Council and to the General Assembly.

Index